COME ALIVE

with GLENCOE'S

TECHNOLOGY TOOLS

Study tools are available online 24 hours a day.

Download tools to help you study anywhere!

Bring the sights and sounds of social studies alive with Section Spotlight Videos!

Keep up-to-date with current events on Glencoe's GA Today Web site.

Find In-Motion Animations, Interactive Graphic Organizers, and more on your StudentWorks™ Plus Online at mybooks.glencoe.com.

QuickPass™
More Than a Textbook

Find it faster

Visit Social Studies ONLINE at glencoe.com and enter a QuickPass™ chapter code to go directly to the chapter resources you need.

GA6EOW6225c1

Enter this code with the appropriate chapter number.

Find what you need.

- StudentWorks™ Plus Online
- Section Spotlight Videos
- Chapter Overview
- Section Audio
- Self-Check Quiz

Find extras to help you succeed.

- Download Study-to-Go™ applications
- Interact with In-Motion Animations
- Access current events articles at GA Today on your book page at glencoe.com
- View video at the Media Library
- Review with ePuzzles and Games
- Explore Student Web Activities
- Multilingual Glossary and more...

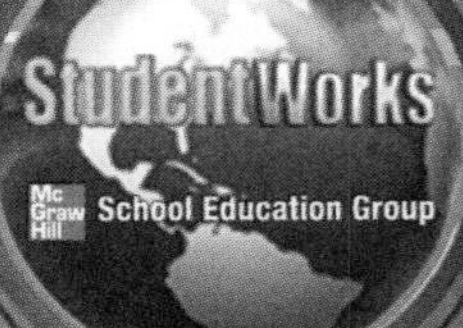

You can easily launch a wide range of digital products from your computer's desktop with the McGraw-Hill Global Gateway widget.

PHOTOLIBRARY.COM/INDEX OPEN; (BKGD)RYAN MCVAY/GETTY IMAGES

Glencoe

Georgia's Exploring Our World

People, Places, and Cultures

Latin America and Canada, Europe, & Australia

Boehm Armstrong Hunkins

Glencoe

About the Authors

NATIONAL GEOGRAPHIC

The National Geographic Society, founded in 1888 for the increase and diffusion of geographic knowledge, is the world's largest nonprofit scientific and educational organization. Since its earliest days, the Society has used sophisticated communication technologies, from color photography to holography, to convey geographic knowledge to a worldwide membership. The School Publishing Division supports the Society's mission by developing innovative education programs—ranging from traditional print materials to multimedia programs including CD-ROMs, videos, and software.

Senior Author

Richard G. Boehm

Richard G. Boehm, Ph.D., was one of seven authors of *Geography for Life,* national standards in geography, prepared under Goals 2000: Educate America Act. He was also one of the authors of the *Guidelines for Geographic Education,* in which the Five Themes of Geography were first articulated. Dr. Boehm has received many honors, including "Distinguished Geography Educator" by the National Geographic Society (1990), the "George J. Miller Award" from the National Council for Geographic Education (NCGE) for distinguished service to geographic education (1991), and "Gilbert Grosvenor Honors" in geographic education from the Association of American Geographers (2002). He was President of the NCGE and has twice won the *Journal of Geography* award for best article. He has received the NCGE's "Distinguished Teaching Achievement" award and presently holds the Jesse H. Jones Distinguished Chair in Geographic Education at Texas State University in San Marcos, Texas.

Francis P. Hunkins

Francis P. Hunkins, Ph.D., is Professor of Education at the University of Washington. He began his career as a teacher in Massachusetts. He received his master's degree in education from Boston University and his doctorate from Kent State University with a major in general curriculum and a minor in geography. Dr. Hunkins has written numerous books and articles.

David G. Armstrong

David G. Armstrong, Ph.D., served as Dean of the School of Education at the University of North Carolina at Greensboro. A social studies education specialist with additional advanced training in geography, Dr. Armstrong was educated at Stanford University, University of Montana, and University of Washington.

Dinah Zike

Dinah Zike, M.Ed., is an award-winning author, educator, and inventor known for designing three-dimensional hands-on manipulatives and graphic organizers known as Foldables®. Dinah has developed educational books and materials and is the author of *The Big Book of Books and Activities,* which was awarded Learning Magazine's Teachers' Choice Award. In 2004 Dinah was honored with the CESI Science Advocacy Award. Dinah received her M.Ed. from Texas A&M, College Station, Texas.

Students with print disabilities may be eligible to obtain an accessible, audio version of the pupil edition of this textbook. Please call Recording for the Blind & Dyslexic at 1-800-221-4792 for complete information.

The McGraw-Hill Companies

Glencoe

Send all inquiries to:
Glencoe/McGraw-Hill, 8787 Orion Place, Columbus, Ohio 43240-4027

ISBN: 978-0-07-895622-5
MHID: 0-07-895622-6

Printed in the United States of America.
4 5 6 7 8 9 QVS 16 15 14 13

Academic Consultants

Pratyusha Basu, Ph.D.
Assistant Professor of Geography
University of South Florida
Tampa, Florida

Sari Bennett, Ph.D.
Director, Center for Geographic Education
University of Maryland, Baltimore County
Baltimore, Maryland

David Berger, Ph.D.
Broeklundian Professor of History
Brooklyn College and the Graduate Center
City University of New York
Brooklyn, New York

Dennis Conway, Ph.D.
Professor of Geography
Indiana University
Bloomington, Indiana

Clifford B. Craig, Ph.D.
Professor of Geography and Earth Resources
Utah State University
Logan, Utah

Richard M. Golden, Ph.D.
Professor of History and Director, Jewish Studies Program
University of North Texas
Denton, Texas

Brooks Green, Ph.D.
Associate Professor of Geography
University of Central Arkansas
Conway, Arkansas

Sumit Guha, Ph.D.
Professor of History
Rutgers University
New Brunswick, New Jersey

Gerald T. Hanson, Ph.D.
Professor of Cultural Geography
University of Arkansas at Little Rock
Little Rock, Arkansas

Darrell P. Kruger, Ph.D.
Professor of Geography
Illinois State University
Normal, Illinois

David A. Lanegran, Ph.D.
John S. Holl Professor of Geography
Macalester College
St. Paul, Minnesota

Elizabeth J. Leppman, Ph.D.
Adjunct Professor of Geography
Eastern Kentucky University
Richmond, Kentucky

Catherine M. Lockwood, Ph.D.
Professor of Geography
Chadron State College
Chadron, Nebraska

Farid Mahdavi, Ph.D.
Department of History
San Diego State University
San Diego, California

Paul Nagel, Ph.D.
Coordinator, Louisiana Geography Education Alliance
Northwestern State University
Natchitoches, Louisiana

Bimal Kanti Paul, Ph.D.
Professor of Geography
Kansas State University
Manhattan, Kansas

Joseph P. Stoltman, Ph.D.
Professor of Geography
Western Michigan University
Kalamazoo, Michigan

George W. White, Jr., Ph.D.
Associate Professor of Geography
Frostburg State University
Frostburg, Maryland

Teacher Reviewers

Desdie Withrow Eberman
Savannah Chatham Public Schools
Savannah, Georgia

Felicia Lester
Atlanta Public Schools
Atlanta, Georgia

Clyde M. Mann, Ed.S.
Dickerson Middle School
Marietta, Georgia

Martha McCarthy
Pierce County Middle School
Blackshear, Georgia

Dayle Earnest Munn
Union Grove Middle School
McDonough, Georgia

Dr. Melissa Haskins-Whitley
Pearson Elementary School
Pearson, Georgia

Reading Consultant

ReLeah Lent
National Education Consultant
Alford, Florida

Contents

Farming in Manitoba, Canada

Contents

Scuba diving along Australia's Great Barrier Reef

Features

Geography & History

TIME Perspectives: Exploring World Issues

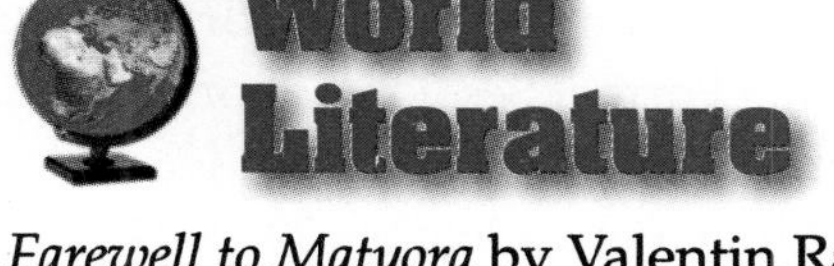

TIME Global Citizens

You Decide

TIME Journal

Primary Sources

Ed. = Editor	Tr. = Translator	V = Volume

UNIT 1

UNIT 2

▲ **Toucan**

◀ **Pan-American Highway, Panama**

UNIT 3

UNIT 4

Skills Handbook

Maps

NATIONAL GEOGRAPHIC Reference Atlas . . . RA1

UNIT 1

Understanding Geography

UNIT 2

Latin America and Canada

NATIONAL GEOGRAPHIC

Canada: Economic Regions

UNIT 3

Europe

UNIT 4

Australia

NATIONAL GEOGRAPHIC

Europe: Currents and Wind Patterns

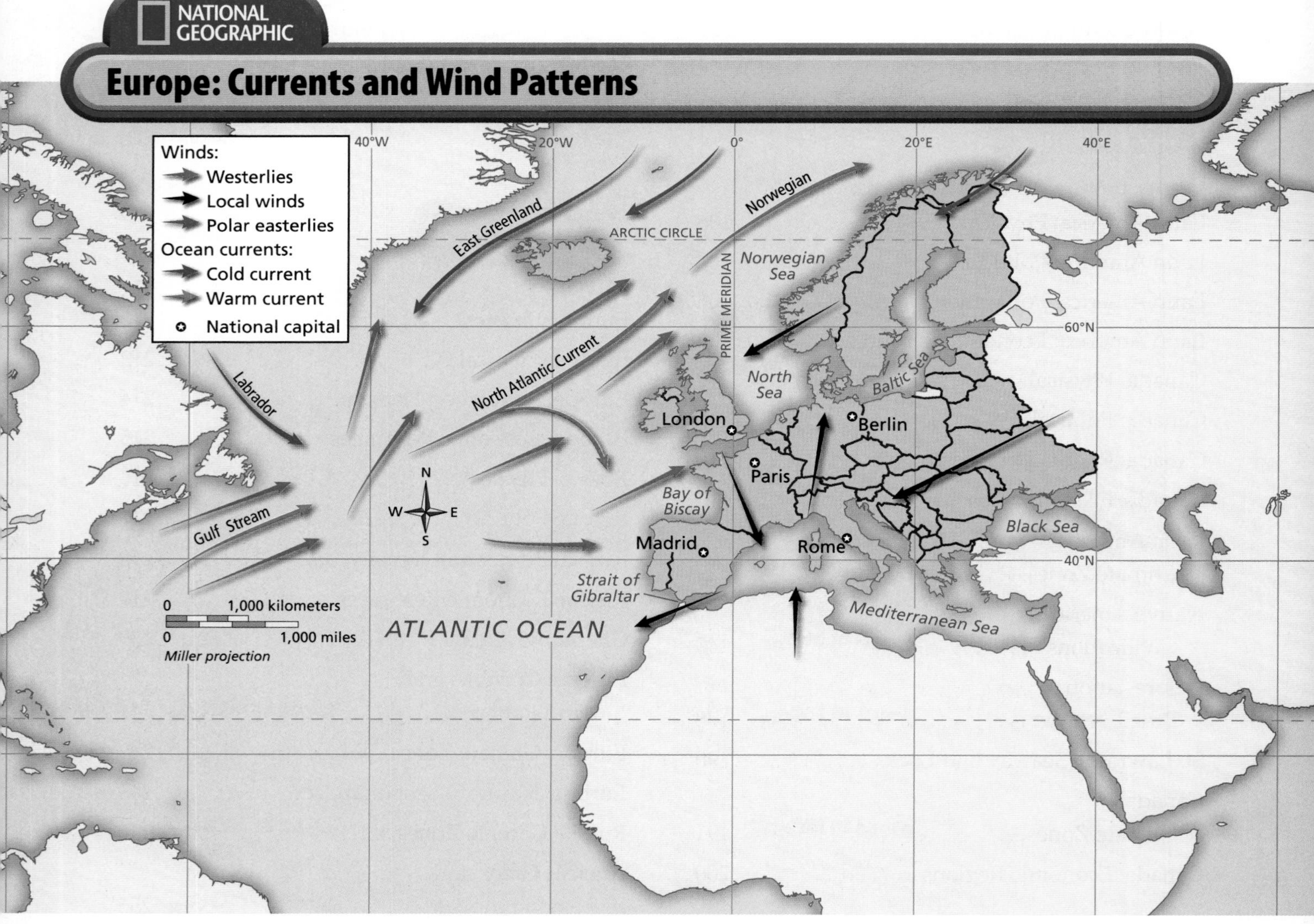

Diagrams, Charts, and Graphs

UNIT 1

Understanding Geography

UNIT 2

Latin America and Canada

Earth's Layers

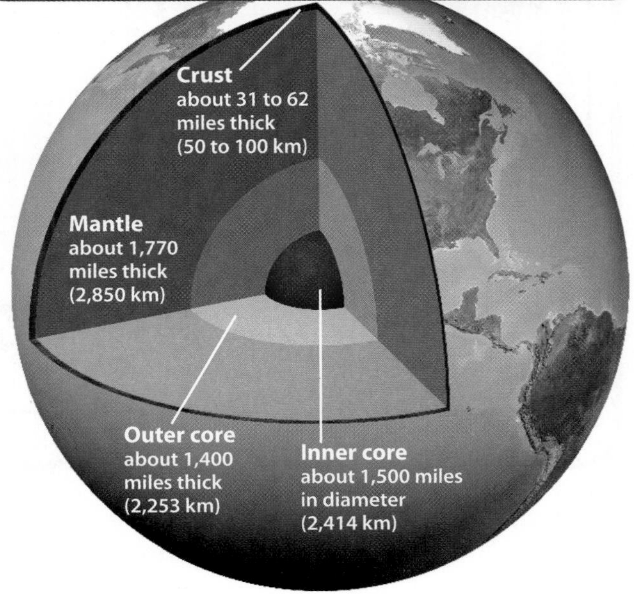

Source: *NGS Almanac of Geography.*

Europe

Australia

Personal Finance Handbook

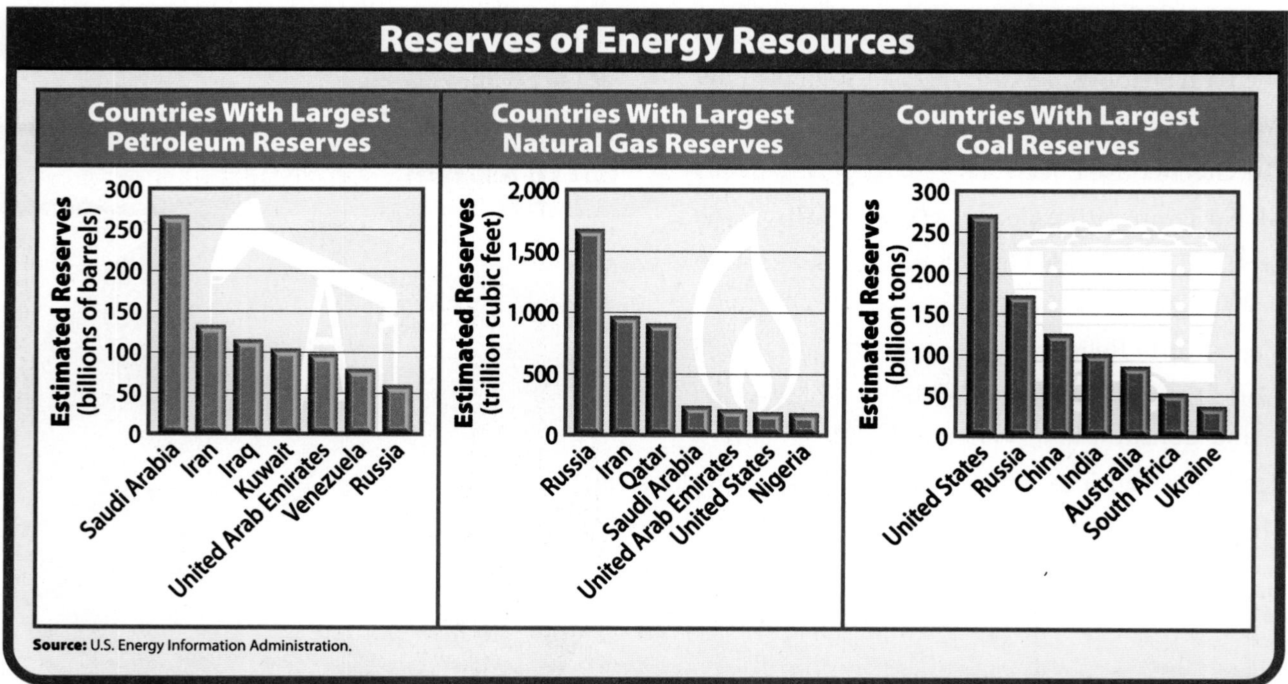

Scavenger Hunt

Georgia's Exploring Our World: People, Places, and Cultures contains a wealth of information. The trick is to know where to look to access all the information in the book. If you complete this scavenger hunt exercise with your teacher or parents, you will see how the textbook is organized and how to get the most out of your reading and study time. Let's get started!

1. How many units and how many chapters are in the book?
2. What does Unit 1 cover?
3. Where can you find facts about each country in each unit?
4. In what three places can you learn about the Big Ideas for each section?
5. What does the Foldables Study Organizer at the beginning of Chapter 2 ask you to do?
6. How are the content vocabulary terms throughout your book highlighted in the narrative?
7. Where do you find graphic organizers in your textbook?

8. You want to quickly find all the maps in the book about the world. Where do you look?
9. Where can you practice specific social studies skills in your textbook?
10. Where can you learn about the different types of map projections?

Reference Atlas

ATLAS KEY

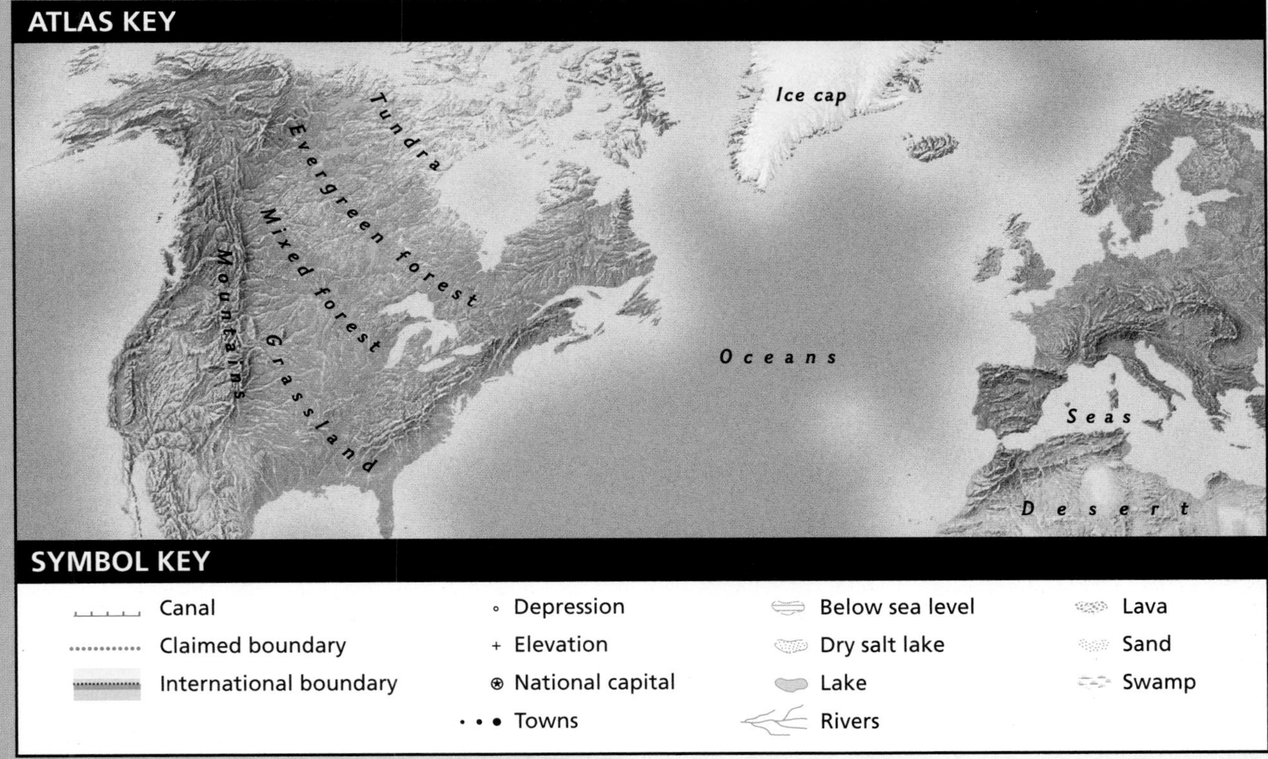

SYMBOL KEY

Canal	Depression	Below sea level	Lava
Claimed boundary	Elevation	Dry salt lake	Sand
International boundary	National capital	Lake	Swamp
	Towns	Rivers	

The maps in this Reference Atlas contain a letter/number grid system to help you determine the location of places. For example, on the next page, if given the coordinates D5, you could find Atlanta. To do so, first locate the letter D along the side of the page, and scan across that "row." Then, locate the number 5, and scan down that "column" until you meet the D row.

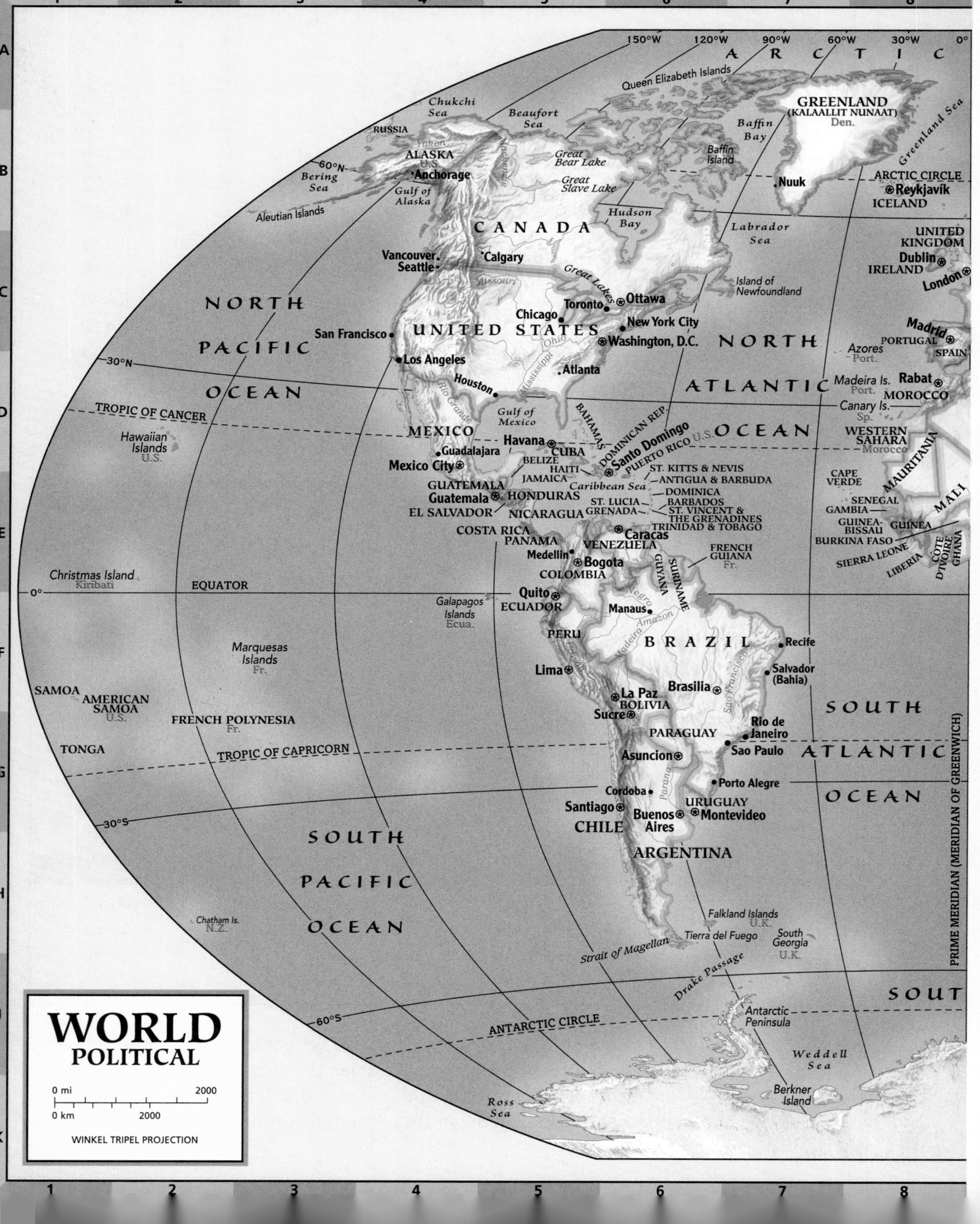

WORLD
POLITICAL
0 mi
2000
0 km
2000
WINKEL TRIPEL PROJECTION
150°W
120°W
90°W
60°W
30°W
0°
60°N
30°N
0°
30°S
60°S
ARCTIC
Queen Elizabeth Islands
GREENLAND
(KALAALLIT NUNAAT)
Den.
Greenland Sea
Chukchi Sea
Beaufort Sea
Baffin Bay
Baffin Island
RUSSIA
Yukon
ALASKA
U.S.
Anchorage
Mackenzie
Great Bear Lake
Great Slave Lake
Bering Sea
Gulf of Alaska
Aleutian Islands
Nuuk
ARCTIC CIRCLE
Reykjavík
ICELAND
Hudson Bay
Labrador Sea
CANADA
UNITED KINGDOM
Dublin
IRELAND
London
Vancouver
Seattle
Calgary
Missouri
Great Lakes
Island of Newfoundland
Ottawa
Toronto
Chicago
New York City
Washington, D.C.
NORTH PACIFIC OCEAN
San Francisco
UNITED STATES
Ohio
Los Angeles
Mississippi
Atlanta
Houston
Rio Grande
NORTH ATLANTIC OCEAN
Madrid
PORTUGAL
SPAIN
Azores
Port.
Madeira Is.
Port.
Rabat
MOROCCO
Canary Is.
Sp.
TROPIC OF CANCER
Gulf of Mexico
BAHAMAS
DOMINICAN REP.
Santo Domingo
PUERTO RICO U.S.
WESTERN SAHARA
Morocco
MAURITANIA
Hawaiian Islands
U.S.
MEXICO
Havana
CUBA
Guadalajara
BELIZE
HAITI
JAMAICA
Mexico City
ST. KITTS & NEVIS
ANTIGUA & BARBUDA
DOMINICA
Caribbean Sea
GUATEMALA
Guatemala
HONDURAS
EL SALVADOR
NICARAGUA
ST. LUCIA
GRENADA
BARBADOS
ST. VINCENT & THE GRENADINES
TRINIDAD & TOBAGO
CAPE VERDE
SENEGAL
GAMBIA
GUINEA-BISSAU
GUINEA
MALI
BURKINA FASO
SIERRA LEONE
LIBERIA
CÔTE D'IVOIRE
GHANA
COSTA RICA
PANAMA
Caracas
VENEZUELA
Medellin
Bogota
COLOMBIA
GUYANA
SURINAME
FRENCH GUIANA
Fr.
Christmas Island
Kiribati
EQUATOR
Quito
ECUADOR
Galapagos Islands
Ecua.
Negro
Manaus
Amazon
PERU
Madeira
BRAZIL
Recife
Marquesas Islands
Fr.
Lima
Salvador (Bahia)
Sao Francisco
Brasilia
La Paz
BOLIVIA
SAMOA
AMERICAN SAMOA
U.S.
FRENCH POLYNESIA
Fr.
Sucre
SOUTH ATLANTIC OCEAN
Rio de Janeiro
PARAGUAY
Sao Paulo
TONGA
TROPIC OF CAPRICORN
Asuncion
Parana
Porto Alegre
Cordoba
URUGUAY
Santiago
Buenos Aires
Montevideo
CHILE
ARGENTINA
SOUTH PACIFIC OCEAN
PRIME MERIDIAN (MERIDIAN OF GREENWICH)
Chatham Is.
N.Z.
Falkland Islands
U.K.
South Georgia
U.K.
Tierra del Fuego
Strait of Magellan
Drake Passage
SOUT
Antarctic Peninsula
ANTARCTIC CIRCLE
Weddell Sea
Berkner Island
Ross Sea

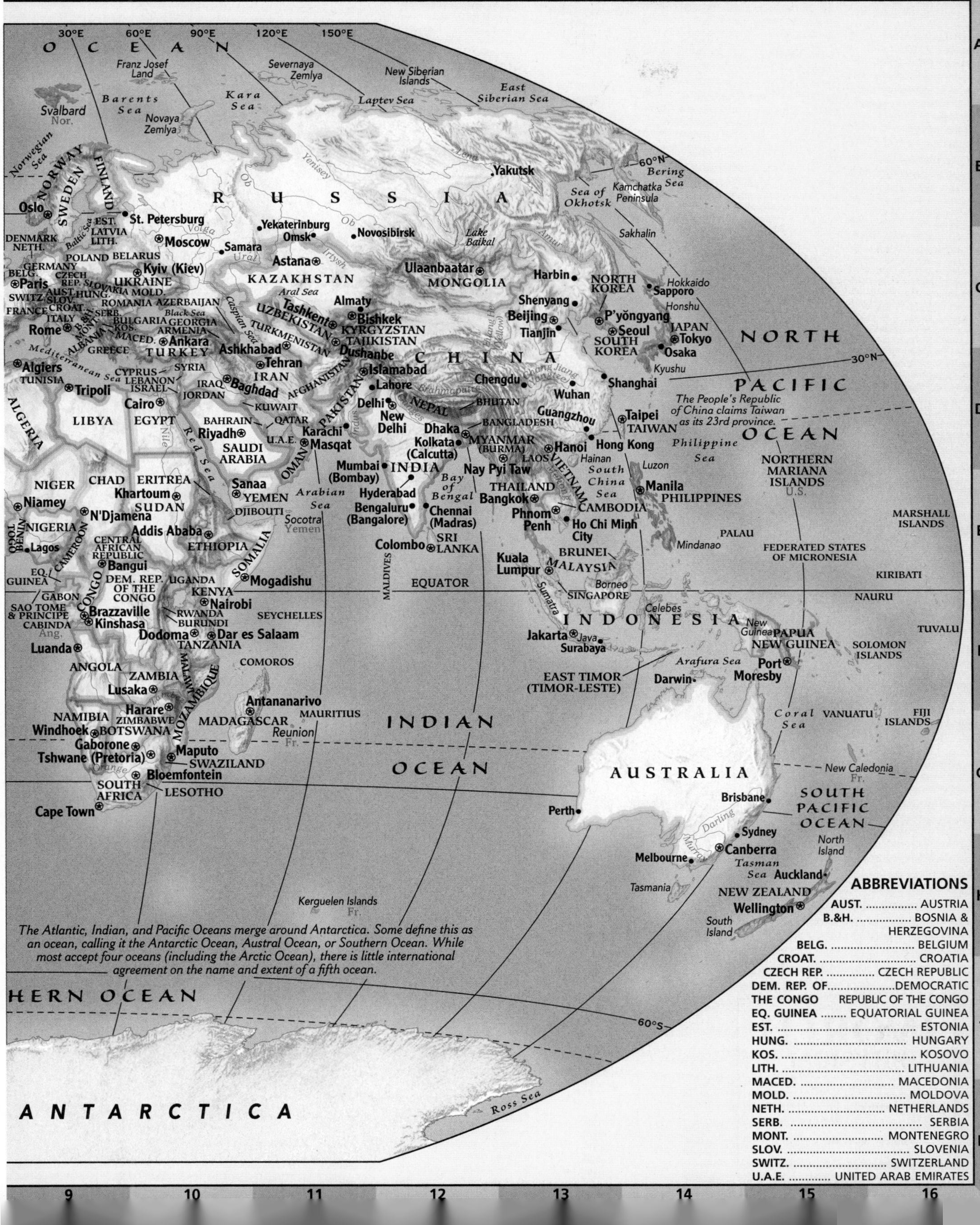
9
10
11
12
13
14
15
16
30°E
60°E
90°E
120°E
150°E
OCEAN
Franz Josef Land
Severnaya Zemlya
New Siberian Islands
East Siberian Sea
Svalbard
Nor.
Barents Sea
Kara Sea
Laptev Sea
Novaya Zemlya
Norwegian Sea
NORWAY
SWEDEN
FINLAND
RUSSIA
Yakutsk
60°N
Bering Sea
Sea of Okhotsk
Kamchatka Peninsula
Oslo
St. Petersburg
EST.
LATVIA
LITH.
Baltic Sea
DENMARK
NETH.
Moscow
Volga
Samara
Ural
Yekaterinburg
Omsk
Novosibirsk
Lake Baikal
Amur
Sakhalin
Ob
Yenisey
Lena
Irtysh
POLAND
BELARUS
GERMANY
BELG.
Paris
CZECH REP.
SLOVAKIA
AUST.
HUNG.
SWITZ.
SLOV.
FRANCE
CROAT.
SERB.
B.&H.
MONT.
ITALY
KOS.
MACED.
ALBANIA
Rome
Kyiv (Kiev)
UKRAINE
MOLD.
ROMANIA
BULGARIA
GREECE
Astana
KAZAKHSTAN
Aral Sea
Ulaanbaatar
MONGOLIA
Harbin
NORTH KOREA
Sapporo
Hokkaido
Honshu
AZERBAIJAN
Black Sea
GEORGIA
ARMENIA
Caspian Sea
Ankara
TURKEY
Tashkent
UZBEKISTAN
Almaty
Bishkek
KYRGYZSTAN
TAJIKISTAN
TURKMENISTAN
Ashkhabad
Dushanbe
Shenyang
Beijing
Tianjin
P'yŏngyang
Seoul
SOUTH KOREA
JAPAN
Tokyo
Osaka
Kyushu
NORTH
Mediterranean Sea
Algiers
TUNISIA
CYPRUS
LEBANON
ISRAEL
SYRIA
IRAQ
Baghdad
JORDAN
Tehran
IRAN
AFGHANISTAN
Islamabad
Lahore
PAKISTAN
CHINA
Huang He (Yellow)
Chang Jiang (Yangtze)
Chengdu
Wuhan
Shanghai
30°N
PACIFIC
Tripoli
ALGERIA
LIBYA
Cairo
EGYPT
Nile
KUWAIT
BAHRAIN
QATAR
Riyadh
U.A.E.
Masqat
OMAN
SAUDI ARABIA
Karachi
Delhi
New Delhi
NEPAL
BHUTAN
Brahmaputra
Ganges
Indus
BANGLADESH
Dhaka
Kolkata (Calcutta)
MYANMAR (BURMA)
Nay Pyi Taw
LAOS
Hanoi
Guangzhou
Hong Kong
Taipei
TAIWAN
The People's Republic of China claims Taiwan as its 23rd province.
OCEAN
Philippine Sea
NORTHERN MARIANA ISLANDS
U.S.
Red Sea
Sanaa
YEMEN
Mumbai (Bombay)
INDIA
Hyderabad
Bengaluru (Bangalore)
Chennai (Madras)
Bay of Bengal
THAILAND
Bangkok
VIETNAM
Mekong
Hainan
South China Sea
Luzon
Manila
PHILIPPINES
NIGER
CHAD
ERITREA
Khartoum
SUDAN
Niamey
N'Djamena
DJIBOUTI
Arabian Sea
Socotra
Yemen
Phnom Penh
CAMBODIA
Ho Chi Minh City
MARSHALL ISLANDS
NIGERIA
BENIN
TOGO
Lagos
CAMEROON
CENTRAL AFRICAN REPUBLIC
Bangui
Addis Ababa
ETHIOPIA
SOMALIA
Colombo
SRI LANKA
MALDIVES
Kuala Lumpur
BRUNEI
MALAYSIA
Mindanao
PALAU
FEDERATED STATES OF MICRONESIA
EQ. GUINEA
GABON
CONGO
DEM. REP. OF THE CONGO
UGANDA
KENYA
Mogadishu
Nairobi
EQUATOR
Sumatra
Borneo
SINGAPORE
KIRIBATI
NAURU
SAO TOME & PRINCIPE
CABINDA
Ang.
Brazzaville
Kinshasa
RWANDA
BURUNDI
SEYCHELLES
Celebes
INDONESIA
New Guinea
PAPUA NEW GUINEA
TUVALU
Luanda
Dodoma
Dar es Salaam
TANZANIA
Jakarta
Java
Surabaya
SOLOMON ISLANDS
ANGOLA
ZAMBIA
COMOROS
MALAWI
Lusaka
Arafura Sea
Port Moresby
EAST TIMOR (TIMOR-LESTE)
Darwin
Harare
ZIMBABWE
MOZAMBIQUE
Antananarivo
MADAGASCAR
MAURITIUS
Reunion
Fr.
NAMIBIA
Windhoek
BOTSWANA
Gaborone
Tshwane (Pretoria)
Maputo
SWAZILAND
Orange
Bloemfontein
INDIAN
OCEAN
Coral Sea
VANUATU
FIJI ISLANDS
New Caledonia
Fr.
AUSTRALIA
SOUTH AFRICA
LESOTHO
Cape Town
Perth
Brisbane
SOUTH PACIFIC OCEAN
Darling
Murray
Sydney
Canberra
Melbourne
North Island
Tasman Sea
Auckland
Tasmania
NEW ZEALAND
Wellington
South Island
Kerguelen Islands
Fr.
The Atlantic, Indian, and Pacific Oceans merge around Antarctica. Some define this as an ocean, calling it the Antarctic Ocean, Austral Ocean, or Southern Ocean. While most accept four oceans (including the Arctic Ocean), there is little international agreement on the name and extent of a fifth ocean.
HERN OCEAN
60°S
Ross Sea
ANTARCTICA
A
B
C
D
E
F
G
H
J
K
ABBREVIATIONS
AUST. .... AUSTRIA
B.&H. .... BOSNIA & HERZEGOVINA
BELG. .... BELGIUM
CROAT. .... CROATIA
CZECH REP. .... CZECH REPUBLIC
DEM. REP. OF THE CONGO .... DEMOCRATIC REPUBLIC OF THE CONGO
EQ. GUINEA .... EQUATORIAL GUINEA
EST. .... ESTONIA
HUNG. .... HUNGARY
KOS. .... KOSOVO
LITH. .... LITHUANIA
MACED. .... MACEDONIA
MOLD. .... MOLDOVA
NETH. .... NETHERLANDS
SERB. .... SERBIA
MONT. .... MONTENEGRO
SLOV. .... SLOVENIA
SWITZ. .... SWITZERLAND
U.A.E. .... UNITED ARAB EMIRATES
9
10
11
12
13
14
15
16

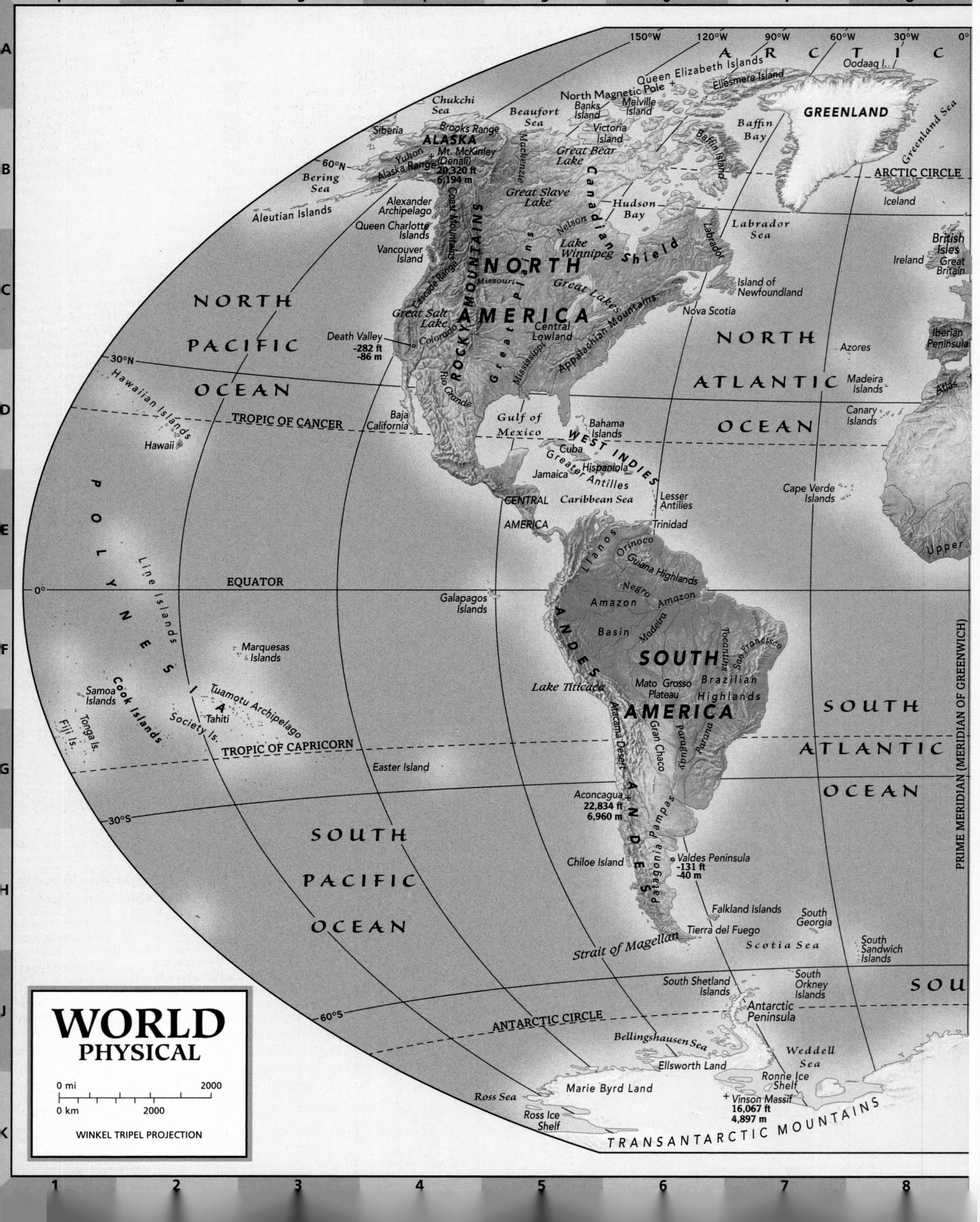
WORLD
PHYSICAL
0 mi
2000
0 km
2000
WINKEL TRIPEL PROJECTION
ARCTIC
NORTH PACIFIC OCEAN
SOUTH PACIFIC OCEAN
NORTH ATLANTIC OCEAN
SOUTH ATLANTIC OCEAN
NORTH AMERICA
SOUTH AMERICA
CENTRAL AMERICA
GREENLAND
ALASKA
POLYNESIA
ROCKY MOUNTAINS
ANDES
Canadian Shield
Great Plains
Mt. McKinley (Denali) 20,320 ft 6,194 m
Death Valley -282 ft -86 m
Aconcagua 22,834 ft 6,960 m
Valdes Peninsula -131 ft -40 m
Vinson Massif 16,067 ft 4,897 m
Queen Elizabeth Islands
Ellesmere Island
Oodaaq I.
North Magnetic Pole
Banks Island
Melville Island
Victoria Island
Chukchi Sea
Beaufort Sea
Siberia
Brooks Range
Yukon
Alaska Range
Mackenzie
Great Bear Lake
Baffin Bay
Baffin Island
Greenland Sea
ARCTIC CIRCLE
Bering Sea
Aleutian Islands
Alexander Archipelago
Queen Charlotte Islands
Vancouver Island
Coast Mountains
Cascade Range
Great Slave Lake
Hudson Bay
Nelson
Lake Winnipeg
Labrador
Labrador Sea
Iceland
British Isles
Ireland
Great Britain
Missouri
Great Lakes
Island of Newfoundland
Nova Scotia
Great Salt Lake
Colorado
Central Lowland
Appalachian Mountains
Mississippi
Rio Grande
Azores
Iberian Peninsula
Madeira Islands
Atlas
Canary Islands
Hawaiian Islands
Hawaii
TROPIC OF CANCER
Baja California
Gulf of Mexico
Bahama Islands
WEST INDIES
Cuba
Hispaniola
Jamaica
Greater Antilles
Caribbean Sea
Lesser Antilles
Trinidad
Cape Verde Islands
Upper
Llanos
Orinoco
Guiana Highlands
Negro
Amazon
Amazon Basin
Madeira
Tocantins
São Francisco
EQUATOR
Galapagos Islands
Line Islands
Marquesas Islands
Lake Titicaca
Mato Grosso Plateau
Brazilian Highlands
Atacama Desert
Gran Chaco
Paraguay
Paraná
Samoa Islands
Cook Islands
Tuamotu Archipelago
Tahiti
Society Is.
Tonga Is.
Fiji Is.
TROPIC OF CAPRICORN
Easter Island
Pampas
Patagonia
Chiloe Island
Falkland Islands
South Georgia
Tierra del Fuego
Strait of Magellan
Scotia Sea
South Sandwich Islands
South Shetland Islands
South Orkney Islands
Antarctic Peninsula
ANTARCTIC CIRCLE
Bellingshausen Sea
Weddell Sea
Ellsworth Land
Ronne Ice Shelf
Marie Byrd Land
Ross Sea
Ross Ice Shelf
TRANSANTARCTIC MOUNTAINS
SOU
PRIME MERIDIAN (MERIDIAN OF GREENWICH)
150°W
120°W
90°W
60°W
30°W
0°
60°N
30°N
0°
30°S
60°S
1 2 3 4 5 6 7 8
A B C D E F G H J K

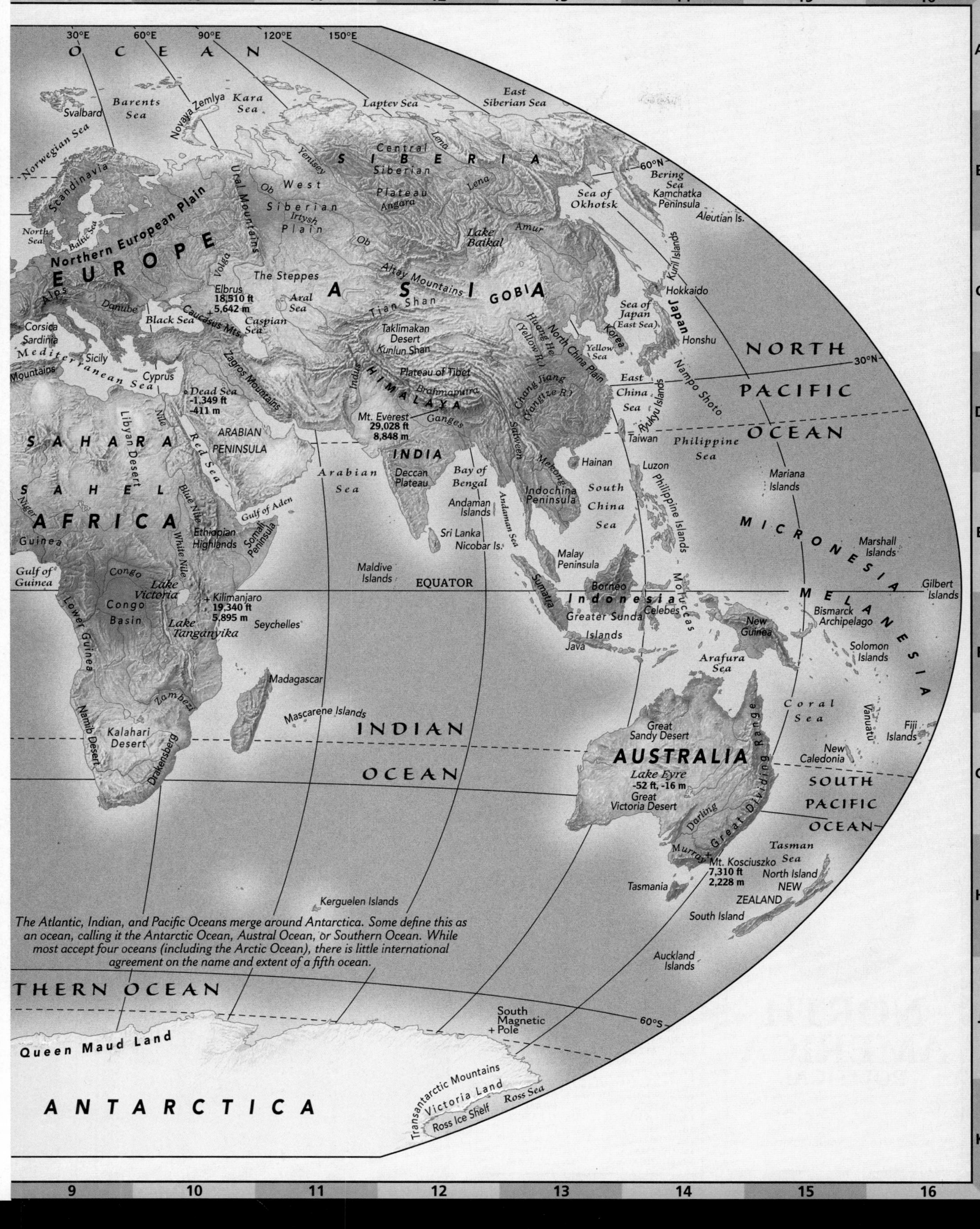

OCEAN
Barents Sea
Kara Sea
Laptev Sea
East Siberian Sea
Svalbard
Novaya Zemlya
Norwegian Sea
Scandinavia
North Sea
Baltic Sea
Northern European Plain
EUROPE
Alps
Danube
Corsica
Sardinia
Sicily
Mediterranean Sea
Mountains
Cyprus
Black Sea
Caucasus Mts.
Elbrus 18,510 ft 5,642 m
Volga
Ural Mountains
SIBERIA
Central Siberian Plateau
Angara
West Siberian Plain
Ob
Irtysh
Yenisey
Lena
Lake Baikal
Amur
Sea of Okhotsk
Bering Sea
Kamchatka Peninsula
Aleutian Is.
Kuril Islands
Hokkaido
Sea of Japan (East Sea)
Japan
Honshu
Korea
Yellow Sea
The Steppes
Aral Sea
Caspian Sea
ASIA
Altay Mountains
GOBI
Tian Shan
Taklimakan Desert
Kunlun Shan
Plateau of Tibet
HIMALAYA
Brahmaputra
Indus
Huang He (Yellow R.)
North China Plain
Chang Jiang (Yangtze R.)
East China Sea
Ryukyu Islands
Nampo Shoto
NORTH PACIFIC OCEAN
Zagros Mountains
Dead Sea -1,349 ft -411 m
ARABIAN PENINSULA
Red Sea
Nile
Libyan Desert
SAHARA
SAHEL
Niger
AFRICA
Blue Nile
White Nile
Ethiopian Highlands
Gulf of Aden
Somali Peninsula
Guinea
Gulf of Guinea
Congo
Congo Basin
Lake Victoria
Lake Tanganyika
Kilimanjaro 19,340 ft 5,895 m
Lower Guinea
Seychelles
Madagascar
Zambezi
Namib Desert
Kalahari Desert
Drakensberg
Mt. Everest 29,028 ft 8,848 m
Ganges
INDIA
Arabian Sea
Deccan Plateau
Bay of Bengal
Andaman Islands
Andaman Sea
Sri Lanka
Nicobar Is.
Maldive Islands
Salween
Mekong
Indochina Peninsula
Hainan
Taiwan
Philippine Sea
Luzon
South China Sea
Philippine Islands
Mariana Islands
MICRONESIA
Marshall Islands
Gilbert Islands
Malay Peninsula
Sumatra
Borneo
Indonesia
Celebes
Moluccas
Greater Sunda Islands
Java
New Guinea
MELANESIA
Bismarck Archipelago
Solomon Islands
Arafura Sea
EQUATOR
Mascarene Islands
INDIAN OCEAN
Great Sandy Desert
AUSTRALIA
Lake Eyre -52 ft, -16 m
Great Victoria Desert
Darling
Murray
Great Dividing Range
Mt. Kosciuszko 7,310 ft 2,228 m
Tasmania
Coral Sea
Vanuatu
Fiji Islands
New Caledonia
SOUTH PACIFIC OCEAN
Tasman Sea
North Island
NEW ZEALAND
South Island
Auckland Islands
Kerguelen Islands
The Atlantic, Indian, and Pacific Oceans merge around Antarctica. Some define this as an ocean, calling it the Antarctic Ocean, Austral Ocean, or Southern Ocean. While most accept four oceans (including the Arctic Ocean), there is little international agreement on the name and extent of a fifth ocean.
THERN OCEAN
South Magnetic Pole
Queen Maud Land
ANTARCTICA
Transantarctic Mountains
Victoria Land
Ross Ice Shelf
Ross Sea
30°E
60°E
90°E
120°E
150°E
60°N
30°N
60°S
9
10
11
12
13
14
15
16
A
B
C
D
E
F
G
H
J
K

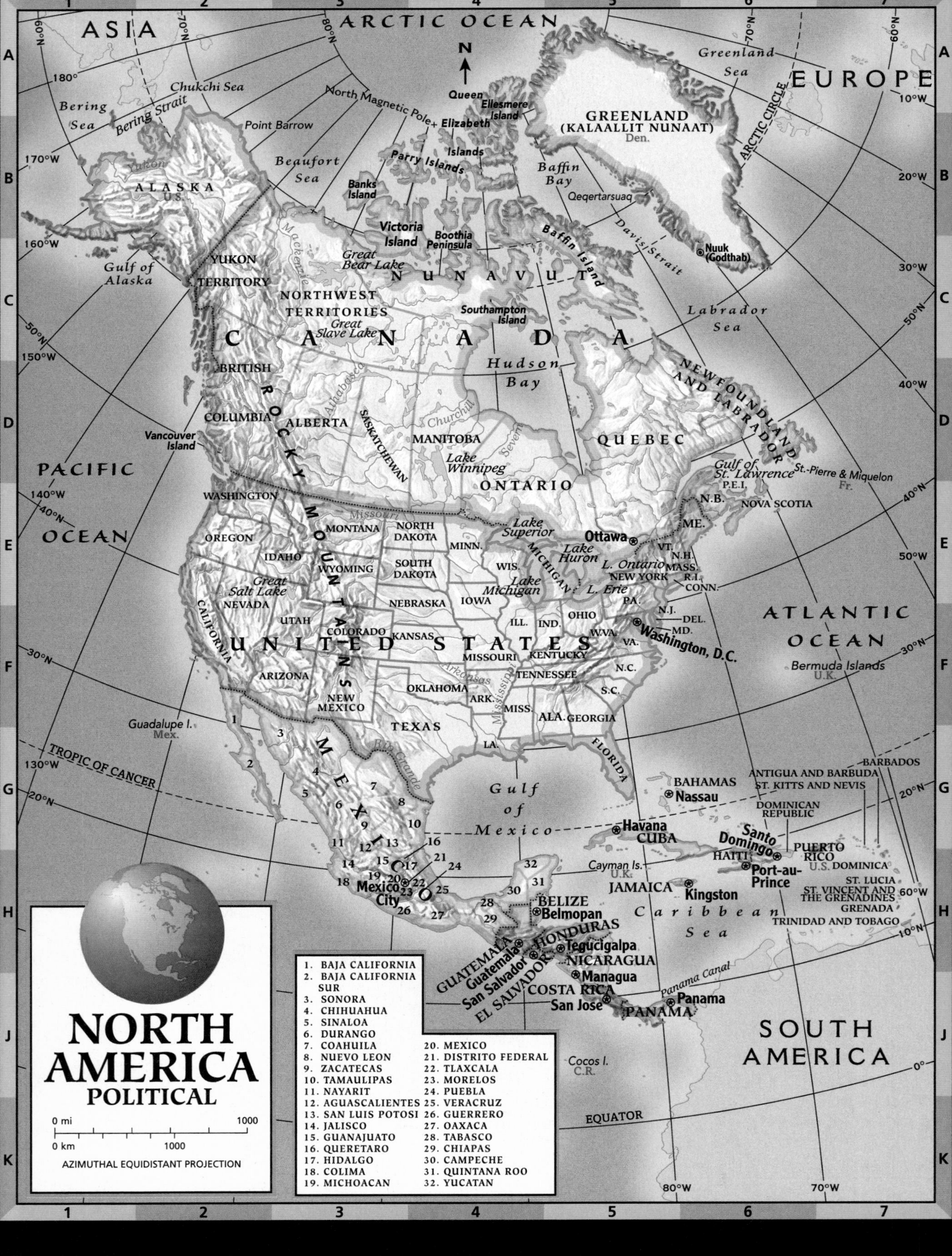
NORTH AMERICA
POLITICAL
0 mi
1000
0 km
1000
AZIMUTHAL EQUIDISTANT PROJECTION
1. BAJA CALIFORNIA
2. BAJA CALIFORNIA SUR
3. SONORA
4. CHIHUAHUA
5. SINALOA
6. DURANGO
7. COAHUILA
8. NUEVO LEON
9. ZACATECAS
10. TAMAULIPAS
11. NAYARIT
12. AGUASCALIENTES
13. SAN LUIS POTOSI
14. JALISCO
15. GUANAJUATO
16. QUERETARO
17. HIDALGO
18. COLIMA
19. MICHOACAN
20. MEXICO
21. DISTRITO FEDERAL
22. TLAXCALA
23. MORELOS
24. PUEBLA
25. VERACRUZ
26. GUERRERO
27. OAXACA
28. TABASCO
29. CHIAPAS
30. CAMPECHE
31. QUINTANA ROO
32. YUCATAN
ARCTIC OCEAN
ASIA
EUROPE
N
Chukchi Sea
Bering Sea
Bering Strait
Point Barrow
North Magnetic Pole
Queen Elizabeth Islands
Ellesmere Island
GREENLAND (KALAALLIT NUNAAT)
Den.
Greenland Sea
ARCTIC CIRCLE
Beaufort Sea
Parry Islands
Banks Island
Victoria Island
Boothia Peninsula
Baffin Bay
Qeqertarsuaq
Baffin Island
Davis Strait
Nuuk (Godthab)
ALASKA
U.S.
Yukon
Mackenzie
Gulf of Alaska
YUKON TERRITORY
NORTHWEST TERRITORIES
Great Bear Lake
NUNAVUT
Great Slave Lake
Southampton Island
Labrador Sea
CANADA
Hudson Bay
BRITISH COLUMBIA
ROCKY MOUNTAINS
ALBERTA
SASKATCHEWAN
Athabasca
Churchill
MANITOBA
Severn
Lake Winnipeg
ONTARIO
QUEBEC
NEWFOUNDLAND AND LABRADOR
Gulf of St. Lawrence
St.-Pierre & Miquelon
Fr.
P.E.I.
N.B.
NOVA SCOTIA
Vancouver Island
PACIFIC OCEAN
WASHINGTON
OREGON
IDAHO
MONTANA
Missouri
NORTH DAKOTA
SOUTH DAKOTA
WYOMING
MINN.
WIS.
Lake Superior
Ottawa
Lake Huron
MICHIGAN
Lake Michigan
L. Ontario
L. Erie
NEW YORK
ME.
VT.
N.H.
MASS.
R.I.
CONN.
PA.
N.J.
DEL.
MD.
Great Salt Lake
NEVADA
CALIFORNIA
UTAH
COLORADO
NEBRASKA
IOWA
ILL.
IND.
OHIO
W.VA.
VA.
Washington, D.C.
KANSAS
MISSOURI
KENTUCKY
UNITED STATES
ATLANTIC OCEAN
Bermuda Islands
U.K.
ARIZONA
NEW MEXICO
OKLAHOMA
Arkansas
TENNESSEE
N.C.
S.C.
ARK.
MISS.
ALA.
GEORGIA
Mississippi
TEXAS
LA.
FLORIDA
Rio Grande
Guadalupe I.
Mex.
TROPIC OF CANCER
MEXICO
Gulf of Mexico
BAHAMAS
Nassau
Havana
CUBA
ANTIGUA AND BARBUDA
ST. KITTS AND NEVIS
BARBADOS
DOMINICAN REPUBLIC
Santo Domingo
HAITI
Port-au-Prince
PUERTO RICO
U.S.
DOMINICA
ST. LUCIA
ST. VINCENT AND THE GRENADINES
GRENADA
TRINIDAD AND TOBAGO
Cayman Is.
U.K.
JAMAICA
Kingston
Mexico City
BELIZE
Belmopan
Caribbean Sea
HONDURAS
Tegucigalpa
GUATEMALA
Guatemala
San Salvador
EL SALVADOR
NICARAGUA
Managua
COSTA RICA
San Jose
Panama Canal
Panama
PANAMA
Cocos I.
C.R.
SOUTH AMERICA
EQUATOR
180°
170°W
160°W
150°W
140°W
130°W
80°W
70°W
60°N
70°N
80°N
50°N
40°N
30°N
20°N
10°N
0°
10°W
20°W
30°W
40°W
50°W
60°W
1
2
3
4
5
6
7
A
B
C
D
E
F
G
H
J
K

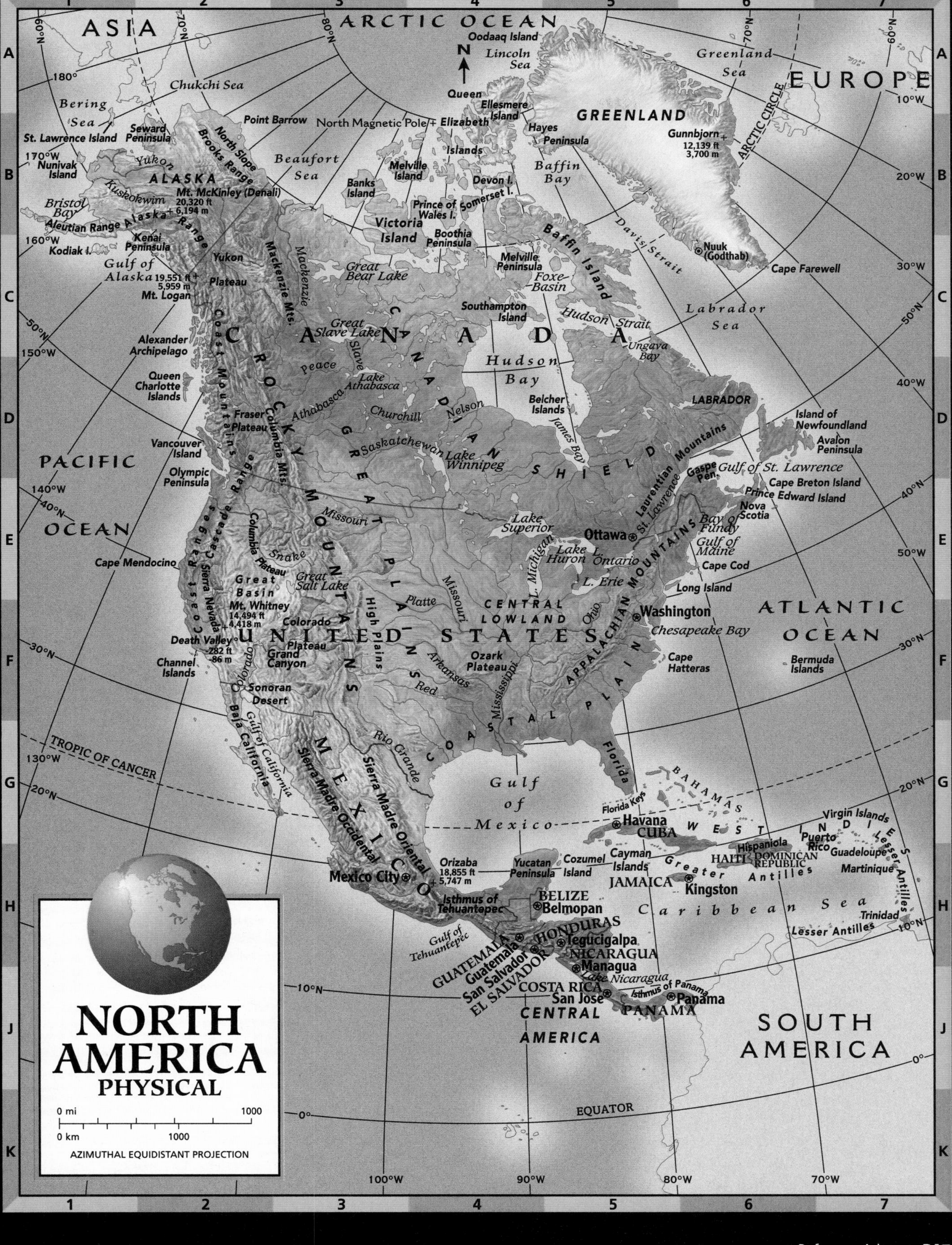
NORTH AMERICA
PHYSICAL
0 mi 1000
0 km 1000
AZIMUTHAL EQUIDISTANT PROJECTION
ASIA
ARCTIC OCEAN
EUROPE
PACIFIC OCEAN
ATLANTIC OCEAN
SOUTH AMERICA
CENTRAL AMERICA
Oodaaq Island
Lincoln Sea
Greenland Sea
Chukchi Sea
Bering Sea
St. Lawrence Island
Seward Peninsula
Point Barrow
North Magnetic Pole
Queen Elizabeth Islands
Ellesmere Island
Hayes Peninsula
GREENLAND
Gunnbjorn 12,139 ft 3,700 m
ARCTIC CIRCLE
Nunivak Island
Yukon
ALASKA
North Slope
Brooks Range
Beaufort Sea
Melville Island
Banks Island
Devon I.
Baffin Bay
Kuskokwim
Mt. McKinley (Denali) 20,320 ft 6,194 m
Bristol Bay
Alaska Range
Aleutian Range
Kenai Peninsula
Kodiak I.
Prince of Wales I.
Somerset I.
Victoria Island
Boothia Peninsula
Baffin Island
Davis Strait
Nuuk (Godthab)
Cape Farewell
Gulf of Alaska
19,551 ft 5,959 m
Mt. Logan
Yukon Plateau
Mackenzie Mts.
Mackenzie
Great Bear Lake
Melville Peninsula
Foxe Basin
Southampton Island
Hudson Strait
Labrador Sea
Alexander Archipelago
CANADA
Great Slave Lake
Slave
Ungava Bay
Peace
Lake Athabasca
Athabasca
Hudson Bay
Queen Charlotte Islands
CANADIAN SHIELD
Churchill
Nelson
Belcher Islands
James Bay
LABRADOR
Island of Newfoundland
Avalon Peninsula
Fraser Plateau
Columbia Mts.
Coast Mountains
ROCKY MOUNTAINS
Vancouver Island
Saskatchewan
Lake Winnipeg
Laurentian Mountains
Gaspe Pen.
Gulf of St. Lawrence
Cape Breton Island
Prince Edward Island
Olympic Peninsula
Cascade Range
GREAT PLAINS
Missouri
Lake Superior
Ottawa
St. Lawrence
Nova Scotia
Bay of Fundy
Gulf of Maine
Cape Cod
Columbia Plateau
Snake
Coast Ranges
Sierra Nevada
Cape Mendocino
Lake Michigan
Lake Huron
L. Ontario
L. Erie
APPALACHIAN MOUNTAINS
Long Island
Great Basin
Great Salt Lake
Mt. Whitney 14,494 ft 4,418 m
High Plains
Platte
CENTRAL LOWLAND
Ohio
Washington
Chesapeake Bay
Colorado Plateau
UNITED STATES
Death Valley -282 ft -86 m
Grand Canyon
Ozark Plateau
Arkansas
Red
Mississippi
Cape Hatteras
Bermuda Islands
Channel Islands
Colorado
Sonoran Desert
COASTAL PLAIN
Baja California
Gulf of California
TROPIC OF CANCER
Rio Grande
Florida
MEXICO
Sierra Madre Occidental
Sierra Madre Oriental
Gulf of Mexico
BAHAMAS
Florida Keys
Havana
CUBA
WEST INDIES
Virgin Islands
Hispaniola
Puerto Rico
HAITI
DOMINICAN REPUBLIC
Guadeloupe
Martinique
Lesser Antilles
Orizaba 18,855 ft 5,747 m
Mexico City
Yucatan Peninsula
Cozumel Island
Cayman Islands
Greater Antilles
JAMAICA
Kingston
Isthmus of Tehuantepec
BELIZE
Belmopan
Caribbean Sea
Trinidad
Gulf of Tehuantepec
GUATEMALA
Guatemala
HONDURAS
Tegucigalpa
NICARAGUA
Managua
San Salvador
EL SALVADOR
Lake Nicaragua
COSTA RICA
San José
Isthmus of Panama
Panama
PANAMA
EQUATOR
180° 170°W 160°W 150°W 140°W 130°W 100°W 90°W 80°W 70°W 60°W 10°W 20°W 30°W 40°W 50°W
60°N 70°N 80°N 50°N 40°N 30°N 20°N 10°N 0°
A B C D E F G H J K
1 2 3 4 5 6 7

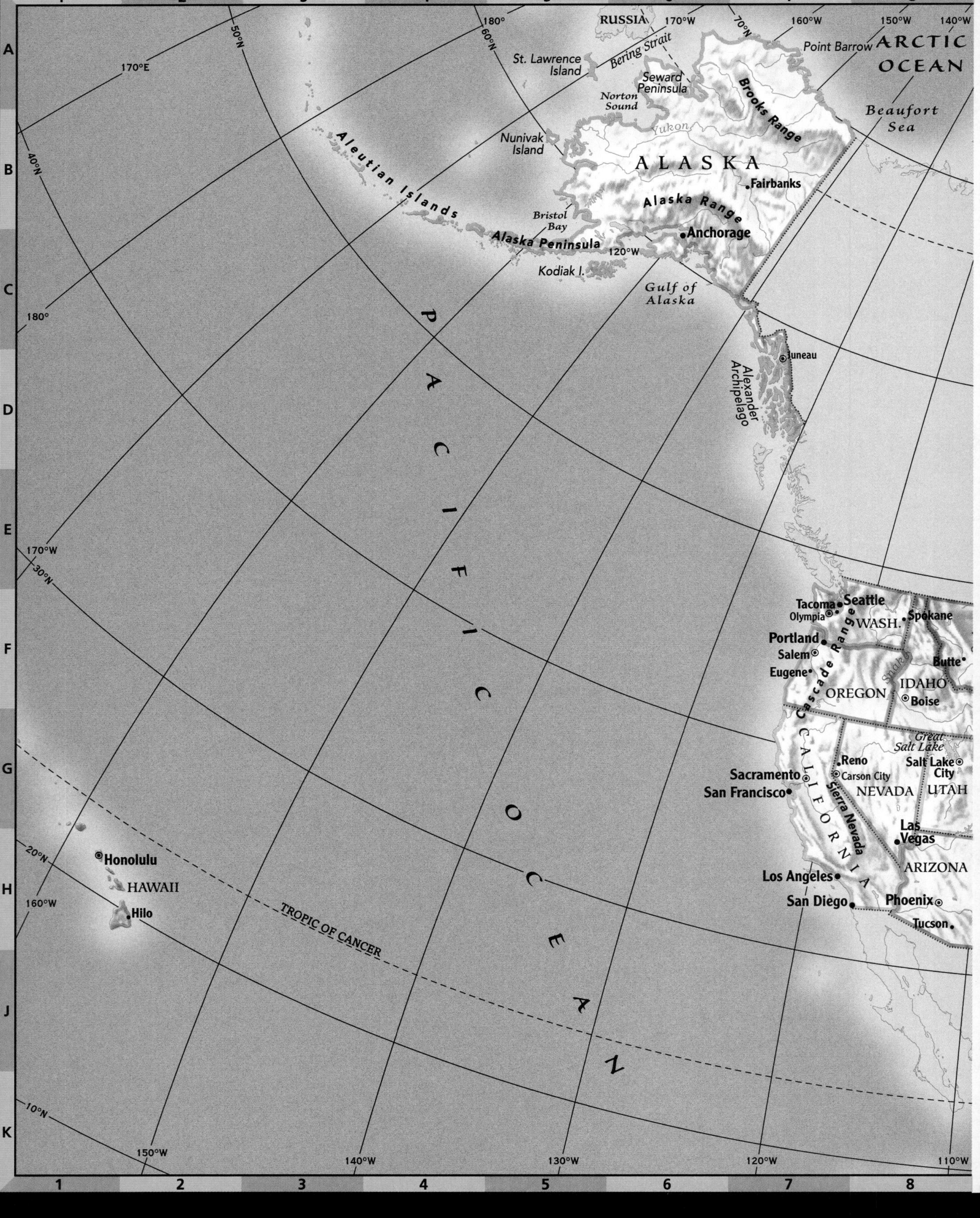
RUSSIA
Bering Strait
St. Lawrence Island
Seward Peninsula
Norton Sound
Brooks Range
Point Barrow
ARCTIC OCEAN
Beaufort Sea
Nunivak Island
Yukon
ALASKA
Fairbanks
Aleutian Islands
Alaska Range
Bristol Bay
Anchorage
Alaska Peninsula
Kodiak I.
Gulf of Alaska
Juneau
Alexander Archipelago
PACIFIC OCEAN
Tacoma
Seattle
Olympia
Spokane
WASH.
Cascade Range
Portland
Salem
Eugene
OREGON
Snake
IDAHO
Boise
Butte
Great Salt Lake
Salt Lake City
UTAH
Reno
Carson City
NEVADA
Sacramento
San Francisco
CALIFORNIA
Sierra Nevada
Las Vegas
ARIZONA
Los Angeles
San Diego
Phoenix
Tucson
Honolulu
HAWAII
Hilo
TROPIC OF CANCER
180°
170°W
160°W
150°W
140°W
170°E
70°N
60°N
50°N
40°N
30°N
20°N
10°N
120°W
130°W
110°W

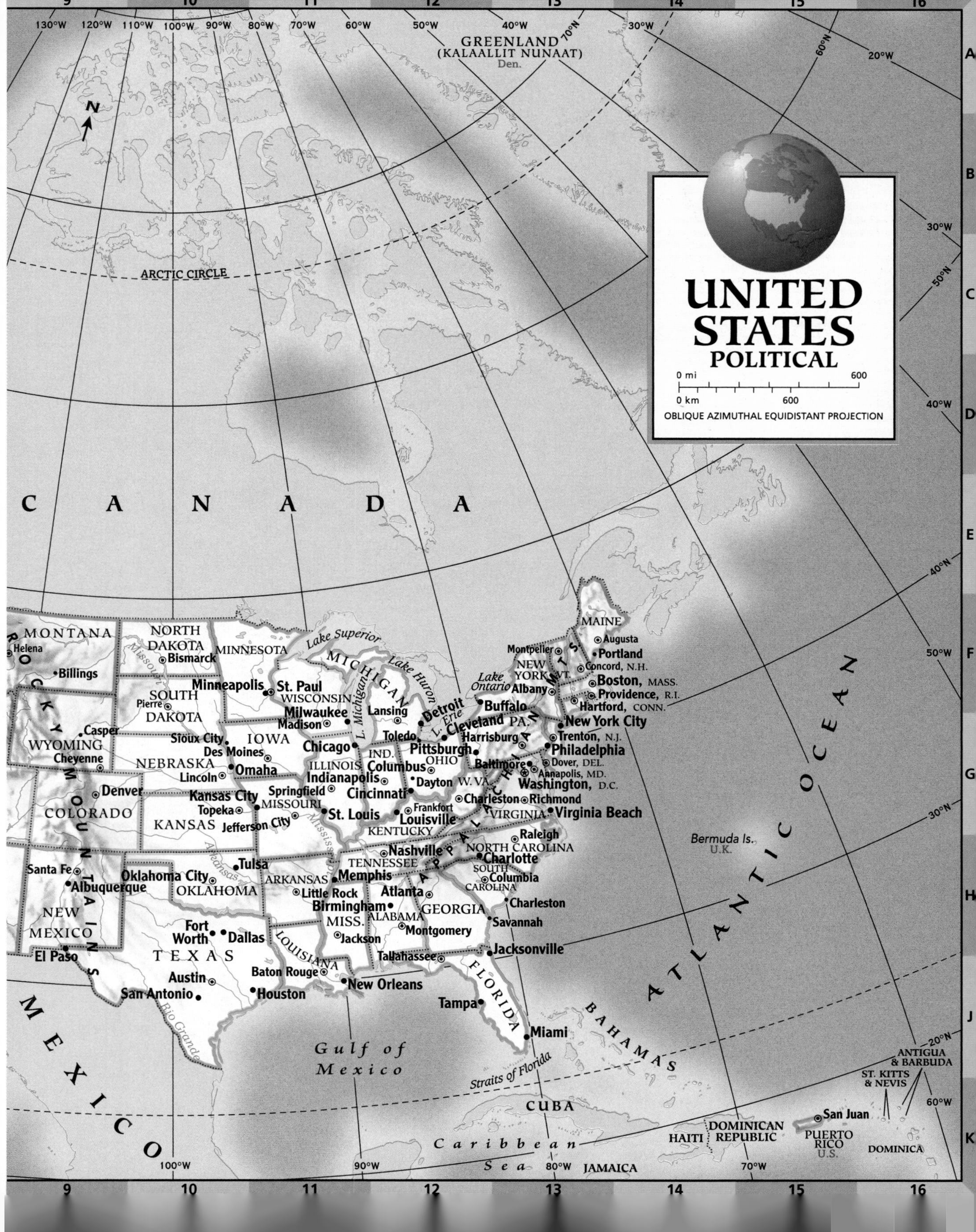
UNITED STATES
POLITICAL
0 mi
600
0 km
600
OBLIQUE AZIMUTHAL EQUIDISTANT PROJECTION
9
10
11
12
13
14
15
16
A
B
C
D
E
F
G
H
J
K
130°W
120°W
110°W
100°W
90°W
80°W
70°W
60°W
50°W
40°W
30°W
20°W
70°N
60°N
50°N
40°N
30°N
20°N
GREENLAND
(KALAALLIT NUNAAT)
Den.
N
ARCTIC CIRCLE
CANADA
MONTANA
Helena
Billings
NORTH DAKOTA
Bismarck
MINNESOTA
Lake Superior
MICHIGAN
Lake Huron
Missouri
SOUTH DAKOTA
Pierre
Minneapolis
St. Paul
WISCONSIN
Milwaukee
Madison
Lansing
L. Michigan
Detroit
L. Erie
Lake Ontario
NEW YORK
Albany
VT.
Montpelier
MAINE
Augusta
Portland
Concord, N.H.
Boston, MASS.
Providence, R.I.
Hartford, CONN.
Buffalo
Cleveland
PA.
New York City
Toledo
Trenton, N.J.
Philadelphia
Harrisburg
Pittsburgh
ROCKY MOUNTAINS
WYOMING
Casper
Cheyenne
Sioux City
IOWA
Des Moines
Chicago
NEBRASKA
Lincoln
Omaha
ILLINOIS
IND.
Columbus
OHIO
Indianapolis
Dayton
Baltimore
Dover, DEL.
Annapolis, MD.
Washington, D.C.
W. VA.
Denver
COLORADO
Kansas City
Springfield
Cincinnati
Charleston
Richmond
Topeka
MISSOURI
St. Louis
Frankfort
Louisville
VIRGINIA
Virginia Beach
KANSAS
Jefferson City
KENTUCKY
APPALACHIAN MTS.
Raleigh
Nashville
NORTH CAROLINA
Charlotte
TENNESSEE
Santa Fe
Albuquerque
Oklahoma City
OKLAHOMA
Tulsa
Arkansas
ARKANSAS
Little Rock
Memphis
Mississippi
SOUTH CAROLINA
Columbia
Charleston
Atlanta
GEORGIA
Birmingham
MISS.
ALABAMA
Savannah
NEW MEXICO
Fort Worth
Dallas
Jackson
Montgomery
El Paso
TEXAS
LOUISIANA
Tallahassee
Jacksonville
FLORIDA
Baton Rouge
Austin
San Antonio
Houston
New Orleans
Tampa
Miami
Rio Grande
MEXICO
Gulf of Mexico
Straits of Florida
BAHAMAS
ATLANTIC OCEAN
Bermuda Is.
U.K.
CUBA
Caribbean Sea
JAMAICA
HAITI
DOMINICAN REPUBLIC
San Juan
PUERTO RICO
U.S.
ANTIGUA & BARBUDA
ST. KITTS & NEVIS
DOMINICA

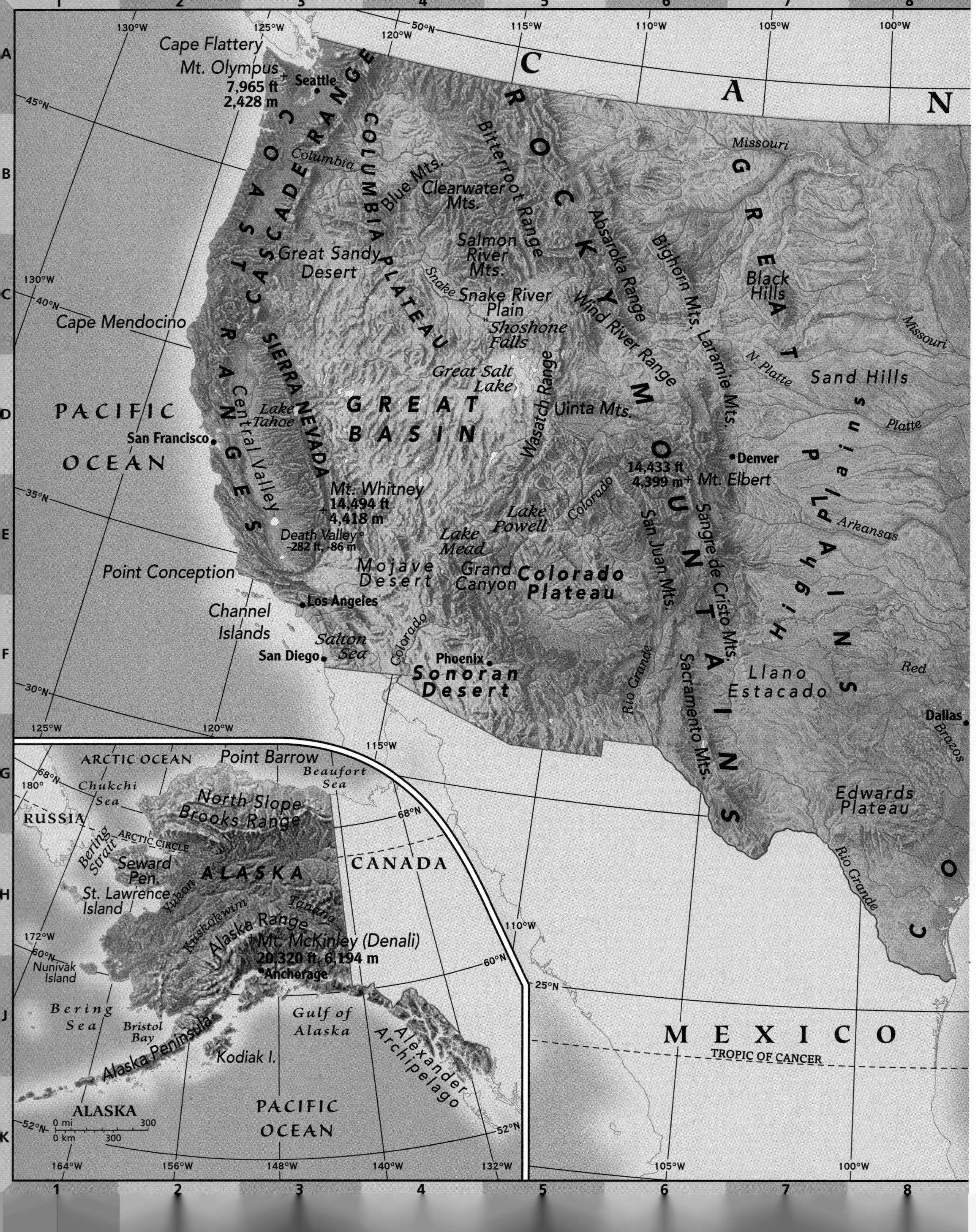

Cape Flattery
Mt. Olympus
7,965 ft
2,428 m
Seattle
CASCADE RANGE
COAST RANGES
COLUMBIA PLATEAU
Columbia
Blue Mts.
Clearwater Mts.
Bitterroot Range
ROCKY MOUNTAINS
Salmon River Mts.
Great Sandy Desert
Snake
Snake River Plain
Shoshone Falls
Absaroka Range
Wind River Range
Bighorn Mts.
Laramie Mts.
Missouri
GREAT PLAINS
Black Hills
N. Platte
Sand Hills
Platte
High Plains
Cape Mendocino
SIERRA NEVADA
Great Salt Lake
Wasatch Range
Uinta Mts.
GREAT BASIN
Lake Tahoe
Central Valley
PACIFIC OCEAN
San Francisco
Denver
14,433 ft
4,399 m
Mt. Elbert
Mt. Whitney
14,494 ft
4,418 m
Colorado
Lake Powell
San Juan Mts.
Sangre de Cristo Mts.
Arkansas
Death Valley
-282 ft, -86 m
Lake Mead
Point Conception
Mojave Desert
Grand Canyon
Colorado Plateau
Los Angeles
Channel Islands
Salton Sea
San Diego
Phoenix
Sonoran Desert
Rio Grande
Sacramento Mts.
Llano Estacado
Red
Dallas
Brazos
Edwards Plateau
CANADA
MEXICO
TROPIC OF CANCER
ARCTIC OCEAN
Point Barrow
Beaufort Sea
Chukchi Sea
RUSSIA
North Slope
Brooks Range
ARCTIC CIRCLE
Bering Strait
Seward Pen.
ALASKA
St. Lawrence Island
Yukon
Tanana
Kuskokwim
Alaska Range
Mt. McKinley (Denali)
20,320 ft, 6,194 m
Anchorage
Nunivak Island
Bering Sea
Bristol Bay
Gulf of Alaska
Alexander Archipelago
Alaska Peninsula
Kodiak I.
PACIFIC OCEAN
0 mi 300
0 km 300

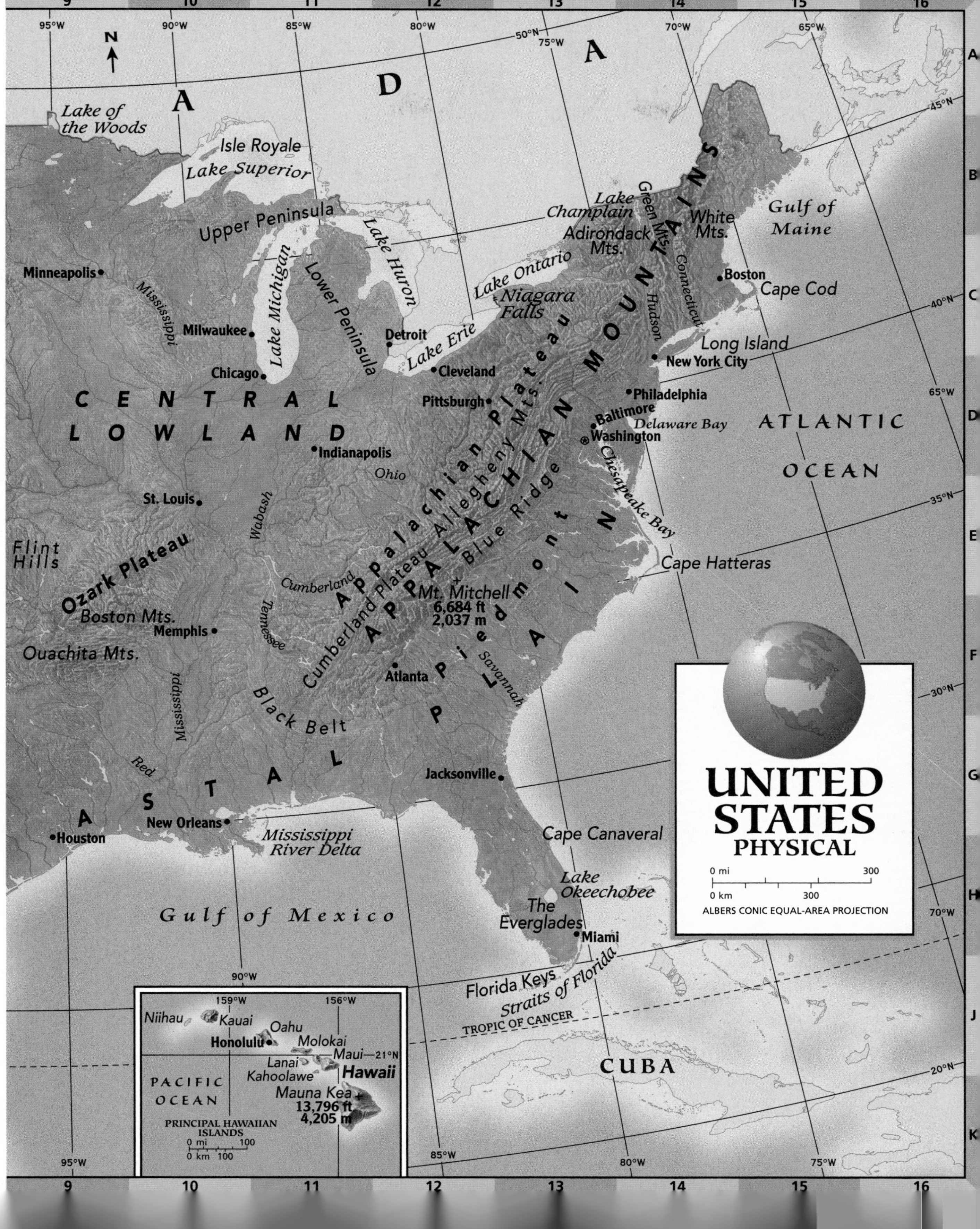
UNITED STATES
PHYSICAL
0 mi 300
0 km 300
ALBERS CONIC EQUAL-AREA PROJECTION
CENTRAL LOWLAND
APPALACHIAN MOUNTAINS
COASTAL PLAIN
ATLANTIC OCEAN
Gulf of Mexico
Gulf of Maine
CUBA
Lake of the Woods
Isle Royale
Lake Superior
Upper Peninsula
Lower Peninsula
Lake Michigan
Lake Huron
Lake Erie
Lake Ontario
Lake Champlain
Niagara Falls
Adirondack Mts.
Green Mts.
White Mts.
Connecticut
Hudson
Boston
Cape Cod
Long Island
New York City
Philadelphia
Baltimore
Washington
Delaware Bay
Chesapeake Bay
Cape Hatteras
Minneapolis
Milwaukee
Chicago
Detroit
Cleveland
Pittsburgh
Indianapolis
St. Louis
Memphis
Atlanta
Jacksonville
New Orleans
Houston
Miami
Mississippi
Ohio
Wabash
Cumberland
Tennessee
Red
Savannah
Appalachian Plateau
Allegheny Mts.
Blue Ridge
Piedmont
Cumberland Plateau
Mt. Mitchell
6,684 ft
2,037 m
Flint Hills
Ozark Plateau
Boston Mts.
Ouachita Mts.
Black Belt
Mississippi River Delta
Cape Canaveral
Lake Okeechobee
The Everglades
Florida Keys
Straits of Florida
TROPIC OF CANCER
Niihau
Kauai
Oahu
Honolulu
Molokai
Maui
Lanai
Kahoolawe
Hawaii
Mauna Kea
13,796 ft
4,205 m
PACIFIC OCEAN
PRINCIPAL HAWAIIAN ISLANDS
0 mi 100
0 km 100
159°W
156°W
21°N
95°W
90°W
85°W
80°W
75°W
70°W
65°W
50°N
45°N
40°N
35°N
30°N
20°N

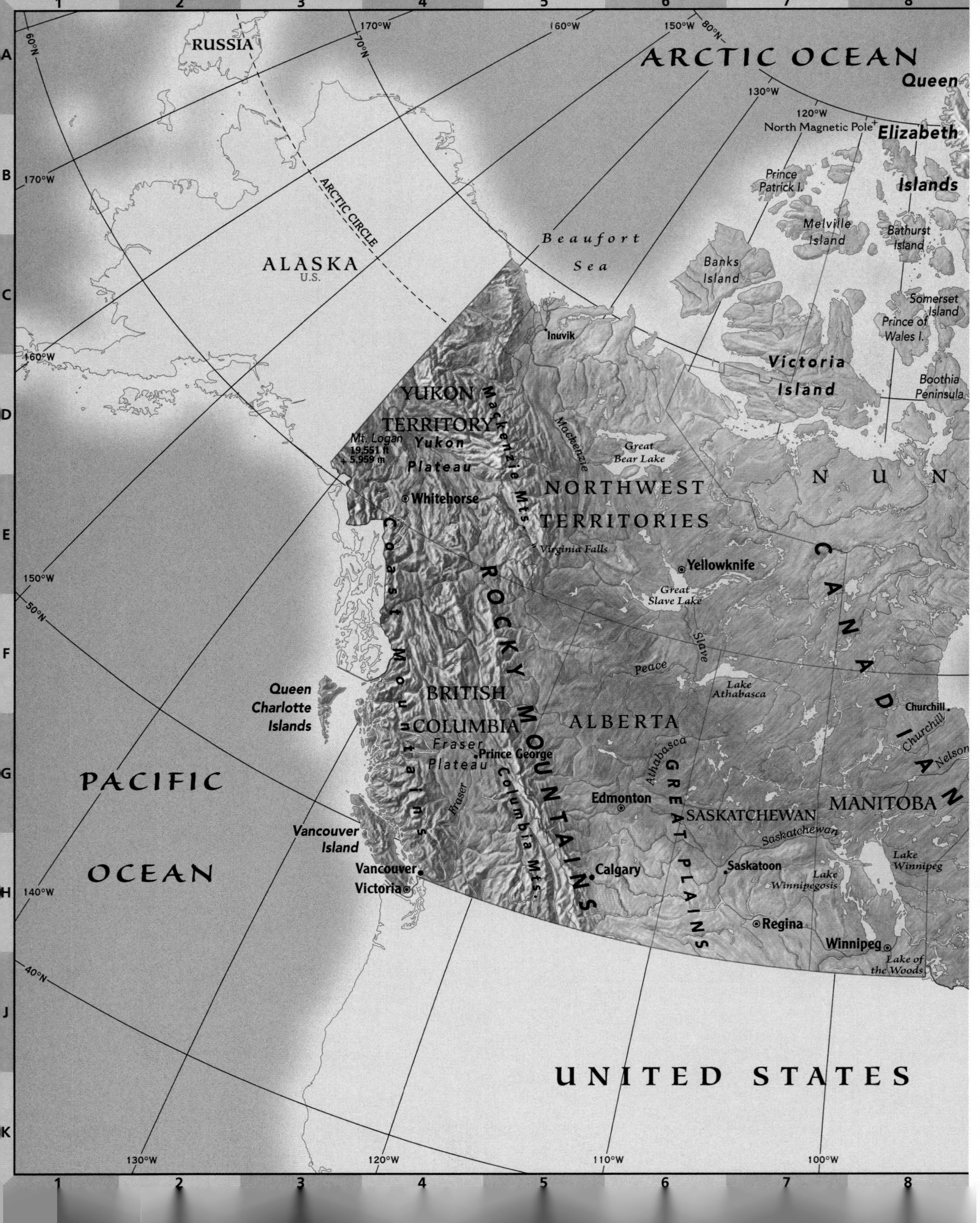

RUSSIA
ARCTIC OCEAN
Queen
Elizabeth
Islands
North Magnetic Pole
Prince Patrick I.
Melville Island
Bathurst Island
Banks Island
Beaufort Sea
ARCTIC CIRCLE
ALASKA
U.S.
Somerset Island
Prince of Wales I.
Inuvik
Victoria Island
Boothia Peninsula
YUKON TERRITORY
Mackenzie Mts.
Mackenzie
Mt. Logan
19,551 ft
5,959 m
Yukon Plateau
Great Bear Lake
NORTHWEST TERRITORIES
NUN
Whitehorse
Coast Mountains
Virginia Falls
Yellowknife
ROCKY MOUNTAINS
Great Slave Lake
CANADIAN
Slave
Peace
Lake Athabasca
Queen Charlotte Islands
BRITISH COLUMBIA
ALBERTA
Churchill
Churchill
Fraser Plateau
Prince George
Athabasca
Nelson
PACIFIC OCEAN
Fraser
Columbia Mts.
Edmonton
GREAT PLAINS
SASKATCHEWAN
MANITOBA
Vancouver Island
Saskatchewan
Lake Winnipeg
Vancouver
Calgary
Saskatoon
Lake Winnipegosis
Victoria
Regina
Winnipeg
Lake of the Woods
UNITED STATES
170°W
160°W
150°W
140°W
130°W
120°W
110°W
100°W
80°N
70°N
60°N
50°N
40°N

CANADA
PHYSICAL/POLITICAL
0 mi
400
0 km
400
AZIMUTHAL EQUIDISTANT PROJECTION
GREENLAND
(KALAALLIT NUNAAT)
Den.
ICELAND
Ellesmere Island
Devon Island
Baffin Bay
Baffin Island
Davis Strait
Melville Peninsula
Foxe Basin
Iqaluit
Southampton Island
Hudson Strait
Labrador Sea
Ungava Bay
Hudson Bay
Belcher Islands
James Bay
NEWFOUNDLAND AND LABRADOR
Cartwright
Schefferville
Happy Valley-Goose Bay
Smallwood Reservoir
Churchill Falls
Island of Newfoundland
St. John's
Avalon Peninsula
QUEBEC
Manicouagan Reservoir
Sept-Îles
Anticosti I.
Gulf of St. Lawrence
St.-Pierre & Miquelon
Fr.
Gaspe Pen.
PRINCE EDWARD ISLAND
Cape Breton I.
Charlottetown
NEW BRUNSWICK
NOVA SCOTIA
ATLANTIC OCEAN
Chicoutimi
Quebec
Fredericton
Saint John
Halifax
Bay of Fundy
St. Lawrence
Rouyn-Noranda
ONTARIO
SHIELD
Lake Nipigon
Thunder Bay
Lake Superior
Sudbury
Montreal
Ottawa
Lake Huron
Lake Michigan
Toronto
L. Ontario
Niagara Falls
London
L. Erie
N
80°N
70°N
60°N
50°N
40°N
90°W
80°W
70°W
60°W
50°W
40°W
30°W
20°W
10°W

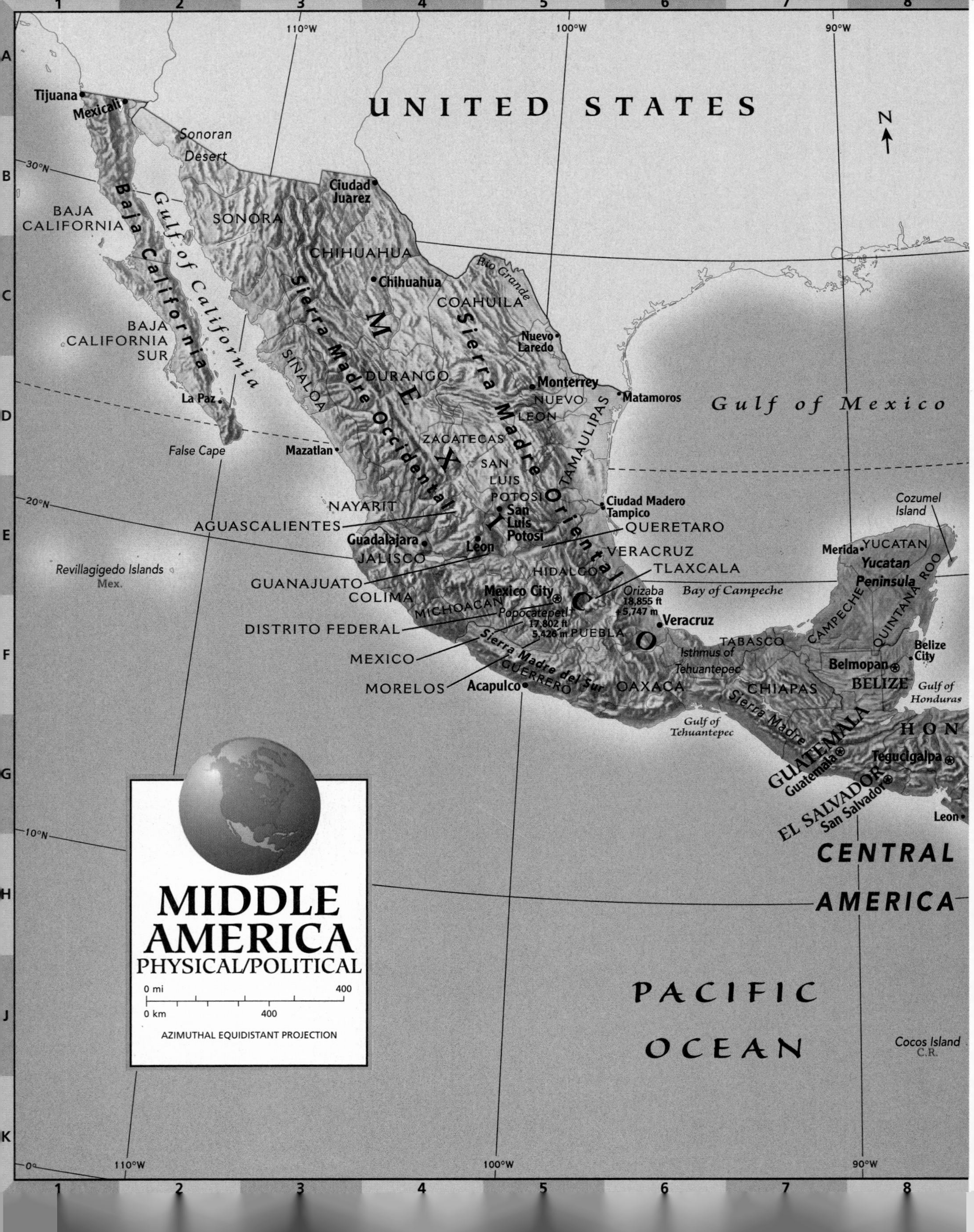

MIDDLE AMERICA
PHYSICAL/POLITICAL
0 mi 400
0 km 400
AZIMUTHAL EQUIDISTANT PROJECTION
UNITED STATES
MEXICO
Gulf of Mexico
PACIFIC OCEAN
CENTRAL AMERICA
Tijuana
Mexicali
Sonoran Desert
BAJA CALIFORNIA
Baja California
Gulf of California
BAJA CALIFORNIA SUR
La Paz
False Cape
Revillagigedo Islands Mex.
SONORA
Ciudad Juarez
CHIHUAHUA
Chihuahua
COAHUILA
Rio Grande
Nuevo Laredo
Monterrey
Matamoros
NUEVO LEON
TAMAULIPAS
SINALOA
DURANGO
Mazatlan
Sierra Madre Occidental
Sierra Madre Oriental
ZACATECAS
SAN LUIS POTOSI
San Luis Potosi
NAYARIT
AGUASCALIENTES
Guadalajara
Leon
JALISCO
GUANAJUATO
COLIMA
MICHOACAN
DISTRITO FEDERAL
MEXICO
MORELOS
Mexico City
Popocatepetl 17,802 ft 5,426 m
Orizaba 18,855 ft 5,747 m
HIDALGO
QUERETARO
VERACRUZ
TLAXCALA
PUEBLA
Ciudad Madero
Tampico
Veracruz
Bay of Campeche
Sierra Madre del Sur
GUERRERO
Acapulco
OAXACA
Isthmus of Tehuantepec
Gulf of Tehuantepec
TABASCO
CHIAPAS
Sierra Madre
CAMPECHE
YUCATAN
Merida
Yucatan Peninsula
QUINTANA ROO
Cozumel Island
Belize City
Belmopan
BELIZE
Gulf of Honduras
GUATEMALA
Guatemala
EL SALVADOR
San Salvador
HON
Tegucigalpa
Leon
Cocos Island C.R.
110°W
100°W
90°W
30°N
20°N
10°N
0°
N

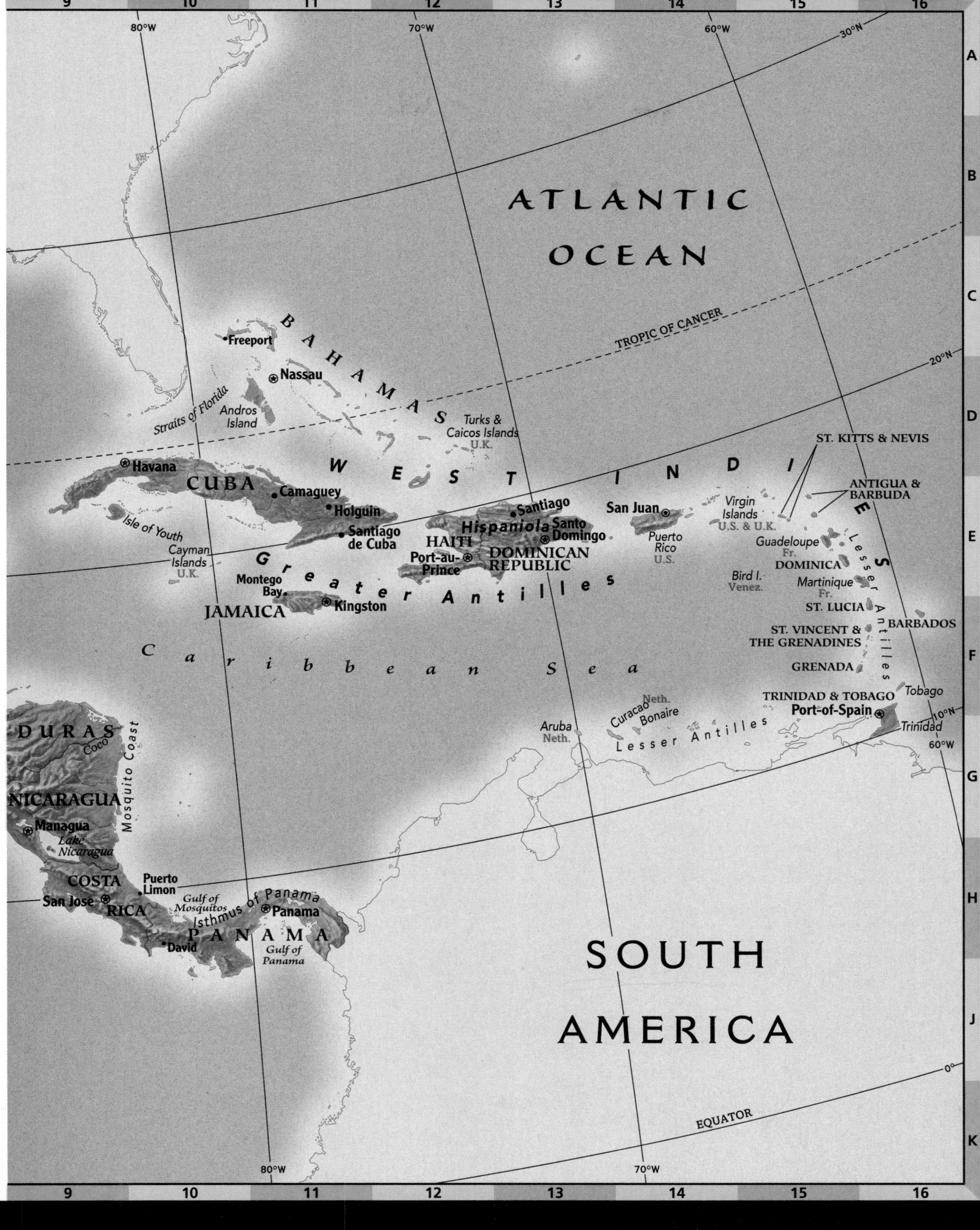

ATLANTIC OCEAN
TROPIC OF CANCER
BAHAMAS
Freeport
Nassau
Andros Island
Straits of Florida
Turks & Caicos Islands U.K.
WEST INDIES
Havana
CUBA
Camaguey
Holguin
Santiago de Cuba
Isle of Youth
Cayman Islands U.K.
Hispaniola
Santiago
Santo Domingo
HAITI
Port-au-Prince
DOMINICAN REPUBLIC
San Juan
Puerto Rico U.S.
Virgin Islands U.S. & U.K.
ST. KITTS & NEVIS
ANTIGUA & BARBUDA
Guadeloupe Fr.
DOMINICA
Martinique Fr.
ST. LUCIA
BARBADOS
ST. VINCENT & THE GRENADINES
GRENADA
Tobago
TRINIDAD & TOBAGO
Port-of-Spain
Trinidad
Lesser Antilles
Bird I. Venez.
Greater Antilles
Montego Bay
Kingston
JAMAICA
Caribbean Sea
Aruba Neth.
Curacao Neth.
Bonaire
Lesser Antilles
DURAS
Coco
Mosquito Coast
NICARAGUA
Managua
Lake Nicaragua
COSTA RICA
San Jose
Puerto Limon
Gulf of Mosquitos
Isthmus of Panama
Panama
PANAMA
David
Gulf of Panama
SOUTH AMERICA
EQUATOR
80°W
70°W
60°W
30°N
20°N
10°N
0°

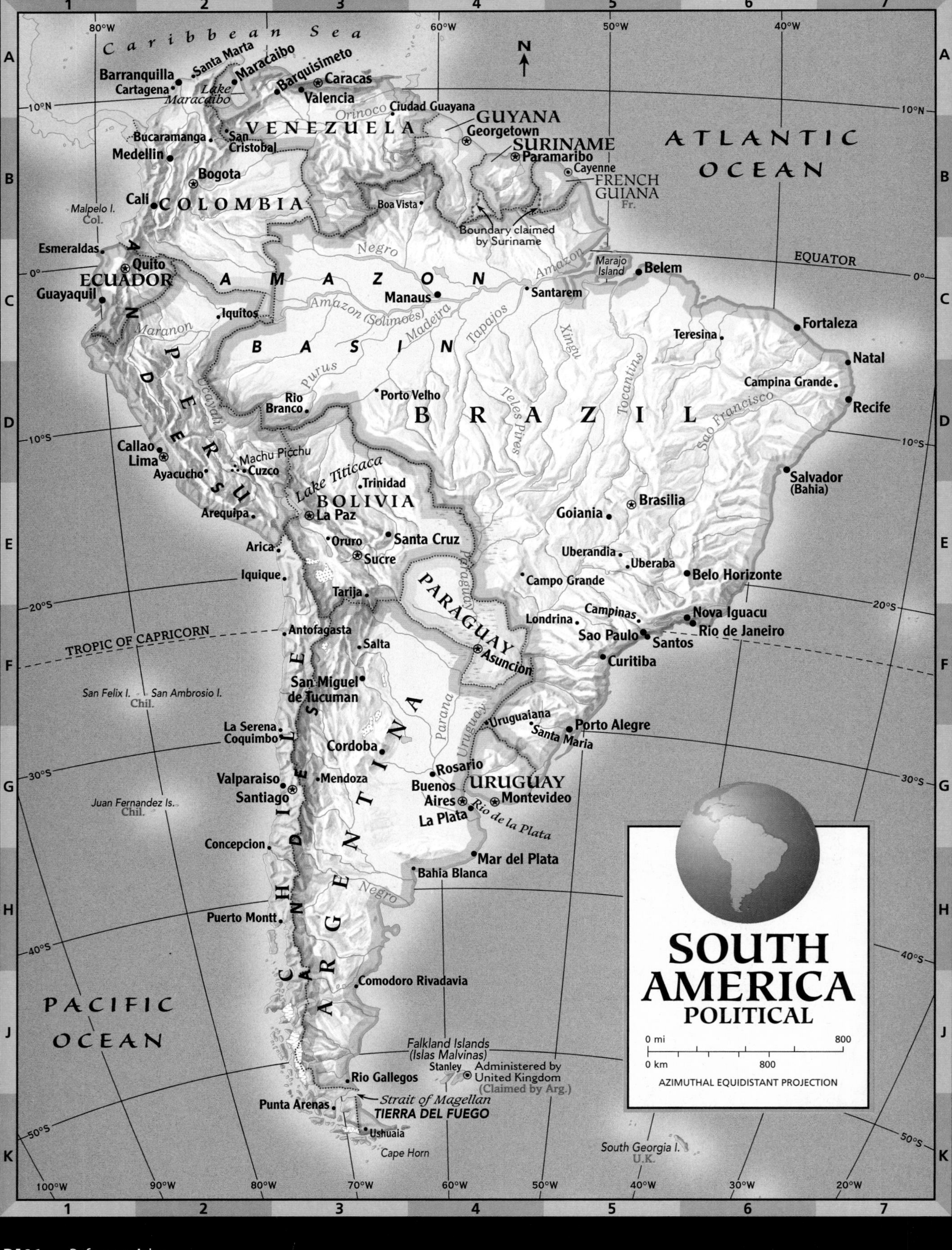
SOUTH AMERICA
POLITICAL
0 mi 800
0 km 800
AZIMUTHAL EQUIDISTANT PROJECTION
Caribbean Sea
ATLANTIC OCEAN
PACIFIC OCEAN
VENEZUELA
GUYANA
SURINAME
FRENCH GUIANA
Fr.
COLOMBIA
ECUADOR
PERU
BRAZIL
BOLIVIA
PARAGUAY
URUGUAY
ARGENTINA
AMAZON BASIN
ANDES
Barranquilla
Cartagena
Santa Marta
Maracaibo
Lake Maracaibo
Barquisimeto
Caracas
Valencia
Ciudad Guayana
Orinoco
Georgetown
Paramaribo
Cayenne
Bucaramanga
San Cristobal
Medellin
Bogota
Cali
Malpelo I.
Col.
Boa Vista
Boundary claimed by Suriname
Esmeraldas
Quito
Guayaquil
Negro
Amazon
Marajo Island
Belem
EQUATOR
Manaus
Santarem
Iquitos
Maranon
Amazon (Solimoes)
Madeira
Tapajos
Xingu
Tocantins
Teresina
Fortaleza
Natal
Campina Grande
Recife
Purus
Porto Velho
Rio Branco
Ucayali
Teles Pires
Sao Francisco
Callao
Lima
Machu Picchu
Cuzco
Ayacucho
Lake Titicaca
Trinidad
Salvador (Bahia)
La Paz
Brasilia
Goiania
Arequipa
Arica
Oruro
Santa Cruz
Sucre
Paraguay
Uberandia
Uberaba
Iquique
Campo Grande
Belo Horizonte
Tarija
Londrina
Campinas
Nova Iguacu
Rio de Janeiro
Sao Paulo
Santos
Antofagasta
TROPIC OF CAPRICORN
Salta
Asuncion
Curitiba
San Miguel de Tucuman
San Felix I.
San Ambrosio I.
Chil.
Parana
Uruguay
Uruguaiana
Santa Maria
Porto Alegre
La Serena
Coquimbo
Cordoba
Rosario
Valparaiso
Mendoza
Santiago
Buenos Aires
Montevideo
Juan Fernandez Is.
Chil.
La Plata
Rio de la Plata
Concepcion
Mar del Plata
Bahia Blanca
Negro
Puerto Montt
Comodoro Rivadavia
Falkland Islands (Islas Malvinas)
Stanley
Administered by United Kingdom
(Claimed by Arg.)
Rio Gallegos
Strait of Magellan
Punta Arenas
TIERRA DEL FUEGO
Ushuaia
Cape Horn
South Georgia I.
U.K.
N
80°W
60°W
50°W
40°W
10°N
0°
10°S
20°S
30°S
40°S
50°S
100°W
90°W
70°W
30°W
20°W
1 2 3 4 5 6 7
A B C D E F G H J K

SOUTH AMERICA
PHYSICAL
0 mi 800
0 km 800
AZIMUTHAL EQUIDISTANT PROJECTION
Caribbean Sea
ATLANTIC OCEAN
PACIFIC OCEAN
Caracas
Lake Maracaibo
VENEZUELA
LLANOS
Orinoco
Angel Falls
Total drop-3,212 ft 979 m
GUYANA
Georgetown
SURINAME
Paramaribo
Cayenne
FRENCH GUIANA
GUIANA HIGHLANDS
Boundary claimed by Suriname
Bogota
COLOMBIA
Malpelo I.
Quito
ECUADOR
EQUATOR
Negro
Amazon
Marajo Island
AMAZON BASIN
Selvas
Madeira
Tapajos
Xingu
Purus
Ucayali
Teles Pires
Tocantins
Sao Francisco
BRAZIL
PERU
Lima
Machu Picchu
Lake Titicaca
BOLIVIA
La Paz
Altiplano
Sucre
Salar de Uyuni
MATO GROSSO PLATEAU
BRAZILIAN HIGHLANDS
Brasilia
Paraguay
PARAGUAY
Asuncion
Iguazu Falls
TROPIC OF CAPRICORN
GRAN CHACO
Parana
Uruguay
San Felix I.
San Ambrosio I.
ANDES
ARGENTINA
PAMPAS
Aconcagua 22,834 ft 6,960 m
Santiago
Juan Fernandez Is.
Buenos Aires
URUGUAY
Montevideo
Rio de la Plata
CHILE
Negro
-131 ft -40 m
Valdes Peninsula
Chiloe Island
PATAGONIA
Gulf of San Jorge
Taitao Peninsula
Wellington I.
Falkland Islands (Islas Malvinas)
Stanley
Strait of Magellan
Tierra del Fuego
Cape Horn
South Georgia I.
N
80°W
60°W
50°W
40°W
100°W
90°W
70°W
30°W
20°W
10°N
0°
10°S
20°S
30°S
40°S
50°S

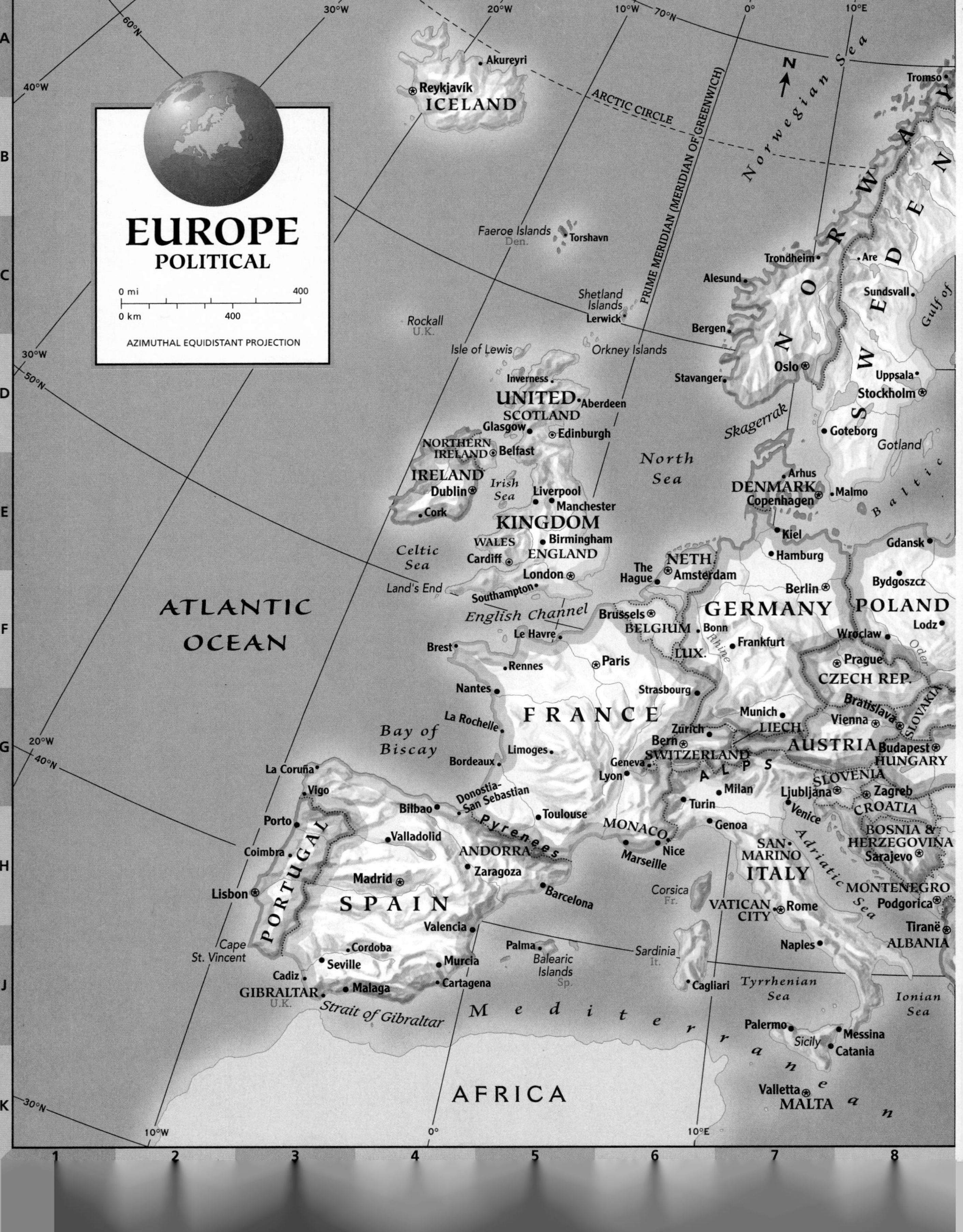

EUROPE
POLITICAL
0 mi 400
0 km 400
AZIMUTHAL EQUIDISTANT PROJECTION
ATLANTIC OCEAN
ICELAND
Reykjavík
Akureyri
ARCTIC CIRCLE
PRIME MERIDIAN (MERIDIAN OF GREENWICH)
Norwegian Sea
Faeroe Islands Den.
Torshavn
Shetland Islands
Lerwick
Orkney Islands
Rockall U.K.
Isle of Lewis
Inverness
UNITED KINGDOM
SCOTLAND
Aberdeen
Glasgow
Edinburgh
NORTHERN IRELAND
Belfast
IRELAND
Dublin
Cork
Irish Sea
Liverpool
Manchester
WALES
ENGLAND
Birmingham
Cardiff
London
Southampton
Celtic Sea
Land's End
English Channel
North Sea
Skagerrak
NORWAY
Trondheim
Alesund
Bergen
Stavanger
Oslo
Tromso
SWEDEN
Are
Sundsvall
Uppsala
Stockholm
Goteborg
Gotland
Malmo
Gulf of
Baltic
DENMARK
Arhus
Copenhagen
Kiel
Hamburg
Gdansk
Bydgoszcz
POLAND
Lodz
Wroclaw
Oder
NETH.
Amsterdam
The Hague
Brussels
BELGIUM
LUX.
GERMANY
Berlin
Bonn
Rhine
Frankfurt
Munich
Prague
CZECH REP.
Bratislava
SLOVAKIA
Vienna
AUSTRIA
Budapest
HUNGARY
LIECH.
Zurich
Bern
SWITZERLAND
Geneva
ALPS
SLOVENIA
Ljubljana
Zagreb
CROATIA
BOSNIA & HERZEGOVINA
Sarajevo
MONTENEGRO
Podgorica
Tiranë
ALBANIA
Le Havre
Brest
Rennes
Paris
Nantes
Strasbourg
FRANCE
La Rochelle
Limoges
Bordeaux
Lyon
Toulouse
MONACO
Nice
Marseille
Bay of Biscay
Donostia-San Sebastian
Bilbao
Pyrenees
ANDORRA
Zaragoza
Barcelona
La Coruña
Vigo
Porto
PORTUGAL
Coimbra
Lisbon
Cape St. Vincent
Valladolid
Madrid
SPAIN
Valencia
Cordoba
Seville
Murcia
Cartagena
Cadiz
Malaga
GIBRALTAR U.K.
Strait of Gibraltar
Palma
Balearic Islands Sp.
Corsica Fr.
Sardinia It.
Cagliari
Milan
Turin
Genoa
Venice
SAN MARINO
ITALY
Adriatic Sea
VATICAN CITY
Rome
Naples
Tyrrhenian Sea
Ionian Sea
Palermo
Sicily
Messina
Catania
Valletta
MALTA
Mediterranean
AFRICA

A commonly accepted division between Asia and Europe—here marked by a gray line—is formed by the Ural Mountains, Ural River, Caspian Sea, Caucasus Mountains, and the Black Sea with its outlets, the Bosporus and the Dardanelles.
Europe-Asia boundary
RUSSIA
ASIA
KAZAKHSTAN
URAL MOUNTAINS
Barents Sea
White Sea
Kola Peninsula
LAPLAND
FINLAND
ESTONIA
LATVIA
LITHUANIA
RUSSIA
BELARUS
UKRAINE
MOLDOVA
ROMANIA
SERBIA
BULGARIA
KOSOVO
MACED.
TURKEY
GREECE
GEORGIA
AZERBAIJAN
CYPRUS
Black Sea
Caspian Sea
Sea of Azov
Aegean Sea
Sea of Marmara
Bosporus
Dardanelles
Caucasus Mountains
Carpathian Mts.
Balkan Mts.
Lake Onega
Lake Ladoga
Murmansk
Kirovsk
Umba
Kem
Arkhangel'sk
Severodvinsk
Tobseda
Pechora
Syktyvkar
Perm
Kirov
Ufa
Kazan
Yaroslavl
Nizhniy Novgorod
Tver
Moscow
Samara
Orenburg
Ryazan
Penza
Oral
Saratov
Smolensk
Bryansk
Kursk
Volgograd
Astrakhan
Stavropol
Grozny
Baku
Rostov
Donetsk
Kharkiv
Poltava
Sumy
Chernihiv
Kyiv (Kiev)
Dnipropetrovsk
Vinnytsya
Lviv
Odesa
Chișinău
Crimea
Kerch
Simferopol
Yalta
Sevastopol
St. Petersburg
Velikiy Novgorod
Helsinki
Turku
Tampere
Pori
Vaasa
Kuopio
Oulu
Kemi
Lulea
Umea
Kiruna
Ivalo
Bothnia
Tallinn
Riga
Daugavpils
Vitsyebsk
Vilnius
Kaunas
Minsk
Homyel
Warsaw
Krakow
Belgrade
Bucharest
Constanta
Varna
Sofia
Pristina
Skopje
Istanbul
Thessaloniki
Athens
Peloponnesus
Crete
Iraklio
Rhodes
Nicosia
Volga
Ural
Dniester
Danube
Sea

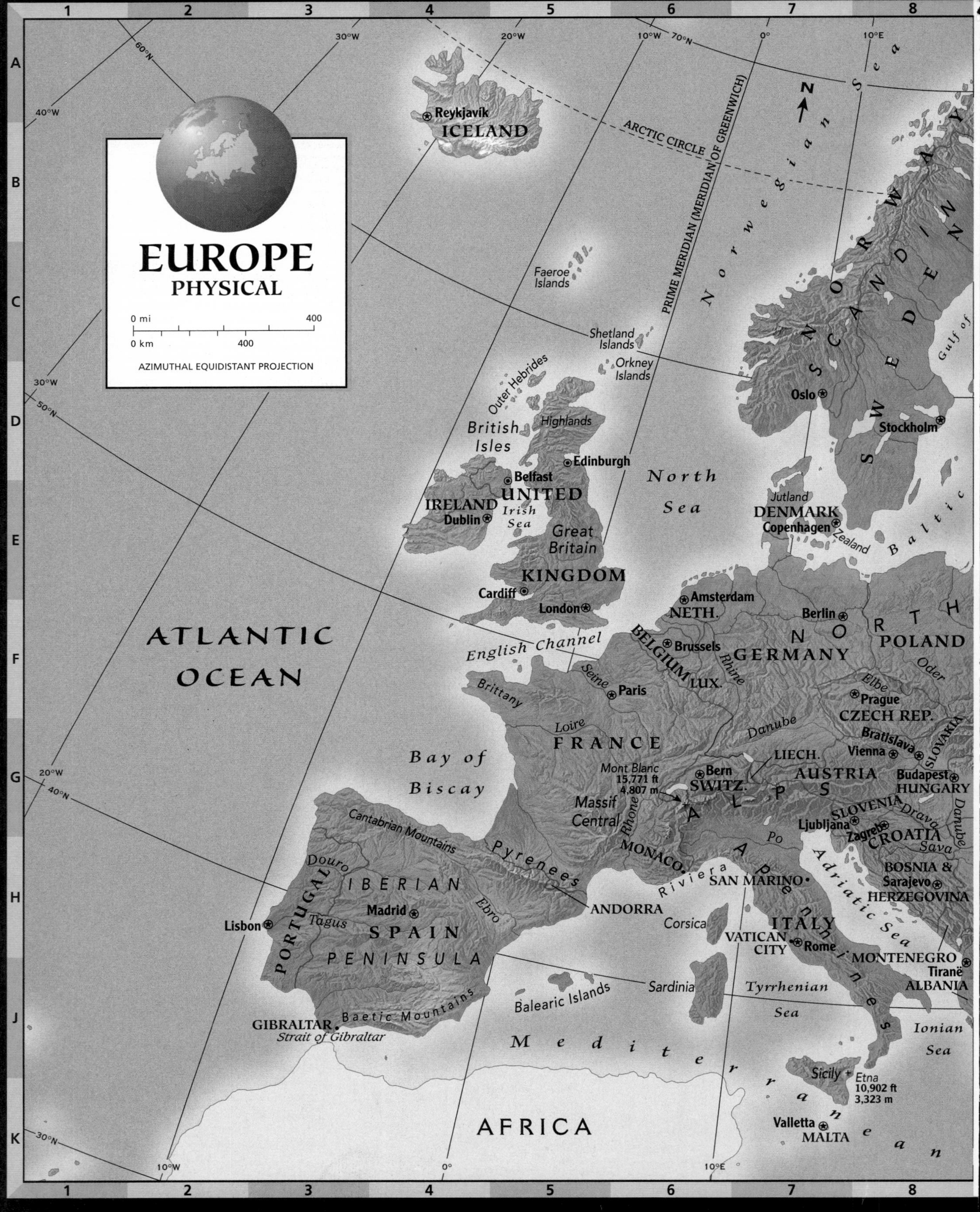

EUROPE
PHYSICAL
0 mi
400
0 km
400
AZIMUTHAL EQUIDISTANT PROJECTION
ATLANTIC
OCEAN
Reykjavík
ICELAND
ARCTIC CIRCLE
PRIME MERIDIAN (MERIDIAN OF GREENWICH)
Norwegian Sea
Faeroe Islands
Shetland Islands
Orkney Islands
Outer Hebrides
British Isles
Highlands
Edinburgh
Belfast
UNITED KINGDOM
IRELAND
Dublin
Irish Sea
Great Britain
Cardiff
London
North Sea
Jutland
DENMARK
Copenhagen
Zealand
Baltic
NORWAY
SWEDEN
SCANDINAVIA
Oslo
Stockholm
Gulf of
Amsterdam
NETH.
Berlin
NORTH
POLAND
Oder
BELGIUM
Brussels
GERMANY
Rhine
LUX.
English Channel
Seine
Paris
Brittany
Elbe
Prague
CZECH REP.
Loire
FRANCE
Danube
Bratislava
SLOVAKIA
Vienna
LIECH.
AUSTRIA
Budapest
HUNGARY
Bay of Biscay
Mont Blanc
15,771 ft
4,807 m
Bern
SWITZ.
ALPS
Massif Central
Rhone
SLOVENIA
Ljubljana
Drava
Danube
Zagreb
CROATIA
Sava
Po
Cantabrian Mountains
Pyrenees
MONACO
Riviera
SAN MARINO
Adriatic Sea
BOSNIA & HERZEGOVINA
Sarajevo
Douro
IBERIAN PENINSULA
PORTUGAL
Lisbon
Tagus
Madrid
SPAIN
Ebro
ANDORRA
Corsica
ITALY
Apennines
VATICAN CITY
Rome
MONTENEGRO
Tiranë
ALBANIA
Sardinia
Tyrrhenian Sea
Balearic Islands
GIBRALTAR
Baetic Mountains
Strait of Gibraltar
Mediterranean
Ionian Sea
Sicily
Etna
10,902 ft
3,323 m
Valletta
MALTA
AFRICA
30°W
20°W
10°W
0°
10°E
70°N
60°N
50°N
40°N
30°N
40°W

Barents Sea
North Cape
Kola Peninsula
White Sea
Pechora
FINLAND
Bothnia
Lake Region
Lake Onega
Lake Ladoga
Northern Dvina
RUSSIA
EUROPEAN PLAIN
URAL MOUNTAINS
Europe-Asia boundary
ASIA
Helsinki
Gulf of Finland
Tallinn
ESTONIA
Kama
Ural
Volga
Riga
LATVIA
Moscow
LITHUANIA
Oka
Vilnius
RUSSIA
CENTRAL RUSSIAN UPLAND
Minsk
BELARUS
Dnieper
Don
Warsaw
KAZAKHSTAN
Caspian Depression
Vistula
Kyiv (Kiev)
UKRAINE
Carpathian Mountains
Dniester
MOLDOVA
Chișinău
Sea of Azov
Crimea
Elbrus
18,510 ft
5,642 m
Caucasus Mountains
Caspian Sea
AZERBAIJAN
Baku
GEORGIA
ROMANIA
Tisza
Belgrade
Bucharest
Danube
BALKAN PENINSULA
Black Sea
SERBIA
BULGARIA
Balkan Mountains
Sofia
KOSOVO
Skopje
MACED.
Bosporus
TURKEY
GREECE
Dardanelles
Sea of Marmara
Aegean Sea
Athens
Peloponnesus
ASIA
Rhodes
Nicosia
CYPRUS
Crete
Sea

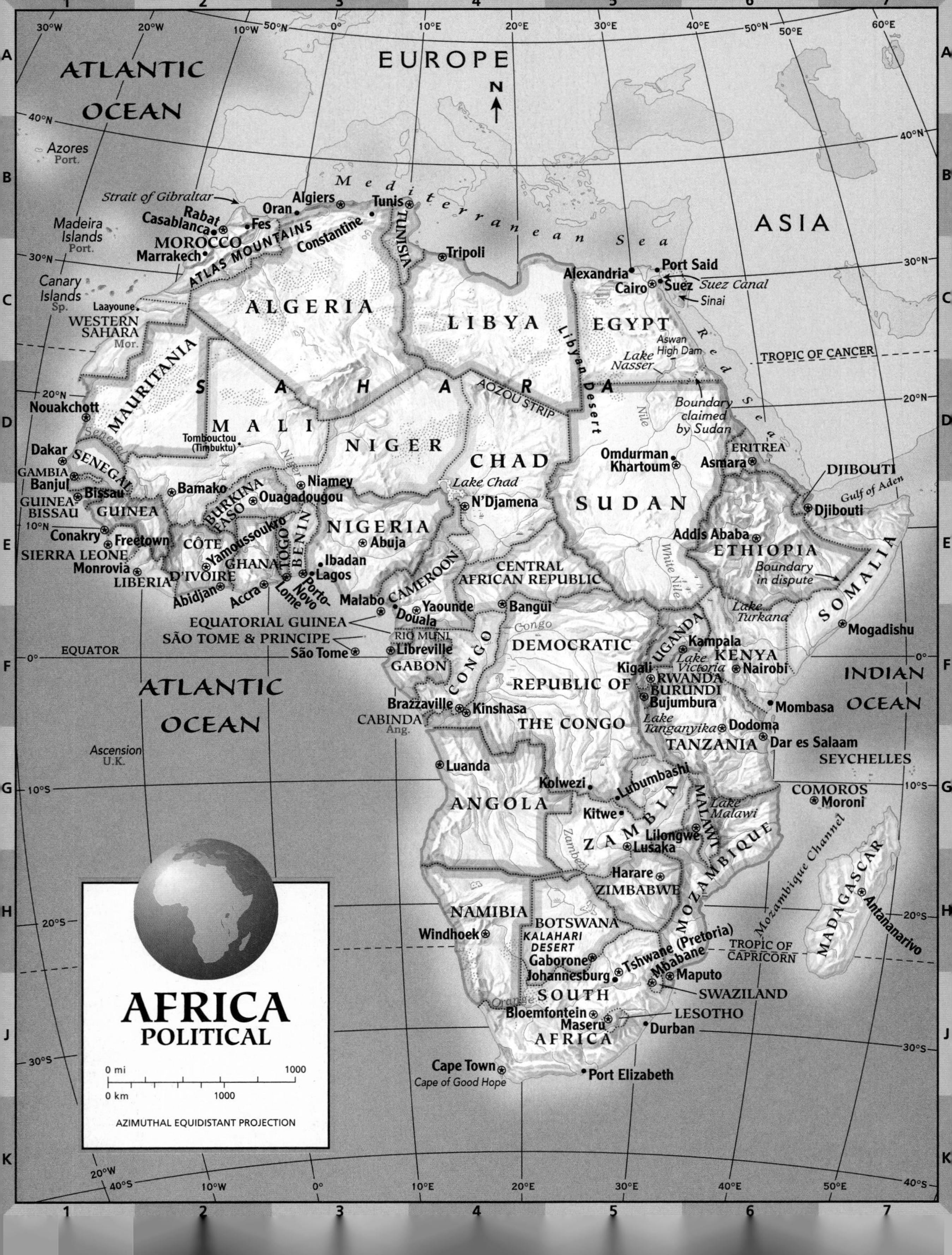
AFRICA
POLITICAL
AZIMUTHAL EQUIDISTANT PROJECTION
0 mi 1000
0 km 1000
ATLANTIC OCEAN
EUROPE
N
ASIA
Azores
Port.
Madeira Islands
Port.
Canary Islands
Sp.
Strait of Gibraltar
Mediterranean Sea
Algiers
Tunis
Oran
Rabat
Fes
Casablanca
MOROCCO
ATLAS MOUNTAINS
Constantine
Marrakech
TUNISIA
Tripoli
Alexandria
Port Said
Cairo
Suez
Suez Canal
Sinai
Laayoune
WESTERN SAHARA
Mor.
ALGERIA
LIBYA
EGYPT
Libyan Desert
Aswan High Dam
Lake Nasser
Red Sea
TROPIC OF CANCER
MAURITANIA
SAHARA
AOZOU STRIP
Boundary claimed by Sudan
Nile
Nouakchott
MALI
Tombouctou (Timbuktu)
Senegal
NIGER
Niger
Dakar
SENEGAL
GAMBIA
Banjul
Bissau
GUINEA-BISSAU
GUINEA
Bamako
BURKINA FASO
Ouagadougou
Niamey
CHAD
Lake Chad
N'Djamena
Omdurman
Khartoum
SUDAN
ERITREA
Asmara
DJIBOUTI
Djibouti
Gulf of Aden
Conakry
Freetown
SIERRA LEONE
Monrovia
LIBERIA
CÔTE D'IVOIRE
Yamoussoukro
GHANA
TOGO
BENIN
NIGERIA
Abuja
Ibadan
Lagos
Porto-Novo
Abidjan
Accra
Lome
Addis Ababa
ETHIOPIA
White Nile
Boundary in dispute
SOMALIA
CENTRAL AFRICAN REPUBLIC
CAMEROON
Malabo
Yaounde
Douala
Bangui
EQUATORIAL GUINEA
RIO MUNI
SÃO TOME & PRINCIPE
São Tome
Libreville
GABON
EQUATOR
Congo
CONGO
DEMOCRATIC REPUBLIC OF THE CONGO
UGANDA
Kampala
Lake Turkana
KENYA
Lake Victoria
Nairobi
Mogadishu
INDIAN OCEAN
Kigali
RWANDA
BURUNDI
Bujumbura
Mombasa
Brazzaville
Kinshasa
CABINDA
Ang.
Lake Tanganyika
Dodoma
TANZANIA
Dar es Salaam
SEYCHELLES
Ascension
U.K.
Luanda
Kolwezi
Lubumbashi
COMOROS
Moroni
ANGOLA
Kitwe
ZAMBIA
MALAWI
Lake Malawi
Lilongwe
Lusaka
Zambezi
MOZAMBIQUE
Mozambique Channel
MADAGASCAR
Antananarivo
Harare
ZIMBABWE
NAMIBIA
BOTSWANA
KALAHARI DESERT
Windhoek
Gaborone
Tshwane (Pretoria)
Mbabane
Maputo
TROPIC OF CAPRICORN
Johannesburg
SWAZILAND
Orange
SOUTH AFRICA
Bloemfontein
Maseru
LESOTHO
Durban
Cape Town
Cape of Good Hope
Port Elizabeth
30°W
20°W
10°W
0°
10°E
20°E
30°E
40°E
50°E
60°E
50°N
40°N
30°N
20°N
10°N
0°
10°S
20°S
30°S
40°S
1 2 3 4 5 6 7
A B C D E F G H J K

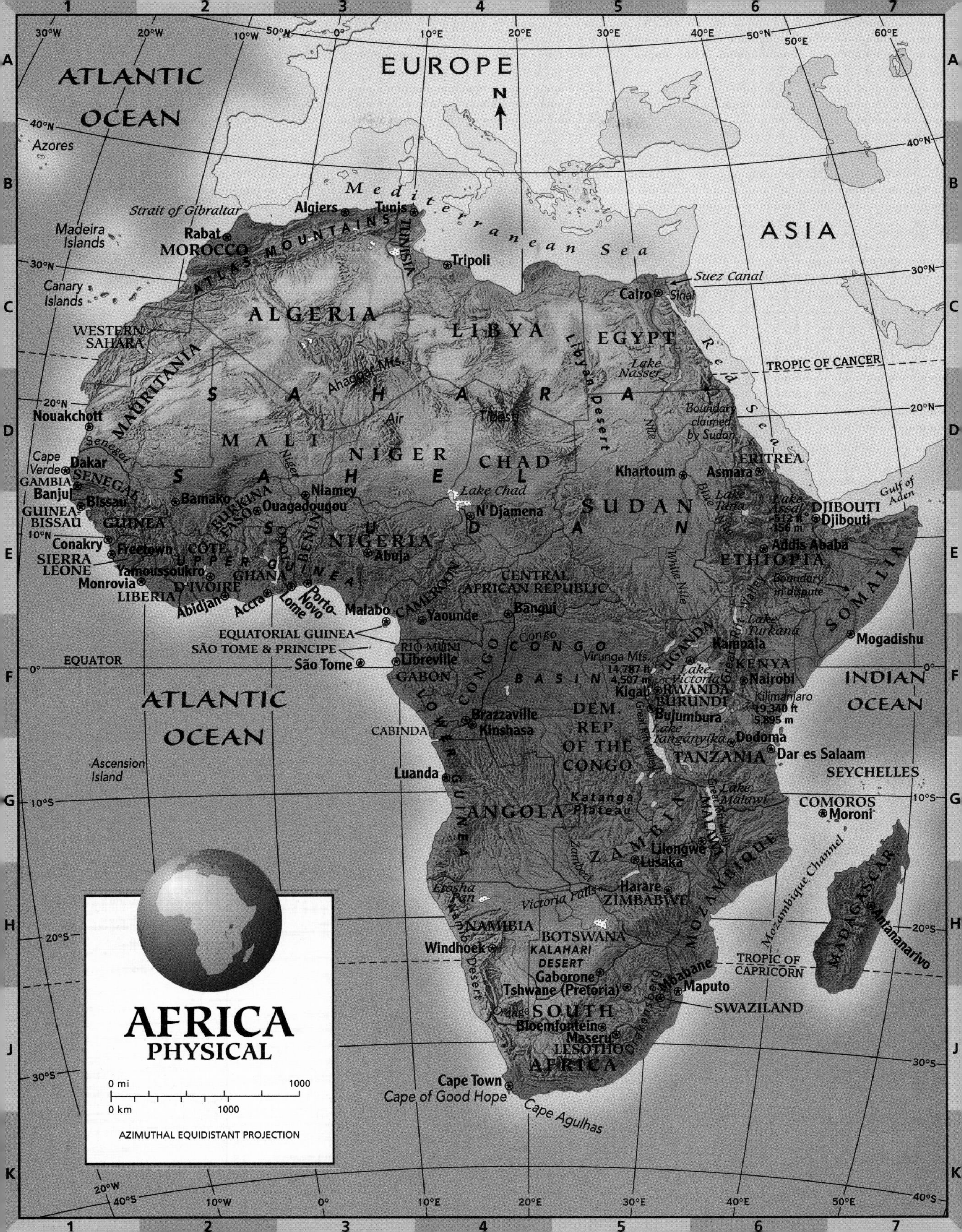
AFRICA
PHYSICAL
AZIMUTHAL EQUIDISTANT PROJECTION
0 mi 1000
0 km 1000
ATLANTIC OCEAN
EUROPE
ASIA
INDIAN OCEAN
Mediterranean Sea
Red Sea
Gulf of Aden
Strait of Gibraltar
Suez Canal
Sinai
Azores
Madeira Islands
Canary Islands
Cape Verde
Ascension Island
ATLAS MOUNTAINS
Ahaggar Mts.
Air
Tibesti
SAHARA
SAHEL
Libyan Desert
Lake Nasser
Nile
Blue Nile
White Nile
Lake Tana
Lake Assal -512 ft -156 m
Boundary claimed by Sudan
Boundary in dispute
TROPIC OF CANCER
EQUATOR
TROPIC OF CAPRICORN
MOROCCO
Rabat
Algiers
Tunis
TUNISIA
Tripoli
ALGERIA
LIBYA
EGYPT
Cairo
WESTERN SAHARA
MAURITANIA
Nouakchott
MALI
NIGER
CHAD
SUDAN
Khartoum
ERITREA
Asmara
DJIBOUTI
Djibouti
ETHIOPIA
Addis Ababa
SOMALIA
Mogadishu
Senegal
Niger
Dakar
SENEGAL
GAMBIA
Banjul
GUINEA-BISSAU
Bissau
GUINEA
Conakry
SIERRA LEONE
Freetown
LIBERIA
Monrovia
CÔTE D'IVOIRE
Yamoussoukro
Abidjan
BURKINA FASO
Ouagadougou
Bamako
Niamey
GHANA
Accra
TOGO
Lome
BENIN
Porto-Novo
NIGERIA
Abuja
Lake Chad
N'Djamena
UPPER GUINEA
CAMEROON
Yaounde
Malabo
EQUATORIAL GUINEA
SÃO TOME & PRINCIPE
São Tome
RIO MUNI
Libreville
GABON
CENTRAL AFRICAN REPUBLIC
Bangui
Congo
CONGO
CONGO BASIN
Brazzaville
Kinshasa
CABINDA
LOWER GUINEA
DEM. REP. OF THE CONGO
Virunga Mts. 14,787 ft 4,507 m
UGANDA
Kampala
Lake Victoria
Lake Turkana
Great Rift Valley
KENYA
Nairobi
Kilimanjaro 19,340 ft 5,895 m
RWANDA
Kigali
BURUNDI
Bujumbura
Lake Tanganyika
TANZANIA
Dodoma
Dar es Salaam
SEYCHELLES
COMOROS
Moroni
Luanda
ANGOLA
Katanga Plateau
ZAMBIA
Lusaka
Zambezi
Lake Malawi
MALAWI
Lilongwe
MOZAMBIQUE
Mozambique Channel
MADAGASCAR
Antananarivo
Etosha Pan
Victoria Falls
Harare
ZIMBABWE
NAMIBIA
Windhoek
Namib Desert
BOTSWANA
KALAHARI DESERT
Gaborone
Tshwane (Pretoria)
Mbabane
Maputo
SWAZILAND
Drakensberg
Orange
SOUTH AFRICA
Bloemfontein
Maseru
LESOTHO
Cape Town
Cape of Good Hope
Cape Agulhas
N

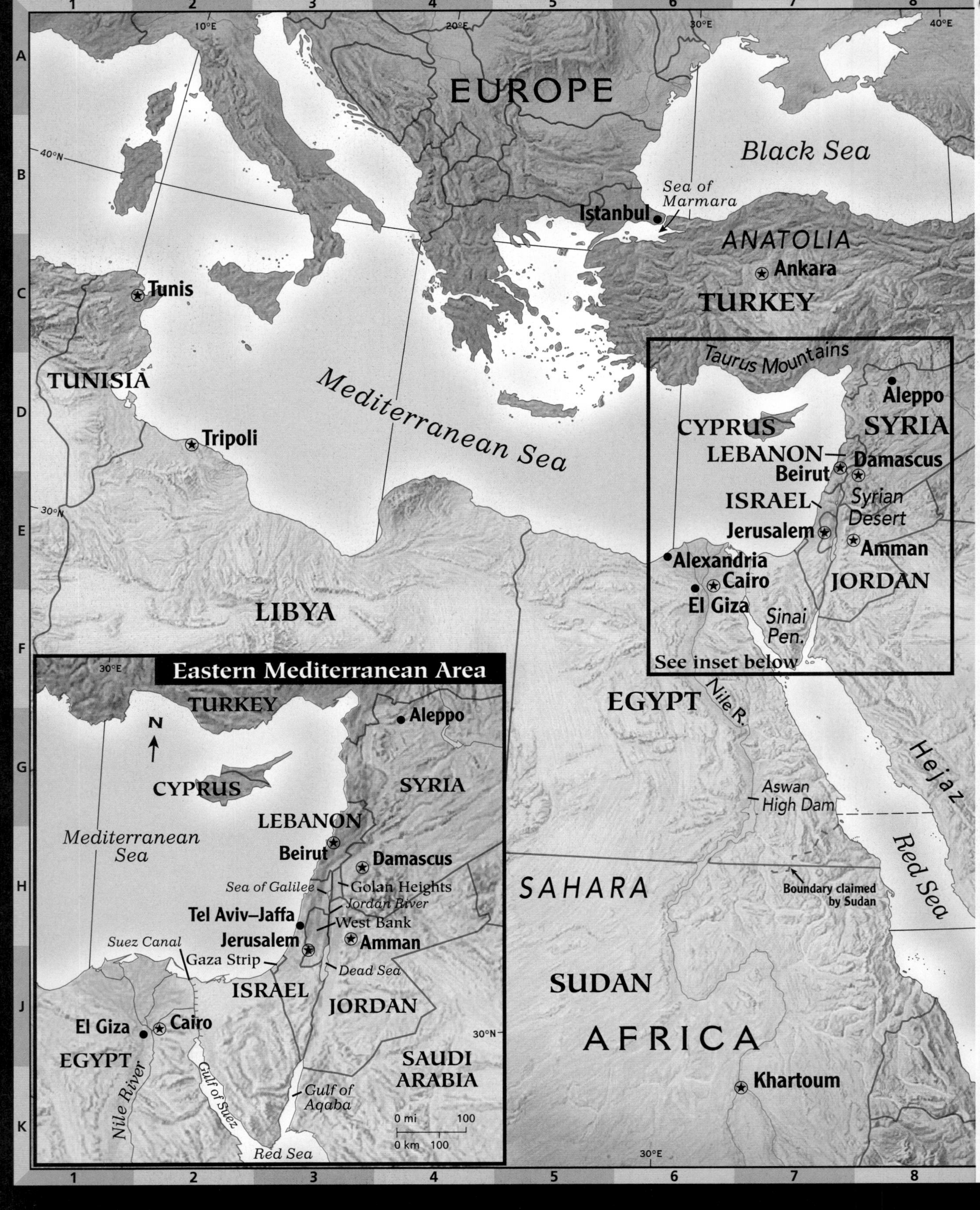
EUROPE
Black Sea
Sea of Marmara
Istanbul
ANATOLIA
Ankara
TURKEY
Tunis
TUNISIA
Tripoli
Mediterranean Sea
Taurus Mountains
Aleppo
SYRIA
CYPRUS
LEBANON
Beirut
Damascus
ISRAEL
Syrian Desert
Jerusalem
Amman
Alexandria
Cairo
El Giza
JORDAN
Sinai Pen.
LIBYA
See inset below
EGYPT
Nile R.
Hejaz
Aswan High Dam
Red Sea
SAHARA
Boundary claimed by Sudan
SUDAN
AFRICA
Khartoum
Eastern Mediterranean Area
TURKEY
N
Aleppo
CYPRUS
SYRIA
LEBANON
Mediterranean Sea
Beirut
Damascus
Sea of Galilee
Golan Heights
Jordan River
Tel Aviv–Jaffa
West Bank
Jerusalem
Amman
Suez Canal
Gaza Strip
Dead Sea
ISRAEL
JORDAN
El Giza
Cairo
EGYPT
SAUDI ARABIA
Nile River
Gulf of Suez
Gulf of Aqaba
0 mi 100
0 km 100
Red Sea
10°E
20°E
30°E
40°E
40°N
30°N

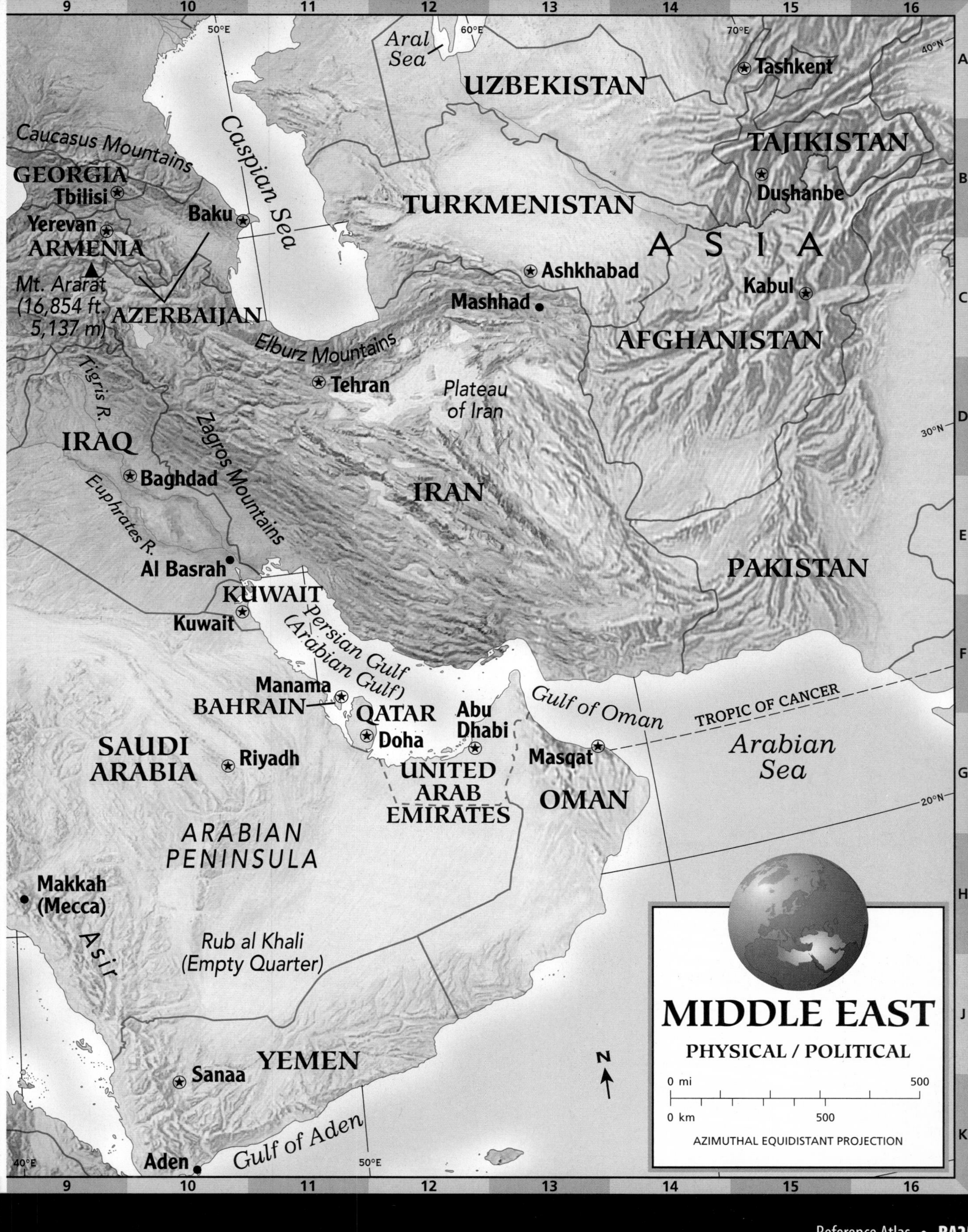
MIDDLE EAST
PHYSICAL / POLITICAL
0 mi
500
0 km
500
AZIMUTHAL EQUIDISTANT PROJECTION
N
UZBEKISTAN
TAJIKISTAN
TURKMENISTAN
AFGHANISTAN
PAKISTAN
IRAN
IRAQ
GEORGIA
ARMENIA
AZERBAIJAN
KUWAIT
BAHRAIN
QATAR
UNITED ARAB EMIRATES
OMAN
SAUDI ARABIA
YEMEN
A S I A
ARABIAN PENINSULA
Aral Sea
Caspian Sea
Caucasus Mountains
Elburz Mountains
Zagros Mountains
Plateau of Iran
Mt. Ararat (16,854 ft. 5,137 m)
Tigris R.
Euphrates R.
Persian Gulf (Arabian Gulf)
Gulf of Oman
Arabian Sea
Gulf of Aden
TROPIC OF CANCER
Rub al Khali (Empty Quarter)
Asir
Tashkent
Dushanbe
Ashkhabad
Mashhad
Kabul
Tbilisi
Yerevan
Baku
Tehran
Baghdad
Al Basrah
Kuwait
Manama
Doha
Abu Dhabi
Masqat
Riyadh
Makkah (Mecca)
Sanaa
Aden
40°N
30°N
20°N
40°E
50°E
60°E
70°E
9
10
11
12
13
14
15
16
A
B
C
D
E
F
G
H
J
K

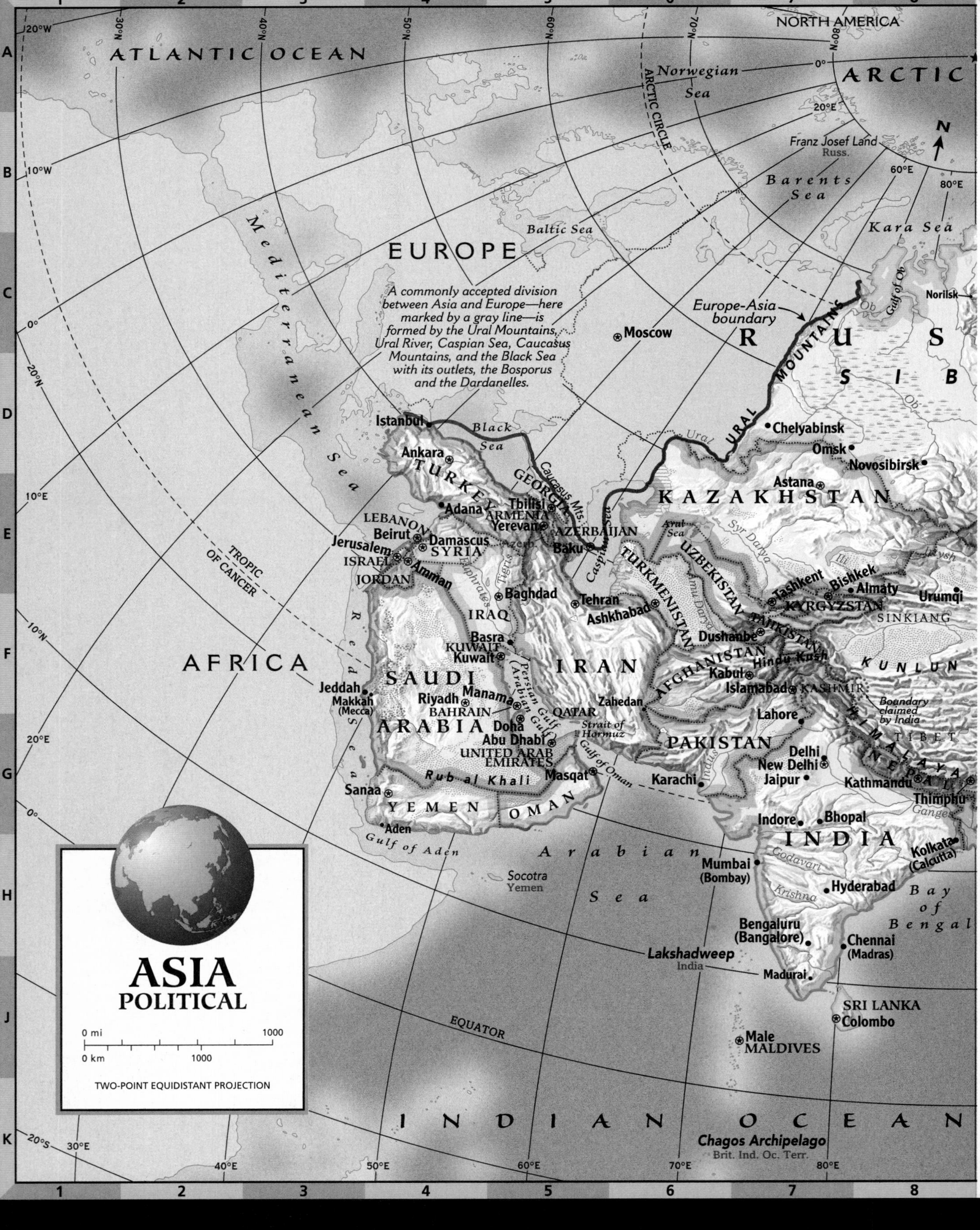
ASIA
POLITICAL
ATLANTIC OCEAN
ARCTIC
NORTH AMERICA
Norwegian Sea
ARCTIC CIRCLE
Franz Josef Land
Russ.
Barents Sea
Kara Sea
Baltic Sea
EUROPE
A commonly accepted division between Asia and Europe—here marked by a gray line—is formed by the Ural Mountains, Ural River, Caspian Sea, Caucasus Mountains, and the Black Sea with its outlets, the Bosporus and the Dardanelles.
Europe-Asia boundary
URAL MOUNTAINS
Gulf of Ob
Ob
Norilsk
Moscow
Mediterranean Sea
Black Sea
Caucasus Mts.
Caspian Sea
Ural
Istanbul
Ankara
TURKEY
GEORGIA
Tbilisi
ARMENIA
Yerevan
AZERBAIJAN
Baku
Adana
LEBANON
Beirut
Damascus
SYRIA
Jerusalem
ISRAEL
Amman
JORDAN
Euphrates
Tigris
Baghdad
IRAQ
Basra
KUWAIT
Kuwait
Tehran
IRAN
Chelyabinsk
Omsk
Novosibirsk
Astana
KAZAKHSTAN
Aral Sea
Syr Darya
Amu Darya
UZBEKISTAN
TURKMENISTAN
Ashkhabad
Tashkent
Bishkek
Almaty
KYRGYZSTAN
Urumqi
SINKIANG
TAJIKISTAN
Dushanbe
AFGHANISTAN
Hindu Kush
Kabul
Islamabad
KASHMIR
Boundary claimed by India
KUNLUN
TIBET
HIMALAYA
NEPAL
Kathmandu
Thimphu
Ganges
Zahedan
Lahore
PAKISTAN
Indus
Karachi
Delhi
New Delhi
Jaipur
Indore
Bhopal
INDIA
Kolkata (Calcutta)
Godavari
Krishna
Mumbai (Bombay)
Hyderabad
Bay of Bengal
Bengaluru (Bangalore)
Chennai (Madras)
Lakshadweep
India
Madurai
SRI LANKA
Colombo
Male
MALDIVES
TROPIC OF CANCER
AFRICA
Red Sea
Jeddah
Makkah (Mecca)
SAUDI ARABIA
Riyadh
Manama
BAHRAIN
Persian Gulf (Arabian Gulf)
QATAR
Doha
Abu Dhabi
UNITED ARAB EMIRATES
Strait of Hormuz
Gulf of Oman
Masqat
Rub al Khali
Sanaa
YEMEN
OMAN
Aden
Gulf of Aden
Socotra
Yemen
Arabian Sea
EQUATOR
INDIAN OCEAN
Chagos Archipelago
Brit. Ind. Oc. Terr.
0 mi
1000
0 km
1000
TWO-POINT EQUIDISTANT PROJECTION

NORTH AMERICA
Bering Strait
Chukchi Sea
North Pole
OCEAN
Wrangel I.
Gulf of Anadyr
Anadyr
Bering Sea
East Siberian Sea
North Land
New Siberian Islands
Laptev Sea
Kolyma Range
Commander Is.
Cherskiy Range
Verkhoyanski Mountains
Kamchatka Peninsula
Magadan
Lena
Aldan
Sea of Okhotsk
Yakutsk
SIBERIA
ASIA
Sakhalin
Kuril Islands
Yenisey
Amur
Lake Baikal
Hokkaido
Sapporo
Irkutsk
MANCHURIA
Vladivostok
Sea of Japan (East Sea)
JAPAN
Herlen
Ulaanbaatar
Changchun
Tokyo
MONGOLIA
Shenyang
NORTH KOREA
Honshu
Kyoto
Osaka
ALTAY MTS.
GOBI
P'yongyang
Seoul
SOUTH KOREA
Hiroshima
Beijing
Qingdao
Kyushu
Shijiazhuang
Yellow Sea
Huang He (Yellow R.)
Xuzhou
Lanzhou
Xian
East China Sea
Shanghai
Nanjing
CHINA
Chang Jiang (Yangtze R.)
Ryukyu Islands
Okinawa
Nanchang
Chengdu
Fuzhou
Taipei
Boundary claimed by China
Changsha
TAIWAN
The People's Republic of China claims Taiwan as its 23rd province.
BHUTAN
BANGLADESH
Guiyang
Dhaka
Irrawaddy
Kunming
Guangzhou
Hong Kong
Macau
Hanoi
Haiphong
MYANMAR (BURMA)
LAOS
Hainan
South China Sea
Nay Pyi Taw
Vientiane
Da Nang
THAILAND
Mekong
VIETNAM
Bangkok
CAMBODIA
Phnom Penh
Ho Chi Minh City
Andaman Islands
India
Andaman Sea
Gulf of Thailand
Nicobar Islands
India
Kuala Lumpur
MALAYSIA
Medan
SINGAPORE
Sumatra
Jambi
Mentawai Islands
Jakarta
Bandar Seri Begawan
BRUNEI
SABAH
SARAWAK
MALAYSIA
Borneo
INDONESIA
GREATER SUNDA ISLANDS
Java Sea
Java
Luzon
Quezon City
Manila
Mindoro
Samar
PHILIPPINES
Leyte
Panay
Negros
Palawan
Mindanao
Philippine Sea
PACIFIC OCEAN
Marcus I.
Jap.
TROPIC OF CANCER
Bonin Is.
Jap.
Volcano Is.
Jap.
Parece Vela
Jap.
EQUATOR
Halmahera
Morotai
Moluccas
Biak
Jayapura
New Guinea
Kepi
Merauke
Ceram
Buru
Celebes
Aru Is.
Dolak
Tanimbar Is.
Dili
EAST TIMOR (TIMOR-LESTE)
Timor Sea
Kupang
AUSTRALIA
80°N
70°N
60°N
50°N
40°N
30°N
20°N
10°N
0°
10°S
20°S
180°
160°E
120°E
100°E
160°W
170°W
180°
170°E
160°E
100°E
110°E
120°E
130°E
140°E
150°E
9
10
11
12
13
14
15
16
A
B
C
D
E
F
G
H
J
K

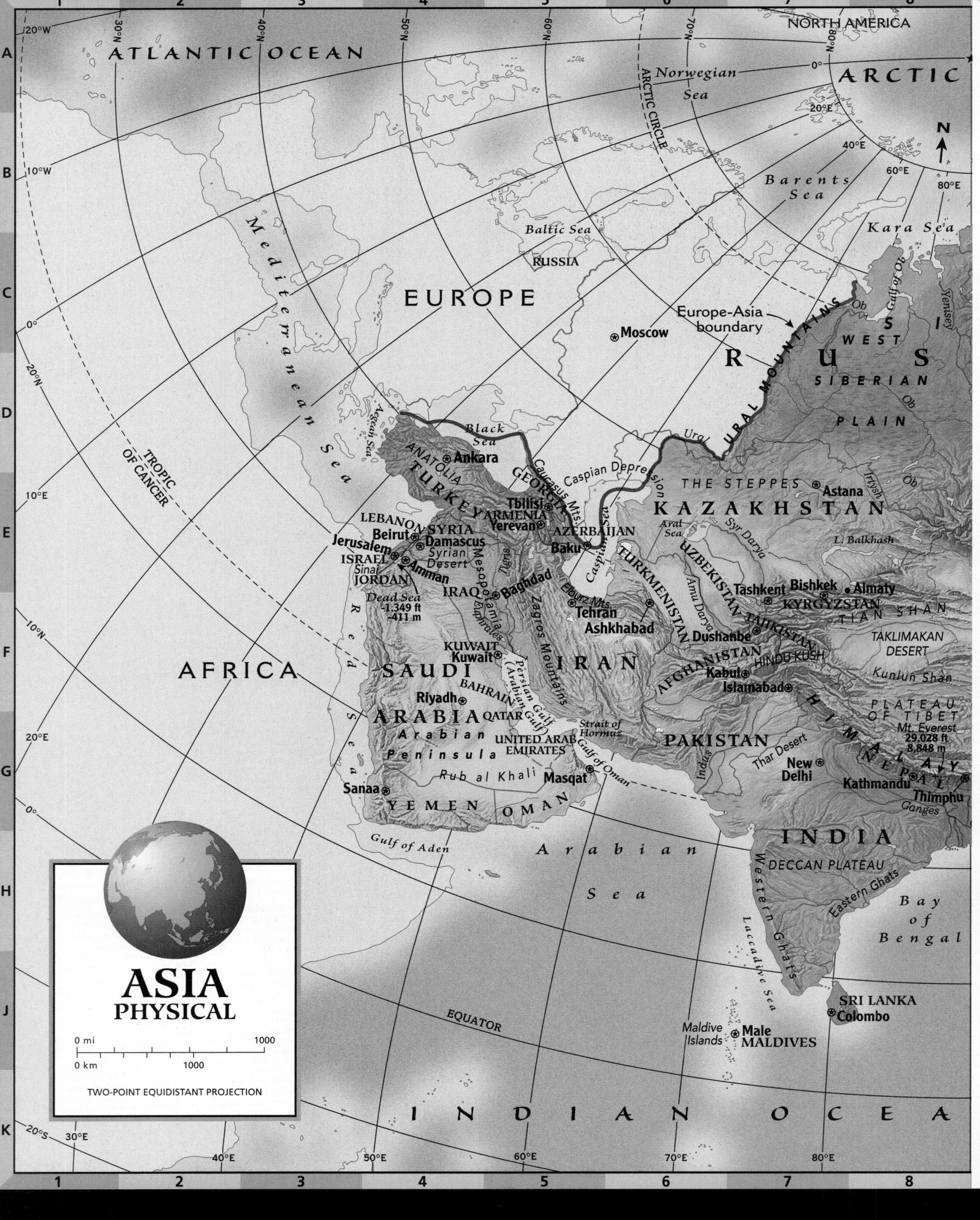
ASIA
PHYSICAL
TWO-POINT EQUIDISTANT PROJECTION
0 mi
1000
0 km
1000
ATLANTIC OCEAN
ARCTIC
NORTH AMERICA
Norwegian Sea
ARCTIC CIRCLE
Barents Sea
Kara Sea
Baltic Sea
RUSSIA
EUROPE
Moscow
Europe-Asia boundary
URAL MOUNTAINS
Ural
WEST SIBERIAN PLAIN
Ob
Gulf of Ob
Yenisey
Irtysh
Mediterranean Sea
Aegean Sea
Black Sea
ANATOLIA
Ankara
TURKEY
GEORGIA
Caucasus Mts.
Caspian Depression
Caspian Sea
Tbilisi
ARMENIA
Yerevan
AZERBAIJAN
Baku
THE STEPPES
Astana
KAZAKHSTAN
Aral Sea
Syr Darya
L. Balkhash
UZBEKISTAN
TURKMENISTAN
Amu Darya
Tashkent
Bishkek
Almaty
KYRGYZSTAN
TIAN SHAN
TAKLIMAKAN DESERT
Ashkhabad
Dushanbe
TAJIKISTAN
LEBANON
SYRIA
Beirut
Damascus
Jerusalem
ISRAEL
Sinai
Syrian Desert
Amman
JORDAN
Dead Sea -1,349 ft -411 m
Mesopotamia
Tigris
Euphrates
IRAQ
Baghdad
Elburz Mts.
Tehran
Zagros Mountains
IRAN
KUWAIT
Kuwait
AFGHANISTAN
HINDU KUSH
Kabul
Islamabad
Kunlun Shan
PLATEAU OF TIBET
Mt. Everest 29,028 ft 8,848 m
HIMALAYA
AFRICA
Red Sea
SAUDI ARABIA
Riyadh
BAHRAIN
QATAR
Persian Gulf (Arabian Gulf)
Strait of Hormuz
UNITED ARAB EMIRATES
Gulf of Oman
Arabian Peninsula
Rub al Khali
Masqat
Sanaa
YEMEN
OMAN
Gulf of Aden
PAKISTAN
Indus
Thar Desert
New Delhi
NEPAL
Kathmandu
Thimphu
Ganges
INDIA
DECCAN PLATEAU
Western Ghats
Eastern Ghats
Bay of Bengal
Arabian Sea
Laccadive Sea
Maldive Islands
Male
MALDIVES
SRI LANKA
Colombo
EQUATOR
TROPIC OF CANCER
INDIAN OCEAN
N
20°W
10°W
0°
10°E
20°E
30°E
40°E
50°E
60°E
70°E
80°E
30°N
40°N
50°N
60°N
70°N
80°N
20°N
10°N
0°
20°S
1
2
3
4
5
6
7
8
A
B
C
D
E
F
G
H
J
K

NORTH AMERICA
Bering Strait
Chukchi Sea
Chukchi Peninsula
Gulf of Anadyr
North Pole
OCEAN
Wrangel Island
East Siberian Sea
Bering Sea
Aleutian Islands
North Land
New Siberian Islands
Laptev Sea
Taymyr Peninsula
Kolyma
Kolyma Range
Commander Islands
Cherskiy Range
Kamchatka Peninsula
Verkhoyanski Mountains
Lena
Aldan
CENTRAL SIBERIAN PLATEAU
SIBERIA
ASIA
Sea of Okhotsk
Sakhalin
Kuril Islands
PACIFIC OCEAN
Angara
Amur
Yablonovyy Range
Lake Baikal
Greater Khingan Range
Manchurian Plain
Sikhote Alin Range
Hokkaido
Yenisey
Sea of Japan (East Sea)
JAPAN
Tokyo
Honshu
Ulaanbaatar
MONGOLIA
GOBI
ALTAY MOUNTAINS
NORTH KOREA
P'yongyang
Seoul
SOUTH KOREA
Beijing
Shikoku
Kyushu
Nampo Shoto
TROPIC OF CANCER
Huang He (Yellow R.)
North China Plain
Yellow Sea
East China Sea
Ryukyu Islands
Qaidam Basin
CHINA
Mekong
Yangtze
Salween
Sichuan Basin
Chang Jiang (Yangtze R.)
Mariana Islands
Gongga Shan 24,790 ft 7,556 m
Taipei
TAIWAN
Philippine Sea
BHUTAN
Brahmaputra
BANGLADESH
Dhaka
Caroline Islands
MYANMAR (BURMA)
Hanoi
LAOS
Luzon
PHILIPPINE ISLANDS
Hainan
South China Sea
Nay Pyi Taw
Vientiane
Manila
PHILIPPINES
THAILAND
EQUATOR
Bangkok
CAMBODIA
VIETNAM
Andaman Islands
Phnom Penh
Sulu Sea
Mindanao
Gulf of Thailand
Andaman Sea
Malay Peninsula
Bandar Seri Begawan
BRUNEI
Celebes Sea
Moluccas
New Guinea
Nicobar Islands
MALAYSIA
Kuala Lumpur
SINGAPORE
Borneo
Celebes
Sumatra
INDONESIA
Arafura Sea
GREATER SUNDA ISLANDS
Java Sea
EAST TIMOR (TIMOR-LESTE)
Dili
Timor Sea
AUSTRALIA
Mentawai Islands
Jakarta
Java
80°N 70°N 60°N 50°N 40°N 30°N 20°N 10°N 0° 10°S 20°S
180° 160°E 120°E 100°E 100°E 110°E 120°E 130°E 140°E 150°E 160°E 170°E 180° 170°W 160°W
9 10 11 12 13 14 15 16
A B C D E F G H J K

TROPIC OF CANCER
NORTH PACIFIC OCEAN
ASIA
NORTHERN MARIANA ISLANDS
U.S.
Saipan
MICRONESIA
GUAM
U.S.
Hagatna
Wake Island
U.S.
Bikini Atoll
MARSHALL ISLANDS
Ratak Chain
Ralik Chain
PALAU
Melekeok
Yap Islands
Truk Islands
Caroline Islands
Palikir
Pohnpei (Ponape)
Majuro
FEDERATED STATES OF MICRONESIA
Tarawa (Bairiki)
Gilbert Islands
EQUATOR
Yaren
NAURU
New Guinea
Mt. Wilhelm
14,793 ft
4,509 m
PAPUA NEW GUINEA
New Britain
MELANESIA
SOLOMON ISLANDS
Solomon Is.
Honiara
TUVALU
Funafuti
Port Moresby
Torres Strait
Santa Cruz Is.
Darwin
Gulf of Carpentaria
Coral Sea
CORAL SEA ISLANDS TERRITORY
Austral.
VANUATU
Port-Vila
Suva
FIJI ISLANDS
NEW CALEDONIA
Fr.
Noumea
Kimberley Plateau
NORTHERN TERRITORY
GREAT DIVIDING RANGE
AUSTRALIA
TROPIC OF CAPRICORN
WESTERN AUSTRALIA
Macdonnell Ranges
QUEENSLAND
Brisbane
GREAT VICTORIA DESERT
SOUTH AUSTRALIA
Lake Eyre
-52 ft
-16 m
Norfolk Island
Austral.
Darling
NEW SOUTH WALES
Lord Howe Island
Austral.
Perth
Great Australian Bight
Sydney
Adelaide
Murray
AUSTRALIAN CAPITAL TERRITORY
Canberra
Mt. Kosciuszko
7,310 ft
2,228 m
VICTORIA
Melbourne
Auckland
North Island
NEW ZEALAND
Tasman Sea
Wellington
INDIAN OCEAN
TASMANIA
Hobart
Mt. Cook
12,316 ft
3,754 m
Christchurch
South Island
Stewart Island

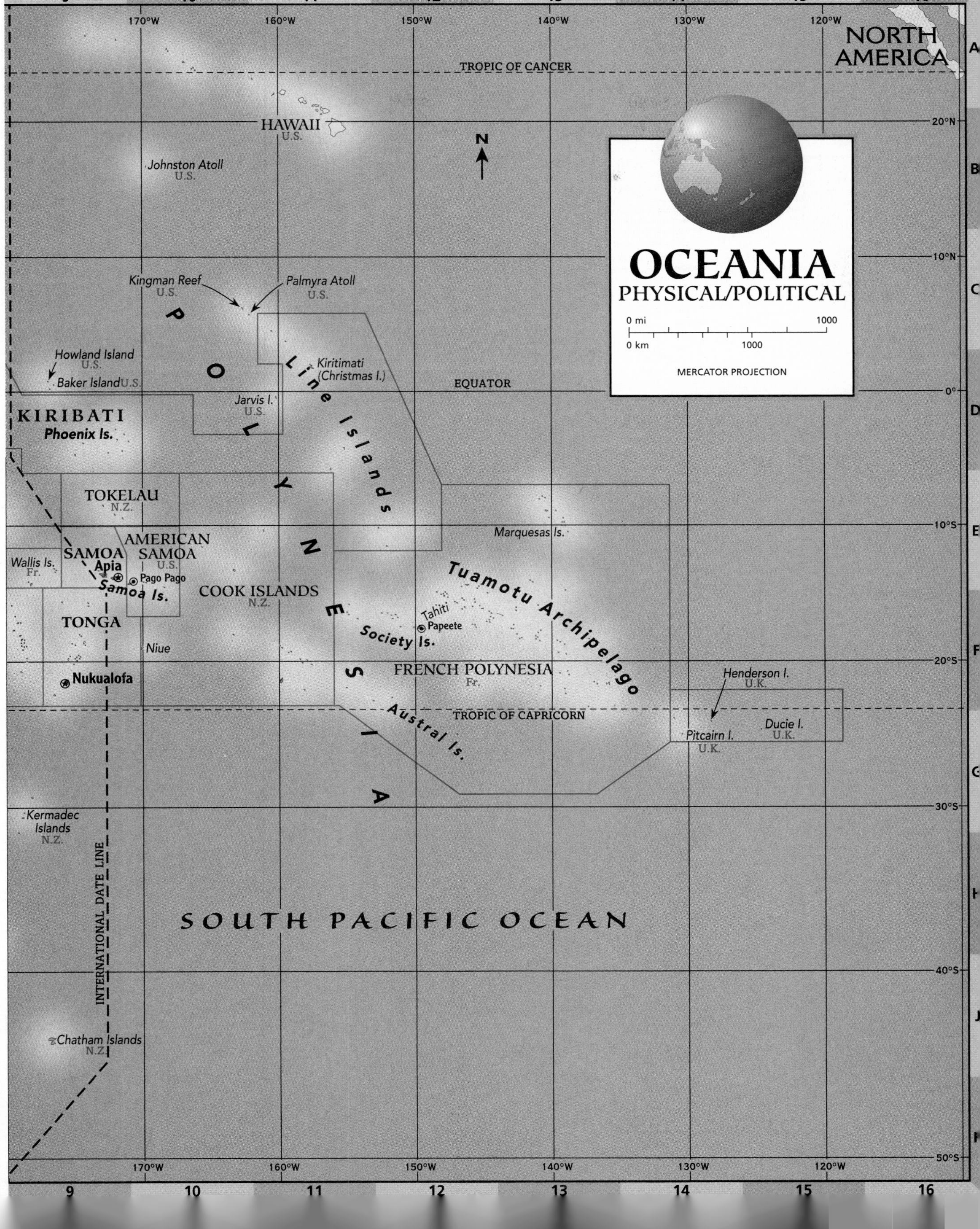

OCEANIA
PHYSICAL/POLITICAL
0 mi 1000
0 km 1000
MERCATOR PROJECTION
NORTH AMERICA
TROPIC OF CANCER
HAWAII
U.S.
Johnston Atoll
U.S.
Kingman Reef
U.S.
Palmyra Atoll
U.S.
POLYNESIA
Howland Island
U.S.
Baker Island U.S.
Kiritimati
(Christmas I.)
Line Islands
EQUATOR
Jarvis I.
U.S.
KIRIBATI
Phoenix Is.
TOKELAU
N.Z.
Marquesas Is.
AMERICAN SAMOA
U.S.
SAMOA
Apia
Wallis Is.
Fr.
Pago Pago
Samoa Is.
COOK ISLANDS
N.Z.
Tuamotu Archipelago
Tahiti
Papeete
Society Is.
TONGA
Niue
Nukualofa
FRENCH POLYNESIA
Fr.
Henderson I.
U.K.
Austral Is.
TROPIC OF CAPRICORN
Ducie I.
U.K.
Pitcairn I.
U.K.
Kermadec Islands
N.Z.
INTERNATIONAL DATE LINE
SOUTH PACIFIC OCEAN
Chatham Islands
N.Z.
170°W
160°W
150°W
140°W
130°W
120°W
20°N
10°N
0°
10°S
20°S
30°S
40°S
50°S

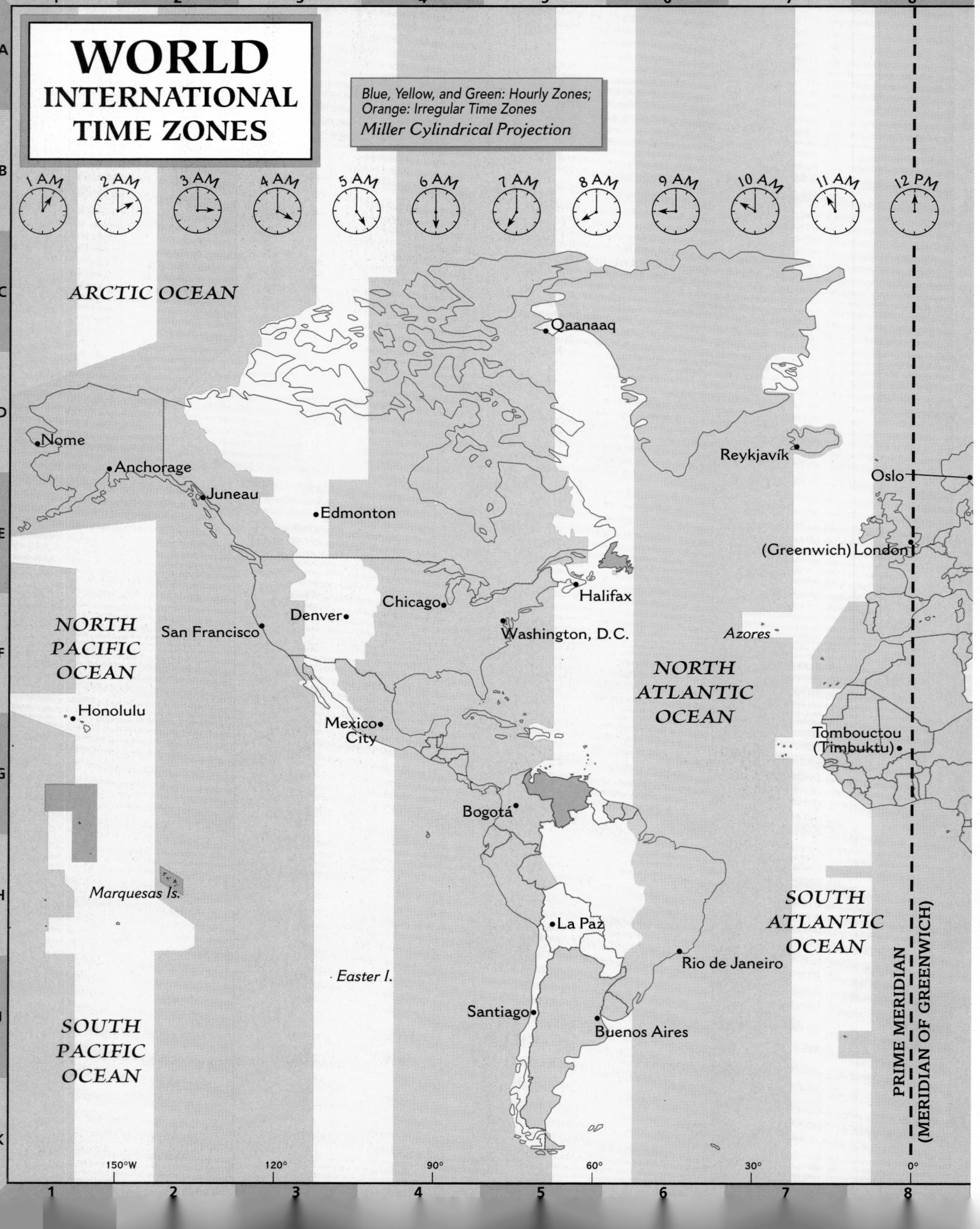
WORLD INTERNATIONAL TIME ZONES
Blue, Yellow, and Green: Hourly Zones; Orange: Irregular Time Zones
Miller Cylindrical Projection
1 AM
2 AM
3 AM
4 AM
5 AM
6 AM
7 AM
8 AM
9 AM
10 AM
11 AM
12 PM
ARCTIC OCEAN
Qaanaaq
Nome
Anchorage
Juneau
Edmonton
Reykjavík
Oslo
(Greenwich) London
Halifax
Chicago
Denver
San Francisco
Washington, D.C.
Azores
NORTH PACIFIC OCEAN
NORTH ATLANTIC OCEAN
Honolulu
Mexico City
Tombouctou (Timbuktu)
Bogotá
Marquesas Is.
La Paz
SOUTH ATLANTIC OCEAN
Rio de Janeiro
Easter I.
Santiago
Buenos Aires
SOUTH PACIFIC OCEAN
PRIME MERIDIAN (MERIDIAN OF GREENWICH)
150°W
120°
90°
60°
30°
0°

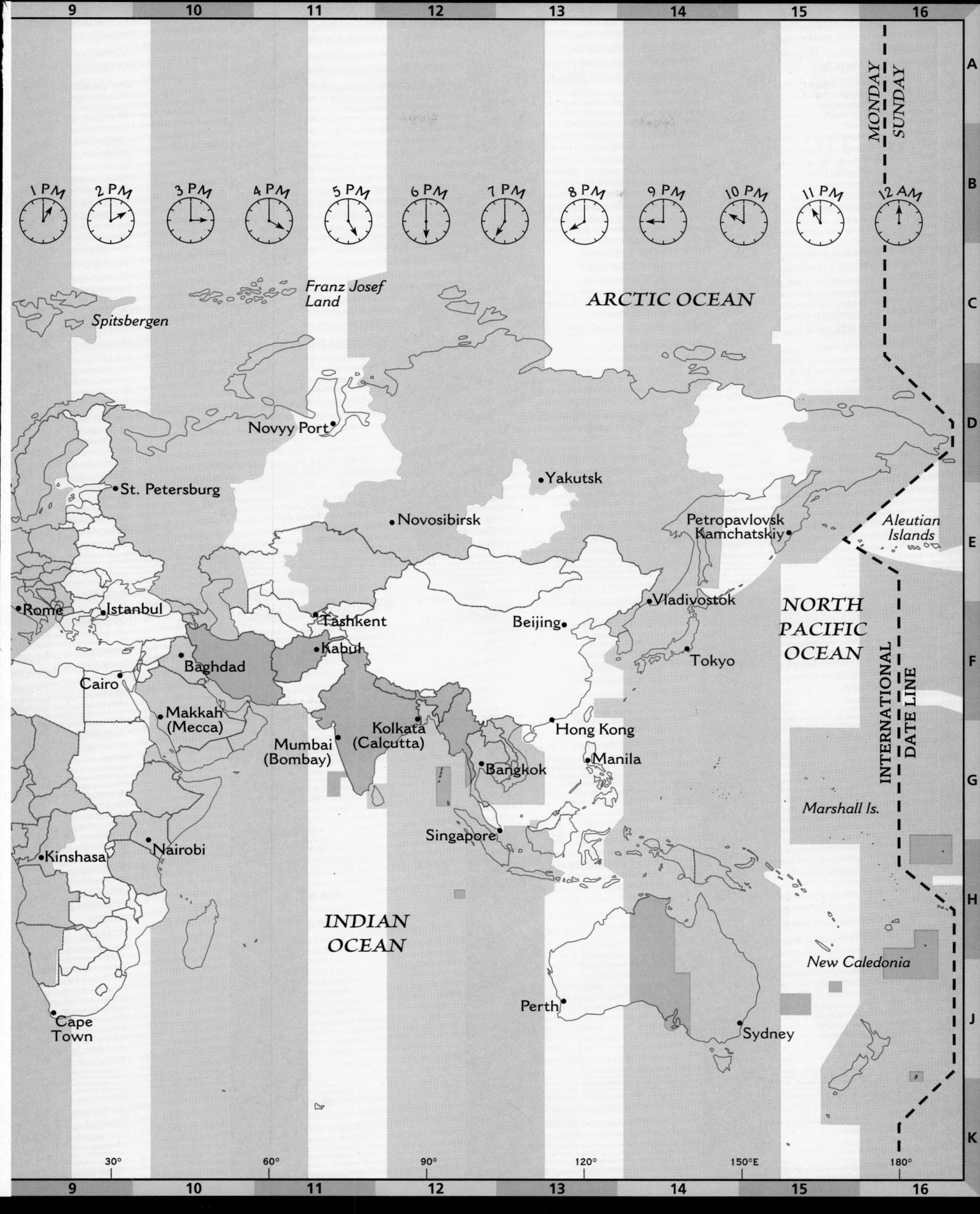
1 PM
2 PM
3 PM
4 PM
5 PM
6 PM
7 PM
8 PM
9 PM
10 PM
11 PM
12 AM
MONDAY
SUNDAY
Franz Josef Land
Spitsbergen
ARCTIC OCEAN
Novyy Port
St. Petersburg
Yakutsk
Novosibirsk
Petropavlovsk Kamchatskiy
Aleutian Islands
Vladivostok
Rome
Istanbul
Tashkent
Beijing
NORTH PACIFIC OCEAN
Kabul
Baghdad
Tokyo
Cairo
INTERNATIONAL DATE LINE
Makkah (Mecca)
Hong Kong
Mumbai (Bombay)
Kolkata (Calcutta)
Manila
Bangkok
Marshall Is.
Singapore
Nairobi
Kinshasa
INDIAN OCEAN
New Caledonia
Perth
Cape Town
Sydney
30°
60°
90°
120°
150°E
180°

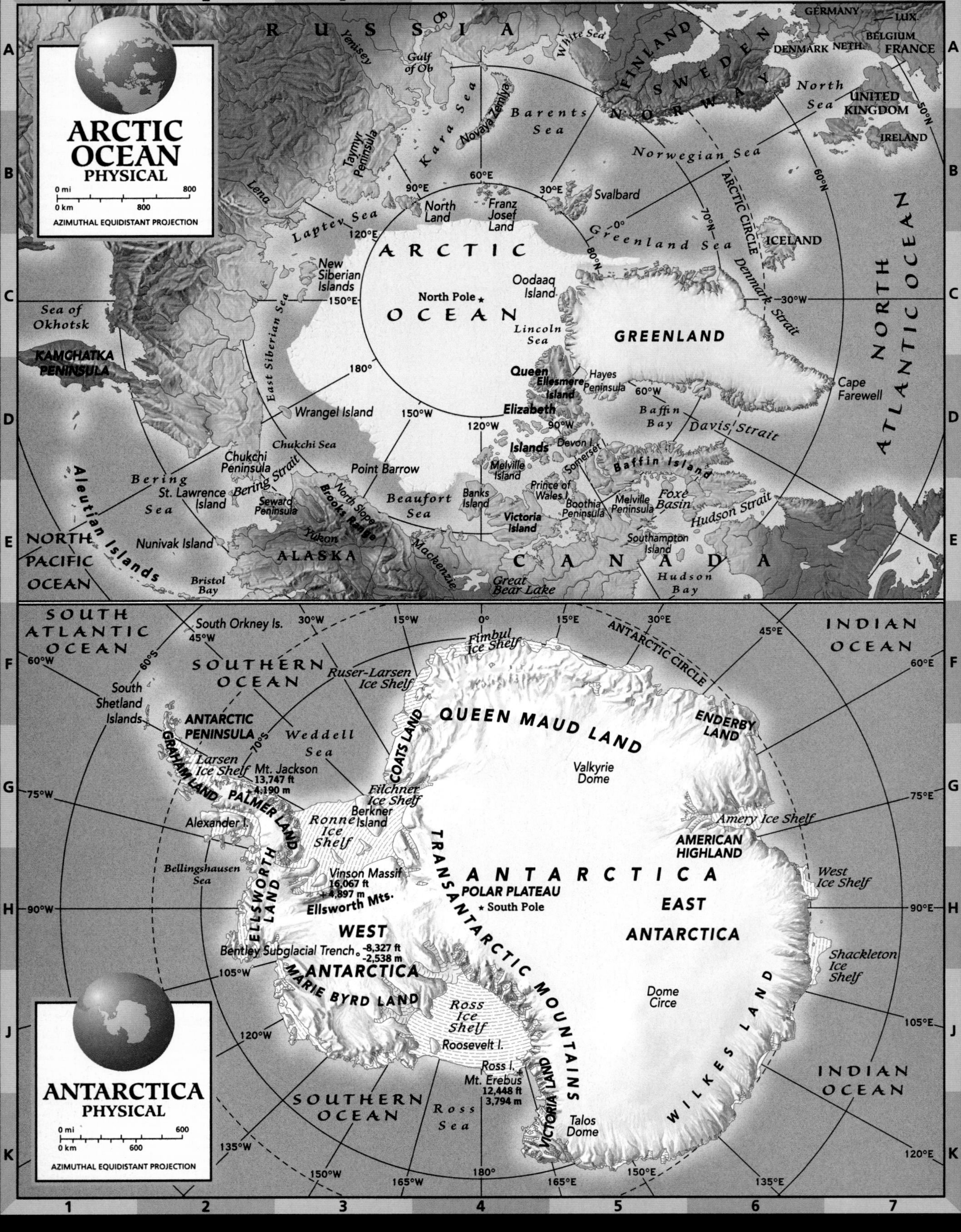
ARCTIC OCEAN
PHYSICAL
0 mi 800
0 km 800
AZIMUTHAL EQUIDISTANT PROJECTION
RUSSIA
Yenisey
Ob
Gulf of Ob
White Sea
FINLAND
SWEDEN
NORWAY
GERMANY
LUX.
BELGIUM
DENMARK
NETH.
FRANCE
North Sea
UNITED KINGDOM
IRELAND
Kara Sea
Novaya Zemlya
Barents Sea
Taymyr Peninsula
Norwegian Sea
ARCTIC CIRCLE
Lena
Laptev Sea
North Land
Franz Josef Land
Svalbard
Greenland Sea
ICELAND
NORTH ATLANTIC OCEAN
ARCTIC OCEAN
New Siberian Islands
North Pole
Oodaaq Island
Denmark Strait
Sea of Okhotsk
East Siberian Sea
Lincoln Sea
GREENLAND
KAMCHATKA PENINSULA
Queen Elizabeth Islands
Ellesmere Island
Hayes Peninsula
Cape Farewell
Wrangel Island
Baffin Bay
Davis Strait
Devon I.
Chukchi Sea
Chukchi Peninsula
Point Barrow
Melville Island
Somerset I.
Baffin Island
Aleutian Islands
Bering Sea
Bering Strait
St. Lawrence Island
Seward Peninsula
Brooks Range
North Slope
Beaufort Sea
Banks Island
Prince of Wales I.
Boothia Peninsula
Melville Peninsula
Foxe Basin
Hudson Strait
Victoria Island
NORTH PACIFIC OCEAN
Nunivak Island
Yukon
ALASKA
Mackenzie
Southampton Island
CANADA
Bristol Bay
Great Bear Lake
Hudson Bay
ANTARCTICA
PHYSICAL
0 mi 600
0 km 600
AZIMUTHAL EQUIDISTANT PROJECTION
SOUTH ATLANTIC OCEAN
South Orkney Is.
ANTARCTIC CIRCLE
Fimbul Ice Shelf
INDIAN OCEAN
SOUTHERN OCEAN
Ruser-Larsen Ice Shelf
South Shetland Islands
ANTARCTIC PENINSULA
QUEEN MAUD LAND
ENDERBY LAND
Weddell Sea
COATS LAND
GRAHAM LAND
Larsen Ice Shelf
Mt. Jackson 13,747 ft 4,190 m
Valkyrie Dome
PALMER LAND
Filchner Ice Shelf
Berkner Island
Alexander I.
Ronne Ice Shelf
Amery Ice Shelf
AMERICAN HIGHLAND
Bellingshausen Sea
ELLSWORTH LAND
Vinson Massif 16,067 ft 4,897 m
ANTARCTICA
West Ice Shelf
POLAR PLATEAU
Ellsworth Mts.
South Pole
EAST ANTARCTICA
WEST ANTARCTICA
TRANSANTARCTIC MOUNTAINS
Bentley Subglacial Trench -8,327 ft -2,538 m
Shackleton Ice Shelf
MARIE BYRD LAND
Ross Ice Shelf
Dome Circe
Roosevelt I.
Ross I.
Mt. Erebus 12,448 ft 3,794 m
VICTORIA LAND
WILKES LAND
SOUTHERN OCEAN
Ross Sea
Talos Dome
INDIAN OCEAN

A WORLD OF EXTREMES

1. **The largest continent** is Asia with an area of 12,262,691 sq. miles (31,758,898 sq. km).
2. **The smallest continent** is Australia with an area of 2,988,888 sq. miles (7,741,184 sq. km).
3. **The largest country** is Russia with an area of 6,592,819 sq. miles (17,075,322 sq. km).
4. **The smallest country** is Vatican City with an area of 1 sq. mile (2.6 sq. km).
5. **The longest river** is the Nile River with a length of 4,160 miles (6,695 km).
6. **The deepest lake** is Lake Baikal with a maximum depth of 5,715 feet (1,742 m).
7. **The highest waterfall** is Angel Falls with a height of 3,212 feet (979 m).
8. **The highest mountain** is Mount Everest with a height of 29,028 feet (8,848 m) above sea level.
9. **The largest desert** is the Sahara with an area of 3,500,000 sq. miles (9,065,000 sq. km).

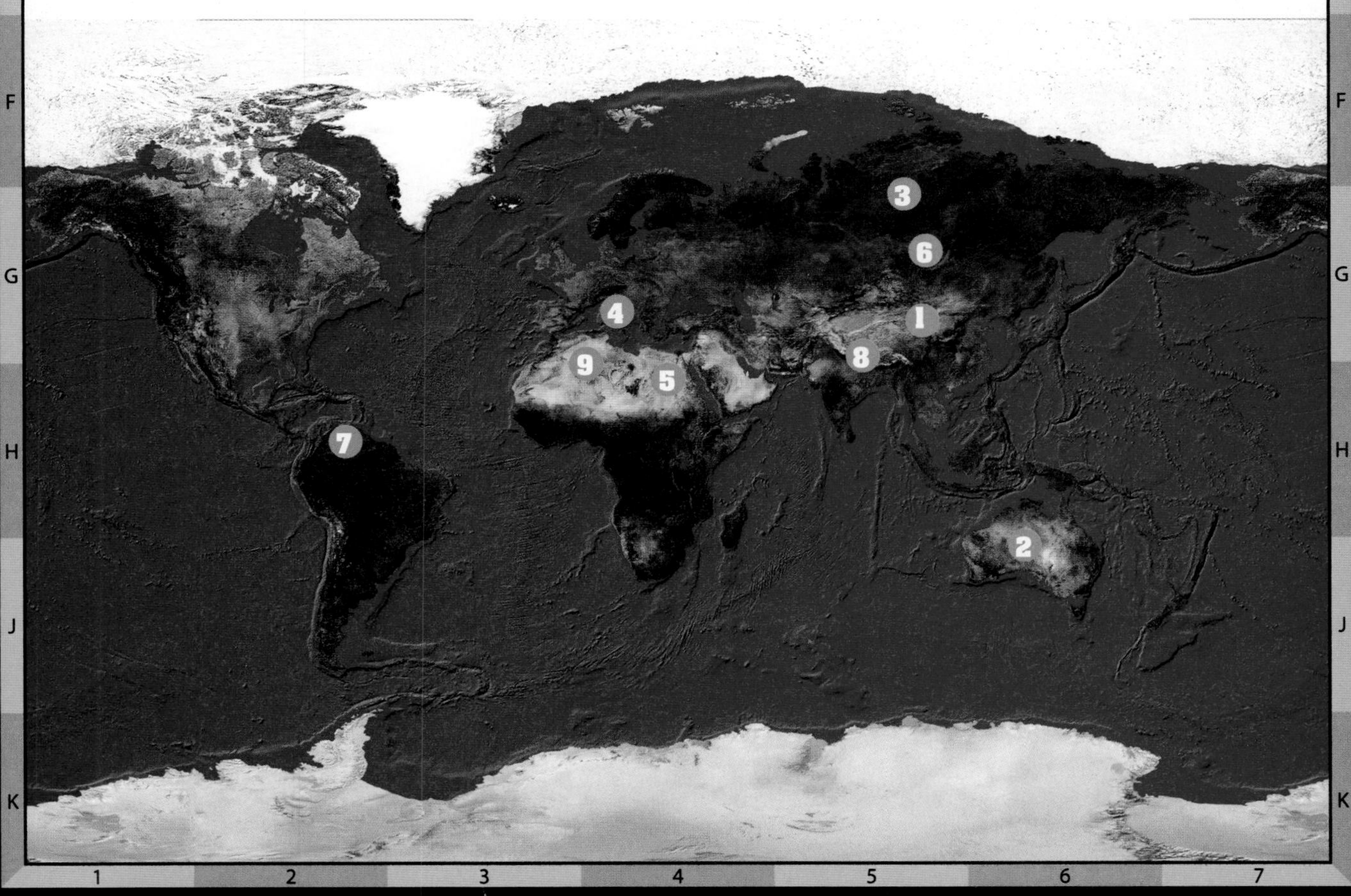

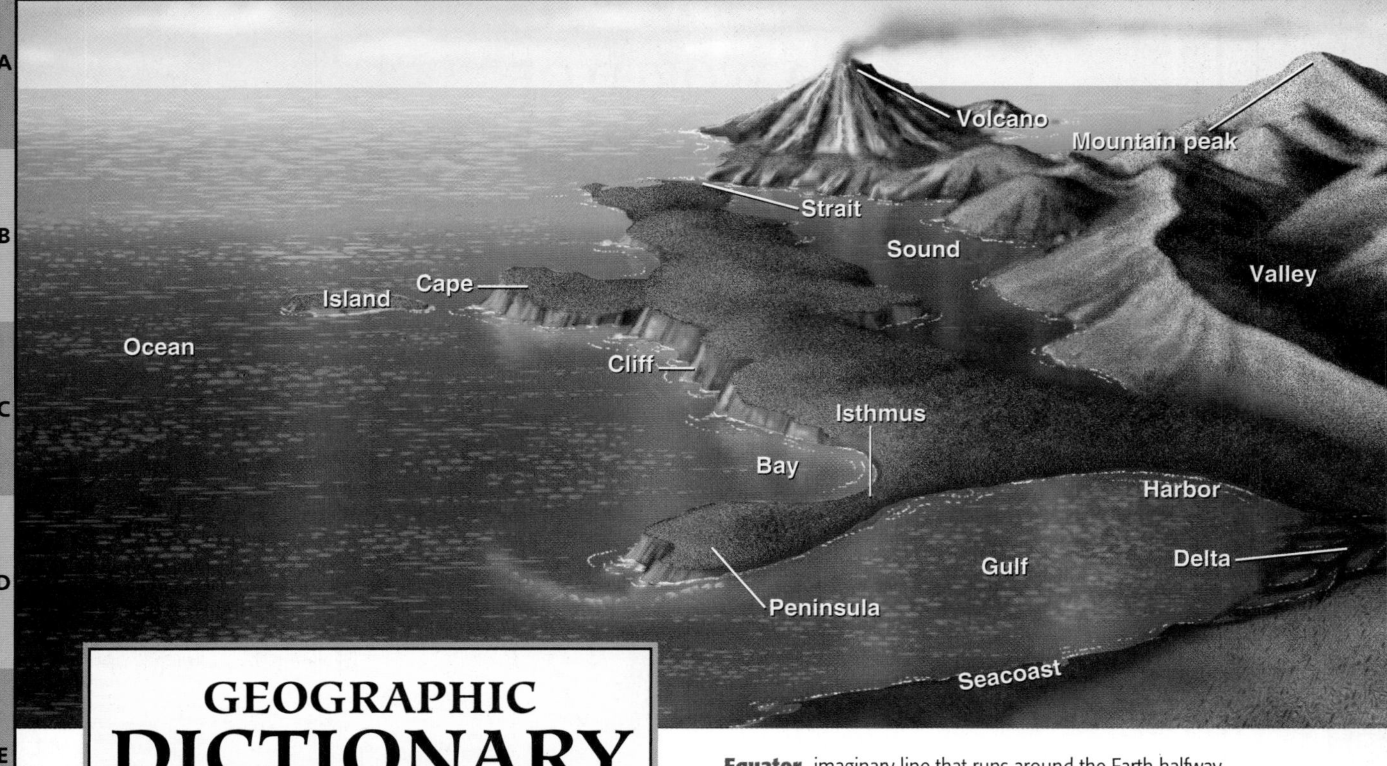

GEOGRAPHIC DICTIONARY

As you read about the world's geography, you will encounter the terms listed below. Many of the terms are pictured in the diagram.

absolute location exact location of a place on the Earth described by global coordinates

basin area of land drained by a given river and its branches; area of land surrounded by lands of higher elevations

bay part of a large body of water that extends into a shoreline, generally smaller than a gulf

canyon deep and narrow valley with steep walls

cape point of land that extends into a river, lake, or ocean

channel wide strait or waterway between two landmasses that lie close to each other; deep part of a river or other waterway

cliff steep, high wall of rock, Earth, or ice

continent one of the seven large landmasses on the Earth

delta flat, low-lying land built up from soil carried downstream by a river and deposited at its mouth

divide stretch of high land that separates river systems

downstream direction in which a river or stream flows from its source to its mouth

elevation height of land above sea level

Equator imaginary line that runs around the Earth halfway between the North and South Poles; used as the starting point to measure degrees of north and south latitude

glacier large, thick body of slowly moving ice

gulf part of a large body of water that extends into a shoreline, generally larger and more deeply indented than a bay

harbor a sheltered place along a shoreline where ships can anchor safely

highland elevated land area such as a hill, mountain, or plateau

hill elevated land with sloping sides and rounded summit; generally smaller than a mountain

island land area, smaller than a continent, completely surrounded by water

isthmus narrow stretch of land connecting two larger land areas

lake a sizable inland body of water

latitude distance north or south of the Equator, measured in degrees

longitude distance east or west of the Prime Meridian, measured in degrees

lowland land, usually level, at a low elevation

map drawing of the Earth shown on a flat surface

meridian one of many lines on the global grid running from the North Pole to the South Pole; used to measure degrees of longitude

mesa broad, flat-topped landform with steep sides; smaller than a plateau

mountain land with steep sides that rises sharply (1,000 feet or more) from surrounding land; generally larger and more rugged than a hill

mountain peak pointed top of a mountain

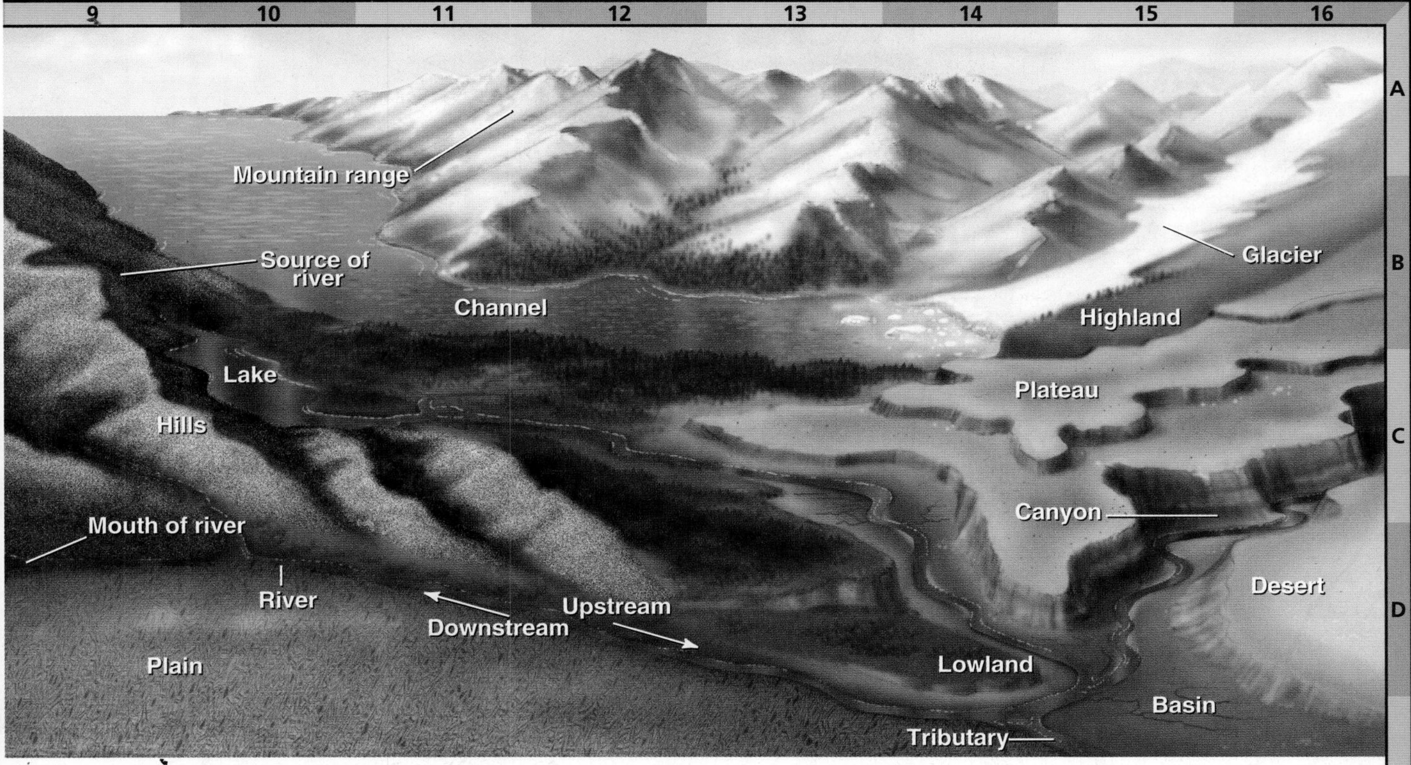

mountain range a series of connected mountains

mouth (of a river) place where a stream or river flows into a larger body of water

ocean one of the four major bodies of salt water that surround the continents

ocean current stream of either cold or warm water that moves in a definite direction through an ocean

parallel one of many lines on the global grid that circles the Earth north or south of the Equator; used to measure degrees of latitude

peninsula body of land jutting into a lake or ocean, surrounded on three sides by water

physical feature characteristic of a place occurring naturally, such as a landform, body of water, climate pattern, or resource

plain area of level land, usually at low elevation and often covered with grasses

plateau area of flat or rolling land at a high elevation, about 300 to 3,000 feet (90 to 900 m) high

Prime Meridian line of the global grid running from the North Pole to the South Pole at Greenwich, England; starting point for measuring degrees of east and west longitude

relief changes in elevation over a given area of land

river large natural stream of water that runs through the land

sea large body of water completely or partly surrounded by land

seacoast land lying next to a sea or an ocean

sound broad inland body of water, often between a coastline and one or more islands off the coast

source (of a river) place where a river or stream begins, often in highlands

strait narrow stretch of water joining two larger bodies of water

tributary small river or stream that flows into a large river or stream; a branch of the river

upstream direction opposite the flow of a river; toward the source of a river or stream

valley area of low land usually between hills or mountains

volcano mountain or hill created as liquid rock and ash erupt from inside the Earth

Use the maps on pages RA2–RA37 to help you answer the following questions.

1. Which physical features are located in G14 on the World Physical map?
2. On the North America Political map, in which section of the grid would you find the Panama Canal?
3. Using the Europe Physical map, determine the length of the Pyrenees Mountains in miles and kilometers.
4. In which direction would you travel to go from Lake Erie to Lake Ontario?

Understanding Geography

CHAPTER 1
Using Geography Skills

CHAPTER 2
Earth's Physical Geography

CHAPTER 3
Earth's Human and Cultural Geography

Hiker on Gros Piton, St. Lucia, in the Caribbean

NATIONAL GEOGRAPHIC

NGS ONLINE For more information about the region, see www.nationalgeographic.com/education.

World Atlas

The World
CLIMATE REGIONS

Map Skills

1 Place What two climate zones are found in Antarctica?

2 Regions In general terms, how would you describe the world climate zones along the Equator?

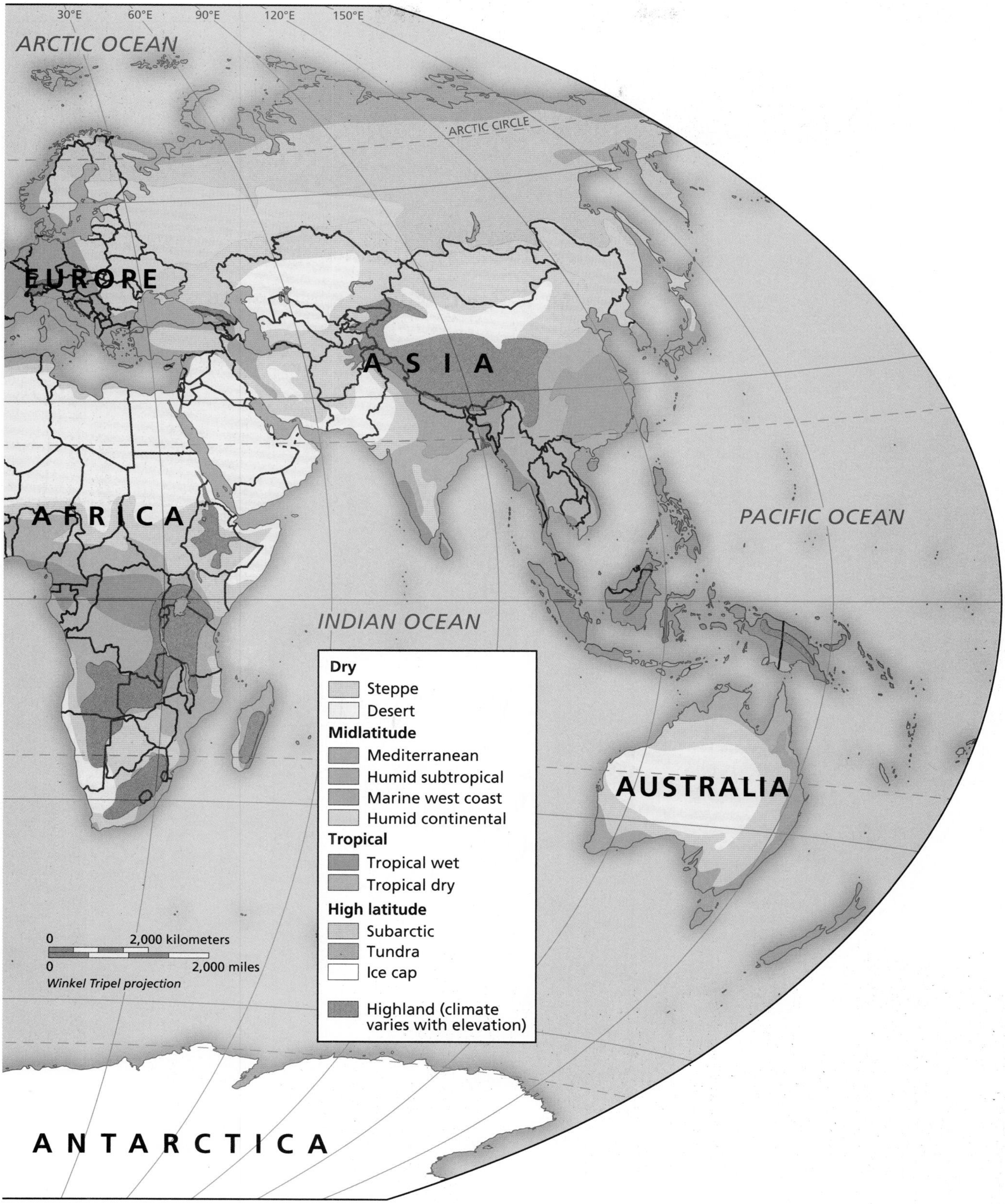

30°E 60°E 90°E 120°E 150°E

ARCTIC OCEAN

ARCTIC CIRCLE

EUROPE

ASIA

AFRICA

PACIFIC OCEAN

INDIAN OCEAN

AUSTRALIA

ANTARCTICA

Dry
- Steppe
- Desert

Midlatitude
- Mediterranean
- Humid subtropical
- Marine west coast
- Humid continental

Tropical
- Tropical wet
- Tropical dry

High latitude
- Subarctic
- Tundra
- Ice cap

- Highland (climate varies with elevation)

0 2,000 kilometers
0 2,000 miles
Winkel Tripel projection

The World
VEGETATION

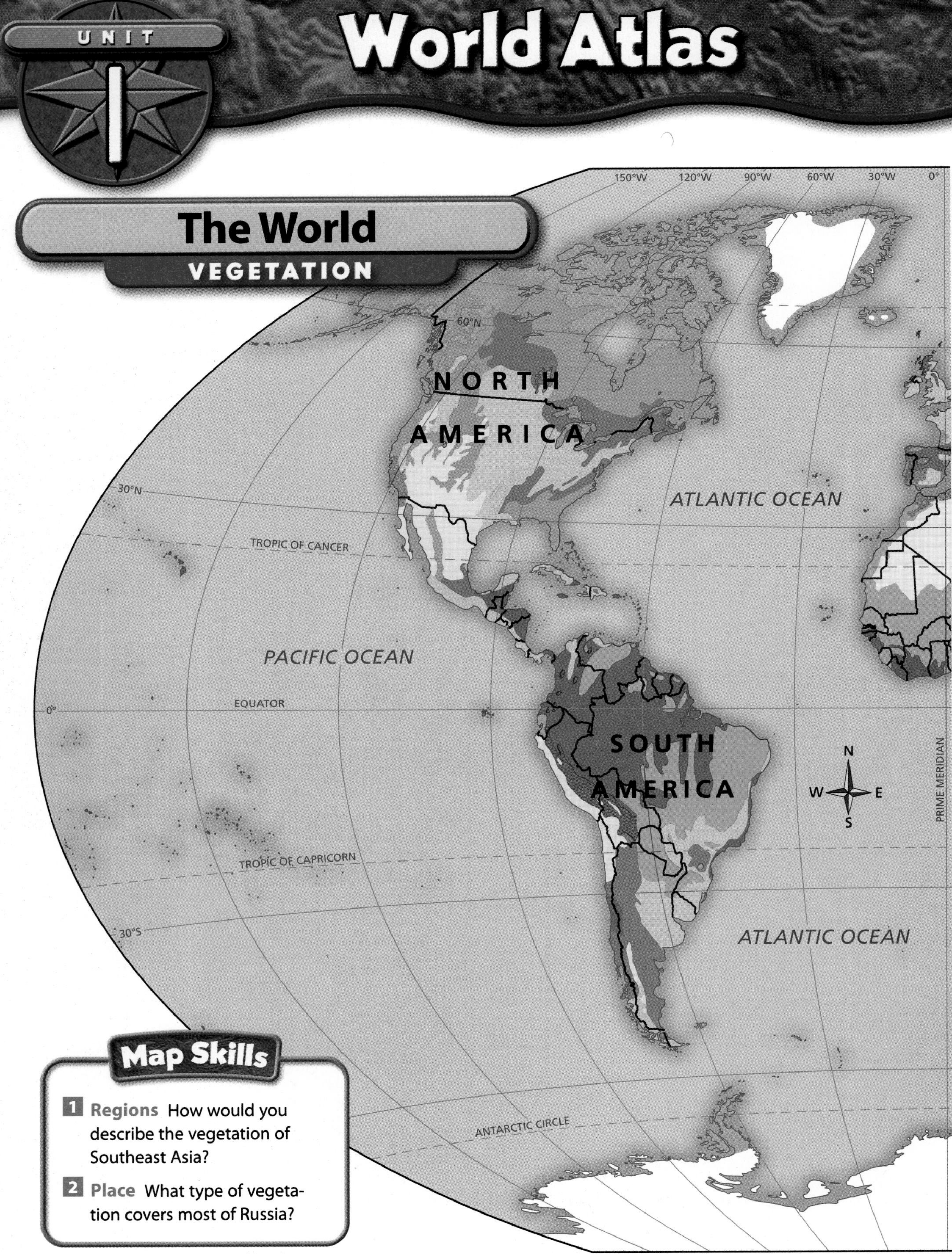

Map Skills

1 Regions How would you describe the vegetation of Southeast Asia?

2 Place What type of vegetation covers most of Russia?

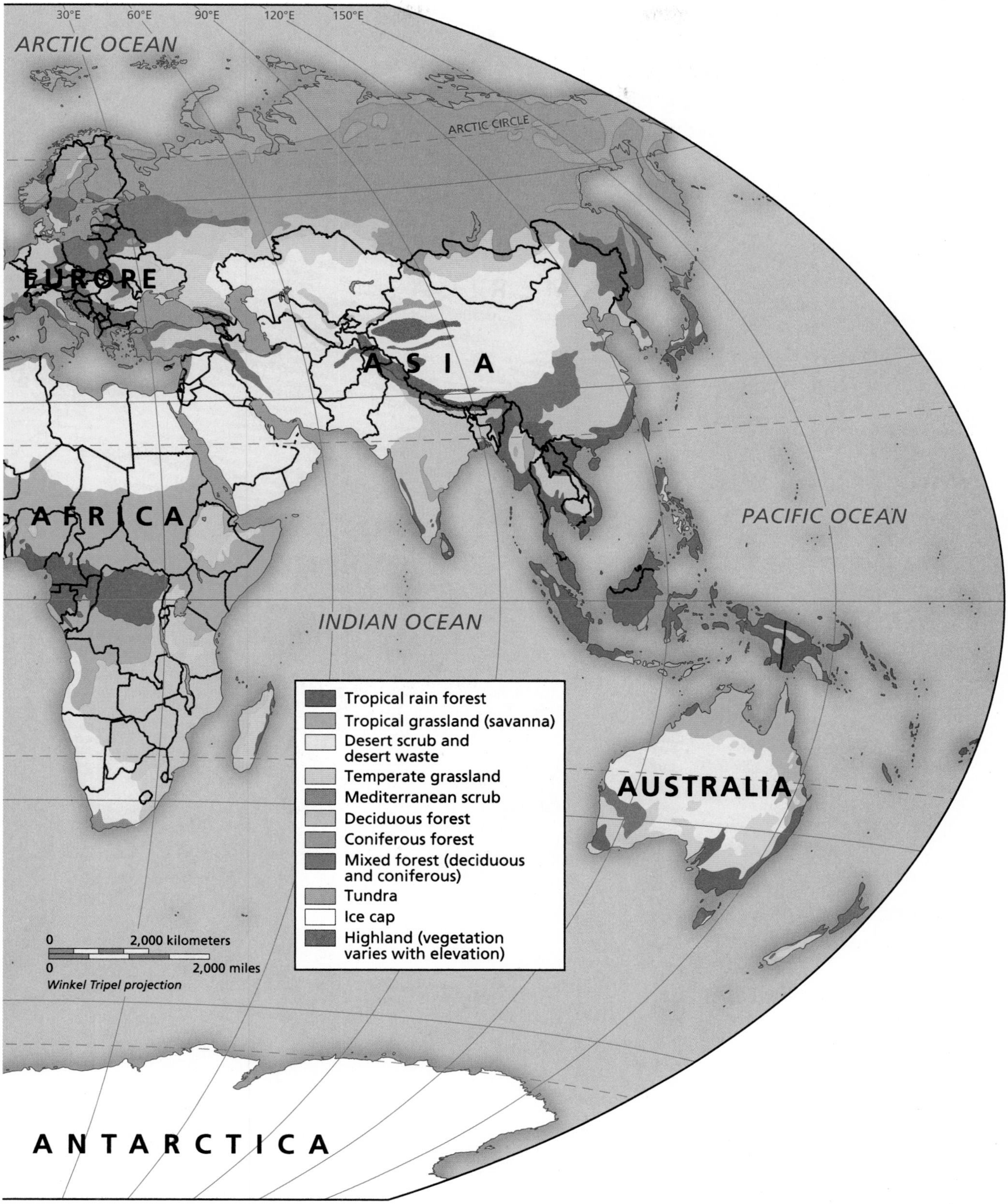

30°E 60°E 90°E 120°E 150°E

ARCTIC OCEAN

ARCTIC CIRCLE

EUROPE

ASIA

AFRICA

PACIFIC OCEAN

INDIAN OCEAN

AUSTRALIA

ANTARCTICA

- Tropical rain forest
- Tropical grassland (savanna)
- Desert scrub and desert waste
- Temperate grassland
- Mediterranean scrub
- Deciduous forest
- Coniferous forest
- Mixed forest (deciduous and coniferous)
- Tundra
- Ice cap
- Highland (vegetation varies with elevation)

0 2,000 kilometers

0 2,000 miles

Winkel Tripel projection

UNIT 1

World Atlas

The World

POPULATION DENSITY

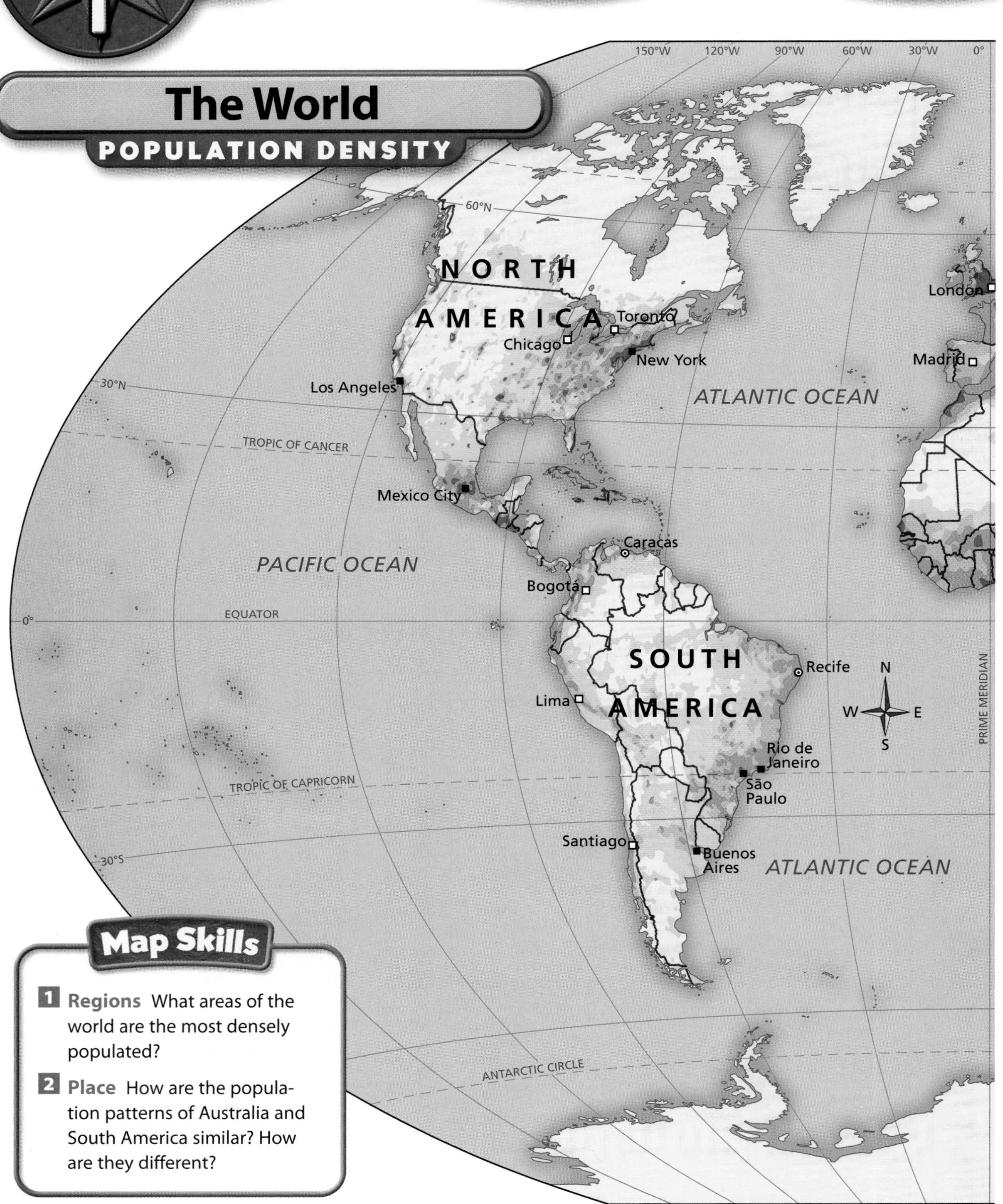

Map Skills

1 Regions What areas of the world are the most densely populated?

2 Place How are the population patterns of Australia and South America similar? How are they different?

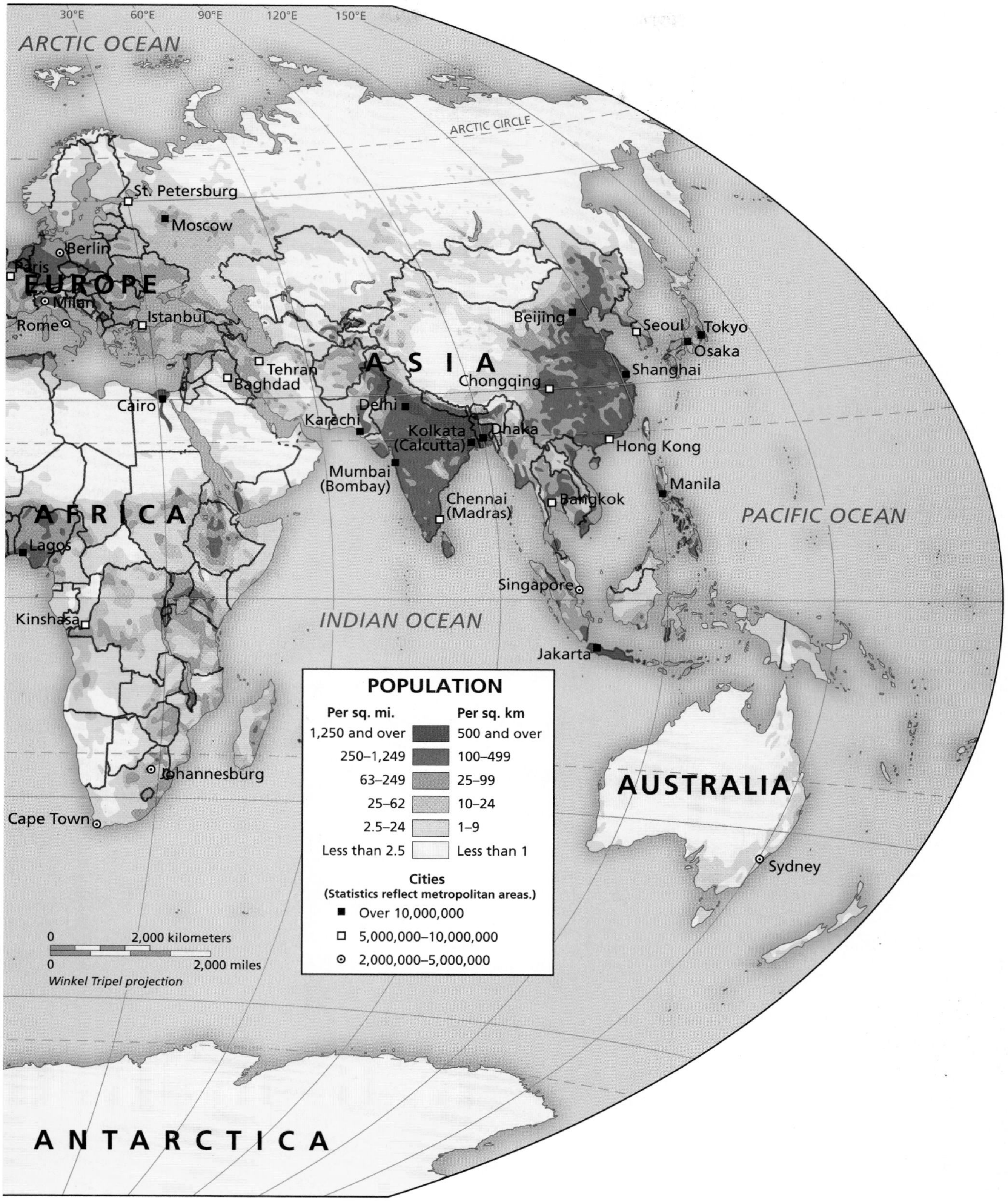

30°E
60°E
90°E
120°E
150°E
ARCTIC OCEAN
ARCTIC CIRCLE
St. Petersburg
Moscow
Berlin
Paris
EUROPE
Milan
Rome
Istanbul
Tehran
Baghdad
Cairo
ASIA
Beijing
Seoul
Tokyo
Osaka
Shanghai
Chongqing
Delhi
Karachi
Kolkata (Calcutta)
Dhaka
Hong Kong
Mumbai (Bombay)
Chennai (Madras)
Bangkok
Manila
PACIFIC OCEAN
AFRICA
Lagos
Singapore
Kinshasa
INDIAN OCEAN
Jakarta
Johannesburg
Cape Town
AUSTRALIA
Sydney
ANTARCTICA

0 2,000 kilometers
0 2,000 miles
Winkel Tripel projection

POPULATION

Per sq. mi.	Per sq. km
1,250 and over	500 and over
250–1,249	100–499
63–249	25–99
25–62	10–24
2.5–24	1–9
Less than 2.5	Less than 1

Cities
(Statistics reflect metropolitan areas.)

- ■ Over 10,000,000
- □ 5,000,000–10,000,000
- ⊙ 2,000,000–5,000,000

UNIT 1

World Atlas

The World

RELIGIONS

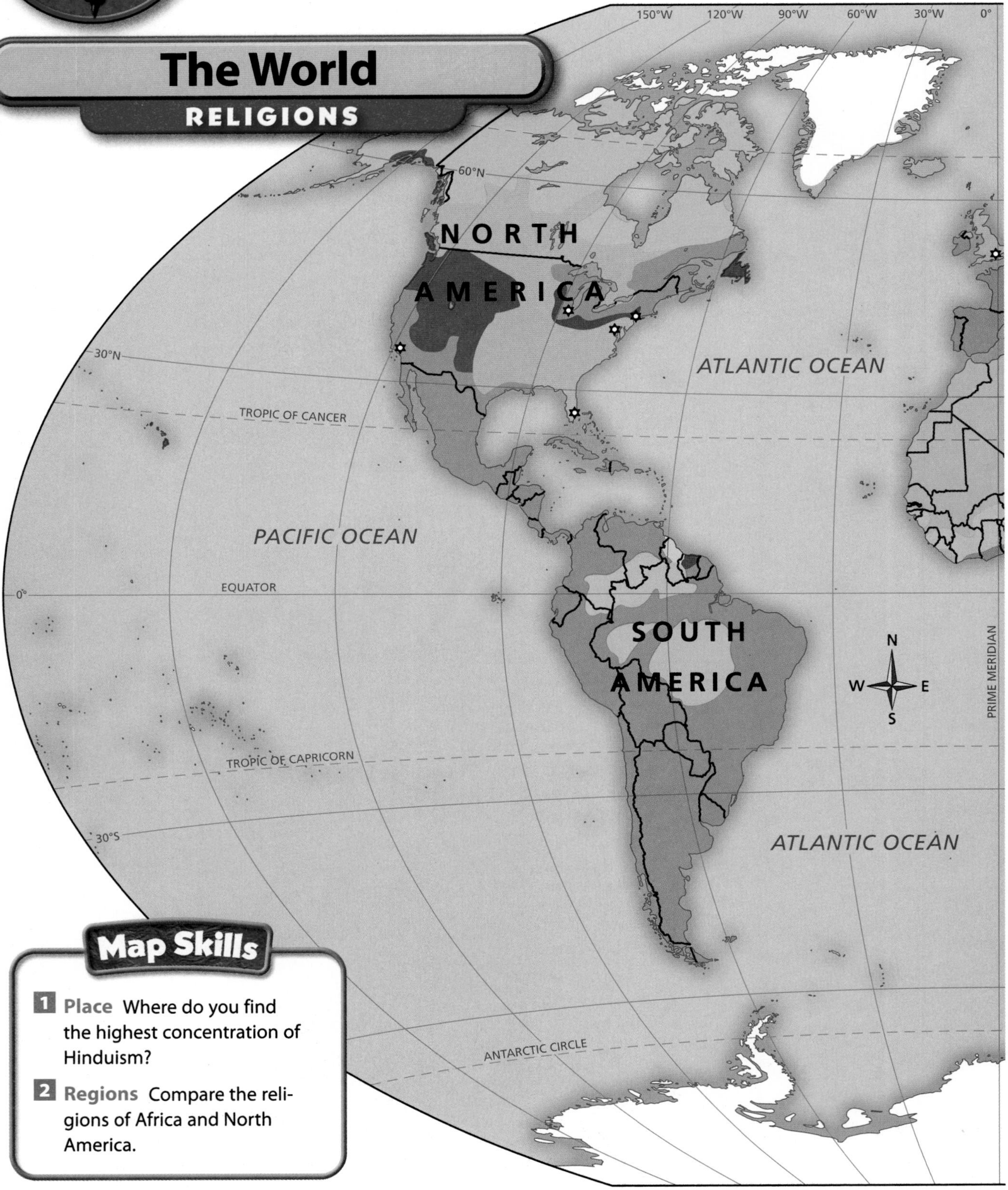

150°W 120°W 90°W 60°W 30°W 0°

60°N
NORTH AMERICA
30°N
ATLANTIC OCEAN
TROPIC OF CANCER
PACIFIC OCEAN
EQUATOR
0°
SOUTH AMERICA
N
W E
S
PRIME MERIDIAN
TROPIC OF CAPRICORN
30°S
ATLANTIC OCEAN
ANTARCTIC CIRCLE

Map Skills

1. **Place** Where do you find the highest concentration of Hinduism?
2. **Regions** Compare the religions of Africa and North America.

NATIONAL
GEOGRAPHIC

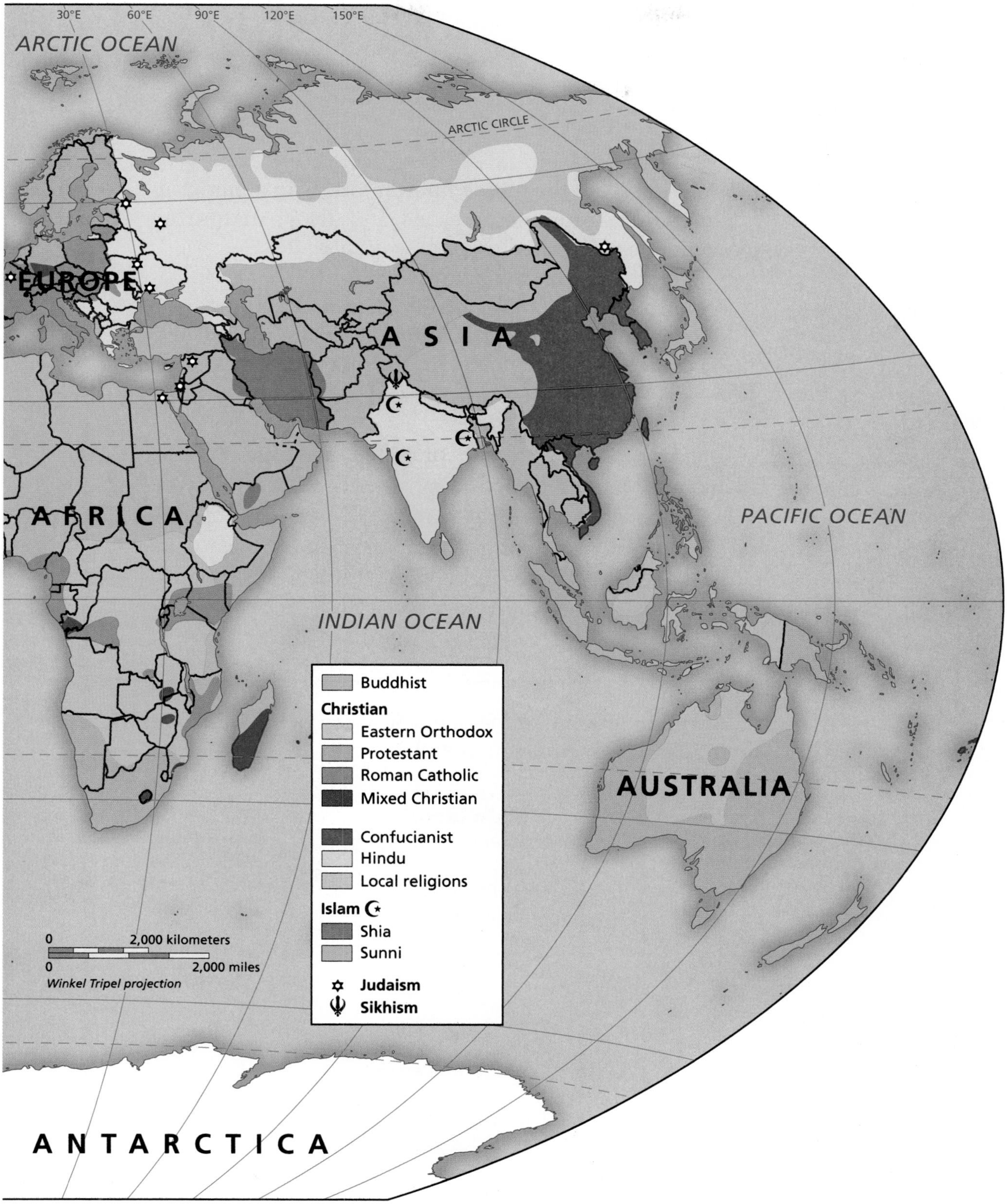

30°E
60°E
90°E
120°E
150°E
ARCTIC OCEAN
ARCTIC CIRCLE
EUROPE
ASIA
AFRICA
PACIFIC OCEAN
INDIAN OCEAN
AUSTRALIA
ANTARCTICA
Buddhist
Christian
Eastern Orthodox
Protestant
Roman Catholic
Mixed Christian
Confucianist
Hindu
Local religions
Islam
Shia
Sunni
Judaism
Sikhism
0 2,000 kilometers
0 2,000 miles
Winkel Tripel projection

Reading Social Studies

Identifying the Main Idea

Learn It!

Main ideas are the most important ideas in a paragraph, section, or chapter. The examples, reasons, and details that further explain the main idea are called *supporting details.*

- Read the paragraph below.
- Notice how the main idea is identified for you.
- Read the sentences that follow the main idea. These are supporting details that explain the main idea.

Main Idea

Supporting Details

> Mountains are huge towers of rock and are the highest landforms. Some mountains may be only a few thousand feet high. Others can soar higher than 20,000 feet (6,096 m). The world's highest mountain is Mount Everest in South Asia's Himalaya ranges. It rises more than 29,028 feet (8,848 m), nearly five and a half miles high!
>
> *—from page 50*

A web diagram like the one below can help you record the main idea and supporting details.

Main Idea: Mountains are huge towers of rock and are the highest landforms.

Supporting Detail: Some mountains may be only a few thousand feet high.

Supporting Detail: Other mountains can soar higher than 20,000 feet (6,096 m).

Supporting Detail: The world's highest mountain, Mount Everest, rises more than 29,028 feet (8,848 m), nearly five and a half miles high.

Reading Tip

Main ideas often appear in the first sentence, but they can also be found in the middle or at the end of the paragraph.

2 Practice It!

Read the following paragraph from this unit.

- Draw a graphic organizer like the one shown below.
- Write the main idea for the paragraph in the center box.
- Write the supporting details in the ovals surrounding the box.

Remember that you do not need to include every word in the sentence when restating the main idea or supporting details.

Read to Write Activity

Read the main idea for Chapter 3, Section 2, and the paragraphs that follow. Using the main idea as a topic sentence, write a paragraph with supporting details. The supporting details should describe the elements that make up a culture.

> People live on a surprisingly small part of the Earth. Land covers only about 30 percent of the Earth's surface, and only half of this land is usable by humans. Deserts, high mountains, and ice-covered lands cannot support large numbers of people.
>
> —*from page 74*

Sparsely settled High Country of British Columbia, Canada

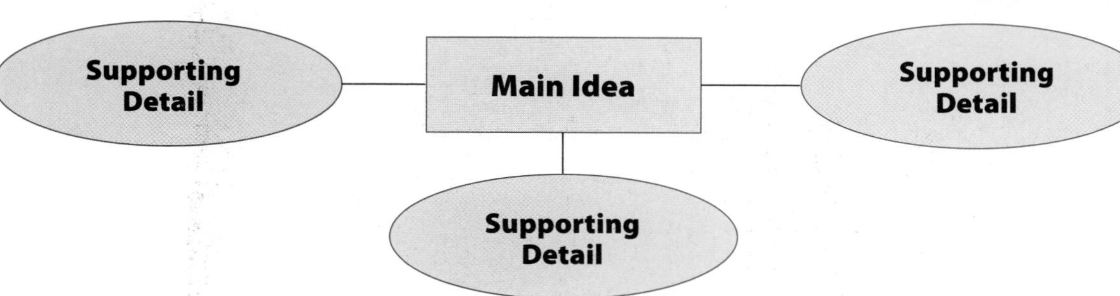

3 Apply It!

Create several web diagrams like the ones found on these pages. As you read Chapters 1, 2, and 3, write the main idea for each section in the center box of the diagram. Write supporting details in ovals surrounding the center box. Use your diagrams to help you study for the chapter assessments.

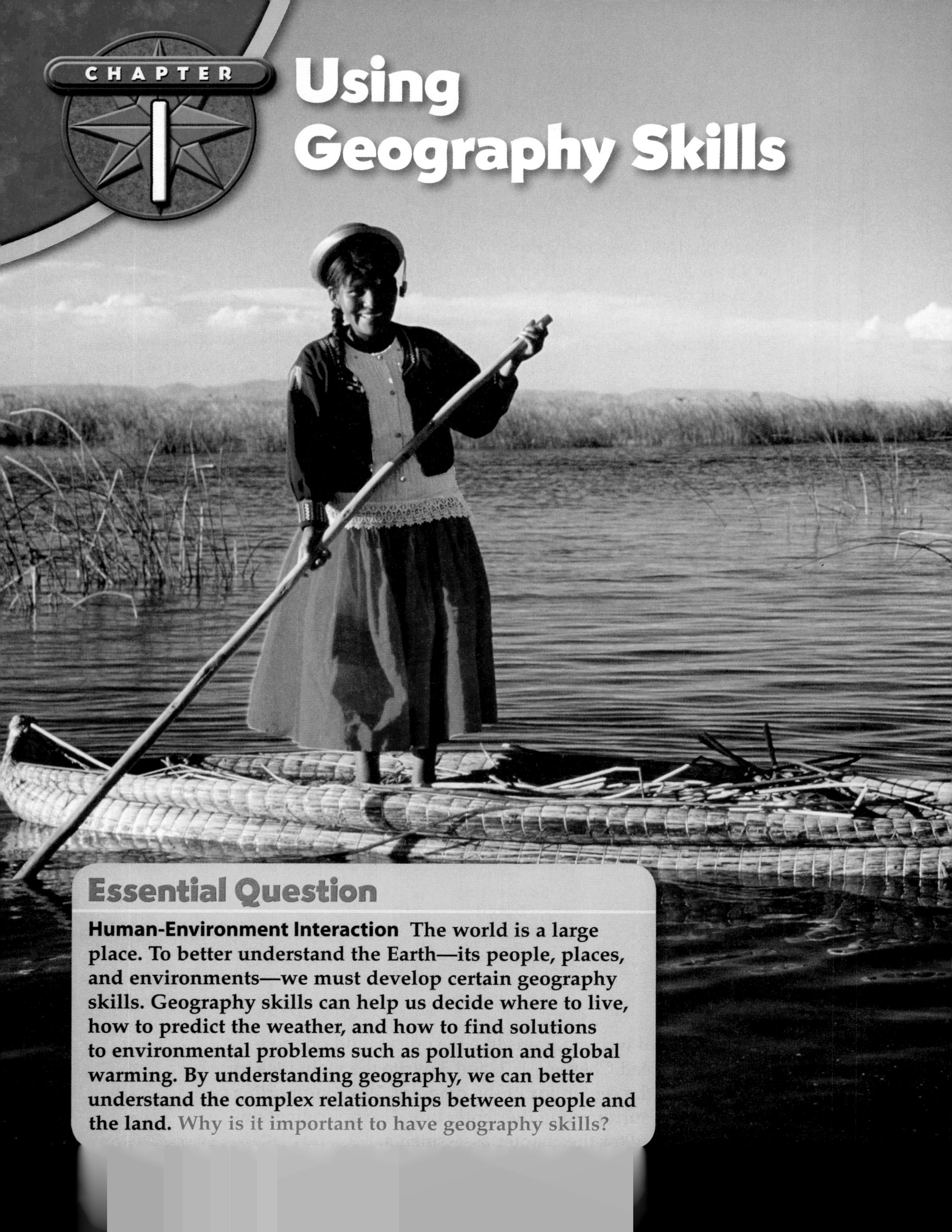

CHAPTER 1 Using Geography Skills

Essential Question

Human-Environment Interaction The world is a large place. To better understand the Earth—its people, places, and environments—we must develop certain geography skills. Geography skills can help us decide where to live, how to predict the weather, and how to find solutions to environmental problems such as pollution and global warming. By understanding geography, we can better understand the complex relationships between people and the land. Why is it important to have geography skills?

Chapter Audio

Section 1: Thinking Like a Geographer

BIG IDEA Geography is used to interpret the past, understand the present, and plan for the future. Geography is the study of the Earth. It is used to analyze the Earth's physical and human features. People can use geographic information to plan, make decisions, and manage resources.

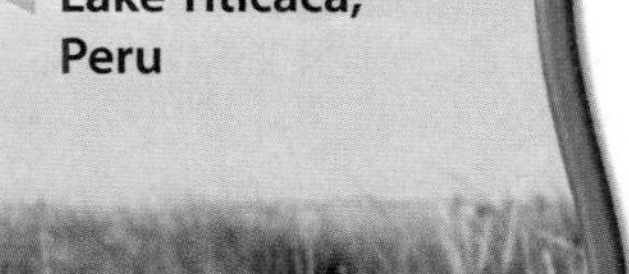

Lake Titicaca, Peru

Section 2: The Earth in Space

BIG IDEA Physical processes shape Earth's surface. Earth has different seasons because of the way it tilts and the way it rotates around the sun. The warmth of the sun's rays makes life on Earth possible.

FOLDABLES™ Study Organizer

Organizing Information Make this Foldable to help you organize information about the uses of geography and about the Earth in space.

Step 1 Fold the sides of an 11x17 sheet of paper to meet in the middle, creating a shutter fold.

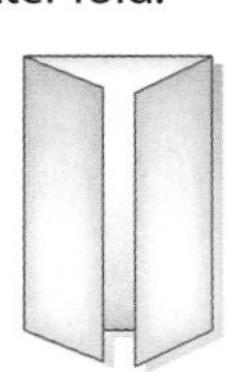

Step 2 Label your Foldable as shown.

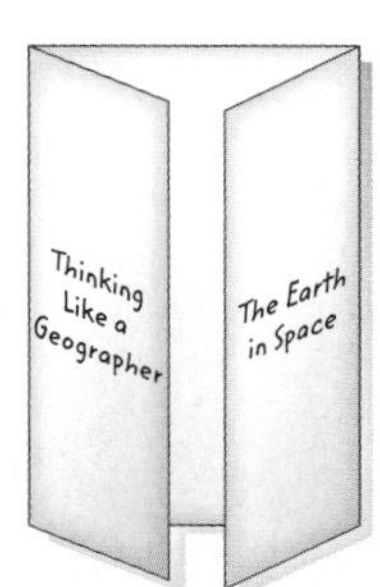

Reading and Writing As you read the chapter, take notes under the appropriate flap of your Foldable. After you have completed your Foldable, use your notes to write a letter encouraging the study of geography by all students.

Visit glencoe.com and enter QuickPass™ code GA6EOW6225c1 for Chapter 1 resources.

Guide to Reading

BIG Idea

Geography is used to interpret the past, understand the present, and plan for the future.

Content Vocabulary

- geography *(p. 15)*
- absolute location *(p. 15)*
- relative location *(p. 15)*
- environment *(p. 15)*
- decade *(p. 16)*
- century *(p. 16)*
- millennium *(p. 16)*
- Global Positioning System (GPS) *(p. 17)*
- Geographic Information Systems (GIS) *(p. 17)*

Academic Vocabulary

- theme *(p. 15)*
- physical *(p. 15)*

Reading Strategy

Identifying Use a chart like the one below to identify two examples for each topic.

Themes of Geography
1.
2.
Types of Geography
1.
2.
Geographer's Tools
1.
2.

Thinking Like a Geographer

Picture This Shaped like a bowl, the top of Mount Sajama in Bolivia holds ice formed during the last Ice Age, about 14,000 years ago. Scientists from Ohio State University's Byrd Polar Research Center collect and transport samples of the ice to a laboratory for study. There, scientists analyze the dust particles, organisms, and gases trapped inside the ice for thousands of years. Their findings give us a better understanding of climate changes during prehistoric times. To learn more about how geographers and other scientists study the Earth, read Section 1.

▼ Carrying ice samples down Mount Sajama

The Five Themes of Geography

Main Idea **Geographers use the Five Themes of Geography to help them study the Earth.**

Geography and You Suppose a teacher tells you to pick a topic for a research paper. How do you organize your ideas? Read to discover how geographers use themes to help them organize ideas about geography.

Geography is the study of the Earth and its people. People who study geography are geographers. Geographers use five **themes,** or topics, to describe places and people. These themes are location, place, human-environment interaction, movement, and regions.

Location

Location is the position of a place on the Earth's surface. Geographers describe location in two ways. **Absolute location** is the exact spot on Earth where a geographic feature, such as a city or mountain, is found. **Relative location** describes where that feature is in relation to the features around it.

Place

Place describes the characteristics of a location that make it unique, or different. A place can be defined by **physical** features, such as landforms, plants, animals, and weather patterns. Other characteristics of a place describe the people who live there—such as what languages they speak.

Human-Environment Interaction

Human-environment interaction describes how people affect their **environment**, or natural surroundings, and how their environment affects them. People affect the environment by using or changing it to meet their needs. Environmental factors that people cannot control, such as temperature and natural disasters, influence how people live.

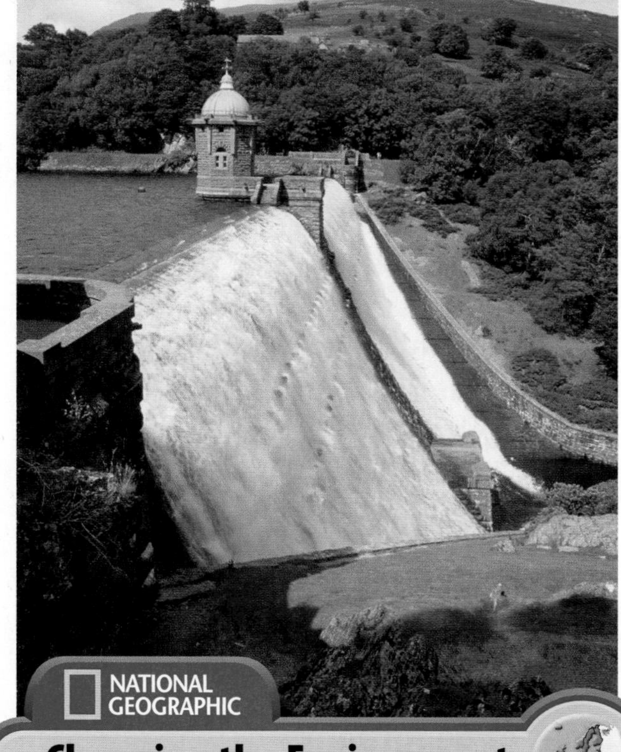

NATIONAL GEOGRAPHIC

Changing the Environment

Dams, like this one in Wales, can be built to control flooding, manage water flow, and supply electricity. ***Human-Environment Interaction*** **How and why do people affect the environment?**

Movement

Movement explains how and why people, ideas, and goods move from place to place. For example, people might leave a country that is involved in a war. Such movements can lead to great cultural change.

Regions

Regions refers to areas of the Earth's surface that have several common characteristics, such as land, natural resources, or population. For example, the alpine region in Europe is a large area known for mining and supplying hydroelectric power.

Reading Check **Explaining** Explain the difference between *place* and *location.*

A Geographer's Tools

Main Idea **Geographers use many different tools to help them study and analyze Earth's people and places.**

Geography and You Suppose a company wanted to build a new shopping center in your community. How would its managers know where to build it? Read to find out how geographers help make such decisions.

Geographers study the physical and human features of Earth. They rely on various tools to study people and places.

Types of Geography

When geographers study physical geography, they examine Earth's land areas, bodies of water, plant life, and other physical features. Physical geographers also study natural resources that are available in an area and the ways people use those resources. They help people make decisions about managing different types of resources such as water, forests, land, and even the wind.

Other geographers study human geography, focusing on people and their activities. Human geographers look at people's religions, languages, and ways of life. They may examine a specific location, or they may study entire countries or continents. They also compare different places to see how they are similar and different. Human geographers help plan cities and aid in international business.

Places in Time

Geographers use knowledge from other subject areas. History, for example, helps them understand how places appeared in the past. Geographers learn about places by studying the changes that have occurred over time.

Surveyors, like this woman in Canada, use specialized equipment to measure land areas. ***Human-Environment Interaction*** **What tasks might geographers hired by the government carry out?**

History is divided into blocks of time known as periods. For example, a period of 10 years is called a **decade.** A period of 100 years is known as a **century.** A period of 1,000 years is a **millennium.**

In Western societies, it is common to group history into four long periods. The first of these periods is called Prehistory. Prehistory refers to the time before people developed writing, about 5,500 years ago. This time is followed by the period known as Ancient History, which lasted until about 1,500 years ago. The next thousand years is called the Middle Ages, or the medieval period. About 500 years ago, Modern History began and continues to the present.

Map Systems

Maps can provide geographers with different types of information about a place. Information for a map can be collected by using modern technology, or tools and methods that help people perform tasks. Satellites circling the Earth provide detailed digital images and photographs to create maps. Satellites can also measure changing temperatures and the amount of pollution in the air or land. This information can then be added to maps.

Another group of satellites makes up the **Global Positioning System (GPS).** This system uses radio signals to determine the exact location of places on Earth. Hikers use GPS equipment to avoid getting lost. GPS is now built into some cars.

Geographic Information Systems (GIS) are computer hardware and software that gather, store, and analyze geographic information and then display it on a screen. It can display maps, but it also can show information that does not usually appear on maps, such as types of vegetation, types of soil, and even water quality.

Careers in Geography

Governments at all levels hire geographers for many kinds of tasks. Geographers help decide how land and resources might be used. For example, they analyze population trends, including why people live in certain areas and not in others.

In the business world, geographers often work as researchers and analysts. They can help companies decide where to locate new buildings. They also provide information about places and cultures where companies do business. Many geographers teach in high schools, colleges, and universities. As more schools recognize the importance of geography education, the demand for geography teachers is expected to grow.

Reading Check **Explaining** How does modern technology make maps more precise?

Section 1 Review

Vocabulary

1. **Explain** the significance of:
   - **a.** geography
   - **b.** absolute location
   - **c.** relative location
   - **d.** environment
   - **e.** decade
   - **f.** century
   - **g.** millennium
   - **h.** Global Positioning System (GPS)
   - **i.** Geographic Information Systems (GIS)

Main Ideas

2. **Explaining** Use a web diagram like the one below to summarize information about the Five Themes of Geography.

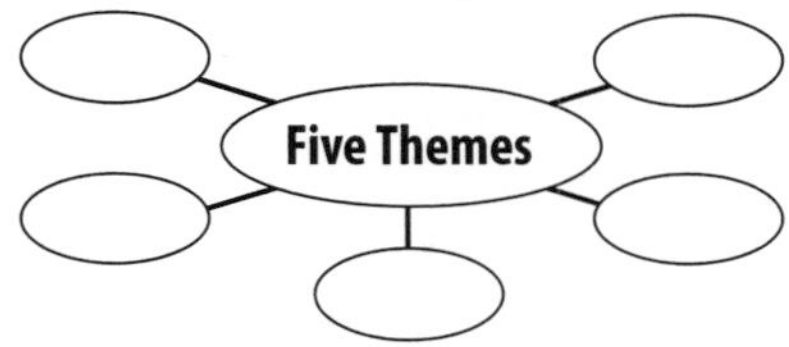

3. **Contrasting** How is physical geography different from human geography?

Critical Thinking

4. **Drawing Conclusions** Describe how helpful you think GIS would be in deciding where to build a gas station.
5. **BIG Idea** What factors might influence where a city would develop?
6. **Challenge** Give three examples of how someone might use geography to plan for the future.

Writing About Geography

7. **Using Your FOLDABLES** Use your Foldable to write a paragraph that describes the uses of geography.

NATIONAL GEOGRAPHIC

Geography Skills Handbook

How Do I Study Geography?

Geographers have created these broad categories and standards as tools to help you understand the relationships among people, places, and environments.

- **5 Themes of Geography**
- **6 Essential Elements**
- **18 Geography Standards**

5 Themes of Geography

1 Location

Location describes where something is. Absolute location describes a place's exact position on the Earth's surface. Relative location expresses where a place is in relation to another place.

2 Place

Place describes the physical and human characteristics that make a location unique.

3 Regions

Regions are areas that share common characteristics.

4 Movement

Movement explains how and why people and things move and are connected.

5 Human-Environment Interaction

Human-Environment Interaction describes the relationship between people and their environment.

6 Essential Elements

18 Geography Standards

I. The World in Spatial Terms

Geographers look to see where a place is located. Location acts as a starting point to answer "Where Is It?" The location of a place helps you orient yourself as to where you are.

1 How to use maps and other tools
2 How to use mental maps to organize information
3 How to analyze the spatial organization of people, places, and environments

II. Places and Regions

Place describes physical characteristics such as landforms, climate, and plant or animal life. It might also describe human characteristics, including language and way of life. Places can also be organized into regions. **Regions** are places united by one or more characteristics.

4 The physical and human characteristics of places
5 How people create regions to interpret Earth's complexity
6 How culture and experience influence people's perceptions of places and regions

III. Physical Systems

Geographers study how physical systems, such as hurricanes, volcanoes, and glaciers, shape the surface of the Earth. They also look at how plants and animals depend upon one another and their surroundings for their survival.

7 The physical processes that shape Earth's surface
8 The distribution of ecosystems on Earth's surface

IV. Human Systems

People shape the world in which they live. They settle in certain places but not in others. An ongoing theme in geography is the movement of people, ideas, and goods.

9 The characteristics, distribution, and migration of human populations
10 The complexity of Earth's cultural mosaics
11 The patterns and networks of economic interdependence
12 The patterns of human settlement
13 The forces of cooperation and conflict

V. Environment and Society

How does the relationship between people and their natural surroundings influence the way people live? Geographers study how people use the environment and how their actions affect the environment.

14 How human actions modify the physical environment
15 How physical systems affect human systems
16 The meaning, use, and distribution of resources

VI. The Uses of Geography

Knowledge of geography helps us understand the relationships among people, places, and environments over time. Applying geographic skills helps you understand the past and prepare for the future.

17 How to apply geography to interpret the past
18 How to apply geography to interpret the present and plan for the future

Understanding the BIG Ideas of Geography

The 15 Big Ideas will help you understand the information in *Georgia's Exploring Our World: People, Places, and Cultures*. The Big Ideas are based on the Essential Elements and the Geography Standards. They help you organize important ideas, and they make it easier to understand patterns and relationships.

The World in Spatial Terms
- Geographers study how people and physical features are distributed on Earth's surface.

Places and Regions
- Places reflect the relationship between humans and the physical environment.
- Geographers organize the Earth into regions that share common characteristics.
- Culture influences people's perceptions about places and regions.

Physical Systems
- Physical processes shape Earth's surface.
- All living things are dependent upon one another and their surroundings for survival.

Human Systems
- The characteristics and movement of people impact physical and human systems.
- Culture groups shape human systems.
- Patterns of economic activities result in global interdependence.
- Geographic factors influence where people settle.
- Cooperation and conflict among people have an effect on the Earth's surface.

Environment and Society
- People's actions can change the physical environment.
- The physical environment affects how people live.
- Changes occur in the use and importance of natural resources.

The Uses of Geography
- Geography is used to interpret the past, understand the present, and plan for the future.

The World in Spatial Terms: Maps help you locate places on Earth's surface.

Physical Systems: Physical processes, such as hurricanes, shape the face of the Earth.

Human Systems: Technology impacts people and economies.

Environment and Society: Recycling is a choice people make to protect Earth's physical environment.

Using the BIG Ideas of Geography

You can find the Big Ideas throughout *Georgia's Exploring Our World: People, Places, and Cultures.*

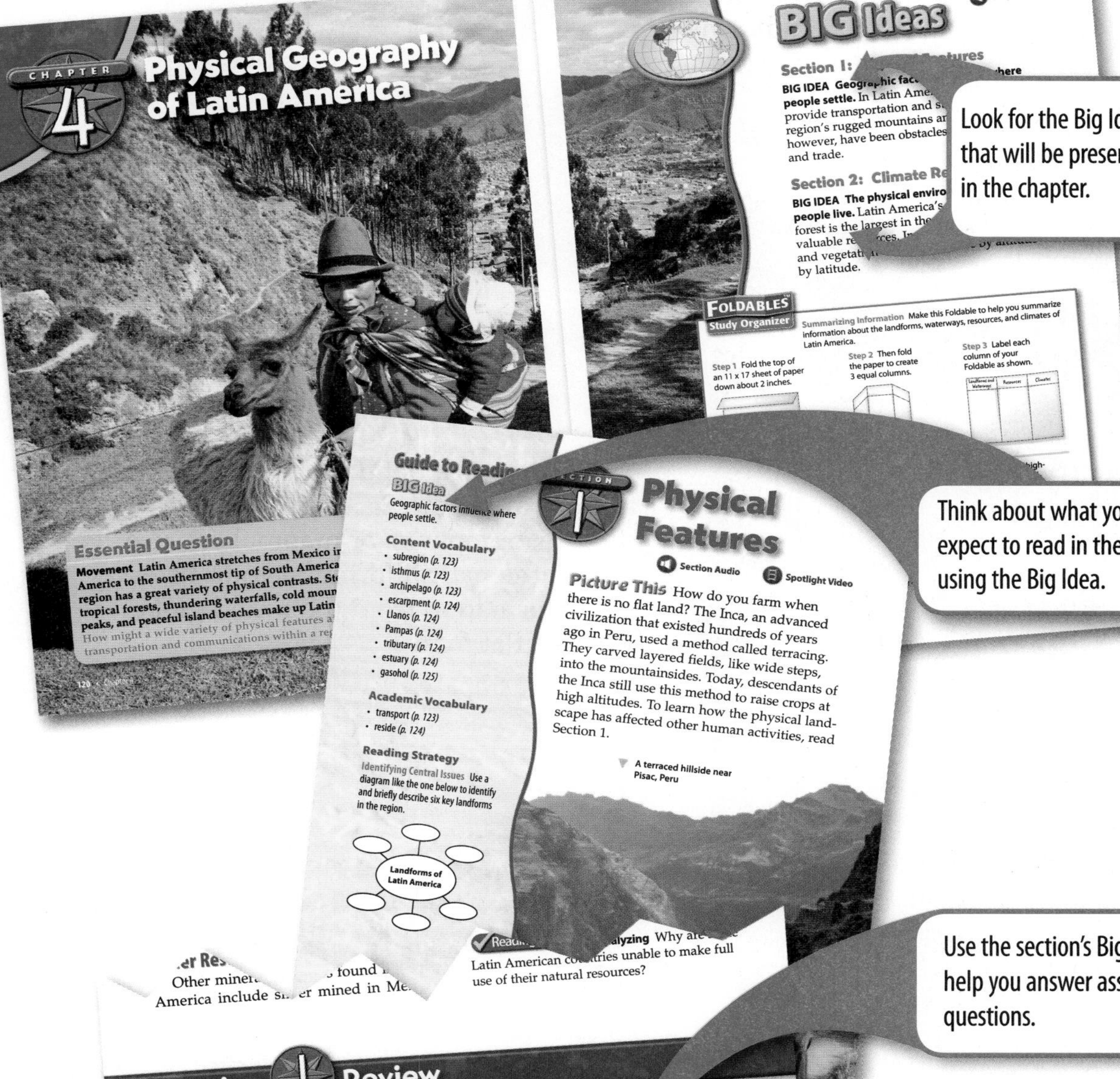

Look for the Big Ideas that will be presented in the chapter.

Think about what you expect to read in the section using the Big Idea.

Use the section's Big Idea to help you answer assessment questions.

Globes and Maps

What Is a Globe? ►

A **globe** is a round model of the Earth that shows its shape, landforms, and directions as they truly relate to one another.

◄ What Is a Map?

A **map** is a flat drawing of all or part of the Earth's surface. Cartographers, or mapmakers, use mathematical formulas to transfer information from the round globe to a flat map.

Globes and Maps ►

Globes and maps serve different purposes, and each has advantages and disadvantages.

	Advantages	Disadvantages
Globes	• Represent true land shape, distances, and directions	• Cannot show detailed information • Difficult to carry
Maps	• Show small areas in great detail • Display different types of information, such as population densities or natural resources • Transport easily	• **Distort,** or change, the accuracy of shapes and distances

Map Projections

When the Earth's surface is flattened on a map, big gaps open up. Mapmakers stretch parts of the Earth to show either the correct shapes of places or their correct sizes. Mapmakers have developed different projections, or ways of showing the Earth on a flat piece of paper. Below are different map projections.

Goode's Interrupted Equal-Area Projection ▼

A map with this projection shows continents close to their true shapes and sizes. This projection is helpful to compare land area among continents.

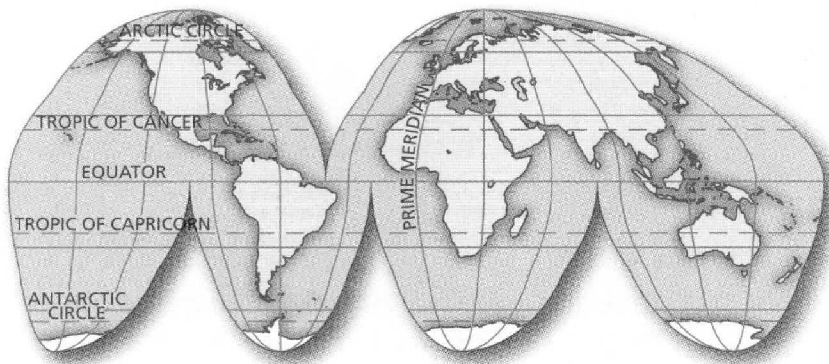

Robinson Projection ▼

The Robinson projection has minor distortions. Continents and oceans are close to their sizes and shapes, but the North and South Poles appear flattened.

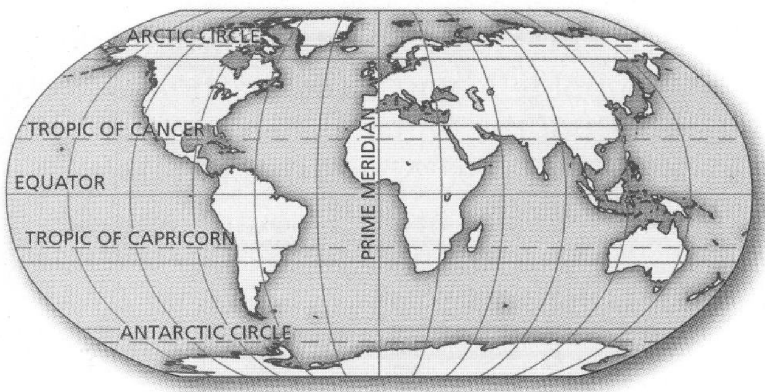

Mercator Projection ▼

The Mercator projection shows land shapes fairly accurately but not size or distance. Areas that are located far from the Equator are quite distorted. The Mercator projection shows true directions, however, making it useful for sea travel.

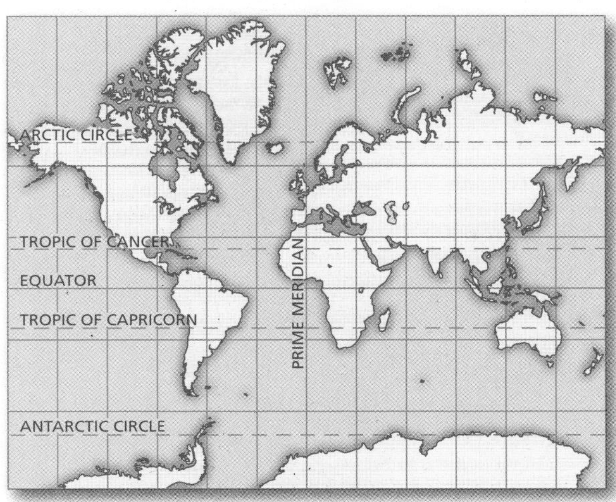

Winkel Tripel Projection ▼

This projection gives a good overall view of the continents' shapes and sizes. Land areas are not as distorted near the poles as they are in the Robinson projection.

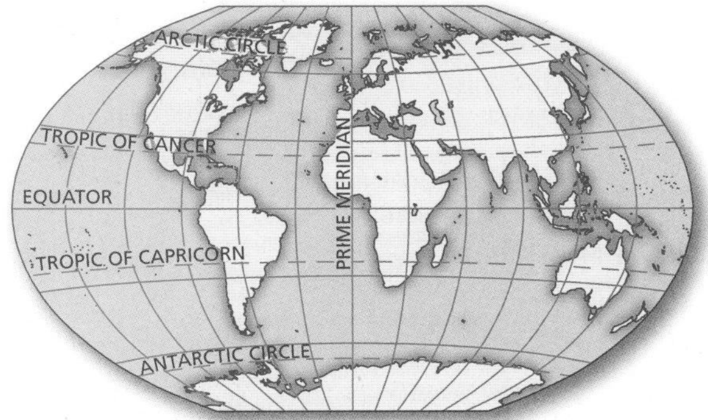

Skills Practice

1. **Comparing and Contrasting** Explain similarities and differences between globes and maps.
2. **Describing** Why do map projections distort some parts of the Earth?

Location

To locate places on Earth, geographers use a system of imaginary lines that crisscross the globe. These lines are called *latitude* and *longitude.*

Latitude ▶

- Lines of **latitude** are imaginary circles that run east to west around the globe. They are known as *parallels*. These parallels divide the globe into units called degrees.
- The **Equator** circles the middle of the Earth like a belt. It is located halfway between the North and South Poles. The Equator is 0° latitude.
- The letter *N* or *S* that follows the degree symbol tells you if the location is north or south of the Equator. The North Pole, for example, is 90°N (north) latitude, and the South Pole is at 90°S (south) latitude.

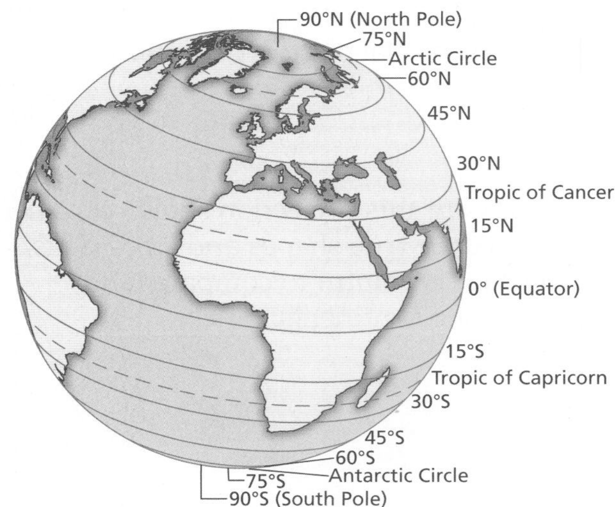

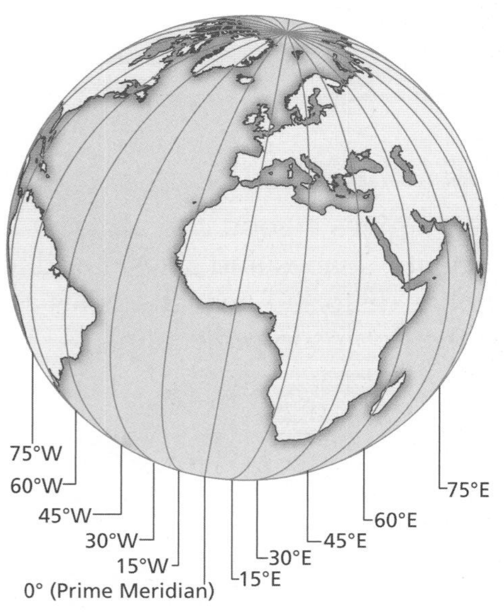

◀ Longitude

- Lines of **longitude,** also known as *meridians*, run from the North Pole to the South Pole. The **Prime Meridian** (also called the Meridian of Greenwich) is 0° longitude and runs through Greenwich, England.
- The letter *E* or *W* that follows the degree symbol tells you if the location is east or west of the Prime Meridian.
- On the opposite side of the Earth is the 180° meridian, also known as the International Date Line.

Absolute Location ▶

A place's exact location can be identified when you use both latitude and longitude. For example, Tokyo, Japan, is 36°N latitude and 140°E longitude.

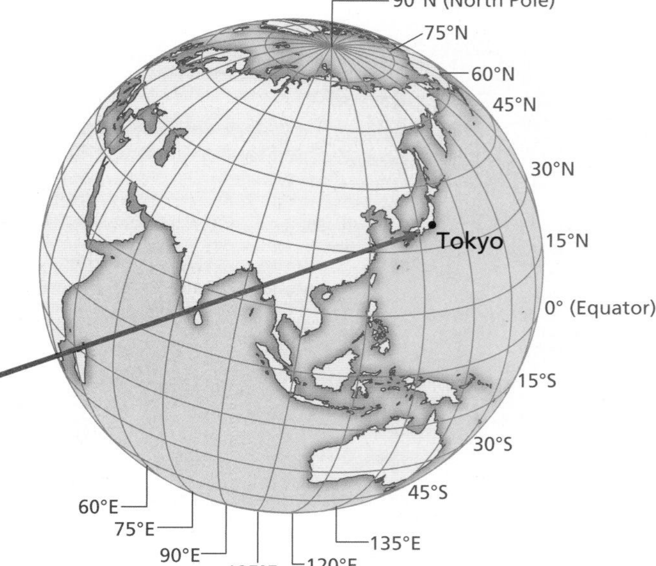

Hemispheres

The Equator divides the Earth into Northern and Southern Hemispheres. Everything north of the Equator is in the Northern Hemisphere. Everything south of the Equator is in the Southern Hemisphere.

Northern Hemisphere

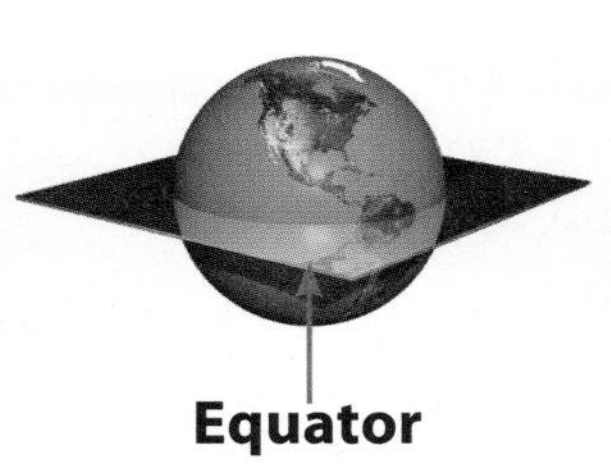

Southern Hemisphere

The Prime Meridian divides the Earth into Eastern and Western Hemispheres. Everything east of the Prime Meridian for 180 degrees is in the Eastern Hemisphere. Everything west of the Prime Meridian for 180 degrees is in the Western Hemisphere.

Eastern Hemisphere

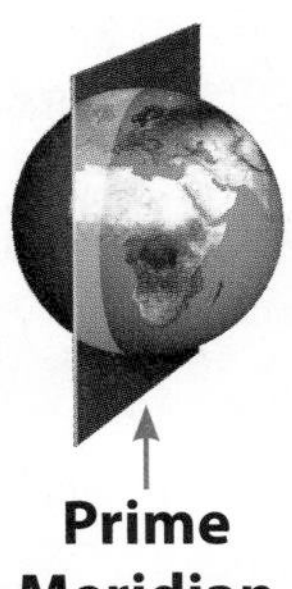

Western Hemisphere

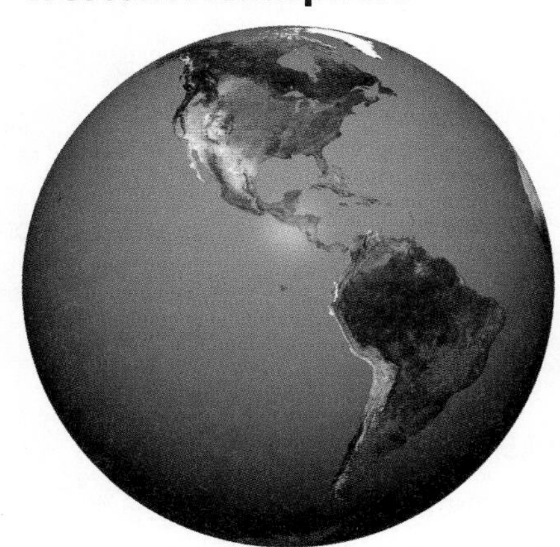

Skills Practice

1. **Identifying** What country is located at 30°S and 120°E?
2. **Analyzing Visuals** In which hemispheres is Europe located?

Parts of a Map

Title
The title tells you what information the map is showing.

Key
The key explains the symbols, colors, and lines on the map. The key is also called a *legend*.

Scale Bar
A measuring line, often called a **scale bar,** helps you figure distance on the map. The map scale shows the relationship between map measurements and actual distances on the Earth.

NATIONAL GEOGRAPHIC

Figure 2 **Europe: Political**

Boundary Lines
Boundary lines show the extent of an area's territory or political influence.

Compass Rose
The compass rose is a symbol that tells you where the **cardinal directions**—north, south, east, and west—are positioned. In between the cardinal directions are **intermediate directions.** They are northeast, southeast, southwest, and northwest.

Cities
Cities are symbolized by a solid circle (●). This symbol is found in the key and on the map.

Capitals
Capitals are symbolized by a star (✪). This symbol is found in the key and on the map.

Using Scale

All maps are drawn to a certain **scale.** The scale of a map is the size of the map compared to the size of the actual land surface. Thus, the scale of a map varies with the size of the area shown.

Small-Scale Maps ▼

A small-scale map, like this political map of Mexico, shows a large land area but little detail.

Large-Scale Maps ▼

A large-scale map, like this map of Mexico City, shows a small land area with a great amount of detail.

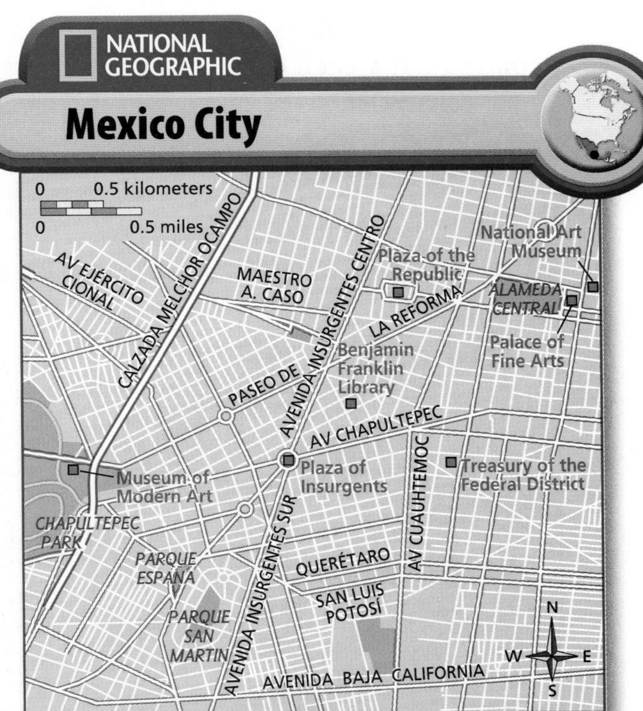

How Do I Use a Scale Bar?

Use the scale bar to find actual distances on a map. The scale bar tells you how many kilometers or miles are represented in that length. You can use a ruler, then, to calculate distances based on the scale bar's length.

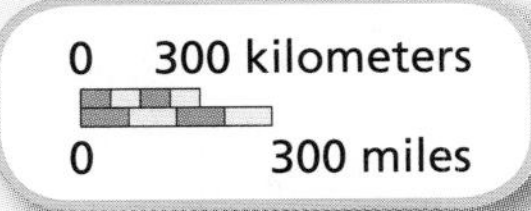

About ½ of an inch equals 300 miles. A little more than ½ of a centimeter is equal to 300 kilometers.

Skills Practice

1. **Defining** What is scale?
2. **Contrasting** What is the difference between a small-scale map and a large-scale map?
3. **Identifying** What are the four cardinal directions? Which direction is Denmark from Germany?
4. **Applying** Which intermediate direction would you travel from the United Kingdom to Iceland?
5. **Applying** About how many miles is it from Berlin to Warsaw? How many kilometers?

Types of Maps

General Purpose Maps

Maps are amazingly useful tools. You can use them to show information and to make connections between seemingly unrelated topics. Geographers use many different types of maps. Maps that show a wide range of information about an area are called **general purpose maps.** Two of the most common general purpose maps are physical maps and political maps.

Physical Maps ▼

Physical maps call out landforms and water features. The map key explains what each color and symbol stands for.

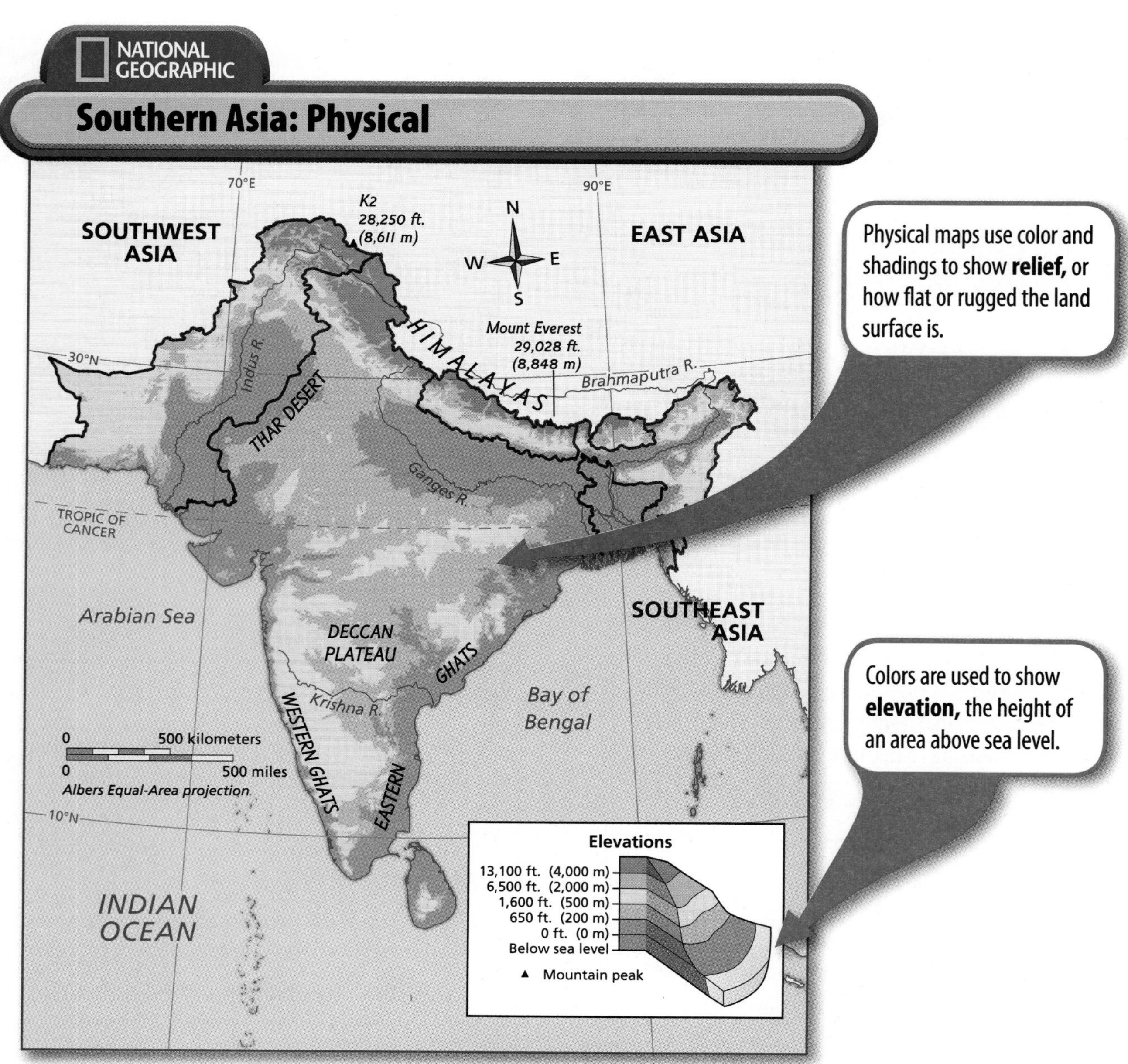

Political Maps ▼

Political maps show the names and political boundaries of countries, along with human-made features such as cities or transportation routes.

NATIONAL GEOGRAPHIC

Southern Asia: Political

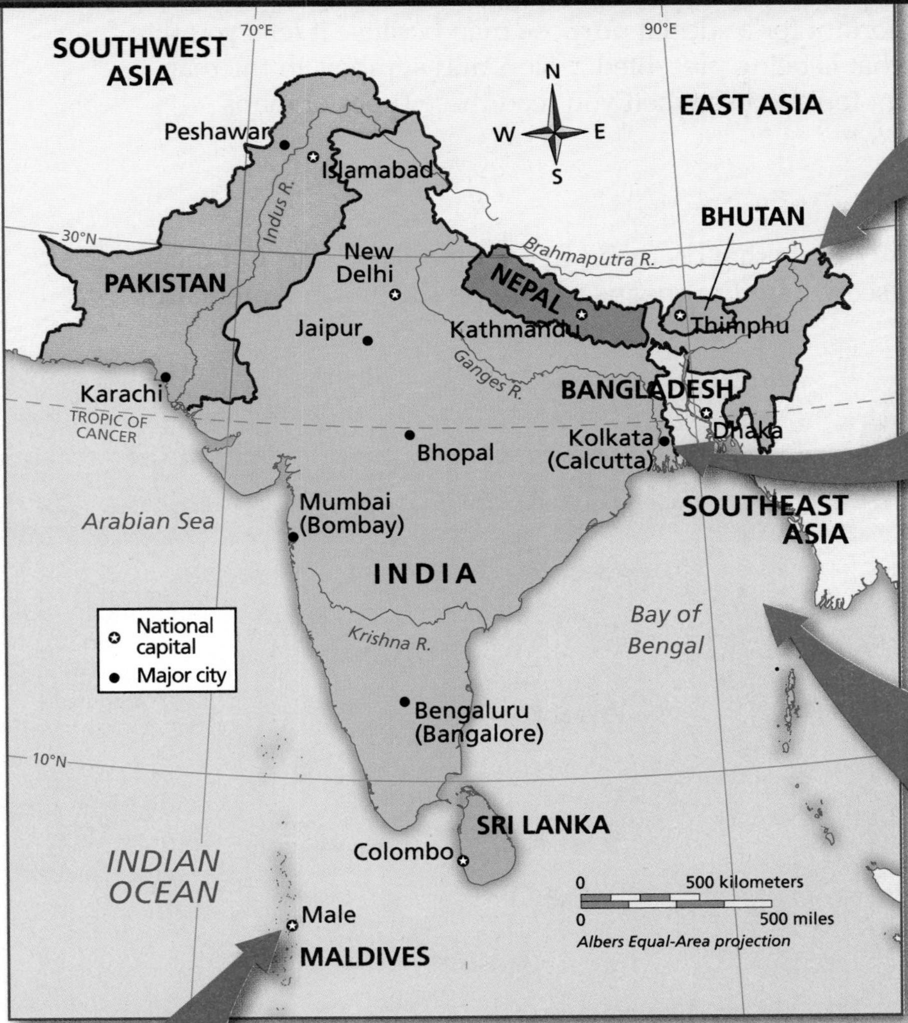

Solid lines outline political boundaries.

Major cities are shown on political maps.

Political maps can include major physical features such as bodies of water and mountains.

Capital cities are identified on political maps.

National capital
Major city

0 500 kilometers
0 500 miles
Albers Equal-Area projection

Skills Practice

1. **Defining** What is elevation?
2. **Describing** What type of map would you use to find the capital of a country?

Types of Maps

Special Purpose Maps

Some maps are made to present specific types of information. These are called **thematic** or **special purpose maps.** These maps usually show specific topics in detail. Special purpose maps may include information about:

- climate
- vegetation
- natural resources
- population density
- historical expansion

Look at some of the types of special purpose maps on these pages. The map's title is especially important for a special purpose map because it tells you the type of information that is being presented. Colors and symbols in the map key are also important tools to use when you read these types of maps.

Historical Maps ▼

Historical maps show events that occurred in a region over time. On the map below, you can see where Europeans settled on the North American continent in the past.

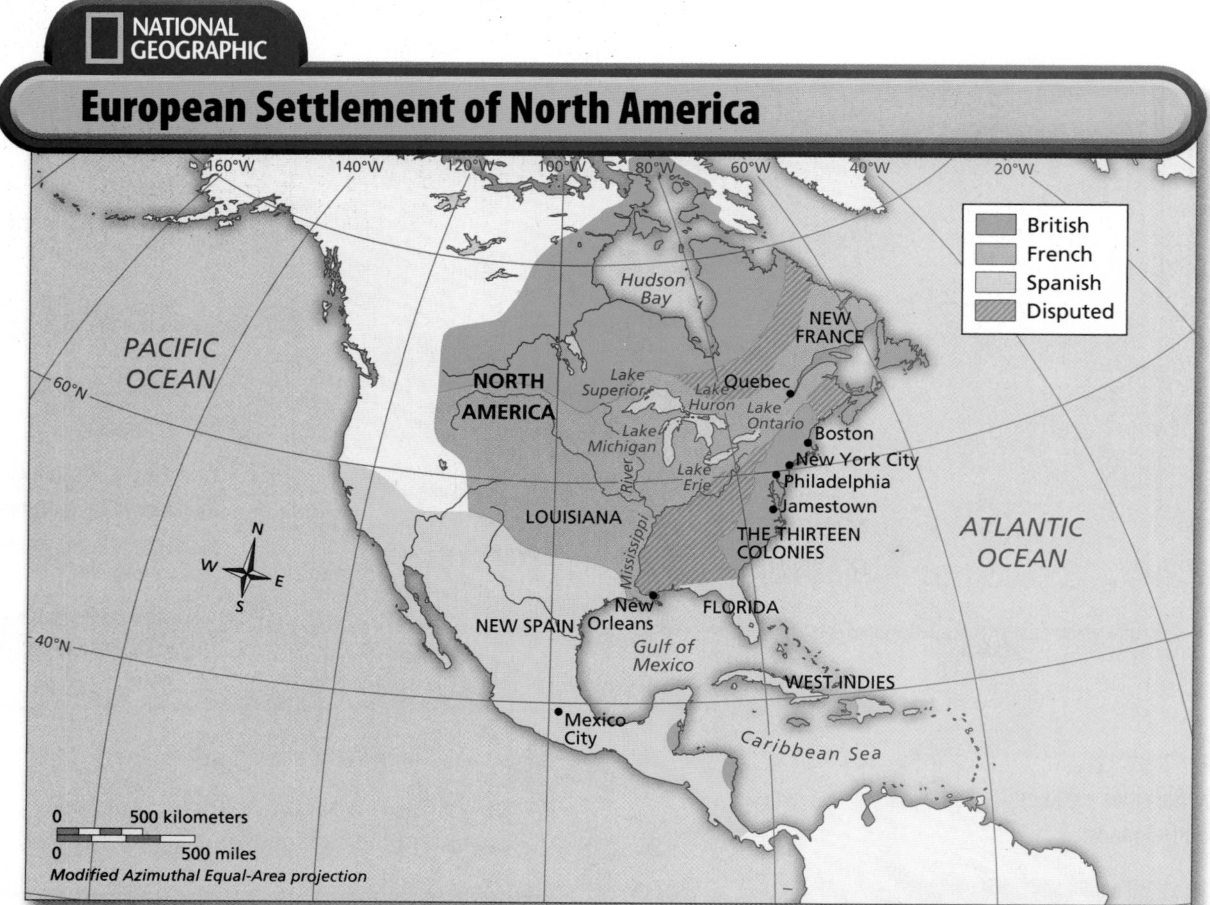

NATIONAL GEOGRAPHIC

Sri Lanka: Contour

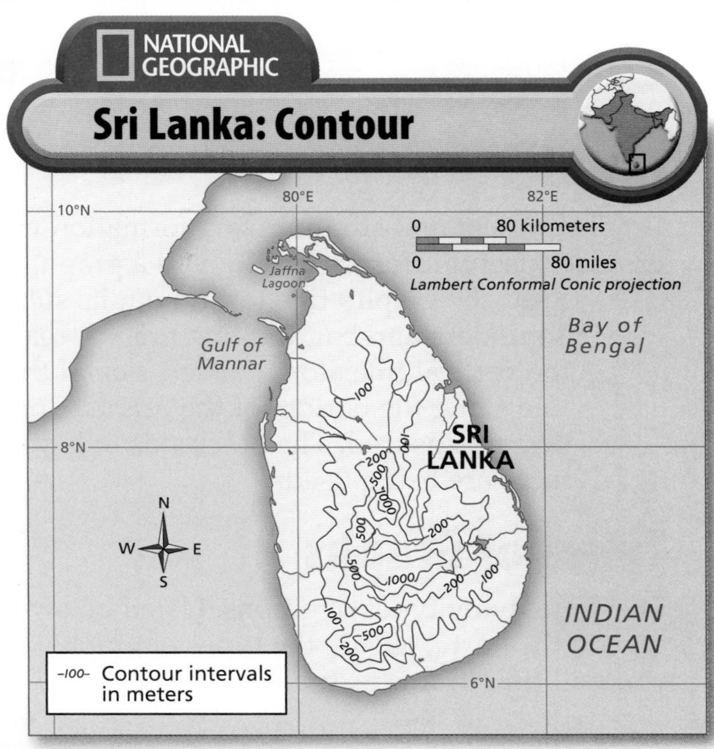

Contour Maps ▶

A contour map has **contour lines**—one line for each major level of elevation. All the land at the same elevation is connected by a line. These lines usually form circles or ovals—one inside the other. If contour lines are close together, the surface is steep. If the lines are spread apart, the land is flat or rises gradually.

NATIONAL GEOGRAPHIC

Africa: Vegetation

20°W 0° 20°E 40°E 60°E

20°N 0° 20°S EQUATOR

Algiers, Cairo, Dakar, Khartoum, Abuja, Addis Ababa, Abidjan, Nairobi, Kinshasa, Luanda, Harare, Antananarivo, Windhoek, Cape Town

ATLANTIC OCEAN

INDIAN OCEAN

- Tropical rain forest
- Tropical grassland (savanna)
- Desert scrub and desert waste
- Temperate grassland
- Mediterranean scrub
- Deciduous forest

0 1,000 kilometers
0 1,000 miles
Lambert Azimuthal Equal-Area projection

◀ Vegetation Maps

Vegetation maps are special purpose maps that show the different types of plants that are found in a region.

Skills Practice

1 Identifying What type of special purpose map might show battles during World War II?

2 Contrasting What is the difference between a general purpose map and a special purpose map?

Graphs, Charts, and Diagrams

Graphs

Graphs present and summarize information visually. Each part of a graph provides useful information. To read a graph, follow these steps:

- Read the graph's title to find out its subject.
- To understand bar and line graphs, read the labels along the **axes**—the vertical line along the left side of the graph and the horizontal line along the bottom of the graph. One axis will tell you what is being measured. The other axis tells you what units of measurement are being used.

Types of Graphs

There are many types of graphs. Listed below and on the next page are the types of graphs you will find in this textbook.

Bar Graphs ▶

Graphs that use bars or wide lines to compare data visually are called bar graphs.

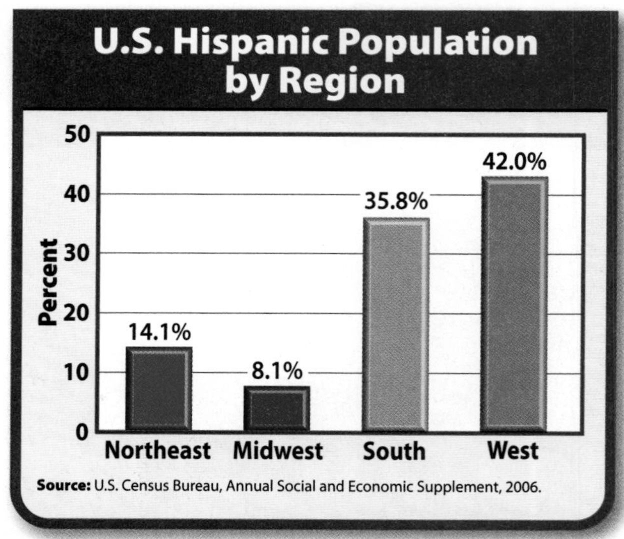

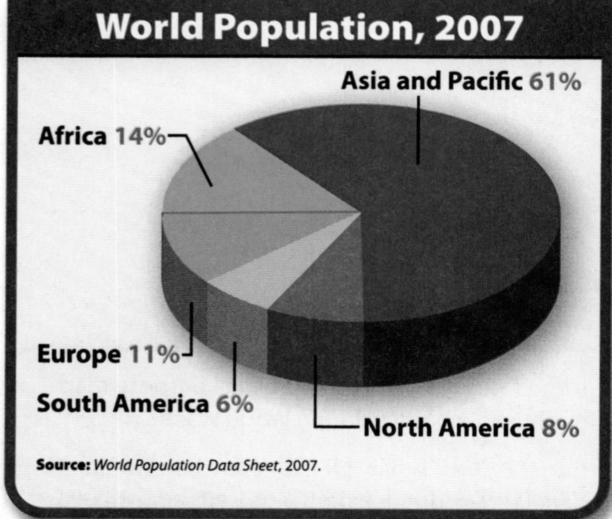

◀ Circle Graphs

You can use circle graphs when you want to show how the whole of something is divided into its parts. Because of their shape, circle graphs are often called *pie graphs.* Each slice represents a part or percentage of the whole pie. The complete circle represents a whole group—or 100 percent.

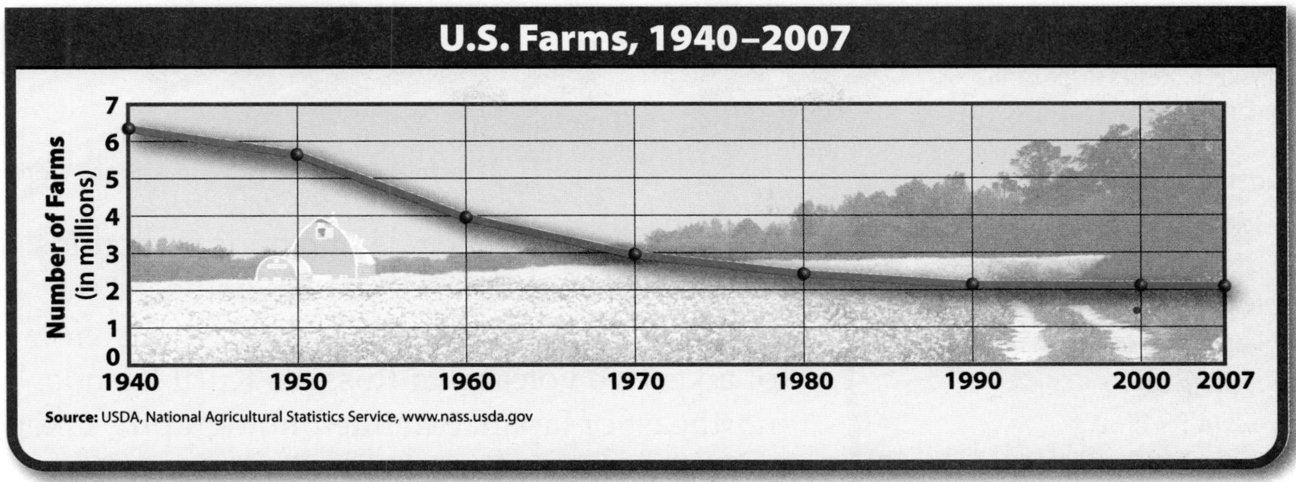

Line Graphs ▲

Line graphs help show changes over a period of time. The amounts being measured are plotted on the grid above each year and then are connected by a line.

Charts

Charts present related facts and numbers in an organized way. They arrange data, especially numbers, in rows and columns for easy reference.

Island Populations

Aruba	71,891
Bermuda	65,773
British Virgin Islands	23,098
Jamaica	2,758,124

Source: *CIA World Factbook*, 2006.

NATIONAL GEOGRAPHIC

The Rain Shadow

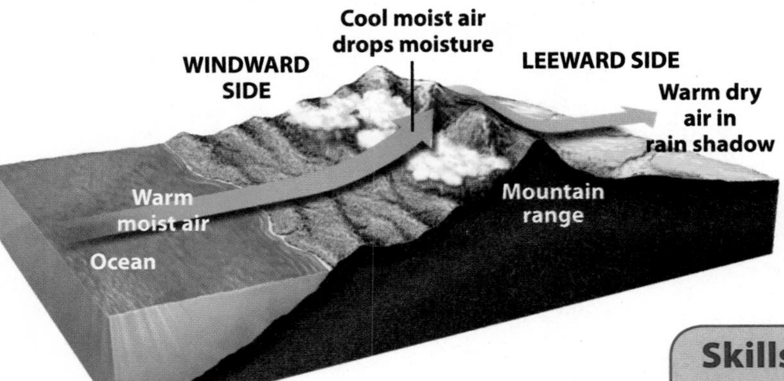

Diagrams

Diagrams are drawings that show steps in a process, point out the parts of an object, or explain how something works.

Skills Practice

1. **Identifying** What percentage does the whole circle in a circle graph represent?
2. **Analyzing Information** What type of graph would best show the number of Republicans and Democrats in the U.S. House of Representatives?

Guide to Reading

BIG Idea

Physical processes shape Earth's surface.

Content Vocabulary

- solar system *(p. 35)*
- orbit *(p. 35)*
- revolution *(p. 36)*
- leap year *(p. 36)*
- rotate *(p. 36)*
- axis *(p. 36)*
- atmosphere *(p. 36)*
- summer solstice *(p. 37)*
- winter solstice *(p. 38)*
- equinox *(p. 38)*
- Tropics *(p. 38)*

Academic Vocabulary

- significant *(p. 37)*
- reverse *(p. 38)*
- identical *(p. 38)*

Reading Strategy

Determining Cause and Effect
Use a diagram like the one below to show the effects of latitude on Earth's temperatures.

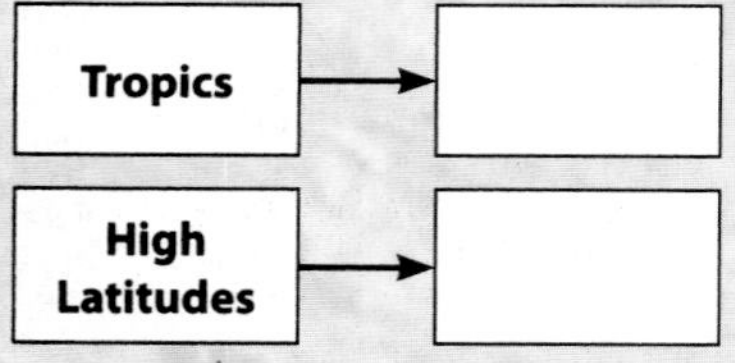

The Earth in Space

Picture This A circle of clouds surrounds a volcanic eruption. Astronauts on board the International Space Station captured this view of an active volcano in Russia's Kuril Islands, northeast of Japan. Satellite photographs, taken over a period of time, help scientists explore the causes and effects of natural occurrences. These images, in addition to other information, help scientists understand how volcanic eruptions and other phenomena affect the Earth's atmosphere. Scientists also continue to explore space and how the Earth's location in the solar system affects our planet. Read the next section to learn how the Earth's rotation, orbit, tilt, and latitude affect life on Earth.

▼ Volcano erupts on a Pacific island

The Solar System

Main Idea **The Earth is one of eight planets in the solar system. It rotates on its axis every 24 hours and takes a year to orbit the sun.**

Geography and You Have you watched a sunrise or sunset and wondered why the sun seems to move across the sky each day? Read to find out about the Earth and its place in our solar system.

The sun provides the heat necessary for life on our planet. Earth, seven other major planets, and thousands of smaller bodies all revolve around the sun. Together with the sun, these bodies form our **solar system.**

Major Planets

The major planets differ from one another in size and makeup. Look at **Figure 1.** It shows that the inner planets—Mercury, Venus, Earth, and Mars—are relatively small and solid. The outer planets—Jupiter, Saturn, Uranus, and Neptune—are larger and composed mostly or entirely of gases. Pluto, once considered a major planet, is now called a minor planet.

Each planet follows its own path, or **orbit**, around the sun. The orbits vary from nearly circular to elliptical, or oval shaped.

Social Studies ONLINE

Student Web Activity Visit glencoe.com and complete the Chapter 1 Web Activity about the solar system.

NATIONAL GEOGRAPHIC

Figure 1 **The Solar System**

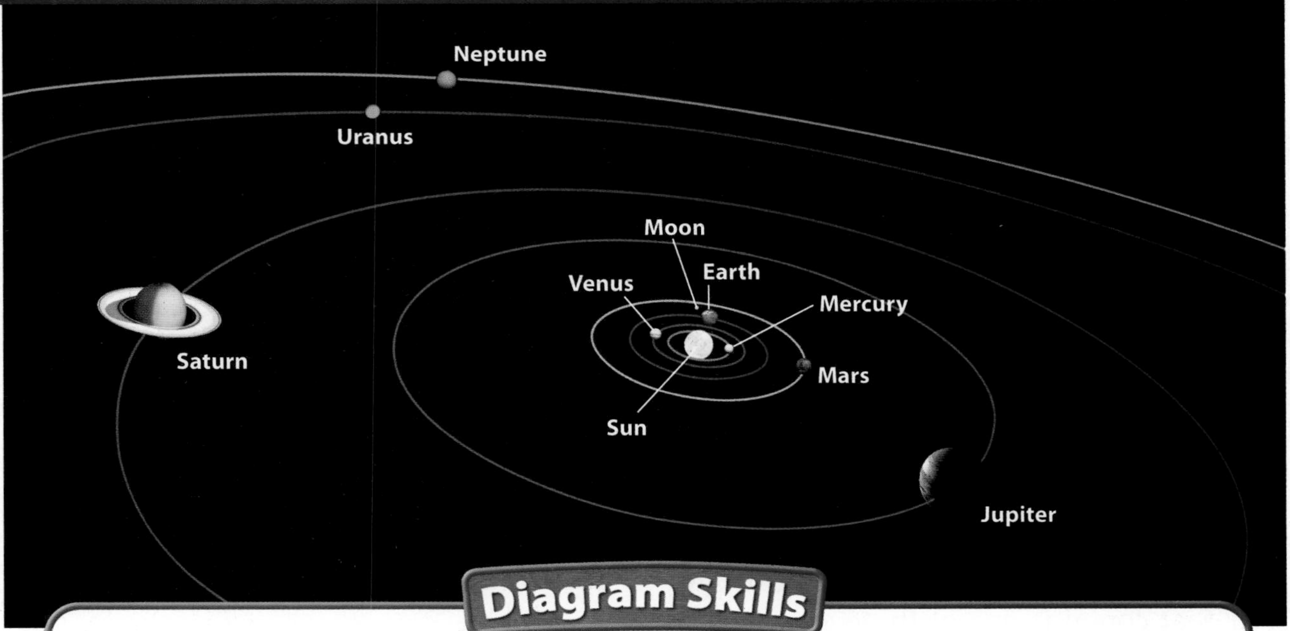

Neptune
Uranus
Moon
Earth
Venus
Mercury
Saturn
Mars
Sun
Jupiter

Diagram Skills

1. **Identifying** Which two planets are closest to the sun?
2. **Identifying** Which planets make up the outer planets?

NATIONAL GEOGRAPHIC

Earth's Movements

Some scientists believe that ancient sites such as Stonehenge, located in southern England, may have helped people track the Earth's revolution around the sun and the change of the seasons. From space, astronauts can see the Earth (inset) in light and shadow at the same time. ***Movement*** **Why do different parts of the Earth experience sunlight or darkness?**

The time necessary to complete an orbit differs, too. Mercury needs only 88 days to circle the sun, but faraway Neptune takes 165 years.

Earth's Movement

Earth takes almost 365¼ days to make one **revolution,** or a complete circuit, around the sun. This period is what we define as one year. Every four years, the extra fourths of a day are combined and added to the calendar as February 29th. A year that contains one of these extra days is called a **leap year.**

As Earth orbits the sun, it **rotates,** or spins, on its axis. The **axis** is an imaginary line that passes through the center of Earth from the North Pole to the South Pole. Earth rotates in an easterly direction, making one complete rotation every 24 hours. As Earth turns, different parts of the planet are in sunlight or in darkness. The part facing the sun experiences daytime, and the part facing away has night.

Why do we not feel Earth moving as it rotates? The reason is that the **atmosphere,** the layer of oxygen and gases that surrounds Earth, moves with it.

Explaining Describe Earth's two principal motions—revolution and rotation.

Sun and Seasons

Main Idea **The tilt of Earth and its revolution around the sun lead to changing seasons during the year.**

Geography and You Did you know that when it is winter in the United States, it is summer in Australia? Read to learn why seasons differ between the Northern and Southern Hemispheres.

Earth is tilted 23½ degrees on its axis. As a result, seasons change as Earth makes its year-long orbit around the sun. To see why this happens, look at **Figure 2.** Notice how sunlight falls directly on the northern or southern half of Earth at different times of the year. Direct rays from the sun bring more warmth than indirect, or slanted rays. When the people in a hemisphere receive direct rays, they enjoy the warmth of summer. When they receive only indirect rays, they experience the cold of winter.

Solstices and Equinoxes

Four days in the year are **significant,** or important, because of the position of the sun in relation to Earth. These days mark the beginnings of the four seasons. On or about June 21, the North Pole is tilted toward the sun. On noon of this day, the sun appears directly overhead at the Tropic of Cancer (23½°N latitude). In the Northern Hemisphere, this day is the **summer solstice**–the day with the most hours of sunlight. It is the beginning of summer—but only in the Northern Hemisphere. In the Southern Hemisphere, that same day is the day with the fewest hours of sunlight and marks the beginning of winter.

NATIONAL GEOGRAPHIC **Maps In MOtion** See StudentWorks™ Plus or glencoe.com.

Figure 2 **The Sun and Earth's Seasons**

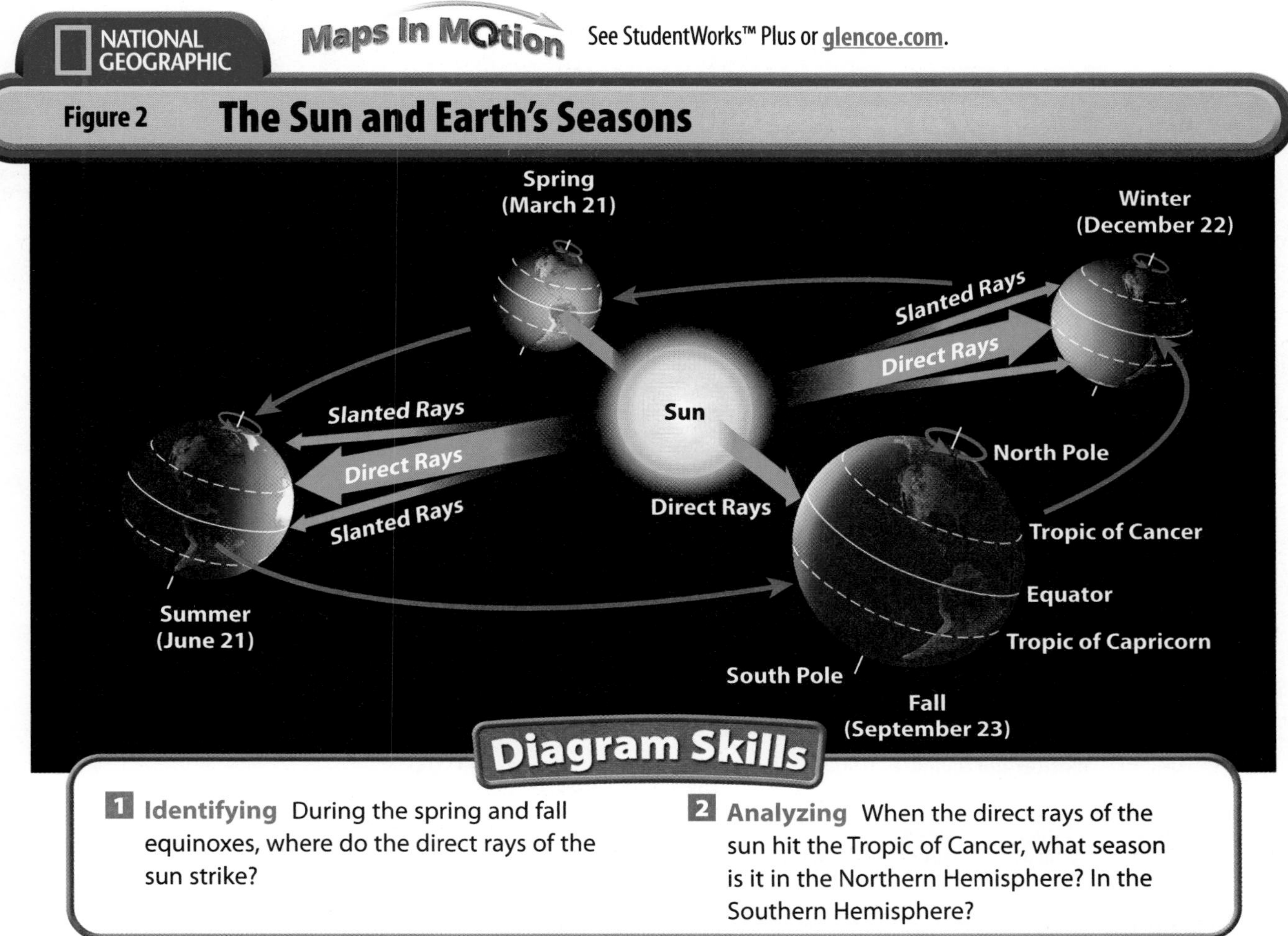

Diagram Skills

1 Identifying During the spring and fall equinoxes, where do the direct rays of the sun strike?

2 Analyzing When the direct rays of the sun hit the Tropic of Cancer, what season is it in the Northern Hemisphere? In the Southern Hemisphere?

Six months later—on or about December 22—the situation is **reversed,** or the opposite. The North Pole is tilted away from the sun. At noon, the sun's direct rays strike the Tropic of Capricorn. In the Northern Hemisphere, this day is the **winter solstice**—the day with the fewest hours of sunlight and the beginning of winter. This same day, however, marks the beginning of summer in the Southern Hemisphere.

Spring and autumn each begin on a day that falls midway between the two solstices. These two days are the **equinoxes,** when day and night are of **identical,** or equal, length in both hemispheres. On or about March 21, the spring equinox occurs. On or about September 23, the fall equinox occurs. On both days, the noon sun shines directly over the Equator.

Effects of Latitude

Earth's temperatures also are affected by the sun. Look again at **Figure 2.** The sun's rays directly hit places in the **Tropics,** the low-latitude areas near the Equator between the Tropic of Cancer and the Tropic of Capricorn. As a result, temperatures in the Tropics tend to be very warm.

At the high latitudes near the North and South Poles, the sun's rays hit indirectly. Temperatures in these regions are always cool or cold. In the midlatitudes—the areas between the Tropics of Cancer and Capricorn and the polar regions—temperatures, weather, and the seasons vary greatly. This is because air masses from both the high latitudes and the Tropics affect these areas.

Reading Check **Analyzing Information** Why are the Tropics the Earth's warmest regions?

Section 2 Review

Vocabulary

1. **Explain** the significance of:
   - a. solar system
   - b. orbit
   - c. revolution
   - d. leap year
   - e. rotate
   - f. axis
   - g. atmosphere
   - h. summer solstice
   - i. winter solstice
   - j. equinox
   - k. Tropics

Main Ideas

2. **Identifying** Name the inner and outer planets, and describe the differences between the two groups.
3. **Comparing** Use a diagram like the one below to compare the days that mark the beginnings of the seasons.

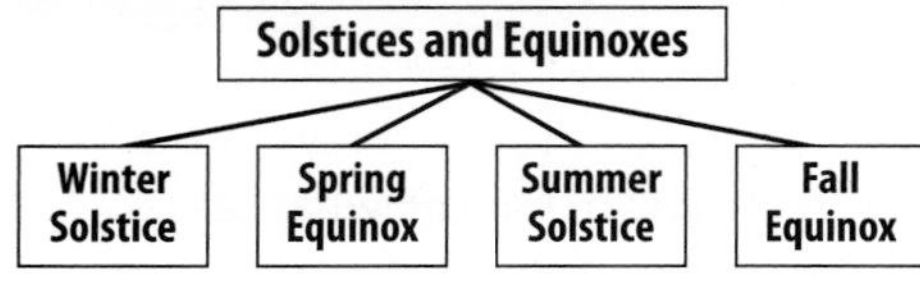

Critical Thinking

4. **Analyzing** Why do we not feel the Earth's movement as it rotates?
5. **BIG Idea** What causes different seasons on Earth?
6. **Challenge** How might latitude affect the population of a region?

Writing About Geography

7. **Expository Writing** Write a paragraph explaining why seasons in the Southern Hemisphere are the opposite of those in the Northern Hemisphere.

Chapter 1 Visual Summary

Themes of Geography

- Geography is the study of the Earth and its people.
- In their study of people and places, geographers use five themes: location, place, human-environment interaction, movement, and regions.

Seven Sisters Waterfall, Norway

Kinds of Geography

- Physical geography examines physical aspects of the Earth, such as land areas, bodies of water, and plant life.
- Human geography focuses on people and their activities, including religions, languages, and ways of life.

Hiker using GPS

Geographers at Work

- To study the Earth, geographers use maps, globes, photographs, the Global Positioning System (GPS), and Geographic Information Systems (GIS).
- People can use information from geographers to plan, make decisions, and manage resources.

Solar System

- The sun, eight planets, and many smaller bodies form our solar system.
- Earth takes almost 365¼ days to make one revolution around the sun.
- Earth spins on its axis, causing day and night.

Sun and Seasons

- The Earth's tilt and its revolution around the sun cause the changes in seasons.
- Four days in the year mark the beginning points of the four seasons.

Luxembourg Palace, Paris, France

The Earth from space

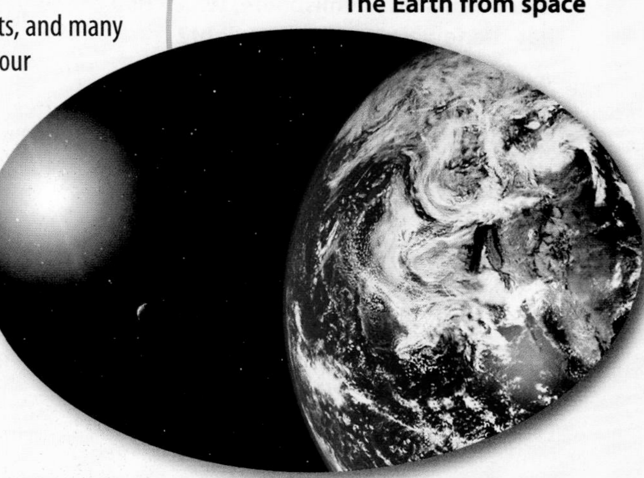

Study anywhere, anytime! Download quizzes and flash cards to your PDA from glencoe.com.

GA CRCT Practice

TEST-TAKING TIP

Read every test question twice before you answer to make certain you know exactly what it is asking.

Directions: Choose the best answer for each question.

1 **Which of the following describes where a geographic feature is located by referring to other features around it?**

A relative location
B absolute location
C the Global Positioning System
D a Geographic Positioning System

2 **When did the period known as Modern History begin?**

A five years ago
B five decades ago
C five centuries ago
D five millennia ago

3 **What is the name of the path that each planet follows around the sun?**

A axis
B orbit
C revolution
D solar system

4 **In the Northern Hemisphere, which day of the year has the fewest hours of sunlight?**

A fall equinox
B winter solstice
C spring equinox
D summer solstice

5 **Which geographic theme is used to describe the characteristics that make a location unique?**

A place
B regions
C location
D movement

6 **Which of the following provide(s) detailed photographs for creating maps?**

A a globe
B a satellite
C a Global Positioning System
D Geographic Information Systems

7 **How often does the Earth circle the sun?**

A every 24 hours
B every 365¼ days
C every 88 years
D every 165 years

8 **Why are temperatures always cool or cold near the North and South Poles?**

A The Poles face the sun in daytime.
B The rays of the sun hit the Poles directly.
C The Poles turn away from the sun at night.
D The Poles receive only slanted rays from the sun.

9 **Which is the BEST reason a globe is more accurate than a map?**

A It shows all of the Earth on one surface.
B It is easier to read the names of places.
C It depicts the true shape of lands on Earth.
D It shows boundaries more clearly.

10 **Look at the diagram.**

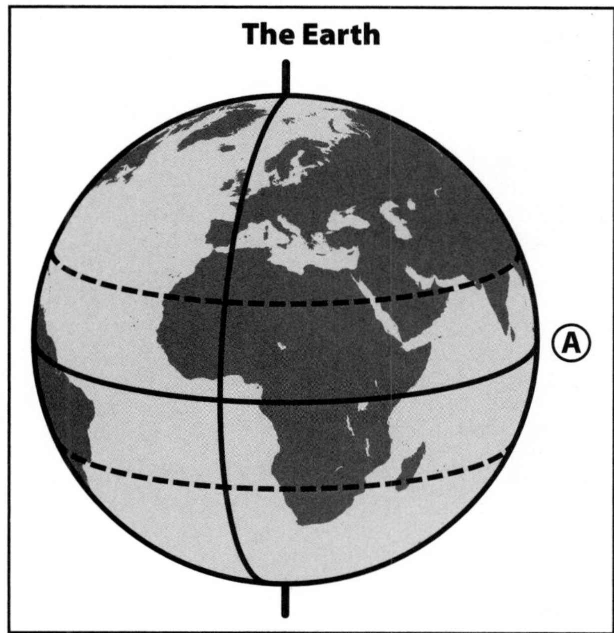

What does Label A show?

A Earth's axis
B the Equator
C the Prime Meridian
D the Tropic of Cancer

11 **Into which of the following does the Equator divide the Earth?**

A the North Pole and South Pole
B the Eastern and Western Hemispheres
C the Tropics of Cancer and Capricorn
D the Northern and Southern Hemispheres

12 **Where do the sun's rays directly hit the Earth?**

A midlatitudes
B high latitudes
C Tropics
D spring equinox

13 **Read the document and answer the questions that follow.**

The following passage explains why scientists no longer consider Pluto a major planet.

> *Once known as the smallest, coldest, and most distant planet from the Sun, Pluto has a dual [double] identity, not to mention being enshrouded [wrapped] in controversy since its discovery in 1930. On August 24, 2006, the International Astronomical Union (IAU) formally downgraded [lowered] Pluto from an official planet to a dwarf planet. According to the new rules a planet meets three criteria: it must orbit the Sun, it must be big enough for gravity to squash it into a round ball, and it must have cleared other things out of the way in its orbital neighborhood. The latter [last mentioned] measure knocks out Pluto and 2003UB313 (Eris), which orbit among the icy wrecks of the Kuiper Belt, and Ceres, which is in the asteroid belt.*
>
> —National Aeronautics and Space Administration, "Pluto"

What was Pluto once known as?

A the largest planet in the solar system
B the most distant planet from the sun
C the oldest planet in the solar system
D a solar system of its own

14 **According to the passage, in which way is Pluto like the major planets?**

A It has several moons which orbit it.
B It reflects the sun's light.
C It is big enough for gravity to mold it into a round ball.
D It orbits the sun in a path by itself.

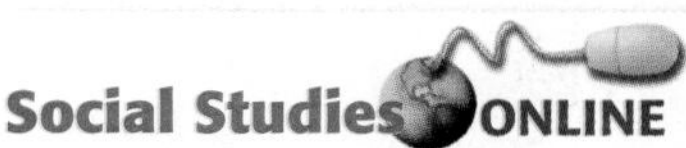

For additional test practice, use Self-Check Quizzes—Chapter 1 at glencoe.com.

Need Extra Help?

If You Missed Questions...	1	2	3	4	5	6	7	8	9	10	11	12	13	14
Go to Page...	15	16	35	38	15	17	36	38	22	25	25	38	35	35

CHAPTER 2

Earth's Physical Geography

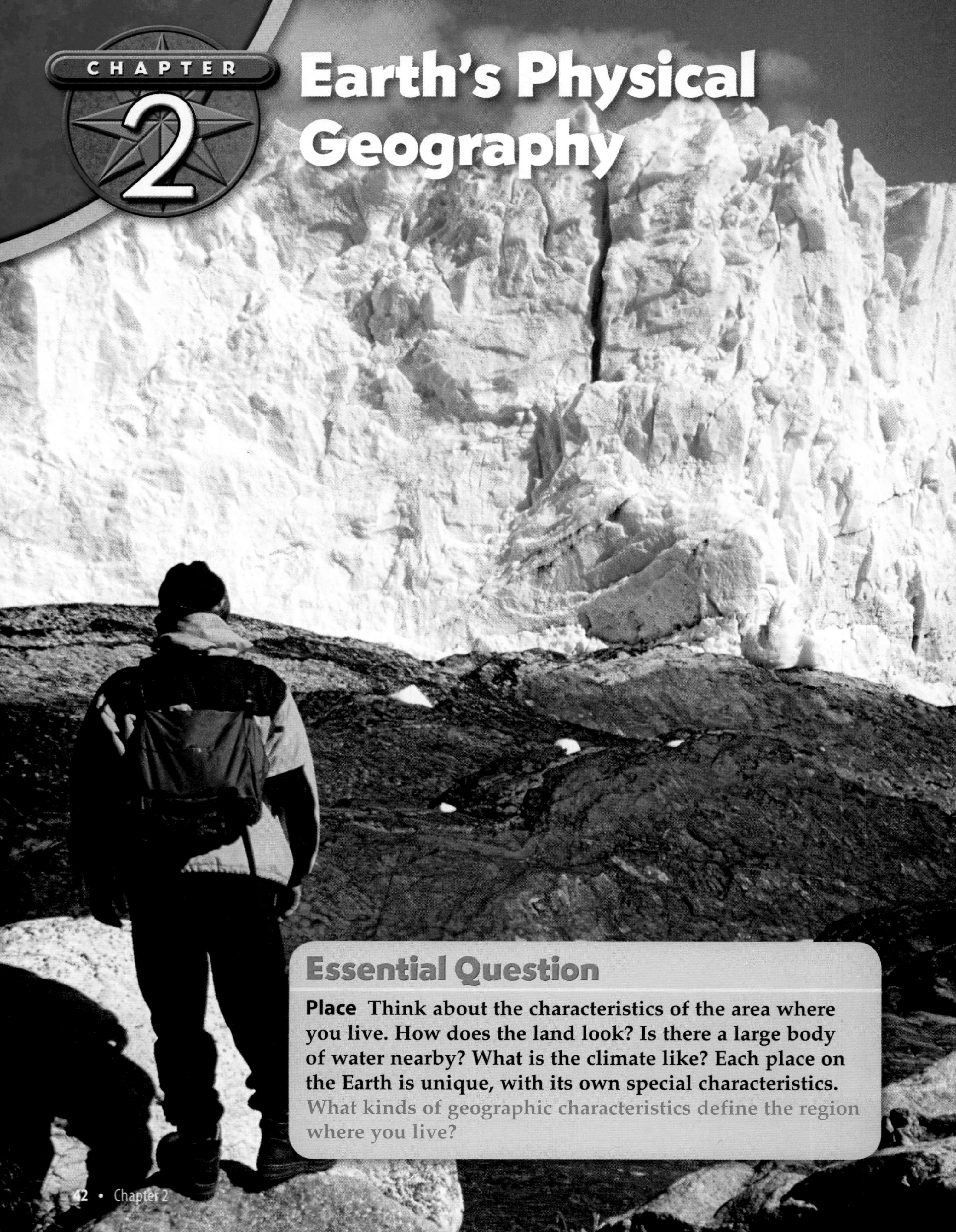

Essential Question

Place Think about the characteristics of the area where you live. How does the land look? Is there a large body of water nearby? What is the climate like? Each place on the Earth is unique, with its own special characteristics. What kinds of geographic characteristics define the region where you live?

Glaciers National Park, Argentina

Section 1: Forces Shaping the Earth

BIG IDEA Physical processes shape the Earth's surface. Forces from within and the actions of wind, water, and ice have shaped Earth's surface.

Section 2: Landforms and Water Resources

BIG IDEA Geographic factors influence where people settle. Physical features determine where people live.

Section 3: Climate Regions

BIG IDEA Geographers organize the Earth into regions that share common characteristics. Geographers use climate to define world regions.

Section 4: Human-Environment Interaction

BIG IDEA All living things are dependent upon one another and their surroundings for survival. Human actions greatly affect the natural world.

Organizing Information Use this four-tab Foldable to help you record what you learn about the Earth's physical geography.

Step 1 Fold the top and bottom of a sheet of paper into the middle.

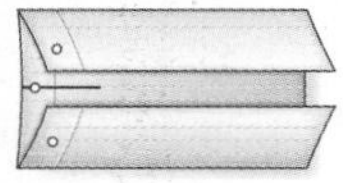

Step 2 Cut each flap at the midpoint to form 4 tabs.

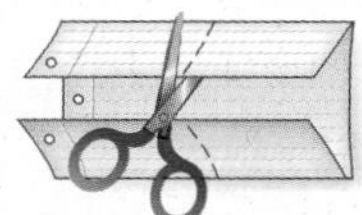

Step 3 Label the tabs as shown.

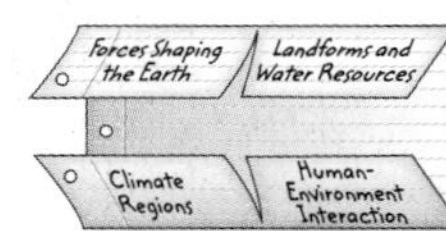

Reading and Writing As you read the chapter, take notes about each section under the appropriate head. Use your Foldable to help you write a summary for each section.

Visit glencoe.com and enter QuickPass™ code GA6EOW6225c2 for Chapter 2 resources.

Guide to Reading

BIG Idea

Physical processes shape the Earth's surface.

Content Vocabulary

- core *(p. 45)*
- mantle *(p. 45)*
- magma *(p. 45)*
- crust *(p. 45)*
- continent *(p. 45)*
- plate tectonics *(p. 46)*
- earthquake *(p. 47)*
- fault *(p. 47)*
- weathering *(p. 47)*
- erosion *(p. 48)*

Academic Vocabulary

- release *(p. 45)*
- constant *(p. 47)*
- accumulate *(p. 48)*

Reading Strategy

Determining Cause and Effect

As you read, use a diagram like the one below to list the forces shaping the Earth and the effects of each.

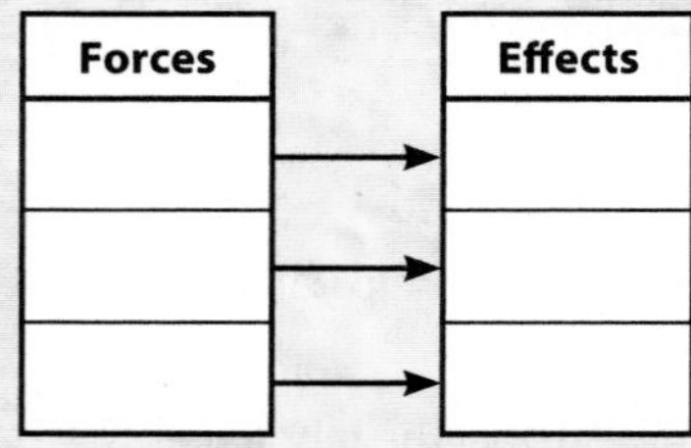

Forces Shaping the Earth

Picture This This spectacular gash is the Mid-Atlantic Ridge Fault in Iceland. A fault is a crack or break in the Earth's crust. Over millions of years, what began as a small crack in the Earth's crust is now the Mid-Atlantic Ridge. The ridge is a very long and mostly underwater mountain range along the Atlantic Ocean floor from Iceland to Antarctica. The ridge's fault line cuts across Iceland, creating the country's many volcanoes and hot springs. Read this section to learn more about processes that have shaped the surface of the Earth.

The Mid-Atlantic Ridge Fault passing through Iceland

Inside the Earth

Main Idea **The Earth is made up of several layers that have different characteristics.**

Geography and You What do you see when you cut a melon in half? Like a melon, the Earth has distinct sections or layers.

The ground feels solid when you walk on it and downright hard if you should happen to fall. Yet Earth is not a large rock, solid through the middle. Beneath our planet's solid shell lies a center that is partly liquid. As **Figure 1** shows, the Earth has different layers, much like a melon or a baseball.

At the center of the Earth is a dense solid **core** of hot iron mixed with other metals and rock. The inner core lies about 3,200 miles (5,150 km) below the surface. Scientists think it is made up of iron and nickel. They also believe the inner core is under tremendous pressure. The next layer, the outer core, is so hot that the metal has melted into a liquid. The temperature in the outer core can reach an incredible 8,500°F (about 4,700°C).

Surrounding the core is the **mantle,** a layer of hot, dense rock about 1,770 miles (2,850 km) thick. Like the core, the mantle has two parts. The section nearest the core is solid. The rock in the outer mantle, however, can be moved, shaped, and even melted. If you have seen photographs of an active volcano, then you have seen this melted rock called **magma.** It flows to the surface during a volcanic eruption. Once it reaches the surface, magma is called lava. This movement of the matter in the mantle **releases** much of the energy generated in the Earth's interior.

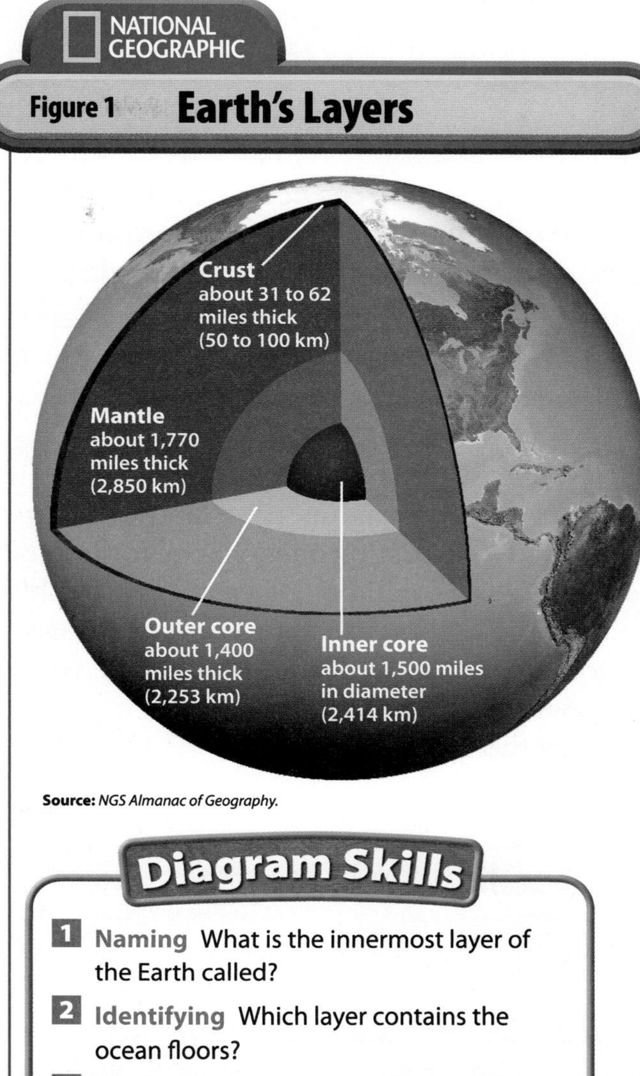

Source: *NGS Almanac of Geography.*

Diagram Skills

1. **Naming** What is the innermost layer of the Earth called?
2. **Identifying** Which layer contains the ocean floors?
3. **Specifying** Which layer is the thickest?

Earth's upper layer is the **crust,** a thin rocky shell that forms the surface. It reaches only 31 to 62 miles (50 to 100 km) deep. The crust includes ocean floors and seven large land areas known as **continents.** The continents are North America, South America, Europe, Asia, Africa, Australia, and Antarctica. The crust is just a few miles thick on the ocean floor, but is much thicker below the continents.

Explaining What is magma, and where does it originate?

Shaping the Earth's Surface

Main Idea **Forces acting both inside and outside the Earth work to change the appearance of the Earth's surface.**

Geography and You Have you been in an earthquake? Or, do you know anyone who has? Read on to discover what causes earthquakes.

The Earth's crust is not a fixed layer. It changes over time as new landforms are created and existing ones change forms. For hundreds of millions of years, the Earth's surface has been in constant motion, slowly transforming. Old mountains are worn down, while new mountains grow taller. Even the continents move.

▲ Mexico is located on top of three tectonic plates that often shift, causing earthquakes. ***Location*** **Where in the world are earthquakes common?**

Plate Movements

The theory of **plate tectonics** explains how the continents were formed and why they move. As **Figure 2** shows, each continent sits on one or more large bases called plates. As these plates move, the continents on top of them move. This movement is called continental drift.

The rate of movement varies from just under 1 inch (2.3 cm) to 7 inches (17 cm) per year. This movement is too slow for people to notice, but over millions of years, it can have dramatic effects.

Look at a map of the world. If you think of the eastern coast of South America as a giant puzzle piece, you will see that it seems to fit into the western coast of Africa. This is because these two continents were once joined together in a gigantic landmass that scientists call Pangaea. About 200 million years ago, however, the continents began to break and move apart because of tectonic activity.

When Plates Meet

The movements of Earth's plates have actually shaped the surface of the Earth. Sometimes the plates pull away from each other. Plates usually pull apart in ocean areas, but this kind of plate activity also occurs in land areas, such as Iceland.

Plates can also collide. When two continental plates collide, they push against each other with tremendous force. This causes the land along the line where the plates meet to rise and form mountains. The Rocky Mountains of North America and the Alps, one of Europe's great mountain range systems, were formed from such collisions.

Collisions of continental and oceanic plates produce a different result. The thinner ocean plate slides underneath the thicker continental plate. The downward

Figure 2 **Tectonic Plate Boundaries**

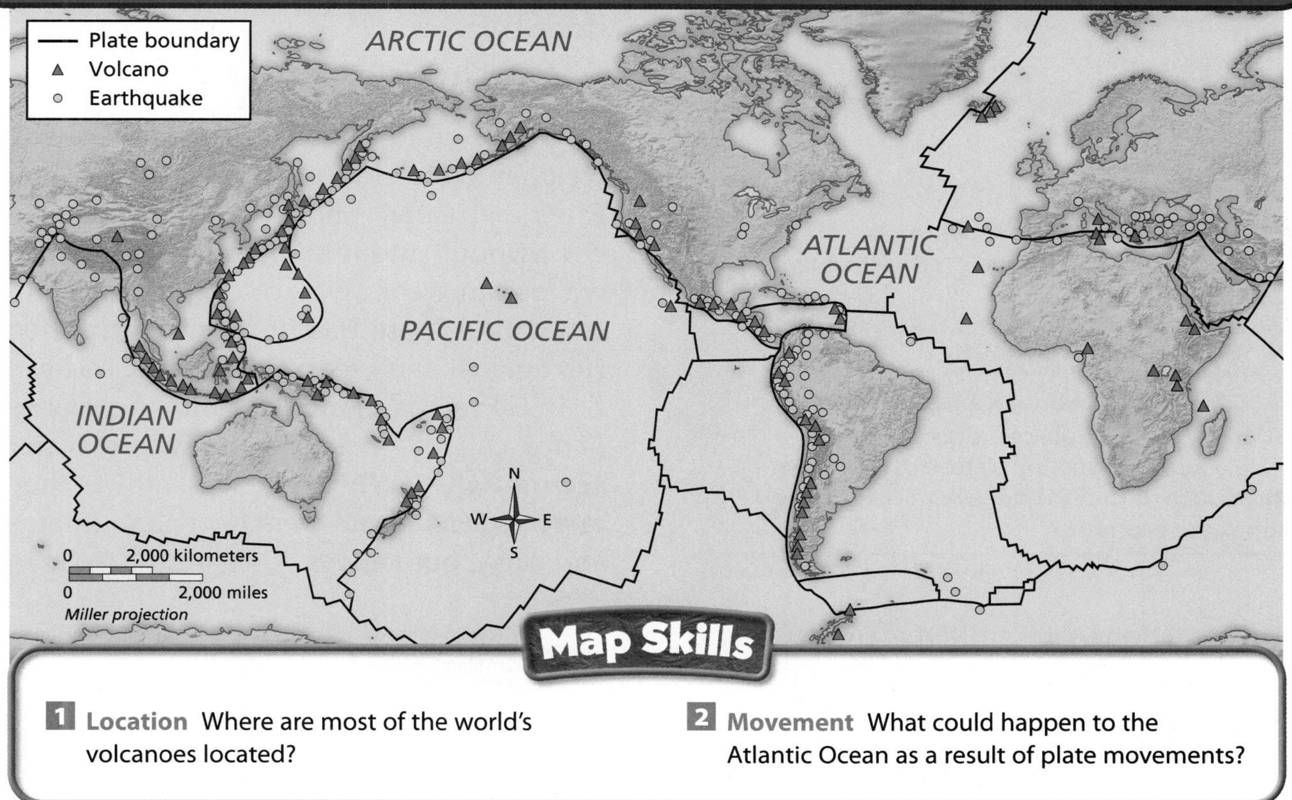

Map Skills

1 Location Where are most of the world's volcanoes located?

2 Movement What could happen to the Atlantic Ocean as a result of plate movements?

force of the lower plate causes magma to build up. Then the magma erupts and slowly hardens, forming volcanic mountains. This is how the Andes of South America were created.

Earthquakes are sudden and violent movements of the Earth's crust. They are common in areas where the collision of ocean and continental plates makes the Earth's crust unstable. For example, so many earthquakes and volcanoes occur around the edge of the Pacific Ocean that people call this region the Ring of Fire.

Sometimes two plates do not meet head-on but move alongside each other. This movement makes cracks in the Earth's crust called **faults.** Movements along faults do not take place **constantly,** but occur in sudden bursts that cause earthquakes. One of the most well-known faults in North America is the Queen Charlotte Fault off Canada's Pacific coast. A number of very destructive earthquakes have occurred in the region, and the threat of more still exists.

Social Studies ONLINE

Student Web Activity Visit glencoe.com and complete the Chapter 2 Web Activity about plate tectonics.

Weathering

The movement of tectonic plates causes volcanoes and earthquakes to change the Earth's landforms. Once created, however, these landforms will continue to change because of other forces that work on the Earth's surface.

One of these forces is called weathering. **Weathering** is when water and ice, chemicals, and even plants break rocks apart into smaller pieces. For example, water can run into cracks of rocks, freeze, and then expand.

Erosion in Bolivia

Strong winds have eroded rocks on Bolivia's Altiplano, a high and dry plateau in the Andes.
Movement **Besides wind, what other forces can cause erosion?**

These actions can split the rock. Chemicals, too, cause weathering when acids in air pollution mix with rain and fall back to Earth. The chemicals eat away rock and stone surfaces.

Erosion

Water, wind, and ice can move away weathered rock in a process called **erosion.** Rivers, streams, and even rainwater can cut through mountains and hills. Ocean waves can wear away coastal rocks. Wind can scatter loose bits of rock, which often rub against and wear down larger rocks.

In cold areas, giant, slow-moving masses of ice called glaciers form where water **accumulates.** When glaciers move, they carry rocks that can wear down mountains and carve out valleys.

Reading Check **Synthesizing** Why are earthquakes common where plates meet?

Section Review

Vocabulary

1. **Illustrate** the meaning of *core, mantle, magma, crust, continent, plate tectonics, earthquake, fault, weathering,* and *erosion* by drawing and labeling one or more diagrams.

Main Ideas

2. **Summarizing** Which layers of the Earth are solid? Which layers are liquid?
3. **Describing** Use a chart like the one below to list and describe the different results when plates meet.

Type of Plate Meeting	Results
1.	1.
2.	2.
3.	3.

Critical Thinking

4. **Drawing Conclusions** Where do you think an earthquake is more likely to occur—along North America's Pacific coast or along North America's Atlantic coast? Why?
5. **BIG Idea** How was the formation of the Alps and the Andes similar and different?
6. **Challenge** How do the shapes of South America and Africa support the theory of plate tectonics? Find another example of land areas that once might have been joined together but separated as plates moved apart.

Writing About Geography

7. **Using Your FOLDABLES™** Use your Foldable to write a paragraph explaining how forces both beneath and on the surface help shape the surface of the Earth.

Guide to Reading

BIG Idea

Geographic factors influence where people settle.

Content Vocabulary

- continental shelf *(p. 50)*
- trench *(p. 50)*
- groundwater *(p. 52)*
- aquifer *(p. 52)*
- water cycle *(p. 53)*
- evaporation *(p. 53)*
- condensation *(p. 54)*
- precipitation *(p. 54)*
- collection *(p. 54)*

Academic Vocabulary

- occur *(p. 50)*
- define *(p. 50)*
- availability *(p. 52)*

Reading Strategy

Identifying Use a diagram like the one below to identify the various bodies of water that can be found on the Earth's surface.

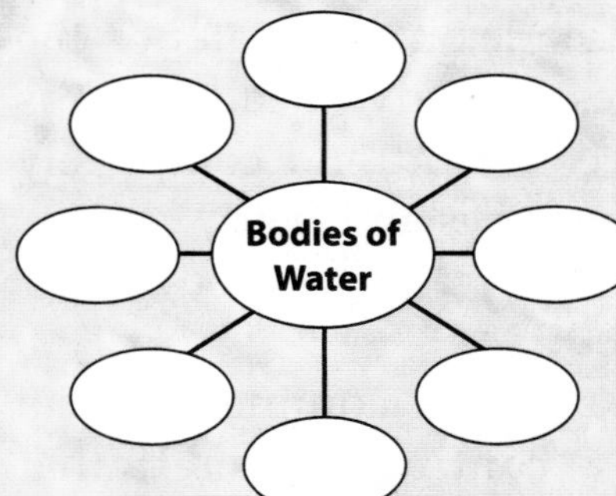

Landforms and Water Resources

 Section Audio  Spotlight Video

Picture This With more than 360 miles (579 km) of coastline, the archipelago of Guadeloupe in the Caribbean Sea is a great spot for fishing. This local fisher uses a large orange net to catch shellfish to feed his family and to sell at a local market. Read this section to learn how landforms and water influence human activities throughout the world.

▼ Fishing in the Caribbean Sea, Guadeloupe

Types of Landforms

Main Idea **Earth has a variety of landforms, and many of the landforms can be found both on the continents and the ocean floors.**

Geography and You Do you know that there are mountains underwater? If the area where you live was underwater, what would it look like?

The Earth has a great variety of landforms—from mountains that soar miles high to lowlands that barely peek above the sea. These landforms appear not only on continents but also under the oceans.

On Land

Mountains are huge towers of rock and are the highest landforms. Some mountains may be only a few thousand feet high. Others can soar higher than 20,000 feet (6,096 m). The world's highest mountain is Mount Everest in South Asia's Himalaya ranges. It rises more than 29,028 feet (8,848 m), nearly five and a half miles high!

Hills are lower and more rounded than mountains. Between mountains and hills lie valleys. A valley is a long stretch of land that is lower than the land on either side. Flatlands **occur** in one of two forms, depending on their height above sea level. Plains are flat lowlands, typically found along coasts and lowland river valleys. Plateaus are flatlands at higher elevations.

Geographers **define** some landforms by their relationship to other landforms or to bodies of water. Look back at the geographic dictionary in the Reference Atlas to see examples of the following landforms.

An isthmus is a narrow strip of land that connects two larger landmasses and has water on two sides. An example is Central America, which connects North and South America. A peninsula, such as Italy, is a piece of land that is connected to a larger landmass on one side but has water on the other three sides. A body of land that is smaller than a continent and completely surrounded by water is an island.

Under the Oceans

Off each coast of a continent lies a plateau called a **continental shelf** that stretches for several miles underwater. At the edge of the shelf, the land drops down sharply to the ocean floor.

On the ocean floor, tall mountains thousands of miles wide line the edges of ocean plates that are pulling apart. Tectonic activity also makes deep cuts in the ocean floor called **trenches.** The Mariana Trench in the western Pacific Ocean is the deepest. It plunges 36,198 feet (11,033 m) below sea level.

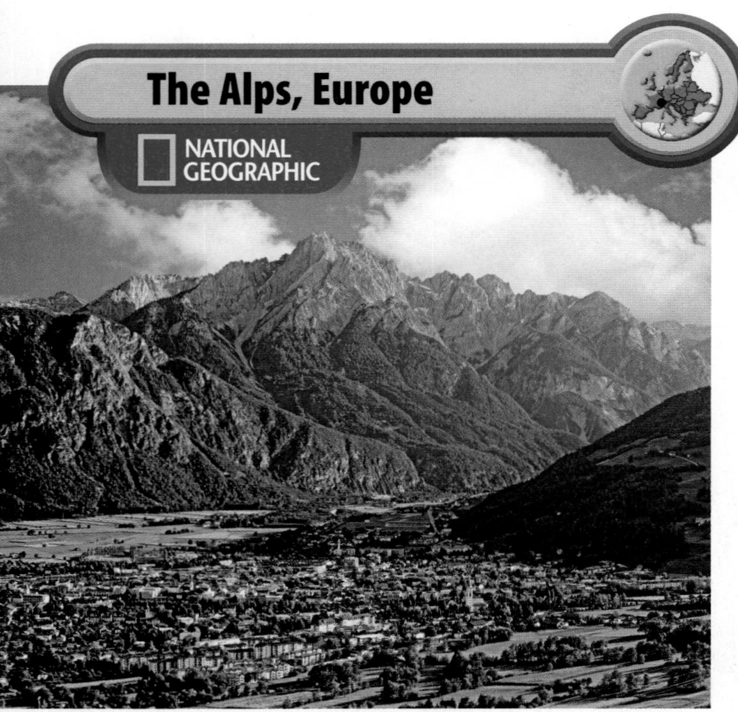

▲ The Alps are the source of many rivers in Europe, including the Rhine and the Po. ***Location*** **Where is Mount Everest, the world's tallest peak, located?**

Farewell to Matyora

By Valentin Rasputin

And so the village had lived on in its lean and simple way, clinging to its spot on the bluff by the left bank [of the Angara River], greeting and seeing off the years, like the water that joined [the villagers] to other settlements and that had helped feed them since time **immemorial.** And just as the flowing water seemed to have no end or limit, the village seemed ageless: some went off to their Maker, others were born, old buildings collapsed, new ones were built. And the village lived on, through hard times and troubles, for three hundred and more years . . . until the rumor thundered down on them that the village would be no more. A dam was being built downriver on the Angara for a hydroelectric power station, and the waters would rise in the rivers and streams, flooding much land, including, first and foremost, Matyora. Even if you were to pile five islands like Matyora one on top of the other, they would still be flooded and you wouldn't be able to show the spot where people once lived. They would have to move. It wasn't easy to believe that it really would come to pass. . . . A year after the first rumors an evaluating **commission** came by [boat] and began assessing the **depreciation** of the buildings and determining how much money they were worth. There was no more doubt about the fate of Matyora, it was living out its last years. Somewhere on the right bank they were building a new settlement for the . . . state-owned farm, into which they were bringing all the neighboring **kolkhozes,** and some that were not so neighboring, and it was decided, so as not to have to deal with rubbish, to set fire to the old villages.

From: *Farewell to Matyora,* by Valentin Rasputin, translated by Antonina W. Bouis, Evanston, Ill.: Northwestern University Press, 1991.

Analyzing Literature

1. **Identifying Central Issues** How is the physical geography of the area changing? Why?
2. **Read to Write** Take the role of a local government official and write an editorial explaining why you either support or oppose the building of the dam.

Valentin Rasputin (1937–)

Born in Siberia, Valentin Rasputin often celebrates the region in his writing. The short novel *Farewell to Matyora* expresses his fear that modern life can erase the traditions of the villagers there.

Background Information

In Soviet times, huge power plants and hydroelectric projects were built to provide energy for heavy industry. Decisions to build factories and power plants were made by the Communist government without consulting the local communities that would be affected by such actions. The government's attempts at modernization often had serious effects on Russia's people.

Reader's Dictionary

immemorial: before memory

commission: official government body

depreciation: lowered value

kolkhozes: government-owned farming villages

Humans and Landforms

Humans settle on all types of landforms. People choose a place to live based on a number of factors. Climate—the average temperature and rainfall of a region—is one factor that people must consider. The **availability** of resources is another factor. People settle where they can get freshwater and where they can grow food, catch fish, or raise animals.

Reading Check **Explaining** What forces form ocean trenches?

Río Colorado, Argentina

NATIONAL GEOGRAPHIC

The Río Colorado forms a delta as it flows into the Atlantic Ocean. River deltas are often rich in wildlife, including birds and mammals. ***Place*** **How are deltas formed?**

The Water Planet

Main Idea **Water covers much of the planet, but only some of this water is usable.**

Geography and You Have you ever watched steam rise from a boiling pot of water? Read to learn how water changes from a solid, to a liquid, to a gas on Earth.

Earth is sometimes called the "water planet" because so much of it—about 70 percent of the surface—is covered with water. Water exists in many different forms. Streams, rivers, lakes, seas, and oceans contain water in liquid form. The atmosphere holds water vapor, or water in the form of gas. Glaciers and ice sheets are masses of water that have been frozen solid.

Salt Water

All of the oceans on Earth are part of a huge, continuous body of salt water. Almost 97 percent of the planet's water is salt water. Oceans have smaller arms or areas that are called seas, bays, or gulfs. These larger bodies of salt water can be linked to oceans by the more narrow bodies called straits or channels.

Freshwater

Only 3 percent of the water on Earth is freshwater. Much of this freshwater is frozen in ice that covers polar regions and parts of mountains. Some is **groundwater,** which filters through the soil into the ground. Groundwater often gathers in **aquifers** (A·kwuh·fuhrz). These are underground layers of rock through which water flows. People can pump the freshwater from aquifers. Only a tiny amount of all

Figure 3 The Water Cycle

Diagram Skills

1 Identifying In which step of the water cycle does water vapor form clouds?

2 Explaining How does the sun's heat drive the water cycle?

the water in the world is found in lakes and rivers. This water is often not safe to drink until it has been purified.

Large inland bodies of water are called lakes. Most lakes are freshwater lakes. Long, flowing bodies of water are called rivers. They begin at a source and end at a mouth. The mouth is the place where a river empties into another body of water, such as an ocean or a lake.

The largest rivers often have many tributaries, which are separate streams or rivers that feed into them. Many rivers form deltas at their mouths. A delta is an area where a river breaks into many different streams flowing toward the sea. Rivers often carry rich soil to their deltas and deposit it, building up the land.

The Water Cycle

The total amount of water on Earth does not change. It does not stay in one place, either. Instead the water moves constantly. In a process called the **water cycle,** the water goes from the oceans, to the air, to the ground, and finally back to the oceans.

Look at **Figure 3** to see how the water cycle works. The sun's heat drives the water cycle because it evaporates the water on the Earth's surface. This **evaporation** changes water from liquid to a gas, called water vapor. Water vapor rises from the Earth's oceans and other bodies of water, and then circulates in the atmosphere. The air's temperature determines how much water the air holds. Warm air holds more water vapor than cool air.

Monroe Lake, Quebec

Fog is a low-lying cloud that can form when moist air blows over a cool surface. ***Place*** **How does air temperature affect water vapor in the air?**

When the air temperature drops low enough, **condensation** takes place. In this process, water changes from gas back to a liquid. Tiny droplets of water form in the air, although they are suspended in clouds.

When conditions in the atmosphere are right, these water droplets fall to the ground as some form of **precipitation.** This can be rain, snow, sleet, or hail. The form of precipitation depends on the temperature of the surrounding air.

Completing the cycle is the process called **collection.** The water collects on the ground and in rivers, lakes, and oceans. There it evaporates to begin the cycle again.

Reading Check **Making Inferences** Why is very little of the Earth's freshwater usable?

Section 2 Review

Vocabulary

1. **Explain** the meaning of the following terms by using each one in a sentence.
   - **a.** continental shelf
   - **b.** trench
   - **c.** groundwater
   - **d.** aquifer
   - **e.** water cycle
   - **f.** evaporation
   - **g.** condensation
   - **h.** precipitation
   - **i.** collection

Main Ideas

2. **Contrasting** How do an isthmus, a peninsula, and an island differ?
3. **Summarizing** Use a diagram like the one below to summarize the water cycle.

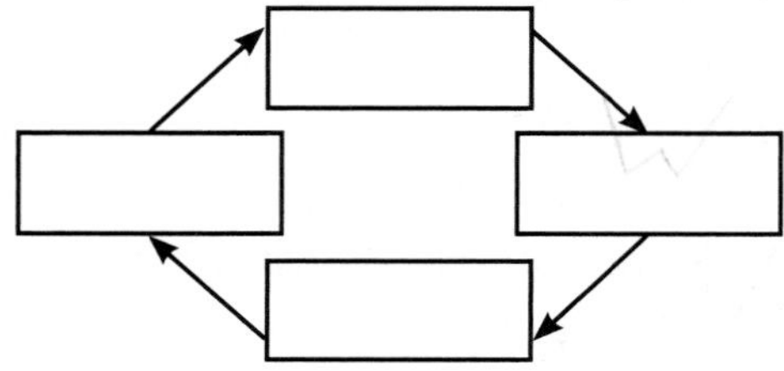

Critical Thinking

4. **Comparing and Contrasting** How are plains and plateaus similar and different?
5. **BIG Idea** Describe several factors that people consider when choosing a place to settle.
6. **Challenge** Which landforms do you think attracted people to settle in the area where you live? Which landforms, if any, may have kept people away?

Writing About Geography

7. **Expository Writing** Write a paragraph describing the major landforms found in the state where you live.

Guide to Reading

BIG Idea

Geographers organize the Earth into regions that share common characteristics.

Content Vocabulary

- weather *(p. 56)*
- climate *(p. 56)*
- prevailing wind *(p. 57)*
- current *(p. 57)*
- El Niño *(p. 58)*
- La Niña *(p. 58)*
- local wind *(p. 59)*
- rain shadow *(p. 59)*
- climate zone *(p. 59)*
- biome *(p. 60)*
- urban climate *(p. 61)*

Academic Vocabulary

- distribute *(p. 56)*
- alter *(p. 57)*

Reading Strategy

Identifying Central Issues Use a diagram like the one below to identify the effects of both El Niño and La Niña.

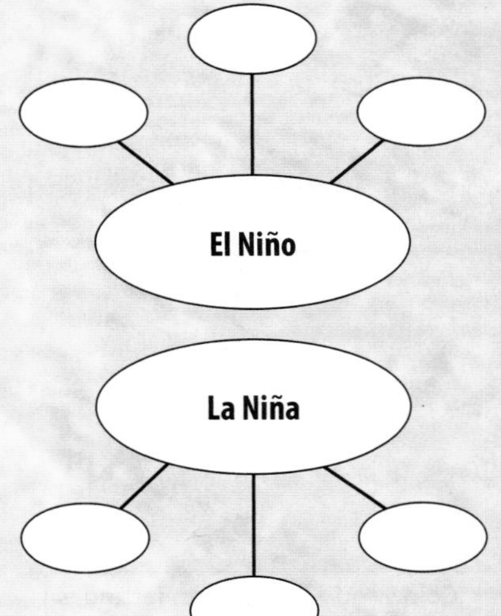

Climate Regions

 Section Audio  Spotlight Video

Picture This A man rushes to escape the swirling winds and pelting rain of a hurricane blowing across the Caribbean island of Cuba. These violent storms draw their power from the warm ocean waters of the Tropics near the Americas. Hurricanes can topple buildings, snap power lines, and uproot trees. The deadliest hurricanes that struck the United States are the Galveston Hurricane (1900), the Great Miami Hurricane (1926), and Hurricane Katrina (2005). Read this section to learn about the variety of climates that are found on Earth.

▼ Fleeing a tropical hurricane in Cuba

Effects on Climate

Main Idea **Sun, wind, and water influence Earth's climate.**

Geography and You What is the weather today in your area? Is it typical of the particular season you are in, or is it unusual? Read to find out about the difference between weather and climate.

When you turn on the television to find out the day's high and low temperatures, you are checking the local weather. **Weather** refers to the changes in temperature, wind direction and speed, and air moisture that take place over a short period of time. When geographers look at the usual, predictable patterns of weather in an area over many years, they are studying **climate**.

The Sun

Earth's climate is linked directly to the sun. As you recall from Chapter 1, the Earth does not heat evenly. The Tropics receive more of the sun's heat energy and the Poles receive less. The movement of air and water over the Earth helps to **distribute** the sun's heat more evenly around the globe.

Maps In MOtion See StudentWorks™ Plus or glencoe.com.

Figure 4 **Prevailing Wind Patterns**

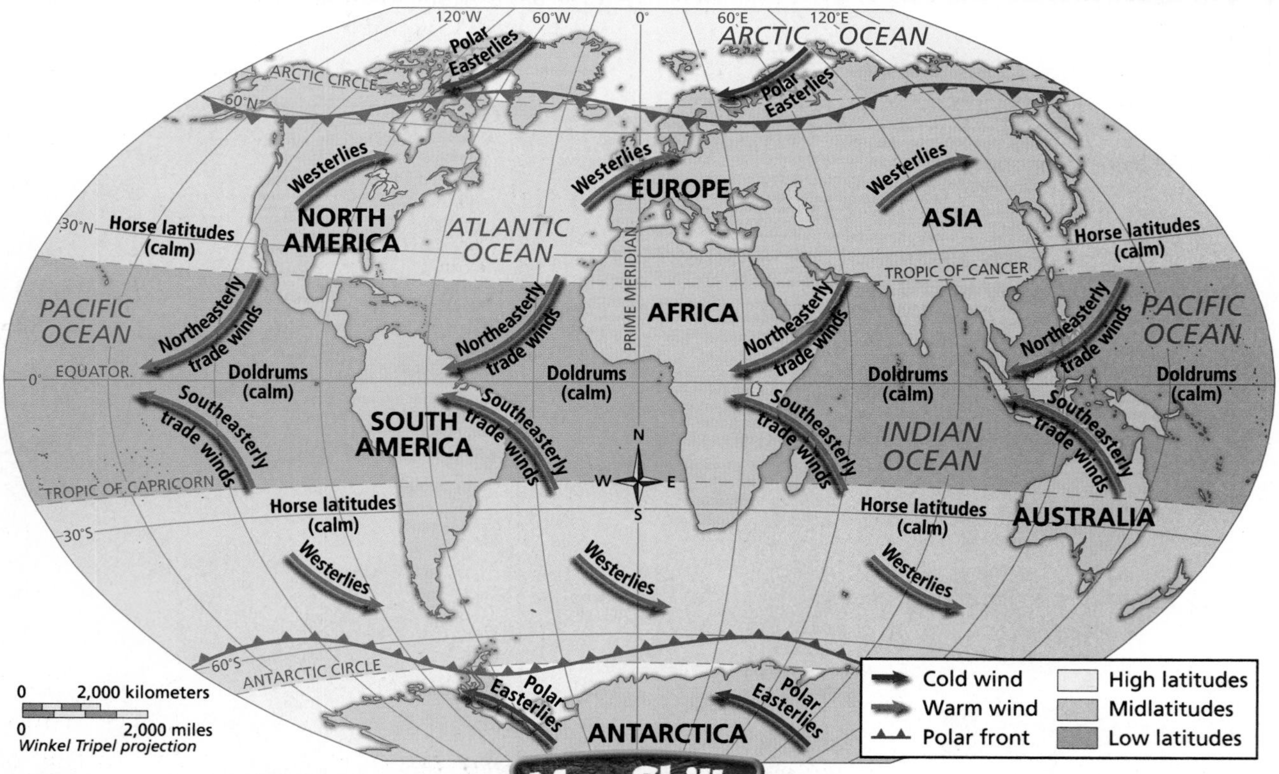

Map Skills

1. **Movement** In which general direction does the wind blow over North America and Europe?
2. **Regions** Which two areas of the world experience calm winds?

Winds

Air in the Tropics, which is warmed by the sun, moves north and south toward the Poles of the Earth. Colder air from the Poles moves toward the Equator. These movements of air are winds. Major wind systems follow patterns that are similar over time. These patterns, shown in **Figure 4,** are called **prevailing winds.**

Because the planet rotates, winds curve across Earth's surface. The winds that blow from east to west between the Tropics and the Equator are called the trade winds. Long ago sailing ships used these winds to carry out trade. The westerlies, which blow over North America, move from west to east in the area between the Tropics and about 60° north latitude.

Storms

When moist, warm air rises suddenly and meets dry, cold air, major storms can develop. In the summer, these storms can include thunder and lightning, heavy rain, and, sometimes, tornadoes. Tornadoes are violent, funnel-shaped windstorms with wind speeds up to 450 miles (724 km) per hour. In the winter, storms can become blizzards that bring much snow.

Other types of destructive storms are hurricanes and typhoons. Hurricanes occur in the western Atlantic and eastern Pacific Oceans. Typhoons occur in the western Pacific Ocean. These storms arise in the warm ocean waters of the Tropics and can reach great size and power. Some are as much as 300 miles (483 km) across and create strong winds and heavy rains.

Ocean Currents

The steadily flowing streams of water in the world's seas are called **currents.** Like winds, they follow patterns, which are shown in **Figure 5,** on the next page.

NATIONAL GEOGRAPHIC

Effects of El Niño

South America can experience dramatic changes in weather due to El Niño and La Niña. Forest fires, like this one in Brazil, occur during periods of drought. ***Place*** **How do El Niño and La Niña differ?**

Currents that carry warm water to higher latitudes can affect the climates in those latitudes. For example, the North Atlantic Current carries warm water from the Tropics to western Europe. Winds blowing over the warm water bring warmth and moisture to western Europe, which enjoys an unexpectedly mild climate.

El Niño and La Niña

Every few years, changes in normal wind and water patterns in the Pacific Ocean cause unusual weather in some places. In one of these events, weakened winds allow warmer waters to reach South America's coast. This change **alters,** or changes, weather there.

These conditions are called **El Niño,** Spanish for "the boy."

In an El Niño, very heavy rains fall on western South America, causing floods. Meanwhile, little rain falls on Australia, southern Asia, and Africa. Also, North America may see severe storms.

In some years the opposite occurs, producing conditions called **La Niña,** Spanish for "the girl." La Niña causes unusually cool waters and low rainfall in the eastern Pacific. In the western Pacific, rains are heavy and typhoons can occur.

Explaining How are winds formed?

Landforms and Climate

Main Idea Landforms, especially mountains, can affect winds, temperature, and rainfall.

Geography and You Have you ever felt a cooling sea breeze on a hot summer's day? Read on to learn how the sea can affect climate.

Sun, wind, and water affect climate, but the shape of the land has an effect on climate as well. The distance between landforms as well as their nearness to water influence climate.

NATIONAL GEOGRAPHIC

Figure 5 **World Ocean Currents**

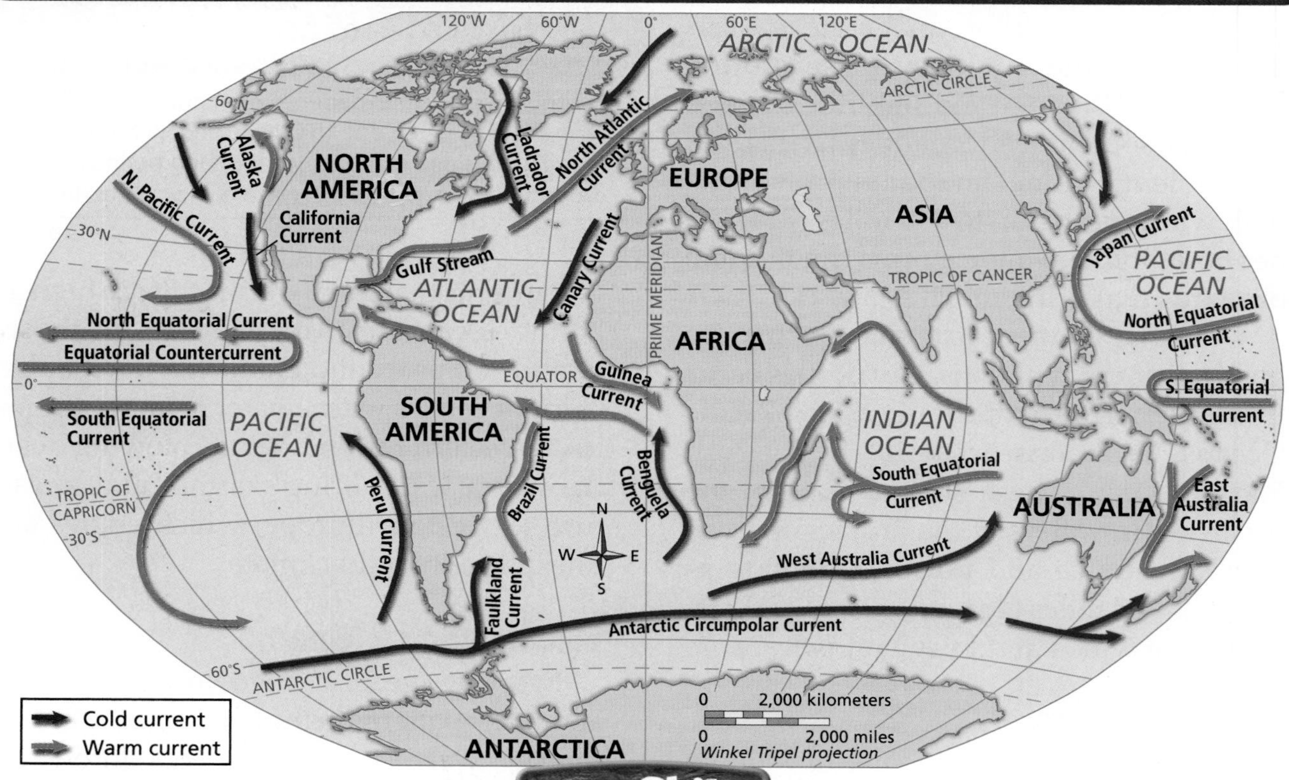

Map Skills

1. **Movement** What kind of climate is the North Atlantic Current likely to bring to Europe?
2. **Regions** Which area generally has warmer waters, western South America or eastern South America?

Landforms and Local Winds

Some landforms cause **local winds**, or wind patterns that are typical only in a small area. Some local winds occur because land warms and cools more quickly than water does. As a result, cool sea breezes keep coastal areas cool during the day. After the sun sets, the opposite occurs. The air over the land cools more quickly than the air over the water. At night, then, a cool breeze blows from the land out to sea.

Local winds also occur near tall mountains. When the air along a mountain slope is warmer than the air in the valley below, it rises and a cool valley breeze moves up the mountain.

Mountains, Temperature, and Rainfall

The slopes of a mountain facing the sun can heat more quickly than nearby land. Higher up in the mountains, however, the air is thin and cannot hold the heat very well. As a result, mountain peaks are cold. This explains why some mountains in the Tropics are covered with snow.

Mountains have an effect on rainfall called a **rain shadow** that blocks rain from reaching interior regions. As warm, moist ocean air moves up the mountain slopes, it cools and releases its moisture. As a result, the side of mountains facing the wind, called the windward side, receives large amounts of rainfall.

As the air passes over the mountain peaks to the other side, called the leeward side, it becomes cool and dry. As a result, the land on the leeward side of the mountains is often very dry. Deserts can develop on the leeward side of mountain ranges.

Reading Check **Determining Cause and Effect** How do mountains cause the rain shadow effect?

Climate Zones

Main Idea **The effects of wind, water, latitude, and landforms combine to create different climate zones.**

Geography and You Suppose you visited two islands that were thousands of miles apart. Read to find out how similar their climates might be.

As you have read, the effects of wind, water, latitude, and landforms combine to shape the climate of an area. Scientists have found that many parts of the world, even though they are very distant from one another, have similar climates. Southern California, for instance, has a warm, dry climate similar to that around the Mediterranean Sea in Europe. These areas have the same **climate zone**, or similar patterns of temperature and precipitation. These regions would also have similar vegetation.

NATIONAL GEOGRAPHIC

Figure 6 The Rain Shadow

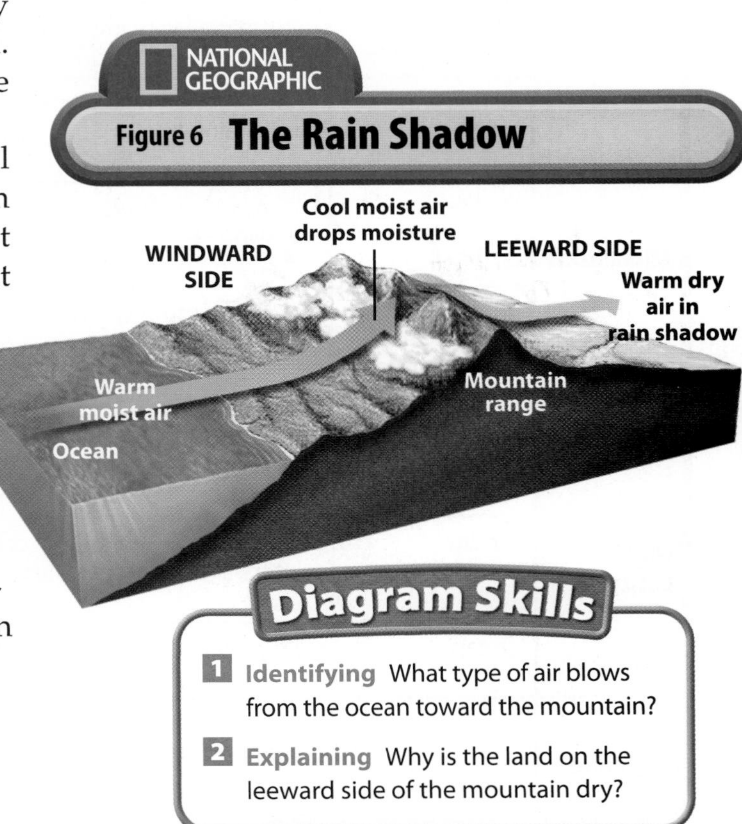

Diagram Skills

1. **Identifying** What type of air blows from the ocean toward the mountain?
2. **Explaining** Why is the land on the leeward side of the mountain dry?

Climate zones include **biomes,** or areas such as rain forest, desert, grassland, and tundra in which particular kinds of plants and animals have adapted to particular climates.

Major Climates

Scientists have identified five major climate zones, which are described in the chart below. Four of these zones have several subcategories. For example, the dry climate zone is subdivided into steppe and desert subcategories. These generally dry climates differ slightly in rainfall and temperature. Locations in the highland zone show great variation. In these areas, altitude, the position of a place toward or away from the sun, and other factors can make large differences in climate even though two locations may be near each other.

World Climate Zones

Category	Subcategory	Characteristics	Vegetation	Example
Tropical	Tropical rain forest	Warm temperatures; heavy rainfall throughout year	Dense rain forests	Amazon basin (South America); Congo basin (Africa)
	Tropical savanna	Warm temperatures throughout year; dry winter	Grasslands dotted by scattered trees	Southern half of Brazil; eastern Africa
Dry	Steppe	Temperatures can be warm or mild; rainfall low and unreliable	Grasses, shrubs	Western Great Plains (United States); Sahel region south of the Sahara (Africa)
	Desert	Temperatures can be warm or mild; rainfall very low and very unreliable	Drought-resistant shrubs and bushes	Sonoran Desert (southwestern United States, Mexico); Sahara (Africa)
Midlatitude	Marine west coast	Cool summers, mild winters; ample rainfall	Deciduous or evergreen forests	Northwestern United States; northwestern Europe
	Mediterranean	Warm, dry summers; mild, wet winters	Shrubs, low trees, drought-resistant plants	Southern California; Mediterranean region (Europe)
	Humid subtropical	Hot, wet summers; mild, wet winters	Mixed forests	Southeastern United States; eastern China
	Humid continental	Hot, wet summers; cold, somewhat wet winters	Deciduous forests	Northeastern United States; eastern Europe; western Russia
High Latitude	Subarctic	Short, mild summers; long, cold winters; light precipitation	Coniferous forests	Most of Alaska, Canada; western Russia
	Tundra	Short, cool summers; long, cold winters; precipitation varies	Low-lying grasses, mosses, shrubs	Extreme north of North America; Europe
	Ice cap	Cold all year long	None to very little	Greenland; Antarctica
Highland		Varies depending on local conditions	Changes with altitude	Northern Rocky Mountains (United States); the Himalaya (Asia)

Urban Climates

Large cities show significant climate differences from surrounding areas in their climate zone. These **urban climates** are marked by higher temperatures and other differences. Paved streets and stone buildings soak up and then release more of the sun's heat energy than areas covered by plants. This absorption leads to higher temperatures—as much as 10° to 20°F (6° to 11°C) higher—than in the nearby countryside. These different heat patterns cause winds to blow into cities from several directions instead of the prevailing direction experienced in rural areas. Some scientists believe cities also have more precipitation than rural areas.

Reading Check **Drawing Conclusions** How do large cities affect climate?

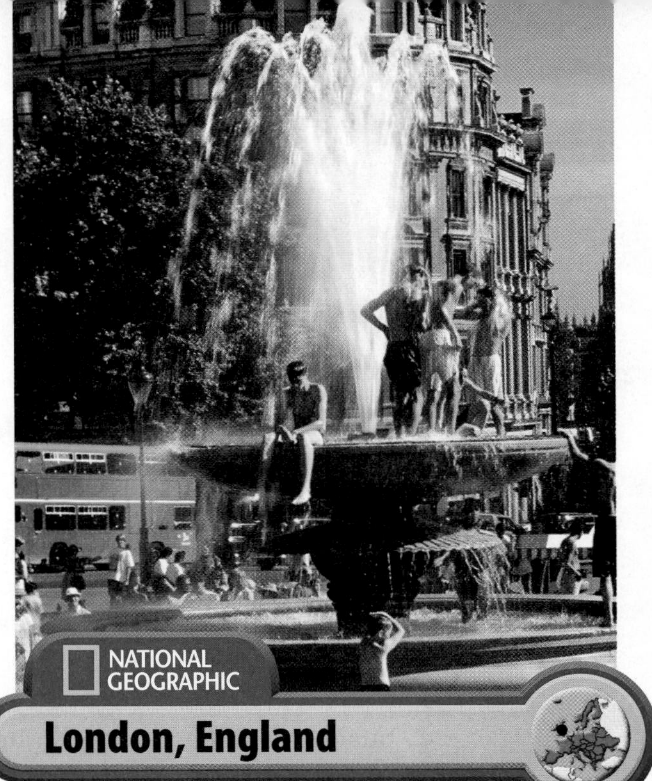

City temperatures can soar in the summer. Buildings and pavement absorb the sun's heat, raising temperatures within the city. ***Location*** **How does urban heat affect winds in the urban area?**

Section 3 Review

Vocabulary

1. **Explain** the meaning of the following terms by writing three paragraphs that include all of the terms: *weather, climate, prevailing wind, current, El Niño, La Niña, local wind, rain shadow, climate zone, biome,* and *urban climate.*

Main Ideas

2. **Explaining** How do wind and water affect the Earth's climates?
3. **Reviewing** Describe two types of local winds and why they form.
4. **Identifying** Use a diagram like the one below to identify the main characteristics of the climate zone in which you live.

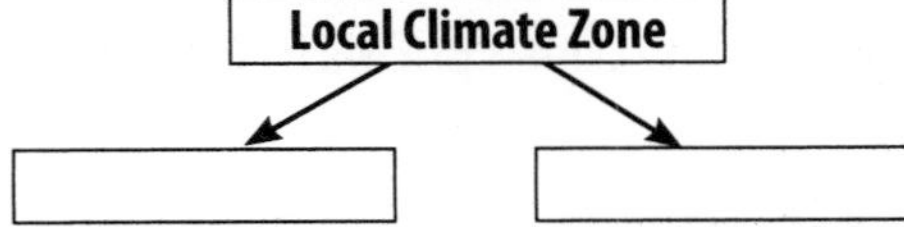

Critical Thinking

5. **BIG Idea** Choose two climate zones, and compare and contrast their characteristics.
6. **Challenge** How might El Niño affect weather conditions in the central United States?

Writing About Geography

7. **Expository Writing** Choose a place in the world you would like to visit because of its climate. Write a paragraph describing the climate of that area.

Geography & History

Invaders From Another Land

When plants and animals move from their natural environment to one in which they do not belong, they can cause great harm.

How They Arrive In the 1800s, a settler in Australia released about a dozen European rabbits onto his land. He brought the rabbits to Australia in order to hunt other animals. Over the years, the number of rabbits grew beyond control. They eventually damaged plant and animal life throughout Australia.

The rabbits brought to Australia are an example of an invasive species. These are plants and animals introduced to new areas where they increase rapidly and crowd out local plants and animal life.

▲ **European rabbit**

Invasive species are a threat in other parts of the world as well as in Australia. Zebra mussels, for example, came to the United States during the 1980s attached to the bottoms of ships. They fell off the ships and spread throughout lakes, rivers, and streams. These mussels have blocked city water treatment systems and destroyed some fish populations.

▲ **Zebra mussels clustered on wood**

Finding a Solution The costs of invasive species can be great. Within a short time of arriving in a new location, invasive species can cause billions of dollars in damage. Costs to the environment are high too. Invasive species can cause the extinction of local animals and plants not used to them.

Experts believe that invasive species are becoming more common. Increasing world trade means more contact among the world's peoples and environments. This contact means more chances for species to move from one place to another. Some governments are working both to keep invasive species from arriving and to restore environments that have been harmed.

The Spread of Zebra Mussels

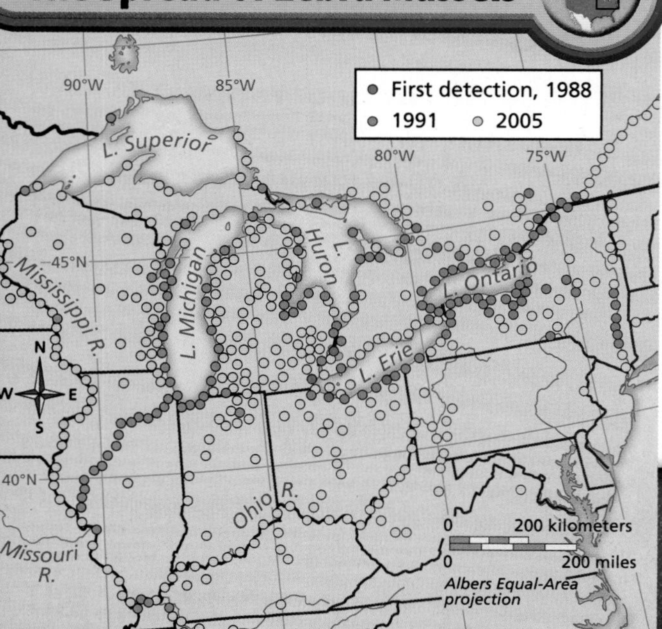

Think About It

1. Why are some plants and animals called *invasive species*?
2. Why are invasive species becoming more common?

Guide to Reading

BIG Idea

All living things are dependent upon one another and their surroundings for survival.

Content Vocabulary

- smog *(p. 64)*
- acid rain *(p. 64)*
- greenhouse effect *(p. 64)*
- crop rotation *(p. 65)*
- deforestation *(p. 65)*
- conservation *(p. 66)*
- irrigation *(p. 66)*
- pesticide *(p. 66)*
- ecosystem *(p. 66)*
- biodiversity *(p. 66)*

Academic Vocabulary

- layer *(p. 64)*
- technique *(p. 65)*

Reading Strategy

Solving Problems Use a chart like the one below to identify environmental problems and what people are doing to solve them.

Problem	Solution
1.	1.
2.	2.
3.	3.

Human-Environment Interaction

 Section Audio  Spotlight Video

Picture This On the Fraser River in Canada's province of British Columbia, newly cut logs float towards the port of Vancouver. The logs are then loaded on ships for export or placed on trucks and taken to lumberyards. Read this section to learn about the effects of human activities on the Earth.

Logs moving on the Fraser River

The Atmosphere

Main Idea **Human activity can have a negative impact on the air.**

Geography and You Have you ever seen a blanket of dirty air hanging over a large city? Read to find out how human actions affect the atmosphere.

Throughout the world, people burn oil, coal, or gas to make electricity, to power factories, or to move cars. These actions often cause air pollution.

Air Pollution

Air pollution has serious effects on people and the planet. Some polluting chemicals combine with ozone, a form of oxygen, to create **smog.** This is a thick haze of smoke and chemicals. Thick smog above cities can lead to serious breathing problems.

Chemicals in air pollution can also combine with precipitation to form **acid rain.** Acid rain kills fish, eats away at the surfaces of buildings, and destroys trees and entire forests. Because the chemicals that form acid rain come from the burning of coal and oil, solving this problem has proved difficult.

Some human-made chemicals, particularly chlorofluorocarbons (CFCs), destroy the ozone **layer.** Ozone forms a shield high in the atmosphere against damaging rays from the sun that can cause skin cancer. Nations today are working to limit the release of CFCs.

The Greenhouse Effect

Like the glass in a greenhouse, gases in the atmosphere trap the sun's warmth. Without this **greenhouse effect,** the Earth would be too cold for most living things. **Figure 7** shows the greenhouse effect.

NATIONAL GEOGRAPHIC

Global Warming

Scientists are concerned that global warming might be harming wildlife, such as this polar bear.
Human-Environment Interaction **What human activities might contribute to global warming?**

Some scientists, however, say that pollution is strengthening the greenhouse effect. They claim that the increased burning of coal, oil, and natural gas has released more gases into the atmosphere. These greenhouse gases have trapped more of the sun's heat near the Earth's surface, raising temperatures around the planet. Such warming could cause climate changes and melt polar ice. Ocean levels could rise and flood low-lying coastal areas.

The issue of global warming is debated. Critics argue that computer models showing global warming are unrealistic. Many nations, however, are addressing the problem. They are trying to use energy more efficiently, burn coal more cleanly, and adopt nonpolluting forms of energy such as wind and solar power.

Reading Check **Explaining** Why do some scientists debate the issue of global warming?

The Lithosphere

Main Idea **Some human activity damages our environment.**

Geography and You How might your community have looked 200 years ago? Read to discover how human actions have affected the land.

The lithosphere is another name for the Earth's crust. It includes all the land above and below the oceans. Human activities, such as farming, logging, and mining can have negative effects on the lithosphere.

Rich topsoil is a vital part of the lithosphere that, if not carefully managed, can be carried away by wind or water. Some farmers use contour plowing to limit the loss of topsoil. With this **technique,** farmers plow along the curves of the land rather than in straight lines, preventing the soil from washing away. **Crop rotation,** or changing what is planted from year to year, also protects topsoil. Planting grasses in fields without crops holds the soil in place.

Deforestation, or cutting down forests without replanting, is another way in which topsoil is lost. When the tree roots are no longer there to hold the soil, wind and water can carry the soil away. Many rain forests, such as the Amazon rain forest, are being cut down at high rates. This has raised concerns because the forests support the water cycle and help replace the oxygen in the atmosphere. Forests also are home to many kinds of plants and animals.

Reading Check **Identifying Central Issues** Why is deforestation a problem?

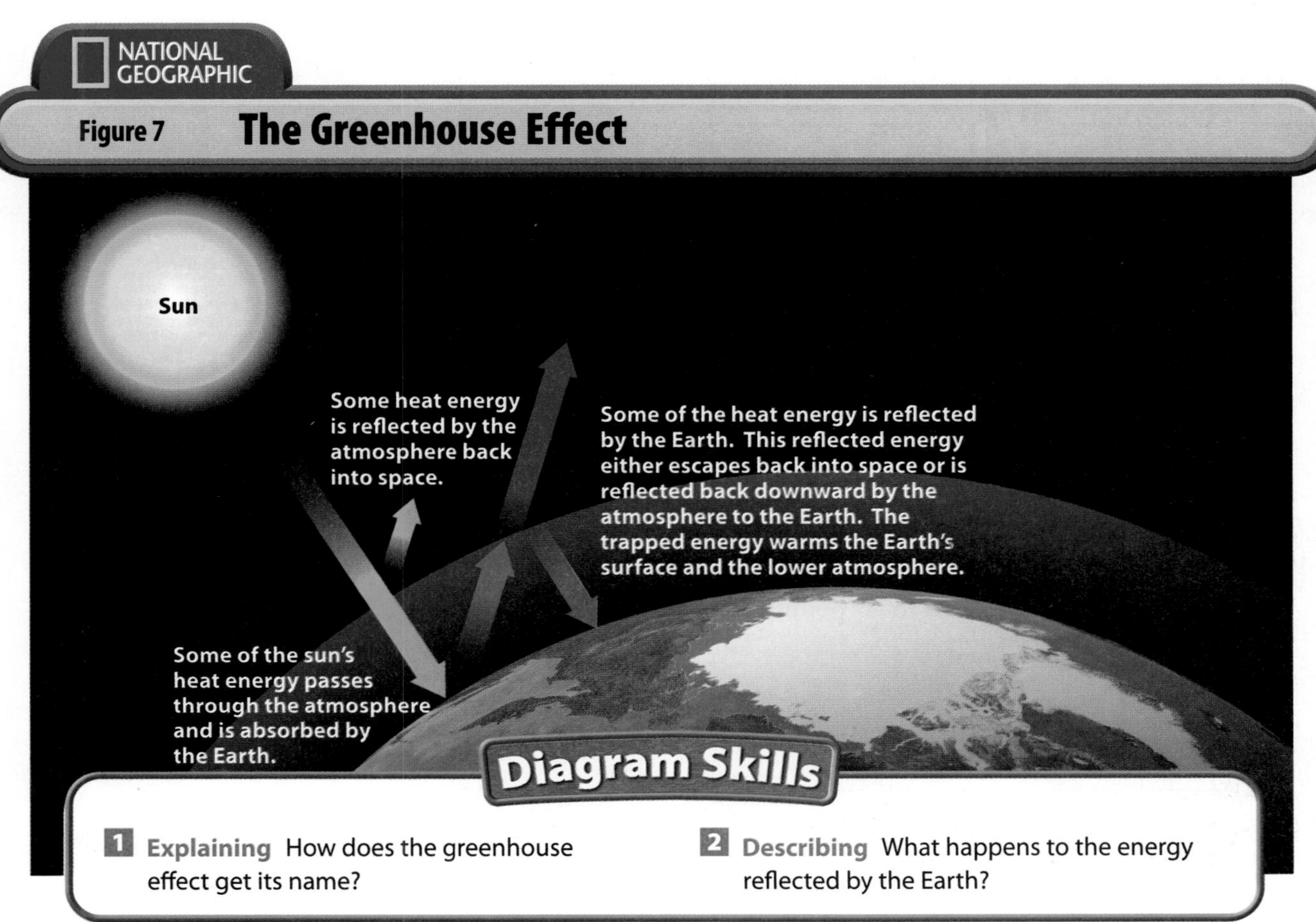

Diagram Skills

1. **Explaining** How does the greenhouse effect get its name?
2. **Describing** What happens to the energy reflected by the Earth?

The Hydrosphere and Biosphere

Main Idea **Water pollution poses a threat to a vital and limited resource.**

Geography and You How much water do you use each day? How much of that water is wasted? Read to find out how people use water resources.

The hydrosphere refers to the Earth's surface water and groundwater. Water is vital to human life. Because the amount of freshwater is limited, people should practice **conservation,** the careful use of a resource, to avoid wasting water.

Throughout the world, farmers use **irrigation,** a process in which water is collected and distributed to crops. Irrigation is often wasteful, however, as much of the water evaporates or soaks into the ground before it reaches the crops. Pollution also threatens water supplies. Chemicals from industrial processes sometimes spill into waterways. **Pesticides,** or powerful chemicals that farmers use to kill crop-destroying insects, can also be harmful.

The biosphere is the collection of plants and animals of all types that live on Earth. The entire biosphere is divided into many **ecosystems.** An ecosystem is a place shared by plants and animals that depend on one another for survival.

Shrinking **biodiversity,** or the variety of plants and animals living on the planet, is also a concern. Changes to the environment can lead to decreasing populations of plants and animals in an ecosystem.

Reading Check **Explaining** Why is the conservation of water important?

Section 4 Review

Vocabulary

1. **Explain** the significance of
   - **a.** smog
   - **b.** acid rain
   - **c.** greenhouse effect
   - **d.** crop rotation
   - **e.** deforestation
   - **f.** conservation
   - **g.** irrigation
   - **h.** pesticide
   - **i.** ecosystem
   - **j.** biodiversity

Main Ideas

2. **Organizing** Use a diagram like the one below to identify problems related to air pollution.

3. **Explaining** How do contour plowing and crop rotation preserve topsoil?

4. **Identifying** What is the biosphere?

Critical Thinking

5. **BIG Idea** What might happen to the animals of the rain forest if large areas of trees are cut down? Why?

6. **Challenge** Do you think countries should cooperate to solve problems like air and water pollution? Why?

Writing About Geography

7. **Persuasive Writing** Write a brief essay identifying the environmental issue you think is most important and what people can do about it.

Visual Summary

Inside the Earth

- Earth has four layers: the inner and outer cores, the mantle, and the crust.
- The continents are on large plates that move.
- Plates colliding or pulling apart reshape the land.

Shaping Landforms

- Water, chemicals, and plants break rock apart into smaller pieces.
- Water, wind, and ice can cause erosion.

Erosion in Switzerland

Types of Landforms

- Mountains, plateaus, valleys, and other landforms are found on land and under oceans.
- Climate and availability of resources affect where humans settle.

Canoeing in British Columbia, Canada

The Water Planet

- About 70 percent of the Earth's surface is water.
- In a process called the water cycle, water travels from the oceans to the air to the ground and back to the oceans.

Climate

- Climate is the usual pattern of weather over a long period of time.
- Sun, winds, ocean currents, landforms, and latitude affect climate.
- Geographers divide the world into different climate zones.

Humans and the Environment

- A delicate balance exists among the Earth's atmosphere, lithosphere, hydrosphere, and biosphere.
- Human actions, such as burning fuels and clearing rain forests, affect the environment.

Hills in Italy

Study anywhere, anytime! Download quizzes and flash cards to your PDA from **glencoe.com**.

CHAPTER 2 ASSESSMENT

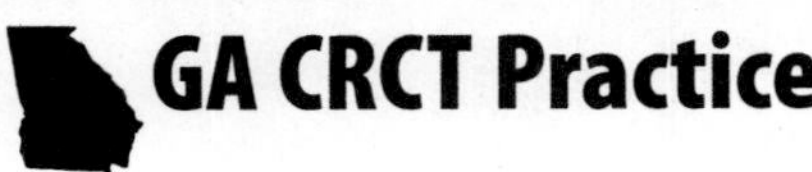

GA CRCT Practice

TEST-TAKING TIP

As you read the first part of a multiple-choice question, try to anticipate the answer before you look at the choices. If your answer is one of the choices, it is probably correct.

Directions: Choose the best answer for each question.

1 Which of the following explains why continents move?

A magma formation
B erosion
C plate tectonics
D mantle disbursement

2 What is the name of the plateau that stretches for several miles underwater along the coastline of each continent?

A continental aquifer
B continental shelf
C continental water cycle
D continental trench

3 Which of the following is used to describe areas that have similar patterns of temperature and precipitation?

A climate zones
B biomes
C El Niño
D currents

4 What forms when chemicals in air pollution combine with precipitation?

A chlorofluorocarbons
B the ozone layer
C the greenhouse effect
D acid rain

5 What is the name of the layer of hot, dense rock that surrounds Earth's core?

A mantle
B crust
C magma
D core

6 Which of the following makes up 97 percent of the planet's water?

A groundwater
B freshwater
C salt water
D frozen in glaciers and ice sheets

7 What is the name for the usual, predictable patterns of weather in an area over many years?

A climate
B current
C El Niño
D biome

8 Which word describes the careful use of resources so that they are not wasted?

A deforestation
B biodiversity
C irrigation
D conservation

9 Which type of storm occurs in the western Pacific Ocean and creates strong winds and heavy rains?

A hurricane
B typhoon
C tornado
D blizzard

10 **Look at the graph.**

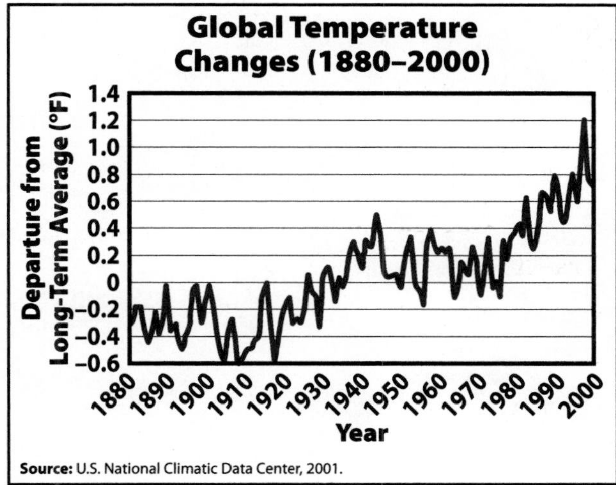

Source: U.S. National Climatic Data Center, 2001.

Based on the graph, what is the overall trend of global temperature change in the twentieth century?

A There has been a stable or flat trend throughout the century.
B There has been an overall upward trend.
C There has been an overall downward trend.
D There was an upward trend early in the century followed by a downward trend.

11 **Use the graph to find the twenty-year period of time when the sharpest increase in global temperatures took place.**

A 1880–1900
B 1910–1930
C 1950–1970
D 1980–2000

12 **What is the difference in temperature from 1880 to 2000?**

A 0.8 degrees
B 1.2 degrees
C 1.4 degrees
D 1.0 degree

13 **Read the passage and answer the questions that follow.**

Under the Kyoto Protocol, industrialized countries are to reduce their combined emissions of six major greenhouse gases during the five-year period 2008–2012 to below 1990 levels. The European Union, for example, is to cut its combined emissions by eight percent, while Japan should reduce emissions by six percent. For many countries, achieving the Kyoto targets will be a major challenge that will require new policies and new approaches. . . .

Developing countries, including Brazil, China, India and Indonesia, are also Parties to the Protocol but do not have emission reduction targets. Many developing countries have already demonstrated success in addressing climate change.

—UNEP, "Kyoto Protocol to Enter into Force 16 February 2005"

According to this passage, what is the purpose of the Kyoto Protocol?

A to create new greenhouse gas policies
B to decrease emissions of greenhouse gases
C to build new industries in certain countries
D to help developing countries stop climate change

14 **How does the Kyoto Protocol affect industrialized nations?**

A They must reduce their emissions to pre-1990 levels.
B They must prevent the release of greenhouse gases completely.
C They must capture and use greenhouse gas emissions for energy purposes.
D They must share greenhouse gas emissions with developing countries.

For additional test practice, use Self-Check Quizzes—Chapter 2 at glencoe.com.

Need Extra Help?

If You Missed Questions...	1	2	3	4	5	6	7	8	9	10	11	12	13	14
Go to Page...	46	50	59	64	45	52	56	66	57	69	69	69	69	69

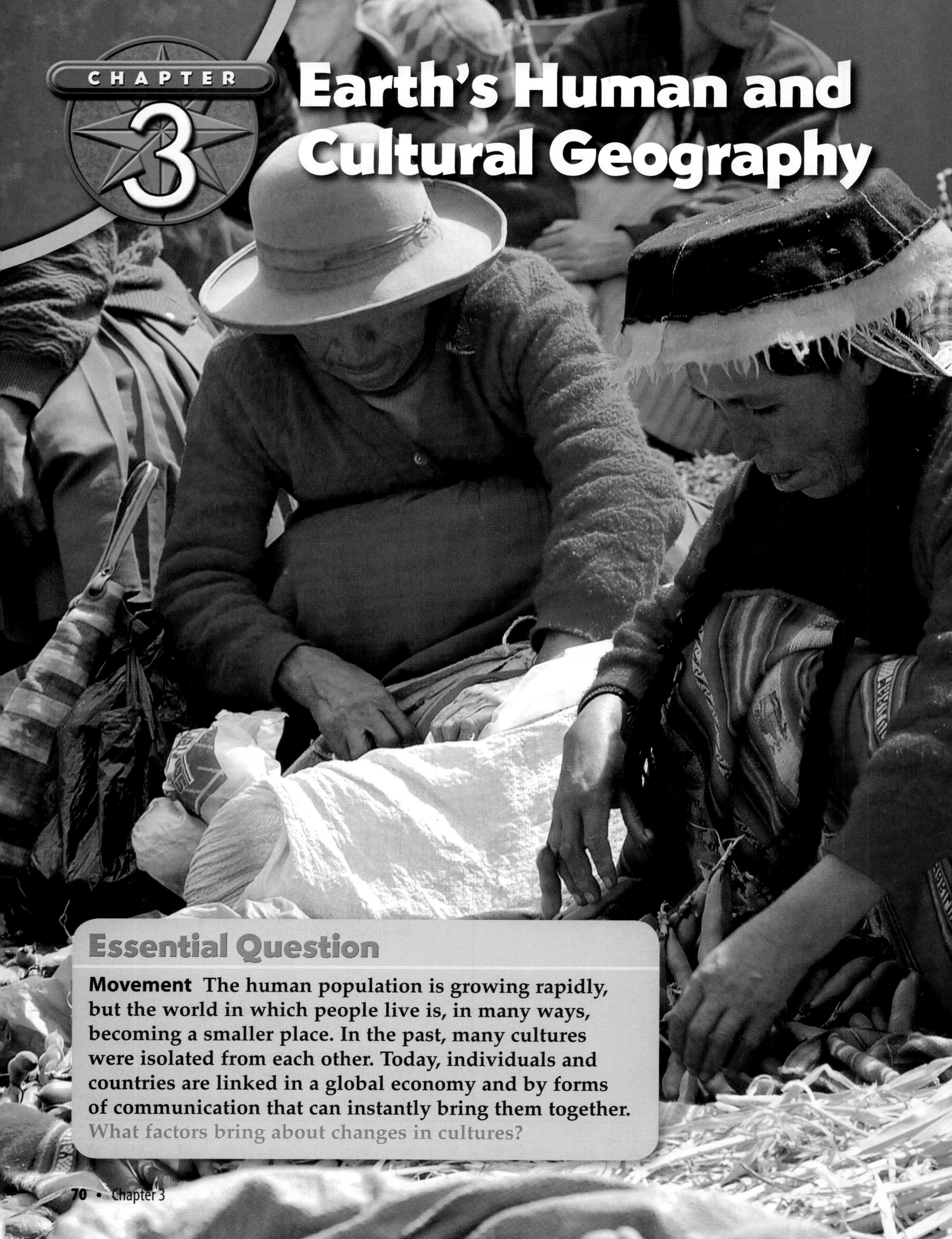

CHAPTER 3

Earth's Human and Cultural Geography

Essential Question

Movement The human population is growing rapidly, but the world in which people live is, in many ways, becoming a smaller place. In the past, many cultures were isolated from each other. Today, individuals and countries are linked in a global economy and by forms of communication that can instantly bring them together. What factors bring about changes in cultures?

Section 1: World Population

BIG IDEA Geographers study how people and physical features are distributed on Earth's surface. Although the world's population is increasing, people still live on only a small part of the Earth's surface.

Section 2: Global Cultures

BIG IDEA Culture influences people's perceptions about places and regions. The world's population is made up of different cultures, each of which is based on common beliefs, customs, and traits.

Section 3: Resources, Technology, and World Trade

BIG IDEA Patterns of economic activities result in global interdependence. Because resources are unevenly distributed, the nations of the world must trade with each other. New technologies make the economies of nations more dependent on one another.

Marketplace, Peru

FOLDABLES™ Study Organizer

Categorizing Information Make this Foldable to organize information about Earth's population; cultures; and resources, technology, and trade.

Step 1 Place two sheets of paper about 1 inch apart.

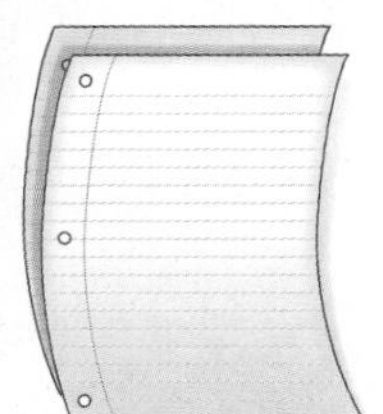

Step 2 Fold the paper to form four equal tabs.

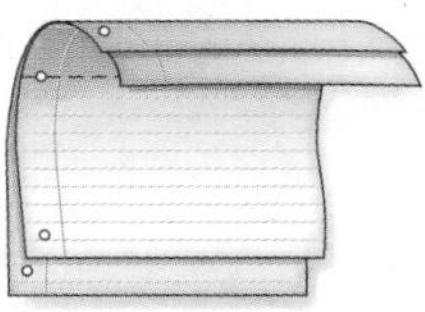

Step 3 Staple the sheets, and label each tab as shown.

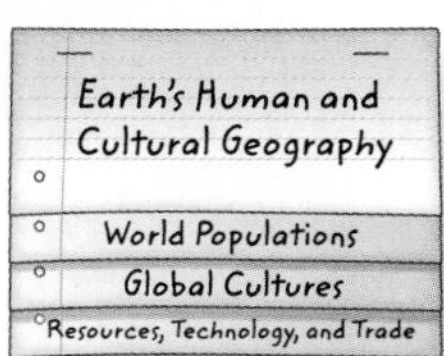

Reading and Writing
As you read the chapter, take notes under the appropriate tab. Write a main idea for each section using your Foldable.

Visit glencoe.com and enter QuickPass™ code GA6EOW6225c3 for Chapter 3 resources.

Guide to Reading

BIG Idea

Geographers study how people and physical features are distributed on Earth's surface.

Content Vocabulary

- death rate *(p. 73)*
- birthrate *(p. 73)*
- famine *(p. 73)*
- population density *(p. 74)*
- urbanization *(p. 75)*
- emigrate *(p. 75)*
- refugee *(p. 76)*

Academic Vocabulary

- technology *(p. 73)*
- internal *(p. 75)*

Reading Strategy

Determining Cause and Effect

Use a diagram like the one below to show the causes and effects of global migration.

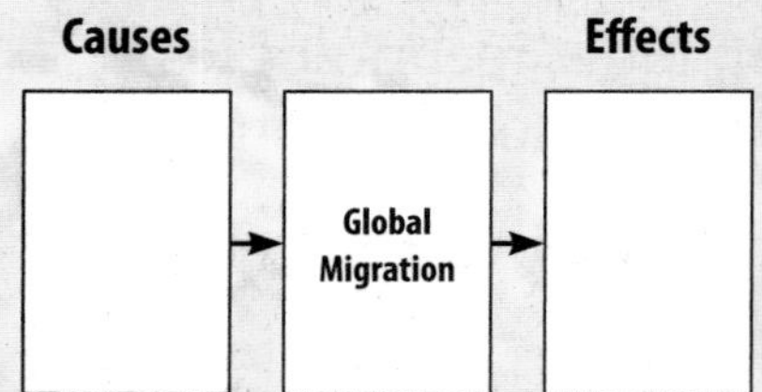

World Population

Section Audio

Spotlight Video

Picture This Tijuana lies on the U.S.-Mexico border near San Diego, California. About 100 years ago, Tijuana was a small town of only 245 residents. Today, Tijuana is Mexico's fourth largest city with about 2 million people. Booming tourism, growing industry, and more than 25 colleges and universities draw people to Tijuana from other parts of Mexico. As more people settle in Tijuana, the city faces crowded neighborhoods, traffic jams, and pollution. Read this section to learn about the world's population and the effects it has on the Earth.

Traffic jam in Tijuana, Mexico

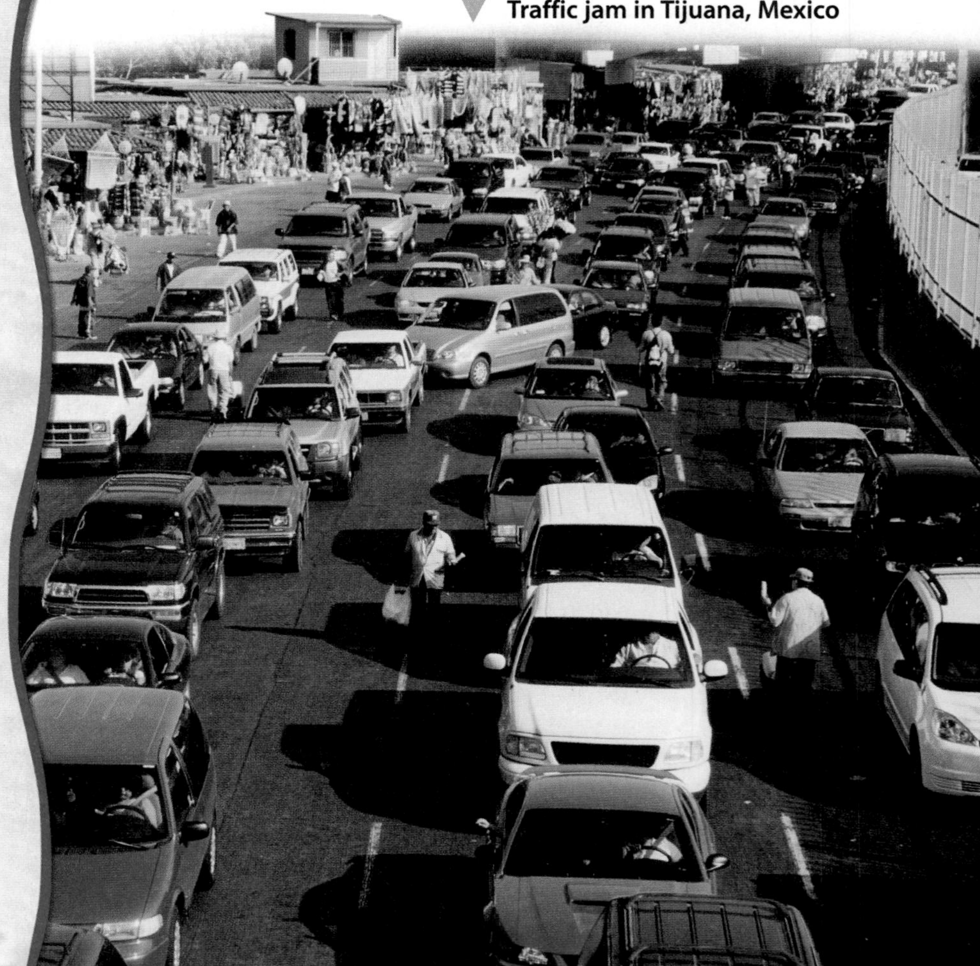

Population Growth

Main Idea **The world's population has increased rapidly in the past two centuries, creating many new challenges.**

Geography and You Has the population in your community increased or decreased in recent years? Are new schools being built, for example? Read to find out why the world's population has grown so fast.

In the past 200 years, the world's population has increased rapidly. Around 1800, a billion people lived on Earth. Today the population is about 7 billion.

Reasons for Population Growth

One reason the population has grown so fast in the last 200 years is that the death rate has gone down. The **death rate** is the number of deaths per year for every 1,000 people. Better health care and living conditions, as well as more plentiful food supplies, have decreased the death rate.

Another reason why the population has grown is high birthrates in Latin America, Asia, and Africa. The **birthrate** is the number of children born each year for every 1,000 people. High numbers of healthy births combined with lower death rates have increased the population growth, especially in these areas of the world.

Challenges of Population Growth

More food is needed for a growing population. Advances in **technology,** such as improved irrigation systems and the creation of hardier plants, will continue to increase food production. On the other hand, warfare and crop failures can lead to **famine**, or a severe lack of food. Some countries may also face shortages of water and housing. Additionally, growing populations require more services, like those provided by hospitals and schools.

Reading Check **Identifying** What has caused population growth in the last 200 years?

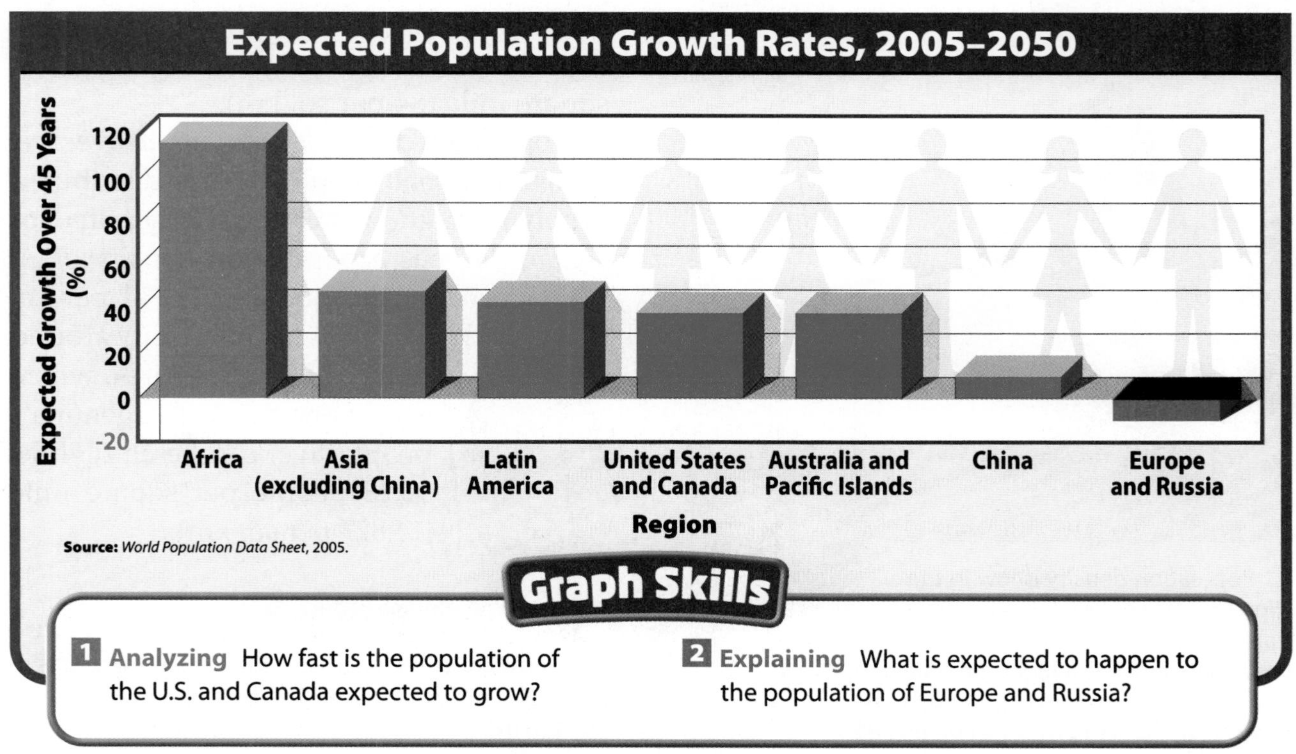

Source: *World Population Data Sheet*, 2005.

Graph Skills

1. **Analyzing** How fast is the population of the U.S. and Canada expected to grow?
2. **Explaining** What is expected to happen to the population of Europe and Russia?

Where People Live

Main Idea The Earth's population is not evenly distributed.

Geography and You Do you live in a city, a suburb, a small town, or a rural area? What are the advantages and disadvantages of your location? Read to find out where the world's people choose to live.

People live on a surprisingly small part of the Earth. Land covers only about 30 percent of the Earth's surface, and only half of this land is usable by humans. Deserts, high mountains, and ice-covered lands cannot support large numbers of people.

Population Distribution

On the usable land, population is not distributed, or spread, evenly. People naturally prefer to live in places that have fertile soil, mild climates, natural resources, and water resources, such as rivers and coastlines. Two-thirds of the world's people are clustered into five regions with these resources—East Asia, South Asia, Southeast Asia, Europe, and eastern North America. In most regions, more people live in cities than in rural areas because of the jobs and resources found there.

Population Density

Geographers have a way to figure out how crowded a country or region is. They measure **population density**—the average number of people living in a square mile or square kilometer. To arrive at this figure, the total population is divided by the total land area.

As you have just read, the world's population is not evenly distributed. Greece and Nicaragua, for example, have about the same total land area, around 50,000 square miles (130,000 sq. km). Nicaragua's population density is about 116 people per square mile (45 per sq. km). Greece, on the other hand, has a density of 218 people per square mile (84 per sq. km).

Population density represents an average. Remember that people are not distributed evenly throughout a country. Argentina, for example, has a population density of 36 people per square mile (14 per sq. km). However, the density around the city of Buenos Aires, where nearly one third of Argentina's people live, can be as high as 5,723 people per square mile (14,827 per sq. km).

Population Density

NATIONAL GEOGRAPHIC

▲ Population density is low in the High Country of British Columbia, Canada. In contrast, Quebec City, Canada (inset), has a high population density. ***Regions*** **In what regions are most of the world's people clustered?**

Reading Check **Determining Cause and Effect** Why does much of the world's population live on a relatively small area of the Earth?

Population Movement

Main Idea **Large numbers of people migrate from one place to another.**

Geography and You Have you and your family ever moved? Read to learn some of the reasons why people all over the world move from one place to another.

Throughout history, millions of people have moved from one place to another. People continue to move today, sometimes as individuals, sometimes in large groups.

Types of Migration

Moving from place to place in the same country is known as **internal** migration. One kind of internal migration is the movement of people from farms and villages to cities. Such migrants are often in search of jobs. This type of movement results in **urbanization,** or the growth of cities. Urbanization has occurred rapidly in Latin America, Asia, and Africa.

Movement between countries is called international migration. Some people **emigrate,** or leave the country where they were born and move to another. They are emigrants in their homeland and immigrants in their new country. **Figure 1** shows the immigrant populations in regions of the world. Immigration has increased greatly in the past 200 years, partly due to better transportation.

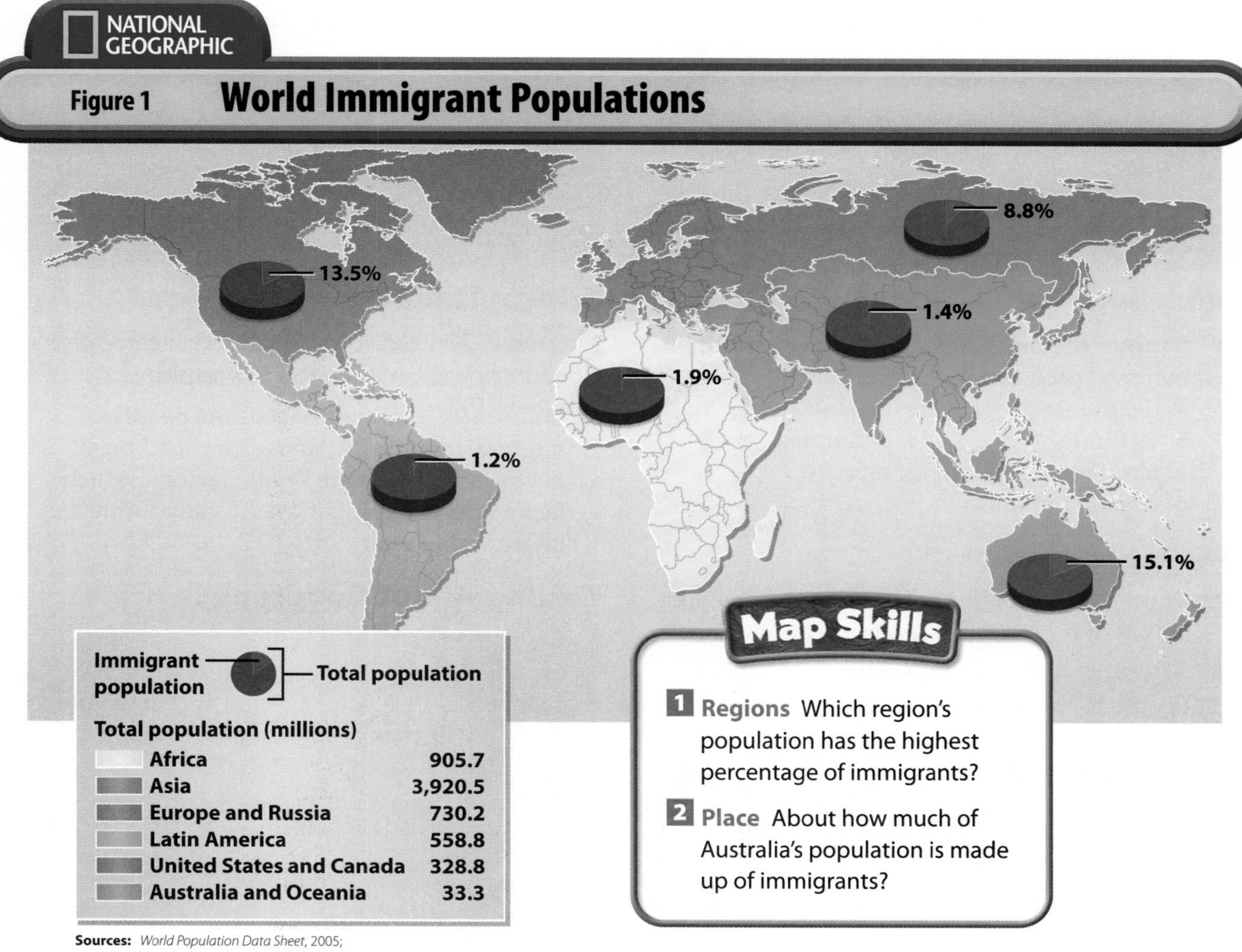

Figure 1 **World Immigrant Populations**

Sources: *World Population Data Sheet*, 2005; World Migrant Stock, United Nations.

Map Skills

1. **Regions** Which region's population has the highest percentage of immigrants?
2. **Place** About how much of Australia's population is made up of immigrants?

Reasons People Move

People migrate for a variety of reasons. Historians say that "push" factors convince people to leave their homes and "pull" factors attract them to another place. A shortage of farmland or few jobs in a region or country may "push" residents to emigrate. The lure of jobs has worked as a "pull" factor, attracting many immigrants to the United States.

People who are forced to flee to another country to escape wars, persecution, or disasters are called **refugees.** For example, 4 million refugees fled war in Europe's Balkan Peninsula in the 1990s.

Impact of Migration

Mass migrations of people have major impacts—both on the region they leave and on the region where they settle. When emigrants leave a country, its population decreases or does not increase as quickly. This can ease overcrowding. However, if skilled or educated workers leave, emigration may hurt the country's economy. Emigration can also divide families.

Migration also affects the country to which people move. Immigrants bring with them new forms of music, art, foods, and language. Some native-born citizens, however, fear or resent immigrants and the changes that they bring. This has led to violence and unjust treatment toward newcomers in some instances.

Making Generalizations Why have so many rural citizens moved to cities in Asia, Africa, and Latin America?

Section 1 Review

Vocabulary

1. **Explain** the meaning of the following terms by using each one in a sentence.
   - a. death rate
   - b. birthrate
   - c. famine
   - d. population density
   - e. urbanization
   - f. emigrate
   - g. refugee

Main Ideas

2. **Making Connections** How might the availability of food affect population growth?
3. **Explaining** What geographic factors lead people to live in certain areas of the world?
4. **Summarizing** Use a diagram like the one below to summarize the positive and negative effects of emigration on a country.

Emigration

Positive Effects | **Negative Effects**

Critical Thinking

5. **BIG Idea** Discuss the factors that can cause a country's population to grow rapidly.
6. **Challenge** Explain the reasons people migrate. Identify which reasons are "push" factors and which are "pull" factors. Which factors do you think most strongly influence migrants? Explain.

Writing About Geography

7. **Expository Writing** Write a paragraph explaining how the Earth's population has changed in the past 200 years and how you think it will change in the next 50 years.

TIME PERSPECTIVES

EXPLORING WORLD ISSUES

THE WORLD GOES GLOBAL

Technology and new methods of trade are affecting how the world interacts.

A local Inuit uses a laptop in the Canadian Arctic.

Around the world, technological advances are changing the way we live and work. Every day, new technologies make it possible for billions of e-mails and trillions of dollars to crisscross national borders. Communication between people and businesses and the movement of goods and money is done more quickly than ever before because of the Internet.

As technology continues to change, what might the world look like ten years from now? Inventions that create faster ways to communicate might make the world seem even smaller than it does today. And as globalization connects the world's economies as never before, people everywhere will learn about other nations and cultures.

WAYNE R. BILENDUKE/GETTY IMAGES

TIME PERSPECTIVES

Workers at a call center in India answer questions from American customers.

A GLOBAL MARKETPLACE

Venugopla Rao Moram is a highly sought after worker. Recently, the computer software engineer who lives in Bangalore, India, was offered five jobs during a two-week period. All of the offers were from companies whose headquarters are located thousands of miles from India.

Luckily, Moram will not have to travel that far to get to work. Computer companies from around the world are opening offices in Bangalore in order to hire Indian workers. Many Indians speak English and are well educated. This makes them valuable to foreign companies that are establishing workplaces in countries where labor is inexpensive. This type of labor helps manufacturers keep their production costs low.

As a result of **globalization**, a trend that is linking the world's nations through trade, thousands of Indians are working for foreign companies. In Moram's case, a business in California hired him to create software that makes the characters in video games jump and run. The software Moram produces becomes part of a product that is assembled in other countries and sold all over the world. All types of products, from toys to clothes to TVs, are being made and traded this way. As a result, economies are becoming much more connected—or global.

The United States and the Global Economy

The United States trades with countries all over the world. It sells, or exports, some products, and buys, or imports, others. Here are the countries the U.S. did the most business with in 2005.

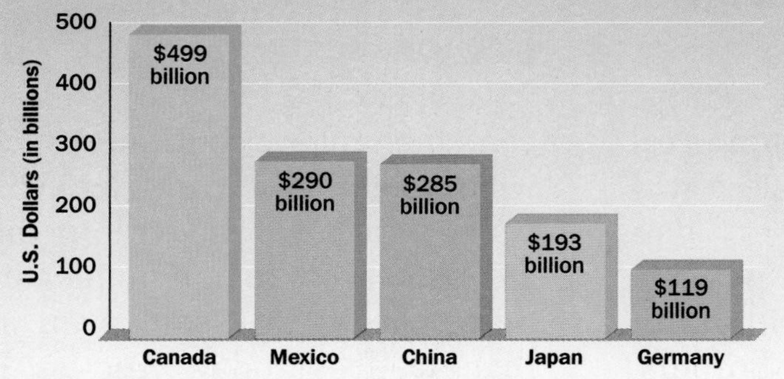

Source: U.S. Census Bureau, Foreign Trade Statistics Division.

INTERPRETING GRAPHS

Making Inferences Why might Canada and Mexico be the United States's top trading partners?

The Internet

The Internet has fueled globalization. The Internet is a giant electronic network that links computers all over the world. It was developed in the late 1960s when the U.S. military worked to connect its computers with those of college researchers so that they could share their ideas more easily. Over time, the Internet became available to everyone, and the way the world interacts changed forever.

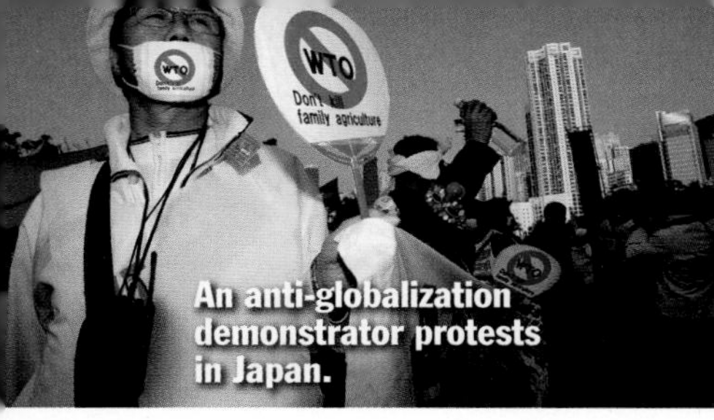

An anti-globalization demonstrator protests in Japan.

People all over the world can trade stocks on the New York Stock Exchange.

A Thai woman uses a bank machine.

The Internet also changed how people and companies buy goods. Today, just like you can shop online for games or CDs, so can businesses. For example, a business in need of computer software can use the Internet to research the products of computer companies from all over the world. With the click of a mouse, the buyer can research and compare prices for software products on a computer company's Web site or at an online store. Then, in seconds, the buyer can purchase the product.

Before the days of the Internet, a company in need of software could not have learned about suppliers and products as easily. As a result, business tended to be conducted more locally and at a slower pace. Today, a buyer can shop and trade online in minutes without leaving his or her desk. Companies can conduct business in less time and from anywhere in the world.

Sharing Globalization's Gains

The impact of globalization has been amazing, but its benefits have not been shared equally. **Developed countries**, or countries in which a great deal of manufacturing is carried out, have more goods to trade than **developing countries** that are still trying to industrialize. Also many companies prefer to build factories in wealthier countries rather than in poor ones, where support systems like roads and airports are often unavailable. As a result, some of the poorer nations in Asia and Africa have had a hard time creating any new jobs.

What steps can be taken to spread the benefits of globalization? International businesses and wealthy developed nations can be part of the solution. By 2005, businesses and governments together had spent about $2.6 trillion to help poorer countries develop their economies. Investing in developing countries could help businesses trade more effectively and grow. There is still much work to be done. Finding ways to help every nation share the gains of globalization is one of biggest challenges the world faces.

Lumber is processed at a Canadian mill for shipment to the United States.

EXPLORING THE ISSUE

1. **Making Inferences** Why do you think companies are concerned about how much money it costs to make a product?

2. **Analyzing Information** How might investing in transportation systems help developing countries?

MUSIC GOES GLOBAL

It has been said that music is the universal language. This has never been more true than in the Internet age. Today, music lovers can listen to music from all over the world. Online music stores and portable music players make it easy to listen to what you want, when you want.

In the past, listeners had much less control over the music they heard. Record producers and companies recorded the music of homegrown musicians, and radio stations played their songs. Artists and songs from different regions of the world were rarely played.

In the Internet age, however, music lovers are being exposed to sounds from around the world. West African drumming or Latin American dance music, for example, is available to anyone online. Listeners can just search for a **genre**, or style of music, and download a song for a small fee.

With such easy access to global sounds, it is not uncommon for a portable player to include a list of songs and artists from several countries. As a result, musicians are working to please the public by blending "international" material and elements into their acts. The American pop singer Christina Aguilera sings in English, but she has also recorded a CD completely in Spanish. Hip-hop artist Wyclef Jean mixes **Creole**, the language of Haiti, into his songs. Madonna has worn traditional costumes from Japan and Scotland during her tours.

In the twenty-first century, musicians and music lovers are no longer tied to the sounds of one nation. In fact, cross-cultural appeal in the music industry is becoming a key to success.

Wyclef Jean uses Haitian elements in his music.

REUTERS/GARY HERSHORN

EXPLORING THE ISSUE

1. **Determining Cause and Effect** How does the Internet help people learn about the music styles of performers from other countries?

2. **Making Inferences** List three reasons why it may be easier to buy music online than in a store that sells CDs.

REVIEW AND ASSESS

Many toys made in China are sold in other countries.

UNDERSTANDING THE ISSUE

1 **Making Connections** How has globalization affected the way some products are produced?

2 **Writing to Inform** Write a short article about how the Internet has changed the way that businesses shop for and buy goods.

3 **Writing to Persuade** Do you think that American musicians who combine music from other countries and cultures can become stars in the United States? Defend your answer in a letter to the president of a record company.

INTERNET RESEARCH ACTIVITIES

4 Go online to research the history of the Internet. Write an essay explaining why the Internet was created. Develop a time line that notes important developments.

5 With your teacher's help, use the Internet to research how many homes have access to the Internet in developed and developing nations. Compare the information and create a bar graph showing the top three countries in both categories.

BEYOND THE CLASSROOM

6 **Organize the class into three teams.** One group should represent developed nations, and another should represent developing nations. Debate this resolution: "Globalization is good for everyone." The third group of students will decide which team has the most convincing arguments.

7 **Take an inventory of your home.** Look for products that were made in other countries. Count the items that were imported from different countries. Make a chart to show how many countries are represented in your home.

The Universal Language

The Internet is changing the way people listen to music. In the Internet age, music lovers around the world are shopping online. Here is a look at the number of people visiting music sites.

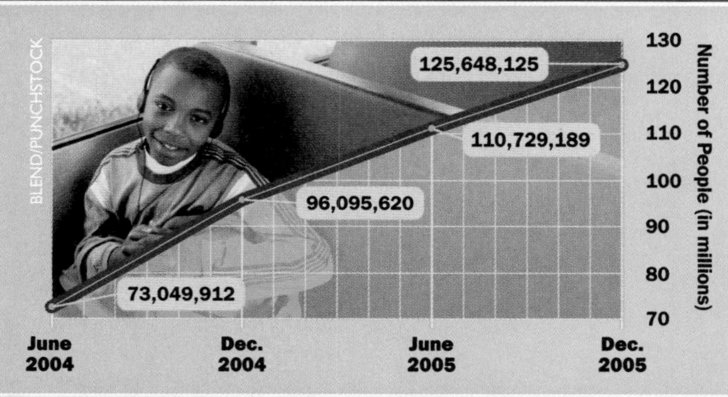

Source: Nielsen/Net Ratings.

Building Graph Reading Skills

1. **Comparing** How many more people visited music Web sites in December 2005 than in December 2004?

2. **Making Inferences** How might the increase of shopping online for music affect traditional music stores?

Guide to Reading

Global Cultures

 Section Audio  Spotlight Video

BIG Idea

Culture influences people's perceptions about places and regions.

Content Vocabulary

- culture *(p. 83)*
- ethnic group *(p. 84)*
- dialect *(p. 84)*
- democracy *(p. 85)*
- dictatorship *(p. 86)*
- monarchy *(p. 86)*
- civilization *(p. 86)*
- cultural diffusion *(p. 87)*
- culture region *(p. 88)*
- globalization *(p. 89)*

Academic Vocabulary

- widespread *(p. 86)*
- unique *(p. 89)*

Reading Strategy

Identifying Use a diagram like the one below to identify the elements of culture.

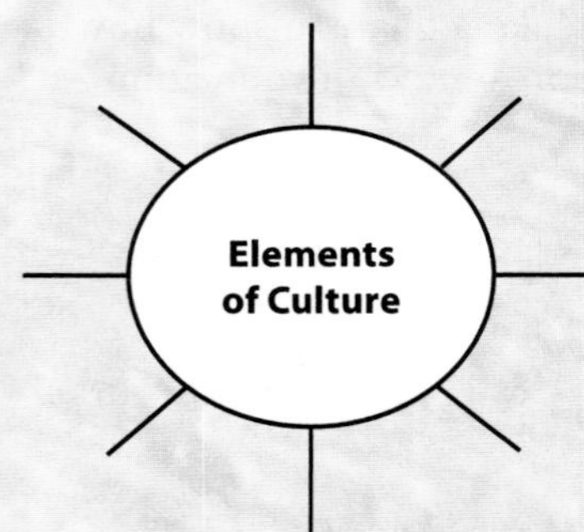

Picture This The eagles that soar above the skies of North America have long been sacred to the native peoples of the area. Many Native Americans, or First Nations people, believe that eagles possess special qualities such as wisdom and courage. Eagle feathers are treated as heirlooms and passed down among families. Each year, First Nations people from all parts of Canada hold pow wows, gathering together to celebrate their language, traditions, and culture. Special dances such as the Eagle Dance and the Feather Dance are an important part of the pow wow. To learn more about how traditions reflect a culture's beliefs, read Section 2.

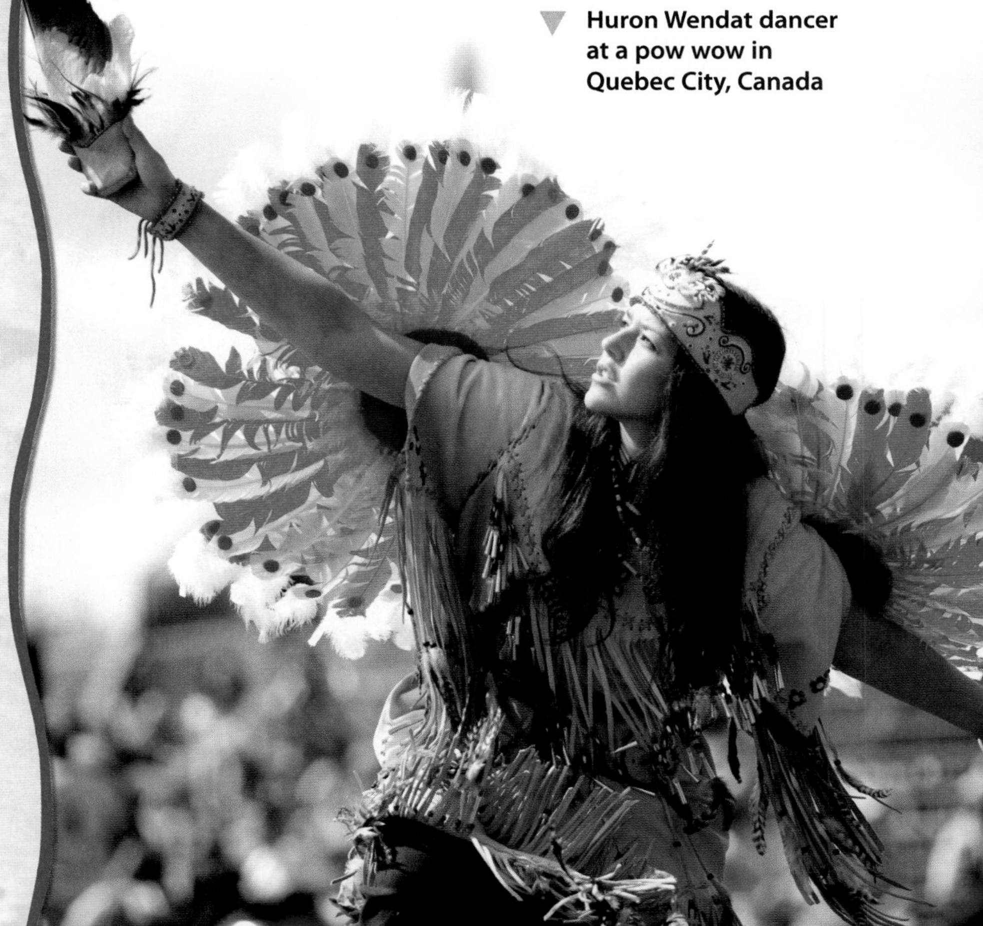

Huron Wendat dancer at a pow wow in Quebec City, Canada

What Is Culture?

Main Idea **Culture refers to the many shared characteristics that define a group of people.**

Geography and You Think about the clothes you wear, the music you listen to, and the foods you eat. Read to learn about the many things that make up culture.

Culture is the way of life of a group of people who share similar beliefs and customs. A particular culture can be understood by looking at various elements: what languages the people speak, what religions they follow, and what smaller groups are part of their society. The study of culture also includes examining people's daily lives, the history they share, and the art forms they have created.

Geographers, anthropologists, and archaeologists all study culture. For example, geographers look at physical objects, such as food and housing. They also study elements such as religion, social groups, types of government, and economies. Anthropologists analyze cultures today to learn how different elements of culture are related. Archaeologists use the physical and historical objects of a culture, such as pottery and tools, to try to understand how people lived in the past. The work of all of these experts helps us better understand the world we live in.

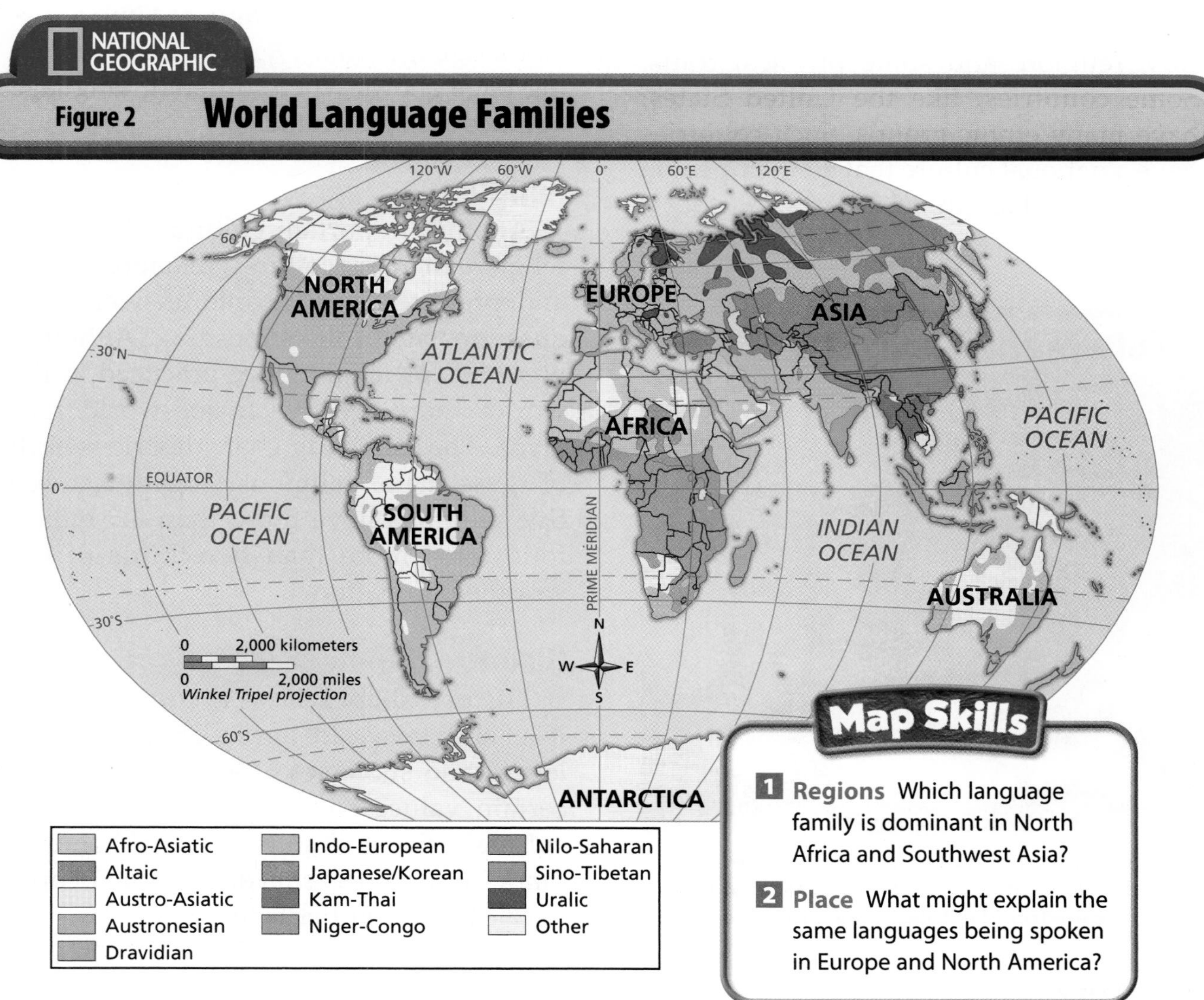

Figure 2 World Language Families

Map Skills

1. **Regions** Which language family is dominant in North Africa and Southwest Asia?
2. **Place** What might explain the same languages being spoken in Europe and North America?

Social Groups

One way scientists study culture is by looking at different groups of people in a society. Each of us belongs to many social groups. For example, are you old or young? Male or female? A student, a worker, or both? Most social groups have rules of behavior that group members learn. The process by which people adjust their behavior to meet these rules is called socialization. Within society, each person has a certain status. Status refers to a person's importance or rank. In all cultures, the family is the most important social group. Although family structures vary from culture to culture, most of us first learn how to behave from our families.

People also belong to an **ethnic group.** This is a group that shares a language, history, religion, and some physical traits. Some countries, like the United States, have many ethnic groups. Such countries have a national culture that all their people share, as well as ethnic cultures.

Family life has long been important to the Inuit people of Nunavut, Canada. ***Place*** **What elements of culture are found in this family gathering?**

In some cases, people come to believe that their own culture is superior to, or better than, other cultures. This attitude is called ethnocentrism. If carried to extremes, ethnocentrism may cause hatred and persecution of other groups.

Language

Sharing a language is one of the strongest unifying forces for a culture. A language, however, may have different variations called dialects. A **dialect** is a local form of a language that may have a distinct vocabulary and pronunciation. Despite different dialects, speakers of the same language can usually understand one another.

More than 2,000 languages are spoken around the world today. Most can be grouped with related languages into a specific language family. **Figure 2** on the preceding page shows where different language families are spoken today.

Religion

Another important cultural element is religion. In many cultures, religious beliefs and practices help people answer basic questions about life's meaning. Although hundreds of religions are practiced in the world, there are five major world religions. The following chart describes each of these major religions. Together, these five religions have more than 4.5 billion followers—more than two-thirds of the world's population.

History

History shapes how a culture views itself and the world. Stories about the challenges and successes of a culture support certain values and help people develop cultural pride and unity. Cultural holidays mark important events and enable people to celebrate their heritage.

Major World Religions

Religion	Major Leader	Followers	Beliefs
Buddhism	**Siddhartha Gautama, the Buddha**	**385.4 million**	Buddhism is based on the teachings of Siddhartha Gautama, known as the Buddha. The Buddha taught that the goal of life is to escape the cycle of birth and death by achieving a state of spiritual understanding called nirvana. Buddhists believe that they must follow an eight-step path to achieve nirvana.
Christianity	**Jesus Christ**	**2.2 billion**	Christianity is based on the belief in one God and the teachings and life of Jesus as described in the New Testament of the Bible. Christians believe that Jesus was the Son of God and was sent to Earth to save people from their sins.
Hinduism	**Unknown**	**875.1 million**	Hinduism is based on the belief in a supreme spiritual force known as Brahman as recorded in sacred texts, including the Upanishads. Hindus believe that to unite with Brahman, they must first pass through many lives, being reborn into new forms. To move closer to Brahman they must make improvements in each of their lives.
Islam	**Muhammad**	**1.4 billion**	Islam is based on the belief in one God, Allah, as revealed through the prophet Muhammad. The Muslim sacred text is the Quran. Muslims follow five major acts of worship known as the Five Pillars of Islam.
Judaism	**Abraham**	**15.2 million**	Judaism is based on the belief in one God and the spiritual and ethical principles handed down by God. These principles, including the Ten Commandments, are presented in Jewish sacred texts collected in the Hebrew Bible.

Source: *The World Factbook*, 2008.

Chart Skills

1 Identifying Which two religions include the belief that people are reborn into new forms?

2 Explaining What help do these religions give to their followers?

Daily Life

Food, clothing, and shelter are basic human needs. The type of food you eat and how you eat it reflect your culture. Do you use chopsticks, a fork, or bread to scoop up your food? The home you live in and the clothing that you wear reflect your culture and your physical surroundings. For example, the clothing people wear in the high, chilly Andes of South America differs greatly from the clothing people wear in the warm outback of Australia.

Arts

Through music, painting, sculpture, dance, and literature, people express what they think is beautiful and meaningful. The arts can also tell stories about important figures and events in the culture.

Government

People need rules in order to live together without conflict. Governments fulfill this need. They can be either limited or unlimited. A limited government restricts the powers of its leaders. For example, in a **democracy**, power is held by the people.

Student Web Activity Visit glencoe.com to learn more about forms of government around the world.

Most democracies today are called representative democracies because the people choose leaders to represent them and make decisions. In unlimited governments, leaders are all-powerful. In a **dictatorship**, for instance, the leader, or dictator, rules by force. Dictators often limit citizens' freedoms.

A **monarchy** is a government led by a king or queen who inherits power by being born into the ruling family. For much of history, monarchies had unlimited power. Today, most monarchies are constitutional monarchies in which elected legislatures hold most of the power.

Economy

People in every culture must earn a living. Geographers study economic activities to see how a culture uses its resources and trades with other places. An economy's success can be seen in people's quality of life—how well they eat and live and what kind of health care they receive.

Reading Check **Describing** Describe three elements that help unify a culture.

The Growth of Industry

NATIONAL GEOGRAPHIC

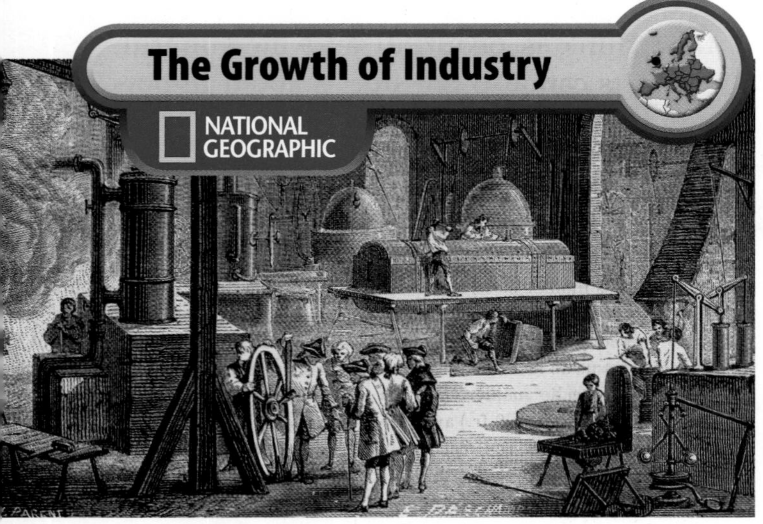

This early factory near Birmingham, England, made steam engines to power other industries. ***Movement*** **What recent technological advancements have led to cultural changes?**

Cultural Change

Main Idea **Cultures are constantly changing and influencing each other.**

Geography and You What influences from other cultures can you see in your community? Read on to see how cultures relate to each other and change.

Over time, all cultures experience change. Sometimes that change results from inventions and innovations, or technological improvements that bring about new ways of life. Sometimes change results from the influence of other cultures.

Inventions and Technology

Thousands of years ago, humans were hunters and gatherers who lived and traveled in small groups. After 8000 B.C., people learned to farm. Planting crops led to more reliable food supplies and larger populations. It also allowed people to settle in one place. Historians call this change the Agricultural Revolution. It had a huge impact on human culture because it led people to create **civilizations**, or highly developed cultures, in river valleys found in present-day Iraq, Egypt, India, and China. The people of these civilizations made a number of important advancements including building cities, forming governments, founding religions, and developing writing systems.

The world remained largely agricultural through the A.D. 1700s. Around that time, some countries began to industrialize, or use machines to make goods. The **widespread** use of machines made economies more productive. Industrial nations produced more food, goods, and wealth, which caused sweeping cultural changes.

The world has changed greatly in the past three decades. Computers have transformed businesses and households. Advances in communications allow people throughout the world to send and receive information almost instantly. Medical technology has dramatically increased human life expectancy. Each of these developments has sparked cultural changes.

Cultural Diffusion

The other major cause of cultural change is influence from other cultures. The process of spreading ideas, languages, or customs from one culture to another is called **cultural diffusion.** In the past, diffusion has taken place through trade, migration, and conquest. In recent years, new methods of communication have also led to cultural diffusion.

Historically, trade began with the exchange of goods, often over great distances. Soon trade also brought new ideas and practices to an area. Phoenician merchants from Southwest Asia brought the use of an alphabet to the Greeks in Europe. Greek traders later passed it on to the Romans. Trade continues to be a major means of cultural diffusion.

The movement of people from one place to another also leads to cultural diffusion. When Europeans arrived in North America, they brought horses, which were new to the continent. Native Americans living on the Great Plains quickly adopted the horse because it made hunting easier.

The conquest of one group by another is a third way culture can spread. Conquerors bring their culture to conquered areas. For example, the Romance languages, such as Italian, French, Spanish, and Portuguese, reflect the influence of the Roman Empire. These languages are based on Latin, the language of ancient Rome. In turn, conquered peoples can influence the culture of the conquerors. Christianity arose among the Jews, a people conquered by the Roman Empire. In time, Christianity became a major religion in the empire.

NATIONAL GEOGRAPHIC

Cultural Influences

Readers around the world, such as these shoppers in Russia, anticipate each new Harry Potter book and movie. The books have been translated into 47 languages. ***Movement*** **What is cultural diffusion?**

Today television, movies, and the Internet contribute to cultural diffusion. For example, movies made in the United States, Mexico, Brazil, and France are seen around the world, introducing people to different ways of life. The Internet allows people to have contact with and be influenced by people from other cultures.

Reading Check **Analyzing Information**
Describe one way that cultural diffusion takes place.

Regional and Global Cultures

Main Idea **As countries and regions share cultural traits, a global culture is emerging.**

Geography and You What do you have in common with a student who lives across town or across the country? Read to learn how similarities help to define cultural regions.

As you recall, geographers use the term *regions* for areas that share common physical characteristics. Likewise, geographers divide the world into several culture regions, as shown in **Figure 3.** A **culture region** is an area that includes different countries that share similar cultural traits.

Culture Regions

The countries in each culture region generally have similar social groups, governments, economic systems, religions, languages, ethnic groups, and histories. One example of a culture region is Latin America. In that area, the major languages are Spanish and Portuguese. Another culture region is Canada and the United States. These countries have similar languages, histories, and ethnic groups.

As you study the world, you will begin to recognize the characteristics shared by the

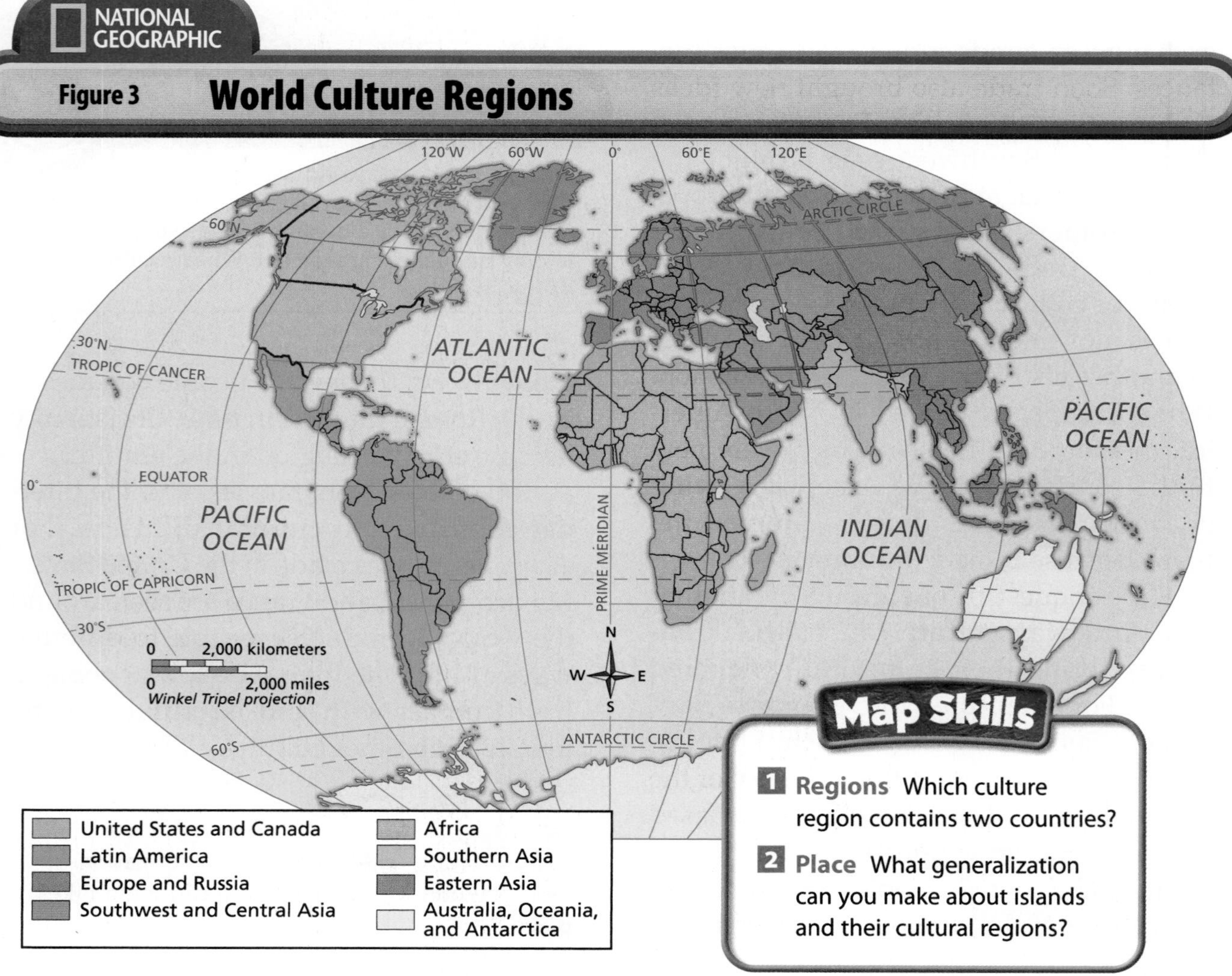

Figure 3 **World Culture Regions**

Map Skills

1. **Regions** Which culture region contains two countries?
2. **Place** What generalization can you make about islands and their cultural regions?

countries in each culture region. Although these countries are similar, they also have **unique** traits that set them apart.

Global Culture

Recent advances in communications and technology have helped break down barriers between culture regions. The result is **globalization**, or the development of a worldwide culture with an interdependent economy.

With globalization, individual economies rely greatly upon one another for resources and markets. Some people believe that as the global culture grows, local cultures will become less important. They point out that globalization might even erase the traditions and customs of smaller groups.

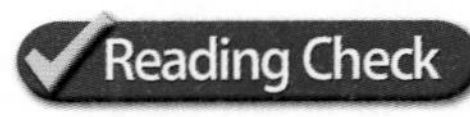

Defining What are culture regions?

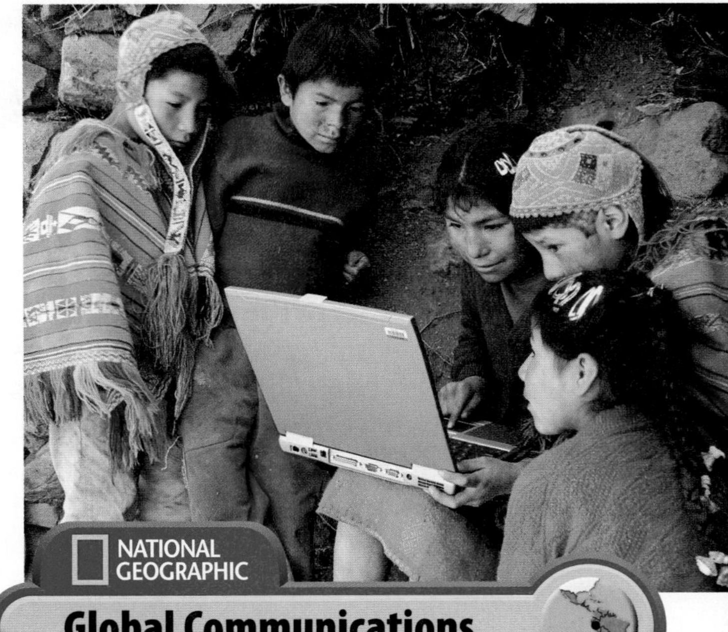

Global Communications

The Internet and other forms of communications have helped link people around the world, such as these children in Peru. ***Movement*** **What might happen as the global culture grows?**

Section 2 Review

Vocabulary

1. **Explain** the meaning of *culture, ethnic group, dialect, democracy, dictatorship, monarchy, civilization, cultural diffusion, culture region,* and *globalization* by writing three to four paragraphs that use all of the terms.

Main Ideas

2. **Explaining** What is an ethnic group, and how do ethnic groups relate to a region's culture?
3. **Summarizing** Use a diagram like the one below to identify the advancements made by the world's earliest civilizations.

4. **Explaining** Why is globalization occurring?

Critical Thinking

5. **BIG Idea** Explain the different ways that cultural change can occur.
6. **Challenge** How do local and national differences affect culture on a regional or global level?

Writing About Geography

7. **Personal Writing** Write a journal entry describing examples of globalization that you have witnessed. Then add your predictions about how globalization might affect your community in the future.

Is Globalization Good for Everyone?

Globalization is sometimes defined as the linking together of the world's nations through trade. This trade among nations allows people from different cultures to interact with each other. As a result, cultures begin sharing traits with others. People disagree about the effects of globalization on economies and cultures. Some people think that globalization helps countries by providing them with jobs and new technologies. However, others believe that globalization destroys the cultural traditions and customs of smaller groups.

For Globalization

> One of the main restraints on liberty has always been "the tyranny [unjust use of power] of place." At its crudest, this has meant restrictions, both political and economic, on where people can live, but it also includes restrictions on where people can go, what they can buy, where they can invest, and what they can read, hear, or see. Globalization by its nature brings down these barriers, and it helps hand the power to choose to the individual.
>
> —John Micklethwait and Adrian Wooldridge
> *A Future Perfect: The Essentials of Globalization*

Against Globalization

For millions of people globalization has not worked. Many have been actually made worse off, as they have seen their jobs destroyed and their lives become more insecure. They have felt increasingly powerless against forces beyond their control. They have seen their democracies undermined, their cultures eroded.

If globalization continues to be conducted in the way that [it] has been in the past, if we continue to fail to learn from our mistakes, globalization will not only not succeed in promoting development but will continue to create poverty and instability.

—Joseph Stiglitz
Globalization and Its Discontents

You Be the Geographer

1. **Identifying** Choose a sentence from each opinion that best summarizes the authors' views about globalization.
2. **Critical Thinking** What does Stiglitz mean when he writes ". . . globalization . . . will continue to create poverty and instability"? Use the definition of *globalization* to explain your answer.
3. **Read to Write** Write one paragraph that identifies how globalization might benefit a nation. Then write a paragraph that describes how globalization might harm a nation.

Guide to Reading

BIG Idea

Patterns of economic activities result in global interdependence.

Content Vocabulary

- natural resource *(p. 93)*
- renewable resource *(p. 93)*
- nonrenewable resource *(p. 93)*
- economic system *(p. 94)*
- developed country *(p. 94)*
- developing country *(p. 94)*
- newly industrialized country *(p. 94)*
- gross domestic product *(p. 95)*
- export *(p. 95)*
- import *(p. 95)*
- tariff *(p. 95)*
- quota *(p. 95)*
- free trade *(p. 96)*
- interdependence *(p. 96)*

Academic Vocabulary

- finite *(p. 93)*
- finance *(p. 95)*

Reading Strategy

Categorizing Information Use a diagram like the one below to list three specific examples of each type of natural resource.

Renewable Resources	Nonrenewable Resources
1.	
2.	
3.	

Resources, Technology, and World Trade

 Section Audio  Spotlight Video

Picture This You have probably seen calculators or other small devices that rely on solar cells instead of batteries. As long as enough light is present, these cells can work a long time. Large panels of solar cells can convert sunlight into electric power for homes and businesses. The worldwide increase in demand for fuel has driven energy costs up. To save money, consumers and businesses are looking to solar power and other energy sources. Read this section to learn more about alternative resources and how the world's people use them.

▼ Solar panels in a sheep pasture in northern Germany

Natural Resources

Main Idea **Earth's resources are not evenly distributed, nor do they all exist in endless supply.**

Geography and You What natural resources can you name? Read to learn about two kinds of natural resources.

Natural resources are materials from the Earth that people use to meet their needs. Soil, trees, wind, and oil are examples of natural resources. Such resources can provide food, shelter, goods, and energy.

Renewable resources are natural resources that cannot be used up or that can be replaced. For example, the sun, the wind, and water cannot be used up, and forests can replace themselves. Some renewable resources, such as rivers, the wind, and the sun, can produce electricity and are important sources of energy.

Most natural resources are **finite,** or limited in supply. They are called **nonrenewable resources.** Once humans use up these resources, they are gone. Minerals like iron ore and gold are nonrenewable, as are oil, coal, and other fossil fuels. Fossil fuels heat homes, run cars, and generate electricity.

Reading Check **Identifying** Which energy resources are renewable? Nonrenewable?

NATIONAL GEOGRAPHIC **Maps In MOtion** See StudentWorks™ Plus or glencoe.com.

Figure 4 **World Energy Production and Consumption**

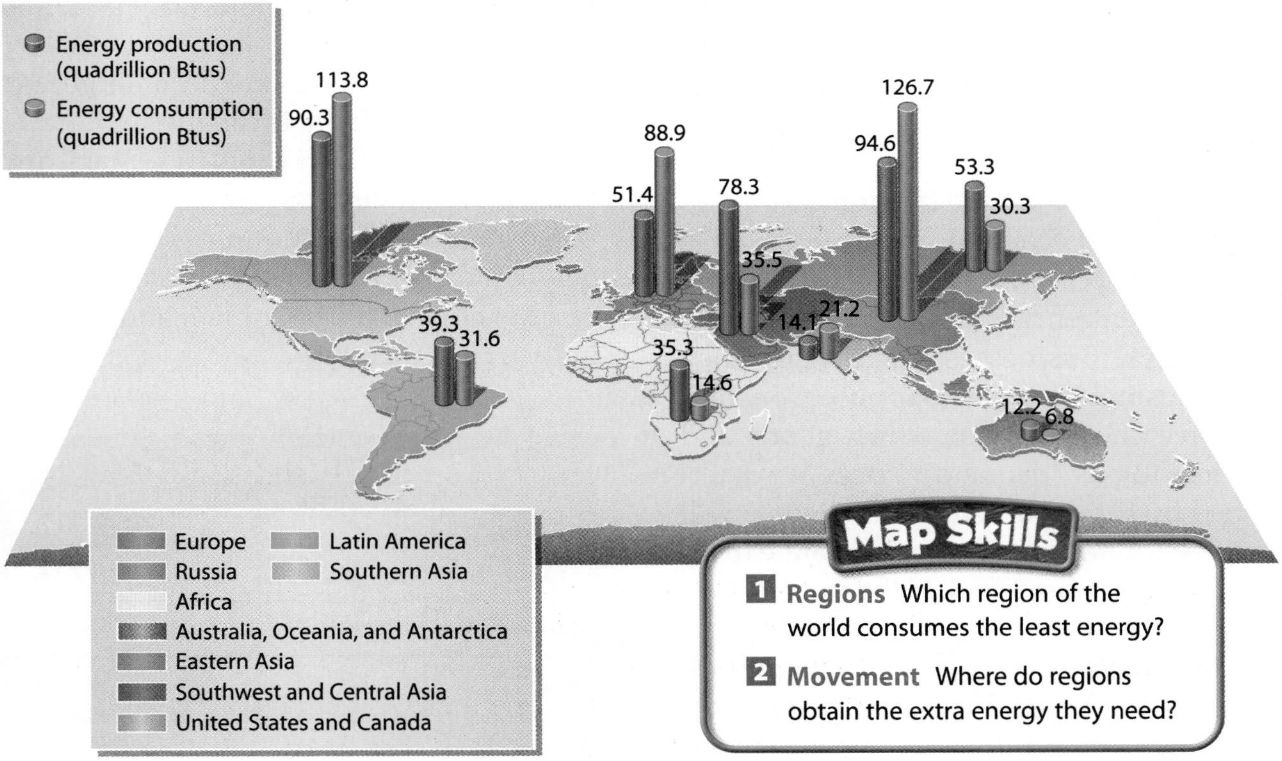

Energy production (quadrillion Btus)
Energy consumption (quadrillion Btus)

90.3 113.8
39.3 31.6
51.4 88.9
78.3 35.5
35.3 14.6
14.1 21.2
94.6 126.7
53.3 30.3
12.2 6.8

Europe
Latin America
Russia
Southern Asia
Africa
Australia, Oceania, and Antarctica
Eastern Asia
Southwest and Central Asia
United States and Canada

Source: Energy Information Administration, 2006.

Map Skills

1. **Regions** Which region of the world consumes the least energy?
2. **Movement** Where do regions obtain the extra energy they need?

Economies and Trade

Main Idea **An economy is the way people use and manage resources.**

Geography and You What kinds of goods and services do the people in your community produce? Read to find out about how economic decisions are made.

Economic Systems

To help make economic decisions, societies develop economic systems. An **economic system** is the method used to answer three key questions: what goods and services to produce, how to produce them, and who will receive them.

There are four kinds of economic systems. In a traditional economy, individuals decide what to produce and how to produce it. These choices are based on custom or habit. In these economies, people often do the same work as their parents and grandparents. Technology is often limited.

In a command economy, the government makes the key economic decisions about resources. It decides the costs of products and the wages workers earn, and individuals have little economic freedom.

In a market economy, individuals make their own economic decisions. People known as entrepreneurs can start and own businesses. Businesses make what they think customers want (supply). Consumers have choices about which goods and services to buy (demand). Prices are determined by supply and demand. People will buy less of an item as it gets more expensive. On the other hand, if the price is low, people will tend to buy more of an item.

Most nations have mixed economies, which is the fourth type of economic system. Cuba, for example, has mostly a command economy, but the government allows some features of a market economy. The United States has mainly a market economy with some government involvement.

Developed and Developing Countries

Geographers look at economies in another way—how developed they are. A **developed country** has a mix of agriculture, a great deal of manufacturing, and service industries. Service industries, such as banking and health care, provide services rather than making products. Developed economies tend to rely on new technologies, and workers have relatively high incomes. Examples of developed countries include the United States, France, and Australia.

Countries with economies that are not as advanced are called **developing countries.** These countries have little industry. Agriculture remains important, and incomes per person are generally low. Developing countries include Moldova, Haiti, and Guatemala.

Still other countries are becoming more industrial. Geographers call these countries **newly industrialized countries.** Brazil and Mexico are moving toward economies like those in developed countries. The chart below shows divisions in the economies of a developed, a developing, and a newly industrialized country.

Economic Divisions

Country	Agriculture	Industry	Services
France	2%	20.4%	77.6%
Haiti	28%	20%	52%
Brazil	6.7%	28%	65.3%

Source: *World Factbook*, 2009.

World Trade

Economies grow when countries produce more goods and services over the long term. Economic growth is measured by **gross domestic product (GDP).** This is the total dollar value of all goods and services produced in a single year. Trade is important for economic growth.

Trade allows nations to **export,** or sell to other countries, the resources they have in abundance or the products made from those resources. They also **import,** or buy from other countries, the resources they do not have or the products they cannot make. To carry out trade, countries have their own currencies, or money. Currencies can be exchanged on the world market with trading partners.

Trade is important for both developed and developing nations. For example, the countries of Europe import what they need—food, energy resources, and minerals—to maintain their successful economies. The developing nations, in turn, rely on the sale of their products and resources to **finance,** or pay for, efforts to further build their economies.

To boost their own economies, some nations use **tariffs,** or taxes, to increase the price of imported goods. The use of tariffs encourages consumers to buy less expensive items that are manufactured in their own country.

Quotas are another barrier to trade. A **quota** is a limit on how many items can be imported from a certain nation.

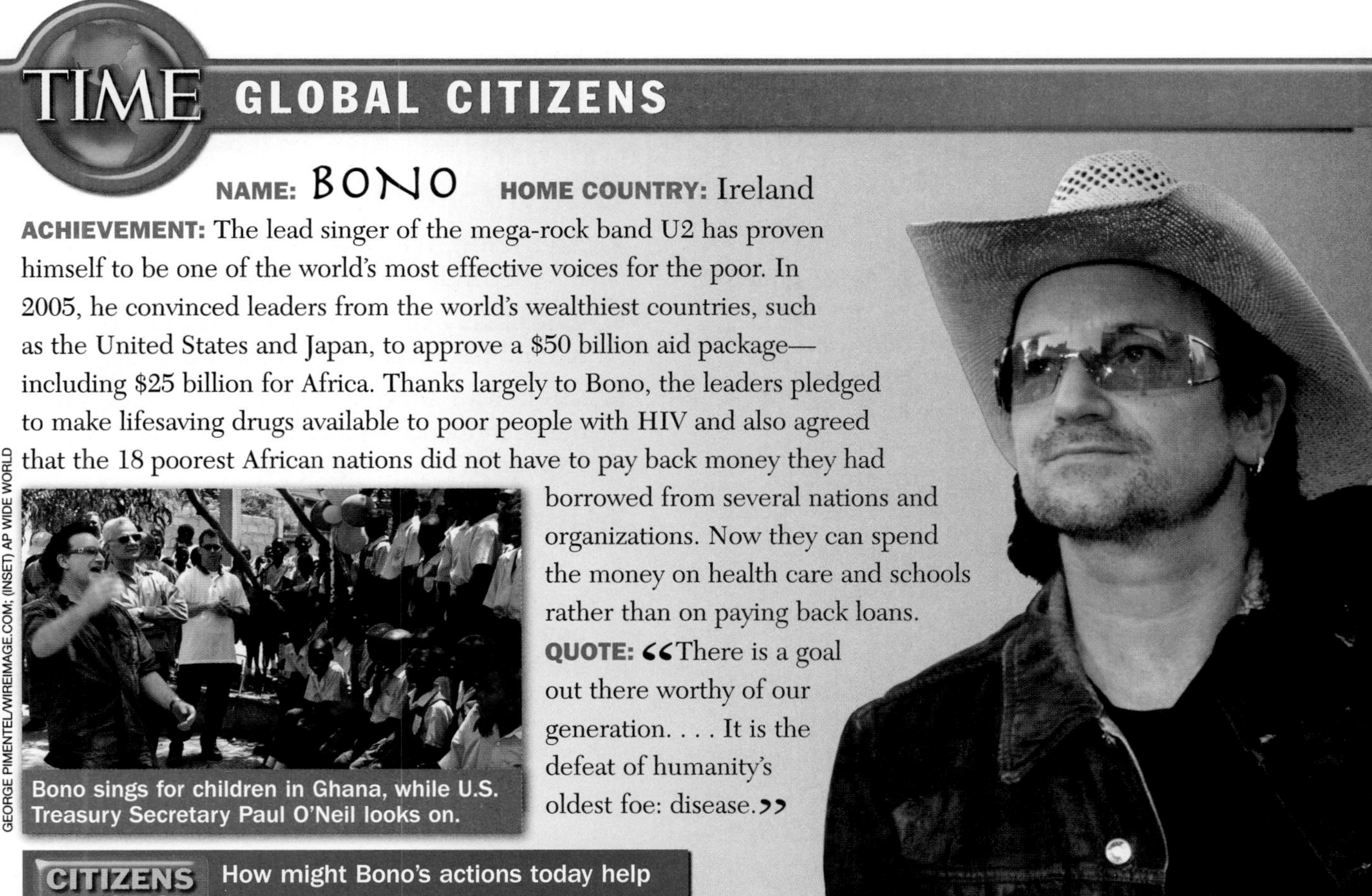

TIME GLOBAL CITIZENS

NAME: BONO **HOME COUNTRY:** Ireland

ACHIEVEMENT: The lead singer of the mega-rock band U2 has proven himself to be one of the world's most effective voices for the poor. In 2005, he convinced leaders from the world's wealthiest countries, such as the United States and Japan, to approve a $50 billion aid package—including $25 billion for Africa. Thanks largely to Bono, the leaders pledged to make lifesaving drugs available to poor people with HIV and also agreed that the 18 poorest African nations did not have to pay back money they had borrowed from several nations and organizations. Now they can spend the money on health care and schools rather than on paying back loans.

QUOTE: "There is a goal out there worthy of our generation. . . . It is the defeat of humanity's oldest foe: disease."

Bono sings for children in Ghana, while U.S. Treasury Secretary Paul O'Neil looks on.

CITIZENS IN ACTION How might Bono's actions today help people 10 years from now?

Free Trade

In recent years, many countries have agreed to get rid of trade barriers. The removal of trade limits so that goods flow freely among countries is called **free trade.** Often countries sign treaties agreeing to free trade. For example, in 1994 Canada, the United States, and Mexico joined together in the North American Free Trade Agreement (NAFTA). This pact removed most trade barriers between the three nations.

Interdependence and Technology

Growing trade among the world's countries has resulted in the globalization of the world's economies. As a result, the world's people and economies have become more interdependent. **Interdependence** means that countries rely on each other for ideas, goods, services, and markets, or places to sell their goods. When economies are linked together, a drought or a war in one region can cause price increases or shortages in another region far away.

Interdependence has come about in part because of new technologies. During the past 200 years, the invention of new technologies has occurred much faster than at any other time in history. Advances in transportation, such as trains and airplanes, and in communication, such as telephones and the Internet, have contributed greatly to globalization.

Reading Check **Explaining** Explain why trade barriers exist, and describe two types of trade barriers.

Section 3 Review

Vocabulary

1. **Explain** the significance of:
   - a. natural resource
   - b. renewable resource
   - c. nonrenewable resource
   - d. economic system
   - e. developed country
   - f. developing country
   - g. newly industrialized country
   - h. gross domestic product
   - i. export
   - j. import
   - k. tarriff
   - l. quota
   - m. free trade
   - n. interdependence

Main Ideas

2. **Explaining** Why do people need natural resources?
3. **Comparing and Contrasting** Use a Venn diagram like the one below to compare and contrast developed and developing countries.

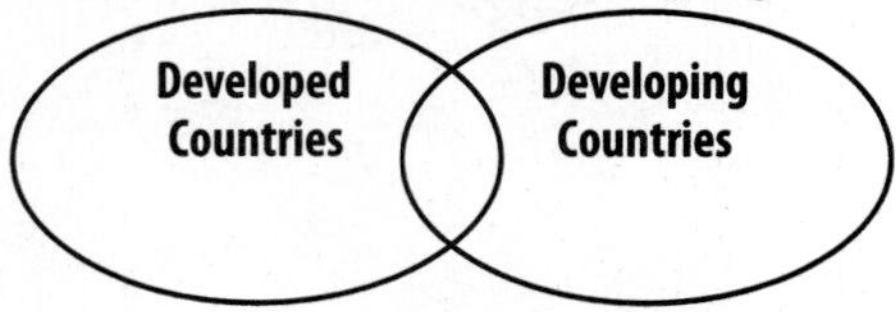

Critical Thinking

4. **Analyzing** Why has the world become more interdependent in recent years?
5. **BIG Idea** Explain how the distribution of natural resources relates to world trade.
6. **Challenge** In what ways might interdependence influence a place's cultural identity? Explain in two paragraphs.

Writing About Geography

7. **Using Your FOLDABLES** Use your Foldable to write a paragraph that predicts how population patterns might affect world resources in the future.

Visual Summary

World Population

- Low death rates and high birthrates have led to rapid population growth.
- Some areas of the world are more densely populated than others.
- Nearly half of the world's population lives in cities.

Commuters, London, England

Culture

- Culture is the way of life of a group of people who share similar beliefs and customs.
- Cultures change over time and influence one another.
- Modern technology has broken down barriers and helped create a global culture.

Oil worker, Mexico

Natural Resources

- Renewable resources either cannot be used up or can be replaced.
- Some resources—such as fossil fuels and minerals—are nonrenewable.

World Economies

- The four kinds of economic systems are traditional, command, market, and mixed.
- Developed countries use advanced technology and are highly productive.
- Developing countries have less advanced technology and are generally less productive.

World Trade

- In recent years, many countries have agreed to eliminate trade barriers.
- Growing trade among countries has made the world's people more interdependent.

Packing pineapples in a plant in Costa Rica

Study anywhere, anytime! Download quizzes and flash cards to your PDA from **glencoe.com**.

CHAPTER 3 ASSESSMENT

GA CRCT Practice

TEST-TAKING TIP

Read each question, then think of the answer before reading the list of choices. You are less likely to be confused or tricked by the choices on the test if you can guess the answer first.

Directions: Choose the best answer for each question.

1 **What is population density?**

A the total number of people living in a square mile or square kilometer
B the average number of people living in a square mile or square kilometer
C the total number of people living in a particular city or state
D the average number of people born each year in a country

2 **What term refers to people who flee to another country to escape wars, persecution, or natural disasters?**

A immigrants
B free traders
C refugees
D importers

3 **Which word describes a group that shares a language, history, and religion as well as some physical traits?**

A democratic
B global
C social
D ethnic

4 **What term describes a country that has a mix of agriculture, manufacturing, and service industries?**

A developed
B underdeveloped
C overdeveloped
D developing

5 **What is one reason for the rapid increase in world population over the last two centuries?**

A increased migration
B increased population density
C improved health care
D urbanization

6 **Which of the following is a "push factor" leading to migration from a region or country?**

A a shortage of jobs
B an abundance of jobs
C low population density
D an abundance of farmland

7 **What type of culture is created when a growing number of countries and regions share similar cultural traits?**

A an isolated culture
B a global culture
C a refugee culture
D an ethnic culture

8 **What do societies develop in order to answer the questions of what goods and services to produce, how to produce them, and who will receive them?**

A quota systems
B trading systems
C manufacturing systems
D economic systems

9 **Which of the following is a nonrenewable resource?**

A water
B sunlight
C oil
D wind

10 Look at the bar graph.

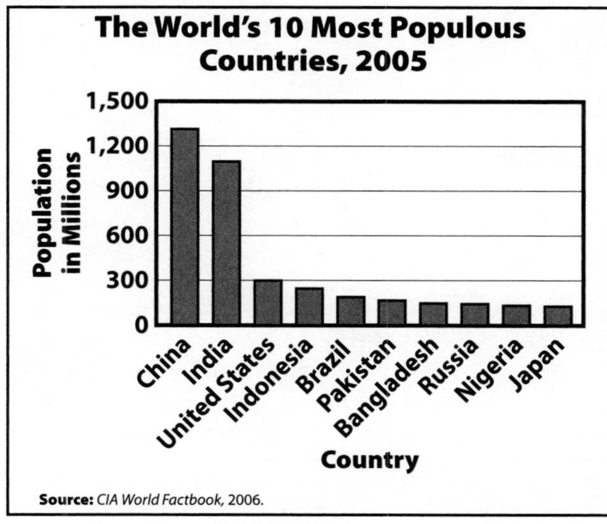

Based on the graph, what continent would likely be the most densely populated?

A North America
B South America
C Asia
D Africa

11 According to the graph, how many Asian countries are more populous than Russia?

A 6
B 5
C 4
D 3

12 Based on the graph, which two countries have the greatest difference in populations?

A India and the United States
B Indonesia and Russia
C China and Brazil
D China and Japan

13 Read the document and answer the questions that follow.

> *[I]magine . . . that the world really is a "global village." . . . Say this village has 1,000 individuals, with all the characteristics of today's human race distributed in exactly the same proportions. . . .*
>
> *Some 150 of the inhabitants live in [a wealthy] area of the village, about 780 in poorer districts. Another 70 or so live in a neighborhood that is [changing]. The average income per person is $6,000 a year. . . . But just 200 people [own] 86 percent of all the wealth, while nearly half of the villagers are eking [scraping] out an existence on less than $2 per day. . . .*
>
> *Life expectancy in the affluent [wealthy] district is nearly 78 years, in the poorer areas 64 years—and in the very poorest neighborhoods a mere 52 years. . . . Why do the poorest lag so far behind? Because in their neighborhoods there is a far higher incidence of infectious diseases and malnutrition, combined with [a serious] lack of access to safe water, sanitation, health care, adequate housing, education, and work.*
>
> —*Kofi Annan,* Millennium Report, 2000

According to the document, how many people from the "global village" live in poorer districts?

A 1,000
B 780
C 150
D 70

14 Why are people who live in the poorest areas more likely to die at an earlier age than those who live in the wealthiest areas?

A They are more likely to become victims of violence.
B Their jobs are physically more difficult.
C Infectious diseases and malnutrition occur more frequently in the poorest areas.
D Wealthy people are able to exercise more.

For additional test practice, use Self-Check Quizzes—Chapter 3 at glencoe.com.

Need Extra Help?

If You Missed Questions...	1	2	3	4	5	6	7	8	9	10	11	12	13	14
Go to Page...	74	76	84	94	73	76	89	94	93	74	74	74	74	74

TIME JOURNAL

It may be the middle of the night where you live, but in many parts of the world, people are well into their day. It's all because of the 24 time zones that divide up Earth. So while one part of the world sleeps, somewhere, kids are at school, workers are at their jobs, and some folks are having dinner. Take a look at what is happening on Earth at exactly the same moment during one day in April.

Monday, 7 a.m. **LOS ANGELES, CALIFORNIA** Some people are just waking up. Others are sitting down to breakfast. Early birds are headed to their jobs hoping to avoid traffic jams on the state's freeways. ▶

◀ **Monday, 10 a.m.** **WASHINGTON, D.C.** Workers are at their desks. And at the White House, the wheels of government have been turning since 7 a.m. or even earlier, where 12-hour workdays are routine.

◀ **Monday, 11 a.m.** **RIO DE JANEIRO, BRAZIL** Almost every day is a beach day in Rio. While beachgoers are enjoying sun and sand, traffic jams clog the city's streets, students are at their desks, and Rio's stores are filled with shoppers.

◀ **Monday, 2 p.m.** **DAKAR, SENEGAL** Outdoor markets are packed in this west African nation. School is winding down for the day, and fishers are returning home with their day's catch from the Atlantic Ocean.

Monday, 4 p.m. **PARIS, FRANCE** School is out and some kids are playing soccer, a favorite pastime. Other students are studying for exams to get into special high schools. Some tourists are having their pictures taken in front of the Eiffel Tower while others are visiting the city's famous museums, perhaps catching a glimpse of the *Mona Lisa.* ▶

Monday, 5 p.m. **CAIRO, EGYPT** This capital city is filled with the sounds of people being called to prayer, vendors selling their goods at outdoor bazaars, and the blare of car and bus horns on traffic-clogged streets. Tourists and residents alike can marvel at the Pyramids of Giza built almost 5,000 years ago. ▼

TOP TO BOTTOM: CREATAS/SUPERSTOCK; AP PHOTO; JIM ZUCKERMAN/CORBIS; KURT SCHOLZ/SUPERSTOCK; LISA ENGLEBRECHT/DANITADELIMONT.COM; GARY COOK/ALAMY; GLOBE: NASA

A DAY IN THE LIFE OF THE WORLD'S PEOPLE

Tuesday, 2 a.m. **WELLINGTON, NEW ZEALAND** What do Kiwis (a nickname for New Zealanders) do when they can't sleep? They might count sheep. That's because the nation's 45 million woolly animals outnumber the island-nation's human inhabitants 11 to 1. ▶

Monday, 10 p.m. **BEIJING, CHINA** The day is winding down for most of the 15 million residents of the nation's capital. China, with its more than one billion people, has one of the world's fastest growing economies. Night workers, including people who work with American companies, are starting their day, keeping to a U.S. time schedule. ▶

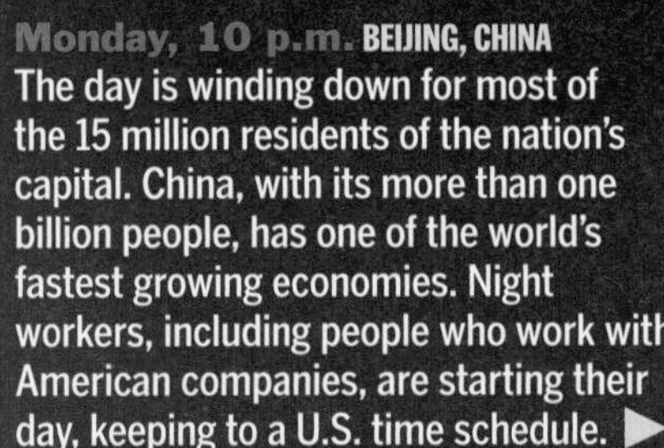

Monday, 6 p.m. **MOSCOW, RUSSIA** This huge country has 11 time zones. The nation, which has turned from communism to democracy, is undergoing a construction boom. Workers are going home for dinner. ▼

◀ **Monday, 8 p.m.** **DHAKA, BANGLADESH** Some residents of this city are sitting down to a dinner of fish or spicy curries. Meanwhile, fans of cricket, a popular sport in this country, are cheering for their favorite team.

TOP TO BOTTOM: ILLUSTRATION BY BOOKMAPMAN; JOSE AZEL/GETTY IMAGES, MACDUFF EVERTON/CORBIS; AP PHOTO; ITAR-TASS/VITALY BELOUSOV/NEWSCOM

Latin America and Canada

CHAPTER 4
Physical Geography of Latin America

CHAPTER 5
History and Cultures of Latin America

CHAPTER 6
Latin America Today

CHAPTER 7
Canada

Rio de Janeiro, Brazil ▶

NATIONAL GEOGRAPHIC

NGS ONLINE For more information about the region, see www.nationalgeographic.com/education.

Regional Atlas

Latin America and Canada

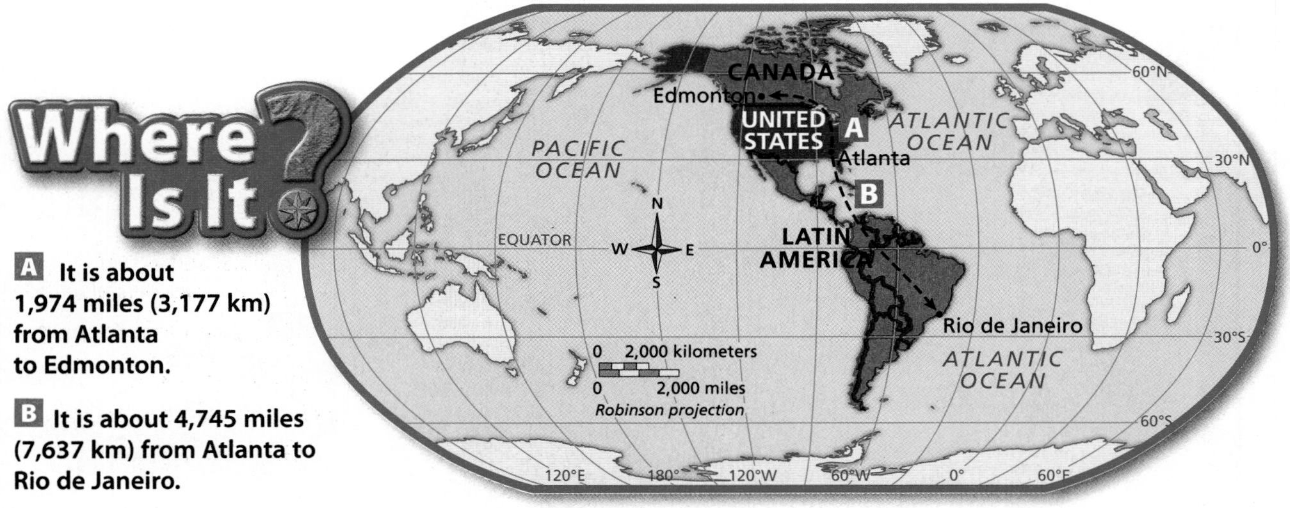

A It is about 1,974 miles (3,177 km) from Atlanta to Edmonton.

B It is about 4,745 miles (7,637 km) from Atlanta to Rio de Janeiro.

The region of Latin America is about two-and-a-half times the size of the continental United States. Its land area is about 7.9 million square miles (20.5 million sq. km). Canada is slightly larger than the United States and is the second-largest country in the world. Its land area is about 3.8 million square miles (10 million sq. km).

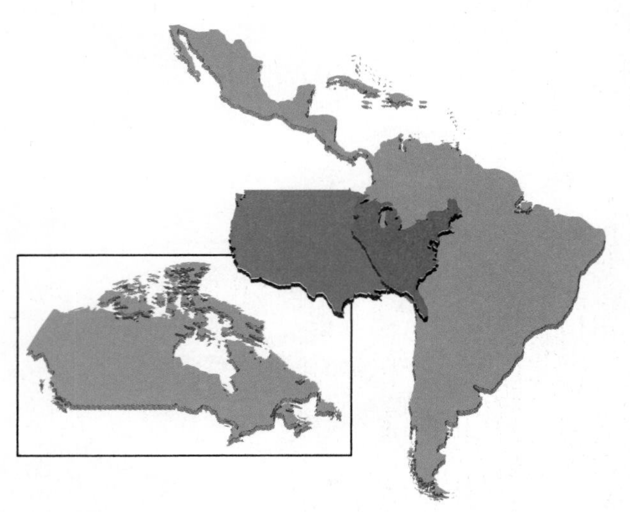

Comparing Population

United States, Selected Countries of Latin America, and Canada

Country	
United States	
Brazil	
Mexico	
Canada	
Peru	
Honduras	

(one figure) = 30,000,000

Source: *World Population Data Sheet,* 2005.

GEO Fast Facts

Largest Island

Baffin Island (Canada)
195,928 sq. mi.
(507,451 sq. km)

Largest Lake

Lake Superior (Canada/United States)
31,800 sq. mi. (82,362 sq. km)

Aconcagua
(Argentina)
22,834 ft.
(6,960 m) high

Longest River

Highest Point

UNIT 2

Regional Atlas

Latin America

PHYSICAL

Map Skills

1. **Regions** What mountain range lines the western coast of South America?
2. **Human-Environment Interaction** Why do you think people would build a canal in Panama to connect the Atlantic and Pacific Oceans?

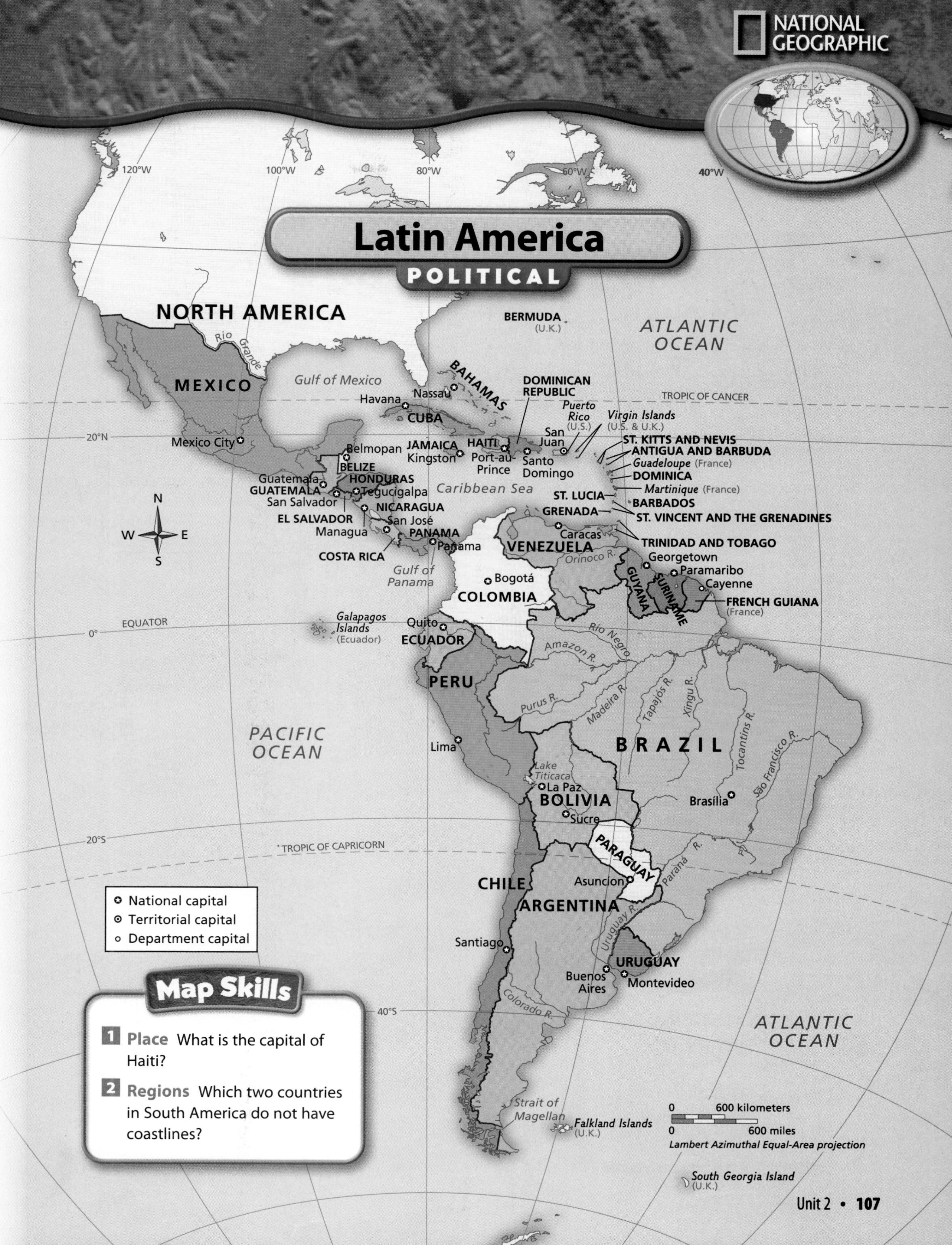

Map Skills

1. **Place** What is the capital of Haiti?
2. **Regions** Which two countries in South America do not have coastlines?

Unit 2 Regional Atlas

Map Skills

1. **Place** What part of Mexico has the highest population density?
2. **Regions** What cities in the region have more than 10 million people?

Map Skills

1. **Regions** How is most of the land used in Argentina?
2. **Location** What energy resources can be extracted from the land in Ecuador and Peru?

Regional Atlas

UNIT 2

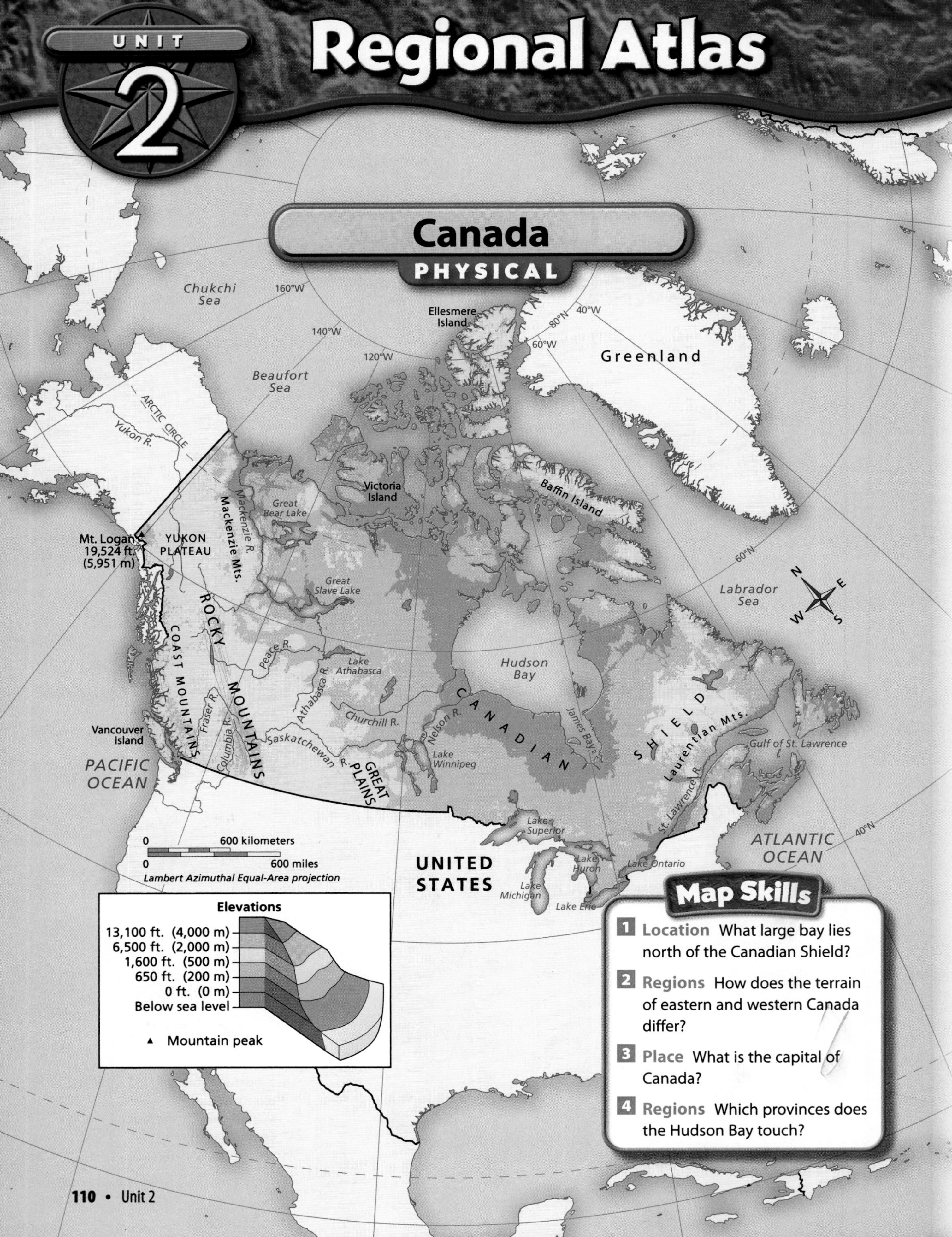

Map Skills

1. **Location** What large bay lies north of the Canadian Shield?
2. **Regions** How does the terrain of eastern and western Canada differ?
3. **Place** What is the capital of Canada?
4. **Regions** Which provinces does the Hudson Bay touch?

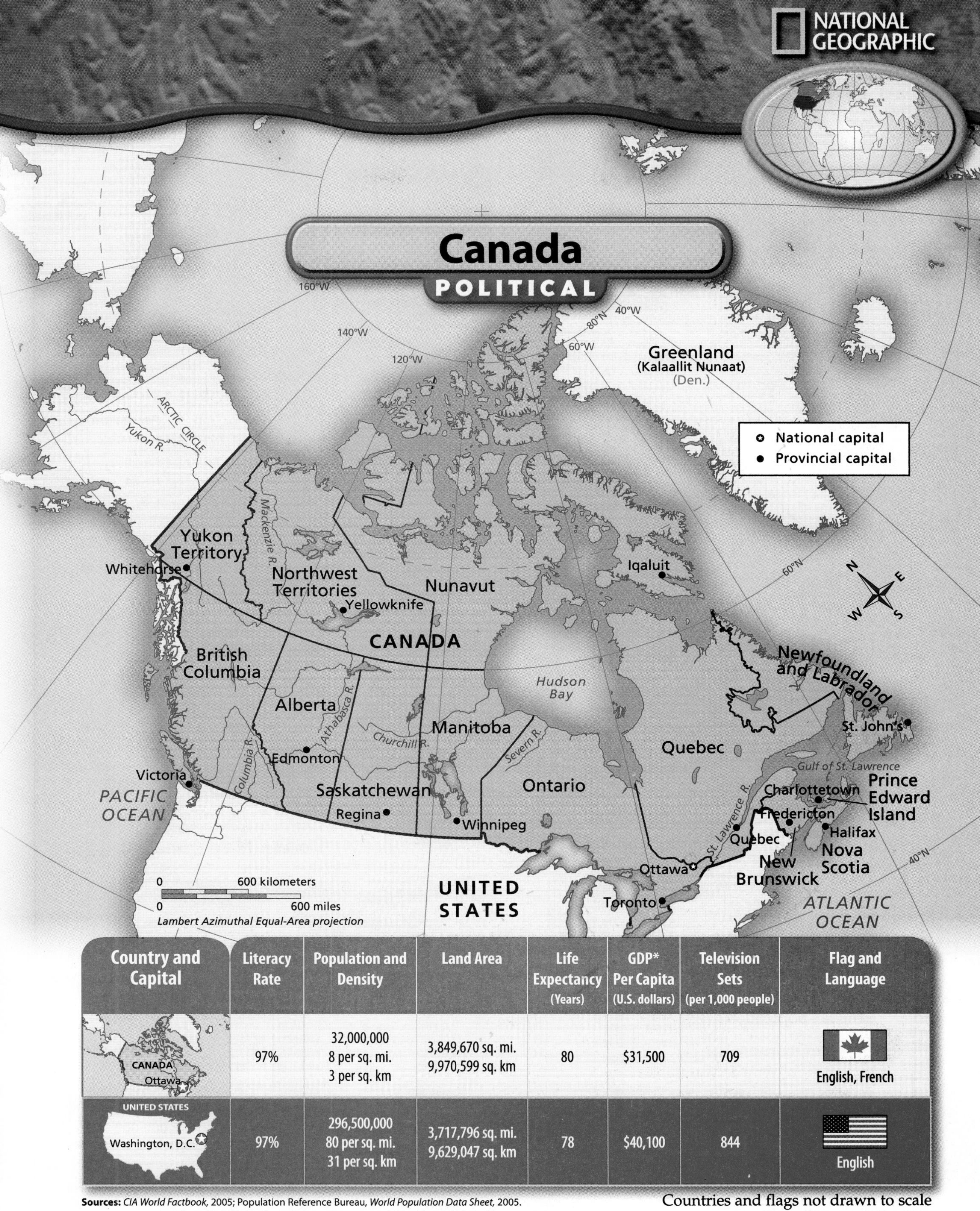

Country and Capital	Literacy Rate	Population and Density	Land Area	Life Expectancy (Years)	GDP* Per Capita (U.S. dollars)	Television Sets (per 1,000 people)	Flag and Language
CANADA Ottawa	97%	32,000,000 8 per sq. mi. 3 per sq. km	3,849,670 sq. mi. 9,970,599 sq. km	80	$31,500	709	English, French
UNITED STATES Washington, D.C.	97%	296,500,000 80 per sq. mi. 31 per sq. km	3,717,796 sq. mi. 9,629,047 sq. km	78	$40,100	844	English

Sources: *CIA World Factbook*, 2005; Population Reference Bureau, *World Population Data Sheet*, 2005.

Countries and flags not drawn to scale

*Gross Domestic Product

For more country facts, go to the **Nations of the World Atlas** at glencoe.com.

UNIT 2

Regional Atlas

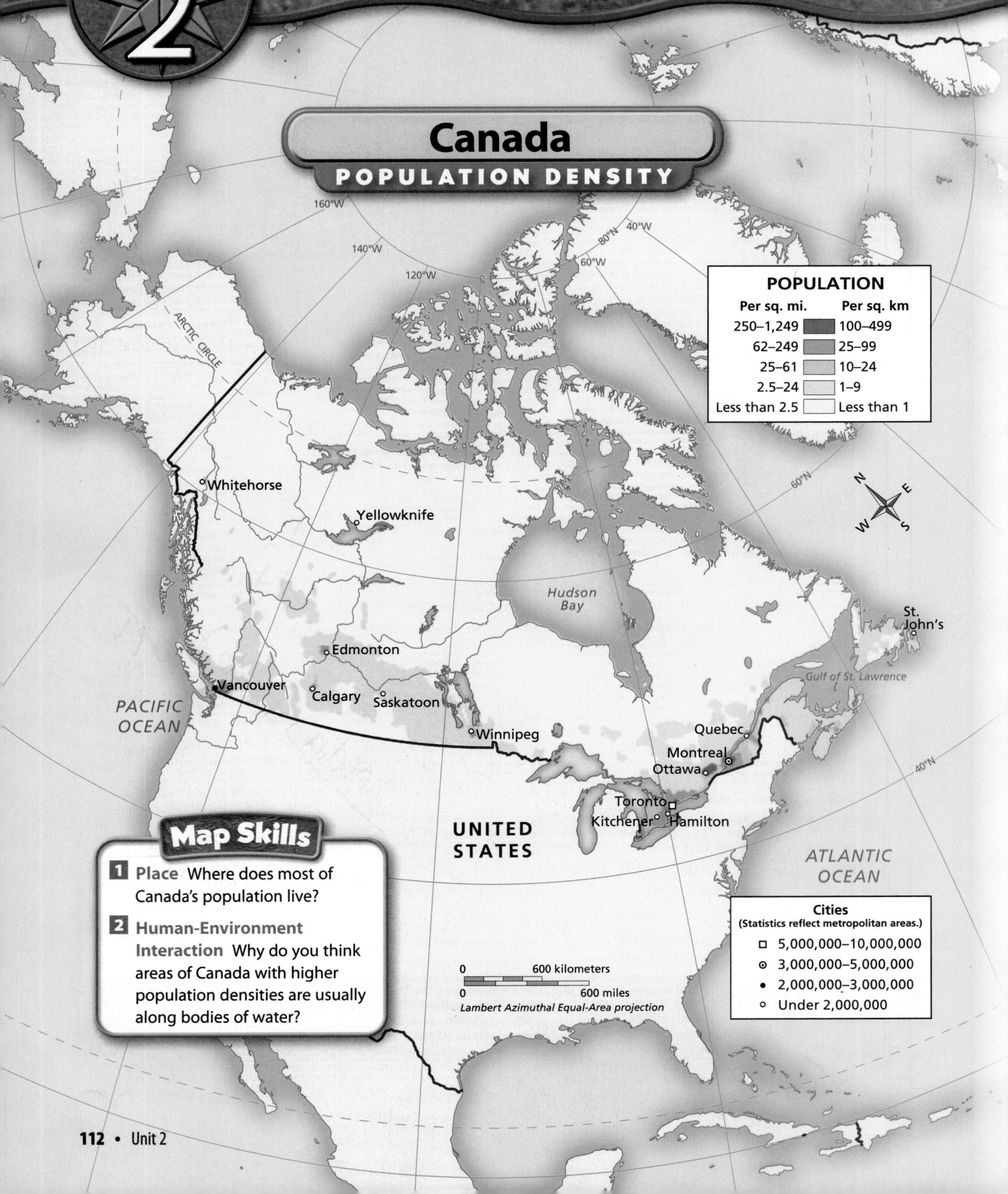

Canada

POPULATION DENSITY

POPULATION

Per sq. mi.	Per sq. km
250–1,249	100–499
62–249	25–99
25–61	10–24
2.5–24	1–9
Less than 2.5	Less than 1

Cities
(Statistics reflect metropolitan areas.)

- □ 5,000,000–10,000,000
- ⊙ 3,000,000–5,000,000
- • 2,000,000–3,000,000
- ○ Under 2,000,000

Map Skills

1. **Place** Where does most of Canada's population live?
2. **Human-Environment Interaction** Why do you think areas of Canada with higher population densities are usually along bodies of water?

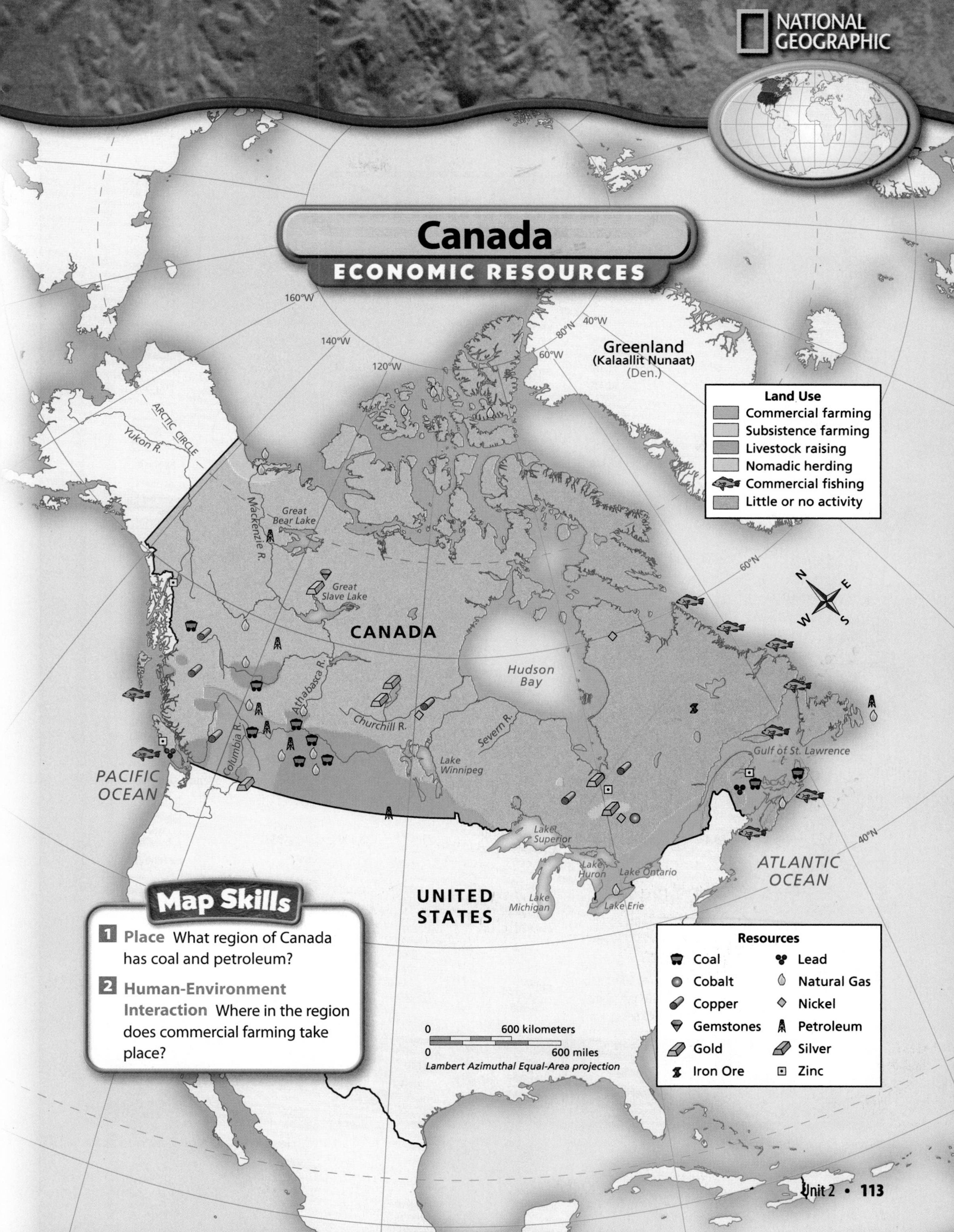

Map Skills

1. **Place** What region of Canada has coal and petroleum?
2. **Human-Environment Interaction** Where in the region does commercial farming take place?

Regional Atlas

Latin America

Country and Capital	Literacy Rate	Population and Density	Land Area	Life Expectancy (Years)	GDP* Per Capita (U.S. dollars)	Television Sets (per 1,000 people)	Flag and Language
ANTIGUA AND BARBUDA St. John's	89%	100,000 588 per sq. mi. 227 per sq. km	170 sq. mi. 440 sq. km	71	$11,000	493	English
ARGENTINA Buenos Aires	97.1%	38,600,000 36 per sq. mi. 14 per sq. km	1,073,514 sq. mi. 2,780,388 sq. km	74	$12,400	293	Spanish
BAHAMAS Nassau	95.6%	300,000 60 per sq. mi. 22 per sq. km	5,359 sq. mi. 13,880 sq. km	70	$17,700	243	English
BARBADOS Bridgetown	97.4%	300,000 1,807 per sq. mi. 698 per sq. km	166 sq. mi. 430 sq. km	72	$16,400	290	English
BELIZE Belmopan	94.1%	300,000 34 per sq. mi. 13 per sq. km	8,865 sq. mi. 22,960 sq. km	70	$6,500	183	English
BOLIVIA La Paz Sucre	87.2%	8,900,000 21 per sq. mi. 8 per sq. km	424,162 sq. mi. 1,098,574 sq. km	64	$2,600	118	Spanish, Quechua, Aymara
BRAZIL Brasília	86.4%	184,200,000 56 per sq. mi. 22 per sq. km	3,300,154 sq. mi. 8,547,359 sq. km	71	$8,100	333	Portuguese
CHILE Santiago	96.2%	16,100,000 55 per sq. mi. 21 per sq. km	292,135 sq. mi. 756,626 sq. km	76	$10,700	240	Spanish
COLOMBIA Bogotá	92.5%	46,000,000 105 per sq. mi. 40 per sq. km	439,734 sq. mi. 1,138,906 sq. km	72	$6,600	279	Spanish
UNITED STATES Washington, D.C.	97%	296,500,000 80 per sq. mi. 31 per sq. km	3,717,796 sq. mi. 9,629,047 sq. km	78	$40,100	844	English

*Gross Domestic Product

Countries and flags not drawn to scale

Latin America

Country and Capital	Literacy Rate	Population and Density	Land Area	Life Expectancy (Years)	GDP* Per Capita (U.S. dollars)	Television Sets (per 1,000 people)	Flag and Language
COSTA RICA San José	96%	4,300,000 218 per sq. mi. 84 per sq. km	19,730 sq. mi. 51,100 sq. km	79	$9,600	229	Spanish
CUBA Havana	97%	11,300,000 264 per sq. mi. 102 per sq. km	42,803 sq. mi. 110,859 sq. km	77	$3,000	248	Spanish
DOMINICA Roseau	94%	100,000 345 per sq. mi. 133 per sq. km	290 sq. mi. 751 sq. km	74	$5,500	232	English
DOMINICAN REPUBLIC Santo Domingo	84%	8,900,000 471 per sq. mi. 168 per sq. km	18,815 sq. mi. 48,731 sq. km	68	$6,300	96	Spanish
ECUADOR Quito	92.5%	13,000,000 119 per sq. mi. 46 per sq. km	109,483 sq. mi. 283,560 sq. km	74	$3,700	213	Spanish
EL SALVADOR San Salvador	80.2%	6,900,000 849 per sq. mi. 328 per sq. km	8,124 sq. mi. 21,041 sq. km	70	$4,900	191	Spanish
FRENCH GUIANA Cayenne	83%	200,000 6 per sq. mi. 2 per sq. km	34,749 sq. mi. 89,999 sq. km	75	$8,300	information not available	French
GRENADA St. George's	98%	100,000 769 per sq. mi. 295 per sq. km	131 sq. mi. 339 sq. km	71	$5,000	376	English
GUATEMALA Guatemala	70.6%	12,700,000 302 per sq. mi. 117 per sq. km	42,042 sq. mi. 108,888 sq. km	66	$4,200	61	Spanish
UNITED STATES Washington, D.C.	97%	296,500,000 80 per sq. mi. 31 per sq. km	3,717,796 sq. mi. 9,629,047 sq. km	78	$40,100	844	English

Sources: *CIA World Factbook,* 2005; Population Reference Bureau, *World Population Data Sheet,* 2005.

For more country facts, go to the **Nations of the World Atlas** at glencoe.com.

Regional Atlas

Latin America

Country and Capital	Literacy Rate	Population and Density	Land Area	Life Expectancy (Years)	GDP* Per Capita (U.S. dollars)	Television Sets (per 1,000 people)	Flag and Language
GUYANA, Georgetown	98.8%	800,000 10 per sq. mi. 4 per sq. km	83,000 sq. mi. 214,969 sq. km	63	$3,800	70	English
HAITI, Port-au-Prince	52.9%	8,300,000 775 per sq. mi. 299 per sq. km	10,714 sq. mi. 27,749 sq. km	52	$1,500	5	French, Creole
HONDURAS, Tegucigalpa	76.2%	7,200,000 166 per sq. mi. 64 per sq. km	43,278 sq. mi. 112,090 sq. km	71	$2,800	95	Spanish
JAMAICA, Kingston	87.9%	2,700,000 636 per sq. mi. 246 per sq. km	4,243 sq. mi. 10,989 sq. km	73	$4,100	191	English
MEXICO, Mexico City	92.2%	107,000,000 142 per sq. mi. 55 per sq. km	756,082 sq. mi. 1,958,243 sq. km	75	$9,600	272	Spanish
NICARAGUA, Managua	67.5%	5,800,000 116 per sq. mi. 45 per sq. km	50,193 sq. mi. 129,999 sq. km	69	$2,300	69	Spanish
PANAMA, Panama	92.6%	3,200,000 110 per sq. mi. 42 per sq. km	29,158 sq. mi. 75,519 sq. km	75	$6,900	192	Spanish
PARAGUAY, Asunción	94%	6,200,000 39 per sq. mi. 15 per sq. km	157,046 sq. mi. 406,747 sq. km	71	$4,800	205	Spanish, Guarani
PERU, Lima	87.7%	27,900,000 56 per sq. mi. 22 per sq. km	496,224 sq. mi. 1,285,214 sq. km	70	$5,600	147	Spanish, Quechua
UNITED STATES, Washington, D.C.	97%	296,500,000 80 per sq. mi. 31 per sq. km	3,717,796 sq. mi. 9,629,047 sq. km	78	$40,100	844	English

*Gross Domestic Product

Countries and flags not drawn to scale

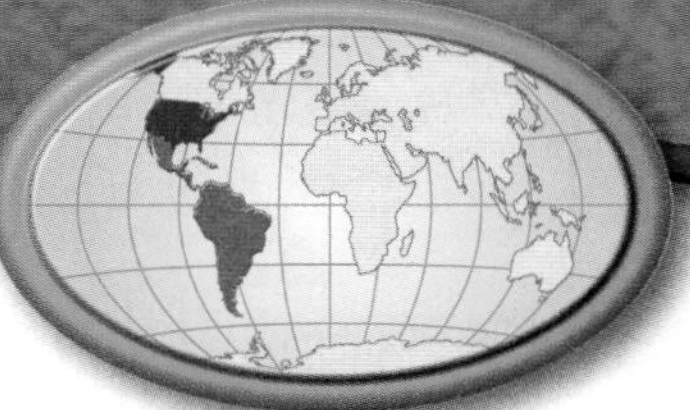

Latin America

Country and Capital	Literacy Rate	Population and Density	Land Area	Life Expectancy (Years)	GDP* Per Capita (U.S. dollars)	Television Sets (per 1,000 people)	Flag and Language
PUERTO RICO San Juan	94.1%	3,900,000 1,128 per sq. mi. 436 per sq. km	3,456 sq. mi. 8,951 sq. km	77	$17,700	information not available	Spanish
ST. KITTS-NEVIS Basseterre	97%	50,000 360 per sq. mi. 139 per sq. km	139 sq. mi. 360 sq. km	70	$8,800	256	English
ST. LUCIA Castries	67%	200,000 837 per sq. mi. 323 per sq. km	239 sq. mi. 619 sq. km	74	$5,400	368	English
ST. VINCENT AND THE GRENADINES Kingstown	96%	100,000 737 per sq. mi. 256 per sq. km	151 sq. mi. 391 sq. km	72	$2,900	230	English
SURINAME Paramaribo	93%	438,000 7 per sq. mi. 3 per sq. km	62,344 sq. mi. 161,470 sq. km	69	$4,300	241	Dutch
TRINIDAD AND TOBAGO Port-of-Spain	98.6%	1,300,000 656 per sq. mi. 253 per sq. km	1,981 sq. mi. 5,131 sq. km	71	$10,500	337	English
URUGUAY Montevideo	98%	3,400,000 50 per sq. mi. 19 per sq. km	68,498 sq. mi. 177,409 sq. km	75	$14,500	531	Spanish
VENEZUELA Caracas	93.4%	26,700,000 76 per sq. mi. 29 per sq. km	352,143 sq. mi. 912,046 sq. km	73	$5,800	185	Spanish
VIRGIN ISLANDS (U.S.) Charlotte Amalie	information not available	108,708 799 per sq. mi. 309 per sq. km	136 sq. mi. 352 sq. km	79	$17,200	information not available	English
UNITED STATES Washington, D.C.	97%	296,500,000 80 per sq. mi. 31 per sq. km	3,717,796 sq. mi. 9,629,047 sq. km	78	$40,100	844	English

Sources: *CIA World Factbook*, 2005; Population Reference Bureau, *World Population Data Sheet*, 2005.

For more country facts, go to the **Nations of the World Atlas** at glencoe.com.

Reading Social Studies

Comparing and Contrasting

Reading Skill

1 Learn It!

When you *compare* people, things, or ideas, you look for the similarities among them. When you *contrast* people, things, or ideas, you identify their differences.

Textbook authors sometimes use this structure to help readers see the similarities and differences between topics.

- Read the following paragraph.
- Then compare and contrast the governments of the United States and Canada.

> Canada, like the United States, is a representative democracy, in which voters choose leaders who make and enforce the laws. Canada is not led by a president. Instead, it has a parliamentary democracy in which voters elect representatives to a lawmaking body called Parliament. These representatives then choose an official called the prime minister to head the government.
>
> —*from pages 195–196*

In a Venn diagram, differences are listed in the outer parts of the circles. Similarities are described where the circles overlap.

Governments of the United States and Canada

United States
The president heads the government.

Similarities
Both governments are representative democracies.

Canada
The prime minister, chosen by Parliament, heads the government.

Reading Tip

As you read, look for signal words that show comparisons, such as *similarly*, *at the same time*, and *likewise*. Contrast signal words include *however*, *rather*, and *on the other hand*.

2 Practice It!

Read the following sentences from this unit that describe environmental challenges in Brazil and Canada.

- Draw a Venn diagram like the one shown below.
- List the differences and similarities between the environmental challenges in the two regions.

Why is the rain forest shrinking? To increase jobs and make products for export, Brazil's government has encouraged mining, logging, and farming in the rain forest. These activities lead to soil erosion and harm the rain forest's ecosystem and biodiversity.

—*from page 178*

The Great Lakes are another [environmental] concern. Ships have accidentally carried some foreign species of fish and shellfish to the lakes. The populations of these creatures have grown rapidly, driving out native fish. Pollution of the lakes also harms their plants and animals.

—*from page 202*

Logging in Brazil's rain forest

Read to Write Activity

Read and take notes about Latin America's physical geography in Chapter 4. Then find similar information about another region in your book. Write an essay that describes the similarities and differences between the two regions.

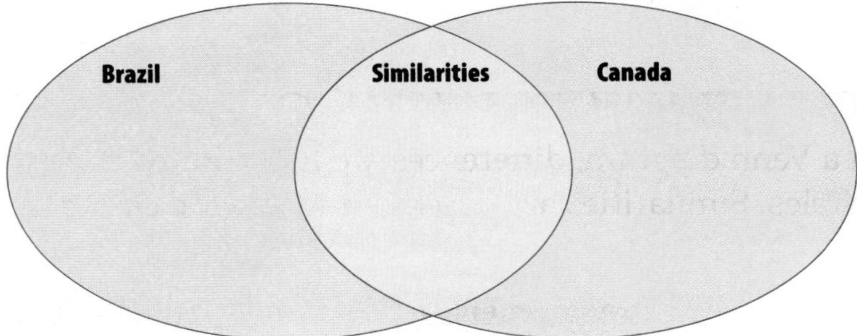

3 Apply It!

As you read Chapters 4, 5, 6, and 7, look for people, things, or ideas that you can compare and contrast. As you read, put notes in a Venn diagram like the one above to help you compare and contrast.

CHAPTER 4

Physical Geography of Latin America

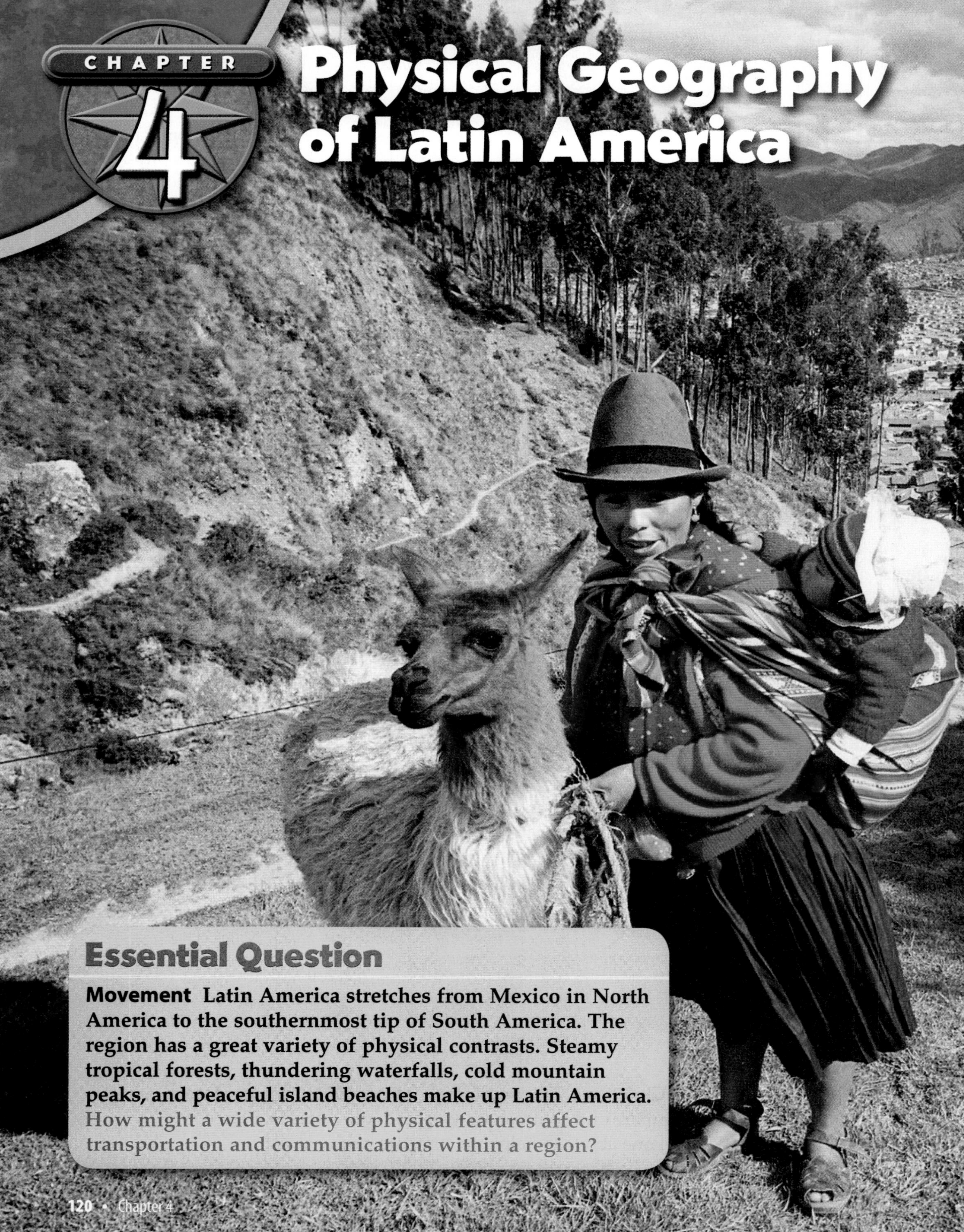

Essential Question

Movement Latin America stretches from Mexico in North America to the southernmost tip of South America. The region has a great variety of physical contrasts. Steamy tropical forests, thundering waterfalls, cold mountain peaks, and peaceful island beaches make up Latin America. How might a wide variety of physical features affect transportation and communications within a region?

Chapter Audio

Section 1: Physical Features

BIG IDEA Geographic factors influence where people settle. In Latin America, vast river systems provide transportation and support fishing. The region's rugged mountains and thick forests, however, have been obstacles to transportation and trade.

Section 2: Climate Regions

BIG IDEA The physical environment affects how people live. Latin America's vast expanse of rain forest is the largest in the world and contains valuable resources. In mountainous areas, climate and vegetation are affected more by altitude than by latitude.

◀ Quechuan Indian woman outside of Cuzco, Peru

FOLDABLES™ Study Organizer

Summarizing Information Make this Foldable to help you summarize information about the landforms, waterways, resources, and climates of Latin America.

Step 1 Fold the top of an 11 x 17 sheet of paper down about 2 inches.

Step 2 Then fold the paper to create 3 equal columns.

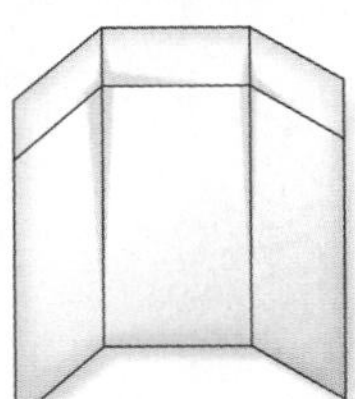

Step 3 Label each column of your Foldable as shown.

Landforms and Waterways | Resources | Climates

Reading and Writing Use the notes from your Foldable to write a travel pamphlet highlighting one of the subregions of Latin America. In your pamphlet, explain why the landforms, waterways, and climates of your chosen area are attractive to tourists.

Visit glencoe.com and enter QuickPass™ code GA6EOW6225c4 for Chapter 4 resources.

Physical Features

Section Audio

Spotlight Video

Guide to Reading

BIG Idea

Geographic factors influence where people settle.

Content Vocabulary

- subregion *(p. 123)*
- isthmus *(p. 123)*
- archipelago *(p. 123)*
- escarpment *(p. 124)*
- Llanos *(p. 124)*
- Pampas *(p. 124)*
- tributary *(p. 124)*
- estuary *(p. 124)*
- gasohol *(p. 125)*

Academic Vocabulary

- transport *(p. 123)*
- reside *(p. 124)*

Reading Strategy

Identifying Central Issues Use a diagram like the one below to identify and briefly describe six key landforms in the region.

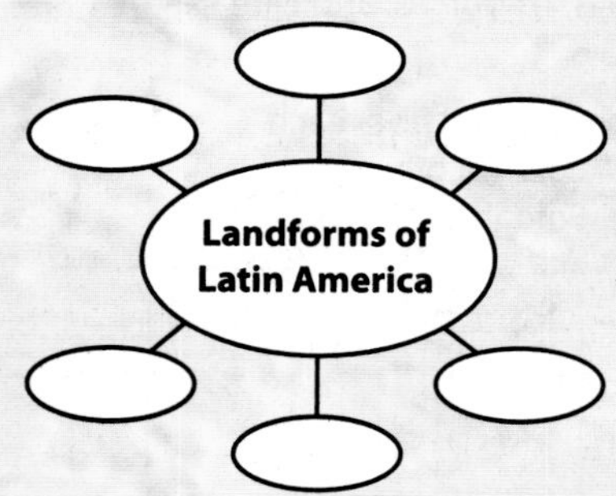

Picture This How do you farm when there is no flat land? The Inca, an advanced civilization that existed hundreds of years ago in Peru, used a method called terracing. They carved layered fields, like wide steps, into the mountainsides. Today, descendants of the Inca still use this method to raise crops at high altitudes. To learn how the physical landscape has affected other human activities, read Section 1.

▼ A terraced hillside near Pisac, Peru

Landforms

Main Idea **Mountains are prominent features in many parts of Latin America.**

Geography and You If you traveled across your state, what geographic features would you see? Read on to learn about the landforms that Latin Americans would encounter if they crossed their region.

Geographers divide the region of Latin America into three **subregions,** or smaller areas. These subregions are Middle America, the Caribbean, and South America.

Middle America

Middle America is made up of Mexico and Central America. Central America is an **isthmus** (IHS·muhs), or a narrow piece of land that links two larger areas of land—North America and South America. Middle America lies where four tectonic plates meet. As a result, it has active volcanoes and frequent earthquakes. Deposits of ash and lava make the soil fertile.

Mexico has mountain ranges along its eastern and western coasts with a high plateau between. Farther south, mountains rise like a backbone through Central America. Lowlands along the coasts are often narrow. Thick forests, rugged mountains, and coastal marshes make it difficult to **transport** goods in Central America.

The Caribbean

The islands of the Caribbean Sea, also known as the West Indies, can be divided into three groups: the Greater Antilles, the Lesser Antilles, and the Bahamas. The Greater Antilles include the largest islands—Cuba, Hispaniola, Puerto Rico, and Jamaica. The Lesser Antilles is an **archipelago** (AHR·kuh·PEH·luh·GOH), or group of islands. It curves from the Virgin Islands to Trinidad. The third group is the Bahamas, another archipelago.

NATIONAL GEOGRAPHIC

Andean Village

In the Andes, most people live in valleys and work fields that have been cut into the hillsides.
Regions **Besides the Andes, what is South America's other major landform?**

Except for the largest islands, most Caribbean islands are small. Cuba alone has about half of the Caribbean's land area. Some islands are very low-lying. Others, formed by volcanoes, have rugged mountains. Some of the volcanoes are still active and can cause great damage. Farmers use the fertile volcanic soil here to grow crops such as sugarcane and tobacco.

South America

The Andes mountain ranges and the vast Amazon Basin are South America's major landforms. The Andes are a cordillera (KAWR·duhl·YEHR·uh), which is a group of mountain ranges that run side by side. They stretch along the Pacific coast of South America for about 5,500 miles (8,851 km). Many peaks in the Andes soar over 20,000 feet (6,096 m). Between the mountain chains lie plateaus and valleys.

That is where most people **reside,** or live, and the land can be farmed.

East of the Andes is the huge Amazon Basin. This low area contains the Amazon River and covers 2.7 million square miles (7.0 million sq. km). Highlands to the north and south border the basin. The Brazilian Highlands are so vast that they cross several climate zones. They end in an **escarpment,** a series of steep cliffs that drop down to the Atlantic coastal plain.

Other lowland plains are found north and south of the Amazon Basin. Tropical grasslands known as the **Llanos** (LAH·nohs) stretch through eastern Colombia and Venezuela. Another well-known plain, the **Pampas,** covers much of Argentina and Uruguay. Like North America's Great Plains, the Pampas is used for cattle herding and grain farming.

Reading Check **Identifying** What areas make up Middle America?

The Pampas

NATIONAL GEOGRAPHIC

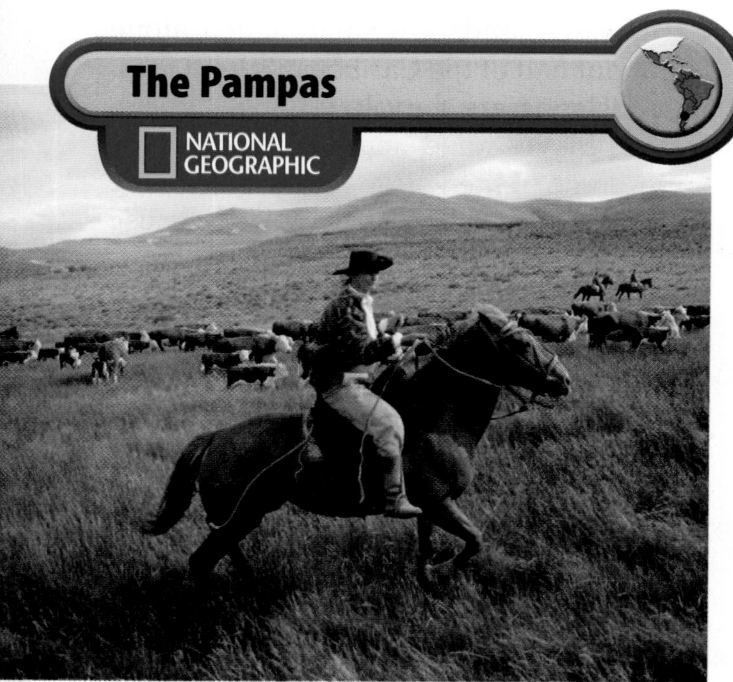

Herding cattle is a major economic activity on the Pampas of Argentina and Uruguay. ***Place*** **What are the Llanos?**

Waterways

Main Idea **Latin America's waterways provide important transportation routes.**

Geography and You What major rivers flow through your part of the country? How are they important to your area? Read on to find out about the amazing Amazon, one of the world's longest rivers.

Latin America has many natural rivers and lakes, most of which are in South America. The people of the region have used these waterways for transportation and water resources for ages.

Rivers

Latin America's longest river is the Amazon, which starts in the Andes and flows east about 4,000 miles (6,437 km) to the Atlantic Ocean. Heavy rains and many tributaries feed the Amazon. A **tributary** is a small river that flows into a larger river. Some ships can follow the Amazon as far west as Peru, more than 2,500 miles (4,023 km) inland. People also rely on the river for its fish.

Three rivers—the Paraná (PAH·rah·NAH), Paraguay (PAH·rah·GWY), and Uruguay (oo·roo·GWY)—form Latin America's second-largest river system. Together, they drain a large portion of central and eastern South America. After winding through inland areas, the three rivers flow into a broad estuary. An **estuary** is an area where river currents and ocean tides meet. This estuary, the Río de la Plata, or "River of Silver," meets the Atlantic Ocean.

Social Studies  **ONLINE**

Student Web Activity Visit glencoe.com and complete the Chapter 4 Web Activity about the Amazon River.

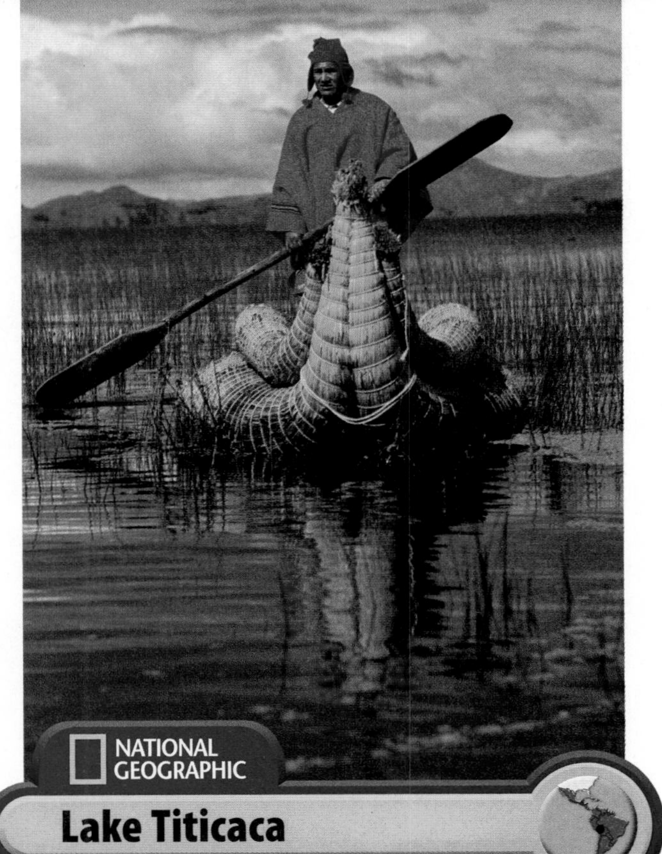

NATIONAL GEOGRAPHIC

Lake Titicaca

For hundreds of years, the native peoples around Lake Titicaca have traveled its waters using boats made from reeds. ***Place*** **What is unique about Lake Titicaca?**

The Orinoco is an important river in northern South America. It carries fertile soil into the Llanos region of Venezuela.

Other Waterways

Lake Maracaibo in Venezuela is Latin America's largest lake. The lake has many of Venezuela's oil fields. Pollution from this oil is a growing problem, though. Lake Titicaca, which lies between Bolivia and Peru, sits at about 12,500 feet (3,810 m) above sea level. It is the world's highest lake that can be used by large ships. The Panama Canal, a human-made waterway, crosses the narrow Isthmus of Panama. Ships use the canal to shorten the travel time between the Atlantic and Pacific Oceans.

Reading Check **Identifying** Why is Lake Maracaibo important to Venezuela?

A Wealth of Natural Resources

Main Idea **Latin America has vast natural resources, but political and economic troubles have kept some countries from fully using them.**

Geography and You Do you use aluminum foil to wrap dinner leftovers? Bauxite, a mineral used to make aluminum, is an important resource on the Caribbean island of Jamaica. Read to find out about the kinds of mineral wealth in Latin America.

Latin America has many natural resources. These include minerals, forests, farmland, and water. Not all of Latin America's countries, however, share equally in this wealth. Remote locations, lack of money for development, and the wide gap between rich and poor have kept many of the region's natural resources from being fully developed.

Brazil's Abundant Resources

Brazil, the largest country in Latin America, possesses a great wealth of natural resources. More than 55 percent of Brazil is covered in forests, including a large area of tropical rain forests. The rain forests provide timber and a range of products such as rubber, palm oil, and Brazil nuts.

Brazil also has great mineral wealth. It has large amounts of bauxite, gold, and tin. Its deposits of iron ore and manganese help support one of the world's largest iron and steel industries. Brazil's oil and natural gas reserves, however, are limited. They provide only some of the energy this huge country needs. To reduce its dependence on oil imports, Brazil uses alcohol produced from sugarcane and gasoline to produce a fuel for cars called **gasohol**.

Energy Resources

In addition to Brazil, other countries of Latin America have energy resources. Venezuela has the region's largest oil and natural gas reserves. Mexico has large amounts of oil and natural gas along the coast of the Gulf of Mexico. Both Mexico and Venezuela use the supplies for their own energy needs as well as for exports.

Bolivia and Ecuador also have valuable oil and natural gas deposits. In Bolivia, however, foreign companies have attempted to control the country's energy resources. Bolivia's government has struggled to prevent this. As a result, production has slowed, and Bolivia has not been able to fully benefit from exports.

Other Resources

Other mineral resources found in Latin America include silver mined in Mexico and Peru. Venezuela has rich iron ore deposits and is a major exporter of the mineral. Colombian mines produce the world's finest emeralds. Chile is the world's largest exporter of copper.

By contrast, the Caribbean islands have relatively few mineral resources, with a few important exceptions. Jamaica has large deposits of bauxite, a mineral used to make aluminum. In addition, Cuba mines nickel, and the Dominican Republic mines gold and silver.

Certain Central American countries, such as Nicaragua and Guatemala, have rich gold deposits. However, political conflicts and transportation difficulties make mining these deposits difficult.

Reading Check **Analyzing** Why are some Latin American countries unable to make full use of their natural resources?

Section Review

Vocabulary

1. **Explain** the significance of:

a. subregion	**d.** escarpment	**g.** tributary
b. isthmus	**e.** Llanos	**h.** estuary
c. archipelago	**f.** Pampas	**i.** gasohol

Main Ideas

2. **Describing** Describe the various mountains found throughout Middle America, the Caribbean, and South America.

3. **Explaining** Use a chart like the one below to note the significance of the listed waterways.

Waterway	Significance
Amazon River	
Paraguay, Paraná, Uruguay system	
Orinoco River	

4. **Identifying** Which Latin American country has the greatest resources? What are they?

Critical Thinking

5. **BIG Idea** What effects can volcanoes have on the peoples and economies of a region?

6. **Challenge** Based on Latin America's natural resources and physical geography, do you think the region will become more important economically in the future? Explain your answer.

Writing About Geography

7. **Using Your FOLDABLES** Use your Foldable to write a paragraph giving examples of how physical geography has affected the lives of people in the region.

NATIONAL GEOGRAPHIC **Geography & History**

The Columbian Exchange

What do corn, beans, and potatoes have in common? All of these foods were first grown in the Americas.

Separate Worlds For thousands of years, people living in the Eastern Hemisphere had no contact with those living in the Western Hemisphere. This changed in 1492 when European explorer Christopher Columbus arrived in the Americas. Columbus's voyages began what became known as "the Columbian Exchange"—a transfer of people, animals, plants, and even diseases between the two hemispheres.

For Better and for Worse The Europeans brought many new things to the Americas. They brought horses, which helped the Native Americans with labor, hunting, and transportation. European farm animals, such as sheep, pigs, and cattle, created new sources of income for people in the Americas. Europeans also brought crops—oats, wheat, rye, and barley. The sugarcane brought by Europeans grew well on plantations in the tropical Americas.

▲ **Tomato sauce on Italian pasta**

Some parts of the Exchange were disastrous, however. Europeans brought diseases that killed millions of Native Americans. Plantation owners put enslaved Africans to work in their fields.

From the Americas, explorers returned home with a wide variety of plants. Spanish sailors carried potatoes to Europe. Nutritious and easy to grow, the potato became one of Europe's most important foods. Corn from the Americas fed European cattle and pigs. Peanuts, tomatoes, hot peppers, and chocolate changed the diets of people in Europe, Asia, and Africa.

▼ **Mexican Indian making chocolate**

Think About It

1. **Place** What foods were unknown in Europe before 1492?
2. **Human-Environment Interaction** Why were some foods adopted from the Americas so important in other parts of the world?

Guide to Reading

BIG Idea

The physical environment affects how people live.

Content Vocabulary

- Tropics *(p. 129)*
- rain forest *(p. 129)*
- canopy *(p. 130)*
- altitude *(p. 131)*

Academic Vocabulary

- facilitate *(p. 129)*
- considerable *(p. 130)*

Reading Strategy

Comparing and Contrasting Use a Venn diagram like the one below to compare and contrast the tropical rain forest and tropical savanna climate zones.

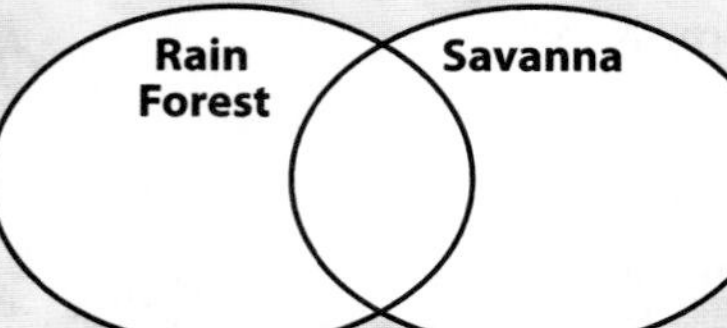

Climate Regions

Picture This These huge, 6-foot-wide water lilies are found deep in Brazilian rain forests near the mighty Amazon River. They are so strong that an average-sized adult could rest his or her full weight on them! The warm temperatures and heavy rains of the rain forest create an ideal growing environment for many exotic plants. To learn more about how climate affects the people, vegetation, and wildlife of Latin America, read Section 2.

▼ Rain forest water lilies

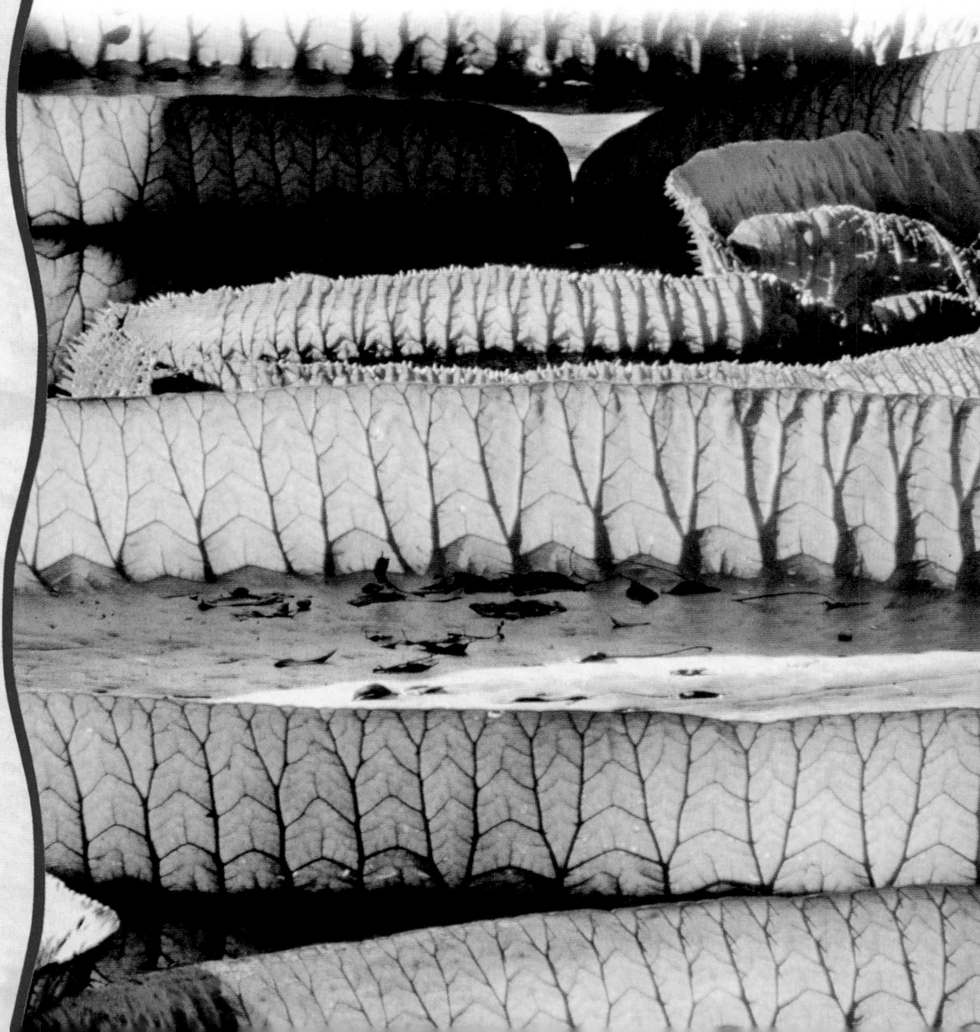

Hot to Mild Climates

Main Idea **Much of Latin America is located in the Tropics and has year-round high temperatures and heavy rainfall.**

Geography and You What might the view be like at the top of a rain forest tree 130 feet up? Read to find out why rain forests thrive in Latin America's tropical areas.

Most of Latin America lies within the **Tropics**—the area between the Tropic of Cancer and the Tropic of Capricorn. This area has generally warm temperatures because it receives the direct rays of the sun for much of the year. Yet even within the Tropics, mountain ranges and wind patterns create a variety of climates in the region. **Figure 1** shows Latin America's different climate zones.

Tropical Climates

A tropical wet climate is found in some Caribbean islands and much of Central America and South America. This climate is marked by year-round hot temperatures and heavy rainfall. Vast areas of rain forest cover much of this climate zone. A **rain forest** is a dense stand of trees and other plants that receive high amounts of precipitation. Warm temperatures and heavy rains **facilitate,** or make possible, the growth of rain forests.

South America's Amazon Basin is home to the world's largest rain forest.

NATIONAL GEOGRAPHIC Maps In MOtion See StudentWorks™ Plus or glencoe.com.

Figure 1 **Latin America: Climate Zones**

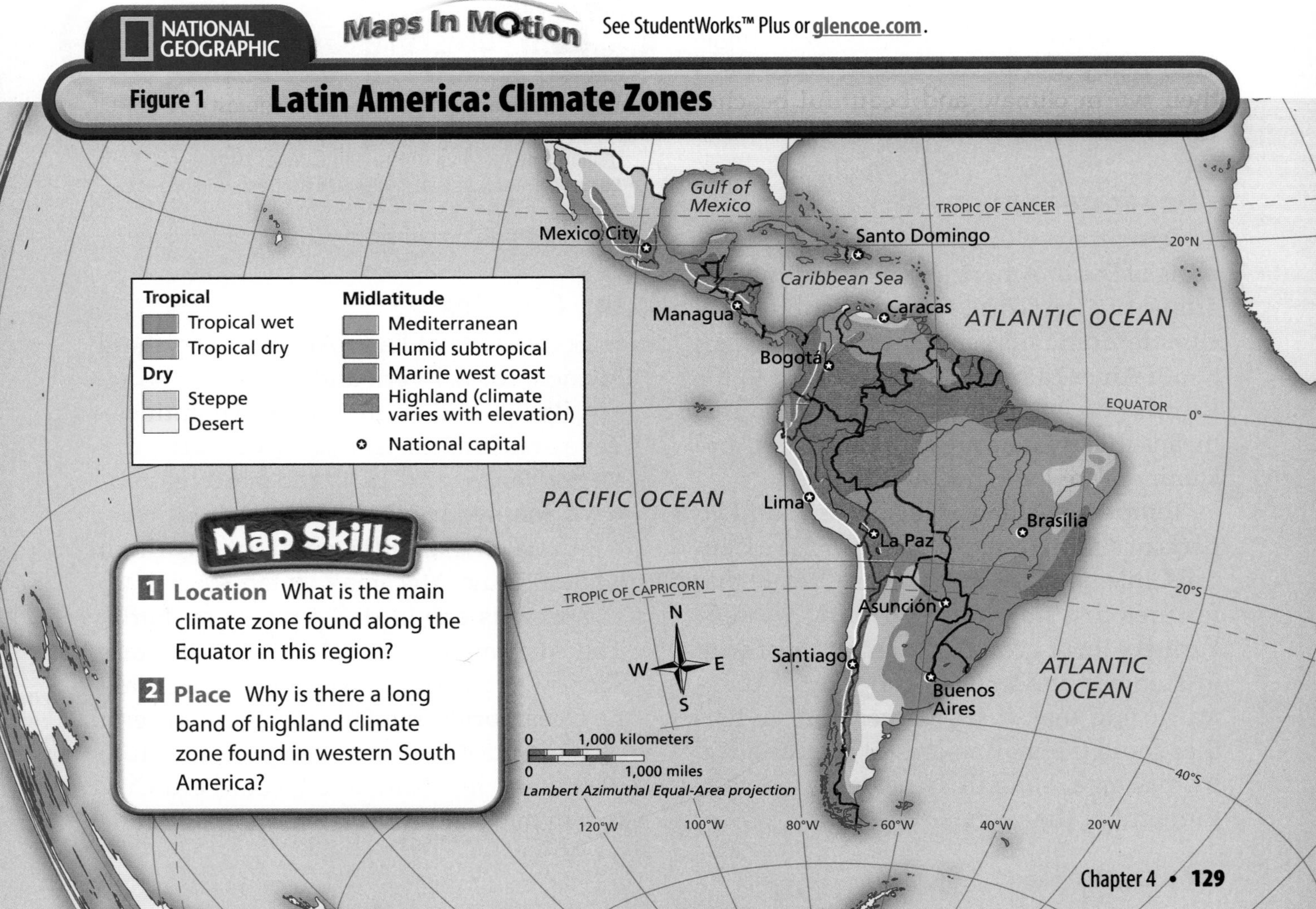

Map Skills

1 Location What is the main climate zone found along the Equator in this region?

2 Place Why is there a long band of highland climate zone found in western South America?

It shelters more species of plants and animals per square mile than anywhere else on Earth. Trees there grow so close together that their tops form a dense **canopy,** an umbrella-like covering of leaves. The canopy may soar to 130 feet (40 m) above the ground. It is so dense that sunlight seldom reaches the forest floor.

A tropical dry climate zone extends over parts of Middle America, most Caribbean islands, and north central South America. This savanna area has hot temperatures and abundant rainfall but also experiences a long dry season.

From June to November, powerful hurricanes often strike the Caribbean islands. The heavy winds and rain of these storms can cause **considerable,** or much, damage. Still, many Caribbean islands have used their warm climate and beautiful beaches to build a strong tourist industry.

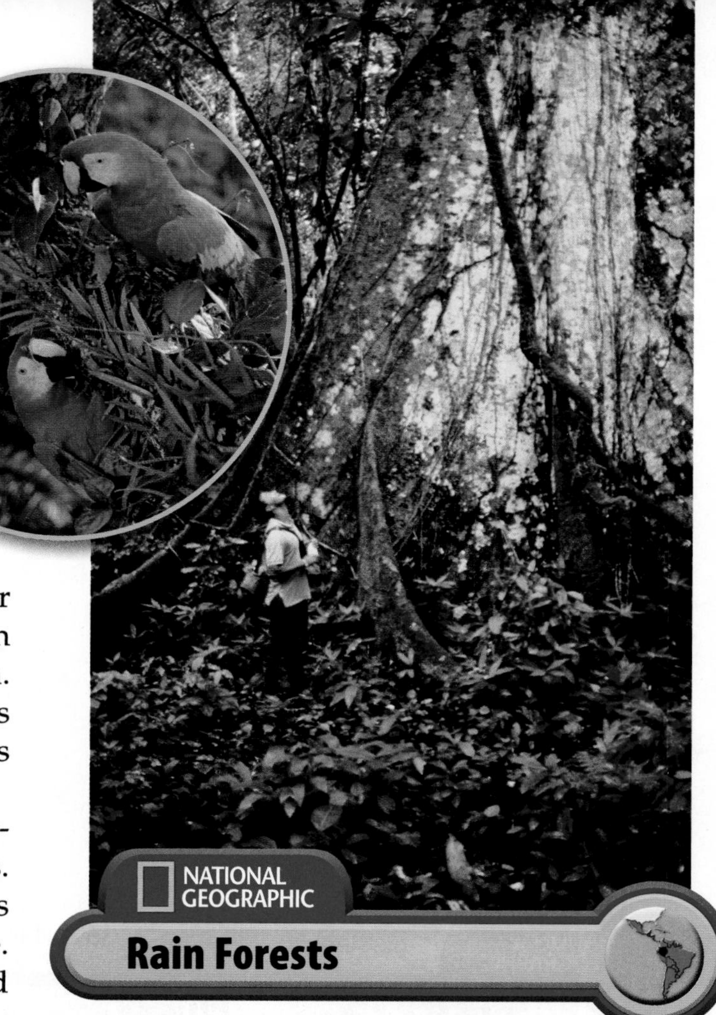

NATIONAL GEOGRAPHIC

Rain Forests

Vegetation can be dense on the rain forest floor. Many species of birds, including colorful macaws (inset), live in the rain forest canopy.
Location **Where is the world's largest rain forest found?**

Temperate Climates

Temperate climates are found in the parts of South America that lie south of the Tropic of Capricorn. A humid subtropical climate dominates much of southeastern South America from southern Brazil to the Pampas of Argentina and Uruguay. This means that winters are short and mild, and summers are long, hot, and humid.

Temperate climates also are found in parts of southwestern South America. Central Chile has a Mediterranean climate that features dry summers and rainy winters. Farmers there grow large amounts of fruit in summer and export it to North America during that area's winter season. Farther south is a marine coastal climate zone. In this area, rainfall is heavier and falls throughout the year.

Dry Climates

Some parts of Latin America—northern Mexico, coastal Peru and Chile, northeastern Brazil, and southeastern Argentina—have dry climates. Grasses cover partly dry steppe lands, and cacti and hardy shrubs have adapted to harsher desert areas.

Along the Pacific coast of northern Chile lies the Atacama (AH·tah·KAH·mah) Desert. It is one of driest places on Earth. The Atacama Desert is located in the rain shadow of the Andes. Winds from the Atlantic Ocean bring rainfall to the regions east of the Andes, but they carry no moisture past them. In addition, the cold Peru Current in the Pacific Ocean does not evaporate as much moisture as a warm current does. As a result, only dry air hits the coast.

El Niño

As you may recall, weather in South America is strongly influenced by the El Niño effect. This is a set of changes in air pressure, temperature, and rainfall that begins in the Pacific Ocean.

When El Niño takes place, the Pacific waters off Peru's coast are unusually warm. As a result, winds blowing toward land carry heavy rains that lead to severe flooding along Peru's coast. El Niño can also bring a long dry season to northeastern Brazil, causing crop failures.

Reading Check **Summarizing** Why do the Tropics tend to have warm temperatures?

Elevation and Climate

Main Idea **In tropical Latin America, altitude causes great changes in climate and vegetation.**

Geography and You Have you ever traveled in the mountains and felt it getting cooler as you went higher? Read to find out how mountains affect climate in tropical areas of Latin America.

As you have read, mountains and highlands cover much of Latin America. **Altitude**, a place's height above sea level, affects climate in these rugged areas. The higher the altitude is, the cooler the temperatures are—even within the warm areas of the Tropics. The Andes, for example, have four altitude zones of climate.

NATIONAL GEOGRAPHIC

Figure 2 **Altitude Climate Zones**

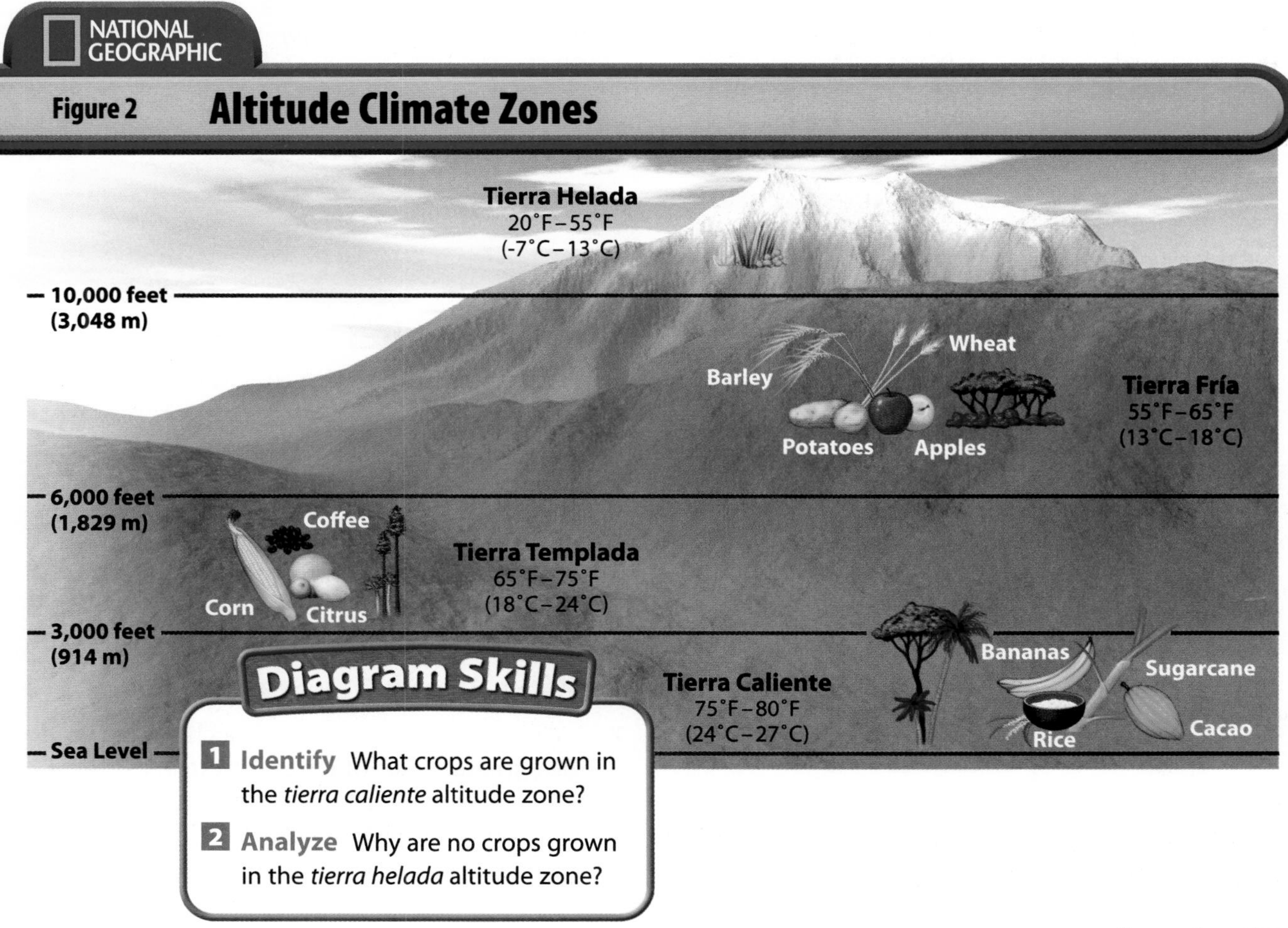

Diagram Skills

1. **Identify** What crops are grown in the *tierra caliente* altitude zone?
2. **Analyze** Why are no crops grown in the *tierra helada* altitude zone?

As **Figure 2** on the previous page shows, terms in the Spanish language are used to label the different zones.

The *tierra caliente,* or "hot land," refers to the hot and humid elevations near sea level. The average temperature range is between 75°F to 80°F (24°C to 27°C). There is little change from one month to another. In the *tierra caliente,* farmers grow a number of different tropical crops, including bananas, sugarcane, and rice.

Higher up the mountains—from 3,000 feet to 6,000 feet (914 m to 1,829 m), the air becomes cooler. Abundant rainfall encourages the growth of forests. This zone of moist, pleasant climates is called the *tierra templada,* or "temperate land." The mild temperatures—between 65°F and 75°F (18°C and 24°C)—make the *tierra templada* the most densely populated of the climate zones. Here, people grow corn and citrus fruits. Coffee, an important export crop in the region, is grown at this level.

The next zone is the *tierra fría,* or "cold land." It begins at 6,000 feet (1,829 m) and stretches up to 10,000 feet (3,048 m). Average yearly temperatures here can be as low as 55°F (13°C). The *tierra fría* has forested and grassy areas. Farming can take place in this zone in the warmer summers. The crops, however, are those that thrive in cooler, more difficult conditions. Potatoes, barley, and wheat are some of the major crops in this zone.

The *tierra helada,* or "frozen land," is the zone of highest elevation. It lies above 10,000 to 12,000 feet (3,048 m to 3,658 m). Conditions here can be harsh. The climate is cold, and the temperature can be as low as 20°F (–7°C). Vegetation throughout this zone is sparse. Relatively few people live at these heights.

Making Generalizations Why do people grow different crops at different altitudes?

Section 2 Review

Vocabulary

1. **Explain** the significance of *Tropics, rain forest, canopy,* and *altitude* by using each word in a sentence.

Main Ideas

2. **Identifying** Use a diagram like the one below to list the effects of El Niño.

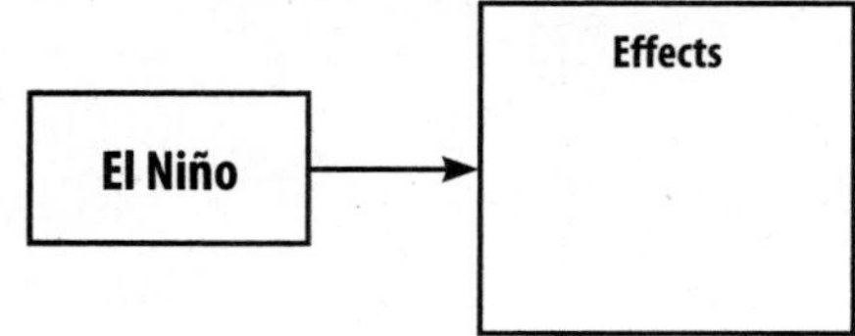

3. **Explaining** Why is the *tierra templada* the most populated altitude zone in the Latin American highlands?

Critical Thinking

4. **BIG Idea** How do some Caribbean countries benefit economically from their environment?
5. **Determining Cause and Effect** Why is the Pacific coast of northern Chile one of the driest places on Earth?
6. **Challenge** Why do parts of Latin America have mild temperatures even though they are located in the Tropics?

Writing About Geography

7. **Expository Writing** Create a chart that lists the climate zones of Latin America, explains where each zone is located, and describes the conditions and vegetation found in each zone.

Visual Summary

Tortola, British Virgin Islands

Landforms

- Geographers divide Latin America into three subregions—Middle America, the Caribbean, and South America.
- Middle America, which joins North America and South America, has central mountains and narrow coastal plains.
- Caribbean islands can be low-lying or mountainous. Many have volcanoes.
- The towering Andes and the vast Amazon Basin are South America's major landforms.
- Highlands border the Amazon Basin. Lowland plains cross parts of Colombia, Venezuela, Uruguay, and Argentina.

Waterways

- Latin America's waterways provide food and transportation.
- The Panama Canal, a human-made waterway, links the Atlantic and Pacific Oceans.
- Large reserves of oil are found near Venezuela's Lake Maracaibo.

An emerald from Colombia

Resources of Latin America

- Venezuela, Mexico, and Bolivia export oil and natural gas.
- Mineral resources from Latin America include iron ore, copper, tin, silver, and emeralds.
- Political conflicts and transportation difficulties keep some countries from fully using their resources.

Fishing on the Amazon River

Climate Regions

- Latin America's tropical rain forest and savanna climates have warm temperatures.
- Rain forests, such as those in the Amazon Basin, have a great variety of plant and animal life.
- The El Niño effect brings heavy rain or drought to parts of South America.
- Climates tend to be drier and cooler at higher elevations, even within the Tropics.

Andes, Chile

Study anywhere, anytime! Download quizzes and flash cards to your PDA from **glencoe.com**.

CHAPTER 4 ASSESSMENT

GA CRCT Practice

TEST-TAKING TIP

For multiple choice questions, try to answer the question first before you read the answer choices. Then, look for your answer among the choices.

Directions: Choose the best answer for each question.

1 **Which of the following make it difficult to transport goods in Central America?**

A active volcanoes
B thick forests and rugged mountains
C frequent flooding and overflowing rivers
D lack of roads

2 **Which natural resource has caused a pollution problem in Venezuela?**

A lumber
B coal
C iron ore
D oil

3 **Which of the following climates is found in most of Brazil?**

A temperate
B Mediterranean
C tropical
D dry

4 **Which two countries have the largest amount of oil and natural gas deposits in the region?**

A Mexico and Venezuela
B Brazil and Peru
C Cuba and Jamaica
D Chile and Colombia

5 **Which of the following statements is true about Cuba's land size?**

A It is the same as Brazil's.
B It is about the same size as Jamaica and Puerto Rico combined.
C It is about half of the Caribbean's total land area.
D It is one of the smallest Caribbean islands.

6 **Some Latin American countries have grown rich from natural resources. Why have other countries with similar resources remained poor?**

A They have a less educated population, and most people herd animals.
B The people who live there are not interested in mining natural resources.
C Those countries use government funds to pay for wars instead.
D The resources are in isolated locations, and there is a lack of money for development.

7 **How can El Niño affect northeastern Brazil's growing season?**

A It can create a long, dry season, causing crop failures.
B It can produce heavy rains that flood fields.
C It can generate high winds that destroy crops.
D It can cause hail storms that destroy the plants.

8 **Most of the Caribbean islands have fewer mineral resources than do Middle and South America. Which of the following does Cuba mine?**

A bauxite
B nickel
C gold
D silver

9 **Why do most people live in the *tierra templada* climate zone of Latin America?**

A It is the best zone in which to grow tropical crops.
B It is the zone that includes the ocean.
C It has mild temperatures throughout the year.
D It receives very little rainfall.

10 **Study the chart.**

Average Monthly Rainfall in Latin America		
	Manaus, Brazil	**Lima, Peru**
January	9.8 in. (24.9 cm)	0.1 in. (0.3 cm)
February	9.0 in. (23.1 cm)	0.0 in. (0.0 cm)
March	10.3 in. (26.2 cm)	0.0 in. (0.0 cm)
April	8.7 in. (22.1 cm)	0.0 in. (0.0 cm)
May	6.7 in. (17.0 cm)	0.2 in. (0.5 cm)
June	3.3 in. (8.4 cm)	0.2 in. (0.5 cm)
July	2.3 in. (5.8 cm)	0.3 in. (0.8 cm)
August	1.5 in. (3.8 cm)	0.3 in. (0.8 cm)
September	1.8 in. (4.6 cm)	0.3 in. (0.8 cm)
October	4.2 in. (10.7 cm)	0.1 in. (0.3 cm)
November	5.6 in. (14.2 cm)	0.1 in. (0.3 cm)
December	8.0 in. (20.3 cm)	0.0 in. (0.0 cm)
Source: BBC Weather Center, 2006.		

During which month does the average rainfall differ the least in Manaus and Lima?

A January
B May
C August
D December

11 **Based on the chart, which of the following statements is true?**

A Lima has a much drier climate than Manaus.
B The rainy season includes March in both cities.
C During Lima's rainy season, it receives more rainfall than Manaus.
D Throughout the year, rainfall averages for both cities are about the same.

12 **Based on the chart, during which two months does Manaus receive a total average of 20.1 inches of rain?**

A January and February
B March and April
C October and November
D January and March

13 **Read the document and answer the questions that follow.**

> *[Bolivian President] Morales, a former coca farmer and union leader, won a resounding victory in the December 2005 elections. As the Movement to Socialism (MAS) candidate, he campaigned in favor of nationalizing, among other sectors of the economy, the gas and oil industries with the cooperation of foreign investors. Experts say that, given such promises, the nationalization was no surprise. But Peter DeShazo, director of the Center for Strategic and International Studies' Americas Program, says the move to occupy the gas fields with military forces lent a dramatic effect. "The confrontational nature of his move was certainly intended to get people's attention," he says, adding that Morales may be looking to garner [gain] votes in July elections of a[n] . . . assembly that will redraft [rewrite] Bolivia's constitution.*
>
> Carin Zissis,
> "Bolivia's Nationalization of Oil and Gas"

What does it mean to "nationalize" the gas and oil industries?

A One large company takes over the smaller companies.
B The government takes control of the industries.
C The country's president becomes the sole owner of the companies.
D New companies are opened and located throughout the nation.

14 **According to the excerpt, who did President Morales send to take over the oil fields?**

A police
B lawmakers
C private citizens
D soldiers

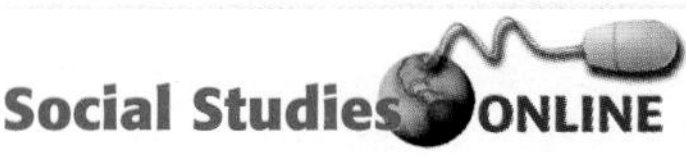

For additional test practice, use Self-Check Quizzes—Chapter 4 at glencoe.com.

Need Extra Help?

If You Missed Questions. . .	1	2	3	4	5	6	7	8	9	10	11	12	13	14
Go to Page. . .	123	125	129	126	123	125	131	126	132	129	129	129	126	126

History and Cultures of Latin America

Essential Question

Regions Common threads of language and religion unite Latin America. Once claimed as European colonies, Latin American countries today are primarily Roman Catholic, and most still use either Spanish or Portuguese as the official language. These two languages are based on Latin, which is how the region gets its name. In what ways can language and religion both unite and divide a region?

Section 1: History and Governments

BIG IDEA All living things are dependent upon one another and their surroundings for survival. Native American civilizations of Latin America developed ways of living that used the resources of their environment. People who lived in different areas depended on trade to obtain the goods they wanted. In colonial times, the people of Latin America exchanged goods with Europeans.

Section 2: Cultures and Lifestyles

BIG IDEA The characteristics and movement of people impact physical and human systems. The different groups who have settled Latin America include Native Americans, Europeans, Africans, and Asians. These groups have influenced the cultures and lifestyles of the region.

Organizing Information Make this Foldable to help you organize information about the history, peoples, cultures, and daily life of Latin America.

Step 1 Fold a sheet of paper in half lengthwise. Leave a ½-inch tab along the left edge.

Step 2 Cut the top layer only to make four equal tabs.

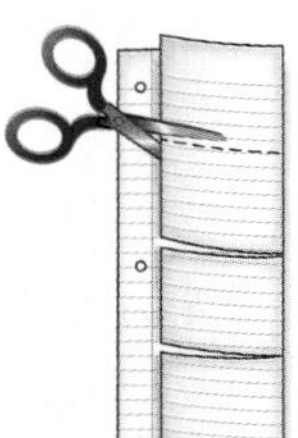

Step 3 Label the tabs as shown.

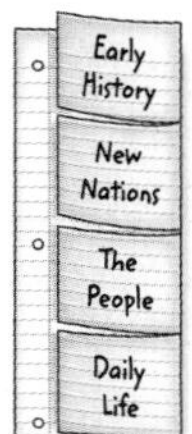

Reading and Writing Use the notes in your Foldable to write a short essay that describes the development of the countries and peoples of Latin America.

◀ Murals by Diego Rivera, Mexico City, Mexico

Visit glencoe.com and enter QuickPass™ code GA6EOW6225c5 for Chapter 5 resources.

Guide to Reading

BIG Idea

All living things are dependent upon one another and their surroundings for survival.

Content Vocabulary

- maize *(p. 139)*
- jade *(p. 139)*
- obsidian *(p. 139)*
- hieroglyphics *(p. 139)*
- empire *(p. 140)*
- cash crop *(p. 141)*
- caudillo *(p. 143)*
- communist state *(p. 145)*

Academic Vocabulary

- complex *(p. 140)*
- transform *(p. 141)*
- stable *(p. 143)*
- revolution *(p. 145)*

Reading Strategy

Identifying Central Issues Use a chart like the one below to organize key facts about the Native American civilizations of the region.

	Key Facts
Olmec	
Maya	
Toltec	
Aztec	
Inca	

History and Governments

 **Section Audio**  **Spotlight Video**

Picture This A Maya village in Guatemala remembers its dead in a spectacular way. For their Day of the Dead celebration—when people remember relatives and friends who have died—villagers create enormous kites of tissue paper, bamboo, and wire. Finished kites can reach 40 feet across! Sailing above local cemeteries, the kites create a symbolic link between the living and the dead. Read this section to learn more about the historical traditions that have shaped Latin America.

▼ **Ready to fly in Guatemala**

Early History

Main Idea **Some Native Americans developed advanced civilizations in the region. Europeans later conquered much of the region and set up colonies.**

Geography and You What sorts of things do you like to read? History books, novels, comics? Read to find out what kinds of things the Maya wrote down.

The first people to arrive in Latin America were the ancestors of today's Native Americans. They came many thousands of years ago. Some settled and farmed. Eventually, some groups developed advanced civilizations. **Figure 1** on the next page shows these Native American civilizations.

Early Native American Civilizations

The Olmec of southern Mexico built Latin America's first civilization, which lasted from 1500 B.C. to 300 B.C. Each Olmec city focused on a certain activity, and they all depended on one another. Some cities were located near farming areas that grew **maize,** or corn, as well as squash and beans. Others controlled important mineral resources such as **jade,** a shiny green semiprecious stone; and **obsidian,** a hard, black, volcanic glass useful in making weapons. Some cities were religious centers with pyramid-shaped stone temples.

A people called the Maya lived in Mexico's Yucatán (YOO·kah·TAHN) Peninsula and surrounding areas between A.D. 300 and A.D. 900. The Maya also built huge, pyramid-shaped stone temples. They were skilled at astronomy and used their knowledge of the stars, moon, and planets to develop a calendar. They also had a number system based on 20. Using **hieroglyphics** (HY·ruh·GLIH·fihks), which is a form of writing that uses signs and symbols, the Maya recorded the history of their kings. About A.D. 900, the Maya civilization mysteriously collapsed. Despite intensive research, historians have not yet been able to determine what happened to the Maya.

NATIONAL GEOGRAPHIC

Maya Architecture

A steep stairway leads to a temple at the top of the Pyramid of the Magician. The Maya built the pyramid about A.D. 800. ***Place*** **How did the Maya record their history?**

Toltec, Aztec, and Inca

As the Maya civilization declined, a people called the Toltec seized what is now northern Mexico. These warriors built the city of Tula, northwest of present-day Mexico City. From Tula, they conquered lands and peoples all the way to the Yucatán Peninsula in the south.

Toltec rulers tightly controlled trade. They held a monopoly (muh·NAH·puh·lee), or sole right, to the trade in obsidian. As a result, the Toltec had the most powerful weapons in the surrounding areas. For many years this weaponry gave them the advantage they needed to maintain their rule.

Around A.D. 1200, the Aztec people from the north moved into central Mexico and captured Tula. They adopted Toltec culture, conquered neighboring peoples, and took control of the region's trade.

NATIONAL GEOGRAPHIC Maps In MOtion See StudentWorks™ Plus or glencoe.com.

Figure 1 **Native American Civilizations**

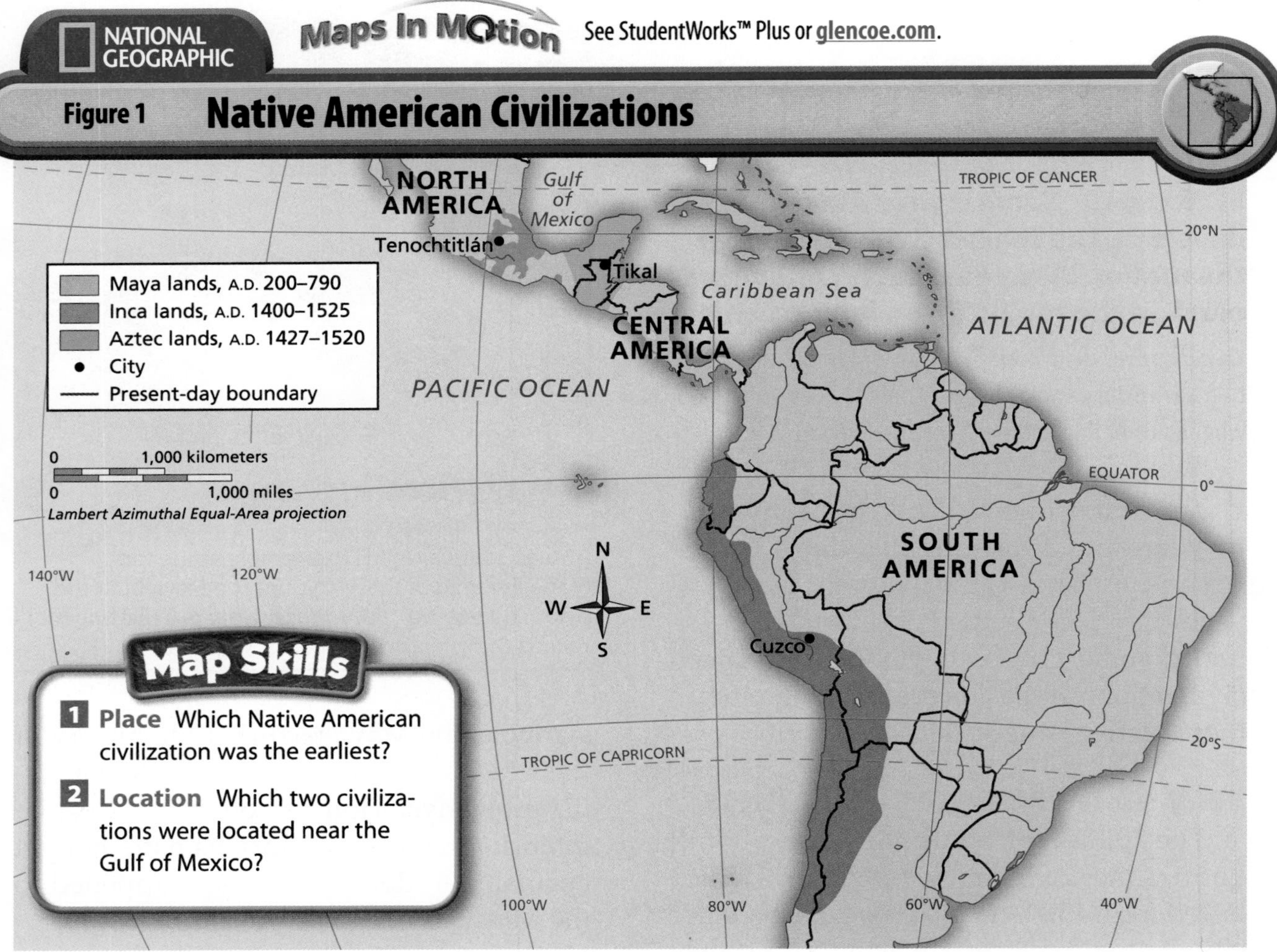

Map Skills

1 **Place** Which Native American civilization was the earliest?

2 **Location** Which two civilizations were located near the Gulf of Mexico?

Tenochtitlán (tay·NAWCH·teet·LAHN), the Aztec capital, was a beautiful city built on an island in a lake. It held about 250,000 people, which was a large population at that time. Tenochtitlán had huge temples, including one that was more than 100 feet (30 m) tall. Roads and bridges joined the city to the mainland, allowing the Aztec to bring food and other goods to their busy markets. Aztec farmers grew their crops on "floating gardens," or rafts filled with mud. The rafts eventually sank to the lake bottom and piled up. Over time, many of these rafts formed fertile islands.

During the 1400s, the Inca had a powerful civilization in South America in what is now Peru. Their empire stretched more than 2,500 miles (4,023 km) along the Andes. An **empire** is a large territory with many different peoples under one ruler. The Inca ruler founded military posts and put in place a **complex,** or highly developed, system of record keeping. Work crews built irrigation systems, roads, and suspension bridges that linked regions of the empire to Cuzco, the capital. You can still see the remains of magnificent fortresses and buildings erected centuries ago by the skilled Inca builders.

European Conquests

In the late 1400s and early 1500s, Spanish explorers arrived in the Americas. They were greatly impressed by the magnificent cities and the great riches of the Native Americans.

In 1519 a Spanish army led by Hernán Cortés landed on Mexico's Gulf coast.

He and about 600 soldiers marched to Tenochtitlán for Aztec gold. Some Native Americans who opposed the harsh rule of the Aztec joined them. Cortés seized the Aztec ruler, Montezuma (MAHN·tuh·ZOO·muh), who later was killed. As the two sides warred, the Aztec's simple weapons were no match for the guns, cannons, and horses of the Spanish. The Spanish also had unseen allies. They brought germs that carried diseases, such as measles and smallpox, that killed many more Aztec than the Spanish weapons. In just two years, Cortés conquered the Aztec.

Another Spanish explorer, Francisco Pizarro, desired the gold and silver of the Inca. In 1531 Pizarro took a small force of Spanish soldiers to South America. The Inca had already been weakened by smallpox and other European diseases. The Spanish attacked the Inca with guns, cannons, and swords, killing many. Pizarro captured the Inca ruler, Atahuallpa (AH·tuh·WAHL·puh) and had him killed. Soon after, Pizarro gained control of the Inca empire.

Colonial Latin America

The Aztec and Inca conquests provided Spain with enormous wealth and control over vast territories. Spain then built an empire that included much of South America, the Caribbean, Middle America, and parts of the present-day United States. Other European countries wanted the same power and influence that Spain had achieved. So, these countries seized different parts of the Americas. Portugal became the colonial ruler of what is today Brazil. France, Britain, and the Netherlands took control of some Caribbean areas and parts of North America.

European rule **transformed,** or greatly changed, the populations of these lands. Europeans settled the land, set up colonial governments, and spread Christianity among the Native Americans. They also used Native Americans as workers to grow **cash crops,** or farm products grown for export.

When hardship and disease greatly reduced the numbers of Native Americans, Europeans brought enslaved Africans to meet the labor shortage. A busy trade eventually resulted. Ships carried enslaved people from Africa and manufactured goods from Europe to the Americas. On the return trip, products including sugar, cotton, tobacco, gold, and silver went from the Americas to Europe. Despite European control, many Native American and African ways survived, leading to a blending of cultures.

Reading Check **Explaining** Why did the Spanish conquer Native American empires?

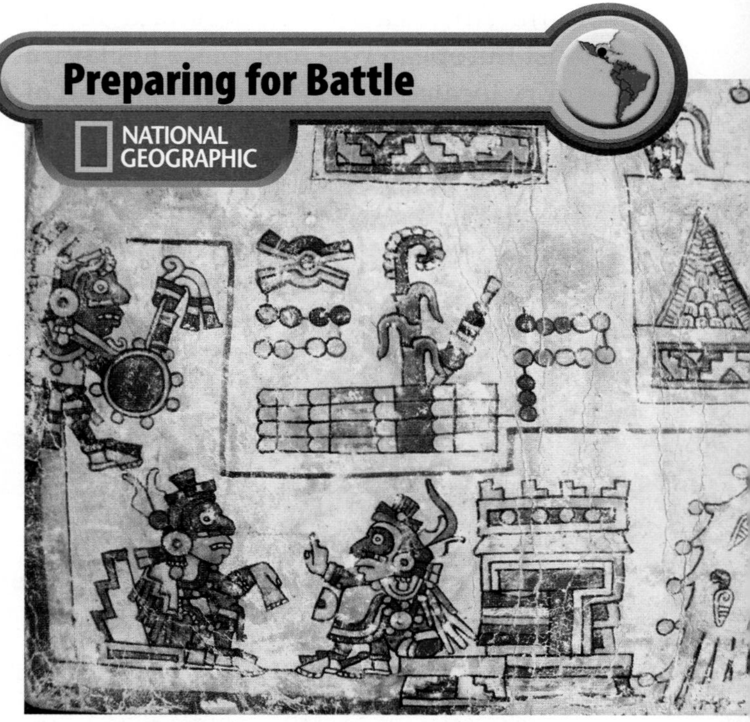

In this drawing, Native American chiefs opposed to the Aztec discuss whether to join with Cortés's forces. ***Regions*** **Why did some Native Americans support the Spanish?**

Forming New Nations

Main Idea **Most of Latin America gained independence in the 1800s, but hardships followed for many of the new nations.**

Geography and You Suppose you have just been elected class president. What challenges would you face? Read to find out what challenges faced new governments in Latin America.

In the late 1700s, revolutions in North America and France stirred the people of Latin America to action. Colonists tried to take charge of their own affairs. While European colonists called for self-rule, Native Americans and enslaved Africans wanted freedom from mistreatment and slavery.

Independence

Latin America's first successful revolt against European rule took place in Haiti, a territory located on the Caribbean island of Hispaniola. There, enslaved Africans under François-Dominique Toussaint-Louverture began a revolt that threw off French rule in 1804. Haiti, which was established as a republic, became the only nation ever created as a result of a successful revolt by enslaved people.

In Spanish and Portuguese Latin America, the fight for freedom increased in the next decade. In Mexico, two Catholic priests, Miguel Hidalgo and José María Morelos, urged poorer Mexicans to fight for freedom from Spanish rule. Both men were defeated and executed.

Despite many battles, Mexicans did not gain their independence until 1821. After a short period of rule under an emperor, Mexico became a republic in 1823. That same year, the countries of Central America won their freedom from Spain.

In northern South America, a wealthy military leader named Simón Bolívar (see·MOHN buh·LEE·VAHR) led the fight for independence. In 1819 Bolívar defeated the Spanish and won freedom for the present-day countries of Venezuela, Colombia, Ecuador, and Bolivia.

While Bolívar fought for self-rule in the north, a soldier named José de San Martín (hoh·SAY day SAN MAHR·TEEN) was fighting for freedom in the south. In 1817 San Martín led his army from Argentina across the Andes Mountains and into Chile. Although the crossing was difficult, San Martín was able to take Spanish forces by surprise, and

c. 1400s, Aztec mask

Atahuallpa, last Inca ruler

he began winning battles. A few years later, the armies of San Martín and Bolívar jointly defeated Spanish forces in Peru.

Political and Economic Challenges

By the end of 1824, all of Spain's colonies in Latin America had won their independence. The 1820s also saw Brazil break away from Portugal without bloodshed. Brazil was the only independent monarchy in Latin America before becoming a republic in 1889.

After winning independence, many of the new Latin American countries passed laws that ended slavery. Some people of African descent made economic and political gains. However, they generally did not have the advantages of Latin Americans of European background. On the other hand, African Latin Americans were better off than Native Americans, most of whom lived in poverty.

Although independent, many Latin American nations hoped their countries would become **stable,** or secure, democracies with prosperous economies. Because of a variety of problems, these goals proved hard to reach.

One major problem was frequent political conflict. Latin Americans quarreled over the role of religion in their society. Individual countries fought over boundary lines, and tensions developed within countries between the rich and poor.

Meanwhile, strong leaders made it difficult for democracy and prosperity to develop. These leaders were known as caudillos (kow·THEE·yohs). **Caudillos** were usually high-ranking military officers or rich men supported by the upper class. They often ruled as dictators. Some built roads, schools, and new cities.

Many caudillos, however, favored the wealthy over the poor. Wealthy Latin Americans owned almost all of the land. The caudillos did nothing to help workers in the countryside. The workers remained landless and struggled to make a living.

Exporting Products

During the late 1800s, Latin America's economy depended on agriculture and mining. At this time, the United States and other industrial countries in Europe began to demand more of Latin America's food products and mineral resources. Businesspeople from these outside countries set up companies throughout Latin America. The companies exported Latin American products such as bananas, sugar, coffee, copper, and oil.

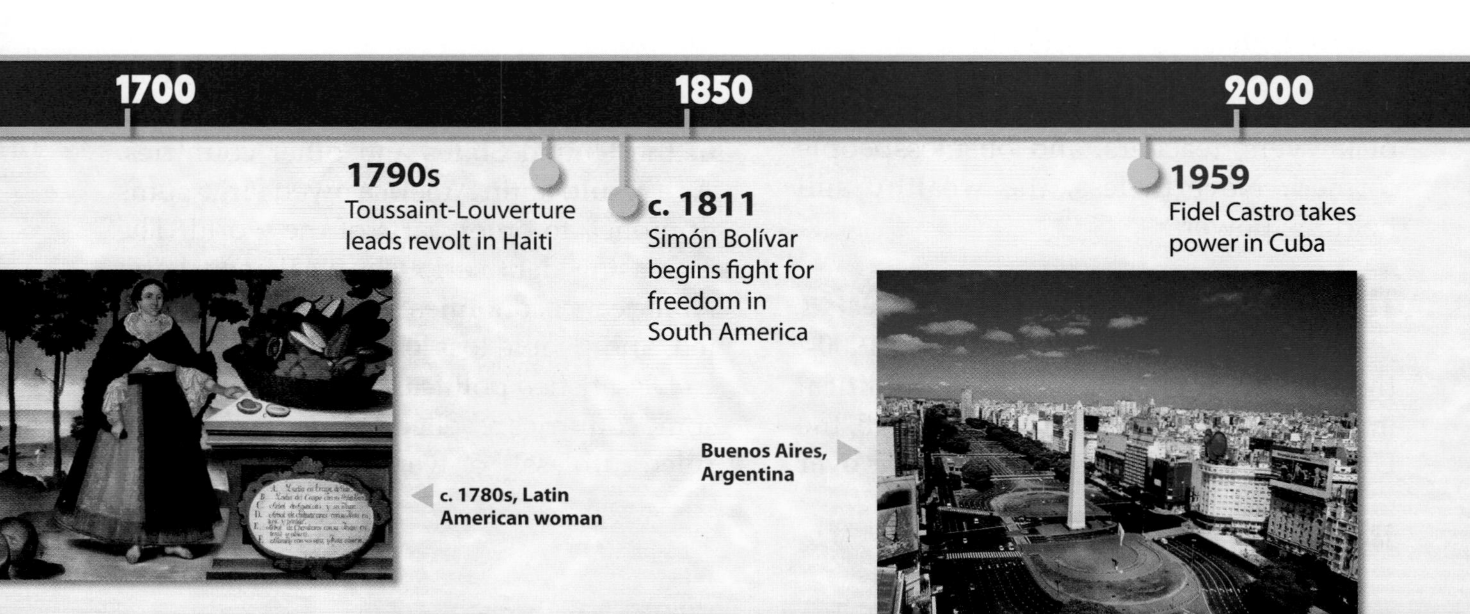

c. 1780s, Latin American woman

Buenos Aires, Argentina

Panama Canal

The Panama Canal was built between 1904 and 1914. Today about 14,000 ships go through the canal each year (inset). ***Place*** **How did the Panama Canal affect the U.S. role in Latin America?**

As the number of exports rose, some Latin American countries chose to grow only one or two key products. Prices and profits increased as a result, but a decline in demand had serious effects. Prices dropped, and people lost income and jobs.

Despite the problems it caused, Latin America's dependence on exports also brought benefits. Foreign investors built ports, roads, and railroads. Cities grew in size and population, and a middle class of lawyers, teachers, and businesspeople formed. Nevertheless, the wealthy still held the power.

The United States and Latin America

During the late 1800s and early 1900s, the United States increased its political influence in Latin America. In 1898 the United States and Spain fought a war over Spanish-ruled Cuba. Spain was defeated, and Cuba became a republic under U.S. protection. The United States also gained control of the Caribbean island of Puerto Rico.

In 1903 the United States helped Panama win its freedom from Colombia. In return, Panama allowed the United States to build the Panama Canal. Over the next 25 years, American troops landed in Haiti, Nicaragua, and the Dominican Republic to protect U.S. political and economic interests.

Many Latin Americans distrusted the United States because of its great wealth and power. They thought the United States might try to control them as their former rulers had. To improve relations, the United States announced the Good Neighbor Policy toward Latin America in the 1930s. Under this policy, the United States promised not to send military forces to Latin America. It also pledged a greater respect for the rights of Latin American countries.

Modern Times

In the mid-1900s, agriculture was still important in Latin America, but many industries had developed there as well. To encourage economic growth, Latin American leaders borrowed heavily from banks in the United States and other countries. As a result, Latin America owed large sums of money to other parts of the world. The increasing debt seriously weakened Latin American economies. Prices rose, wages fell, and people lost jobs.

Dissatisfied political and social groups in some countries rebelled against leaders who ruled ruthlessly or were in power too long.

For example, in 1959 a young lawyer named Fidel Castro carried out a **revolution,** or a sudden, violent change of government, in Cuba. Instead of favoring democracy, Castro set up a **communist state,** in which the government controlled the economy and society.

At the same time, other countries were divided by civil wars among political, ethnic, or social groups. In El Salvador, fighters supported by Castro battled government troops armed by the United States. Thousands of people died before a settlement ended the fighting.

Difficult economic and political reforms made during the 1980s helped strengthen many Latin American countries. These changes were often very harsh, which turned many Latin Americans against dictators. During the 1990s, democratic movements succeeded in several countries.

Today's Latin American governments face many challenges. Population is growing rapidly, but resources are limited. Growing trade in illegal drugs has increased crime and corruption. Differences between rich and poor still create social tensions. In the early 2000s, angry voters in Venezuela, Bolivia, Peru, Mexico, and Chile elected new leaders. These leaders promised significant changes that would weaken the power of the wealthy and benefit the poor.

Analyzing Information Why were economies in Latin America hurt by focusing on one or two products?

Section Review

Vocabulary

1. **Explain** the significance of:
   - **a.** maize
   - **b.** jade
   - **c.** obsidian
   - **d.** hieroglyphics
   - **e.** empire
   - **f.** cash crop
   - **g.** caudillo
   - **h.** communist state

Main Ideas

2. **Comparing and Contrasting** Use a Venn diagram like the one below to show similarities and differences between the Aztec and Inca civilizations.

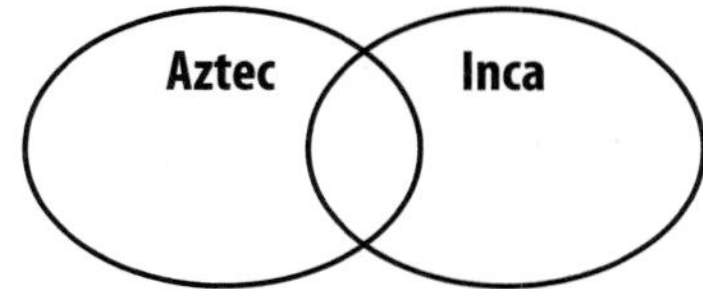

3. **Explaining** What was the social status of African Americans and Native Americans in the newly independent countries of Latin America?

Critical Thinking

4. **Drawing Conclusions** How did European colonial rule change the populations of the region?
5. **BIG Idea** How were the economies of Latin American colonies and European countries connected by trade?
6. **Challenge** Write a paragraph explaining whether you think U.S. involvement in Latin America has helped or hurt the region.

Writing About Geography

7. **Using Your FOLDABLES** Use your Foldable to write a paragraph that explains how political unrest in much of Latin America can be tied to social and economic challenges in the region.

The Darien Gap: Should a Highway Be Built?

The Pan-American Highway extends from Alaska to the tip of South America. The road stops short in Panama, at Darien National Park. In Colombia, the road starts again, where it continues for the length of South America. Roads have not been built through the Darien Gap because of its unique environment. Supporters of a road believe that it will help the region's economy and that the rain forest can still be preserved. Others, however, think that the forest could be lost forever.

Construction

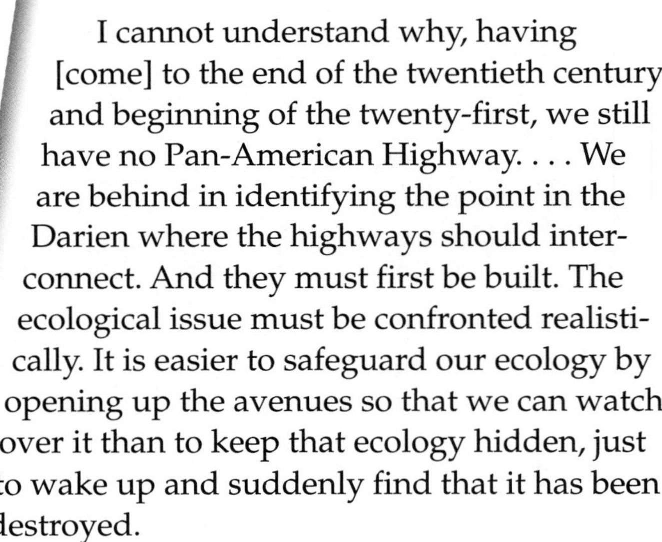

I cannot understand why, having [come] to the end of the twentieth century and beginning of the twenty-first, we still have no Pan-American Highway. . . . We are behind in identifying the point in the Darien where the highways should interconnect. And they must first be built. The ecological issue must be confronted realistically. It is easier to safeguard our ecology by opening up the avenues so that we can watch over it than to keep that ecology hidden, just to wake up and suddenly find that it has been destroyed.

—Alvaro Uribe Vélez
President of the
Republic of Colombia

Against Construction

I get very angry, seeing how the Panamanian economy . . . places value on felled trees and does not recognize the terrible damage to an area suffering constant deforestation. . . . One of the most comforting and encouraging sights that you can see today in the Darien is the presence of eco-tourists. . . . The worst enemy of a rain forest is the road. . . .

We should look at the Darien rain forest as a highly productive mine of eco-dollars. That is really the value of it. . . . If the Darien were to be lost, Panama would lose its soul, because nature is the base of everything.

—Hernan Arauz
Panamanian naturalist guide

You Be the Geographer

1. **Analyzing** What argument does Vélez make for building the highway?
2. **Critical Thinking** What does Arauz claim is an encouraging sight in the Darien Gap? Why do you think he feels that way?
3. **Read to Write** Write a paragraph describing how a road might benefit trade between North America and South America.

Cultures and Lifestyles

 Section Audio  Spotlight Video

Guide to Reading

BIG Idea

The characteristics and movement of people impact physical and human systems.

Content Vocabulary

- migration *(p. 149)*
- mestizo *(p. 151)*
- pidgin language *(p. 151)*
- carnival *(p. 154)*
- mural *(p. 154)*

Academic Vocabulary

- element *(p. 149)*
- comment *(p. 154)*
- style *(p. 154)*

Reading Strategy

Summarizing Use a diagram like the one below to summarize the cultures of Latin America by adding one or more facts to each of the outer boxes.

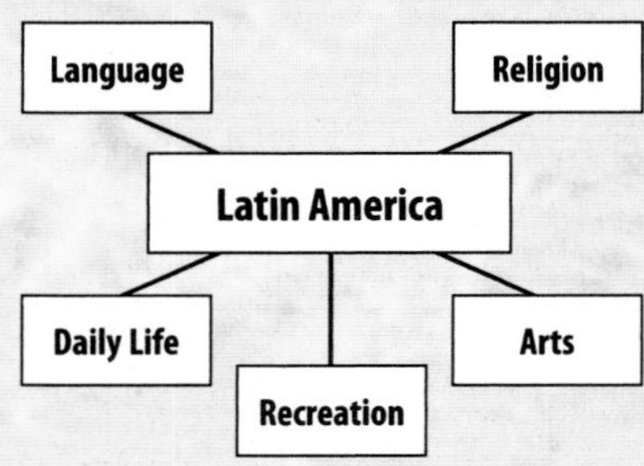

Picture This Teenage girls celebrate their African heritage during Trinidad's Children's Carnival Competition. Carnival is celebrated in the days before Lent begins. Lent is a time of prayer and fasting in the Roman Catholic Church. During carnival, both young people and adults dress in costumes. Costumes include characters from nursery rhymes and movie superheroes. As you read this section, you will learn about the different cultures of the people of Latin America.

▼ Celebration in Port-of-Spain, Trinidad

The People

Main Idea **Latin Americans come from a variety of cultures, but many share common characteristics.**

Geography and You Does anyone in your neighborhood speak a foreign language? Read to discover the mix of languages and cultures in Latin America.

Latin Americans come from many different backgrounds. Native Americans, Europeans, Africans, and others all have left their mark. Most Latin Americans today practice the Roman Catholic faith and speak either Spanish or Portuguese.

NATIONAL GEOGRAPHIC

A Young Population

About 30 percent of people in Latin America are age 15 and younger. In the United States, 21 percent are 15 and younger. ***Regions*** **Which area of Latin America has the highest birthrate?**

Population Patterns

Latin America has a high population growth rate. The region's highest birthrates are in Central America, except for Costa Rica, whose birthrate is relatively low. As a result, the Central American countries are growing most quickly in population. In fact, Guatemala and Honduras are expected to double in population by 2050.

Latin America's varied climates and landscapes affect where people live. Temperature extremes, rain forests, deserts, and mountains are common in many parts of Latin America. In these areas, harsh living conditions and poor soil limit where people live. As a result, most Latin Americans live in more favorable climates along the coasts of South America or in an area reaching from Mexico into Central America. These areas provide fertile land and easy access to transportation.

Migration

Migration, or the movement of people, has greatly shaped Latin America's population. In the past, Europeans, Africans, and Asians came to Latin America in large numbers, either willingly or by force. Today, people from places as far away as Korea and Syria come to Latin America looking for jobs or personal freedom.

In addition to people immigrating into the region, some leave Latin America for other parts of the world. Many Latin Americans move north to the United States to escape political unrest or to find a better way of life. Some go through the process of legally entering the United States, while others enter illegally. All of these new arrivals bring **elements,** or parts, of their culture with them. Most stay in close contact with family and friends in their home countries. Many also plan to return when economic conditions in their home countries improve.

Social Studies ONLINE

Student Web Activity Visit glencoe.com and complete the Chapter 5 Web Activity about Latin American populations.

Latin Americans also move within their country or the region. As in many parts of the world, Latin America's rural areas have increased greatly in population. In certain areas, this growth has resulted in a shortage of fertile land. Smaller farms cannot always support large families. People often leave to find jobs elsewhere, usually in cities. The result is urbanization, or the movement of people from the countryside to the cities.

Growth of Cities

In the past, most Latin Americans lived in the countryside and worked the land. Today most of them live in rapidly growing cities. Some of the largest urban areas in the world are in Latin America, including Mexico City, Mexico; São Paulo (sow POW·loo) and Rio de Janeiro (REE·oo dee zhah·NAY·roo) in Brazil; and Buenos Aires, Argentina.

The number of urban dwellers, however, varies throughout the region. In South America, about 80 percent of people live in cities—about the same as in the United States. In Central America and the Caribbean, only about 65 percent of people are urban dwellers.

Most Latin Americans leave villages for the cities to find better jobs, schools, housing, and health care. In many cases, people do not find what they seek. As city populations grow, jobs and housing become scarce. At the same time, rural dwellers often lack the education and skills to find good jobs. There have been too few schools and health care centers to serve the growing number of city dwellers. Unable to return to the countryside, many people have been forced by poverty to live in crowded neighborhoods with poor housing, lack of sanitation, and rising crime.

Once the capital city of Brazil, Rio de Janeiro remains an important center for trade and industry. ***Place*** **What percentage of South Americans live in cities?**

Ethnic Groups and Languages

Latin America's people include Native Americans, Europeans, Africans, Asians, and mixtures of these groups. The blend of ethnic groups varies from area to area.

Most of Latin America's Native Americans live in Mexico, Central America, and the Andes countries of Ecuador, Peru, and Bolivia. Great Native American empires thrived in these places before Europeans arrived there. Today, Native Americans work to keep their languages and traditions alive while adopting features of other cultures.

Since the 1400s, millions of Europeans have settled in Latin America. Most settlers have been Spanish or Portuguese. Over the years, other Europeans—Italians, British, French, and Germans—have come as well. In the 1800s, many Spanish and Italian immigrants settled in Argentina, Uruguay, and Chile. As a result, these three nations today are mainly populated by people of European descent.

African Latin Americans form a high percentage of the populations in the Caribbean islands and northeastern Brazil. They are descended from enslaved Africans whom Europeans brought as laborers during colonial days. Over the years, Africans have added their rich cultural influences to the food, music, and arts of Latin America.

Large Asian populations live in the Caribbean islands and some countries of South America. Most Asians came during the 1800s to work as temporary laborers. They remained and formed ethnic communities. In Guyana about one-half of the population is of South Asian or Southeast Asian ancestry. Many people of Chinese descent make their homes in Peru, Mexico, and Cuba. About 1 million people of Japanese descent live in Brazil, making Brazil home to the largest number of Japanese in one place outside of Japan.

Over the centuries, there has been a blending of the different ethnic groups throughout Latin America. In countries such as Mexico, Honduras, El Salvador, and Colombia, **mestizos,** or people of mixed Native American and European descent, make up the largest part of the population. In Cuba, the Dominican Republic, and Brazil, people of mixed African and European descent form a large percentage of the population.

Because Spain once ruled most of Latin America, Spanish is the most widely spoken language in the region. In Brazil, which was once a colony of Portugal, most people speak Portuguese. Native American languages are still spoken in many countries. For example, Quechua (KEH·chuh·wuh), spoken centuries ago by the Inca, is an official language of Peru and Bolivia. In the Caribbean, where the British and French once ruled many islands, English and French are widely spoken. In some countries, people have developed a **pidgin language** by combining parts of different languages. An example is Creole, spoken in Haiti. Most Creole words are from French, but sentence structure, or organization, reflects African languages.

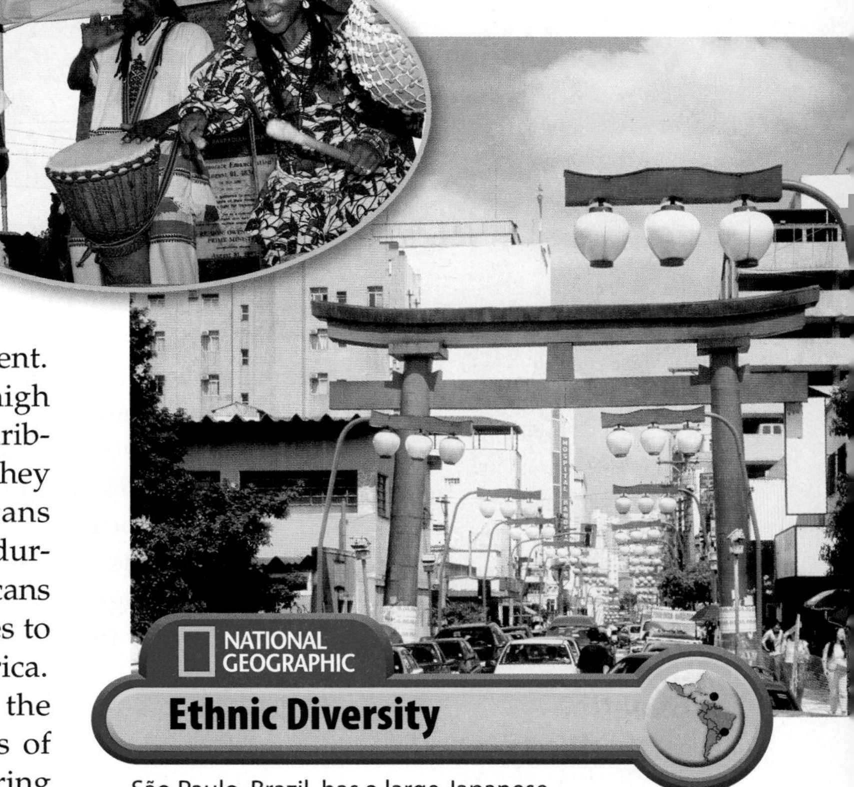

NATIONAL GEOGRAPHIC

Ethnic Diversity

São Paulo, Brazil, has a large Japanese community. Drummers in Barbados (inset) celebrate their African heritage. ***Place*** **What Latin American nations have populations that are mainly of European background?**

Reading Check **Analyzing** What challenges do Latin America's growing cities face?

Mexican Folktale

Folktales are stories that have no known author. They are the literature of the common people of a country or region. They express the views these people have about life, what is important to society, and how individuals are expected to behave.

Background Information

The folktales of Mexico reflect Mexican society. Like that society, they include a mix of Spanish and Native American cultures. Some tales point out the tensions between different social and ethnic groups. This folktale reflects basic Mexican values, including the respect that children owe to their parents.

Reader's Dictionary

crystal: expensive, high-quality glass

weevil: a kind of beetle

The Hard-Hearted Son

Mexican Folktale

There was an old couple who had a married son. They were very poor, and one day they went to visit their son to see if he would give them some corn and ask them to dinner. His corn bins were full, and his table was laid out with many good things. For dessert there was candy in a large dish made of **crystal.**

When he saw his parents coming, he told his wife, "There come those old people! Put the cover on the candy dish and hide the food, so we won't have to ask them to dinner."

The wife did so, and when his parents came in and saw it all, they asked their son for a few handfuls of corn. But he told them he didn't have anything, that he hadn't harvested his crop yet. "It's all right," his parents said. "God bless you and give you more." And they left.

When [the son and his wife] sat down to dinner, they found the food had spoiled. The man went to his corn bins and found it all eaten by **weevils.** He came back, and when he was going to eat the candy, a serpent came out and wound itself about his neck and strangled him.

It [wasn't] his parents' curse; rather, [it was] a punishment for his greed and hard-heartedness.

Analyzing Literature

1. **Making Inferences** What message does this tale give about how children should behave?
2. **Read to Write** Think about a kind of behavior or attitude that you think is important for people to have. Write a brief story like this one to illustrate why people should behave that way or have that attitude.

Daily Life

Main Idea Many aspects of daily life in Latin America reflect the region's blend of cultures.

Geography and You Do you enjoy eating tomatoes, potatoes, and chocolate? These foods were first eaten in Latin America. Read to find out about other features of Latin American daily life.

Religion and family play an important role in Latin American life. The region's history and politics are reflected in celebrations and art.

Religion

Religion has long played an important role in Latin American cultures. During colonial times, most Latin Americans became Christians, and Christianity still has the most followers. Roman Catholics form the largest Christian group. In recent years, however, Protestant missionaries have encouraged many people to convert, or to change their beliefs, to Protestant forms of Christianity.

Other faiths are also practiced in the region. For example, many traditional Native American and African religions thrive, often mixed with Christianity and other faiths. Islam, Hinduism, and Buddhism, brought by Asian immigrants, are practiced in the Caribbean region and coastal areas of South America. Judaism has followers in the largest Latin American cities.

Family

Family life is important in Latin America. Often several generations live together, and adults are expected to care for their aged parents. Adult brothers and sisters often live near each other, and their children—who are cousins—can form close relationships. Traditionally, the father is the family leader and the chief decision maker. In some parts of the Caribbean, however, the mother is the leader of the family.

NATIONAL GEOGRAPHIC

Colonial Church, Brazil

In Brazil, many churches—such as this one in the town of Tiradentes—were built during the 1700s under Portuguese rule. ***Regions*** **How is Christianity changing in Latin America?**

Recreation and Celebrations

Most Latin Americans are devoted sports fans. Soccer is popular throughout the region, and Brazil and Argentina have produced outstanding players and world championship teams. Cuba was the second country in the world—after the United States—to play baseball. This sport has taken hold throughout the Caribbean, Central America, and northern South America. Several countries have their own leagues, and many skilled players have gone to play in the United States. In Caribbean countries that were once ruled by the British, cricket is a favorite sport.

Religious and patriotic holidays are celebrated throughout Latin America. Each spring, many countries hold a large festival called **carnival** on the last day before the Christian holy period called Lent. The celebration is marked by singing, dancing, and parades. The carnival held in Rio de Janeiro, Brazil, is famous for its color and excitement. On the Mexican holiday known as the Day of the Dead, people honor family members who have died.

Feasting is an important part of Latin American celebrations. The foods of Latin America blend the traditions of the region's many peoples. Corn and beans—crops grown by Native Americans since ancient times—are important in Mexico and Central America. Beans and rice are a standard meal in the islands of the Caribbean and in Brazil. Fresh fish from the sea is also popular in those areas. Beef is the national dish in Argentina, Uruguay, and Chile.

The Arts

Culture in Latin America shows the influence of its ethnic mix. Cuban music is famous for its use of African rhythms. During the 1930s, Mexican artists, such as Diego Rivera, painted **murals,** or large paintings on walls, that recall the artistic traditions of the ancient Maya and Aztec. In Latin America, many writers have used their work to **comment** on, or talk about, social and political conflicts.

Latin American artists have influenced those in other countries. The music of Cuba and Brazil has shaped American jazz. Latin American writers of the late 1900s invented a **style,** or form, of writing called magic realism that combined fantastic events with the ordinary. This style was adopted by European and Asian writers.

Reading Check **Identifying** What sports are popular in Latin America?

Section 2 Review

Vocabulary

1. **Explain** the significance of:
   - **a.** migration
   - **b.** mestizo
   - **c.** pidgin language
   - **d.** carnival
   - **e.** mural

Main Ideas

2. **Describing** Describe patterns of migration in Latin America in the past and today.
3. **Summarizing** Use a diagram like the one below to summarize key facts about religion in Latin America.

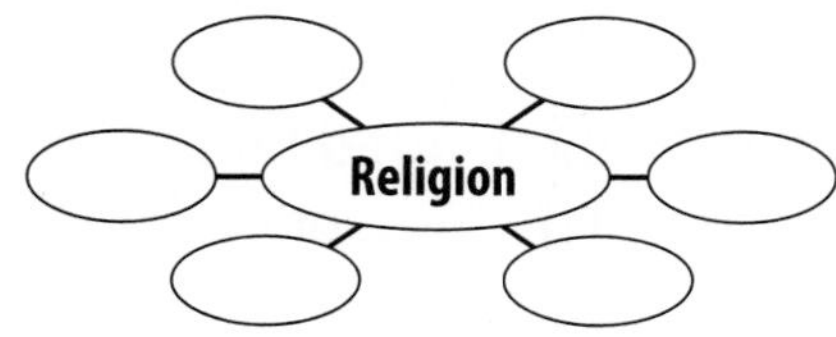

Critical Thinking

4. **BIG Idea** How do pidgin languages show the blending of different cultures in Latin America?
5. **Identifying Central Issues** In what parts of the region do most Latin Americans live? Why?
6. **Challenge** How has the region been influenced by other regions of the world?

Writing About Geography

7. **Expository Writing** Make a map of Latin America. Add labels that highlight facts about the population patterns, religions, and cultures of different countries and areas within the region. Then write a short paragraph describing the patterns you see.

Visual Summary

Native American Civilizations

- The Olmec built the first civilization in Latin America.
- The Maya created a calendar and a complex number system.
- The Aztec set up a large empire in central Mexico.
- The Inca developed a network of roads to unite their territories.

Aztec stone calendar

Colonial Rule

- Spanish explorers conquered the Aztec and Inca Empires.
- Spain and Portugal ruled most of Latin America from the 1500s to the early 1800s.
- Colonial rule brought a mixing of different cultures.

Hernán Cortés

Forming New Nations

- Most Latin American countries achieved independence during the 1800s.
- Dictators, the military, or wealthy groups ruled Latin American countries, while most people remained poor and powerless.
- Many Latin American countries developed more democratic systems in the 1900s.

People

- About 80 percent of South Americans live in urban areas.
- Most people in Latin America are of European, Native American, or African background.
- Most Latin Americans speak Spanish or Portuguese, and most practice the Roman Catholic faith.

Culture

- Family life is important to most Latin Americans.
- Soccer and baseball are major sports in Latin America.
- Food, arts, and music reflect the diverse ethnic mixture of the region.
- Religious and patriotic holidays are important throughout Latin America.

Baseball players, Dominican Republic

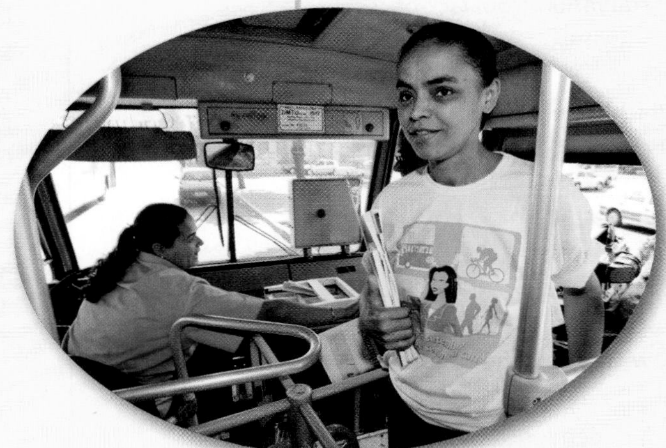

Bus rider in Brasília, Brazil

Study anywhere, anytime! Download quizzes and flash cards to your PDA from glencoe.com.

CHAPTER 5 ASSESSMENT

GA CRCT Practice

TEST-TAKING TIP

Do not keep changing your answers on a test. Your first choice is usually the correct one, unless you misread the question.

Directions: Choose the best answer for each question.

1 **In some Latin American countries, people of mixed Native American and European descent make up most of the population. What are these people called?**

A creoles
B pidgin
C mestizos
D immigrants

2 **Why do most people in Latin America speak languages that are based on Spanish and Portuguese?**

A Spain and Portugal once ruled the region.
B Most of the people in the region once lived in Spain and Portugal.
C Spanish and Portuguese nuns taught their language to Latin American children.
D French and English were too difficult to learn.

3 **Which of the following contributed to the decline of the Aztec in Mexico?**

A war with Inca
B natural disaster
C starvation from lack of resources
D disease

4 **Which form of government did Cuba establish after the 1959 revolution led by Fidel Castro?**

A republic
B communist
C parliamentary
D monarchy

5 **How was Haiti freed from French rule in 1804?**

A Simón Bolívar and his army led the fight for independence.
B François-Dominque Toussaint-Louverture led enslaved Africans in a revolt.
C Miguel Hidalgo encouraged the Haitians to fight for freedom.
D Haitians recruited Spanish soldiers to fight with them.

6 **Who was the ruler of the Inca before Francisco Pizarro?**

A Montezuma
B Tenochtitlán
C Cuzco
D Atahuallpa

7 **After winning their independence, what issues created conflict among many Latin American nations?**

A slavery
B the economy
C religion and boundaries between countries
D natural resources

8 **Which is the largest Asian group living in Brazil?**

A Japanese
B Chinese
C Korean
D Vietnamese

9 **In some Latin American countries, people speak a language that is a combination of different languages. What is the name of this language?**

A mestizo
B Quechua
C pidgin
D Creole

10 **What is the name of the large festival held in many Latin American countries on the last day before the Christian holy period called Lent?**

A carnival
B the Day of the Dead
C Independence Day
D Simón Bolívar Day

11 **Look at the chart.**

Internet and Cell Phone Users in Central America			
	Population	Internet Users	Cell Phone Users
Belize	287,730	35,000	93,100
Honduras	7,326,496	223,000	1,282,000
Guatemala	12,293,545	756,000	3,168,300
Costa Rica	4,075,261	1,000,000	1,101,000
Source: *CIA World Factbook.*			

Divide the population by the number of cell phone users to determine the number of people per cell phone in each country. Based on the results, which of the following statements is true?

A Honduras has the most cell phones in proportion to its population.
B The more people there are per cell phone, the fewer the number of cell phones there are available.
C Costa Ricans spend most of their time talking on cell phones.
D The more people there are per cell phone, the more cell phones there are available.

12 **Divide the number of Internet users by the population. Which country has the most Internet users in proportion to its population?**

A Belize
B Honduras
C Guatemala
D Costa Rica

13 **What can you MOST LIKELY determine about the economic wealth of the countries based on the amount of cell phone and Internet users?**

A There is no difference in the economic wealth of the countries.
B The countries with more users are likely to be developing.
C The countries with fewer users are likely to be wealthier.
D The countries with more users are likely to be wealthier.

14 **Read the document and answer the questions that follow.**

The following passage was written by a Catholic priest who visited the Yucatán Peninsula in the 1560s.

Before the Spaniards subdued [overcame] the country the Indians lived together in well ordered communities; they kept the ground in excellent condition, free from noxious [harmful] vegetation and planted with fine trees. The habitation was as follows: in the center of the town were the temples, with beautiful plazas, and around the temples stood the houses of the chiefs and the priests, and next those of the leading men. Closest to these came the houses of those who were wealthiest and most [respected], and at the borders of the town were the houses of the common people. The wells, where they were few, were near the houses of the chiefs; their plantations were set out in the trees for making wine, and sown with cotton, pepper and maize. They lived in these communities for fear of their enemies, lest [for fear that] they be taken in captivity; but after the wars with the Spaniards they dispersed [scattered] through the forests.

—Diego de Landa,
Yucatán Before and After the Conquest

According to the priest, what was located at the center of the community?

A wells for water
B houses of the wealthy
C temples
D crops

15 **How did the priest feel about the communities of the Yucatán Peninsula?**

A He was impressed by their organization and beauty.
B He was afraid of them.
C He was jealous of their wealth.
D He was angry about the loss of rain forests.

For additional test practice, use Self-Check Quizzes—Chapter 5 at glencoe.com.

Need Extra Help?

If You Missed Questions. . .	1	2	3	4	5	6	7	8	9	10	11	12	13	14	15
Go to Page. . .	151	151	141	145	142	141	143	151	151	154	149	149	149	140	140

TIME JOURNAL

"Hello! My name is Miguel.

I'm 14 years old and I live in San Cristóbal Ecatepec, a town near Mexico City, the capital of Mexico. I live in a small house with my mother, sister, and grandmother. Read about my day."

6:15 a.m. I wake up and get dressed then have breakfast with my family. This morning, my two young cousins come over to eat with us. We have quesadillas, which are corn tortillas with melted cheese. My grandmother also puts out a plate of bananas and papayas.

6:45 a.m. I comb my hair, brush my teeth, and put my books in my backpack. It's time to leave for school, even though it's still pretty dark outside. I walk to school with my sister, Areli (ah•ray•LEE).

7:00 a.m. The sun is starting to come up as we arrive at José María Morelos y Pavón Middle School. The school is named for a famous leader in Mexico's struggle for independence from Spain. (We have learned about him in history class!)

7:10 a.m. English is my first class of the day. Our teacher, Mr. Aranda, encourages us to speak mostly English during class.

7:45 a.m. It is time for my least favorite class—math. Today, though, I get a break. The local police visit our school to lead an assembly on crime prevention. They talk to us about staying safe and drug-free.

8:45 a.m. In physical education class, we play *fútbol*, or soccer. Then I move on to music, where I practice my skills on the recorder. I am learning to play a song from a musical.

10:30 a.m. During a short recess, I sit outside and talk with my friends Alejandra, Ismael, and José.

10:45 a.m. I go to history class, then to Spanish. I am working hard for a good grade in both classes. In Mexico, we are graded on a 10-point scale. A passing grade is a 6 or higher.

12:45 p.m. It is time for my elective class—family values. It's about respecting family and friends, and doing community volunteer work.

1:00 p.m. The school day is over. While I walk home, I chat with my dad on my cell phone. He and my mother are separated, so he does not live with us. I see him often though.

1:10 p.m. I change clothes and feed my dogs. Then I help my grandmother with lunch. I squeeze oranges for juice while she makes chicken and rice. My mom comes home for lunch from her job as a secretary.

2:30 p.m. I ride my bike to the hardware store that my family owns. My grandmother and uncles work there. In the back of the store, my Uncle Ricardo raises roosters. I help my uncle by feeding the birds and cleaning their cages.

4:30 p.m. I go back home and play soccer outside with my cousins. Then I start my homework.

6:30 p.m. For dinner, we have *pollo con mole*. It is chicken in a delicious black sauce made with chocolate and spices. Later, I watch some TV (I like to watch reality shows).

10:00 p.m. I am tired, so I go to bed.

ILLUSTRATIONS BY BOOKMAPMAN

WHAT'S THE WORD? Miguel works on a team project in Spanish class.

MAKING MUSIC Miguel plays the recorder in music class. He also knows how to play the flute.

AT HOME Miguel, his sister, cousins, and grandmother spend time together.

ALL SMILES In his spare time, Miguel Rodriguez (mee·GELL rod·REE·guez) helps care for his uncle's roosters.

ADRIANA ZEHBRAUSKAS / POLARIS (4)

What's Popular in Mexico

DANITA DELIMONT/ALAMY

Murals Mexico's early inhabitants, the ancient Maya, painted scenes from their daily lives on rock walls. Today, large murals or wall paintings are still a popular art form.

Turning 15 In Mexican tradition, a girl's fifteenth birthday calls for a special celebration. The event is called *quince años*, or "fifteen years."

Mariachi music Lively mariachi bands often play at Mexican festivals and weddings. The musicians play violins, guitars, and trumpets and often dress like traditional Mexican cowboys called *charros*.

KEN WELSH/AGE FOTOSTOCK

Say It in Spanish

There are still several native Indian languages spoken in Mexico, but the national language is Spanish. It was brought to Mexico in the sixteenth century by Spanish settlers. Try these everyday Spanish expressions.

Hello
Hola (OH · lah)

Good-bye
Adios (ah · dee · OHS)

My name is _______.
Me llamo (may YAH · moh) _______.

LUC NOVOVITCH/ALAMY

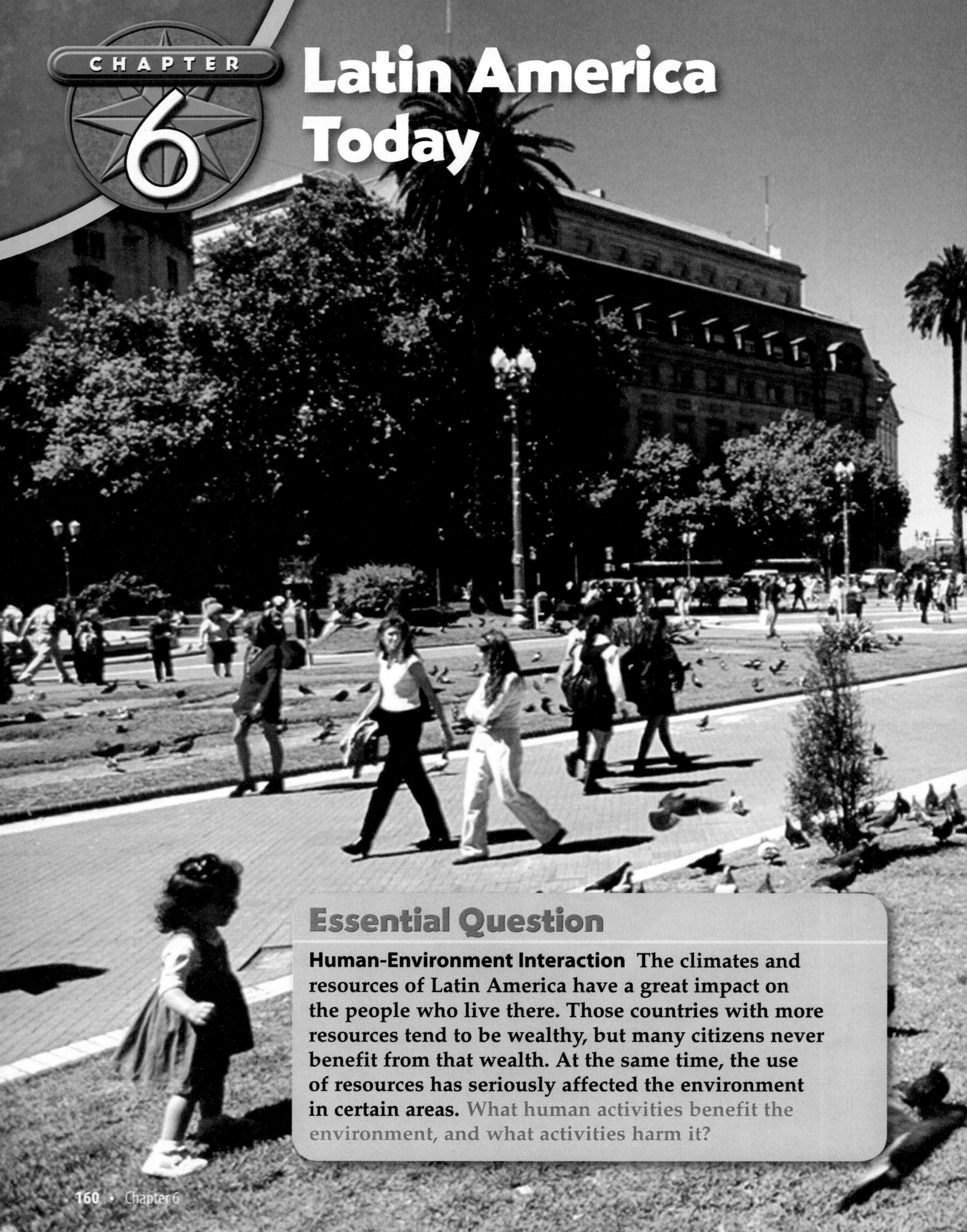

CHAPTER 6 Latin America Today

Essential Question

Human-Environment Interaction The climates and resources of Latin America have a great impact on the people who live there. Those countries with more resources tend to be wealthy, but many citizens never benefit from that wealth. At the same time, the use of resources has seriously affected the environment in certain areas. What human activities benefit the environment, and what activities harm it?

Section 1: Mexico

BIG IDEA Patterns of economic activities result in global interdependence. Many Mexicans now depend on factory jobs. Those who cannot find work at home sometimes migrate to the United States in search of work.

Section 2: Central America and the Caribbean

BIG IDEA The physical environment affects how people live. Many Caribbean islands have limited resources. Their warm climate and beautiful beaches, however, make tourism an important industry.

Section 3: South America

BIG IDEA People's actions can change the physical environment. The Amazon Basin holds the world's largest rain forest. People are now using the rain forest's resources to boost economic growth. Their actions greatly affect the Amazon Basin's fragile environment.

FOLDABLES™ Study Organizer

Organizing Information Make this Foldable to help you organize information about the countries of Latin America today.

Step 1 Place two 11x17 pieces of paper together.

Step 2 Fold the papers in half to form a booklet.

Step 3 Label your booklet as shown.

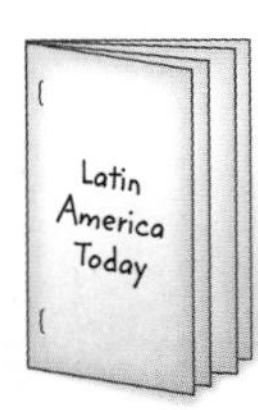

Reading and Writing As you read the chapter, take notes about each Latin American country. Use your notes to write five quiz questions for each section of the chapter.

Plaza de Mayo, Buenos Aires, Argentina

Visit glencoe.com and enter *QuickPass*™ code GA6EOW6225c6 for Chapter 6 resources.

Guide to Reading

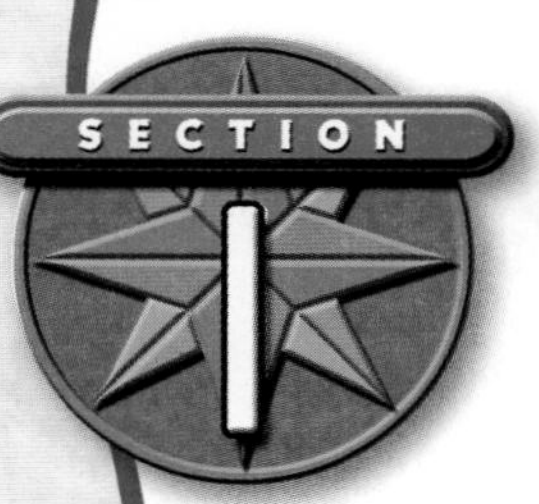

BIG Idea

Patterns of economic activities result in global interdependence.

Content Vocabulary

- plaza *(p. 163)*
- vaquero *(p. 164)*
- maquiladora *(p. 165)*
- subsistence farm *(p. 165)*
- plantation *(p. 165)*
- migrant worker *(p. 166)*

Academic Vocabulary

- reveal *(p. 164)*
- assemble *(p. 165)*

Reading Strategy

Summarizing Use a chart like the one below to organize key facts about Mexico's economic regions.

Region	Key Facts
North	
Central	
South	

SECTION 1

Mexico

Section Audio   Spotlight Video

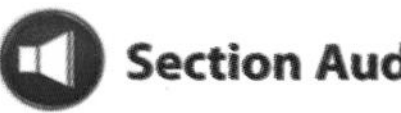

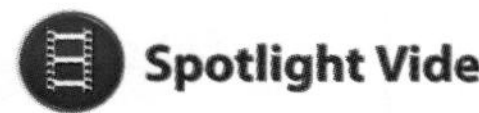

Picture This They may not look like soccer balls, but these piles of plastic panels will be stitched together by workers in San Miguelito, Mexico, to create thousands of balls for the popular sport. The soccer balls are then sold to large companies that export them. Read this section to learn about Mexico's economy today and how it is connected to other regions of the world.

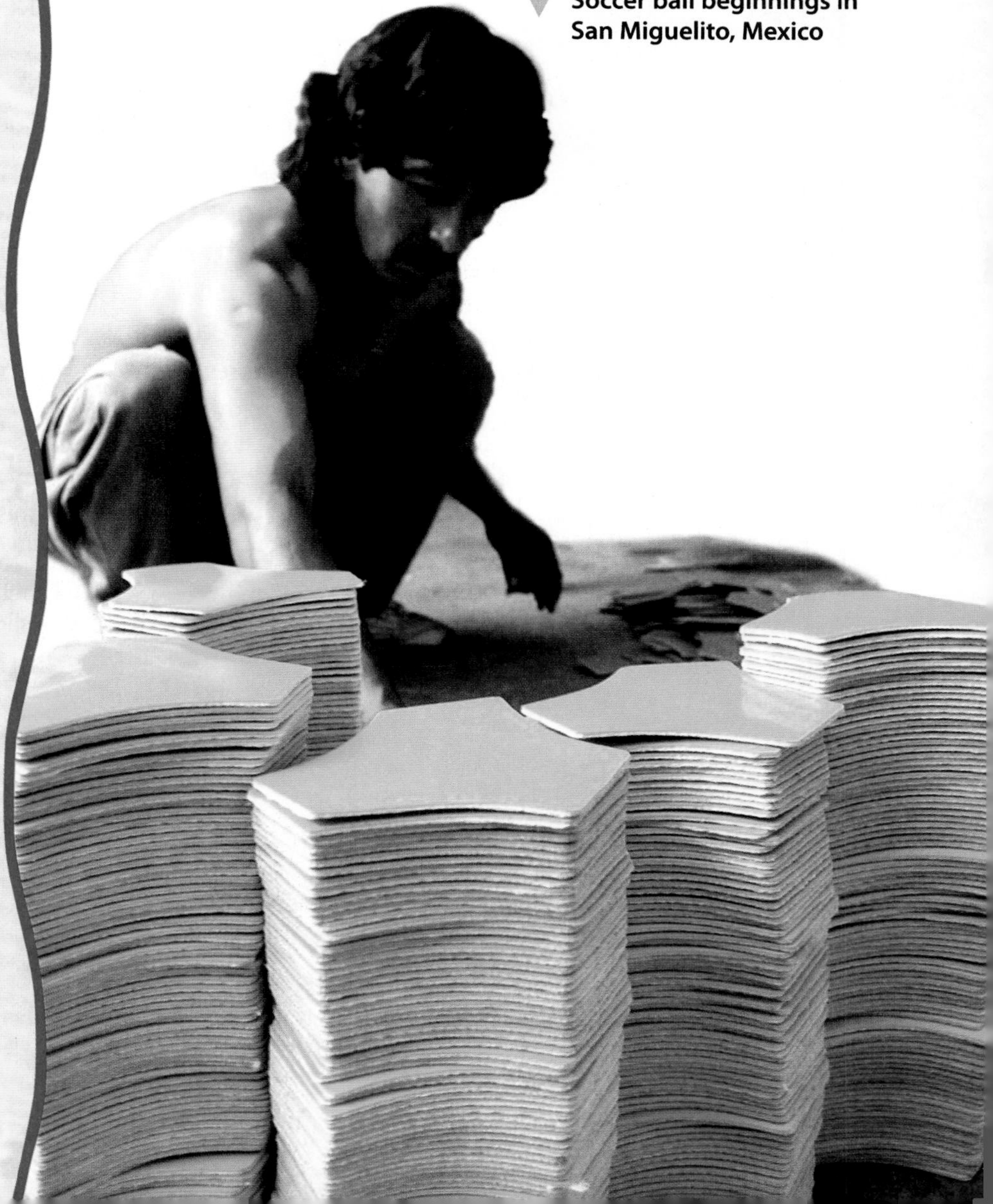

Soccer ball beginnings in San Miguelito, Mexico

Mexico's People, Government, and Culture

Main Idea **Mexico's culture reflects its Native American and Spanish past as well as modern influences.**

Geography and You Do you like tacos or enchiladas? These are tasty Mexican dishes. Read to learn about Mexico's people and culture.

Mexico, officially named the United Mexican States, is the United States's nearest southern neighbor. It is the third-largest country in area in Latin America, after Brazil and Argentina. Mexico also ranks second in population.

Mexico's People

Mexico's people reflect the blending of Spanish and Native American populations over the centuries. About two-thirds of Mexicans are mestizos. A quarter of Mexico's people are mostly or completely Native American.

In Mexico, rural traditions remain strong, but about 75 percent of Mexicans now live in cities. The largest city is Mexico City, the country's capital. With nearly 22 million people, Mexico City is one of the world's largest and most crowded urban areas.

Mexican cities show the influence of Spanish culture. Many of them are organized around large **plazas**, or public squares. City plazas serve as centers of public life. The main government buildings and the largest church are located alongside each city's plaza. Newer sections of the cities have glass office buildings and modern houses. In poorer sections, homes are built of boards, sheet metal, or even cardboard.

Plaza in Mexico City

The plazas of Mexican cities are popular places to gather. The church on this plaza in Mexico City was built in 1536. ***Place*** **About what percentage of Mexico's people live in cities today?**

Mexico's Government

Mexico, like the United States, is a federal republic, where power is divided between national and state governments. A strong president leads the national government. He or she can serve only one six-year term but has more power than the legislative and judicial branches.

After a revolution in the early 1900s, one political party ruled Mexico for many decades. Then, in the 1990s, economic troubles and the people's lack of political power led to calls for change. In 2000 Mexican voters elected a president from a different political party for the first time in more than 70 years. In the next presidential election six years later, the vote count was too close to call. An election court finally ruled Felipe Calderón president of Mexico, despite bitter protests from supporters of the opposing candidate.

Mexican Culture

Mexican culture **reveals** both European and Native American influences. Folk arts, such as wood carving, are deeply rooted in Native American traditions. Favorite sports, such as soccer, were brought from Europe. Carved and painted religious statues display the mixing of the two cultures.

Mexican artists and writers have created many national treasures. In the early 1900s, Diego Rivera and his wife, Frida Kahlo, became well-known for their paintings. Carlos Fuentes and Octavio Paz have written works about the values of Mexico's people.

Mexicans enjoy celebrations called fiestas (fee·EHS·tuhs) that include parades, fireworks, music, and dancing. Food is an important part of Mexican fiestas. Tacos and enchiladas are now as popular in the United States as they are in Mexico.

Reading Check **Identifying** What are the sources of Mexico's culture?

Mexican Fiesta

▲ Women wearing traditional clothes dance in a parade at a fiesta in Oaxaca, Mexico. ***Place*** **In what other ways do Mexicans celebrate at a fiesta?**

Mexico's Economy and Society

Main Idea **While Mexico's economy is improving, the country still faces significant challenges from poverty, overcrowded cities, and environmental issues.**

Geography and You Have you seen the brown haze of smog? Read to find out how economic growth in Mexico City has contributed to the increase of smog there.

With many resources and workers, Mexico has a growing economy. Mexico has tried to use its resources to improve the lives of its people. Although these efforts have brought some gains for Mexicans, they have also created some challenges for the future.

Economic Regions

Mexico's physical geography and climate together give the country three distinct economic regions. These regions are the North, Central Mexico, and the South.

Mexico's North has large stretches of land that are too dry and rocky to farm without irrigation. So farmers have built canals to carry water to their fields. As a result, they are able to grow cotton, grains, fruits, and vegetables for export. Areas in the North have grasslands that support cattle ranches. Mexican cowhands called **vaqueros** (vah·KEHR·ohs) developed tools and methods for raising cattle during Spanish colonial times. Their skills were later passed on to American cowhands. Vaqueros still carry on this work today.

In addition to farming and ranching, the North profits from rich deposits of copper, zinc, iron, lead, and silver. Manufacturing is located in cities near or along the Mexico–United States border, such as Monterrey and Tijuana (tee·HWAH·nah). In the North, many companies from the United States and elsewhere have built **maquiladoras** (muh·KEE·luh·DOHR·uhs). These are factories in which workers **assemble** parts made in other countries. The finished products are then exported to the United States and other countries.

Central Mexico holds more than half of Mexico's people. Although it is situated in the Tropics, this area has a high elevation. Temperatures are mild, and the climate is pleasant year-round. Fertile soil created by volcanic eruptions over the centuries allows for productive farming.

Large industrial cities, such as Mexico City and Guadalajara (GWAH·thuh·lah·HAH·rah), prosper in central Mexico. Workers in these cities make cars, clothing, household items, and electronic goods. The coastal area along the Gulf of Mexico is a center of Mexico's energy industry. This is because of the major oil and gas deposits that lie offshore.

Mexico's South is the poorest economic region. The mountains towering in the center of this region have poor soil. **Subsistence farms,** or small plots where farmers grow only enough food to feed their families, are common here. In contrast, coastal lowlands have good soil and abundant rain. Wealthy farmers grow sugarcane or bananas on **plantations,** large farms that raise a single crop for sale. Both coasts in the South have beautiful beaches. Tourists flock to resort cities, such as Acapulco and Cancun.

Student Web Activity Visit glencoe.com and complete the Chapter 6 Web Activity about economic changes in Mexico.

Making Cars in Mexico

Workers build a new car at an assembly plant in central Mexico. American and Japanese companies have located hundreds of plants in Mexico. ***Regions*** **What agreement has helped Mexico's economy?**

Economic and Social Changes

For years Mexico's economy relied on agriculture. Today, Mexico still exports food products, but it relies less on farming and more on manufacturing. Much of the change has come about because of Mexico's closer ties with its northern neighbors: the United States and Canada. In 1994, Mexico, the United States, and Canada entered into the North American Free Trade Agreement (NAFTA). Under NAFTA, the three countries decided to end barriers to trade among themselves. Mexico's currency, the peso, is widely traded throughout the Americas.

Mexico's growing industries now provide a wide range of goods, such as steel, cars, and consumer goods. Many service industries, such as banking and tourism, also contribute to Mexico's economy. The growing economy is encouraging Mexican entrepreneurs to start new businesses. Such businesses often involve consulting or technology.

Economic advances have raised the standard of living, especially in the North. The speed of growth also has brought concerns about damage to the environment, as well as dangers to workers' health and safety.

As Mexico's economy has grown, pollution has increased. For example, the mountains that surround Mexico City trap car fumes and factory smoke. As a result, the city is often covered by unhealthy smog, a thick haze of fog and chemicals.

Population and Ethnic Challenges

Mexico's population has grown rapidly in recent decades. As a result, many people have moved to cities for work. Because many jobs pay low wages, people live in crowded slums, or poor sections of cities.

Many Mexicans who cannot find work at home become **migrant workers.** These are people who travel to find work when extra help is needed to plant or harvest crops. These workers cross Mexico's long border into the United States. Despite low pay, they can earn more there than in Mexico. Many poorer Mexicans depend on money sent from relatives working in the United States.

Some of these workers come to the United States illegally. To reduce illegal entry, the United States has tightened border controls. This has increased tensions with Mexico.

Many of Mexico's Native Americans are poor and live in rural areas. In the 1990s, a group called the Zapatistas rose against the Mexican government in southern Mexico. They demanded changes to help Native Americans. Today, the struggle between the Zapatistas and the government remains unresolved. The Zapatistas still control some towns in the region.

Determining Cause and Effect Why have many Mexicans migrated to the United States?

Section Review

Vocabulary

1. **Explain** the significance of:
   - **a.** plaza
   - **b.** vaquero
   - **c.** maquiladora
   - **d.** subsistence farm
   - **e.** plantation
   - **f.** migrant worker

Main Ideas

2. **Describing** Describe Mexico's form of government and recent events concerning the government.
3. **Identifying** Use a diagram like the one below to explain the challenges facing Mexico.

Critical Thinking

4. **Determining Cause and Effect** Why is irrigation needed to farm parts of the northern region?
5. **BIG Idea** Compare Mexico's three economic regions.
6. **Challenge** What problems might people in northern Mexico face if maquiladoras are closed, even if they do not work in the maquiladoras?

Writing About Geography

7. **Persuasive Writing** Choose one of the challenges facing Mexico. Write a newspaper editorial in which you suggest steps Mexico's government could take to improve the situation.

Guide to Reading

Central America and the Caribbean

BIG Idea

The physical environment affects how people live.

Content Vocabulary

- literacy rate *(p. 169)*
- command economy *(p. 170)*
- remittance *(p. 170)*
- commonwealth *(p. 170)*

Academic Vocabulary

- shift *(p. 169)*
- fee *(p. 169)*

Reading Strategy

Comparing and Contrasting Use a Venn diagram like the one below to compare and contrast Guatemala and Costa Rica.

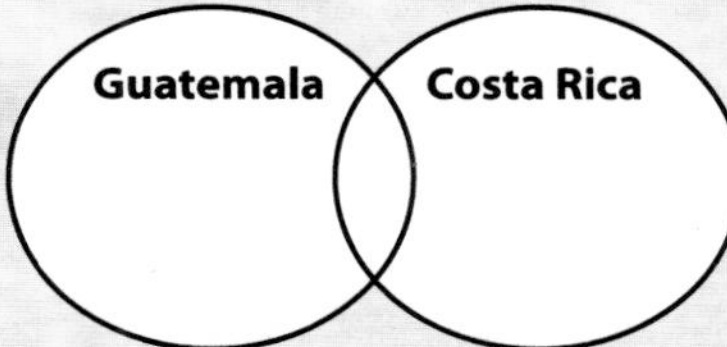

 Section Audio  Spotlight Video

Picture This What is it like to glide along a cable 230 feet (70 m) above a lagoon? Tourists can use this method to enjoy the spectacular views of Tiscapa Lagoon and the surrounding forest in Nicaragua. Opportunities like this show why ecotourism is fast replacing coffee, meat, and seafood as Nicaragua's primary source of income. Read this section to learn more about Central America and the Caribbean today.

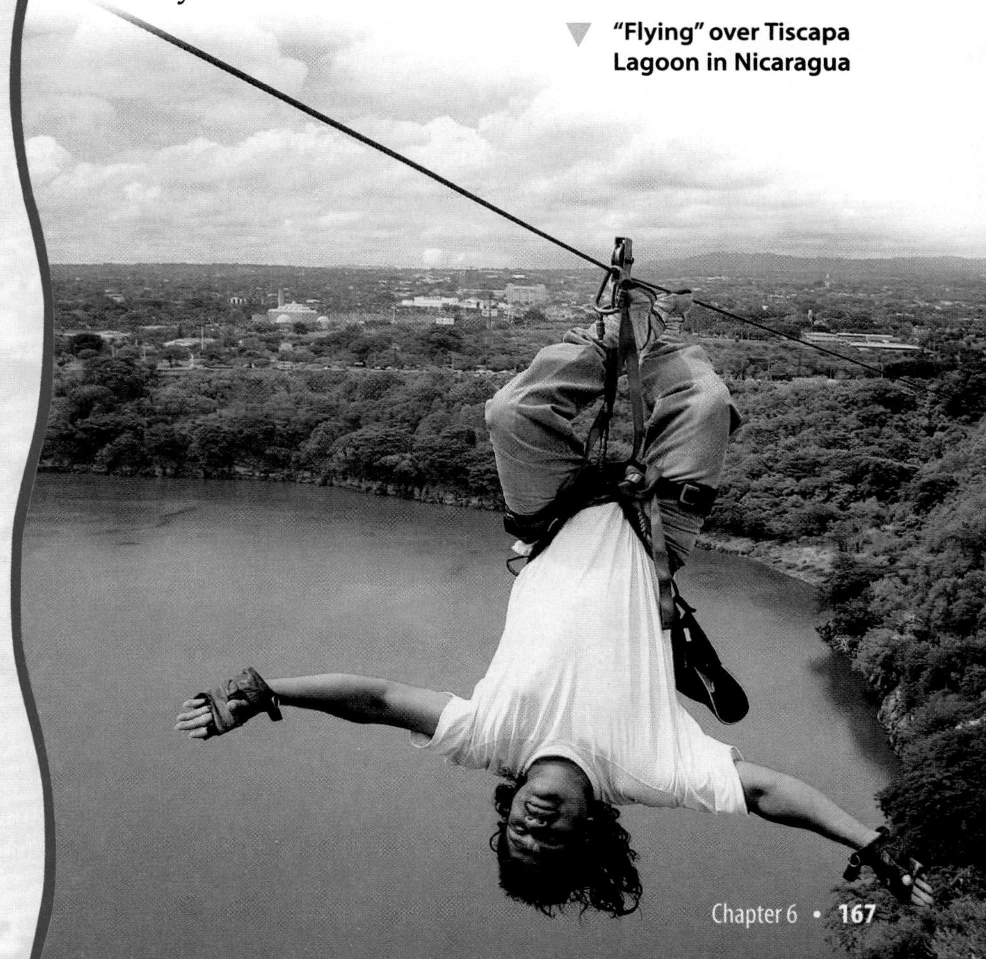

"Flying" over Tiscapa Lagoon in Nicaragua

Countries of Central America

Main Idea **Farming is the main economic activity in Central America, where many people are poor.**

Geography and You Do you enjoy eating bananas at breakfast? They might have come from Central America. Read to find out about other ways in which Central Americans use their land and resources.

Central America is made up of seven countries: Belize, Guatemala, El Salvador, Honduras, Nicaragua, Costa Rica, and Panama. Most people in Central America depend on farming. For many decades, they have produced crops, such as bananas, sugarcane, and coffee, for export. In some Central American countries, conflict between ethnic or political groups has slowed their economies.

Guatemala

Guatemala is a country of rugged mountains, thick forests, and blue lakes. About half of its people are descended from the ancient Maya. Other Guatemalans are of mixed Maya and Spanish origin. Maya languages and Spanish are spoken.

Guatemala has fertile volcanic soil. Most of the land is owned by a small group of people who hold most of the wealth and power. During the late 1990s, rebel groups fought the government for control of the land.

TIME GLOBAL CITIZENS

NAME: MARIE CLAIRE PAIZ **HOME COUNTRY:** Guatemala

ACHIEVEMENT: Biologist Marie Claire Paiz directs a major preservation project for The Nature Conservancy in the Maya Forest, one of the world's largest rain forests. Here, for more than 1,000 years, ancient Maya flourished on both sides of the Usumacinta River, which divides Guatemala and Mexico. Maya ruins and writings that date back to 2300 B.C. attract tourists and scientists. Today, however, the forest is being destroyed by farmers clearing the land. And the possible construction of a hydroelectric dam threatens to flood the area. Paiz works to educate Latin Americans about the importance of the site's cultural heritage and what they can do to protect it.

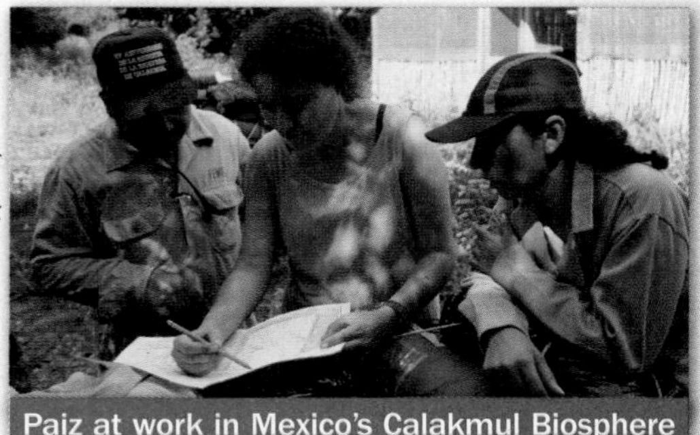

Paiz at work in Mexico's Calakmul Biosphere Reserve near the border of Guatemala.

QUOTE: "I hope that through conservation work, the wonders shared by Guatemala and Mexico can endure."

Paiz believes that it is important for human-made structures and nature to exist in harmony. How would that benefit both nature and humans?

When the conflict ended, more than 200,000 people had been killed or were missing.

Guatemala has shown recent signs of economic change. In the past, many farmers produced only bananas and coffee. Today they are **shifting** production to crops that have higher values, such as other fruits, flowers, and spices. In the early 2000s, Guatemala and its Central American neighbors agreed to free trade with the United States. Central Americans hope that this removal of trade barriers will enable them to sell more of their goods to the United States.

Costa Rica

Costa Rica has long stood out from its war-torn neighbors. A stable democracy is in place, and the country has not been involved in a war since the 1800s. As a result, Costa Rica has no army—only a police force to keep law and order.

Costa Rica also has fewer poor people than other Central American countries. One reason is that Costa Rica has a higher literacy rate. **Literacy rate** is the percentage of people who can read and write. Workers with reading skills can be more productive and earn higher incomes.

Panama

Panama lies on the narrowest part of Central America. The country is best known for the Panama Canal, which shortens distance and travel time between the Atlantic and Pacific Oceans. In 1999 the United States gave Panama control of the canal. Today, Panama profits from **fees,** or set charges, that ships pay to use the canal. Due to the commerce brought by the canal, Panama is an important banking center.

Reading Check **Determining Cause and Effect** How does literacy rate affect income?

Countries of the Caribbean

Main Idea **Although most Caribbean island countries are poor, several are turning to tourism to help their economies grow.**

Geography and You Do many tourists visit the area where you live? Read to find out what attracts tourists to the Caribbean.

The warm weather and sandy beaches of some Caribbean island nations, such as the Bahamas and Virgin Islands, attract many tourists. Those countries' economies rely on tourism. Many countries in the area, however, face economic and political challenges.

Havana, Cuba

NATIONAL GEOGRAPHIC

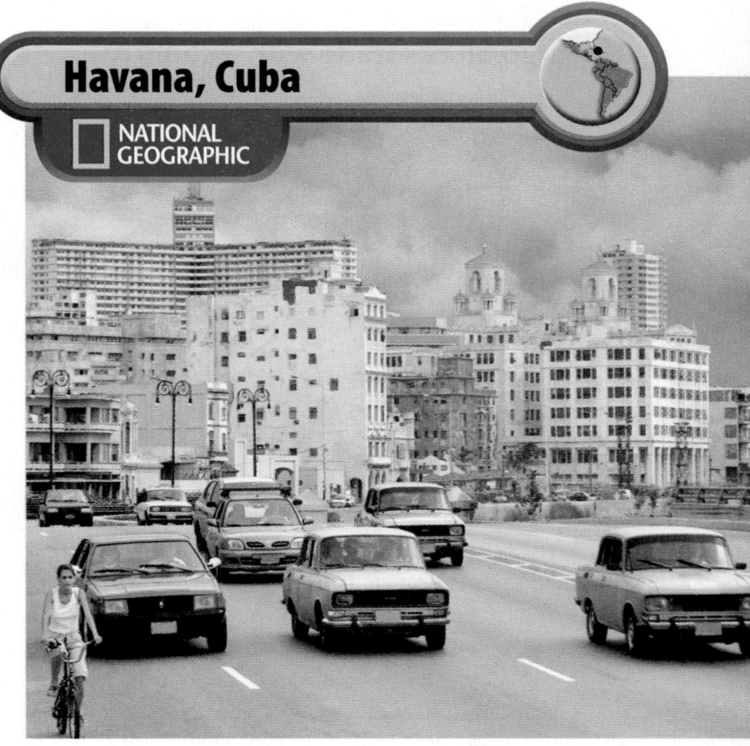

Cars zoom down the Malecón, a famous avenue that runs along the coastline in Havana. ***Regions*** **What major economic challenge do Cuba and other Caribbean nations face?**

Cuba

Cuba lies about 90 miles (145 km) south of Florida. It has a **command economy,** which means that the government decides how resources are used and what goods and services are produced. Cubans are trying to develop tourism and industries, but the economy has struggled since the early 1990s. Many Cubans lack food and clothing.

Cuba, officially the Republic of Cuba, is an autocracy, or a government controlled by one person. In 2008 Cuba's aging dictator Fidel Castro stepped down and was replaced by his brother. Cuba's communist government tightly controls society. People can vote, but the Communist Party is the only legal party. People who criticize the government are often arrested and jailed. The United States has condemned these actions. Since the early 1960s, the United States has had an embargo on Cuba. An embargo blocks trade with a country.

Haiti

Located on the western half of the island of Hispaniola, Haiti has had a troubled history. Conflicts among political groups have made for an unstable government. In addition, most of Haiti's people are poor. A major source of income is **remittances,** or money sent back home by Haitians who work in other countries.

Puerto Rico

Puerto Rico is a **commonwealth,** or a self-governing territory, of the United States. Its people are American citizens. Puerto Rico has a higher standard of living than most Caribbean islands. Its industries produce medicines, machinery, and clothes. Farmers grow sugarcane and coffee. Puerto Rico makes more money from tourism than does any other Caribbean island.

✓ Reading Check **Drawing Conclusions** Is Cuba's command economy effective?

Section 2 Review

Vocabulary

1. **Explain** the meaning of *literacy rate, command economy, remittance,* and *commonwealth* by using each term in a sentence.

Main Ideas

2. **Analyzing** How is Costa Rica different from its Central American neighbors?
3. **Comparing** Use a chart like the one below to examine the economies of Cuba, Haiti, and Puerto Rico.

Country	Economy
Cuba	
Haiti	
Puerto Rico	

Critical Thinking

4. **Contrasting** How does Cuba's government contrast with Costa Rica's?
5. **BIG Idea** Why are many people on the Caribbean islands poor?
6. **Challenge** Do you think farmers in Guatemala will earn more money by growing different crops? Why?

Writing About Geography

7. **Expository Writing** Write a paragraph explaining how specific countries in this region have achieved some economic success and how they have done it.

TIME PERSPECTIVES

EXPLORING WORLD ISSUES

PROTECTING NATURAL RESOURCES

People are learning how to profit from the land without harming it.

Activists camp out in an Ecuadorian forest to protest an oil pipeline being built through it.

For decades many natural environments and wildlife species have been damaged by human activity. Farmers and loggers in Brazil and Ecuador have cut down or set fire to countless trees in order to acquire the land for farming and other economic activities. Miners in Bolivia have also cleared land in search of minerals. As a result, thousands of miles of forests have disappeared and wildlife populations have suffered. Human activities have also hurt other environments. In Chile, fish farms that raise salmon in large tanks have harmed marine ecosystems.

In recent years, however, people have been working to protect but still profit from natural resources. Governments and citizens are working to limit the damage to forests and wildlife. Industries are developing alternative energy sources that are less harmful to natural environments. But is it too late?

AP PHOTO/DOLORES OCHOA

TIME PERSPECTIVES

Colorful macaws live in the Amazon rain forest.

ENVIRONMENT-FRIENDLY SOLUTIONS

South America has some of the world's largest and most beautiful forests. From the Amazon rain forest to the woodlands of the Andes mountain ranges, the region's green lush forests are home to many species of wildlife.

In recent decades, however, this fragile environment has changed. Since the 1960s, loggers, miners, and farmers have been clearing the trees from this region's forests. Some people cut down trees to produce wood and paper. Others burn the trees to clear land for mining, farming, and industry. The process of clearing an area of forest is called **deforestation**.

The Destruction of the Amazon Rain Forest

Since 1970, more than 232,000 square miles (600,000 square km) of the Amazon rain forest has been cleared. Here is a look at the amount of deforestation in recent years.

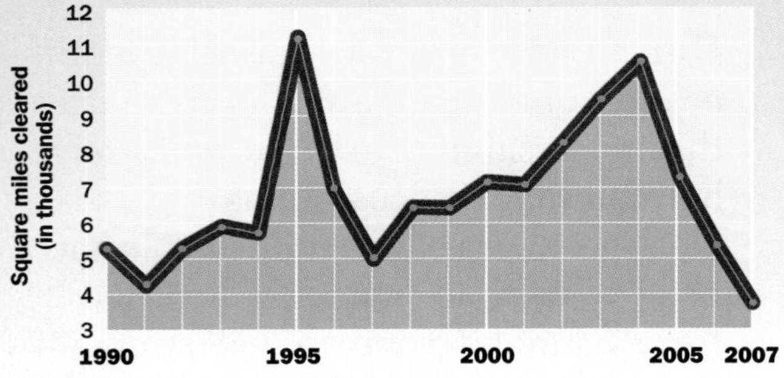

Source: National Institute of Space Research.

INTERPRETING GRAPHS

Analyzing Information During which four-year period did the largest amount of deforestation occur? About how many total square miles were cleared during this time?

Deforestation is a major challenge for South America and the world. Developing countries in this region need the land for industries that will help their economies grow. But deforestation destroys ecosystems and wildlife habitats. Deforestation also contributes to global warming. The burning of wooded areas sends large amounts of carbon dioxide into the atmosphere and speeds up the rate of global warming.

There is much work to be done to protect these lush forests. After years of neglect, the region's governments and citizens are beginning to realize how much is at stake. In recent years, people have been working to reverse decades of damage.

Amazon Alert!

The Amazon rain forest covers about 2.7 million square miles (7 million sq. km) of land in South America—mostly in Brazil. Parrots, jaguars, and piranhas are just some of the thousands of animals that make their home in the Amazon and the many rivers that run through it.

For decades, this tropical environment has been shrinking. In addition to farmers, cattle ranchers, and others clearing the land, the rain forest has also been cut down to make way for roads and highways that crisscross through the center of it. Since 1970, more than 232,000 square miles (600,000 sq. km) of the rain forest has been destroyed.

At a Brazilian ranch, cattle graze on cleared land.

This land was deforested by Brazilian farmers in order to grow soybeans.

The beauty and ecological diversity of the rain forest are at risk.

Stopping the Damage

Brazil's government has been working to preserve the Amazon rain forest. In order to slow the rate of deforestation, Brazil is studying ways to make land that has been cleared more productive. If deforested land can grow more crops or feed more cattle, it will lessen the need for more deforestation.

Legal limits on the amount of land that can be cleared have also been created. However, these laws have not always been enforced. In recent years, though, Brazilian officials are doing a better job at imposing and enforcing laws that protect the Amazon rain forest. Now companies and individuals who ignore the limits are punished with large fines.

Saving Wildlife Populations

Citizens throughout South America are also taking action to protect wildlife. In Chile, fish are often raised on fish farms in giant tanks, called cages. Breeding fish in captivity raises production. Chile is one of the world's biggest exporters of cage-bred salmon. In 2007 the country exported 1.3 million tons of fish (1.2 metric t).

But success has created its share of problems. Fish raised in crowded cages pollute the ocean floor and are prone to illness. Critics of the farms say that the fish are given large amounts of antibiotics and other chemicals to keep them from getting sick. When people eat the fish, the drugs may be passed on to them, which can be unhealthy.

Juan Carlos Cárdenas is the director of Centro Ecocéanos, an organization that works to protect marine life. For years, the center has been working to improve the production methods of Chile's fishing industry. The center teaches local fisheries how to catch more fish using traditional methods. It also conducts research and educates the public about how fish farms affect ecosystems.

Cárdenas says there is still much work to do. He is encouraged that consumers are learning about the health risks associated with eating cage-bred fish. Cárdenas hopes that if people buy fewer farmed fish, the lower sales will force the fish industry to make changes in how it operates.

A Chilean worker observes tanks full of farmed salmon.

REUTERS/CARLOS BARRIA

EXPLORING THE ISSUE

1. **Identifying Cause and Effect** How does deforestation speed up the process of global warming?

2. **Finding Solutions** Human activity can threaten the environment. What can you do in your community to help protect your natural environment?

A SWEET RIDE IN BRAZIL

Brazil's "Flex car" has a sweet tooth. *Flex* is short for "flexible," which describes the kinds of fuel the car uses. The Flex car looks and works like a regular vehicle, but it can run on gasoline or ethanol. Many Brazilians are filling up their gas tanks with ethanol—a fuel that is produced from sugarcane. The alternative fuel is pressed from sugarcane and then blended with gasoline. This "gasohol" mixture could eventually take the place of fossil fuels to keep cars running.

Ethanol-powered cars are not new in Brazil. The country developed them—and the fuel they operate on—in the 1980s, when the cost of buying oil from foreign nations began to soar. Over time, ethanol-powered cars zoomed onto the fast track. By 1988, more than 88 percent of cars sold each year in Brazil were running on a combination of ethanol and gasoline. Throughout Brazil there are now about 29,000 ethanol stations.

Today, Brazil is the world's largest producer of ethanol, and Flex cars are seen everywhere. In 2006 sales of Flex vehicles were higher than sales of cars that ran only on gasoline. Flex car technology is also spreading to other Brazilian industries. Small planes, such as crop dusters, are using ethanol because it is more widely available than conventional aviation fuel.

Added Mileage

Flex cars are also good for the environment and the economy. The ethanol they run on is cleaner than gasoline, so Flex cars create less air pollution. And ethanol is less expensive. Its price is almost half that of gasoline.

As gasoline prices continue to skyrocket, the nations of the world are expected to follow Brazil's example. In 2006 President George W. Bush called for the United States to develop more ethanol. "There is an enormous demand from abroad to know more," said the president of Brazil's carmakers' association. "This is an opportunity for Brazil." Perhaps it will be an opportunity for the rest of the world to have a sweet ride, too.

REUTERS/JAMIL BITTAR

A Flex car

EXPLORING THE ISSUE

1. **Explaining** Why did Brazil develop ethanol as an alternative fuel?
2. **Identifying Cause and Effect** How might Brazil's success with ethanol inspire other nations to develop and use alternative fuels?

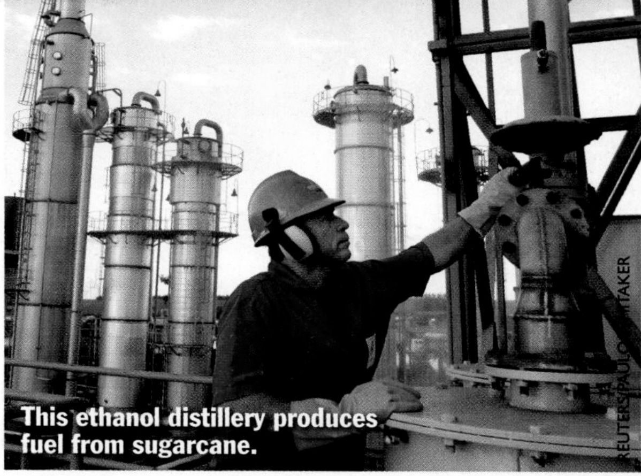

This ethanol distillery produces fuel from sugarcane.

REVIEW AND ASSESS

UNDERSTANDING THE ISSUE

1 **Making Connections** How does deforestation affect wildlife?

2 **Writing to Inform** In a short article, explain some of the ways governments are working to preserve the natural environments in their countries.

3 **Writing to Persuade** In a letter to an editor of a newspaper, discuss your beliefs about driving vehicles that use alternative fuels.

INTERNET RESEARCH ACTIVITIES

4 Go to www.savethehighseas.org, the Web site of the Deep Sea Conservation Coalition. Click the "About Us" link and scroll down to the "Coalition Steering Group Members." Read about some of the organizations and how they work to protect marine ecosytems. Write a short essay describing one of these activities.

5 With your teacher's help, do an online search on alternative fuel sources, such as ethanol or solar power. Read about how the nations of the world are developing these energy sources. Write a brief article that explains your findings.

BEYOND THE CLASSROOM

6 **Work in groups** to create and display an ecological mural on paper that illustrates how people can protect natural environments in your community.

7 **At your school or local library,** research what other countries are doing to decrease their dependency on foreign oil imports. Do you think their strategies will succeed? Why or why not?

Major Producers of Ethanol

Ethanol can be made from sugarcane and corn. As oil prices soar, the nations of the world are expected to produce more ethanol. Here is a look at major producers in 2006.

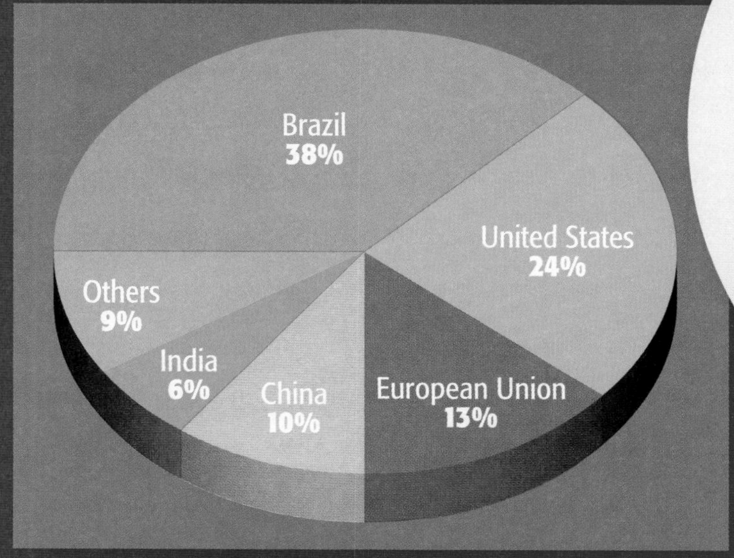

Source: University of York Science and Education Group, United Kingdom.

Building Graph Reading Skills

1. **Analyzing Data** What percentage of the world's ethanol is produced by the United States and the European Union?

2. **Identifying Cause and Effect** Brazil is the world's largest producer of ethanol. As the world searches for less expensive energy sources, how might Brazil's top ranking help its economy grow?

Guide to Reading

BIG Idea

People's actions can change the physical environment.

Content Vocabulary

- selva *(p. 177)*
- favela *(p. 177)*
- gaucho *(p. 179)*
- national debt *(p. 180)*
- default *(p. 180)*
- sodium nitrate *(p. 182)*

Academic Vocabulary

- maintain *(p. 178)*
- issue *(p. 178)*

Reading Strategy

Identifying Central Issues Use a diagram like the one below to describe Brazil's economy. Write the main idea on the line to the left and supporting details on the lines to the right. You can add as many additional lines as you have details.

South America

Spotlight Video

Picture This This giant dish is like an "eye" studying the universe. The Swedish ESO (European Southern Observatory) Sub-millimeter Telescope, or SEST, is not like some telescopes that use light from stars or planets to "see" them. SEST is able to study distant objects by gathering radio waves that radiate from them. The telescope is located in the southern Atacama Desert in Chile, where the clear sky conditions are ideal for this type of research. To learn more about South America today, read Section 3.

Learning about the universe in Chile

Brazil

Main Idea **Brazil is a leading economic power, but concerns have grown about its use of the Amazon rain forest.**

Geography and You Did you know that some of the best farmland in the United States was once forestland? The forests were cleared by farmers. Read to find out how and why Brazil's forests are being cut down.

Brazil is the fifth-largest country in the world and the largest in South America. The country is known for its Amazon rain forest, which Brazilians call the **selva.** This resource is threatened by economic growth.

Brazil's People

With 187 million people, Brazil has the largest population of all Latin American countries. Brazil's culture is largely Portuguese because they were the first and largest European group to settle Brazil. Today Brazilians are of European, African, Native American, Asian, or mixed ancestry. Almost all of them speak a Brazilian form of Portuguese, which includes many words from Native American and African languages.

Most of Brazil's people live in cities along the Atlantic coast. São Paulo and Rio de Janeiro are among the largest cities in the world. In recent years, millions of Brazilians have moved from rural areas to coastal cities to find better jobs. Many of these migrants have settled in favelas. **Favelas** are overcrowded slum areas that surround many Brazilian cities. To reduce city crowding, the government now encourages people to move back to less-populated, inland areas. In 1960 Brazil moved its capital from Rio de Janeiro to the newly built city of Brasília 600 miles (966 km) inland. With more than 2 million people, Brasília is a modern and rapidly growing city.

NATIONAL GEOGRAPHIC

Harvesting Sugarcane

A truck is loaded with sugarcane at a farm in southeastern Brazil. ***Human-Environment Interaction*** **In what unique way does Brazil make use of its sugarcane?**

Brazil's Economy

Brazil has a mixed economy. Most businesses are in private hands, but the government owns some firms. In recent years, the government has sold off many of these firms. By reducing its involvement, the government aims to promote competition and strengthen the economy.

Brazil is one of the world's leading food producers. It grows more coffee, oranges, and cassava than any other country. Brazil's farm output has grown greatly in recent years. This is partly because people have cleared land from the rain forest for farms. Also, farmers now use machinery to do many tasks. Finally, farmers have planted crops that have been scientifically changed to produce larger harvests.

Brazil also has valuable mineral resources, such as iron ore, bauxite, tin, manganese, gold, silver, and diamonds. Offshore deposits of oil, as well as hydroelectric power from rivers, supply energy. Brazil also uses sugarcane to make a substitute for gasoline.

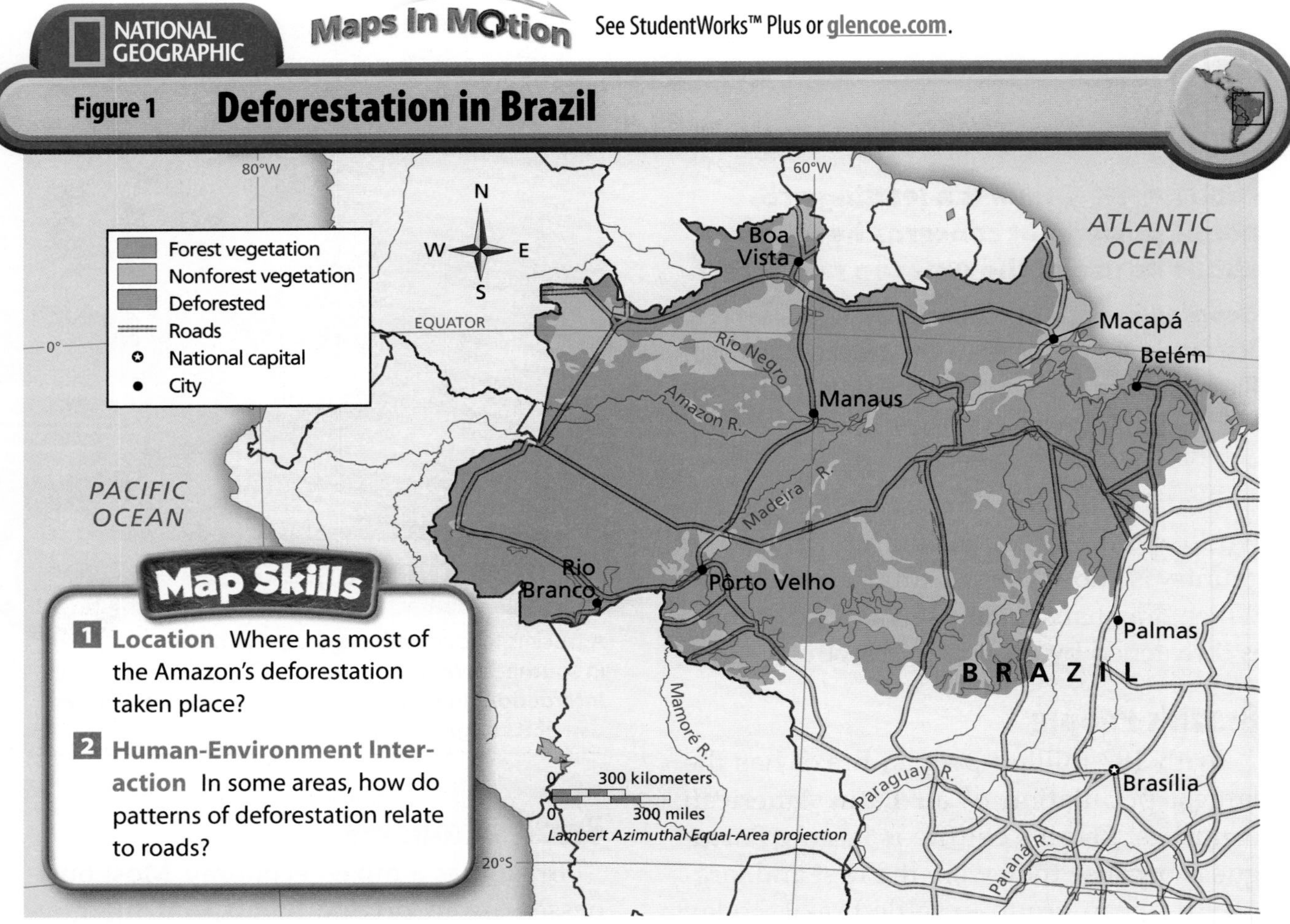

Brazil has successful industries too. Most manufacturing takes place in São Paulo and other southeastern cities. Factory workers produce heavy industrial goods, such as machinery, airplanes, and cars. They also make food products, medicines, paper, and clothing.

The Rain Forest

Brazil's greatest natural resource is the Amazon rain forest. It is the world's largest rain forest area, yet it also has the highest rate of deforestation. Each year, the land deforested in the Amazon rain forest is equal in size to Ohio. **Figure 1** shows how much of the rain forest has been lost.

Why is the rain forest shrinking? To increase jobs and make products for export, Brazil's government has encouraged mining, logging, and farming in the rain forest. These activities lead to soil erosion and harm the rain forest's ecosystem and biodiversity.

As deforestation takes place, roads are built, bringing companies, farmers, and change. Native Americans who live in the rain forest find it difficult to follow their traditional cultures as this occurs.

In addition, tropical forests give off huge amounts of oxygen and play a role in **maintaining,** or keeping up, the Earth's climate patterns. Forests also provide shelter to many wildlife species that may not survive if deforestation continues. Thus, although the rain forest belongs to Brazil, the effects of deforestation are felt worldwide. Because deforestation is a global **issue,** or problem, other nations have convinced Brazil to protect at least part of the rain forest from economic development.

Brazil's Government

Brazil declared independence from Portugal in 1822. During most of the 1800s, emperors ruled the country. Today Brazil is a democratic federal republic, in which people elect a president and other leaders. Brazil has many political parties, not just two main ones, as does the United States.

The national government of Brazil is much stronger than its 26 state governments. Like the United States, Brazil's national government has three branches. The president heads the executive branch, which carries out the laws. The National Congress, which is similar to the U.S. Congress, makes the laws. A Supreme Federal Tribunal, or court, heads a judicial system that interprets the laws.

Reading Check **Analyzing Information** Why has Brazil's agricultural output greatly increased?

NATIONAL GEOGRAPHIC

Brazil's Government

▲ Brazil's President Luiz Inacio Lula da Silva (left) talks with Governor Rosinha Garotinho of the state of Rio de Janeiro. ***Place*** **How is Brazil's government like that of the United States?**

Argentina

Main Idea **Argentina has experienced harsh military rule but now has a democratic government.**

Geography and You How would you feel if the government seized a member of your family and you never saw him or her again? Read to find out how Argentina went through a period of violent rule in recent decades.

Argentina is South America's second-largest country after Brazil. It is about the size of the United States east of the Mississippi River. The Andes tower over western Argentina. South and east of the Andes lies a dry, windswept plateau called Patagonia. The center of Argentina has vast treeless plains known as the Pampas. More than two-thirds of Argentina's people live in this central area.

Argentina's People

About 85 percent of Argentina's people are of European ancestry, especially Spanish and Italian. European cultural traditions are stronger in Argentina than in most other Latin American countries.

The majority of people in Argentina are city dwellers. In fact, more than one-third of the country's population lives in the capital, Buenos Aires. This bustling city is a seat of government, a busy port, and a center of culture. Buenos Aires resembles a European city with its parks, beautiful buildings, wide streets, and cafés. It has been nicknamed "the Paris of the South."

Argentina's Economy

Argentina's economy depends heavily on farming and ranching. Huge ranches cover the Pampas. There, **gauchos** (GOW·chohs), or cowhands, raise livestock. Gauchos are Argentina's national symbol.

NATIONAL GEOGRAPHIC

Beef Cattle in Argentina

Beef plays an important role in Argentina's foreign trade. Earnings from exports of animal products were about 1.9 billion dollars a year in the early 2000s. ***Location*** **Where are most of Argentina's livestock raised?**

They are admired for their independence and horse-riding skills. The livestock that the gauchos herd and tend are a vital part of the economy. Beef and beef products are Argentina's chief exports.

Argentina is one of the most industrialized countries in South America. Most factories are in or near Buenos Aires. They produce food products, cars, chemicals, and textiles. Zinc, iron ore, and copper are mined in the Andes. Oil fields lie in the Andes as well as in Patagonia.

Despite these resources, Argentina's economy has struggled. To help its economy grow, Argentina borrowed money from foreign banks during the late 1900s. However, this led to a high **national debt,** or money owed by the government. A few years ago, Argentina had to default on its debts to the foreign banks. To **default** is to miss a debt payment to the company or person who lent the money. People in other countries stopped investing money in Argentina's businesses. This caused a severe economic slowdown in Argentina. Recently the economy has recovered, and the government has paid off part of the debt.

Argentina's Government

After independence in the early 1800s, Argentina was torn apart by civil war. By the mid-1850s, a strong national government had emerged, and Argentina prospered. During the early 1900s, though, the economy suffered, and the military took over. One of the military leaders, Juan Perón, became a dictator in the late 1940s. Perón tried to improve the economy and to help the workers. At the same time, he restricted freedom of speech and freedom of the press. These actions made people unhappy. In 1955 a revolt drove Perón from power and restored democracy.

Military officers again took control in the 1970s. They ruled harshly and secretly seized and killed thousands of people they thought opposed their policies. The families of these people did not know what had happened to them. It was a time of fear.

In 1982 Argentina suffered defeat in a war with the United Kingdom over control of the Falkland Islands. The Falklands, known to Argentinians as the Malvinas, lie in the Atlantic Ocean. After their defeat, military leaders gave up power, and elected leaders won control of the government.

Today, Argentina is a democratic federal republic. It has a central government and 23 state governments. A legislature with two houses makes the laws. A Supreme Court heads a system of judges. The nation is led by a powerful president elected every four years. In 2007, Cristina Fernandez was elected Argentina's first woman president.

Reading Check **Explaining** Why are food products among the leading manufactured items in Argentina?

Other Countries of South America

Main Idea **Economic growth for other countries of South America has been hindered by political and social troubles.**

Geography and You Can you recall hard times and good times in your life? Read on to learn which nations in South America are experiencing hard times and which are experiencing good times.

Many countries in South America face the same challenges as Brazil and Argentina. Some, such as Venezuela, Colombia, and Chile, have relatively strong economies. Others, however, face more difficult economic hardships.

Venezuela

Venezuela lies along the Caribbean Sea in northern South America. It is one of the world's leading producers of oil and natural gas. Although it relies mainly on oil production, Venezuela also benefits from mining bauxite, gold, diamonds, and emeralds. The country's factories make steel, chemicals, and food products. Farmers grow sugarcane and bananas or raise cattle. Most Venezuelans are poor, and some live in slums that sprawl over the hills around the capital, Caracas.

In 1998 Venezuelans elected a former military leader, Hugo Chávez, as president. Chávez promised to use oil money to better the lives of Venezuela's poor. His strong rule, however, split the country into opposing groups. Chávez also tried to spread his influence overseas. He became friendly with Cuba's leader, Fidel Castro, and frequently criticized the United States.

Colombia

Venezuela's neighbor, Colombia, has coasts on both the Caribbean Sea and the Pacific Ocean. The Andes rise in the western part of Colombia. Nearly 80 percent of Colombia's people live in the valleys and highland plateaus of the Andes. Bogotá (BOH·goh·TAH), the capital and largest city, lies on one of these plateaus.

Colombia has many natural resources, such as coal, oil, and copper. It is the world's leading supplier of emeralds. Colombian coffee, a major export, is famous for its rich flavor. Colombia also exports bananas, sugarcane, rice, and cotton.

Despite these economic strengths, Colombia has much political unrest. Wealth remains in the hands of a few, and many people are poor. Since the 1970s, rebel forces have fought the government and now control parts of the country.

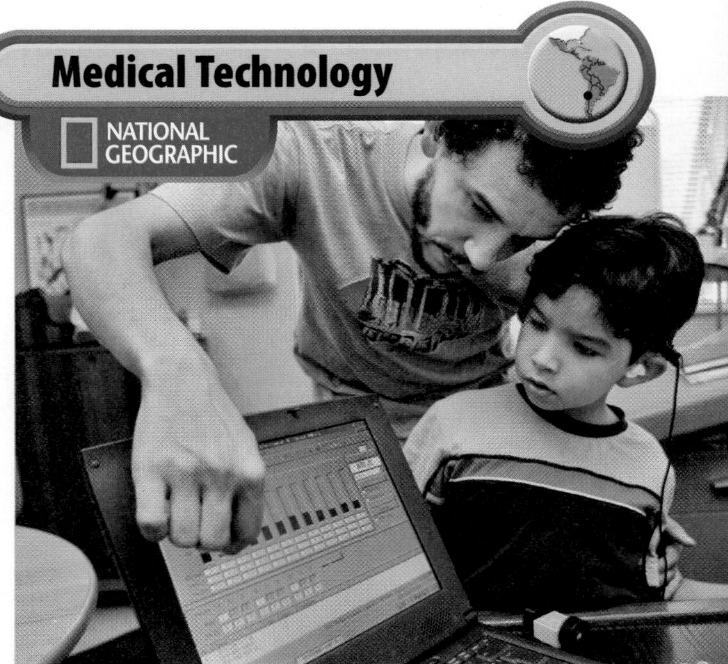

A six-year-old boy hears for the first time as a result of new medical equipment provided by Chile's government. ***Regions*** **In addition to Chile, what other South American countries have relatively strong economies?**

Drug dealers are a major problem in Colombia. The dealers pay farmers to grow coca leaves, which are used to make the illegal drug cocaine. Much of the cocaine is smuggled into the United States and Europe. Drug dealers have used their profits to build private armies. The United States has lent Colombia support in an effort to break the power of the drug dealers.

Chile

Chile lies along the southern Pacific coast of South America. It has an unusual ribbonlike shape that is 2,652 miles long (4,268 km) and an average of 110 miles (177 km) wide. Chile's landscapes range from extremely dry desert in the north to ice formations in the south.

In recent years, Chile has had strong economic growth. Mining forms the backbone of Chile's economy. Chile is a major world producer of copper. It also mines and exports gold, silver, iron ore, and **sodium nitrate,** a mineral used in fertilizer and explosives.

Agriculture is also a major economic activity. Farmers produce wheat, corn, beans, sugarcane, and potatoes. The grapes and apples you eat in winter may come from Chile's summer harvest. Many people also raise cattle, sheep, and other livestock. Northern Chile's fishing industry is the largest in South America.

Like Argentina, Chile has emerged from a long period of military rule. During that time, the government treated its opponents harshly. Today, Chile is a democracy. In 2006 Michelle Bachelet was elected the country's first woman president.

Reading Check **Identifying** What resource is especially important to Venezuela?

Section 3 Review

Vocabulary

1. **Explain** the significance of:
   a. selva **b.** favela **c.** gaucho **d.** national debt **e.** default **f.** sodium nitrate

Main Ideas

2. **Explaining** In what ways has Brazil improved its economy?
3. **Sequencing** Use a diagram like the one below to show changes in Argentina's government following independence.

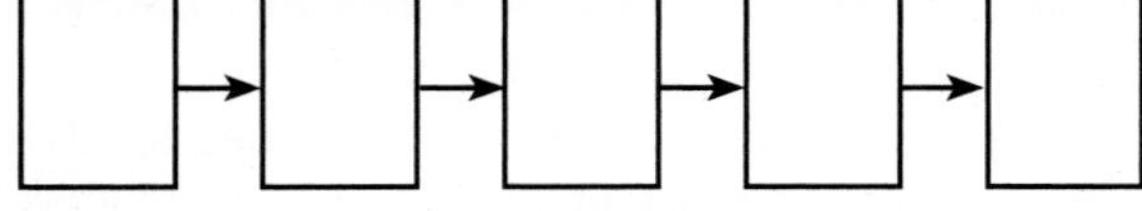

4. **Describing** Describe the problem of illegal drugs in Colombia.

Critical Thinking

5. BIG Idea How are Brazilians changing the rain forest, and why does that matter to people in other areas of the world?
6. **Challenge** Do you think Venezuela is likely to suffer from focusing on one major product? Why or why not?

Writing About Geography

7. **Using Your** FOLDABLES Use your Foldable to write a paragraph comparing the roles that two governments of South America play in economic affairs. Be sure to analyze how effective you think their governments are.

Visual Summary

Mexico

- Mexico City is one of the world's largest cities.
- Mexico's culture reflects both European and Native American influences.
- Industry and farming dominate Mexico's North; agriculture and tourism lead in the South.
- Many Mexicans have migrated to cities and to the United States to find jobs.

Subsistence farming, Mexico

Central America and the Caribbean

- Civil wars have slowed economic growth in parts of Central America.
- Costa Rica's citizens have a high literacy rate and enjoy a stable government.
- The Panama Canal enables ships to pass between the Atlantic and Pacific Oceans.
- Many Caribbean islands' economies rely on tourism.

Logs from Amazon forest, Brazil

Brazil

- Brazil is the biggest and most populous country in South America.
- Brazil's people, who speak Portuguese, are a mix of many different ethnic backgrounds.
- Brazil has many resources and a productive economy.
- Economic development threatens the Amazon rain forest.

Cruise ship docked in the British Virgin Islands

Argentina

- A large grassland called the Pampas covers much of Argentina.
- Argentina's economy depends on farming and ranching.
- More than a third of Argentina's people live in the capital, Buenos Aires.
- After years of military rule, Argentina is today a democracy.

Oil rig in Venezuela

Other Countries of South America

- Venezuela has relied on oil wealth to build a stronger economy.
- Colombia has been weakened by political unrest and illegal drug trade.
- Chile's economy depends on the export of copper and agricultural products.

Study anywhere, anytime! Download quizzes and flash cards to your PDA from **glencoe.com**.

CHAPTER 6 ASSESSMENT

GA CRCT Practice

TEST-TAKING TIP

When you begin to take a test, look through it first. Find out how many questions there are or how many sections are included. Are some questions worth more points than others? As you answer the questions, pace yourself accordingly.

Directions: Choose the best answer for each question.

1 **Mexico, like the United States, is a federal republic. Which of the following sentences describes a federal republic?**

A Power is held by one person.
B Power is held by a small group of people.
C Power is divided between national and state governments.
D Power is divided among the wealthy members of the population.

2 **Which cultures have influenced Mexico the most?**

A European and Russian
B European and Native American
C Native American and Slavic
D Spanish and French

3 **What was the purpose of the North American Free Trade Agreement (NAFTA)?**

A to stop immigration from Mexico to the United States and Canada
B to create plantations in southern Mexico that supply crops for Canada and the United States
C to stop global warming
D to end trade barriers among Canada, the United States, and Mexico

4 **Which group continues to fight for the rights of poor Native Americans in Mexico?**

A Zapatistas
B vaqueros
C maquiladoras
D migrant workers

5 **Cuba has a command economy. Which of the following statements is an accurate description of a command economy?**

A People decide how resources are used and what goods and services are produced.
B The government decides how resources are used and what goods and services are produced.
C People and the government decide how resources are used and what goods and services are produced.
D Trading partners decide how resources are used and what goods and services are produced.

6 **Why has Brazil become one of the world's leading food producers?**

A The government has taken control of farms.
B People have cleared land from the rain forest in order to build farms.
C Brazil's farmers are planting more crops because people are eating more.
D Brazil uses fertilizers made with sugarcane.

7 **Argentina is one of the most industrialized countries in South America. Where are most of its mineral resources mined?**

A the Pampas
B the Himalaya
C the Alps
D the Andes

8 **Which South American country is one of the world's leading producers of oil and natural gas?**

A Venezuela
B Bolivia
C Peru
D Argentina

9 **Look at the graph.**

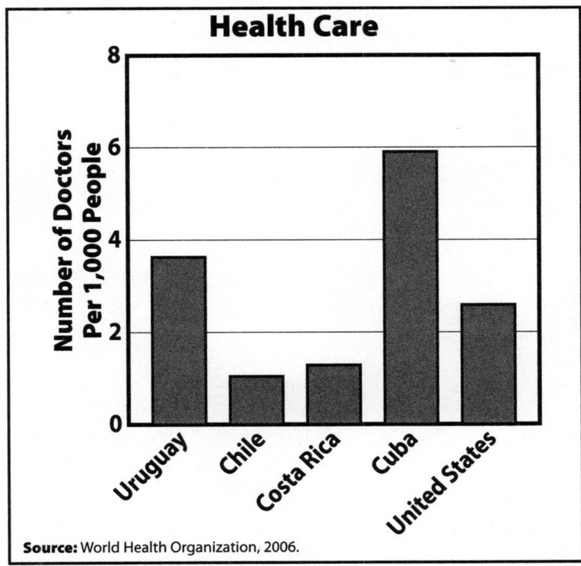

Which country has the fewest doctors per thousand people?

A Cuba
B Uruguay
C Chile
D Costa Rica

10 **Which statement does the graph support?**

A Uruguay and Costa Rica have about the same number of doctors per 1,000 people.
B Chile has more disease than the other countries.
C Most of the people living in Chile are doctors.
D Cuba has more doctors per 1,000 people than either the United States or Uruguay.

11 **Read the passage below.**

> *Since 1972 the Mil Hojas pasta factory [in Argentina] has churned out delicacies like ravioli and Italian desserts. But Mil Hojas' fortunes—along with those of the national economy—began to decline with the late 1990s as deep recession set in.*
>
> *The factory owners decided to abandon it amid a national epidemic of bankruptcies. Mil Hojas, like many other factories in Argentina, was to permanently close its doors.*
>
> *That was when its workers decided to act. They took back, or "recovered" Mil Hojas, transforming it into what today is a thriving cooperative, as Argentina emerges from one of the worst economic crises in its history.*
>
> *Today, thousands of workers are reactivating previously closed factories on their own terms and . . . breathing life into the national economy.*
>
> —Eduardo Stanley, "Argentina's Recovered Factories: A Story of Economic Success"

Which statement best summarizes the main idea of the passage?

A Food factories in Argentina, like Mil Hoja, have closed because food can be made more cheaply in other countries.
B Argentina's government has taken over failing businesses and made them profitable again.
C Factory owners have caused numerous bankruptcies in Argentina.
D Argentina's economy is strengthening as workers become owners of previously closed factories.

For additional test practice, use Self-Check Quizzes—Chapter 6 at glencoe.com.

Need Extra Help?

If You Missed Questions. . .	1	2	3	4	5	6	7	8	9	10	11
Go to Page. . .	163	164	165	166	170	177	180	181	32	32	179

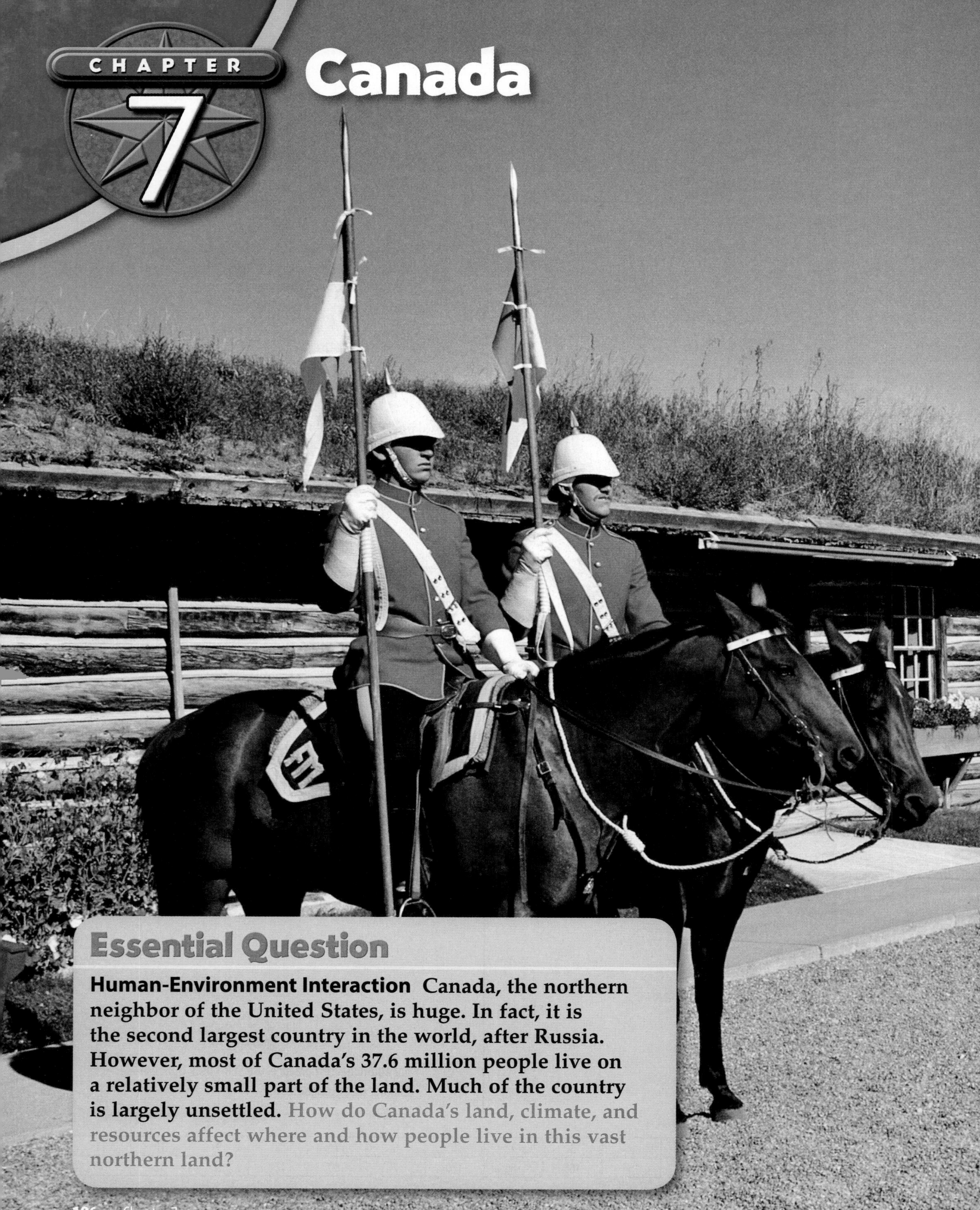

CHAPTER 7

Canada

Essential Question

Human-Environment Interaction **Canada, the northern neighbor of the United States, is huge. In fact, it is the second largest country in the world, after Russia. However, most of Canada's 37.6 million people live on a relatively small part of the land. Much of the country is largely unsettled.** How do Canada's land, climate, and resources affect where and how people live in this vast northern land?

Fort McLeod, Alberta, Canada

Section 1: Physical Geography and Climate

BIG IDEA Geographers study how people and physical features are distributed on Earth's surface. Because of landforms and climate, Canada's people can only live in a small part of the country.

Section 2: History and Culture

BIG IDEA Culture influences people's perceptions about places and regions. Canada's history has shaped the way Canadians feel about their nation.

Section 3: Canada Today

BIG IDEA Patterns of economic activities result in global interdependence. Canada is one of the world's wealthiest nations, and its economy is closely linked to the economy of the United States.

FOLDABLES™ Study Organizer

Summarizing Information Make this Foldable to help you summarize information about the physical and human geography of Canada.

Step 1 Fold the top of an 11 x 17 sheet of paper down about 2 inches.

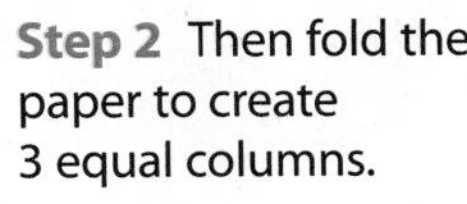

Step 2 Then fold the paper to create 3 equal columns.

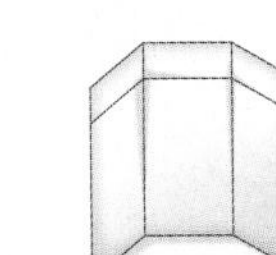

Step 3 Label each column of your Foldable as shown.

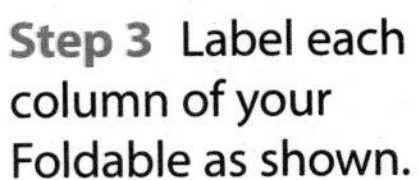

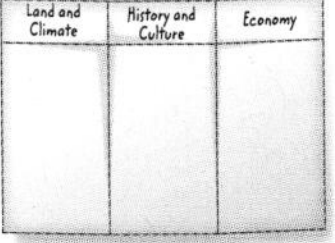

Reading and Writing Using the notes in your Foldable, write several short journal entries from an imaginary trip through Canada, describing the landforms, cultural features, and economic activities you encounter.

Visit glencoe.com and enter QuickPass™ code GA6EOW6225c7 for Chapter 7 resources.

Guide to Reading

BIG Idea

Geographers study how people and physical features are distributed on Earth's surface.

Content Vocabulary

- prairie *(p. 189)*
- navigable *(p. 190)*
- glacier *(p. 190)*
- divide *(p. 190)*

Academic Vocabulary

- constrain *(p. 189)*
- route *(p. 190)*

Reading Strategy

Analyzing Information Use a chart like the one below to list key facts about four regions of Canada.

	Land and Water	Climate	Resources
East			
West			
Central			
North			

Physical Geography and Climate

Picture This Long ago, ice canoeing was a way to deliver supplies across the icy Saint Lawrence River during winter. Ice canoes were small enough to dodge floating ice and light enough to carry over solid ice. Traveling between the river's islands was dangerous, difficult work, but it was necessary to carry vital items such as medicine and mail. Today, ice canoes are used for sport. Many Canadian teams compete in ice races at winter festivals. Learn more about Canada's climate in Section 1.

▼ Ice canoe racing in Toronto, Canada

Landforms and Bodies of Water

Main Idea **The region rises in elevation from east to west.**

Geography and You Do you live in an area that is flat, hilly, or mountainous? Read to find out about the major landforms of Canada.

Canada sits on the northern border of the United States and stretches up to the Arctic Ocean. It has coasts along the Atlantic Ocean in the east and the Pacific Ocean in the west.

Landforms of Canada

Canada has four main regions. In the east, highlands rise. The country's center is covered by a massive plateau surrounded by lowlands. The western region has mountains, plateaus, and valleys. The far north is dotted by islands.

The highlands of eastern Canada are an extension of the Appalachian Mountains found in the eastern United States. Erosion has worn down the peaks of this old range. As a result, the Appalachian Mountains in Canada are mainly low mountains or hills. The highest mountains in this area reach only about 4,000 feet (1,219 m) high. The thin, rocky soil in this part of the country **constrains,** or limits, farming.

Dominating central Canada are a plateau and a lowland plain. The higher land is a feature called the Canadian Shield. This horseshoe-shaped area of rocky hills, lakes, and evergreen forests wraps around Hudson Bay. With poor soil and a cold climate, the Canadian Shield cannot be farmed. It does, however, contain many mineral deposits.

A second, broader horseshoe of lowlands wraps around the Canadian Shield.

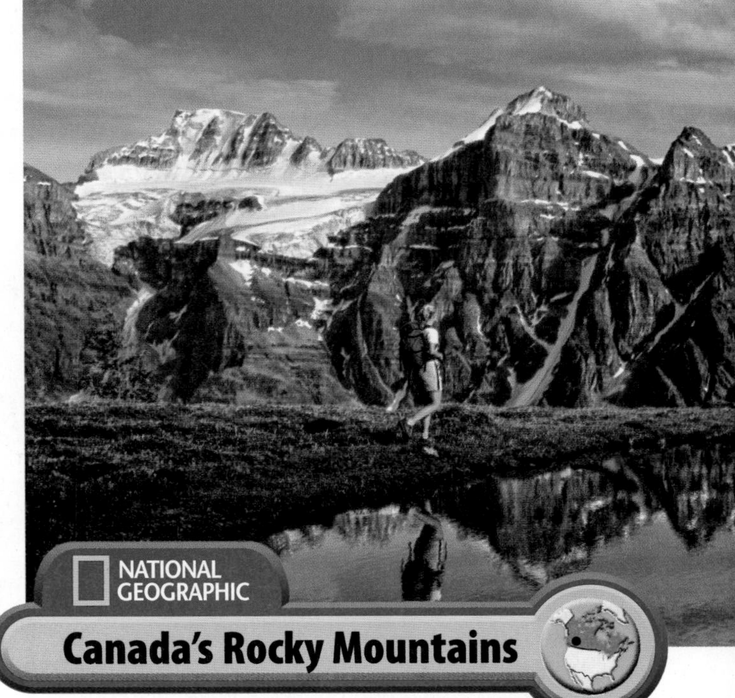

NATIONAL GEOGRAPHIC

Canada's Rocky Mountains

Banff National Park in Alberta, Canada, is the country's oldest national park and a popular location for hikers. ***Place*** **How do Canada's eastern and western mountain ranges differ?**

In the east, this area reaches down to the St. Lawrence River and the Great Lakes. Good soil here supports farming. The western lowlands stretch south to the United States, west to the Rocky Mountains, and north to the Arctic Ocean. The southernmost area is a **prairie,** or rolling inland grasslands. This area has rich soil that is well-suited for growing wheat.

West of these plains is a cordillera, which is a group of mountain ranges that run side by side. The eastern edge of this cordillera is the Rocky Mountains. High plateaus and basins separate these mountains from another range, the Coast Mountains, to the west. A narrow lowland plain stretches along the Pacific coast. Both of these mountain ranges have peaks much higher than those in eastern Canada.

The few thousand islands of Canada's Arctic north reach from the top of Hudson Bay to near the North Pole. These frigid lands are mostly barren.

FIGURE 1 **St. Lawrence Seaway and Locks**

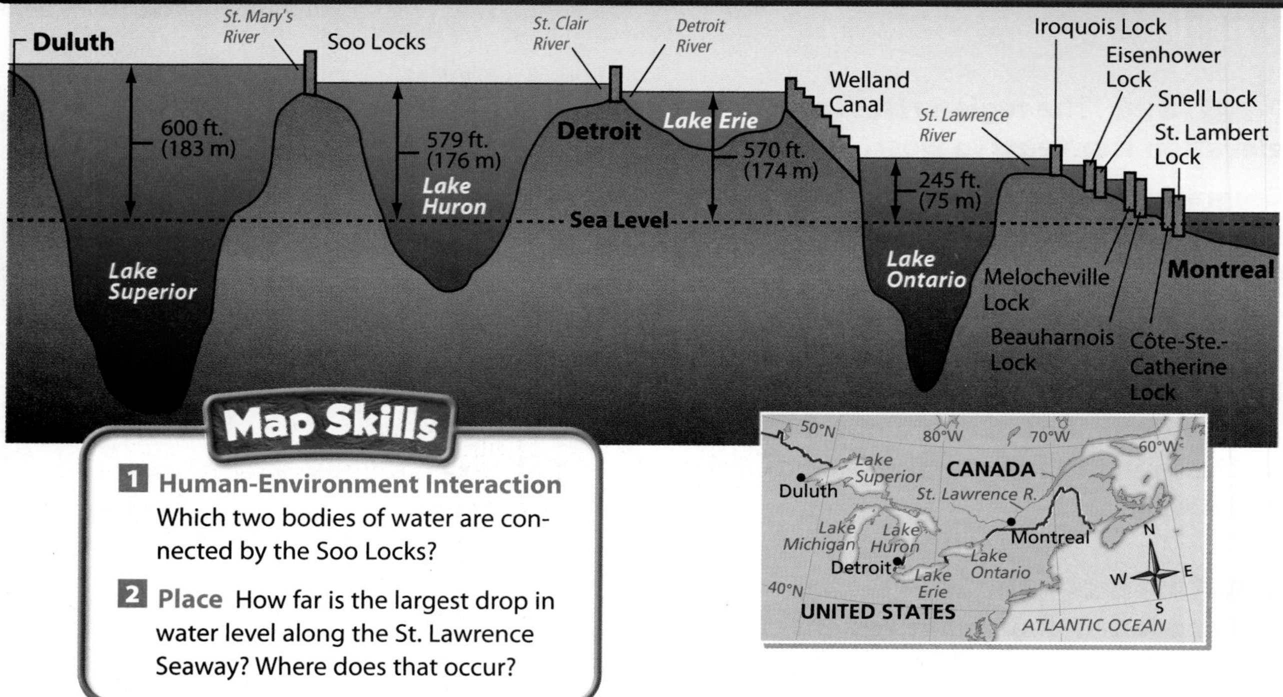

Map Skills

1. **Human-Environment Interaction** Which two bodies of water are connected by the Soo Locks?
2. **Place** How far is the largest drop in water level along the St. Lawrence Seaway? Where does that occur?

Bodies of Water

Canada has many freshwater lakes and rivers. Many of its rivers are **navigable,** or wide and deep enough to allow the passage of ships.

The Great Lakes—the world's largest group of freshwater lakes—lie on central Canada's southern border. Thousands of years ago, **glaciers,** or giant sheets of ice, formed lakes Ontario, Erie, Huron, Superior, and Michigan. Canada shares all but Lake Michigan with the United States.

The waters of these connected lakes flow into the St. Lawrence River, which empties into the Atlantic Ocean. The St. Lawrence is one of Canada's most important rivers. The cities of Quebec, Montreal, and Ottawa developed along the river and its tributaries. They depend on the St. Lawrence for transportation.

For many years, rapids, waterfalls, and other obstructions kept ships from navigating the entire **route,** or journey, from the Great Lakes to the ocean. Then, in the mid-1900s, the United States and Canada built the St. Lawrence Seaway. As shown in **Figure 1,** the Seaway links the Great Lakes and the Atlantic. Ships now carry raw materials and products from cities such as Windsor and Toronto to the rest of the world.

In western Canada, the high ridge of the Rockies is called the Continental Divide. A **divide** is a high point that determines the direction that rivers flow. East of the Continental Divide, rivers flow east or north. They empty into interior lakes, the Arctic Ocean, Hudson Bay, or the Atlantic Ocean. West of the divide, rivers flow west. Some, like the Yukon, end in the Bering Sea. Others, like the Fraser, reach the Pacific Ocean.

Determining Cause and Effect How did the Great Lakes form?

Canada's Climate

Main Idea **Most people in Canada live in temperate climate regions.**

Geography and You What is the climate like in your area? Read to find out about the different climate regions in Canada.

Canada has several climate zones. As you see in **Figure 2,** though, most of the country lies in the coldest climate zones. In these zones, winters are long and cold, and summers are brief and cool. The extreme cold of the tundra prevents the growth of most plants. In the subarctic region, dense forests of evergreen trees thrive.

Most Canadians live in southern Canada and on the west coast. These areas have more temperate climates.

In southeastern Canada, warm summer winds from the west raise temperatures and allow farming. In the winter, the cold air blasts down from the Arctic and brings plentiful snow.

The prairie lands of south central Canada have either a dry steppe climate or a humid continental climate. The steppe areas are dominated by short grasses. Other areas receive more moisture and provide good land for farming.

The Pacific coast of British Columbia is affected by moist ocean winds. This area has a marine west coast climate of year-round mild temperatures and abundant rainfall. It is common to see evergreen forests, ferns, and mosses growing here.

Reading Check **Identifying** What type of vegetation is found in Canada's subarctic region?

NATIONAL GEOGRAPHIC **Maps In MOtion** See StudentWorks™ Plus or glencoe.com.

Figure 2 **Canada: Climate Zones**

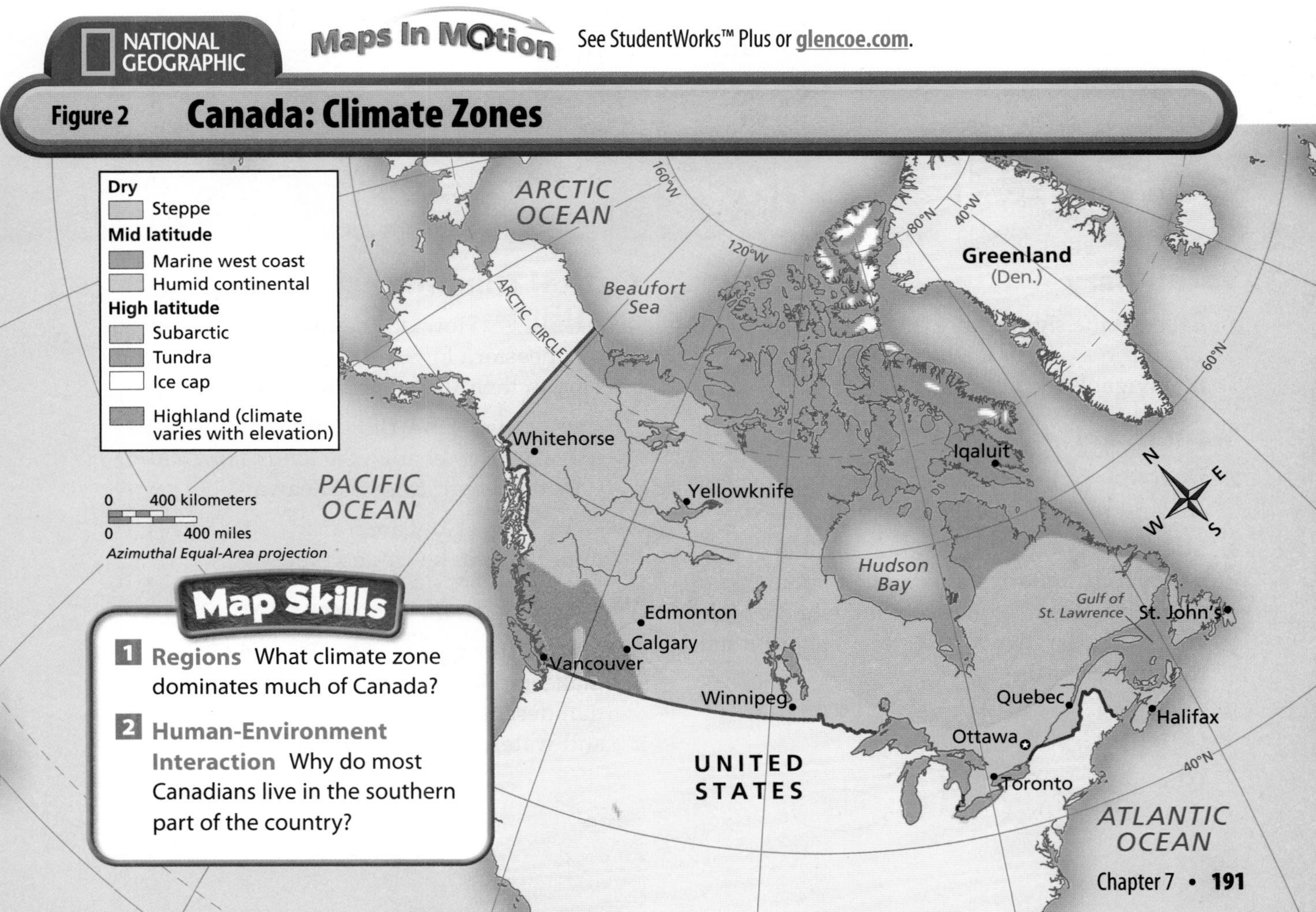

Map Skills

1. **Regions** What climate zone dominates much of Canada?
2. **Human-Environment Interaction** Why do most Canadians live in the southern part of the country?

Natural Resources

Main Idea **Energy and other resources helped Canada build a strong economy.**

Geography and You Where does the paper used for this book come from? Read to learn about the products made from Canada's natural resources.

Canada's energy resources include oil, natural gas, and coal. The country exports much of this energy to the United States. Most of Canada's oil and natural gas reserves lie in or near the province of Alberta. Canada also has significant amounts of coal, mainly in British Columbia.

Another energy source is hydroelectric power. Niagara Falls is a major source of this power for Canada and the United States. The falls lie on the Niagara River, which connects Lake Erie to Lake Ontario.

Mineral resources are also plentiful in Canada. Parts of eastern Canada have large iron ore deposits. The Rocky Mountains yield gold, silver, and copper. Deep within the Canadian Shield are iron ore, copper, nickel, gold, and uranium. These minerals helped create a large manufacturing region in southern Ontario and Quebec.

Timber is another important resource in Canada. Lumber and wood products, such as paper, are major Canadian exports.

Fishing is a major economic activity in the coastal provinces. The Grand Banks, off Canada's southeast coast, was once a rich fishing grounds. Overfishing has dramatically reduced stocks of fish, however. As a result, Canada banned the fishing of some species in this area.

Reading Check **Describing** Describe Canada's energy resources and where they are located.

Section Review

Vocabulary

1. **Explain** the significance of:
   a. prairie
   b. navigable
   c. glacier
   d. divide

Main Ideas

2. **Describing** Describe the physical characteristics and resources of the Canadian Shield.
3. **Summarizing** Use a diagram like the one below to summarize information about one of Canada's climate zones. Write the name of the zone in the large oval and details about it in the smaller ovals.

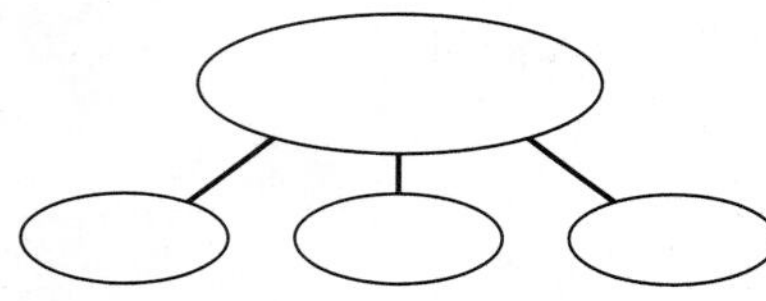

Critical Thinking

4. **BIG Idea** How do the eastern highlands, the southeastern lowlands, and the prairies compare in their usefulness for farming?
5. **Explaining** How did building the St. Lawrence Seaway change the land? How did Canada benefit from the Seaway?
6. **Challenge** How are Canada's resources important to the United States?

Writing About Geography

7. **Using Your FOLDABLES** Use your Foldable to make and write captions for a map of Canada that describes the importance of landforms and waterways on people's lives.

Guide to Reading

BIG Idea

Culture influences people's perceptions about places and regions.

Content Vocabulary

- colony *(p. 194)*
- dominion *(p. 195)*
- representative democracy *(p. 195)*
- parliamentary democracy *(p. 195)*
- federalism *(p. 196)*
- bilingual *(p. 196)*
- indigenous *(p. 196)*

Academic Vocabulary

- economy *(p. 195)*
- generate *(p. 197)*
- participate *(p. 197)*

Reading Strategy

Making a Time Line Use a diagram like the one below to list key dates in the history of Canada.

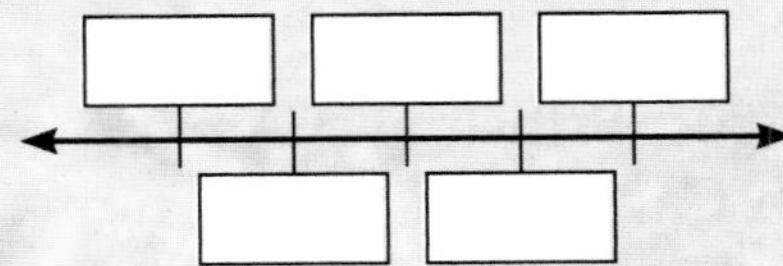

History and Culture

 Section Audio  Spotlight Video

Picture This This towering sculpture is a totem pole that stands with others like it in a park in Vancouver, Canada's major Pacific coastal city. Totem poles are carved from tall cedar trees and painted by First Nation peoples of the Pacific Northwest. The colorful figures of each totem pole represent animals and ancestors and often tell a story about a particular clan, or family group. Read Section 2 to learn more about the unique history and cultures of Canada.

▼ A totem pole in Vancouver's Stanley Park

The History of Canada

Main Idea **Canada gradually won independence from British rule during the late 1800s and early 1900s.**

Geography and You Do people of varying ethnic backgrounds live in your area? Read to learn how different peoples have helped build Canada.

Canada was originally settled by Native American groups. They lived by hunting animals and gathering plants to eat. Many groups later learned to farm the land. The first Europeans to arrive in the area in about A.D. 1000 were Viking explorers from Scandinavia. They settled only briefly on the Newfoundland coast before leaving the Americas.

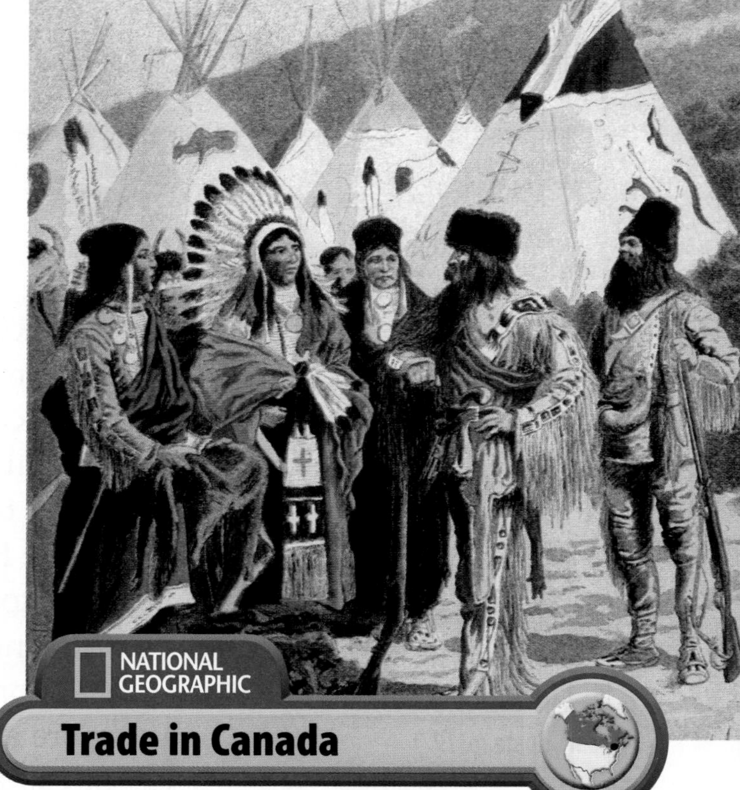

NATIONAL GEOGRAPHIC

Trade in Canada

As Europeans explored Canada, they made treaties and traded with the Native Americans who lived there. ***Place*** **What two European nations colonized Canada?**

Early Settlement

In the 1500s and 1600s, both England and France claimed large areas of Canada. They set up **colonies**, which are overseas settlements tied to a parent country. The French colony was called New France. It covered the area around the St. Lawrence River and the Great Lakes. The main cities in the colony were Quebec and Montreal.

Some French colonists settled on land and farmed. Others traded with Native Americans for beaver furs, which were then sold in Europe. The fur trade was very important to New France.

During the 1600s and 1700s, the English and French fought each other for territory around the globe. In 1707, England and Scotland united to form Great Britain. This union laid the foundation for the British Empire. In the 1760s, the British defeated France in a war and gained control of most of New France.

In the late 1700s, British and American settlers came to Canada in greater numbers than before. They built farms along the Atlantic coast and in what is now Ontario. French-speaking Canadians lived mostly in present-day Quebec. Tragically, warfare and diseases had nearly destroyed many Native American cultures by this time.

The Road to Independence

For many decades, Great Britain held various colonies in eastern Canada. These colonies constantly quarreled with one another over government policies. They feared that the United States would try to capture them, however. This fear forced

Social Studies ONLINE

Student Web Activity Visit glencoe.com and complete the Chapter 7 Web Activity about Native American groups in Canada.

them together. In 1867, most of the colonies united as the Dominion of Canada. As a **dominion,** Canada had its own government to run local affairs. Great Britain, though, controlled Canada's relations with other countries.

Under Canada's central government, the colonies became provinces, which are like states. At first, there were four provinces—Quebec, Ontario, Nova Scotia, and New Brunswick. Over the next hundred years, several nearby British-ruled areas joined Canada. They included Manitoba, British Columbia, Saskatchewan (suh·SKA·chuh·wuhn), and Alberta in the west, and Prince Edward Island and Newfoundland along the Atlantic coast. Along with these 10 provinces, Canada today has 3 territories—the Yukon Territory, the Northwest Territories, and Nunavut (NOO·nah·VOOT).

During the 1900s, many immigrants arrived, and Canada's population grew. So did its **economy,** or way of producing goods. In 1982, the British granted Canada full independence. That year, Canadians gained the right to change their constitution without British approval.

Canada's government promised to protect the French language and culture in Quebec. However, the English-speaking minority there was wealthier and controlled the economy. French speakers complained that they were treated unfairly.

Late in the 1900s, French-speaking leaders in Quebec launched a new political party. This party urged the people of Quebec to declare independence from Canada. While that step has never been taken, political unrest in Quebec continues to be a problem for Canada.

Reading Check **Summarizing** How did Canada become independent?

The Government of Canada

Main Idea Canadians have individual rights under their democratic government.

Geography and You Do you think democracy is a good government system? Why? Read to discover how Canada's government is set up.

Canada, like the United States, is a **representative democracy,** in which voters choose leaders who make and enforce the laws. Canada, however, is a **parliamentary democracy.** Voters elect representatives to a lawmaking body called Parliament. These representatives then choose an official called the prime minister to head the government.

Voting in Canada

NATIONAL GEOGRAPHIC

Citizens in Canada vote regularly to choose members of the legislative assembly known as the House of Commons. Members of the other assembly, the Senate, are chosen by government officials. ***Place*** **What is the head of Canada's government—who is chosen by Parliament—called?**

Officially, Canada is still ruled by the British monarch. In reality, however, Canadians are left to run their own affairs.

The structure of Canada's government reflects the idea called federalism. In **federalism,** power is divided between the federal, or national, government and smaller units that make up the nation, the provinces.

Canada's people have the right to vote for local officials, the leaders of their province, and members of Parliament. Under the Charter of Rights and Freedoms, which is similar to the U.S. Bill of Rights, Canadians also enjoy certain liberties, such as freedom of religion.

Reading Check **Explaining** How is Canada's government a federal system?

Quebec's French Culture

NATIONAL GEOGRAPHIC

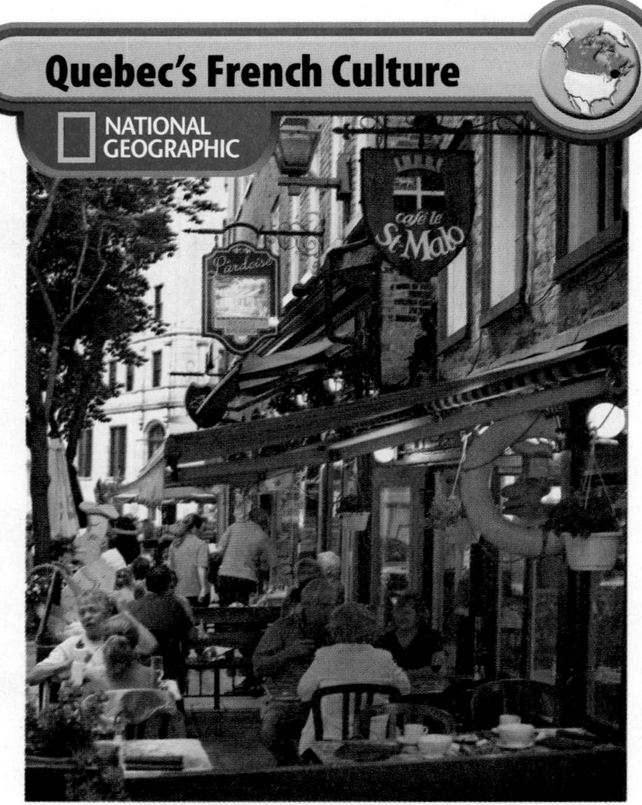

▲ The French-speaking city of Quebec, founded in 1608, is one of Canada's oldest settlements. ***Regions*** **What percentage of Canadians are of French ancestry?**

Cultures and Lifestyles of Canada

Main Idea **Canada is a nation of immigrants with many different cultures.**

Geography and You Have you played hockey or seen a hockey game? Hockey is a Canadian sport. Read to find out about the variety of Canadian cultures.

Canada has had difficulty building a strong national identity. Canada's vast size and many cultures cause some Canadians to feel more closely attached to their own region or group than to the country.

Mix of Cultures

About one-fourth of Canadians are of French ancestry. Most of them live in Quebec. People of British ancestry form another fourth of Canada's population. They live mainly in Ontario, along the east coast, and in British Columbia. Canada is a **bilingual** country, which means it has two official languages. Those languages are English and French. People of other European backgrounds form about 15 percent of Canada's population.

Canada also is home to people of Asian, African, and Latin American backgrounds. More than one million people are indigenous Canadians. **Indigenous** (ihn·DIH·juh·nuhs) refers to people who are descended from an area's first inhabitants. Many people in Canada call these groups the "First Nations."

One of these First Nations, the Inuit (IH·nu·wuht), wanted self-rule while remaining part of Canada. In 1999 the Canadian government created the territory of Nunavut for them. The name means "Our Land" in the Inuit language. There, the Inuit govern themselves.

Arts and Daily Life

Canadian art reflects both European and indigenous influences. The beauty of Canada's landscape has long been a favorite subject for many artists. Nature and history have been popular subjects for Canadian writers.

Centuries ago, indigenous peoples used song and dance as part of their religious rituals. European music, such as Irish and Scottish ballads, gained popularity after the 1700s. In recent decades, pop and rock have become as popular in Canada as in the United States.

Movies are also a major part of Canadian culture. The film industry **generates,** or makes, $5 billion each year.

Like Americans, Canadians are very mobile. Millions of them use cars to commute to work every day. Many city dwellers use public transportation, such as buses and trains, to travel locally.

Certain foods are regional favorites throughout Canada. Seafood dishes are popular in the Atlantic Provinces, while French cuisine is preferred in Quebec. Foods in Ontario reflect the different immigrant groups that settled there. British Columbia is known for its locally caught salmon and for Asian foods.

Canadians are enthusiastic about hockey—a sport that began in Canada—as well as lacrosse, which began as a Native American game. Many Canadians **participate,** or take part in, outdoor sports such as fishing and skiing.

Canadians celebrate the founding of their country on July 1. They also have a Thanksgiving holiday in October. As in the United States, different ethnic groups celebrate their heritage on special days.

✓ Reading Check **Explaining** Why was the territory of Nunavut created?

Section 2 Review

Vocabulary

1. **Explain** the meaning of *colony, dominion, representative democracy, parliamentary democracy, federalism, bilingual,* and *indigenous* by using each word in a sentence.

Main Ideas

2. **Identifying** What economic activities were pursued by the colonists of New France?
3. **Summarizing** Use a diagram like the one below to provide key details about the culture of Canada.

Critical Thinking

4. **Analyzing Information** Why did Canada's colonies come together in the mid-1800s?
5. **Challenge** How is Canada's government similar to and different from the government of the United States?
6. **BIG Idea** Explain why many people in Quebec have wanted to form a separate nation.

Writing About Geography

7. **Expository Writing** Write a paragraph explaining Canada's changing relationship with Great Britain over time.

Canada Today

Guide to Reading

BIG Idea

Patterns of economic activities result in global interdependence.

Content Vocabulary

- free market economy *(p. 199)*
- profit *(p. 199)*
- stock *(p. 199)*
- newsprint *(p. 200)*
- trade surplus *(p. 201)*
- acid rain *(p. 202)*

Academic Vocabulary

- reluctant *(p. 200)*
- restriction *(p. 201)*

Reading Strategy

Categorizing Information Use a diagram like the one below to list the economic regions in Canada and provide several key facts about each.

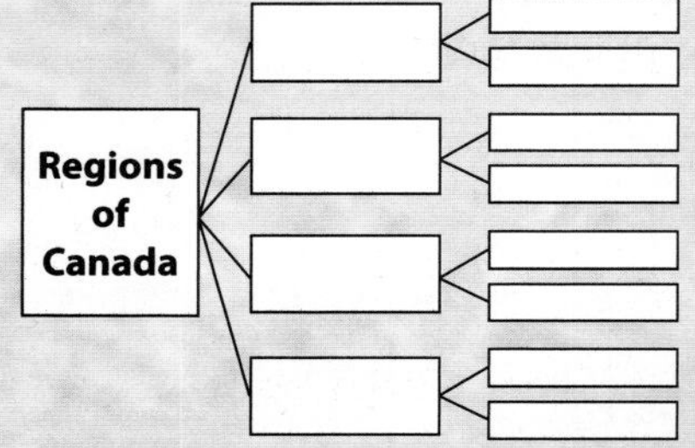

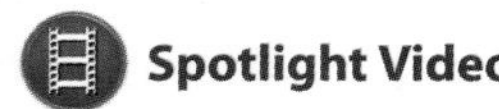

Picture This On a bright, cold winter day, skaters glide across an ice rink at Toronto's Nathan Phillips Square. In spring, the ice rink is transformed into a beautiful reflecting pool. It mirrors the graceful arches above it as well as Toronto's modern curve-shaped city hall in the distance. Nearby is the CN Tower, a symbol of Canada and one of the world's tallest buildings at a height of 1,815 feet (553 m). Learn more about Canada today in Section 3.

▼ Skating in downtown Toronto, Canada

Canada's Economy

Main Idea **Canada can be organized into economic regions.**

Geography and You Have you worked hard to build or make something? Did you feel a sense of accomplishment when you finished? Read to learn how Canadians have worked to build their economy.

The economic system of Canada is similar to that of the United States. Canadians have made their system work somewhat differently, however.

A Mixed Economy

Like the United States, Canada has a free market economy. In a **free market economy,** people are free to buy, sell, and produce whatever they want, with limited government involvement. They also can work wherever they want. A free market economy has two key groups: business owners and consumers.

Business owners who start their own businesses are called entrepreneurs. They develop an idea for a product to make or a service to provide. Then they form a company and gather resources to make that good or provide the service. They take a risk in the hopes of making a **profit,** or the money business owners keep after all expenses are paid.

Consumers shop for the best products and services at the best possible price. It is their demand for goods and services that drives the economy. Most consumers are also workers. Business owners hire them to do the work needed to provide the goods and services they supply.

People also take part in a free market by investing in businesses. People can buy **stock,** which represents part ownership in a company. When a company succeeds, it may pay some of its profits out to the people who own stock.

NATIONAL GEOGRAPHIC

Vancouver Harbor

Vancouver, Canada's busiest Pacific port, handles more than $75 billion of trade per year. ***Place*** **What sort of economy does Canada have?**

In a pure free market economy, the government plays a very small role. Most nations, though, have mixed economies. They mix some features of the free market system with more government control. That is true in Canada, where the government plays more of an economic role than does the government of the United States. For instance, the national and provincial governments of Canada provide health care to their people, a service not currently provided by the U.S. government for all Americans. Canada's government also regulates broadcasting, transport industries, and power companies.

Canada's Economic Regions

Resources are needed to produce a good or service, but some resources are more available in one region than another.

As a result, different regions have come to specialize in making products using their available resources. Canada consists of four economic regions.

Fishing was for many years a major industry in the Atlantic Provinces of Newfoundland and Labrador, Nova Scotia, Prince Edward Island, and New Brunswick. Overfishing, however, has greatly reduced fish populations and weakened the industry. The city of Halifax, in Nova Scotia, is a major shipping port in this region. The natural beauty of the Atlantic Provinces helps make tourism important in the region, also.

NATIONAL GEOGRAPHIC

Figure 3 Canada: Economic Regions

Map Skills

1. **Regions** Which of Canada's regions includes the least territory?
2. **Movement** Which region would make use of the St. Lawrence Seaway?

Canada's Central and Eastern Region includes the provinces of Quebec and Ontario. The paper industry is important in Quebec, as is the creation of hydroelectric power. Montreal is a major port and leading financial and industrial center. Quebec's economy has suffered in recent years. Because of the uncertainty over its independence, many outside businesses have been **reluctant,** or hesitant, to invest in Quebec's economy.

Ontario has the largest population and greatest wealth of Canada's provinces. It is a major agricultural, manufacturing, forestry, and mining center. Ontario's capital, Toronto, is Canada's largest city and a center of finance and business. Because of recent immigration, Toronto is now home to people from about 170 countries. Ottawa, the nation's capital, is also located in Ontario.

In the West region, farming and ranching are major economic activities in Manitoba, Saskatchewan, and Alberta. These provinces produce large amounts of wheat for export. Alberta also has large reserves of oil and natural gas.

Another province in the West, British Columbia, has extensive forests. These forests help make Canada the world's largest producer of **newsprint,** the type of paper used for printing newspapers. Mining, fishing, and tourism also support British Columbia's economy. The city of Vancouver is Canada's main Pacific port.

The three territories of Canada's vast North cover about one-third of the country. Many of the 25,000 people in this area are indigenous peoples. The main resources in the North are minerals such as gold and diamonds.

Reading Check **Explaining** How has political uncertainty affected Quebec's economy?

Canada and the World

Main Idea **Canada trades with countries throughout the world.**

Geography and You Think about all the trucks or trains you have seen carrying products to stores or to ports. Read to see how Canada is involved in world trade.

Because of its large economy, Canada trades with many countries. Much of Canada's trade, however, is with its neighbor to the south—the United States.

Trade With the United States and Mexico

Canada, like the United States, supports free trade. This means the removal of trade **restrictions,** or barriers, so that goods flow freely among countries. In 1994 Canada joined with the United States and Mexico in the North American Free Trade Agreement (NAFTA). In this agreement, the countries promised to take away most barriers to trade among them.

Partly as a result of NAFTA, Canada sends nearly 80 percent of its exports to the United States. It also buys more than 50 percent of its imports from that country. Canada is the chief trading partner of the United States.

Canada enjoys a **trade surplus.** This means that the country earns more from exports than it spends for imports. This trade surplus exists for two reasons. Canada's smaller population and its own energy resources limit the amount of expensive energy it must buy from other countries. Also, Canada's export earnings have grown in recent years.

Relations With Other Countries

Canada and the United States have the longest undefended border between two countries in the world. That border is peaceful because relations between Canada and the United States are very close. The two national governments cooperate on many matters.

The two countries do differ on some policies. In 2003 Canada opposed the U.S. decision to invade Iraq. It urged the United States to try to settle the matter in the United Nations (UN). The United Nations is the world organization that promotes cooperation among nations.

Canada has a strong role in the United Nations. It, along with the United States, provides much of the money that funds the organization. Canada also takes part in UN agencies the provide aid to people in areas affected by war and natural disaster. The nation also offers its soldiers to serve in UN forces that act as peacekeepers in troubled areas of the world.

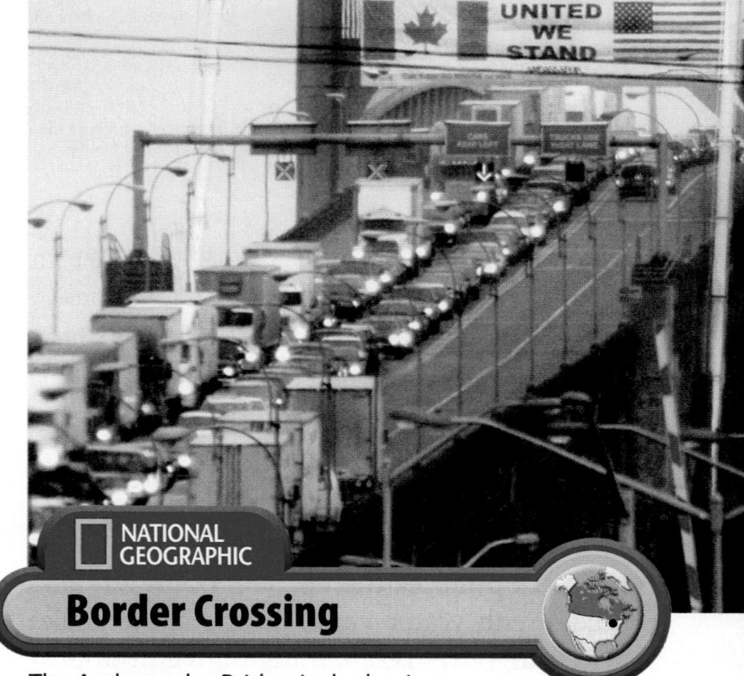

NATIONAL GEOGRAPHIC

Border Crossing

The Ambassador Bridge is the busiest international border crossing in North America. More than 10,000 trucks cross the bridge daily between Detroit, Michigan, and Windsor, Canada.

Regions **What did NAFTA establish?**

Reading Check **Explaining** Why does Canada have a trade surplus?

Environmental Issues

Main Idea Canada faces some important environmental issues.

Geography and You Have you seen instances of air or water pollution in your area? Read to learn how Canada is trying to face environmental challenges.

Burning coal, oil, and natural gas to power factories, produce electricity, and fuel cars pollutes the air. The pollution also mixes with water vapor in the air to make **acid rain**, or rain containing high amounts of chemical pollutants. Acid rain damages trees and harms rivers, lakes, and the stone used in buildings. Canada has acted to reduce the amount of chemicals released into the air.

The Great Lakes are another concern. Ships have accidentally carried some foreign species of fish and shellfish to the lakes. The populations of these creatures have grown rapidly, driving out native fish. Pollution of the lakes also harms their plants and animals. Canadian and American leaders are working together to solve these problems.

Making use of Canada's resources has also caused problems. Companies have built roads and mines in the Canadian Shield to collect the minerals there. Obtaining those minerals, however, has sometimes led to environmental damage.

As you have read, Canada's timber industry is important. The amount of land covered by forests has been decreasing over the years, though. The government has been pushing timber companies to take steps to prevent permanently damaging Canada's forests by harvesting trees more carefully.

Reading Check **Explaining** Why is the area of the Canadian Shield threatened with environmental damage?

Section 3 Review

Vocabulary

1. **Explain** the significance of:
   - **a.** free market economy
   - **b.** profit
   - **c.** stock
   - **d.** newsprint
   - **e.** trade surplus
   - **f.** acid rain

Main Ideas

2. **Describing** Why is Canada's economic system called a mixed economy?
3. **Summarizing** Use a chart like the one below to list important facts about the economies of three regions of Canada. Then identify a physical characteristic of that region related to the fact you listed.

Economic Fact	Physical Characteristic
1.	1.
2.	2.
3.	3.

Critical Thinking

4. **Drawing Conclusions** Which economic region of Canada do you think faces the most challenging problems? Why?
5. **BIG Idea** Describe the trade relationship Canada has with the United States.
6. **Challenge** Why do Canada and the United States need to work together on some environmental issues?

Writing About Geography

7. **Persuasive Writing** Write a letter to a government official urging him or her to take action on a specific environmental issue facing Canada.

Visual Summary

Geography of Canada

- Canada has four physical regions: eastern highlands, a central plateau and lowlands, mountains and plateaus in the west, and islands in the north.
- The Great Lakes and St. Lawrence Seaway support trade from Canada's interior with other parts of the world.
- Abundant mineral resources are found in the Canadian Shield and western provinces.
- Most Canadians live in the southern, more temperate areas of the country.

Farming in Manitoba, Canada

Canadian History and Government

- France and then Britain acquired control of the area that today is Canada.
- In 1867 the Dominion of Canada was founded.
- Some people in French-speaking Quebec want their province to be independent.
- Canada has a parliamentary democracy. Legislative members choose a prime minister to head the government.

Toronto, Canada

Canadian Culture

- Canadian culture reflects the diversity of the many peoples who settled the country.
- Canadian art often draws on nature and the history of the country.

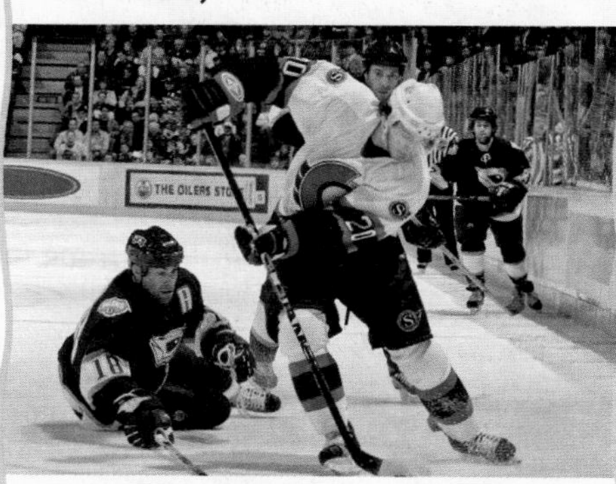

Hockey, Canada

Canada Today

- Canada's main economic regions are the Atlantic Provinces, the Central and Eastern Region, the West, and the North.
- Ontario is Canada's most populous and prosperous province.
- Canada has joined with the United States and Mexico to promote free trade among the three countries.
- Canada's government is taking steps to reduce air and water pollution.

Canadian wheelchair athlete

Study anywhere, anytime! Download quizzes and flash cards to your PDA from glencoe.com.

CHAPTER 7 ASSESSMENT

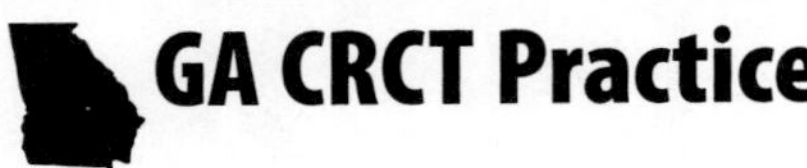

TEST-TAKING TIP

Do not be afraid to skip questions on a multiple-choice test. Make a small pencil mark by the number of the question that you skipped so you can find it quickly when you go back to answer it.

Directions: Choose the best answer for each question.

1 **The Canadian Shield wraps around Hudson Bay. Which of the following describes this area?**

A fertile farmland and mild climate
B poor soil and cold climate
C few lakes and forests
D rich soil and prairies

2 **Which river is vital to Canada's economy?**

A Yukon River
B Mississippi River
C St. Lawrence River
D Fraser River

3 **Why do most Canadians live in Southern Canada and on the west coast?**

A These regions have temperate climates.
B There are more rivers located in Southern Canada and the west coast than anywhere else in Canada.
C The government offered people tax incentives to move there.
D It is easy for ships to travel to the Great Lakes from Southern Canada and the west coast.

4 **Which natural resource provides power for Canada and the United States?**

A St. Lawrence Seaway
B Niagara Falls
C Rocky Mountains
D Appalachian Mountains

5 **Which country won control of most of Canada in the 1760s?**

A Portugal
B Spain
C France
D Great Britain

6 **Canada was a dominion before it won its independence. What was the role of Canada's government in this dominion?**

A France had to approve all decisions made by Canada's government.
B Canada's government was not allowed to make any decisions without British approval.
C Canada could run its own affairs, but Britain controlled Canada's relationships with other countries.
D The Canadian government had to pay taxes to Britain.

7 **Canada is a parliamentary democracy. Who heads the government in a parliamentary democracy?**

A prime minister
B president
C queen
D dictator

8 **Why did a French-speaking political party emerge in Quebec in the late 1900s?**

A They wanted to overthrow the queen of England.
B The French who lived in Quebec felt they were being treated unfairly by the wealthy English-speaking minority.
C The new political party wanted to reduce the amount of pollution in Quebec.
D They wanted health care for all French-speaking citizens.

9 **Which of the following statements BEST summarizes the definition of a free market economy?**

A The prime minister tells people what to produce and sell.
B People are free to produce and sell whatever they want, but they must give their profits to the government.
C The government tells people what to produce and sell.
D People are free to buy, sell, and produce whatever they want with limited government involvement.

10 **Study the circle graph.**

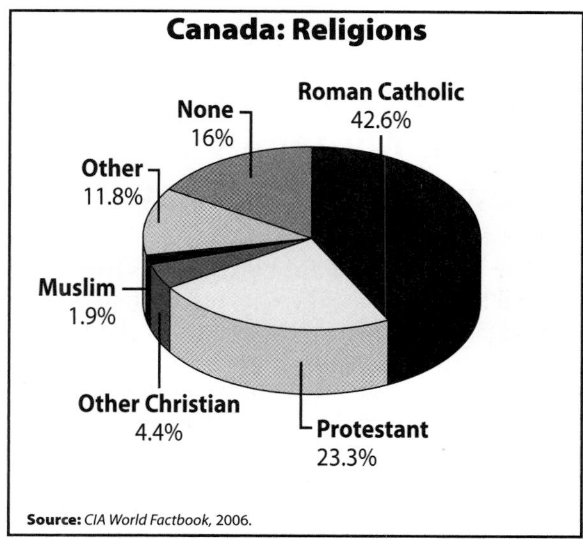

Which is the largest religious group in Canada?

A Protestant
B Muslim
C Roman Catholic
D Greek Othodox

11 **Which statement best summarizes the information shown in the circle graph?**

A A majority of Canadians are Christian.
B There are no Buddhists living in Canada.
C All Canadians are deeply religious.
D Canadians are very intolerant of religious differences.

12 **Which statement best reflects why there are a large number of Christians in Canada?**

A Many Christians in France and England fled to Canada to escape religious persecution.
B French and British settlers who came to Canada were mostly Christian.
C Canada was founded by a Roman Catholic pope.
D Followers of Martin Luther settled Canada.

13 **Read the document and answer the questions that follow.**

> Guarantee of Rights and Freedoms
>
> *1. The* Canadian Charter of Rights and Freedoms *guarantees the rights and freedoms set out in it subject only to such reasonable limits prescribed by law as can be demonstrably justified in a free and democratic society.*
>
> Fundamental Freedoms
>
> *2. Everyone has the following fundamental freedoms:*
> *a) freedom of conscience and religion;*
> *b) freedom of thought, belief, opinion and expression, including freedom of the press and other media of communication;*
> *c) freedom of peaceful assembly; and*
> *d) freedom of association.*
>
> Democratic Rights
>
> *3. Every citizen of Canada has the right to vote in an election of members of the House of Commons or of a legislative assembly and to be qualified for membership therein.*

Which of the following is a fundamental freedom found in the *Canadian Charter of Rights and Freedoms?*

A freedom to choose one's own healthcare plan
B freedom to carry a firearm without a permit
C freedom of wealth
D freedom of religion

14 **Which statement best summarizes the freedoms of Canadian citizens?**

A They are similar to those freedoms that American citizens enjoy.
B They limit citizen participation in Canada's government.
C Canadian citizens have limited freedoms.
D Canadian citizens are only allowed to vote in local elections.

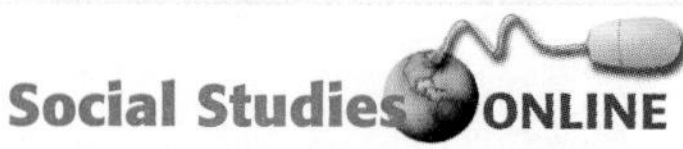

For additional test practice, use Self-Check Quizzes—Chapter 7 at glencoe.com.

Need Extra Help?

If You Missed Questions...	1	2	3	4	5	6	7	8	9	10	11	12	13	14
Go to Page...	189	190	191	192	194	195	195	195	199	196	196	196	196	196

TIME JOURNAL

"Hello! My name is Taylor.

I'm 13 years old and live in Ashcroft, British Columbia. British Columbia is one of Canada's 10 provinces. My family runs a horse ranch and lodge there. Here's how I spend my day."

7:15 a.m. I wake up to the sound of my alarm clock. I shower and put on jeans, a T-shirt, and my tan cowboy boots. Then I head to the kitchen and say good morning to my parents and older brother, Daniel.

7:45 a.m. My mom has made pancakes and bacon for breakfast, and it smells great. I dig in. A hot breakfast is a nice treat. On most days, I just have cereal and toast.

8:25 a.m. Everyone goes their separate ways. My dad leaves for work in town. My brother goes off to high school, and my mom gets ready to work in the ranch office. I walk down our rural road and wait for the school bus.

9:00 a.m. My school day begins with math class. It's okay, but I am happy when the bell rings because I have English next. I love reading and writing and would like to become an author.

10:30 a.m. I stop at my locker, then go to French class. French is the official language in Quebec, Canada's biggest province. We speak English throughout the rest of Canada, but many kids study French as a second language.

11:40 a.m. It's time for lunch. Sometimes I walk to my friend's house for lunch (she lives near the school). Today, I stay at school and buy a grilled cheese sandwich and an apple.

12:20 p.m. In physical education class, we play basketball. In Canada, kids take "phys. ed." until tenth grade. We learn everything from softball to gymnastics.

1:20 p.m. I head to the school wood shop for woodworking class. I put on my safety goggles and use a power tool to carve a wooden sign. In a few weeks, woodworking will be over and I will start a new class—health.

3:00 p.m. I take the bus back home. There, I feed the horses and tackle some other ranch chores. In the summer, when the ranch is full of guests, I will be much busier! Then I will have to set up for meals and wash dishes.

4:45 p.m. I have some free time before dinner, so I grab my helmet, get my horse from the stable, and go riding.

6:15 p.m. Tonight, my grandfather and two uncles join us for dinner. They live in a separate house here on the ranch, so we see them all the time. We eat thick steaks and salad.

7:30 p.m. I help clear the table then do my homework. For one assignment, I have to use the family computer to log on to the Internet.

10:00 p.m. I read in my room for a while then get ready for bed. I'm tired!

ILLUSTRATIONS BY BOOKMAPMAN

SCHOOL TIME Taylor and her classmates share a laugh. Each semester Taylor studies four or five subjects. She gets three minutes between classes to get to her next lesson.

HORSING AROUND Ranching and tourism are big business in Taylor's village. Taylor's family owns a guest ranch. One of Taylor's chores is to feed the horses.

GREAT OUTDOORS Hiking is a popular pastime around Ashcroft. Here, Taylor and her dog take a break at a scenic spot overlooking the Thompson River.

FROM A STUDENT IN CANADA

ON THE RANCH Taylor Nichols spends her time going to school, riding horses, and helping out on her family's ranch. Taylor lives in Canada's westernmost province.

ARON HUEY / POLARIS (4)

What's Popular in Canada

Ice hockey Canadians are passionate about this national sport. At the professional level, there are intense team rivalries, like the one between the Toronto Maple Leafs and the Montreal Canadiens.

AP PHOTO/RYAN REMIORZ

Doughnuts Canada has more doughnut shops per person than any other country in the world! Apple fritters are a big favorite.

MELANIE ACEVEDO

Maple syrup Canada produces 85 percent of the world's maple syrup. Syrup makers tap the maple trees in early March. In one season, a single tree can make one liter of syrup.

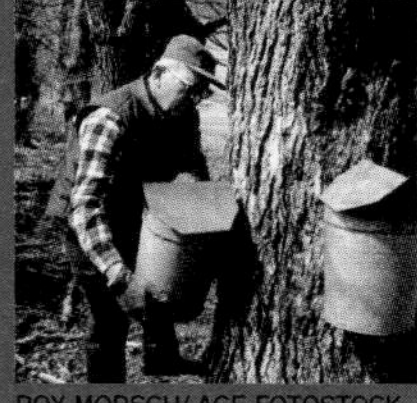

ROY MORSCH/ AGE FOTOSTOCK

Say It in Canadian Slang

English and French are the national languages of Canada. In fact, all official signs, including road signs across the country, are printed in both languages. But Canada also has its share of unusual slang expressions. Try these examples.

How are you doing?
Whadda'yat? (This expression is from eastern Canada.)

A Canadian dollar
Loonie (The nickname comes from the picture of a loon that appears on the coin.)

Very good
Skookum
(SKOO·kum)

PURESTOCK / ALAMY

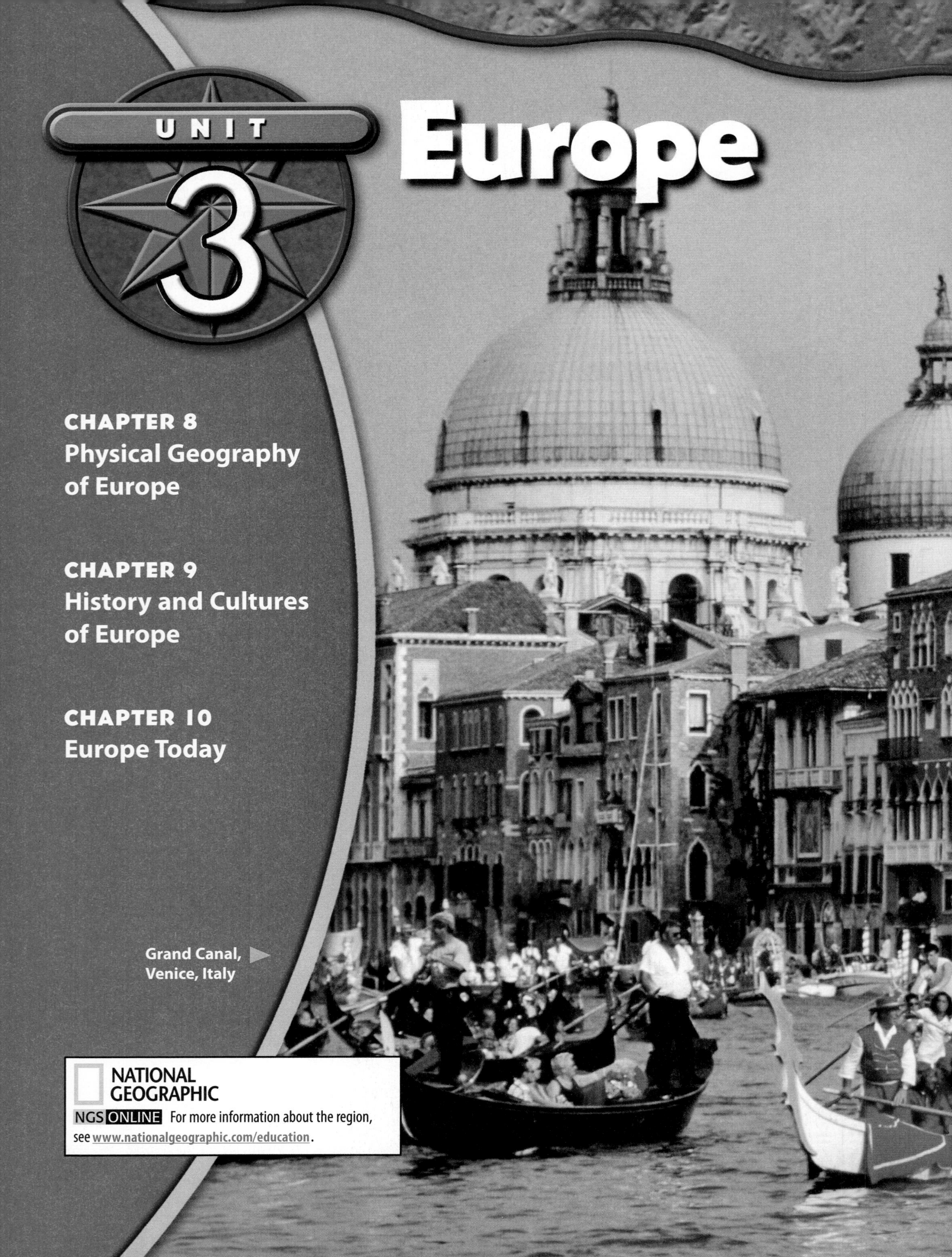

UNIT 3

Europe

CHAPTER 8
Physical Geography of Europe

CHAPTER 9
History and Cultures of Europe

CHAPTER 10
Europe Today

Grand Canal, Venice, Italy

NATIONAL GEOGRAPHIC

NGS ONLINE For more information about the region, see www.nationalgeographic.com/education.

VENEZIA

Regional Atlas

Europe

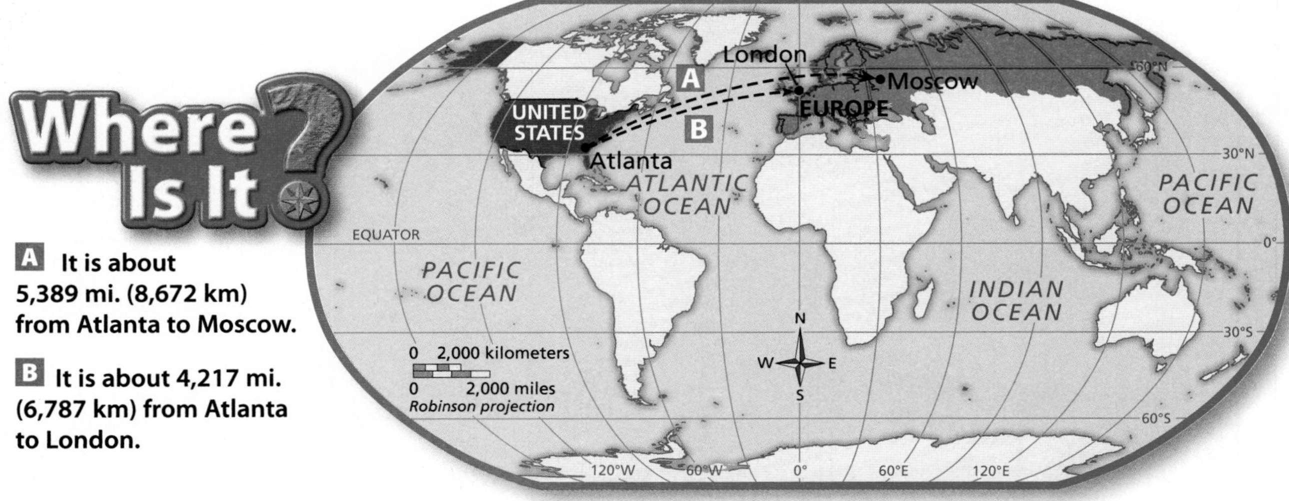

A It is about 5,389 mi. (8,672 km) from Atlanta to Moscow.

B It is about 4,217 mi. (6,787 km) from Atlanta to London.

At about 8.9 million square miles (23 million sq. km), Europe and Russia are almost three times the size of the continental United States. More than 580 million people—almost twice the population of the United States—live in this area.

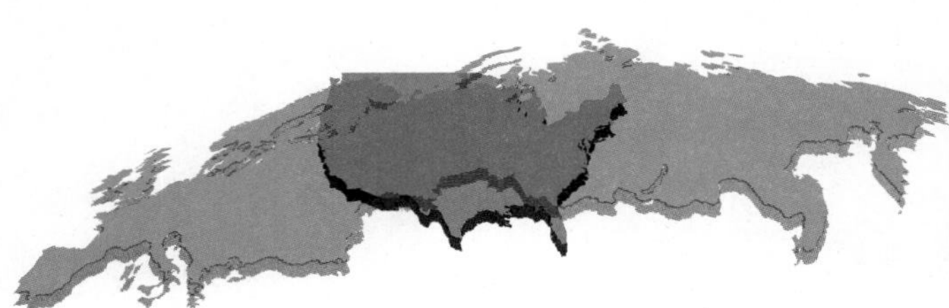

Comparing Population

United States and Selected Countries of Europe

Country	Population (each symbol = 30,000,000)
United States	10 symbols
Russia	5 symbols (last partial)
Germany	3 symbols (last partial)
United Kingdom	2 symbols
Italy	2 symbols
Ukraine	2 symbols (last partial)
Czech Republic	partial symbol

= 30,000,000

Source: *World Population Data Sheet*, 2005.

GEO Fast Facts

Largest Island

Great Britain 80,823 sq. mi. (209,331 sq. km)

Longest River

Ob-Irtysh River (Russia) 3,461 mi. (5,569 km) long

Highest Point

Mount Elbrus (Russia) 18,510 ft. (5,642 m) high

Deepest Lake

Lake Baikal (Russia) 5,175 ft. (1,742 m) deep

Unit 3 Regional Atlas

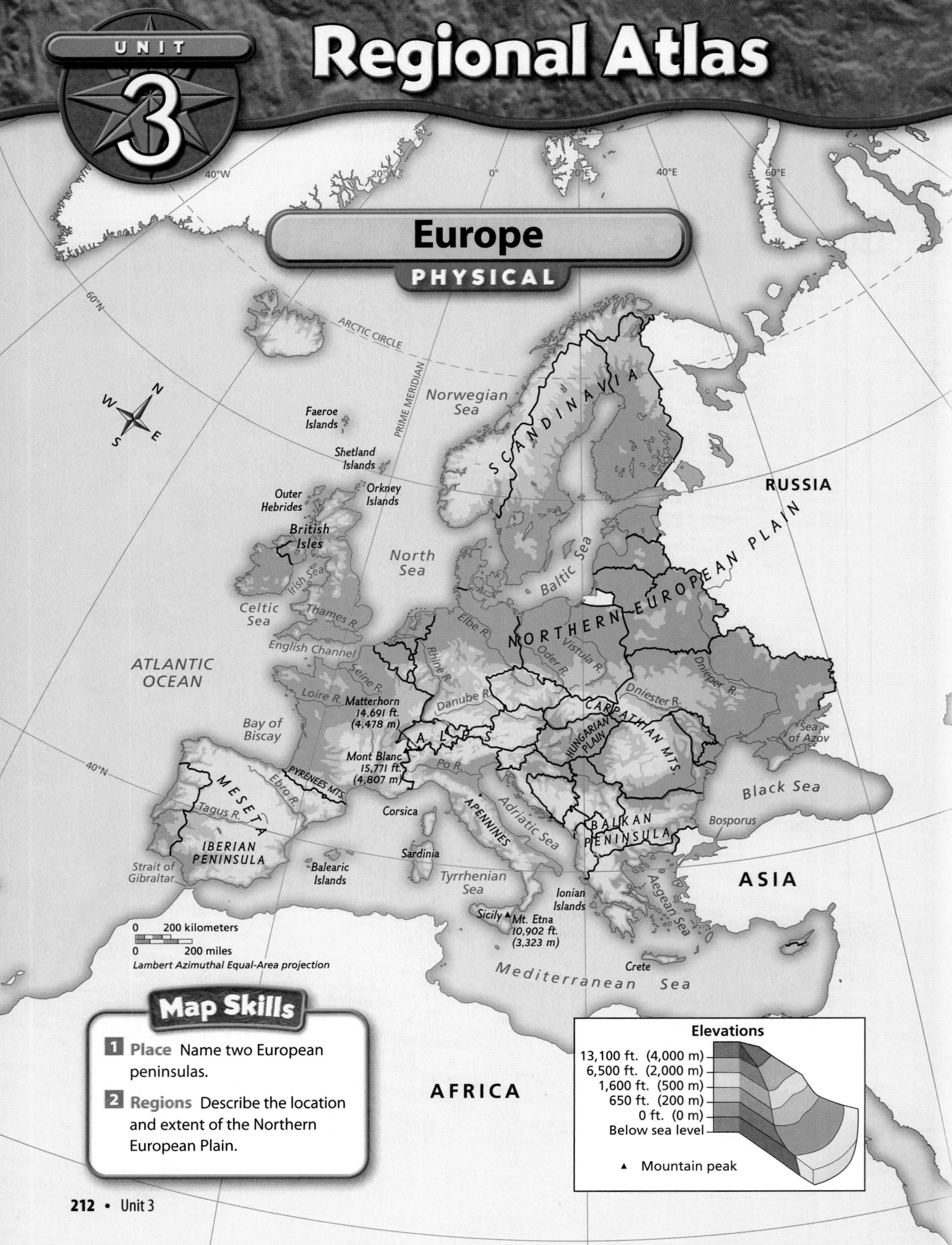

Map Skills

1. **Place** Name two European peninsulas.
2. **Regions** Describe the location and extent of the Northern European Plain.

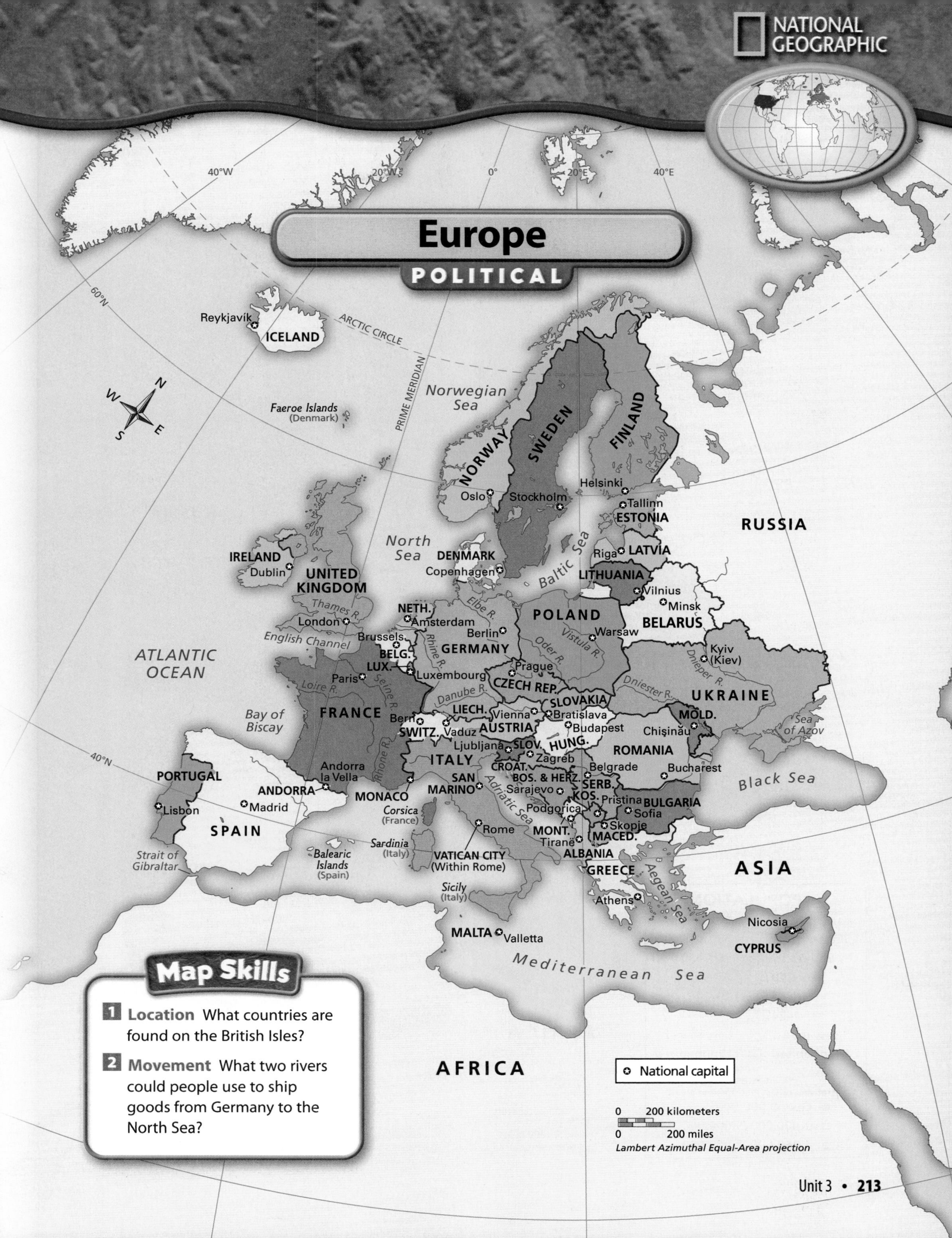

Map Skills

1 Location What countries are found on the British Isles?

2 Movement What two rivers could people use to ship goods from Germany to the North Sea?

Regional Atlas

UNIT 3

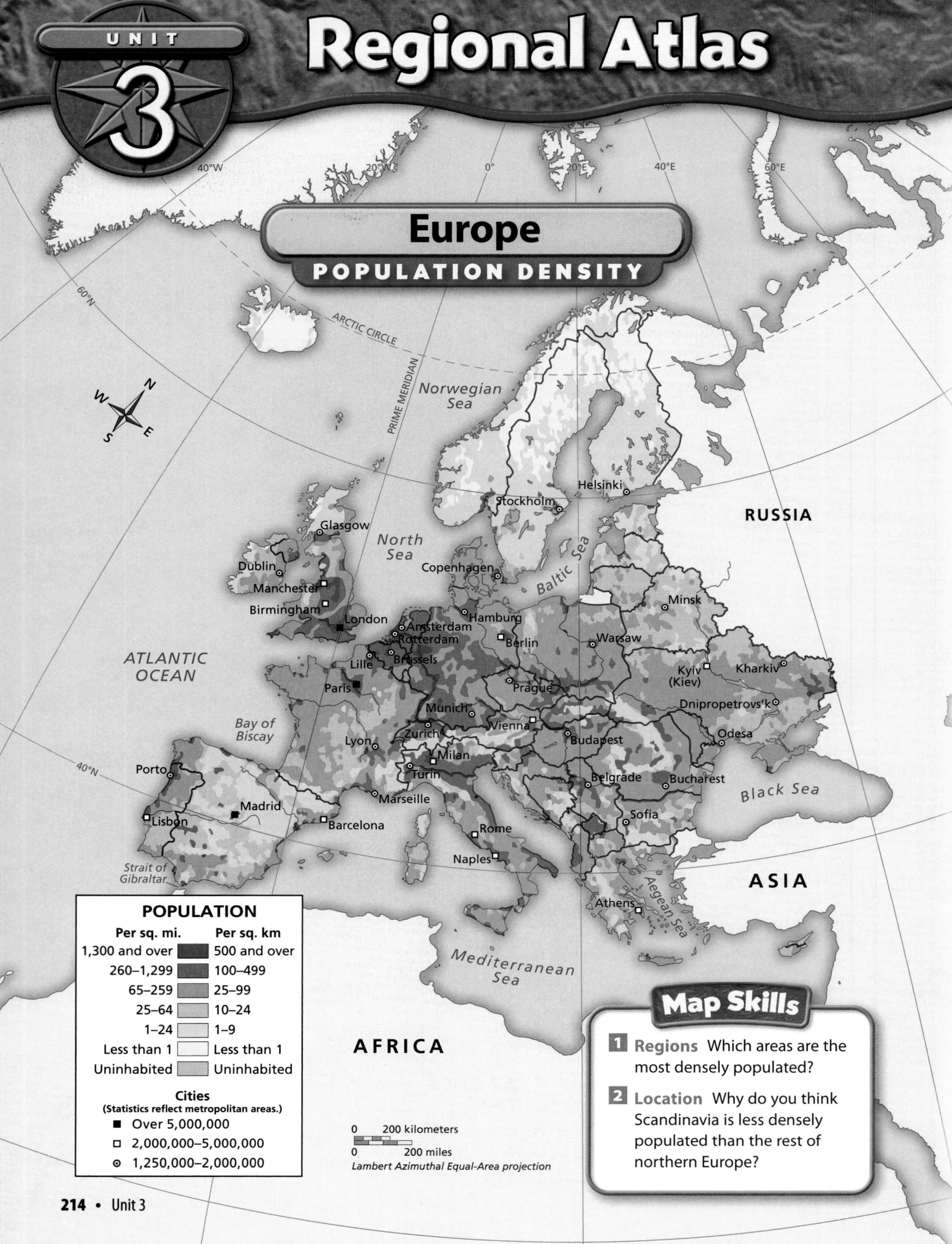

Map Skills

1. **Regions** Which areas are the most densely populated?
2. **Location** Why do you think Scandinavia is less densely populated than the rest of northern Europe?

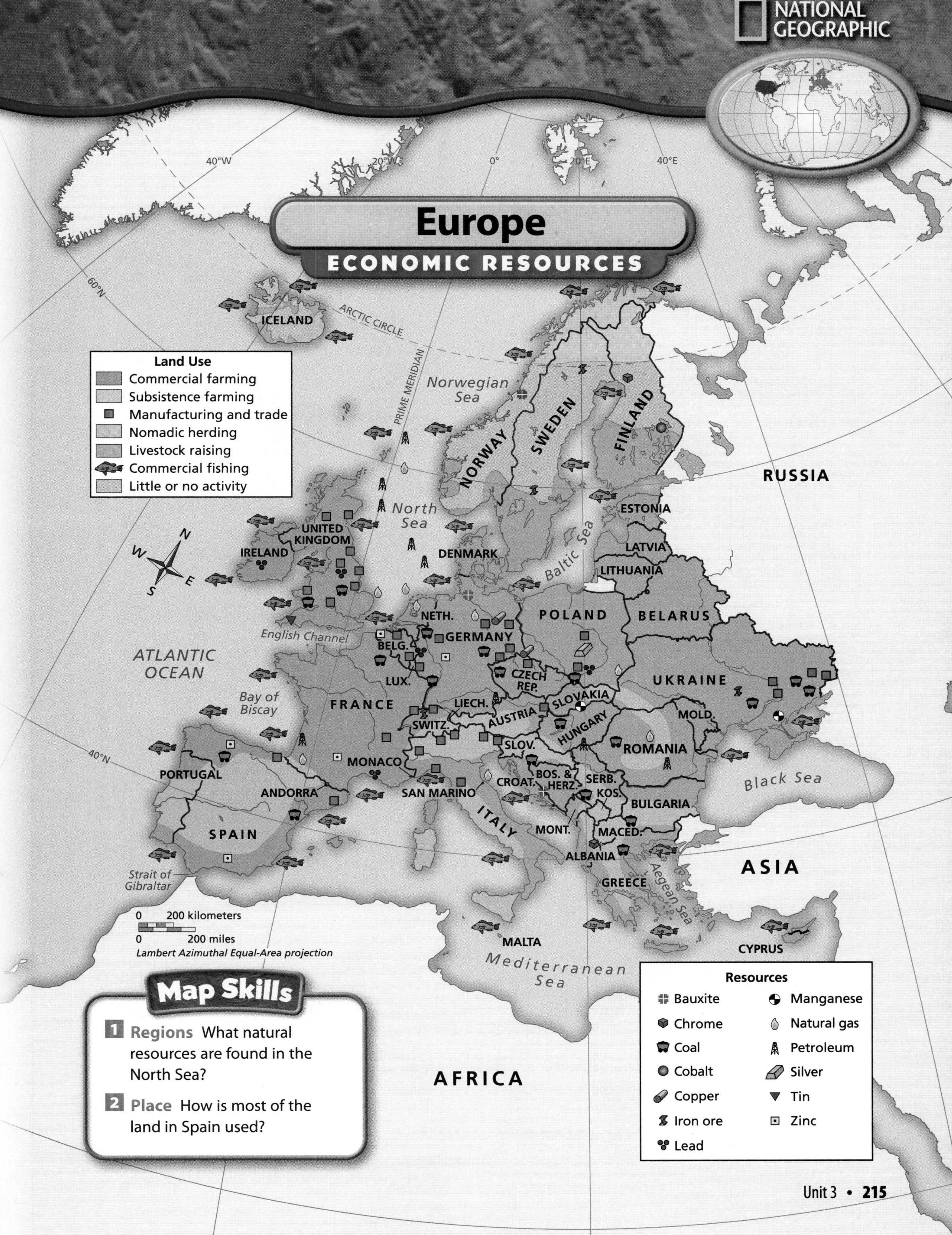

Map Skills

1. **Regions** What natural resources are found in the North Sea?
2. **Place** How is most of the land in Spain used?

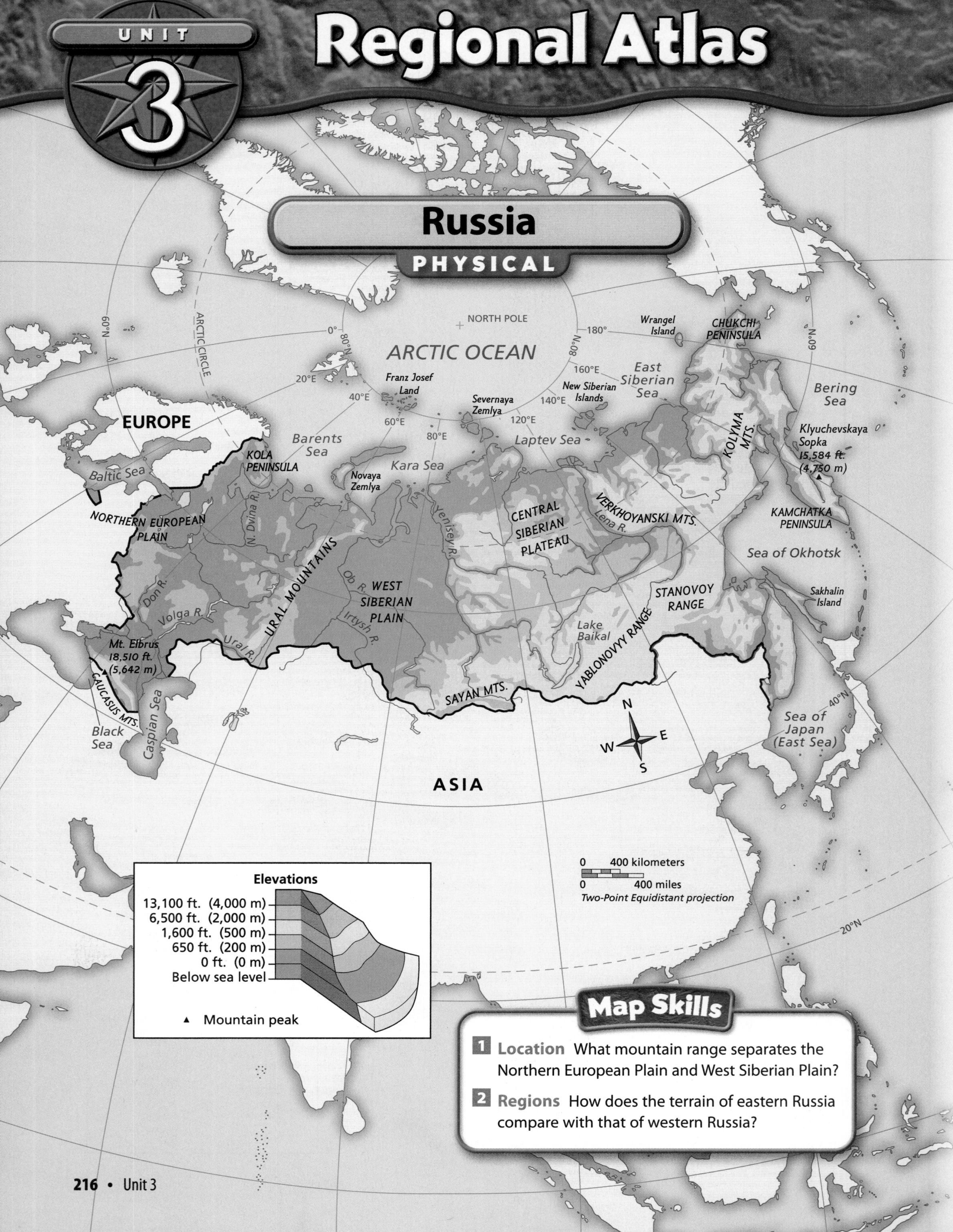

Map Skills

1 Location What mountain range separates the Northern European Plain and West Siberian Plain?

2 Regions How does the terrain of eastern Russia compare with that of western Russia?

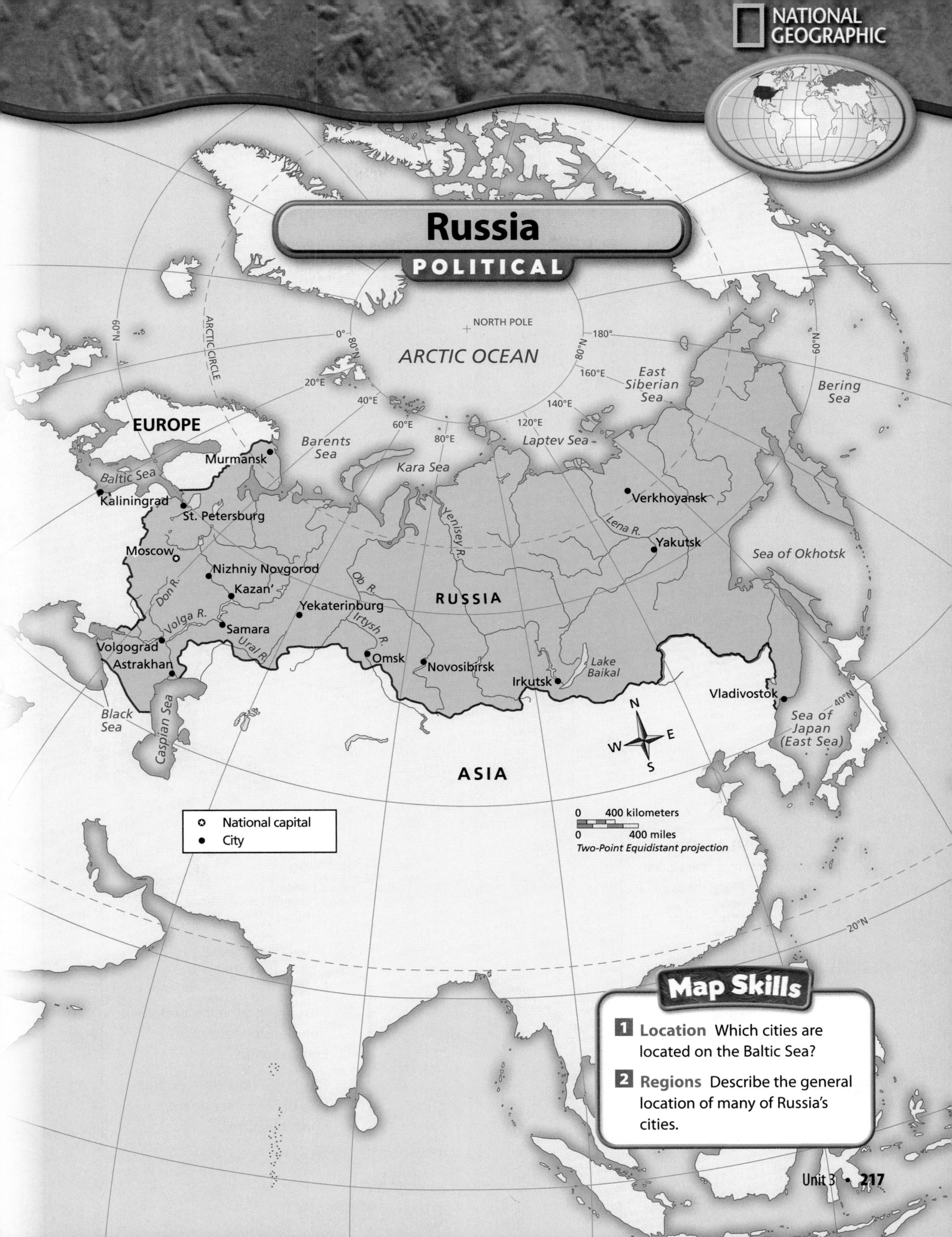

Map Skills

1. **Location** Which cities are located on the Baltic Sea?
2. **Regions** Describe the general location of many of Russia's cities.

Regional Atlas

UNIT 3

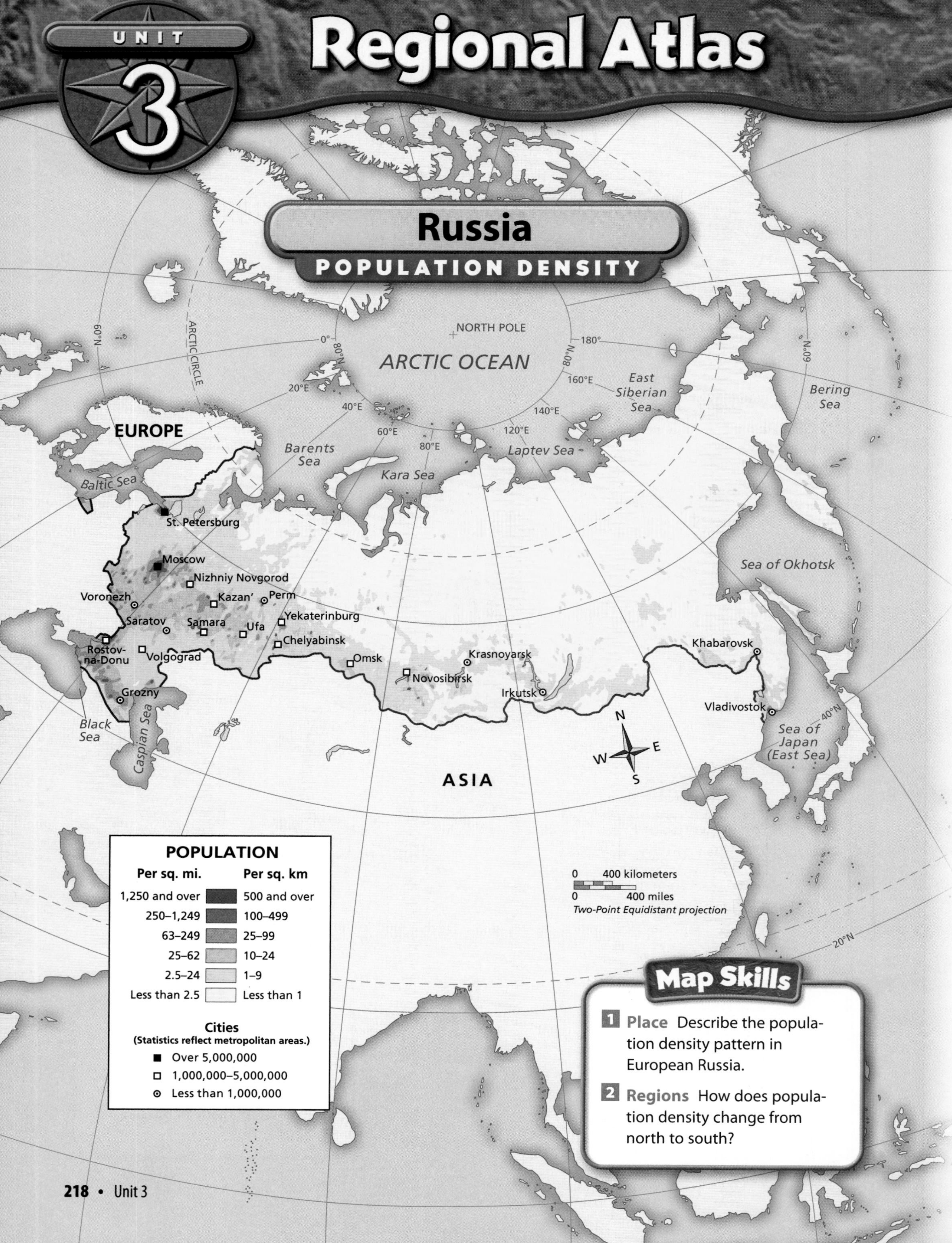

POPULATION Per sq. mi.	Per sq. km
1,250 and over	500 and over
250–1,249	100–499
63–249	25–99
25–62	10–24
2.5–24	1–9
Less than 2.5	Less than 1

Cities
(Statistics reflect metropolitan areas.)

- ■ Over 5,000,000
- □ 1,000,000–5,000,000
- ⊙ Less than 1,000,000

Map Skills

1. **Place** Describe the population density pattern in European Russia.
2. **Regions** How does population density change from north to south?

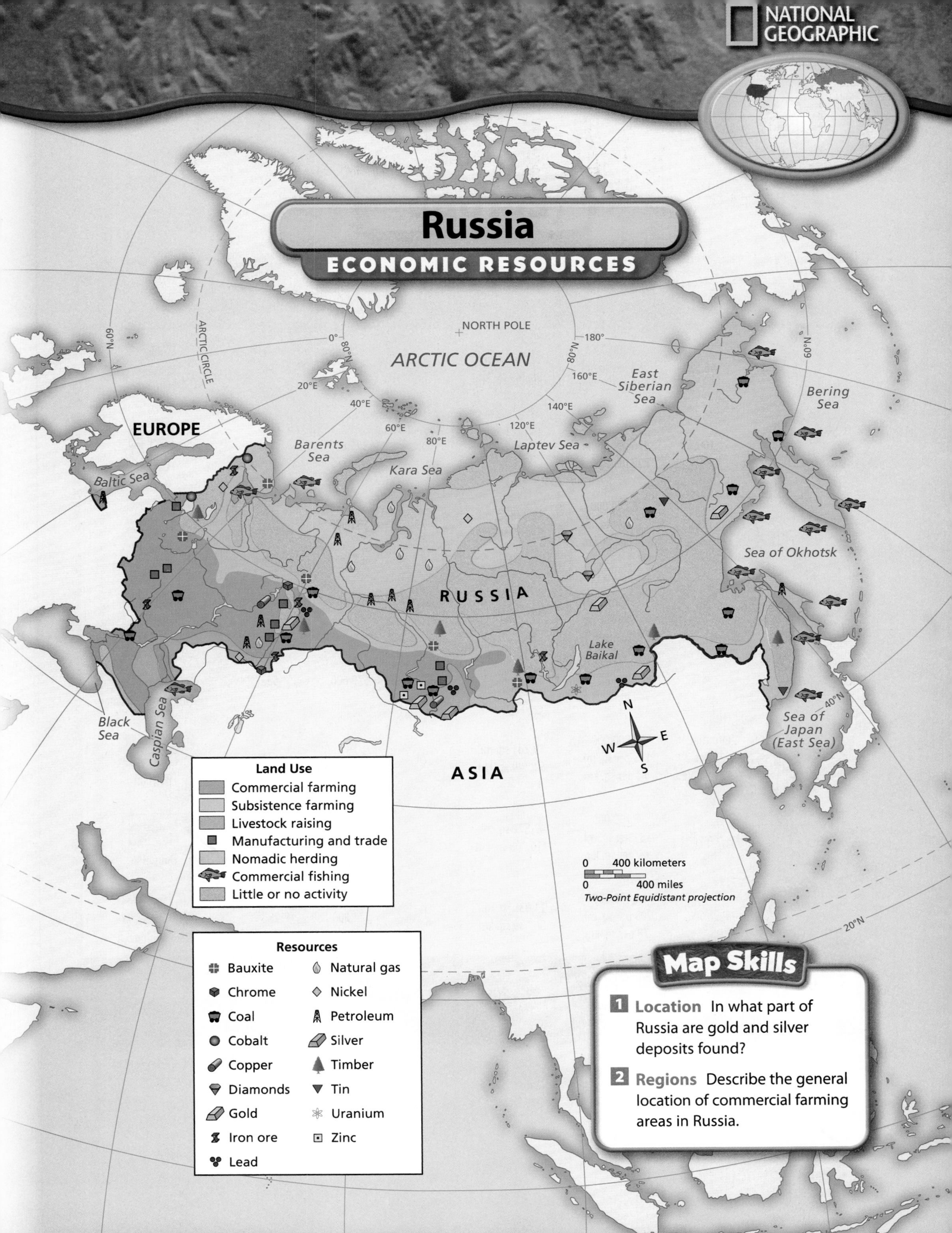
NATIONAL GEOGRAPHIC
Russia
ECONOMIC RESOURCES
NORTH POLE
ARCTIC OCEAN
ARCTIC CIRCLE
60°N
0°
80°N
180°
20°E
40°E
60°E
80°E
120°E
140°E
160°E
East Siberian Sea
Bering Sea
Barents Sea
Kara Sea
Laptev Sea
EUROPE
Baltic Sea
RUSSIA
Sea of Okhotsk
Lake Baikal
Black Sea
Caspian Sea
Sea of Japan (East Sea)
40°N
20°N
ASIA
N
E
S
W
Land Use
Commercial farming
Subsistence farming
Livestock raising
Manufacturing and trade
Nomadic herding
Commercial fishing
Little or no activity
Resources
Bauxite
Chrome
Coal
Cobalt
Copper
Diamonds
Gold
Iron ore
Lead
Natural gas
Nickel
Petroleum
Silver
Timber
Tin
Uranium
Zinc
0 400 kilometers
0 400 miles
Two-Point Equidistant projection
Map Skills
1 Location In what part of Russia are gold and silver deposits found?
2 Regions Describe the general location of commercial farming areas in Russia.

Regional Atlas

Europe

Country and Capital	Literacy Rate	Population and Density	Land Area	Life Expectancy (Years)	GDP* Per Capita (U.S. dollars)	Television Sets (per 1,000 people)	Flag and Language
Tiranë, ALBANIA	86.5%	3,200,000 286 per sq. mi. 111 per sq. km	11,100 sq. mi. 28,749 sq. km	74	$4,900	146	Albanian
ANDORRA, Andorra la Vella	100%	100,000 426 per sq. mi. 222 per sq. km	174 sq. mi. 451 sq. km	information not available	$26,800	440	Catalan
Vienna, AUSTRIA	98%	8,200,000 252 per sq. mi. 98 per sq. km	32,378 sq. mi. 83,859 sq. km	79	$31,300	526	German
Minsk, BELARUS	99.6%	9,800,000 122 per sq. mi. 47 per sq. km	80,154 sq. mi. 207,598 sq. km	69	$6,800	331	Belarusian
Brussels, BELGIUM	98%	10,500,000 887 per sq. mi. 344 per sq. km	11,787 sq. mi. 30,528 sq. km	79	$30,600	532	Dutch, French, German
BOSNIA AND HERZEGOVINA, Sarajevo	information not available	3,800,000 195 per sq. mi. 74 per sq. km	19,741 sq. mi. 51,129 sq. km	74	$6,500	112	Bosnian
BULGARIA, Sofia	98.6%	7,700,000 181 per sq. mi. 69 per sq. km	42,822 sq. mi. 110,908 sq. km	72	$8,200	429	Bulgarian
Zagreb, CROATIA	98.5%	4,400,000 203 per sq. mi. 78 per sq. km	21,830 sq. mi. 56,539 sq. km	75	$11,200	286	Croatian
UNITED STATES, Washington, D.C.	97%	296,500,000 80 per sq. mi. 31 per sq. km	3,717,796 sq. mi. 9,629,047 sq. km	78	$40,100	844	English

*Gross Domestic Product

Countries and flags not drawn to scale

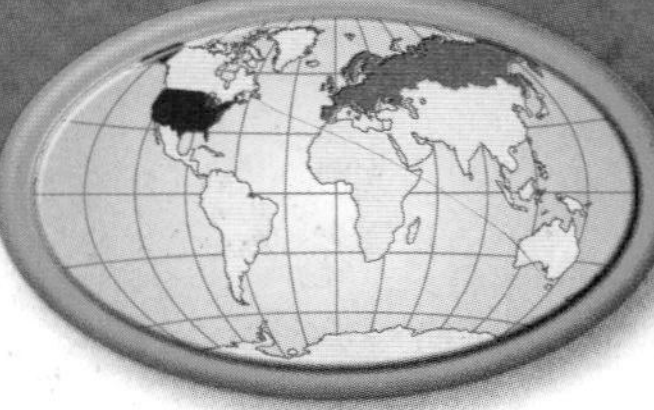

Europe

Country and Capital	Literacy Rate	Population and Density	Land Area	Life Expectancy (Years)	GDP* Per Capita (U.S. dollars)	Television Sets (per 1,000 people)	Flag and Language
CYPRUS Nicosia	97.6%	1,000,000 270 per sq. mi. 108 per sq. km	3,571 sq. mi. 9,249 sq. km	77	$20,300	154	Greek
CZECH REPUBLIC Prague	99.9%	10,200,000 335 per sq. mi. 129 per sq. km	30,448 sq. mi. 78,860 sq. km	75	$16,800	487	Czech
DENMARK Copenhagen	100%	5,400,000 326 per sq. mi. 125 per sq. km	16,637 sq. mi. 43,090 sq. km	77	$32,200	776	Danish
ESTONIA Tallinn	99.8%	1,300,000 77 per sq. mi. 29 per sq. km	17,413 sq. mi. 45,099 sq. km	72	$14,300	567	Estonian
FINLAND Helsinki	100%	5,200,000 40 per sq. mi. 15 per sq. km	130,560 sq. mi. 338,149 sq. km	79	$29,000	643	Finnish, Swedish
FRANCE Paris	99%	60,700,000 285 per sq. mi. 110 per sq. km	212,934 sq. mi. 551,497 sq. km	80	$28,700	620	French
GERMANY Berlin	99%	82,500,000 598 per sq. mi. 231 per sq. km	137,830 sq. mi. 356,978 sq. km	79	$28,700	581	German
GREECE Athens	97.5%	11,100,000 218 per sq. mi. 84 per sq. km	50,950 sq. mi. 131,960 sq. km	76	$21,300	480	Greek
UNITED STATES Washington, D.C.	97%	296,500,000 80 per sq. mi. 31 per sq. km	3,717,796 sq. mi. 9,629,047 sq. km	78	$40,100	844	English

Sources: *CIA World Factbook*, 2005; Population Reference Bureau, *World Population Data Sheet*, 2005.

For more country facts, go to the **Nations of the World Atlas** at glencoe.com.

Regional Atlas

Europe

Country and Capital	Literacy Rate	Population and Density	Land Area	Life Expectancy (Years)	GDP* Per Capita (U.S. dollars)	Television Sets (per 1,000 people)	Flag and Language
HUNGARY, Budapest	99.4%	10,100,000 281 per sq. mi. 109 per sq. km	35,919 sq. mi. 93,030 sq. km	68	$14,900	447	Hungarian
ICELAND, Reykjavík	99.9%	300,000 8 per sq. mi. 3 per sq. km	39,768 sq. mi. 102,999 sq. km	81	$31,900	505	Icelandic
IRELAND, Dublin	98%	4,100,000 151 per sq. mi. 58 per sq. km	27,135 sq. mi. 70,279 sq. km	78	$31,900	406	English, Irish
ITALY, Rome	98.6%	58,700,000 505 per sq. mi. 195 per sq. km	116,320 sq. mi. 301,267 sq. km	77	$27,700	492	Italian
KOSOVO, Pristina	information not available	2,100,000 506 per sq. mi. 195 per sq. km	4,203 sq. mi. 10,887 sq. km	information not available	$1,800	information not available	Albanian, Serbian
LATVIA, Riga	99.8%	2,300,000 92 per sq. mi. 36 per sq. km	24,942 sq. mi. 64,599 sq. km	72	$11,500	757	Latvian
LIECHTENSTEIN, Vaduz	100%	40,000 645 per sq. mi. 248 per sq. km	62 sq. mi. 161 sq. km	80	$25,000	469	German
LITHUANIA, Vilnius	99.6%	3,400,000 135 per sq. mi. 52 per sq. km	25,174 sq. mi. 65,200 sq. km	72	$12,500	422	Lithuanian
LUXEMBOURG, Luxembourg	100%	500,000 501 per sq. mi. 193 per sq. km	999 sq. mi. 2,587 sq. km	78	$58,900	599	Luxembourgish, German, French
UNITED STATES, Washington, D.C.	97%	296,500,000 80 per sq. mi. 31 per sq. km	3,717,796 sq. mi. 9,629,047 sq. km	78	$40,100	844	English

*Gross Domestic Product
Kosovo's information is based on 2008 data.

Countries and flags not drawn to scale

Europe

Country and Capital	Literacy Rate	Population and Density	Land Area	Life Expectancy (Years)	GDP* Per Capita (U.S. dollars)	Television Sets (per 1,000 people)	Flag and Language
MACEDONIA, Skopje	information not available	2,000,000 201 per sq. mi. 78 per sq. km	9,927 sq. mi. 25,711 sq. km	71	$7,100	273	Macedonian
MALTA, Valletta	92.8%	400,000 3,278 per sq. mi. 1,246 per sq. km	124 sq. mi. 321 sq. km	79	$18,200	549	Maltese, English
MOLDOVA, Chişinău	99.1%	4,200,000 323 per sq. mi. 125 per sq. km	13,012 sq. mi. 33,701 sq. km	65	$1,900	297	Moldovan
MONACO, Monaco	99%	30,000 30,000 per sq. mi. 11,538 per sq. km	1 sq. mi. 2.6 sq. km	information not available	$27,000	758	French
MONTENEGRO, Podgorica	97%	650,000 122 per sq. mi. 47 per sq. km	5,333 sq. mi. 13,812 sq. km	73	$2,200	277	Montenegrin, Serbian, Albanian
NETHERLANDS, Amsterdam	99%	16,400,000 1,023 per sq. mi. 395 per sq. km	13,082 sq. mi. 33,883 sq. km	79	$29,500	540	Dutch
NORWAY, Oslo	100%	4,600,000 37 per sq. mi. 14 per sq. km	125,050 sq. mi. 323,878 sq. km	80	$40,000	653	Norwegian
POLAND, Warsaw	99.8%	38,200,000 306 per sq. mi. 118 per sq. km	124,807 sq. mi. 323,249 sq. km	71	$12,000	387	Polish
UNITED STATES, Washington, D.C.	97%	296,500,000 80 per sq. mi. 31 per sq. km	3,717,796 sq. mi. 9,629,047 sq. km	78	$40,100	844	English

Sources: *CIA World Factbook,* 2005; Population Reference Bureau, *World Population Data Sheet,* 2005.

For more country facts, go to the **Nations of the World Atlas** at glencoe.com.

Regional Atlas

Europe

Country and Capital	Literacy Rate	Population and Density	Land Area	Life Expectancy (Years)	GDP* Per Capita (U.S. dollars)	Television Sets (per 1,000 people)	Flag and Language
PORTUGAL Lisbon	93%	10,600,000 298 per sq. mi. 115 per sq. km	35,502 sq. mi. 91,951 sq. km	78	$17,900	567	Portuguese
ROMANIA Bucharest	98.4%	21,600,000 235 per sq. mi. 91 per sq. km	92,042 sq. mi. 238,388 sq. km	68	$7,700	312	Romanian
RUSSIA Moscow	99.6%	143,000,000 22 per sq. mi. 8 per sq. km	6,592,819 sq. mi. 17,075,322 sq. km	66	$9,800	421	Russian
SAN MARINO San Marino	96%	30,000 1,304 per sq. mi. 500 per sq. km	23 sq. mi. 60 sq. km	81	$34,600	875	Italian
SERBIA Belgrade	96%	8,000,000 269 per sq. mi. 104 per sq. km	29,913 sq. mi. 77,474 sq. km	75	$7,700	information not available	Serbian
SLOVAKIA Bratislava	information not available	5,400,000 285 per sq. mi. 110 per sq. km	18,923 sq. mi. 49,010 sq. km	70	$14,500	418	Slovak
SLOVENIA Ljubljana	99.7%	2,000,000 256 per sq. mi. 99 per sq. km	7,819 sq. mi. 20,251 sq. km	77	$19,600	362	Slovenian
SPAIN Madrid	97.9%	43,500,000 225 per sq. mi. 87 per sq. km	193,363 sq. mi. 500,808 sq. km	80	$23,300	555	Spanish
SWEDEN Stockholm	99%	9,000,000 52 per sq. mi. 20 per sq. km	173,730 sq. mi. 449,959 sq. km	81	$28,400	551	Swedish
UNITED STATES Washington, D.C.	97%	296,500,000 80 per sq. mi. 31 per sq. km	3,717,796 sq. mi. 9,629,047 sq. km	78	$40,100	844	English

*Gross Domestic Product
Serbia's information is based on 2008 data.

Countries and flags not drawn to scale

Europe

Country and Capital	Literacy Rate	Population and Density	Land Area	Life Expectancy (Years)	GDP* Per Capita (U.S. dollars)	Television Sets (per 1,000 people)	Flag and Language
Bern SWITZERLAND	96%	7,400,000 464 per sq. mi. 179 per sq. km	15,942 sq. mi. 41,290 sq. km	80	$33,800	457	German, French, Italian
Kyiv (Kiev) UKRAINE	93%	47,100,000 202 per sq. mi. 70 per sq. km	233,089 sq. mi. 603,698 sq. km	63	$6,300	433	Ukrainian
UNITED KINGDOM London	information not available	60,100,000 636 per sq. mi. 245 per sq. km	94,548 sq. mi. 244,878 sq. km	78	$29,600	661	English
VATICAN CITY	99.7%	1,000 1,000 per sq. mi. 385 per sq. km	1 sq. mi. 2.6 sq. km	information not available	information not available	information not available	Italian, Latin
UNITED STATES Washington, D.C.	97%	296,500,000 80 per sq. mi. 31 per sq. km	3,717,796 sq. mi. 9,629,047 sq. km	78	$40,100	844	English

Sources: *CIA World Factbook*, 2005; Population Reference Bureau, *World Population Data Sheet*, 2005.

For more country facts, go to the **Nations of the World Atlas** at glencoe.com.

▼ L'Arc de Triomphe, Paris, France

Reading Social Studies

Making Inferences

Reading Skill

1 Learn It!

It is impossible for authors to write every detail about a topic in a textbook. Because of this, good readers must make inferences to help them understand what they are reading. To infer means to evaluate information and form a conclusion.

- Read the excerpt below about the effects of the Crusades on Europe.
- Think about what you already know about the topic.
- Then, look for clues that might explain what is happening in the passage even though it might not be stated.
- What inference can you make about the importance of the Crusades in the development of Europe?

Clues

Feudalism weakened as kings took land from nobles who had gone off to fight. Europe's kingdoms grew stronger. Many of them, such as France, later became modern Europe's nation-states. A nation-state is a country made up of people who share a common culture or history.

—from page 259

What you already know:
Europe today contains a number of nations.

Clues in the text:
- Feudalism weakened and nobles lost power after the Crusades. Kingdoms grew in strength.
- Many kingdoms later became modern Europe's nation-states.

Inference:
The years following the Crusades were important to the political structure of modern Europe.

Reading Tip

Making inferences is an everyday part of life. For example, if you look at the sky and see dark clouds, you may infer that it is going to rain. As you read, use the facts in the text to make inferences by thinking beyond the words on the page.

Read to Write Activity

In Chapter 9, Section 1, read the paragraphs titled "An Economic Revolution." Then take notes about the Industrial Revolution. Write a statement in which you make an inference about what life was like for a teenager during the Industrial Revolution.

2 Practice It!

Read the following paragraph from this unit.

- Draw a diagram like the one shown below.
- Write what you know about the United Kingdom's constitutional monarchy, along with facts from the text.
- Make an inference about the power of the king or queen in the United Kingdom.

> The government of the United Kingdom is a constitutional monarchy. A king or queen serves as head of state and takes part in ceremonies, but elected officials actively run the government.
>
> —*from page 286*

What you already know:

Clues in the text:

Inference:

Queen Elizabeth II of the United Kingdom and members of the royal family

3 Apply It!

For each chapter in this unit choose a topic, and create a diagram like the one above. Write related information that you already know, along with facts from the text, in the diagrams. Make inferences using this information. Read your facts to a partner, and ask your partner to make inferences from them. Are your inferences the same?

Physical Geography of Europe

Essential Question

Regions Europe's landforms include high, snowcapped mountains; broad, fertile plains; expansive forests; and a variety of waterways. A number of oceans and seas border Europe's countries. The region also has many important rivers. How do people use waterways?

Section 1: Physical Features

BIG IDEA Geographic factors influence where people settle. Europe has a variety of landforms and plentiful natural resources that have attracted a large population. Most people live on Europe's plains, where industry and agriculture flourish. Such successes, however, have contributed to environmental problems in the region.

◀ Bridges span the Vltava River in Prague, Czech Republic.

Section 2: Climate Regions

BIG IDEA The physical environment affects how people live. Much of Europe has a mild climate. Russia's east, however, is far from the moderating influence of the Atlantic Ocean. Climates there can be harsh. Still, many Europeans are concerned that the climate is warming, which may have dangerous consequences.

FOLDABLES™ Study Organizer

Summarizing Information Make this Foldable to help you gather notes and summarize information about Europe's physical features, climate, and environmental issues.

Step 1 Mark the midpoint of the side edge of a sheet of paper.

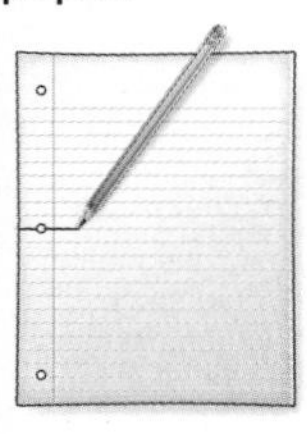

Step 2 Fold the top and bottom of the paper into the middle to make a shutter fold.

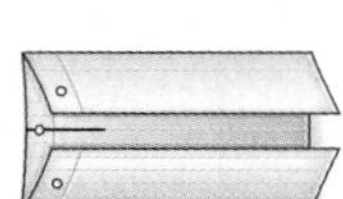

Step 3 Fold the paper in half from side to side.

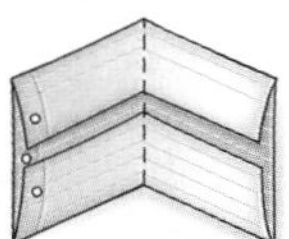

Step 4 Open and cut along the inside fold lines to form four tabs.

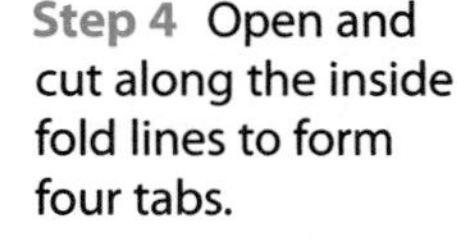

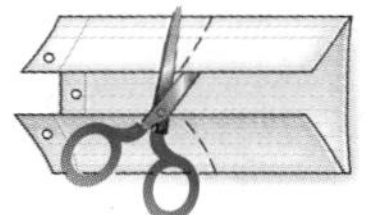

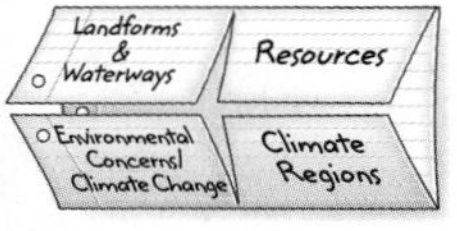

Step 5 Label the tabs as shown.

Reading and Writing As you read the chapter, fill in the Foldable. When you have finished the chapter, use your Foldable to write a list of the 10 most important facts about Europe's physical geography.

Visit glencoe.com and enter QuickPass™ code GA6EOW6225c8 for Chapter 8 resources.

Guide to Reading

BIG Idea

Geographic factors influence where people settle.

Content Vocabulary

- landlocked *(p. 231)*
- pass *(p. 233)*
- navigable *(p. 234)*
- fossil fuel *(p. 235)*
- softwood *(p. 236)*
- infrastructure *(p. 237)*

Academic Vocabulary

- access *(p. 231)*
- benefit *(p. 231)*
- affect *(p. 231)*
- inhibit *(p. 237)*
- impact *(p. 237)*

Reading Strategy

Organizing Information Use a diagram like the one below to organize key facts about each of Europe's major landforms (Islands and Peninsulas, Plains, Mountains and Highlands).

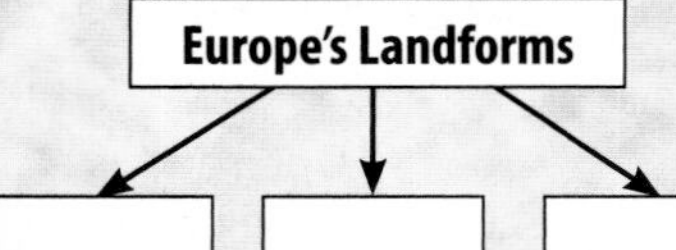

Physical Features

Picture This Snowdrifts? No, these snow-like mounds were formed about 1,500 years ago during a volcanic eruption on the island of Lipari, off the coast of Sicily, in Italy. The mounds are made of pumice, a stone formed from the cooling of lava, which rained down on the island during the eruption. Today the volcano is quiet, but Lipari hums with the sounds of open-pit pumice mines. Pumice is used to polish smooth surfaces. The stone is often used to give "stonewashed" jeans their worn look. In Section 1, you will learn about the different European landforms and the effect they have had on people living in the region.

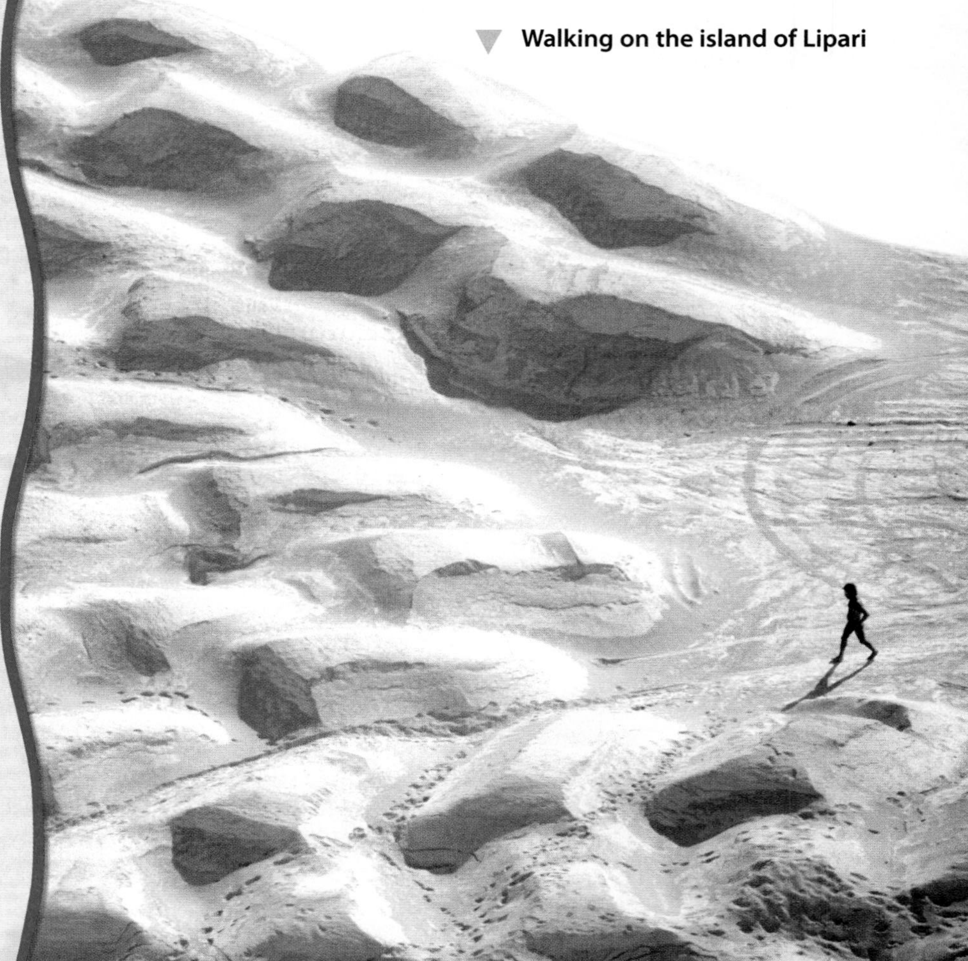

▼ Walking on the island of Lipari

Landforms and Waterways

Main Idea **Europe's landforms and waterways have greatly influenced where and how Europeans live.**

Geography and You What landforms can you find near your community? In Europe you would find impressive mountains, shimmering seas, and rolling farmland. Read to learn more about the variety of landscapes.

While Europe is a continent, it is not a separate landmass. Europe and Asia share a common landmass called Eurasia. Russia straddles both continents.

Other than Russia, most of Europe lies within 300 miles (483 km) of a coast. Only a few countries are **landlocked,** meaning they do not border on an ocean or a sea. Rivers give these inland countries **access** to coastal ports, however.

This nearness to water has shaped the lives and history of Europe's people. Europeans developed skills in sailing and fishing, which encouraged trade and helped Europe's economy grow. Closeness to the sea also enables people to move easily between Europe and other continents. This fact has had important effects on Europe's history and culture.

Russia does not **benefit** much from its closeness to the sea because the waters of the Arctic Ocean are frozen much of the year. Also, much of Russia's interior is inland, far from oceans or seas.

Peninsulas and Islands

Look at the physical map in this unit's Regional Atlas. You can see that Europe is a huge peninsula, with many smaller peninsulas branching out from it. Europe also includes many islands. Some of these major islands—Great Britain, Ireland, and Iceland—lie in the Atlantic Ocean. Other large islands, such as Sicily, Crete, and Cyprus, are located in the Mediterranean Sea.

The large number of peninsulas and islands has **affected** Europe's history. Europe's many seas, rivers, and mountains separated groups of people. As a result, many different cultures developed. Today, Europe is home to more than 40 independent countries. That is a remarkable number of neighbors squeezed together on a relatively small continent.

Plains

Europe's major landform is the Northern European Plain. This large lowland area stretches like a rumpled blanket across the northern half of mainland Europe.

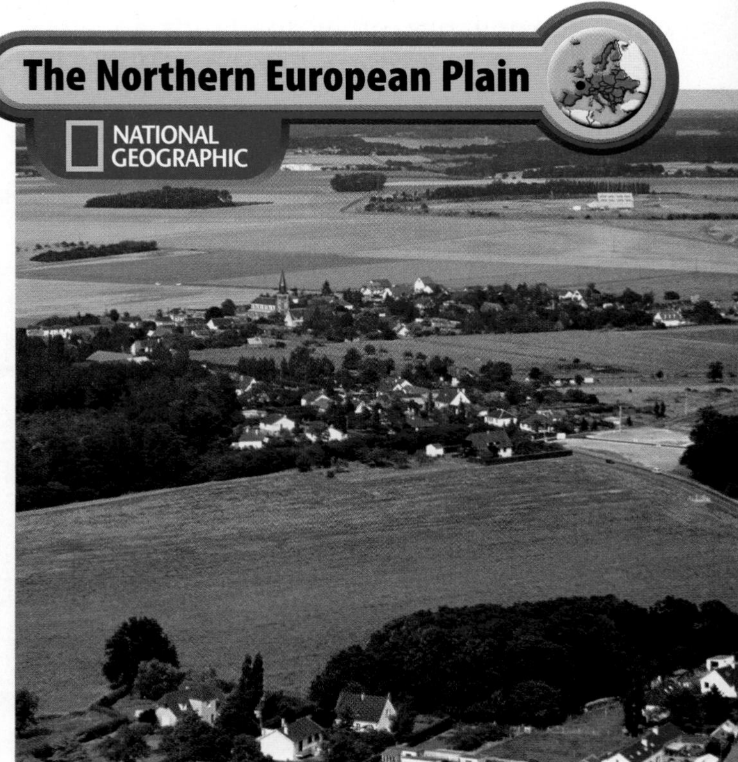

▲ Rich farmland in the region of Normandy in France is part of the Northern European Plain. ***Regions*** **Describe the Northern European Plain.**

It has rolling land with isolated hills. The Northern European Plain reaches from Russia westward to France and also extends to the British Isles.

The plain's rich soil makes its farms highly productive. Farmers grow a great variety of grains, fruits, and vegetables. Some farmers raise dairy cattle to produce milk used in making cheese and other dairy products.

The Northern European Plain also has important energy and mineral resources. Deposits of coal, iron ore, and other minerals lie underground. These resources aided Europe's industrial growth.

Because the plain is so rich agriculturally and industrially, it is densely populated. Today, most of Europe's people live in this area. The landscape is dotted with villages, towns, and cities, including the busy capital cities of Moscow, Berlin, Paris, and London.

Europe has other lowlands in addition to the Northern European Plain. For example, narrow plains rim the coasts of southern Europe. Two larger lowlands in the east—the Hungarian Plain, east of the Alps, and the Ukrainian Steppe, a broad, grassy plain north of the Black Sea—have rich soil that supports farming.

Eastern Russia includes the area called Siberia. Northern Siberia is a vast treeless plain that remains frozen much of the year. The few people who live there fish, hunt seals and walruses, or herd reindeer.

Mountains and Highlands

Highlands mark the northern border of the Northern European Plain. Steeper mountains lie south of the plain. Europe's highest mountain ranges form the Alpine Mountain System, which stretches from Spain to the Balkan Peninsula. The system takes its name from the Alps of south-central Europe. It also includes the Pyrenees, which lie between France and Spain, and the Carpathians, in east-central Europe.

NATIONAL GEOGRAPHIC

The Alps

▲ Rugged beauty and good skiing conditions make the Alps a popular tourist destination. ***Place*** **What mountain ranges form the Alpine Mountain System?**

NATIONAL GEOGRAPHIC

Spain's Meseta

▲ The name "Meseta" comes from the Spanish word *mesa* or "table." Although wheat and other grains are grown on the Meseta, lack of rainfall and extreme temperatures make it difficult to farm. ***Regions*** **Where are Europe's highest mountain ranges located?**

The highest mountain in the Alpine Mountain System is Mont Blanc in the French Alps. It rises to 15,771 feet (4,807 m). Most of Europe's mountains, though, are not very tall compared to those of Asia.

The highest peak in Europe is not in the Alps. Instead, it is farther east, near Asia, in the Caucasus Mountains. This high peak, which is in Russia, is called Mt. Elbrus, and it stands 18,510 feet (5,642 m) high. The Caucasus Mountains are located near a fault line. As a result, this area is prone to earthquakes. Another Russian mountain system, the Urals, divides Europe from Asia. Worn down by erosion, the Urals are not very high.

Europe's mountains have helped isolate certain countries and peoples. Switzerland, for example, is located high in the Alps. While European wars have raged around it, the country has remained free from conflict and invasion for many centuries. Europe's mountains have never completely blocked movement, however. **Passes,** or low areas between mountains, allow the movement of people and goods.

Less dramatic than the mountains are three older, eroded highland areas. One area extends from Sweden through northern Great Britain to Iceland. Stripped of soil by glaciers, the land here is poor for farming, so many people raise sheep. A second highland area, the Central Uplands, contains much of Europe's coal. The area reaches from southern Poland to France. The third highland, the Meseta in Spain, is a plateau on which people grow grains and raise livestock.

Waterways

In addition to plains and mountains, Europe has an abundance of rivers, lakes, and other waterways. Europe's major rivers flow from inland highlands and mountains into the oceans and seas surrounding the region.

Many European rivers are **navigable**, or wide and deep enough for ships to use. People and goods can sail easily from inland areas to the open sea and, from there, around the world. The Danube and the Rhine, two of Europe's longest rivers, are important for transporting goods. Canals link these rivers, further improving Europe's water transportation network.

Rivers carry rich soil downstream, creating productive farmland along their banks and at their mouths. For this reason, river valleys have long been home to large numbers of people. Today, fast-flowing rivers are also used to generate electricity to support these large populations.

Russia's Volga, like the Rhine and Danube, creates a rich farming region and is used to transport goods. Many of Russia's Siberian rivers flow north across marshy lowlands. Eventually, they empty into the frigid Arctic Ocean. The Lena (LEE·nuh), Yenisey (YIH·nih·SAY), and the Ob' (AWB) are among the longest rivers in the world. Because they can freeze, however, they cannot always be used for transportation like other European rivers.

Lakes cover only a small fraction of Europe. They are valuable for recreation, though, and for tourism. Most lakes are located on the Northern European Plain and in Scandinavia. The highland lakes in northern Great Britain and the Alps, however, are among the most beautiful and frequently visited. People visit these lakes to boat, fish, swim, and appreciate nature.

NATIONAL GEOGRAPHIC

Hydroelectric Power

This hydroelectric power plant is located on the Danube River between Austria and Germany.
Human-Environment Interaction **How do Europeans use their rivers?**

Lake Baikal, in Asian Russia, is the world's deepest freshwater lake. The lake holds one-fifth of the world's supply of unfrozen freshwater. Baikal is home to many kinds of aquatic life, including Baikal seals, or nerpa, the only seals that live in freshwater.

Russia's economy relies heavily on the Caspian Sea. This sea—the largest inland body of water in the world—is really a saltwater lake. The Caspian Sea is an important resource for fishing. Major oil and gas deposits are located near and under it.

Reading Check **Explaining** How have Europeans improved their water transportation network?

Student Web Activity Visit glencoe.com and complete the Chapter 8 Web Activity about the Northern European Plain.

Europe's Resources

Main Idea **Europe has valuable resources that strengthen its economy.**

Geography and You Think of the products that you use every day. What are these products made of? As you read, think about how Europe's natural resources benefit people around the world.

Europe is a leader in the world economy. Part of this success comes from Europe's rich supply of natural resources.

Energy Resources

Europe has a variety of energy resources. As you can see in the graphs below, Russia is a leader in reserves of some **fossil fuels**—oil, natural gas, and coal. Earnings from oil sales have helped boost the Russian economy in recent years. Pipelines carry Russian oil and gas to some nations in Europe.

Outside of Russia, the most productive oil fields lie beneath the North Sea. These areas are controlled by Norway and the United Kingdom, which then sell oil to other countries. The North Sea oilfields provide Norway with almost all of the oil it needs. The United Kingdom, though, imports about as much oil as it exports.

Most other European nations also must import oil to supply their energy needs. To discourage dependence on oil, European governments tax gasoline heavily. Because of these taxes, drivers in Europe pay high gasoline prices.

Coal has been a major energy source in Europe for many decades. By burning coal, Europeans fueled the development of modern industry in the 1800s.

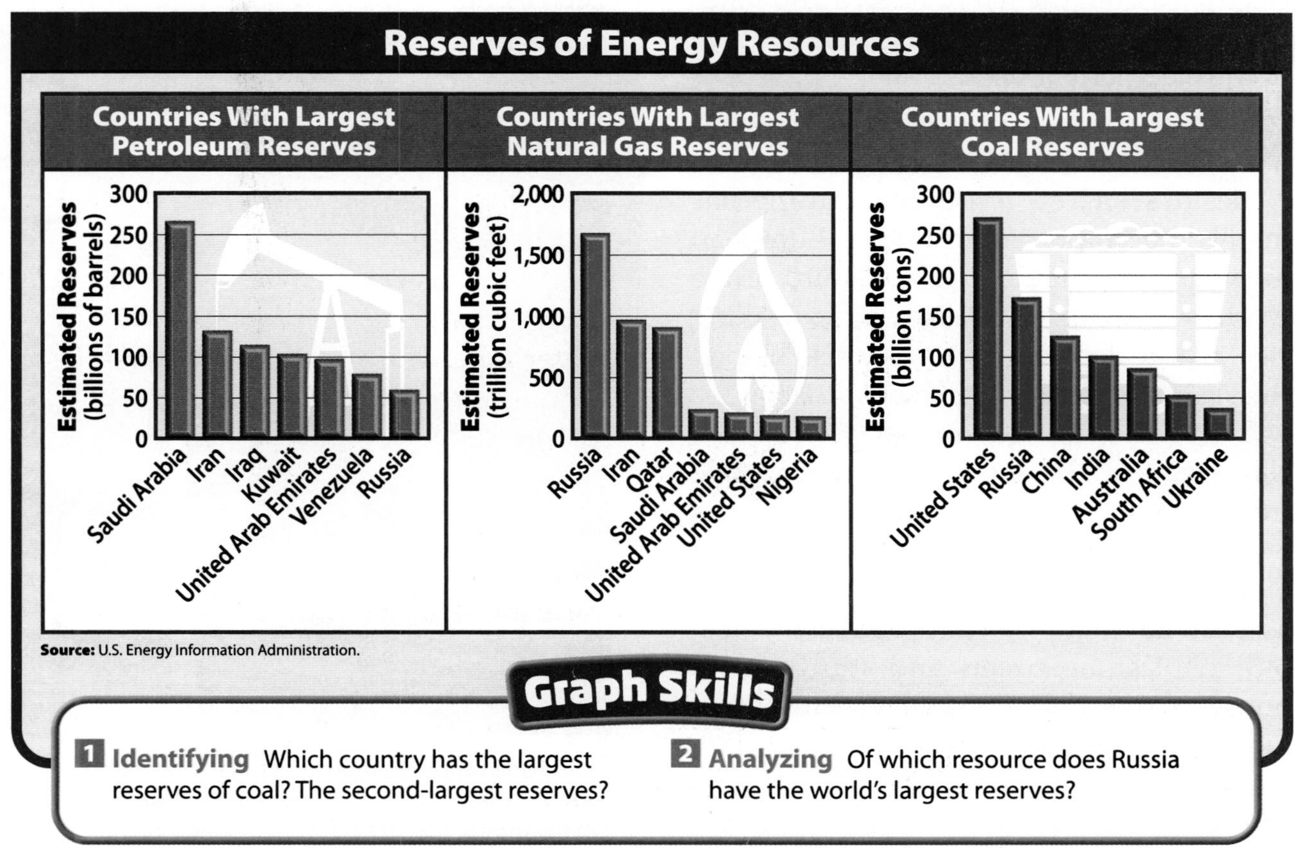

Graph Skills

1 Identifying Which country has the largest reserves of coal? The second-largest reserves?

2 Analyzing Of which resource does Russia have the world's largest reserves?

Factories benefited from Europe's large coal deposits. Coal was used to power textile mills that made cloth, steel mills, and chemical plants. Coal also fueled railroad trains that became a major source of transportation in the 1800s.

Coal remains important today. Almost half of the world's coal comes from Europe. Coal mining provides jobs for people from the United Kingdom in the west to Ukraine, Poland, and the Czech Republic in Eastern Europe, as well as in Russia. As you will read in the next section, though, burning coal has some negative results.

Europe also relies on "clean" energy sources that cause less pollution than burning coal or oil. In the highlands and mountains, swift-flowing rivers make hydroelectric power. Germany, Spain, and Denmark are leaders in building wind farms, which use large turbines to create electricity from the wind. France also relies on nuclear power plants to generate much of the electricity it uses.

Other Natural Resources

Besides energy resources, Europe has many other important resources. European mines produce more than one-third of the world's iron ore, which is used in making steel. Large deposits of iron ore also helped Russia develop a strong steel industry.

The United Kingdom exports a special clay used to make fine china dishes. Marble from Italy and granite from Norway and Sweden provide fine building materials. Stone has long been an important resource as seen in many of Europe's centuries-old cobblestone streets and sturdy stone houses. Other important mineral resources include copper and gold found in Russia.

Forests once covered a large part of Europe. Long ago, however, people cleared the land for farms, using the wood for building and for fuel. Forests are still a major resource in Russia. Trees cover much of Siberia, and Russia produces about a fifth of the world's **softwood.** This evergreen tree wood is used in buildings and for furniture. Sweden and Finland also produce much lumber.

Fertile soil is another valuable resource, providing Europe with some of the world's best farmland. European farmers grow large amounts of grains, including nearly all of the world's rye, most of its oats, and nearly half of its wheat. Europe also grows more potatoes than any other region in the world.

The waters around Europe contain yet another resource—fish. From the Mediterranean Sea to the North Atlantic, Europeans catch many varieties of fish. Overfishing is a problem in some of the region's seas, however. As a result, the supply of fish is decreasing.

▲ Europe produces more electricity from wind turbines than any other world region. ***Human-Environment Interaction*** **Why is wind power considered a "clean" energy source?**

NATIONAL GEOGRAPHIC

Air Pollution

Air pollution from industrial plants, such as this one in Wales, can destroy forests in Poland (inset). ***Human-Environment Interaction*** **What is acid rain, and why is it harmful?**

While Russia has many resources, its large size and cold climate **inhibit,** or limit, the ability to use them all. Many resources in Siberia are difficult to use for two reasons. First, the region lacks **infrastructure.** Infrastructure is the system of roads and railroads for transporting materials. Second, Siberia's cold climate can freeze equipment. Some advances in technology, however, have made it easier to obtain Siberia's resources. For example, a pipeline now carries natural gas from Siberia to Europe. If this trend continues, Russia will benefit from its many resources.

Reading Check **Describing** Where are Europe's most productive oil fields?

Environmental Issues

Main Idea **Europe's plentiful resources have helped its economy, but environmental problems are a growing concern.**

Geography and You Do you recycle at home and try to use energy wisely? As you read, see how Europeans are taking similar steps to protect their resources.

By taking advantage of its natural resources, Europe has become an economic powerhouse. The **impact** on the environment, however, has sometimes been harmful. For instance, in deforested areas of Southern Europe, tree roots no longer hold the soil in place. Valuable topsoil can be washed away.

Air Pollution and Acid Rain

Industrial growth in Europe has also hurt the environment—and created health risks. For example, car exhaust and smoke from burning oil and coal create air pollution. This pollution causes breathing problems, eye irritation, and lung disease.

Air pollution has another serious effect. When pollutant particles mix with precipitation, acid rain falls to Earth. Acid rain can make trees vulnerable to attack from insects and disease. Forests in eastern Europe are especially threatened. In that region, lignite coal is a major fuel source because it is cheap. It burns poorly, however, and pollutes heavily. The resulting acid rain has destroyed many forest areas in Hungary, Poland, the Czech Republic, and Slovakia.

Acid rain falls on Europe's waterways as well as on its forests. As acids build up in lakes, rivers, and streams, fish and other wildlife are poisoned and die.

Acid rain is also a problem for Europe's historic buildings. The famous Tower of London, Germany's Cologne Cathedral, and ancient buildings and monuments dating from Greek and Roman times all show damage from acid deposits.

Water Pollution

Water pollution is another challenge for Europe. Sewage, garbage, and industrial waste have all been dumped into the region's seas, lakes, and rivers. As populations and tourism have increased, the problem has worsened.

Runoff from farms is also a problem for Europe's waters. Runoff is precipitation that flows over the ground, often picking up pesticides and fertilizers along the way. When chemicals from runoff enter a river, they encourage the growth of algae. Algae rob the river of so much oxygen that fish cannot survive. Runoff spilling into the Danube River, for example, has killed much of its marine life.

Finding Solutions

European leaders are trying to solve environmental problems in a number of ways. Many are working to prevent air pollution and acid rain by limiting the amount of chemicals that factories and cars can release into the air. Norway and Sweden are adding lime to their lakes. This substance stops the damage caused by acid rain and allows fish to multiply again.

Europeans are also making their lakes and rivers cleaner by treating waste and sewage. In addition, some countries encourage farmers to use less fertilizer to reduce damaging runoff.

In Russia, past leaders paid little attention to the environment. As a result, pollution is a serious problem there. Other countries are giving Russia help to improve its sewage systems and clean up heavily polluted sites.

Reading Check **Explaining** How does runoff contribute to water pollution?

Section Review

Vocabulary

1. **Explain** the significance of:
   a. landlocked **c.** navigable **e.** softwood
   b. pass **d.** fossil fuel **f.** infrastructure

Main Ideas

2. **Summarizing** Use a diagram like the one below to explain the importance of rivers.

3. **Analyzing** Why are Europe's clean energy sources important to the region?
4. **Explaining** Why and where is acid rain especially a problem?

Critical Thinking

5. **BIG Idea** Which resources helped industry and farming develop in Europe?
6. **Challenge** Describe how Europe's landforms and bodies of water influenced where people settled.

Writing About Geography

7. **Expository Writing** Write a paragraph explaining which physical feature you think has most helped Europe's economy to prosper.

NATIONAL GEOGRAPHIC **Geography & History**

Disaster at Chernobyl

In the modern world, we depend on technology to survive. What happens when technology goes wrong?

The Accident On April 26, 1986, the world saw its worst nuclear disaster. That day, a reactor at the Chernobyl nuclear power plant in Ukraine exploded. Dangerous radioactive material shot into the sky. The explosion also caused a fire that raged for 10 days, pouring out more radioactive dust and ash. During that time, radioactive material—called fallout—fell to the Earth over large parts of Ukraine and Belarus, as well as other parts of Europe.

The Impact Fewer than a hundred people died from the high levels of radiation that resulted from the explosion and fire. About 4,000 more, however, are expected to die from cancers caused by the accident. Fortunately, these numbers are far below what had originally been feared.

▲ **Abandoned amusement park, Pripyat', Russia**

Nevertheless, more than 20 years after the accident, its effects are ongoing. Around the area contaminated by fallout, officials created an exclusion zone of about 1,545 square miles (4,002 sq. km). People are prohibited from living within this zone. More than 350,000 people were forced to leave their homes following the accident. The disaster scarred the land as well. More than 1.8 million acres (728,435 hectares) of farmland and 1.7 million acres (687,966 hectares) of forest were abandoned because of contamination from fallout.

Meanwhile, a threat remains at Chernobyl. A protective concrete shell, built around the reactor to contain the contamination, could collapse. Also, rainwater leaks into the shell. When the water seeps back into the ground, it carries radioactive material with it, further poisoning the land.

Think About It

1. **Movement** How many people were forced to leave the contaminated area?
2. **Human-Environment Interaction** What effect did the accident have on the environment?

Guide to Reading

BIG Idea

The physical environment affects how people live.

Content Vocabulary

- deciduous *(p. 243)*
- coniferous *(p. 243)*
- mistral *(p. 245)*
- sirocco *(p. 245)*
- permafrost *(p. 247)*
- taiga *(p. 247)*

Academic Vocabulary

- major *(p. 241)*
- feature *(p. 242)*
- period *(p. 247)*

Reading Strategy

Categorizing Information Use a chart like the one below to describe Europe's climate zones.

Climate Zone	Characteristics
1.	1.
2.	2.
3.	3.
4.	4.

Climate Regions

Section Audio

Spotlight Video

Picture This For many Russians, ice fishing is a favorite pastime. In this photo, an ice fisher is shielded from the cold winds blowing along the Tom River in Siberia. The fisher must often reach into the icy water and remove slush from the hole to keep it from freezing over. Read this section to learn how Europe's many climate zones have influenced its people.

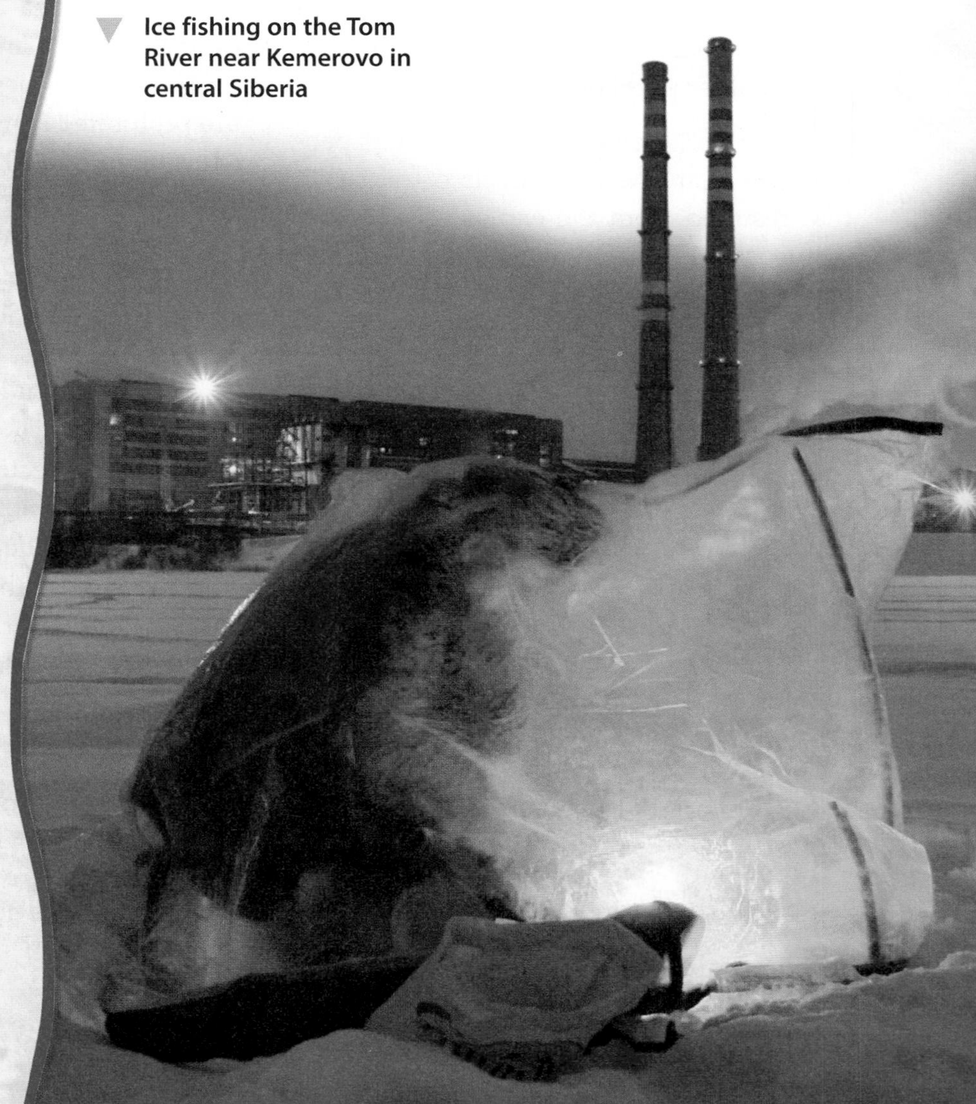

Ice fishing on the Tom River near Kemerovo in central Siberia

Wind and Water

Main Idea **Wind patterns and water currents shape Europe's climate.**

Geography and You Doesn't a cool breeze feel great on a hot day? Read to learn how winds are helpful to Europe too.

Look at the physical map of the world in the Reference Atlas. Because Europe is farther north than the United States, you might expect Europe's climate to be colder than ours. In fact, much of Europe enjoys a milder climate. Why?

As **Figure 1** shows, the North Atlantic Current carries warm waters from the Gulf of Mexico toward Europe. Winds from the west pass over this water and carry more warmth to Europe. These prevailing winds, known as westerlies, are a **major** influence on warming the European climate.

Other wind patterns also affect the climate in parts of Europe. For example, warm winds from Africa contribute to the high temperatures in southern Europe. Blustery winter winds from Asia lower temperatures throughout much of eastern Europe.

The water surrounding Europe also affects the region's climate. Winds blowing off the water cool the hot land in the summer and warm the cold land in the winter. For this reason, coastal areas tend to have a more moderate climate than inland areas.

Reading Check **Explaining** Why does northwestern Europe have a mild climate?

NATIONAL GEOGRAPHIC Maps In MOtion See StudentWorks™ Plus or glencoe.com.

Figure 1 **Europe: Currents and Wind Patterns**

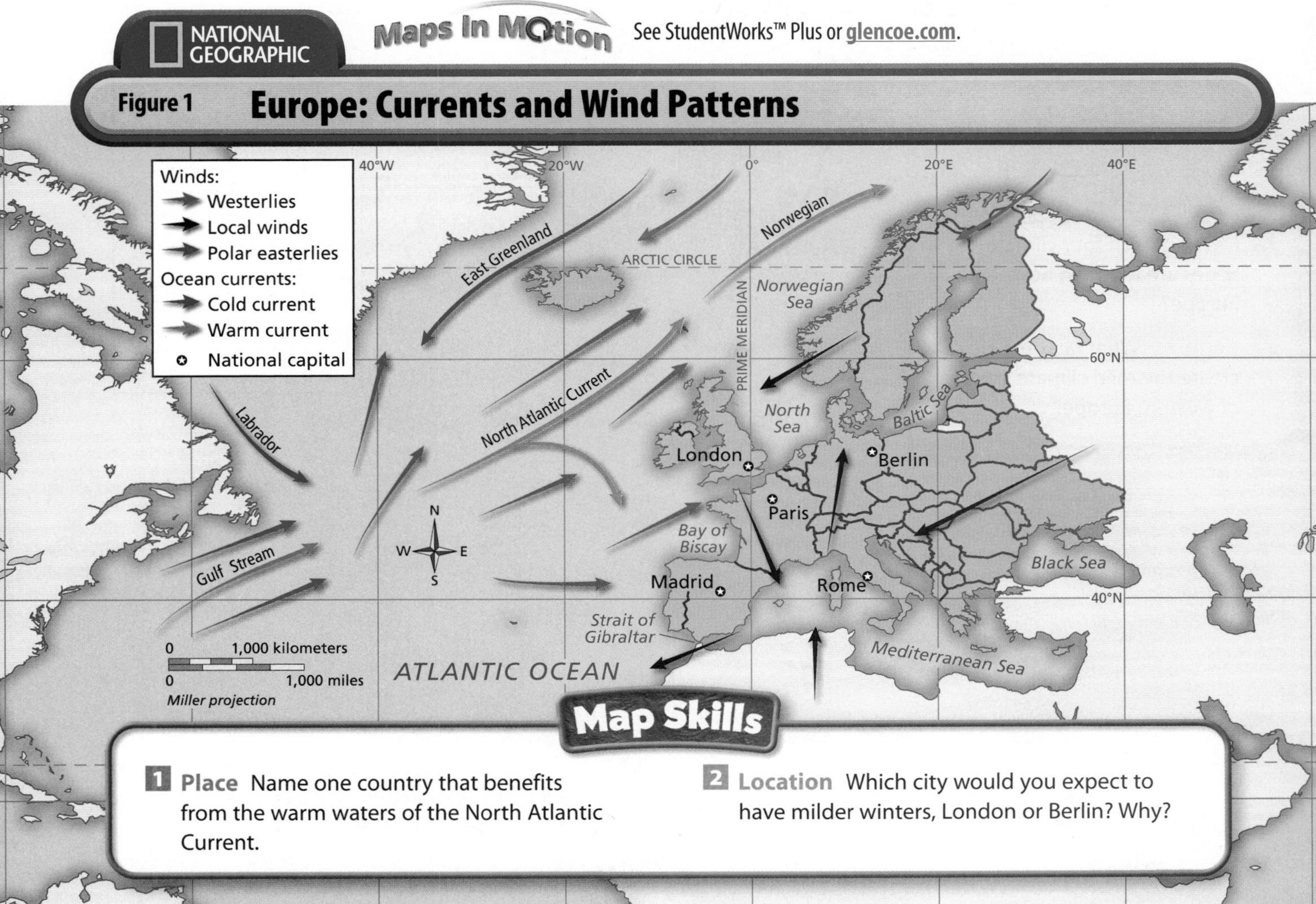

Map Skills

1 **Place** Name one country that benefits from the warm waters of the North Atlantic Current.

2 **Location** Which city would you expect to have milder winters, London or Berlin? Why?

Climate Zones

Main Idea **Europe has eight climate zones, each with different vegetation.**

Geography and You What is your ideal climate? Chances are, you can find it in Europe! Read to learn how Europe's climate varies from area to area.

Most of Europe falls into three main climate zones—marine west coast, humid continental, and Mediterranean. **Figure 2** also shows five other climate zones that appear in smaller areas—subarctic, tundra, highland, steppe, and humid subtropical.

Marine West Coast

Much of northwestern and central Europe has a marine west coast climate. This climate has two **features,** one of which is mild temperatures. The North Atlantic Current carries so much warmth that southern Iceland has mild temperatures, even though it is near the Arctic Circle. Because of the mild temperatures, this climate zone has surprisingly long growing seasons. In the United Kingdom, for example, farmers have a window of 250 or more days for planting and harvesting—nearly 60 more days than in eastern Canada—which is located at the same latitude.

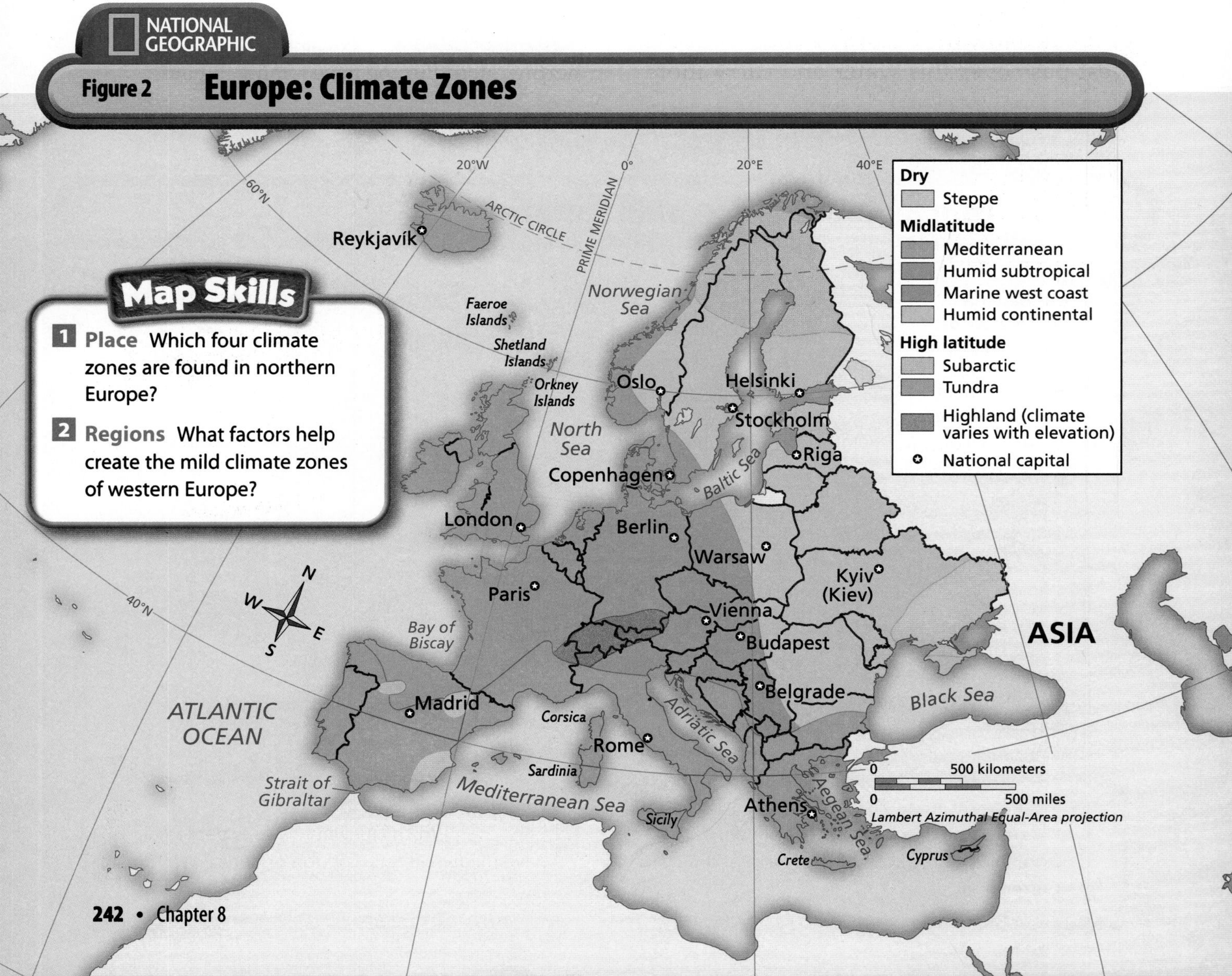

Although temperatures stay mild, differences do exist across the region. In the north, summers are shorter and cooler. Also, the farther away you get from water, the wider the range of temperatures will be. For example, in the coastal city of Brest, France, a December day might be only 20 degrees cooler than a July day. However, in Strasbourg, France, which is more than 400 miles (644 km) from the Atlantic Ocean, the temperature can differ by 40 degrees between summer and winter.

The second feature of the marine west coast climate, besides mild temperatures, is abundant precipitation. This typically falls in autumn and early winter. Although the zone as a whole gets plenty of rain, certain mountainous areas stay dry because of the rain shadow effect. For example, the coastal area of Norway, on the western edge of highlands, receives a yearly average of 90 inches (229 cm) of precipitation. The eastern slopes of those same highlands receive only one-third that amount.

Forests thrive in much of Europe's marine west coast climate zone. Some forests consist of **deciduous** trees, which lose their leaves in the fall. **Coniferous** trees, also called evergreens, grow in cooler areas of the marine west coast climate zone.

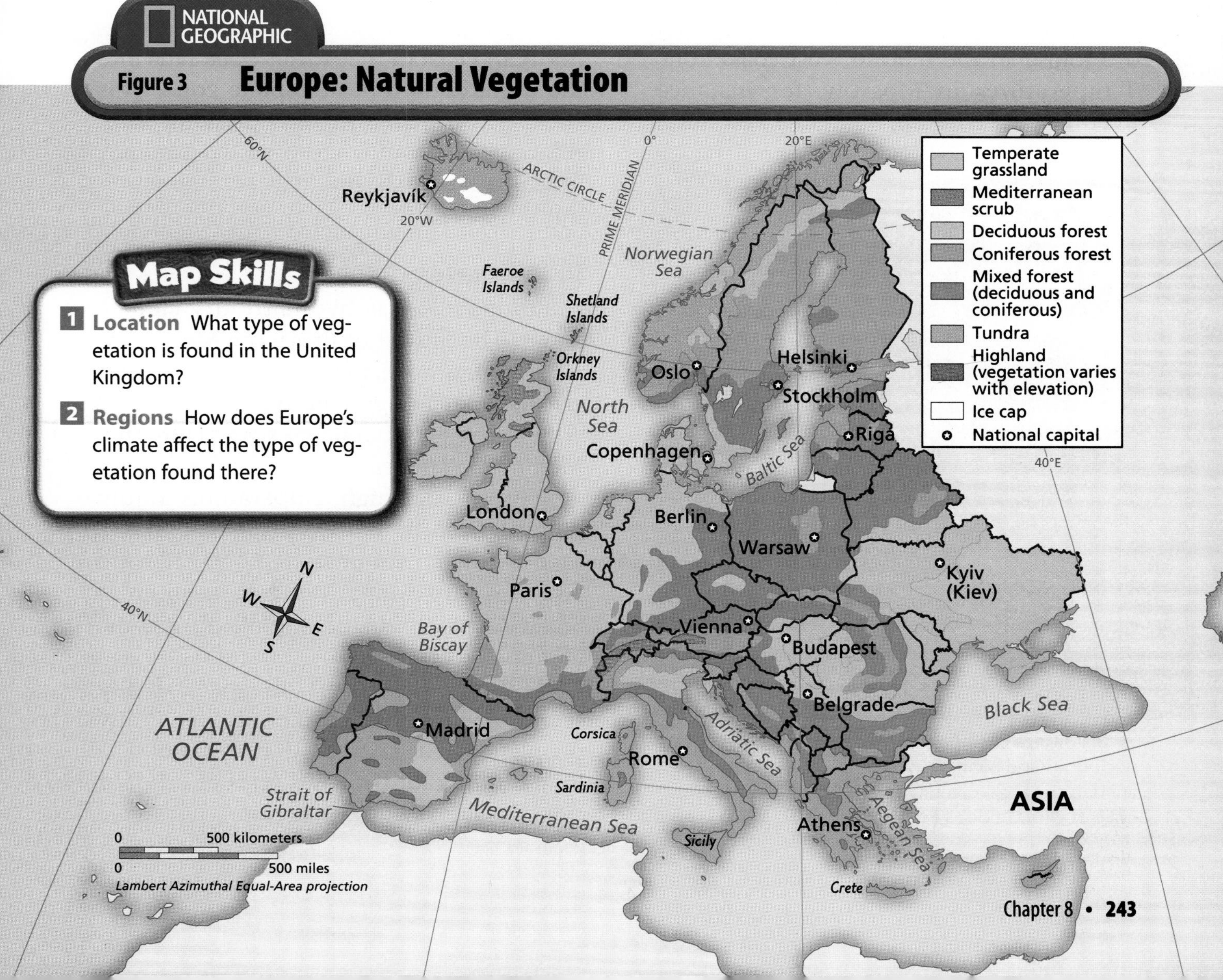

They dominate the landscape in southern Norway, Sweden, and parts of eastern Europe.

Although forests no longer blanket the continent, many people still earn their living from forest-related industries. They cut timber and produce lumber, paper, charcoal, and turpentine.

Humid Climates

Europe has two humid climate zones that are located along the southern and eastern edges of the marine west coast zone. The largest is the humid continental zone that covers eastern Europe and some parts of northern Europe. Cool, dry winds from the Arctic and Asia give this zone cooler summers and colder winters than are found in the marine west coast zone. Temperatures in Moscow, for instance, average only 66°F (19°C) in July and fall as low as 16°F (-9°C) in January. Cold Russian winters have played an important role in Russia's history. During World War II, bitter cold halted the German army's advance into Russia. Better-prepared Russian troops forced the Germans to retreat.

Because of drier winds, the humid continental zone gets less rain and snow than the marine west coast zone. Nonetheless, some low-lying areas are wet and marshy. This is because the precipitation that does fall can be slow to evaporate in the cool climate. The humid continental zone supports mixed forests of deciduous and evergreen trees. However, only evergreens grow farther north and in higher elevations.

A small crescent of land that arches north and east of the Adriatic Sea falls into the humid subtropical climate zone. This zone is warmed by winds blowing from Africa, to the south, and over the Mediterranean Sea. It has hot, wet summers and mild, wet winters.

▲ Bialowieza National Park in eastern Poland contains deciduous and coniferous trees. The park is home to animals such as wolves, lynx, and bison. ***Place*** **What type of climate does Poland have?**

Dry Climates

Europe also has two fairly dry climate zones. The largest of these, the Mediterranean climate zone, includes much of southern Europe. The climate type is so linked with this region that it was named after the Mediterranean Sea.

With average high temperatures in July ranging from 83°F to 98°F (28°C to 37°C), Mediterranean summers are hot. They are also very dry. Many Mediterranean areas receive just a trace of rainfall during the summer.

Because of the heat, the pace of life seems to slow down in the summer. Many people take August vacations. Others take long midday lunches and relax at outdoor cafes for hours in the evening.

Greek Herder

Herding goats and sheep is a common economic activity in areas with a Mediterranean climate. ***Regions*** **What types of vegetation grow in Europe's Mediterranean climate zone?**

Winters in the Mediterranean zone are mild and wet. With temperatures in the 50s Fahrenheit (low teens Celsius), nobody worries about snow. Rainfall, however, averages 3 to 4 inches (7.6 to 10.2 cm) per month, so an umbrella comes in handy.

The mountains of southern Europe affect the Mediterranean climate zone. The Pyrenees and Alps block chilly northern winds from reaching Spain and Italy. Some mountains also create rain shadows. Winds coming over the mountains from the west bring more rain to the western slopes. The eastern side stays drier. The effect is dramatic in Spain, where the northwest region is cool, wet, and green. Inland Spain, on the other hand, is hot, dry, and brown.

In southern France, the lack of a mountain barrier allows a cold, dry wind to blow in from the north. This wind, the **mistral** (MIHS·truhl), occurs in winter and spring. It also creates waves, making southern France a popular site for windsurfing.

Countries in the Mediterranean climate zone are also affected by hot, dry winds from Africa to the south. In Italy, these winds are called **siroccos** (suh·RAH·kohs). They pick up moisture as they cross the Mediterranean, bringing uncomfortably humid conditions to southern Europe.

Because of the Mediterranean zone's low rainfall, plants that grow there must be drought resistant. Vegetation includes low-lying shrubs and grasses, as well as the olive trees and grapevines that the region is known for. Forests are rare, and stands of trees appear only on rainy mountainsides or along rivers.

Europe's other dry climate zone is the steppe zone that stretches from the southern part of Ukraine into Russia. Steppes are dry, treeless grasslands, much like prairies but with shorter grass. Here the climate is not dry enough to be classified as desert, but not wet enough for forests to flourish.

Highland

The highland zone is found in the higher altitudes of the Alps and Carpathians where the climate is generally cool to cold. However, temperatures and precipitation vary greatly from place to place, depending on three factors—wind direction, orientation to the sun, and altitude. As an example, consider two peaks in the Swiss Alps—Säntis and Saint Gall. Säntis receives more than twice the precipitation of Saint Gall even though the two mountains are only 12 miles (19 km) apart. The difference is due to altitude—Säntis is about three times higher than Saint Gall.

Sturdy trees add color to the highland zone, but they grow only so far up the mountainsides. The point at which they stop growing is called the timberline. Above the timberline, where the sun barely warms the ground, only scrubby bushes and low-lying plants can survive.

Subarctic and Tundra

On its northern fringe, Europe has two zones of extreme cold. These are the tundra and subarctic climate zones. In **Figure 2,** you can see that the subarctic climate zone covers much of the northern parts of Norway, Sweden, and Finland. In **Figure 4,** you can see that the tundra zone covers the far north of Russia, the area above the Arctic Circle. To the south, and covering most of Asian Russia, lies the subarctic zone.

Why does most of Russia have cold climates? Far to the east of the North Atlantic Current, Russia receives little benefit from its warm air. Most of Russia also lies at high latitudes. As a result, most of this vast nation receives very little of the sun's heat even during summer, giving it a fairly cold climate. Russia's landforms contribute to its cold climate as well. In the far north, low elevations allow the southerly flow of icy Arctic air. In the south and east, mountains block warm air coming from the south. Because of these factors, large parts of Russia experience only winter- and summerlike conditions.

NATIONAL GEOGRAPHIC Maps In MOtion See StudentWorks™ Plus or glencoe.com.

Figure 4 **Russia: Climate Zones**

Map Skills

1 Regions What four climate zones does Russia have?

2 Location Which Russian city is in the tundra climate zone?

Russia's Siberian Taiga

▲ The taiga is a belt of coniferous trees that extends across northern Eurasia and North America. Russia's taiga includes a variety of birds and animals, along with resources such as lumber, oil, and natural gas. ***Regions*** **What is permafrost?**

Spring and autumn are not full seasons in Russia. Instead, they are simply brief **periods** of changing weather.

Europe's coldest climate, the tundra, is found in the northernmost reaches of Norway, Sweden, Finland, and Russia. The tundra is an area of vast treeless plains near the North Pole. This climate zone has short, cool summers and long, snowy winters. Summer temperatures reach only about 40°F (4°C) and frigid winter temperatures plunge as low as -25°F (-32°C).

In the tundra climate zone, it is so cold that moisture in the soil cannot evaporate. Cold temperatures and lack of precipitation result in **permafrost,** a permanently frozen layer of soil beneath the surface. Only mosses, lichens, and small shrubs can survive in the tundra.

Because of Earth's tilt, the sun shines on the far north for up to 20 hours per day in late spring and early summer. As a result, the nights are extremely short. In the middle of winter, however, conditions are reversed. The days are short, and nights can last as long as 20 hours. Some people are so affected by the scarce light in winter that they lose energy and feel depressed.

South of the tundra lies the subarctic climate zone. Slightly warmer temperatures here support a greater variety of vegetation than in the tundra. As a result, evergreens grow in this region at low altitudes. In fact, the **taiga,** the world's largest coniferous forest, stretches about 4,000 miles (6,436 km) across Russia's subarctic zone. This forest is so vast, it is roughly the size of the United States.

Climate Change

Most scientists agree that the world's climate is growing warmer. Average temperatures have been inching upward for several decades. Measurements and photos show that glaciers are steadily eroding. In 2003 western Europe suffered its worst heat wave since the Middle Ages.

People debate whether this global warming is just part of nature's cycle or is instead related to human activities. Many scientists, though, believe that burning fossil fuels, such as coal and oil, contributes to the greenhouse effect. Gases build up in the atmosphere and trap large amounts of warm air near Earth's surface.

People also debate what this warming means for the planet. Many European leaders are worried. They fear that melting glaciers will produce higher ocean levels that will flood low-lying areas, such as the Netherlands and coastal cities like Venice, Italy. Such flooding would affect millions of people.

As a result, European officials are taking action. They are trying to slow global warming by encouraging changes in energy use. Most European governments have signed the Kyoto Treaty. This is an international agreement to limit the output of greenhouse gases. The period in which countries were supposed to begin working toward the goals set in this treaty began in 2008.

Meanwhile, leaders from Europe and other areas continued to discuss the problem and possible solutions. Another international meeting to address the issue of climate change took place in Copenhagen, Denmark, in 2009.

Reading Check **Explaining** How do mountains affect southern Europe's Mediterranean climate zone?

Section 2 Review

Vocabulary

1. **Explain** the meaning of *deciduous, coniferous, mistral, sirocco, permafrost,* and *taiga* by using each term in a sentence.

Main Ideas

2. **Identifying** What factors affect Europe's climates?
3. **Summarizing** Using a diagram like the one below, identify each of Europe's climate zones and the vegetation found in each zone.

Critical Thinking

4. **Comparing and Contrasting** How are Norway and Spain similar in climate? How are they different?
5. **BIG Idea** How does the North Atlantic Current affect farming in the marine west coast climate zone?
6. **Challenge** Describe how latitude and altitude affect climate and vegetation in Europe.

Writing About Geography

7. **Using Your FOLDABLES** Use your Foldable to write a paragraph comparing and contrasting the climate of Russia to the climate of Europe.

Visual Summary

Landforms

- The Northern European Plain is a rich farming region and has a high population density.
- Mountains separate much of northern and southern Europe.
- Uplands regions are found in northwest and central Europe and in Spain.

Berlin, Germany, on the Northern European Plain

Waterways

- Waterways have had a major impact on Europe's population and ways of life.
- Rivers provide transportation, good soil for farming, and hydroelectric power.
- Many of Russia's rivers flow north into the Arctic Ocean and freeze in winter, making them less useful than other rivers of Europe.

European Resources

- Europe's energy resources include coal, petroleum, natural gas, and hydroelectric and wind power.
- Russia's large size and cold climate make it difficult for Russians to use all of their resources.
- Fishing is important to coastal Europe.

Fishers in Spain

Environmental Issues

- The European environment has been damaged by deforestation, pollution, and acid rain.
- Europeans are working to protect and improve their environment through recycling and limiting forms of chemical pollution.

Tulip harvest in the Netherlands

Climate Regions

- Europe's nearness to water and its wind patterns greatly affect its climates.
- Europe has eight main climate zones.
- Much of Russia is covered by cold, high latitude climates and is sparsely settled as a result.
- Europeans are concerned about the negative effects of global warming.

Reindeer on Norwegian tundra

Study anywhere, anytime! Download quizzes and flash cards to your PDA from glencoe.com.

GA CRCT Practice

TEST-TAKING TIP

Eliminate answers that you know for certain are incorrect. Then choose the most likely answer from those remaining.

Directions: Choose the best answer for each question.

1 **Acid rain has destroyed forests, poisoned fish and wildlife, and damaged historic buildings in Europe. What causes acid rain?**

A It occurs when water from polluted streams and rivers evaporates into the atmosphere and is then released as rain.
B It is created when particles escape from nuclear power plants and are drawn into rain clouds.
C It is created when air pollution mixes with precipitation.
D It naturally occurs when volcanoes erupt and release minerals into the atmosphere.

2 **Why are the Danube and the Rhine Rivers important to Europe?**

A They are well-stocked with a variety of fish that are a part of the European diet.
B They are used for transporting goods from inland areas to the ocean.
C Farmers use the water from these rivers to irrigate their crops.
D They supply drinking water to people in nearby cities and towns.

3 **Which of the following can be found in plentiful supply in Russia?**

A natural resources
B cars
C wind farms
D immigrants

4 **Why does much of Europe enjoy a milder climate than the United States?**

A Europe is closer to the Equator than the United States.
B Mountain ranges that surround Europe block the polar easterlies.
C Warm winds blow from Asia to Europe.
D Westerly winds carry warm air to Europe when they pass over warm water that flows from the Gulf of Mexico into the North Atlantic Current.

5 **Why does Russia have cold climates?**

A Most of the country is located near the North Pole.
B Most of the country sits at high latitudes, and warm air from the south is blocked by tall mountains.
C Cold air from Norway, Sweden, and Finland combines with icy Arctic air to blow over Russia throughout the year.
D It receives very little light or heat because of its position when Earth is tilted away from the sun.

6 **Many scientists believe that the world's climate is growing warmer. What do they think contributes to this greenhouse effect?**

A the burning of fossil fuels
B extreme weather events such as hurricanes
C the sun's increasing heat
D volcanic eruptions

7 **What role has coal played in Europe's industry and economy?**

A Europe has had to buy coal from foreign nations since the 1800s to keep its industries operating.
B It was used to power factories, plants, and trains and still provides mining jobs today.
C Coal has been used as a fertilizer that increases production of fruits and vegetables.
D Europe uses oil and natural gas to fuel its industries, so it exports nearly all of its coal supply.

8 **How many independent countries are in Europe?**

A more than 100
B about 10
C about 40
D about 25

9 **Look at the bar graph and answer the questions that follow.**

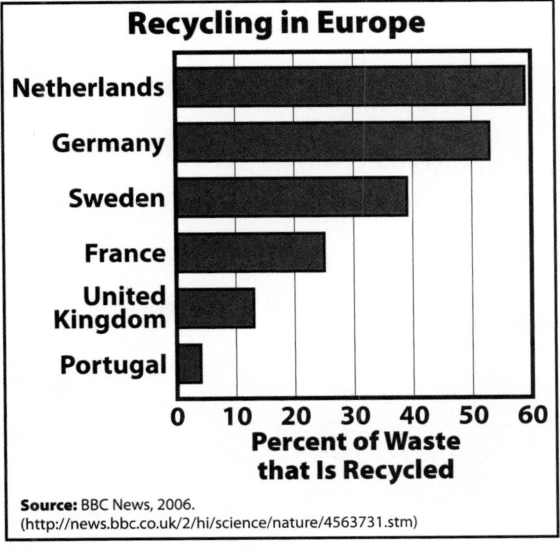

Which two European countries recycle more than 50 percent of their waste?

A Sweden and Portugal
B Netherlands and Germany
C Sweden and the United Kingdom
D France and Germany

10 **Which country recycles twice the amount of waste that France does?**

A United Kingdom
B Sweden
C Germany
D Netherlands

11 **Based on the graph, which of the following statements is most accurate?**

A Most European countries recycle more than half their waste.
B The six countries represented in the graph pollute more than any other European nations.
C The Netherlands relies more on recycling to manage waste than does Sweden.
D The Netherlands produces more waste than the other five countries represented on the graph.

12 **Read the passage and answer the questions that follow.**

Natalia Ivanova was a schoolteacher when the nuclear reactor in Chernobyl exploded. She was told to gather the children of the village so they could be evacuated. Parents were not allowed to leave with their children.

> *It was terrible having to knock on the door or window in the middle of the night to tell the parents that their children should be evacuated the next morning. We said it was because of the radioactivity, which could have bad consequences for all of them. We arranged a place for everyone to gather to be put on buses. It was a dreadful sight.*
>
> —Natalia Ivanovna Ivanova, "Return to Chernobyl: 20 Years 20 Lives"

What did Natalia do following the accident?

A She drove a bus to pick up the children who were to be evacuated.
B She gathered a group of friends and fled the area.
C She helped take care of the sick and wounded.
D She went door-to-door to tell parents that their children were to be evacuated.

13 **Based on the passage, what did Natalia believe was "a dreadful sight"?**

A the effect of radioactivity on the people of the village
B all the children gathered to get on evacuation buses
C the large group of journalists trying to interview the villagers
D the cloud of radioactivity that was coming closer

For additional test practice, use Self-Check Quizzes—Chapter 8 at glencoe.com.

Need Extra Help?

If You Missed Questions...	1	2	3	4	5	6	7	8	9	10	11	12	13
Go to Page...	237	234	237	241	246	248	235	231	237	237	237	239	239

History and Cultures of Europe

Essential Question

Regions Europe is rich in history and culture. Like the United States, most countries in Europe are industrialized and have high standards of living. Unlike the United States, however, the people of Europe do not share a common language and government. What forces have helped unify Europeans at different times?

Chapter Audio

Ruins of a Greek amphitheater in Sicily

Section 1: History and Governments

BIG IDEA The characteristics and movement of people impact physical and human systems. Over the centuries, migrations and wars have brought different groups to power in Europe. As modern nations have taken the place of empires and kingdoms, ways of living and thinking have also changed.

Section 2: Cultures and Lifestyles

BIG IDEA Culture groups shape human systems. Europe is a region of many peoples with different ethnic backgrounds, languages, religions, and traditions. Despite their differences, Europeans lead similar lifestyles and share a rich cultural heritage.

Organizing Information Make this Foldable to help you organize information about Europe's history, population, and cultures.

Step 1 Place three sheets of paper on top of one another about 1 inch apart.

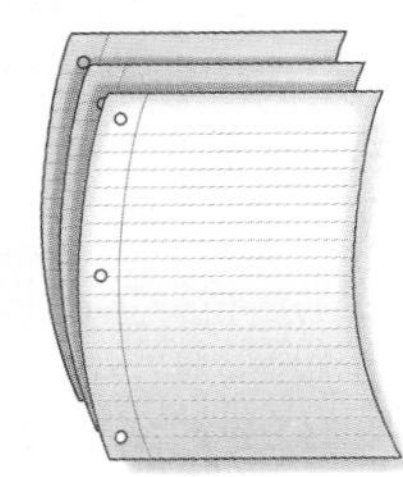

Step 2 Fold the papers to form six equal tabs.

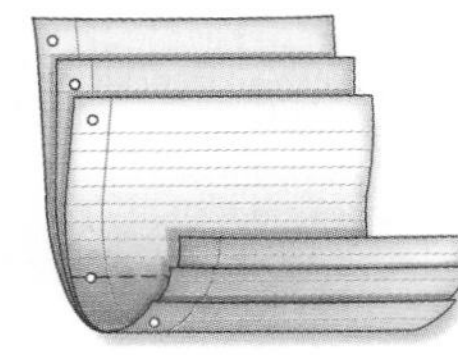

Step 3 Staple the sheets, and label each tab as shown.

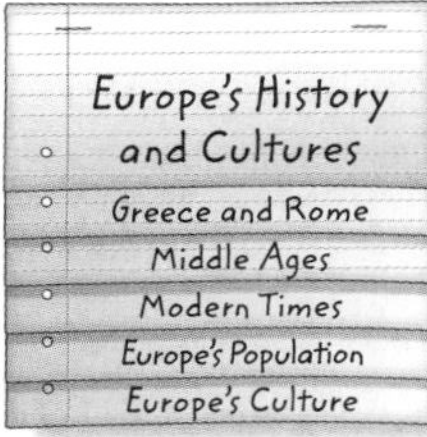

Reading and Writing As you read, use your Foldable to write down facts related to each period of European history, Europe's population, and European cultures. Then use the facts to write brief summaries for each of the tabs on the Foldable.

Visit glencoe.com and enter ***QuickPass***™ code GA6EOW6225c9 for Chapter 9 resources.

History and Governments

Guide to Reading

BIG Idea

The characteristics and movement of people impact physical and human systems.

Content Vocabulary

- classical *(p. 255)*
- city-state *(p. 255)*
- democracy *(p. 255)*
- republic *(p. 256)*
- emperor *(p. 257)*
- pope *(p. 258)*
- feudalism *(p. 258)*
- czar *(p. 260)*
- revolution *(p. 261)*
- communist state *(p. 262)*
- Holocaust *(p. 263)*
- Cold War *(p. 263)*

Academic Vocabulary

- dominant *(p. 256)*
- authority *(p. 260)*
- eliminate *(p. 263)*
- currency *(p. 265)*

Reading Strategy

Making a Time Line Use a time line like the one below to list at least five key events and dates in Europe's history.

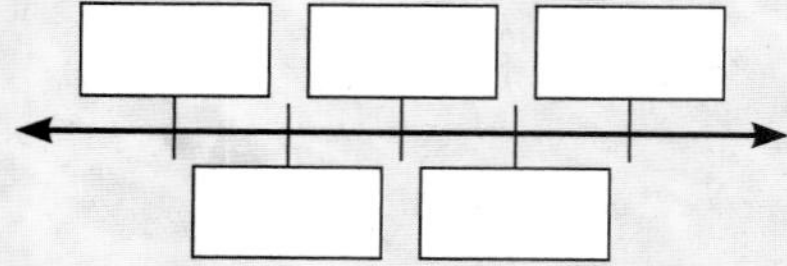

Picture This Who is that giant? Is it a warrior? A farmer? A king? One thing is certain—at almost 230 feet (70 m) high, the Long Man of Wilmington, in England, is one of the world's largest carved figures. Originally a chalk outline that became overgrown by grass, the Long Man was restored in 1969 with 770 concrete blocks. As scientists study the earth around the giant, they will be better able to judge when it was made—and maybe even why it was made! Read this section to learn more about the history of Europe.

Ancient Long Man in hills of southern England

Ancient Europe

Main Idea **Ancient Greece and Rome laid the foundations of European civilization.**

Geography and You Do you get to vote on family decisions or elect leaders to your student government? Read to find out how voting rights arose with the ancient Greeks and Romans.

The story of European civilization begins with the ancient Greeks and Romans. More than 2,500 years ago, these peoples settled near the Mediterranean Sea. Eventually their cultures spread throughout Europe and beyond. Even today, the influence of the **classical** world—meaning ancient Greece and Rome—lingers.

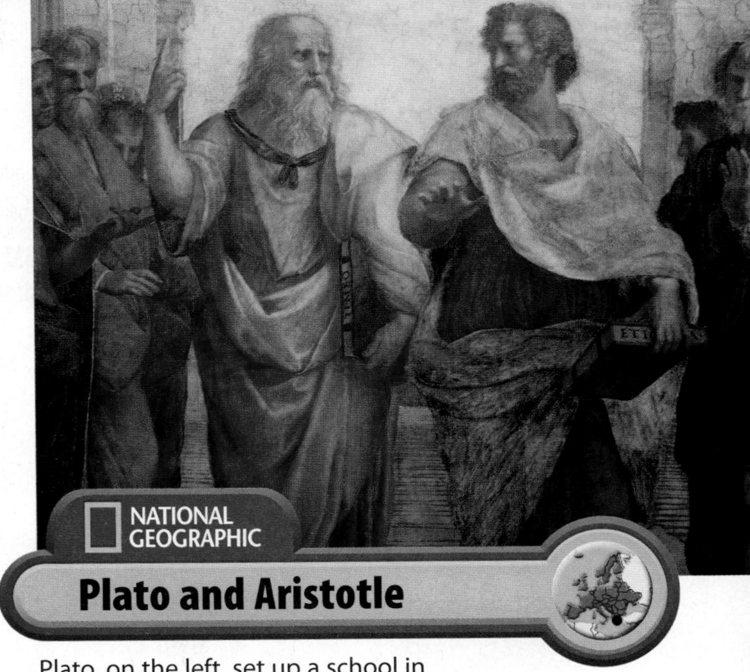

NATIONAL GEOGRAPHIC

Plato and Aristotle

Plato, on the left, set up a school in ancient Greece. His most famous student was Aristotle, another great Greek thinker. ***Place*** **In which Greek city-state did democracy develop?**

Ancient Greece

Physical geography naturally shaped the development of ancient Greece. The people felt deep ties to the land, which is ruggedly beautiful. At the same time, Greece's many mountains, islands, and the surrounding seas isolated early communities and kept them fiercely independent.

The earliest Greek civilizations began among farming and fishing peoples who lived near the Aegean Sea. These civilizations became wealthy through trade. After warfare led to their decline, independent territories called **city-states** developed throughout Greece. Each city-state was made up of a city and its surrounding area. Although separated by geography, the Greek city-states shared the same language and culture.

One of the most prosperous and powerful city-states was Athens. The people of Athens introduced the world's first **democracy**, a political system in which all citizens share in running the government. Although women and enslaved persons could not vote because they were not citizens, Athenian democracy set an example for later civilizations. Learning and the arts also thrived in Athens. Among the city-state's great thinkers were Socrates, Plato, and Aristotle. Their ideas about the world and humankind had a major influence on Europe.

During the mid-300s B.C., warfare weakened the Greek city-states. Soon an invader from the north, Philip II of Macedonia, conquered Greece. Philip's son earned the name Alexander the Great by making even more conquests. As shown in **Figure 1** on the next page, his empire included Egypt and Persia and stretched eastward into India. Trade boomed, Greek culture mixed with Egyptian and Persian cultures, and scientific advances spread. Alexander died young, however, and his empire quickly broke into several smaller kingdoms. By about 130 B.C., the Romans had conquered most of the Greek kingdoms.

NATIONAL GEOGRAPHIC **Maps In MOtion** See StudentWorks™ Plus or glencoe.com.

Figure 1 Ancient Greek and Roman Empires

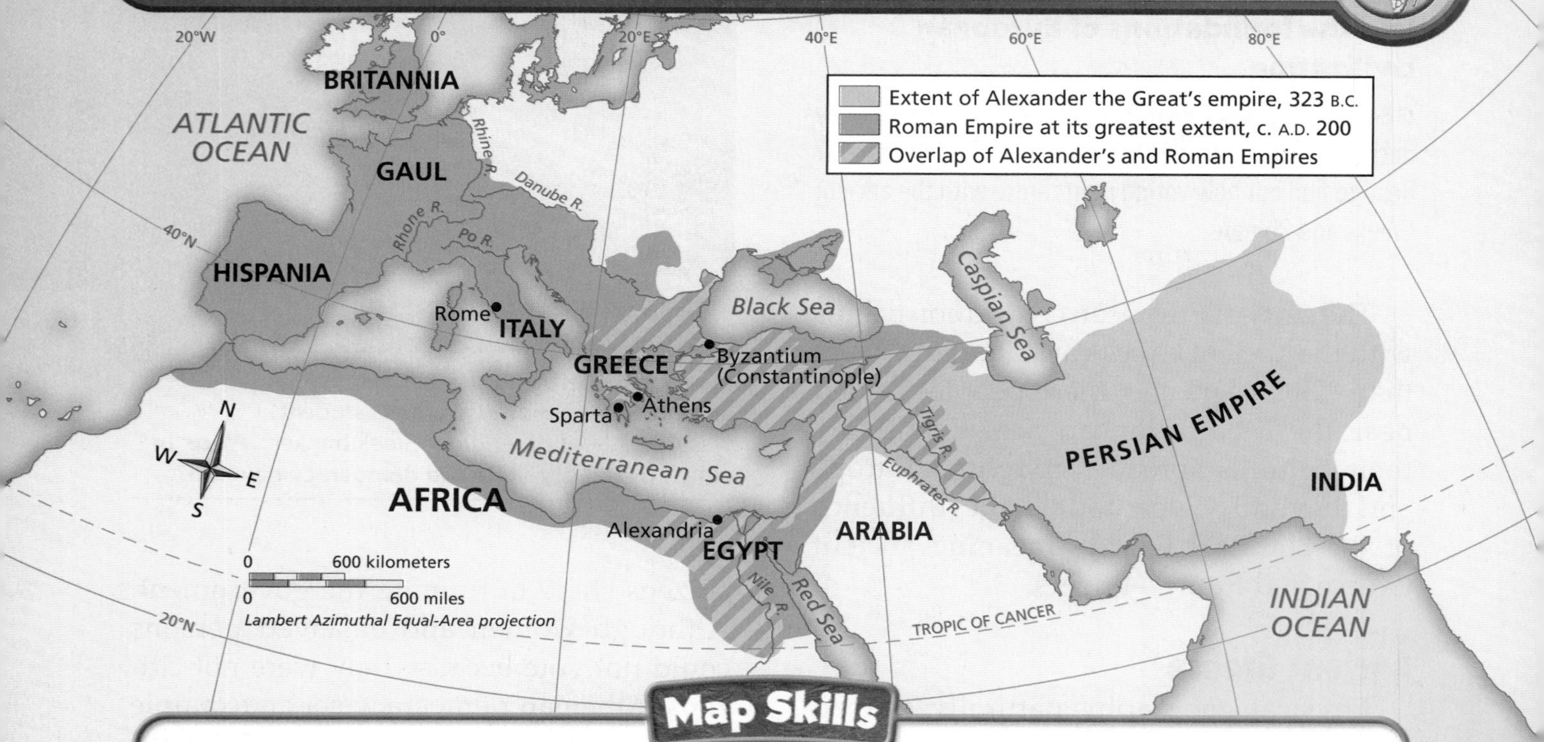

Extent of Alexander the Great's empire, 323 B.C.
Roman Empire at its greatest extent, c. A.D. 200
Overlap of Alexander's and Roman Empires

Map Skills

1 Regions Name two areas that were part of both empires.

2 Place The Romans called the Mediterranean Sea "our sea." Why was that name appropriate?

The Roman Empire

While Greece ruled the eastern Mediterranean, Rome became a **dominant** power on the Italian Peninsula. Rome began as a monarchy but changed to a republic in 509 B.C. In a **republic,** people choose their leaders. Rome was led by two consuls who were elected by the citizens. The consuls reported to and were advised by the Senate, an assembly of rich landowners who served for life. One of the government's great achievements was the development of a code of laws. Written on bronze tablets known as the Twelve Tables, the laws stated that all free citizens had the right to be treated equally. Roman law led to standards of justice still used today. For example, a person was regarded as innocent until proven guilty. Also, judges were expected to examine evidence in a case.

About 200 B.C., Roman armies began seizing territory throughout the Mediterranean region. Instead of ruling only by force, though, the Romans allowed many of the people they conquered to become Roman citizens. By granting people citizenship, the Romans were able to build a strong state with loyal members.

Social Studies  ONLINE

Student Web Activity Visit glencoe.com and complete the Chapter 9 Web Activity on ancient Rome.

As the Roman Republic expanded, it evolved into the massive Roman Empire. The first **emperor,** or all-powerful ruler, was Augustus, who gained that position in 27 B.C. His rule brought order to Rome's vast lands. His rule began a period of about 200 years called the *Pax Romana,* marked by peace, artistic growth, and expanding trade.

Christianity

During the *Pax Romana,* Christianity was developing in Palestine in the eastern part of the Roman Empire. There, a Jewish teacher, Jesus of Nazareth, preached a message of love and forgiveness. Jesus soon attracted followers as well as enemies. Fearing public unrest, the Roman authorities had Jesus executed. Yet within days, Jesus' followers, known as Christians, reported that he had risen from the dead. They took this as proof that Jesus was the son of God.

Eager to spread Jesus' teachings, two early Christian leaders, Peter and Paul, established the Christian Church in Rome. Roman officials at first persecuted, or mistreated, Christians. Despite this abuse, the new religion grew in popularity. In A.D. 392, Christianity became Rome's official religion.

Rome's Decline

By the late A.D. 300s, the Roman Empire was in decline. Rivals struggled to become emperor, and Germanic groups attacked from the north. About A.D. 395, the empire was divided into eastern and western parts. The eastern part remained strong and prosperous. Known as the Byzantine Empire, it lasted another thousand years. The western part was occupied by Germanic groups. In A.D. 476, Germanic leaders overthrew the last emperor in Rome and brought the Western Roman Empire to an end.

Despite its fall, Rome had great influence on Europe and the West. It helped spread classical culture and Christianity. Roman law shaped the legal systems in many countries. The Roman idea of a republic later influenced the founders of the United States. The Latin language of Rome became the basis for many modern European languages known as the Romance languages, such as Italian, French, and Spanish. Ancient Rome also influenced architectural styles in the Western world. For example, the U.S. Capitol and many other buildings have domes and arches inspired by Roman architecture.

Reading Check **Analyzing** Describe ancient Rome's influences on the modern world.

Roman Influences

NATIONAL GEOGRAPHIC

▲ The style of the U.S. Capitol was influenced by Roman architecture. Barbara Mikulski (inset) is a member of the U.S. Senate, which has powers similar to the ancient Roman Senate. ***Place Who made up the Roman Senate?***

Expansion of Europe

Main Idea During the Middle Ages, European society, religion, and government underwent great changes.

Geography and You Are there still parts of the world left to explore? Read to learn about changes in Europe, including how Europeans began to explore the far reaches of the world in the 1400s.

After Rome's fall, Europe entered the Middle Ages, a 1,000-year period between ancient and modern times. Christianity strongly influenced society during this period. In the 1300s, though, interest in education, art, and science exploded. Questions began to arise about earlier beliefs and practices. By the 1500s, Europe was experiencing changes that gave birth to the modern period.

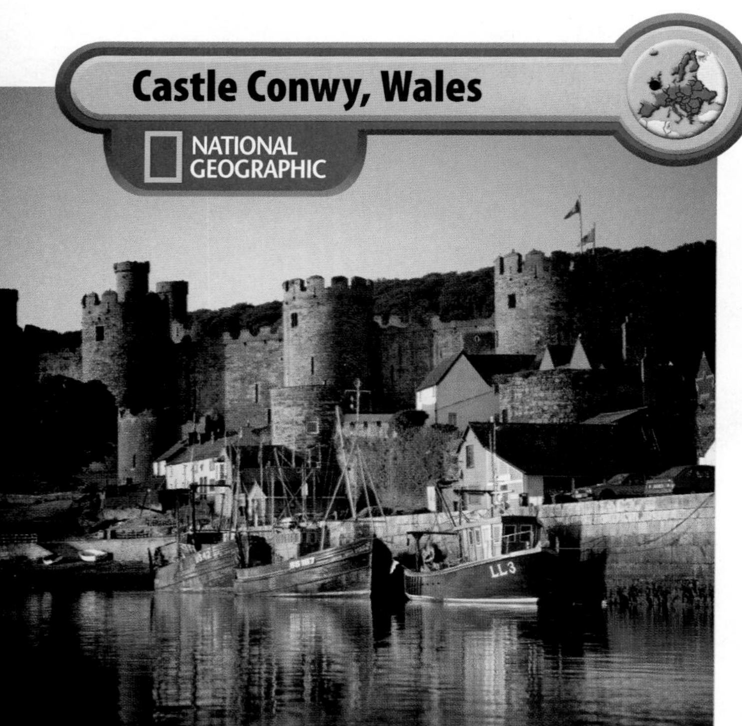

▲ During the Middle Ages, nobles were forced to build thick-walled castles for protection against invaders. ***Place*** **How can you tell that this castle was built for defense?**

A Christian Europe

During the Middle Ages, Christianity held a central place in people's lives. Two separate branches of the religion had formed, though. The Roman Catholic Church, based in Rome, was headed by a powerful **pope.** The Eastern Orthodox Church was centered in the Byzantine Empire. The Roman Catholic Church spread Roman culture and law to the Germanic groups living in western and central Europe. Eastern Orthodoxy was spread by missionaries. Missionaries are people who move to another area to spread their religion. They traveled from the Byzantine Empire and passed on their beliefs to Russians and other Slavic groups in eastern Europe.

The Middle Ages

About A.D. 800, a Germanic king named Charlemagne united much of western Europe. After his death, this empire broke up. To bring order, a new political and social system arose by the 1000s. Under this system, called **feudalism**, kings gave land to nobles. The nobles in turn provided military service, becoming knights, or warriors, for the king. This new system brought some order, but life was hard for most people. Most Europeans were poor peasants. They farmed the lands of kings, nobles, and church leaders, who housed and protected them but who also limited their freedom.

The Crusades

In feudal times, the Christian faith united Europeans. Yet the religion of Islam, founded in the A.D. 600s by an Arab named Muhammad, was on the rise. Followers of Islam, called Muslims, spread through Southwest Asia to North Africa and parts of Europe. They also gained control of Palestine, alarming Christians who considered this the Holy Land.

Beginning in the 1000s, nobles from western Europe gathered volunteers into large armies to win back the Holy Land. These religious wars, called the Crusades, were only partly successful. Muslims eventually recaptured much of the region. Later, in the 1400s, Muslims were forced from Spain, where they had controlled parts of the country since the A.D. 700s.

The Crusades led to greater trade for Europe and more wealth for European kings who collected taxes on that trade. Feudalism weakened as kings took land from nobles who had gone off to fight. Europe's kingdoms grew stronger. Many of them, such as France, later became modern Europe's nation-states. A nation-state is a country made up of people who share a common culture or history.

Meanwhile, in the 1300s, people all across Europe battled the bubonic plague, also known as the Black Death. Almost a third of Europe's population died from the disease, leading to a shortage of labor. Workers therefore gained more freedoms, further weakening feudalism.

NATIONAL GEOGRAPHIC

The Northern Renaissance

Several great Renaissance artists were from northern Europe, including Jan van Eyck, who painted this portrait of a married couple. ***Location*** **Why did the Renaissance begin in Italian city states?**

The Renaissance

As parts of Europe recovered from the Black Death, interest in art and learning revived. Ways of thinking changed so much between about 1350 and 1550 that this period is called the Renaissance, from the French word for "rebirth."

The Renaissance thrived in Italian city-states, such as Florence, Rome, and Venice. Merchants in these city-states had gained great wealth through trade with Asia and the Mediterranean world. They then used this wealth to support scholars and artists. Poets, sculptors, and painters, such as Michelangelo and Leonardo da Vinci, created stunning masterpieces. People also took an interest in the cultures of ancient Greece and Rome. Another important element of the Renaissance was humanism, a way of thinking that gave importance to the individual and human society. Humanism held that reason, as well as faith, was a path to knowledge. Over time, Renaissance ideas and practices spread from Italy to other parts of Europe.

The Reformation

During the 1500s, the Renaissance idea of humanism led people to think differently about religion and the role of the church in people's lives. Some people felt there were problems in the Roman Catholic Church that needed to be corrected. They criticized some of the practices and beliefs of the church.

In 1517 Martin Luther, a German religious leader, set out to reform, or correct, certain church practices. The pope in Rome, however, did not accept Luther's ideas, and Luther broke away from the Roman Catholic Church. Luther's ideas sparked a religious movement called the Reformation, which led to a new form of Christianity called Protestantism. Wars between Roman Catholics and Protestants shattered the religious unity of Europeans.

In western Europe, the power of monarchs grew as the **authority** of church leaders was challenged. In Russia, power also became more centralized as Ivan IV declared himself **czar** (ZAHR), or emperor, in 1547. The czars that followed him expanded Russia's territory, extending their power from eastern Europe all the way to the Pacific Ocean.

European Explorations

As Europe's kingdoms grew stronger, European seafarers began a series of ocean voyages that led to a great age of exploration and discovery. During the 1400s, Portugal wanted an easier way to get exotic spices from India and other parts of East Asia. Under the guidance of a gifted leader named Prince Henry the Navigator, Portuguese sailors developed new trade routes by sailing south around the continent of Africa to Asia. Sailing for Spain in 1492, the Italian-born explorer Christopher Columbus tried to find a different route to Asia. Instead of sailing south around the coast of Africa, Columbus attempted to sail west, across the Atlantic Ocean. Columbus's voyage took him to the Americas, continents unknown in Europe at the time.

In the Americas, Spain found gold and other resources and grew wealthy as a result of its overseas expeditions. Soon, other European countries sent forth their own explorers. Portugal, France, the Netherlands, and England all quickly claimed lands in the Americas. These countries founded colonies, or overseas settlements, there. Europeans also set up colonies or trading posts throughout Asia and Africa. While they sought more resources and new markets for their goods, Europeans also wished to spread the Christian religion. Trade with their colonies around the world brought European nations great wealth and power. Sadly, though, the Europeans often destroyed the local cultures in the lands they claimed.

Reading Check **Determining Cause and Effect** What changes did the Black Death bring to Europe?

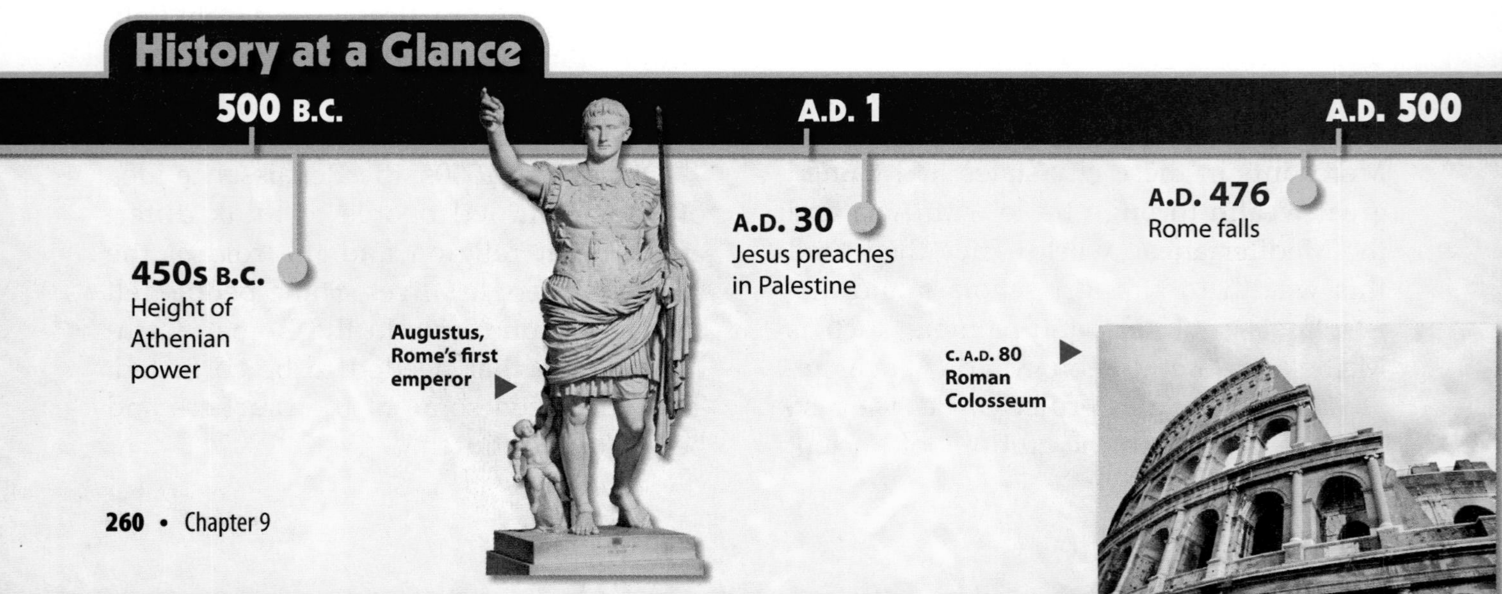

Modern Europe

Main Idea **From the 1600s to the 1800s and beyond, new ideas and discoveries helped Europe become a global power.**

Geography and You How would your life be different without computers, cell phones, or other modern technologies? Read on to discover how new technology changed Europe after 1600.

From the 1600s to the 2000s, Europe experienced rapid change. New machines helped economies grow. Powerful new weapons, however, made for deadly wars.

The Enlightenment

After the Renaissance, educated Europeans turned to science as a way to explain the world. Nicolaus Copernicus, a Polish mathematician, concluded that the sun, not the Earth, is the center of the universe. An Italian scientist named Galileo Galilei believed that new knowledge could come from carefully observing and measuring the natural world. These and other ideas sparked a **revolution,** or sweeping change, in the way people thought. During this Scientific Revolution, many Europeans relied on reason, rather than faith or tradition, to guide them. Reason, they believed, could bring both truth and error to light. As a result, the 1700s became known as the Age of Enlightenment.

Englishman John Locke was an important Enlightenment thinker. He said that all people have natural rights, including the rights to life, liberty, and property. He also said that when a government does not protect these rights, citizens can overthrow it. The American colonists later used Locke's ideas to support their war for independence from Britain in 1776.

Inspired by the American example, the people of France overthrew their king and set up a republic in 1789. Their republic did not last long, however. A brilliant general named Napoleon Bonaparte gained power and made himself emperor. His armies conquered much of Europe, until several countries united to defeat him in 1815.

Other revolutions continued to erupt in Europe in the 1800s. By 1900, most countries had made some changes, such as limiting the powers of rulers and guaranteeing some rights to citizens. Russia saw fewer changes, though. There, the czars began to modernize the economy, building industries. Most Russians remained poor, however, and unrest spread.

Coin from the Crusades

c. 1503 Renaissance artist Da Vinci's *Mona Lisa*

An Economic Revolution

Meanwhile, an economic revolution was also transforming Europe. The Industrial Revolution began in Britain. As it spread, it changed the way that people across Europe lived and worked.

Instead of making goods by hand, people began using machines and building factories. Machines could produce goods faster and at lower cost. People could now afford more things, such as comfortable cotton clothes. Travel improved, too, thanks to new inventions such as the railroad. Machines also helped farmers grow more food, which led to population growth. Additionally, farms required less labor.

Many people left farms to find work in cities. Cities became crowded, industries spewed out pollution, and diseases spread. Urban life remained grim for many Europeans until the mid-1800s. In the long run, though, the achievements of the Industrial Revolution benefited most people.

▲ The Industrial Revolution led to new advances in the weapons of war. During World War I, weapons such as airplanes, tanks, and submarines were widely used by armies for the first time. ***Regions*** **What events led to World War I?**

Industrial advances also helped European countries grow more powerful. They developed new weapons and competed aggressively for colonies in Africa and Asia. In 1914 European competition erupted into a four-year war. When this conflict, called World War I, finally ended in 1918, millions were dead.

Revolution in Russia

In 1914 Russia joined France and Britain to fight Germany and Austria in World War I. Poorly prepared, Russia suffered military defeats, losing millions of men between 1914 and 1916. Many Russians blamed Czar Nicholas II for this catastrophe—and for shortages of food that left them hungry. In early 1917, the people staged a revolution that forced the czar to step down from the throne. A new, temporary government took power.

Later that year, Vladimir Lenin led a second revolt that overthrew the temporary government. He set up a **communist state** in which the government controlled the economy and society. Lenin and his followers created a new nation—the Union of Soviet Socialist Republics (U.S.S.R.), or the Soviet Union.

Lenin said that he wanted to make everyone in Soviet society more equal. So he ended private ownership, bringing all farms and factories under the control of the government. Lenin's policies were continued by Joseph Stalin, who ruled the Soviet Union after Lenin's death in 1924. A harsh dictator, Stalin prevented the Soviet people from practicing their religions and had religious property seized. His secret police killed or imprisoned anyone who disagreed with his policies.

Soviet leaders set up a command economy, in which the government ran all areas of economic life. They decided what crops farmers should grow and what goods factories should produce.

They also combined small farms into large, factorylike farms run by the government. The leaders hoped these farms would be more efficient and reduce the need for farmworkers. Thousands of former peasants could then be put to work in factories. These leaders hoped to increase the Soviet Union's industrial output.

Soviet economic plans had mixed success. Industrial output increased, but the farms did not produce enough food for the Soviet people. Also, strict government control had drawbacks. The government **eliminated,** or did away with, competition, allowing only certain factories to make certain goods. This led to a lack of efficiency and poor-quality goods.

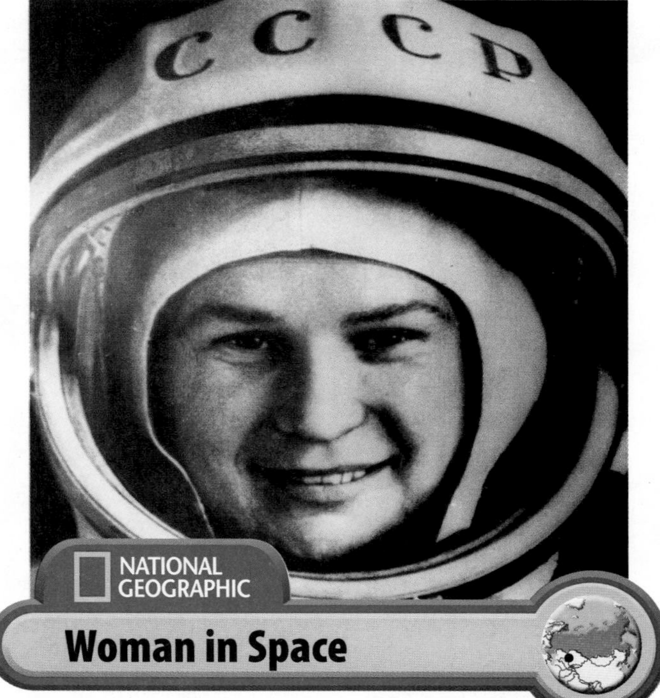

Woman in Space

In 1963 Valentina Tereshkova of the Soviet Union became the first woman to travel in space. ***Place*** **With whom did the Soviet Union compete in space exploration?**

Wars Hot and Cold

The 1930s brought hard times to Europe. The world was caught in a major economic slowdown called the Great Depression. Factories shut down, and millions of workers lost their jobs.

Unrest spread. In 1933 dictator Adolf Hitler took power in Germany, taking advantage of that unrest. Hitler led a movement called Nazism that wanted a strong government and military for Germany. Hitler rebuilt Germany's army and air force. He broke agreements that the country had made in the Treaty of Versailles, which ended World War I.

In 1939 Germany invaded Poland, and World War II began. By the time the war ended in 1945, much of Europe was in ruins, with millions of people dead or homeless. A major horror of the war was the **Holocaust**, the mass murder of 6 million European Jews by Hitler's followers.

The Soviet Union and the United States had been allies during the war, but their differing political and economic views caused them to become bitter rivals afterward. From the late 1940s until about 1990, these superpowers, the two most powerful nations in the world, engaged in a struggle for world influence. Because this struggle never became "hot," with actual combat between the two opponents, the conflict was called the **Cold War**. As part of the Cold War, the two superpowers competed to produce military weapons and to explore outer space.

Each superpower became the center of a group of nations. The United States was allied with most of western Europe's democracies. The Soviet Union was joined with the nations of Eastern Europe, which had also adopted Communist governments. Germany was split in two. The western part was allied with the United States. East Germany sided with the Soviet Union.

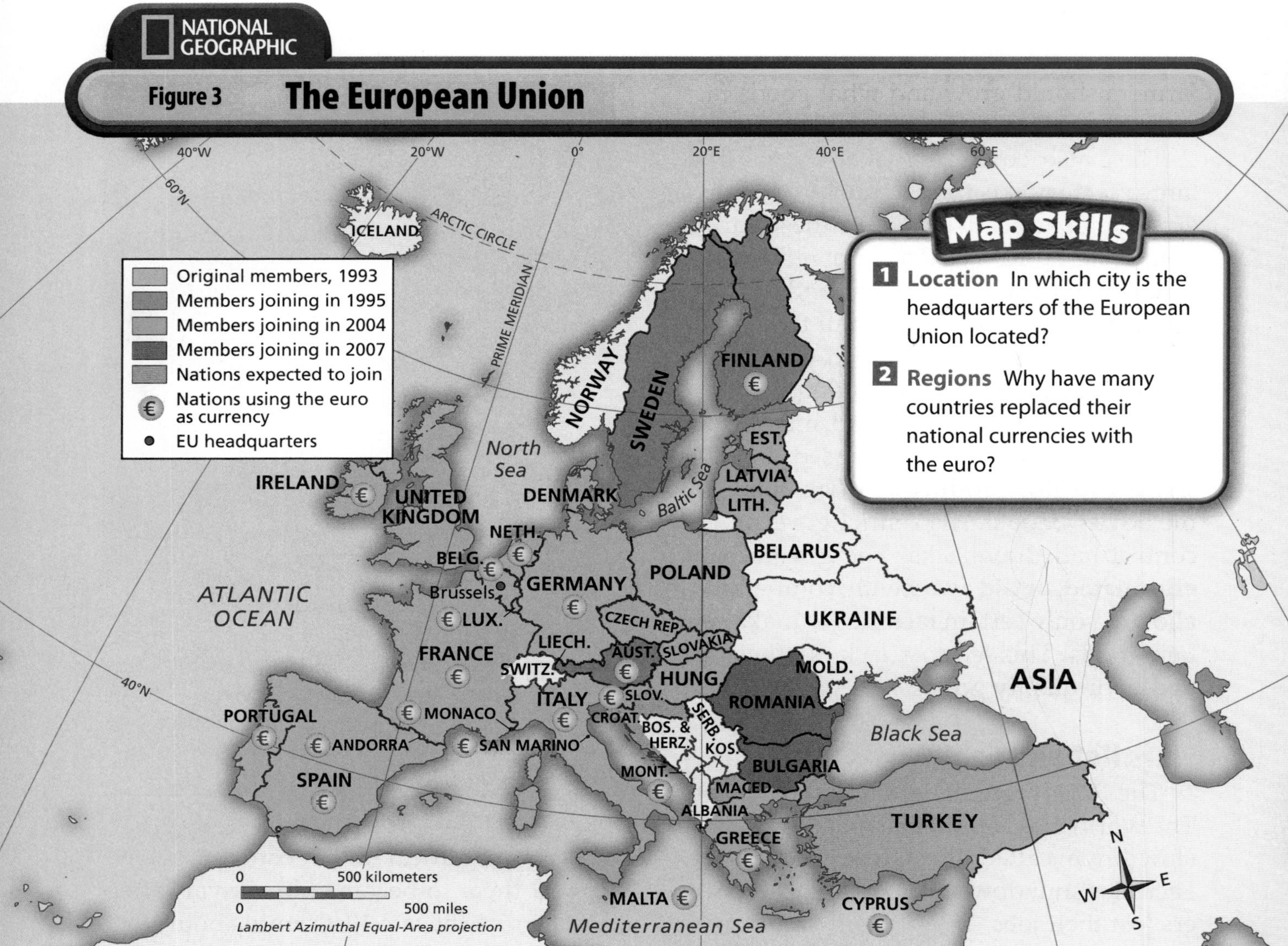

Reform and Change in the East

In the postwar years, the economies of Western European nations grew. People prospered and enjoyed comfortable lives. In Eastern Europe, though, consumers could not always buy goods they wanted. In addition, goods that were available often had poor quality. Along with these frustrations, many people in Eastern Europe also wanted more freedom.

A new leader named Mikhail Gorbachev (mih·KAH·el gawr·buh·CHAWF) came to power in the Soviet Union in 1985. He tried to reform the Soviet government to boost the economy. He also tried giving the Soviet people more political freedom. Instead of strengthening the country, these changes made people doubt communism even more.

In 1989 people in Eastern European countries forced several Communist governments from power. They set up new democracies. They adopted new economic systems that rejected government planning. A year later, East and West Germany merged to become one democratic state.

As communism ended in Eastern Europe, unrest grew among the Soviet Union's ethnic groups. Gorbachev was criticized by Communist hard-liners and reformers alike. The hard-liners wanted to stop the changes and maintain their rule.

Reformers wanted Gorbachev to make even more changes. The reformers were led by a popular politician named Boris Yeltsin (buhr·YEES YEHLT·suhn).

In August 1991, hard-line Communists attempted a coup (KOO), an overthrow of the government by military force. The attempt failed, however, and the hard-liners gave up. Within a few months, Russia and all the other Soviet republics declared independence. By the end of 1991, the Soviet Union no longer existed.

Boris Yeltsin became the first president of the newly-independent Russia. At first, he had some success in building democracy and a market economy. His successor, Vladimir Putin (vlah·DEE·meer POO·tuhn), however, sought greater power and increased government controls.

A New Era for Europe

In 1993 several democracies in Western Europe formed the European Union (EU). The goal of the organization is a united Europe. As shown in **Figure 3,** other countries joined the EU in later years, including many eastern European nations that previously had communist governments. The EU did away with tariffs and other trade barriers and allows goods, services, and workers to move freely among member countries. It has also created a common **currency,** or form of money, called the euro. With the euro, member countries can trade more easily with each other because there is no need to exchange the money of two different countries.

Reading Check **Describing** What was the Age of Enlightenment?

Section Review

Vocabulary

1. **Explain** the significance of:

a. classical	**e.** emperor	**i.** revolution
b. city-state	**f.** pope	**j.** communist state
c. democracy	**g.** feudalism	**k.** Holocaust
d. republic	**h.** czar	**l.** Cold War

Main Ideas

2. **Describing** Describe the political system of ancient Athens.
3. **Explaining** How did the Crusades help lead to the creation of modern Europe's nation-states?
4. **Summarizing** Use a diagram like the one below to summarize the changes brought about by the Industrial Revolution.

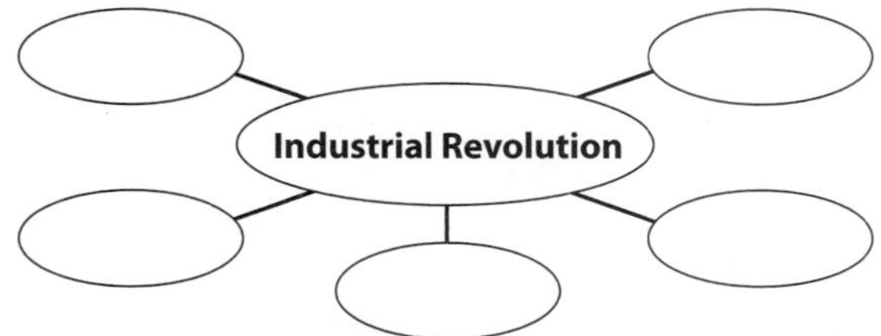

Critical Thinking

5. **Analyzing** How did Rome build a large, strong empire?
6. **Analyzing** Was the Soviet economy a success? Why or why not?
7. **Challenge** Which of Europe's revolutions do you think was most important for the creation of modern Europe? Explain your answer.
8. **BIG Idea** Provide an example of how political or social ideas, such as democracy or Christianity, spread in Europe.

Writing About Geography

9. **Using Your FOLDABLES** Use your Foldable to write a summary describing how governments in Europe have changed over time.

Learning in School: Should All Students Speak the Same Language?

In Europe, migration between countries is common. As a result, many students do not speak the local language where they live. Some educators believe that all students should speak the nation's official language in school. For example, in Berlin, Germany, several schools allow only the German language to be spoken during class, on school property, and on school trips. However, others disagree, arguing that students should be allowed to learn in their own languages.

Speaking the Same Language

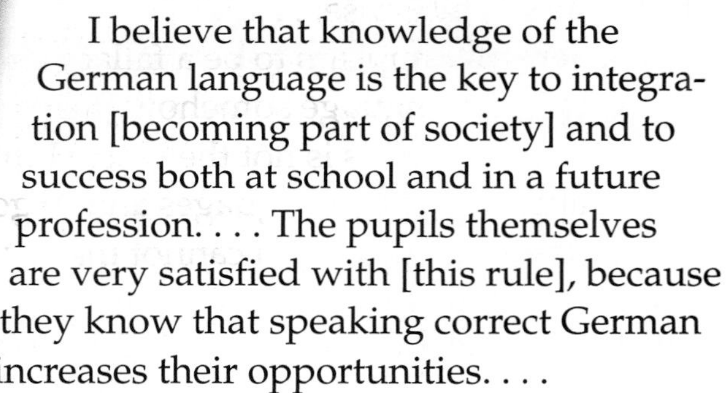

I believe that knowledge of the German language is the key to integration [becoming part of society] and to success both at school and in a future profession. . . . The pupils themselves are very satisfied with [this rule], because they know that speaking correct German increases their opportunities. . . .

When children start school and don't speak the language correctly, they . . . receive worse grades. That continues throughout their schooling and in the end they aren't able to get a vocational [job] training place. That's why we are in favour of introducing language tests starting from the age of four and thereby promoting language skills from kindergarten on.

—Armin Laschet
Minister for Generations, Family, Women, and Integration
North Rhine-Westphalia, Germany

Speaking the Same Language

Banning pupils from speaking their [traditional] languages in the schoolyard is not the answer, even if it were workable, which it is not. Other means of developing their linguistic [language] skills, such as pre-school instruction in German, are much more likely to be effective and should be fully supported.

. . . It is perfectly acceptable to ban other languages within the classroom. But outside the classroom pupils should be free to speak whichever language they like. Banning pupils' [traditional] languages sends a message that they are somehow "second class" citizens, which is likely to promote resentment rather than integration. . . .

Many children of immigrants choose to communicate in German in any case. . . .

There also appears to be a fallacy [mistaken belief] that speaking another language somehow [takes away] from pupils' ability with German. This is not the case. Humans have an almost unlimited ability to learn languages and in general there is no reason why the average person cannot master two or more languages.

—David Gordon Smith
Editor, Expatica: Germany

You Be the Geographer

1. **Identifying** What reasons do Laschet and Smith give to support their opinions?
2. **Critical Thinking** What might be some challenges for a student who speaks a different language than that of the other students in his or her class?
3. **Read to Write** Write a paragraph that explains your own opinion about students speaking only one language at school.

Guide to Reading

BIG Idea

Culture groups shape human systems.

Content Vocabulary

- ethnic group *(p. 269)*
- welfare state *(p. 269)*
- fertility rate *(p. 269)*
- urbanization *(p. 270)*
- secular *(p. 272)*
- oral tradition *(p. 274)*
- nationalism *(p. 275)*

Academic Vocabulary

- bond *(p. 269)*
- primary *(p. 271)*
- attitude *(p. 272)*
- promote *(p. 276)*

Reading Strategy

Organizing Information Use a diagram like the one below to list key facts about Europe's population patterns.

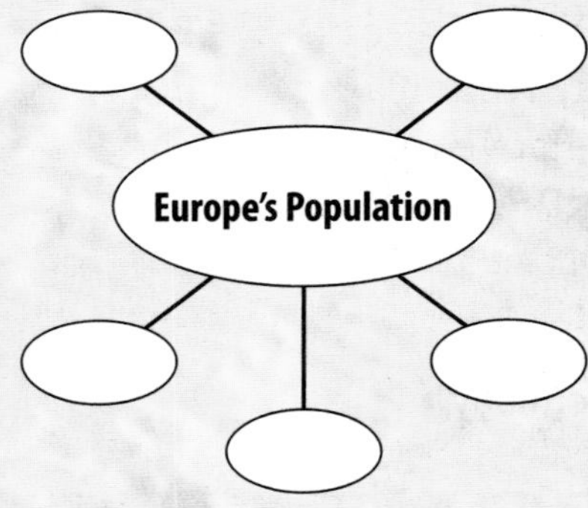

Cultures and Lifestyles

 Section Audio  Spotlight Video

Picture This Bog snorkeling? For more than twenty years, competitors wearing snorkels and flippers have met in the small town of Powys, Wales, to swim in its slimy bog. The challenge is to swim the fastest without using any standard swimming strokes. The just-for-fun event has attracted swimmers from as far away as South Africa and Australia. Read Section 2 to learn more about the cultures and lifestyles of Europeans.

Decorated in blue paint, this swimmer hopes to win first place.

Population Patterns

Main Idea **Ethnic differences and population changes pose challenges for Europe.**

Geography and You How do you treat a new person who joins your class? What kind of challenges does he or she face? Read to discover how Europe is responding to its new immigrant populations.

Europe's people are crowded into a relatively small space. The population is not distributed evenly, however, and it continues to undergo change.

NATIONAL GEOGRAPHIC

A Changing Population

These schoolgirls in London represent Europe's growing immigrant population and ethnic diversity. ***Movement*** **From where have people immigrated to Europe?**

A Rich Ethnic Mix

Today Europe is home to many ethnic groups. An **ethnic group** is a group of people with shared ancestry, language, and customs. Europe's ethnic mix has resulted from migrations, wars, and changing boundaries over the centuries.

Many Europeans identify strongly with their particular country or ethnic group. Having a common heritage or culture creates **bonds** among people. National and ethnic loyalties, however, have also led to conflict. By 2008, disputes among ethnic groups had split Yugoslavia into seven separate countries. In some of these new countries, ethnic hatred sparked the worst fighting in Europe since World War II.

Despite divisions, Europeans have a growing sense of unity. They realize that because their countries are linked by geography, cooperation can help bring peace and prosperity. In addition, the people share many values that go beyond ethnic or national loyalties. For example, Europeans value democracy and human rights. They also believe that a government must care for its citizens. Many European countries are **welfare states** in which the government is the main provider of support for the sick, the needy, and the retired.

Population Changes

Because of recent immigration, Europe's population is still undergoing change. Since World War II, many people from Asia, Africa, and Latin America have settled in Europe. Tensions have risen as immigrants and local residents compete for jobs, housing, and social services. As a result, immigrants have not always felt welcome in many places in Europe.

European countries deal with immigrants in various ways. Some want immigrants to adapt quickly, so they require newcomers to learn the national language. Other countries pass laws to keep immigrants from settling within their borders. Still others try to improve educational and job opportunities for newcomers.

You might be surprised to learn that although the number of immigrants is increasing, the region's overall population is decreasing. Europe has a low **fertility rate,** which is the average number of children born to each woman.

As a result, Europe is expected to have 10 percent fewer people by 2050. In Russia alone, the population is expected to drop by nearly 20 percent. This decline in population means there will be fewer workers to keep Europe's economy growing. Meanwhile, Europeans tend to be living longer now. As a result, young workers will face higher taxes to support the aging population.

Reading Check **Making Generalizations** How do national and ethnic loyalties benefit and harm Europeans?

NATIONAL GEOGRAPHIC

European Fashion

With their generally high incomes, many Europeans can afford the latest fashions, like the one worn by this model at a fashion show in Paris. ***Regions*** **How might a shrinking population affect Europe's economy?**

Life in Europe

Main Idea **European lifestyles today reflect the region's urban society and level of wealth.**

Geography and You Does the idea of living in a city appeal to you? Read to discover how cities play an important part in the lives of Europeans.

Customs, languages, and religions have always differed among Europeans. In recent decades, however, differences in lifestyles among Europe's peoples have lessened as a result of industrial and economic growth, urban growth, and improved standards of living. Today, most Europeans are well-educated city dwellers with comfortable incomes.

Cities

Beginning in the late 1700s, the Industrial Revolution changed Europe from a rural, farming society to an urban, industrial society. Rural villagers moved in large numbers to urban areas. This concentration of people in towns and cities is known as **urbanization**. Many of Europe's cities grew quickly and became some of the world's largest.

Today, three of every four Europeans live in cities. Moscow, London, and Paris rank among the largest urban areas on the globe. Other large cities include Madrid, Spain; Rome, Italy; and Berlin, Germany.

Many European cities blend the old and the new. Ancient landmarks often stand near modern highways and skyscrapers. European cities are also crisscrossed by public transportation systems that bring people to jobs and urban attractions. In recent decades, however, more Europeans have bought cars and have chosen to live in suburbs outside the cities.

Transportation

Most of Europe's transportation systems are government owned. Standards differ from country to country, but overall, Europe boasts one of the world's most advanced transportation networks. The rail system links cities and towns across the continent. Trains travel underwater between England and France via a 31-mile (50-km) tunnel under the English Channel, known as the Chunnel. France developed the use of high-speed trains, which cause less damage to the environment than most other forms of transportation. Trains are the **primary** means of transportation in Russia.

Highways also allow high-speed, long-distance travel. Trucks use these roads to carry most of Europe's freight. Russia's highways lag behind those of other countries, though the government is building a highway across the country.

Canals and rivers are also used to transport goods. The Main-Danube Canal in Germany links hundreds of inland ports between the North Sea and the Black Sea. Europe's long coastline is dotted with other important ports, such as Rotterdam, in the Netherlands. This is one of the busiest ports in the world.

Airports connect European cities too. Planes fly both people and goods to their destinations all around Europe.

Education and Income

Europeans take schooling seriously. They tend to be well educated and have some of the highest literacy rates in the world. More than three-quarters of young people complete high school.

Because of their high levels of education, Europeans earn more money than people in many other parts of the world. There are differences, however, from place to place. Incomes are higher in northern and western Europe than in southern and eastern Europe. Many eastern European countries are still struggling to rebuild economies that were damaged by conflicts or slowed by years of Communist rule. Throughout Europe, service industries, such as banking, provide more jobs than any other economic activity.

NATIONAL GEOGRAPHIC

Leisure Time in Europe

Europeans enjoy dining with friends at outdoor cafés, such as this one on the island of Capri, Italy. ***Regions*** **What other leisure activities are popular with Europeans?**

Income can also vary greatly within a country. For example, unemployment and poverty are common in southern Italy. Mountains and a lack of natural resources in the area have slowed the development of industry. Workers are better off in northern and central Italy, where rich farmland and modern industries provide many jobs.

Leisure

Their relatively high incomes allow many Europeans to enjoy their leisure time. They have a generous amount of it too!

In a number of European countries, workers receive four weeks of paid vacation each year. Many Europeans use this vacation time to travel. France and Italy are popular vacation spots because of their lively cities, beautiful countryside, mild climate, and fine food.

Europeans also take full advantage of their natural surroundings. The region's mountains, seas, lakes, and rivers provide great opportunities for recreation. Winter sports such as ice skating and skiing had their beginnings in Scandinavia about 5,000 years ago. In summer, Europeans lace up their hiking boots, hop on their bikes, or take to the water. Many Europeans are also passionate about playing and watching rugby and soccer, which they call football.

Reading Check **Making Connections** What type of industry provides the most jobs in Europe?

Football in Europe

▲ Many Europeans, like these Romanians, enjoy playing soccer. Rules for the game were first established in England in the 1800s. ***Regions*** **What winter sports developed in Europe?**

Religion and the Arts

Main Idea **Religion, especially Christianity, has had an important effect on European society and arts.**

Geography and You If you enjoy creative writing or making art or music, what ideas inspire you? Read on to find out how religion, nature, and other influences shaped the arts in Europe.

As in other parts of the world, religion has shaped European culture, including its arts. Today, though, European art reflects a variety of influences.

Religion

For centuries, Christianity was a major influence in European life. Since the 1700s, however, European **attitudes** have become more **secular,** or nonreligious. Today many Europeans do not belong to a particular religious group. Still, Christian moral teachings, such as respect for human life and compassion for others, remain core values throughout the region.

Most of Europe's Christians are Roman Catholic. As you can see in **Figure 4,** Roman Catholics are heavily concentrated in the southern part of western Europe and in some eastern European countries. Protestants are dominant in northern Europe. Eastern Orthodox churches are strongest in the southern part of eastern Europe.

Judaism and Islam have also influenced European culture. Judaism, like Christianity, reached Europe during Roman times. Despite eras of persecution, Jews have made major contributions to European life. Today, Jewish communities thrive in all major European cities. Thousands of Muslim immigrants are also settling in the region.

In the past, religious differences sometimes led to conflict in Europe. After the Reformation of the 1500s, disagreements between Roman Catholics and Protestants heightened the already existing rivalries between European rulers. As a result, a number of religious wars swept through Europe. In the 1900s, Adolf Hitler's hatred of Jews led to the tragedy of the Holocaust.

For years, hostility between Catholics and Protestants created conflict in Northern Ireland, a part of the United Kingdom. Since 1998, both sides have agreed to share political power, but the situation remains unstable.

Religious and ethnic differences were also at the heart of troubles on the Balkan Peninsula. There, Roman Catholic, Eastern Orthodox, and Muslim groups fought over land and political power during the 1990s. Today, though, Europeans of different faiths mainly live together peacefully.

In Russia, religion has a distinct history. Russia was one of the lands that adopted Eastern Orthodox Christianity hundreds of years ago. The church flourished in Russia for many centuries.

NATIONAL GEOGRAPHIC

Figure 4 **Europe's Religions**

Map Skills

1. **Place** Which religions are found in France?
2. **Regions** Why do you think most Christians in southern Europe are Catholic?

In 1936 Communist leaders destroyed the cathedral that stood on this site in Moscow. It was rebuilt in the 1980s. ***Regions*** **What is Russia's major religion today?**

Under communism, however, Russia's people were not allowed to practice religion. The Soviet government taught in its schools that there is no god or other supreme being. By the late 1980s, however, the Soviets began to relax this ban on religions. Today people enjoy religious freedom, and about half of the population practices a faith. Eastern Orthodox Christianity is the country's major religion. Russia also has many Muslims, who live mainly in the Caucasus region. Smaller numbers of Roman Catholics, Protestants, and Jews also live in Russia.

Arts

The arts have flourished in Europe for centuries. In ancient times, the Greeks and Romans constructed stately temples and public buildings with huge, graceful columns. Greek playwrights wrote comedies and dramas whose themes still influence plays today. The Greek epic poems told, in thousands of lines of powerful poetry, the adventures of heroic figures. Greek and Roman writers also wrote important works of history and philosophy.

During the Middle Ages, a new style of building known as Gothic architecture arose. Europeans built majestic churches called cathedrals, designing them with pointed arches and large, stained-glass windows.

Religion also inspired European art, literature, and music. From ancient times to the Middle Ages, artists and writers focused on holy or heroic subjects. Composers wrote pieces to accompany religious services. In eastern Europe, Christian art included icons, or symbolic religious images painted on wood. Some of the most famous paintings produced by European artists show scenes from the Bible or the lives of religious figures.

During the 1500s and 1600s, Renaissance artists continued to create religious art, but their art also portrayed life in the everyday world. Renaissance artists tried to make their works more realistic. When you study a painting by Leonardo da Vinci or a statue by Michelangelo, you will see lifelike figures. In the writings of England's William Shakespeare or Spain's Miguel de Cervantes, you will encounter believable characters with timeless problems.

Artistic creativity continued to soar in Europe. In the 1600s and 1700s, new types of music, such as opera and symphony, emerged. The 1700s also gave birth to a new literary form, the novel. By this time, more and more Europeans had received an education, and they became a ready audience for novels.

Some European artistic creations draw on different groups' strong **oral tradition**, or passing stories by word of mouth from generation to generation. Folk tales and fairy tales that were once transmitted in this way later became the basis of famous operas, ballets, or movies. Examples of such works are the stories of Cinderella and Sleeping Beauty.

The Arts in Modern Europe

Nationalism, or feelings of loyalty toward one's country, is also reflected in many artists' works over the years. Russian author Leo Tolstoy's masterpiece *War and Peace* describes the Russians' defense against an invasion by Napoleon Bonaparte in 1812. The novel celebrates the nation's victory over the French forces. Tolstoy was just one of several Russian writers who helped make the 1800s the "golden age" of Russian literature. Other nations produced famous novelists in the 1800s as well, including Britain's Charles Dickens and France's Victor Hugo.

In the early 1800s, musicians, writers, and artists developed a new style known as Romanticism, which aimed to stir strong emotions. This style drew inspiration not from religion but from nature and history. Later, the Impressionist movement began. Impressionist painters used bold colors and brushstrokes to create "impressions" of the natural world.

Another new art that took shape in the 1800s was the dance form known as ballet. In the late 1800s, the Russian Peter Ilich Tchaikovsky (chy·KAWF·skee) wrote some of the world's favorite ballets, including *Swan Lake* and *The Nutcracker.* Today, Russia's Bolshoi and Kirov are among the world's most famous ballet companies.

For centuries, artists relied on kings and queens or wealthy nobles to support their work. Monarchs collected works of art from the best artists of their time.

NATIONAL GEOGRAPHIC

Russian Treasures

The State Russian Museum in St. Petersburg holds more than 400,000 exhibits of Russian art from the last 1,000 years. Ornate Fabergé eggs (inset) were handcrafted for the czar's family and others. ***Regions*** **For what other arts is Russia known?**

These collections later became the basis of some of Europe's finest art museums. The Louvre (LOOV·ruh) in Paris, France; the Prado (PRAH·doh) in Madrid, Spain; and the Hermitage in St. Petersburg, Russia, are among the world's most famous museums.

In the 1900s, the religious influence on European arts lessened. At the same time, European artists moved away from portraying the world as it appeared to the human eye. They turned to abstract painting to express feelings and ideas. Architects began to create sleek, modern buildings using a variety of new materials such as glass and concrete.

The 1900s also saw the birth of new artistic forms, such as film. European directors have been among the world's most creative and influential. Later in the 1900s, new kinds of music, such as rock and roll, caught on. British rock and roll bands such as The Beatles gained worldwide fame and influence. The popularity of these bands helped link people all over the world.

During the Communist era in Russia and Eastern Europe, artists did not enjoy freedom of expression. They were required to **promote** government policies in their works. They also had to tell the government-approved version of history. Alexander Solzhenitsyn (SOHL·zhuh·NEET·suhn) was sent to Soviet prison camps because he wrote about the harsh conditions of Communist society. Later, the government forced him to leave the country.

The fall of communism ushered in a new period of artistic freedom in Russia and eastern Europe. Artists in these countries today are generally free to write about any idea or topic. Recently, however, the Russian government placed new limits on freedom of speech.

Reading Check **Analyzing** How has religion influenced the arts in Europe?

Section 2 Review

Vocabulary

1. **Explain** how the terms *ethnic group, welfare state, fertility rate, urbanization, secular, oral tradition,* and *nationalism* relate to Europe's people or culture by using each in a sentence.

Main Ideas

2. **Describing** How does Europe's generally high level of education affect life there?
3. **Identifying** Use a chart like the one below to identify Europe's major religions, including the major forms of Christianity, and where each religion is generally located in Europe.

Major Religion	Where Found

Critical Thinking

4. **Challenge** Will immigration benefit Europe in the future? Explain your answer.
5. **Drawing Conclusions** What factors have slowed economic development in certain areas of Europe?
6. **Contrasting** How were the arts in Europe different in the 1900s then they had been in earlier periods?
7. **BIG Idea** What factors help unify Europe's different ethnic groups today?

Writing About Geography

8. **Expository Writing** Write a paragraph comparing European and American cultures.

Visual Summary

Ancient Europe

- The Greek city-state of Athens introduced the world's first democracy.
- Rome influenced later civilizations through its legal system, its language, and its role in the spread of Christianity.
- Invasions by Germanic peoples led to the Roman Empire's decline.

Caesar Augustus

Europe's Expansion

- Christianity shaped Europe's society and culture during the Middle Ages.
- The Renaissance, which began in Italy, brought about a new interest in learning.
- European countries controlled various parts of the world as a result of overseas explorations.

Map of the world, c. 1620

Modern Europe

- Through revolutions people challenged the power of kings and demanded certain rights.
- In the 1800s, many people left farms to find work in cities.
- Two costly wars in the 1900s led Europeans to seek peace and greater unity.
- The collapse of communism around 1990 changed life in Russia and eastern European countries.

Eurostar train, London

Population Patterns

- Europe is densely populated in many areas.
- Europe's population is aging, and the total population is declining.
- Many people have immigrated to Europe from Asia, Africa, and Latin America.

Playing chess in Prague, Czech Republic

Life and Culture

- Europeans tend to live in urban areas and have relatively high levels of education and income.
- With more leisure time, Europeans enjoy sports such as soccer.
- European society and culture have become more secular.

Study anywhere, anytime! Download quizzes and flash cards to your PDA from glencoe.com.

CHAPTER 9 ASSESSMENT

GA CRCT Practice

TEST-TAKING TIP

Do not pick an answer choice just because it sounds good. Sometimes a choice is meant to sound correct, but it is actually wrong. Read all of the answer choices very carefully before you select the best one.

Directions: Choose the best answer for each question.

1 **Why did the Portuguese want to find a route around Africa to Asia?**

A to avoid war with Russia
B to search for gold in East Asia
C to transport its army to India
D to get exotic spices from India

2 **Which of the following statements explains why Russia's Czar Nicholas II was overthrown in 1917?**

A Nicholas wanted to create a communist state.
B Russians blamed Nicholas for their military defeats during World War I.
C Nicholas prevented Russians from practicing their own religions.
D Russians believed that he was too old to lead the country after the war.

3 **Which of the following is a characteristic of a command economy?**

A The government only interferes in business when market prices increase.
B People make all business decisions with little interference from the government.
C The government tells people what types of goods they will produce.
D The government creates different industries to compete against each other.

4 **Which of the following is an effect of the world-wide depression that occurred in the 1930s?**

A Adolf Hitler became dictator of Germany.
B Vladimir Lenin led a revolt that overthrew the Russian government.
C Joseph Stalin used force to stop the Soviet people from practicing their religions.
D The European Union formed.

5 **What two superpowers fought the Cold War?**

A the Soviet Union and China
B the Soviet Union and Poland
C the United States and the European Union
D the United States and the Soviet Union

6 **Which of the following statements describes why several Eastern European Communist governments were overthrown in 1989?**

A People did not want to use the euro.
B The United States encouraged people to overthrow their governments to defeat the Soviet Union in the Cold War.
C Many people in Eastern Europe wanted better consumer goods and more freedoms.
D People in Eastern Europe did not want to belong to the European Union.

7 **Which of the following is an advantage of the European Union?**

A There is only one prime minister who makes decisions for all the countries.
B Goods, services, and workers can move freely among member countries.
C Member countries have the same laws.
D All European Union workers make the same wage.

8 **Europeans have some of the highest literacy rates in the world. Which of the following is an effect of these high literacy rates?**

A Europeans earn more money than people in other parts of the world.
B There are more schools in Europe than in any other world region.
C European doctors and scientists are the smartest people in the world.
D Europeans work so hard that they never take vacation time.

9 **Look at the chart and answer the questions that follow.**

European Oil Exports, Select Countries	
Country	**Total Oil Exported (barrels per day)**
Croatia	43,750
European Union	2,196,000
Germany	582,900
Luxembourg	168
Norway	2,383,000
Russia	6,845,000
Spain	226,900
Source: *CIA World Factbook*, 2009.	

Which country exports the largest amount of oil in a day?

A Norway
B Germany
C European Union
D Russia

10 **Which countries export the least amount of oil in a day?**

A Germany and Spain
B Croatia and Luxembourg
C Spain and Luxembourg
D Germany and Croatia

11 **Based on the chart, which of the following statements is most accurate?**

A Luxembourg's economy is heavily dependent on oil exports.
B Spain's economy is more dependent on oil exports than Norway's.
C Oil exports are important to Russia's economy.
D The European Union economy does not rely heavily on oil exports.

12 **Read the passage and answer the questions that follow.**

In November, 2009, world leaders gathered in Berlin to mark the twentieth anniversary of the fall of the Berlin Wall. Many of the leaders gave speeches about why the event was significant.

> *I am the President of France, you are Germans and twice over the course of the 20th century, we fought against one another and triggered terrible tragedy. If Europe stands for freedom, then it is above all the peoples of Germany and France . . . who have an immense responsibility for friendship, fraternity and solidarity.*
>
> *If I am happy to be here, it is because the fall of the Berlin Wall was a liberation, and the fall of the Berlin Wall serves for us all today as a call to fight oppression and to tear down all the walls that still separate the world, that divide cities, regions and nations. This is the message that a unified Europe proudly embodies and delivers to the world.*
>
> *We are brothers, we are Berliners.*
>
> —French president Nicolas Sarkozy

According to Sarkozy, why is the fall of the Berlin Wall still important to people today?

A It is a warning that tensions still exist between France and Germany.
B It serves to remind people that they will never gain freedom.
C It is a memorial to the end of all hostilities between nations.
D It is a reminder that people can remove the divisions that exist between them.

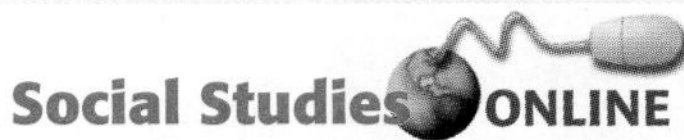

For additional test practice, use Self-Check Quizzes—Chapter 9 at glencoe.com.

Need Extra Help?

If You Missed Questions. . .	1	2	3	4	5	6	7	8	9	10	11	12
Go to Page. . .	260	262	262	263	263	264	265	271	271	271	271	264

"Hello! My name is Kade.

I am 13 years old and live in Paris, the capital of France. My family moved here from Guinea, a country in Africa. Like other immigrant families, we blend some of our own traditions with France's rich culture. Here's how I spend my day."

8:45 a.m. My mom wakes me up. I sleep late today because school does not start until 10 o'clock on Mondays! (On other days, it begins at 8 o'clock.) I shower and get dressed.

9:15 a.m. I eat breakfast with my parents and little brother and sister. We have warm chocolate milk, which we drink out of bowls. We also have flaky rolls called croissants. Croissants are delicious. I like them best when they are filled with chocolate.

9:40 a.m. I meet my friends and walk to school. We can see the Eiffel Tower from our building.

10:00 a.m. It's the start of a long day—and a long week. Like many French kids, I go to school six days a week. Wednesdays and Saturdays are half days, though. I look forward to them!

10:15 a.m. In history, my first class, we are learning about ancient Greece. Then I study geography. Our geography classroom is decorated with flags from all over the world.

12:00 p.m. In music class, I take an exam on the flute. I hope I did well!

1:00 p.m. It's time for *déjeuner* (day•zhuh•NAY), or lunch. Many students go home for lunch, but I buy my meal in the cafeteria. Today I choose a grapefruit, chicken nuggets, and pasta.

2:00 p.m. I go to the computer lab for technology class. After that, we have a short recess period. My friends and I play dodgeball. I enjoy sports. I think I would like to be a handball instructor one day.

3:00 p.m. In English class, we practice saying sentences that begin with the phrase, "Do you like…?" My English is already strong because we often speak it at home, but this lesson is fun.

4:00 p.m. School is over. I walk back home with my friends. Today, some of them come to my apartment. We watch music videos and listen to CDs. I like most kinds of music, including rock and reggae.

6:00 p.m. My dad will be home from work soon. He designs and sells clothing. My mom is starting to prepare dinner. I help her out by picking up my brother from school.

6:30 p.m. I do my homework.

7:30 p.m. Dinner is ready. We are having rice with fish and vegetables in a spicy sauce. It is a dish that is popular in Guinea. Now my family has brought it to France!

8:30 p.m. I play and watch cartoons with my little brother and sister.

9:30 p.m. I brush my teeth and go to bed. I listen to music until I get sleepy. I use earphones so I do not wake my sister.

ILLUSTRATIONS BY BOOKMAPMAN

BEFORE CLASS Kade meets up with her friends. French students go to school six days a week.

DODGEBALL At Kade's school, this sport is popular at recess. Soccer is still the number one sport in France, as it is in most of Europe.

MAP TIME Kade's teacher checks her work. Geography is a required subject in France, a nation that borders several countries.

BACKPACKED Kade Diallo (kahd dee•AH•low) passes the Eiffel Tower on her way to school. The teen moved to France with her parents and brother and sister in search of better economic opportunities.

RICHARD HARBUS/POLARIS (4)

What's Popular in France

STEVEN MARK NEEDHAM/ PICTUREARTS/NEWSCOM

Cheese France produces hundreds of varieties. The average French person eats about 50 pounds of cheese each year.

Cycling Every July, France hosts a three-week, 2,000-mile bicycle race called the Tour de France. More people come to watch the race than any other sporting event in the world.

FRANCK FIFE/AFP/NEWSCOM

Fashion France is home to some of the world's top clothing designers. Styles that start in workrooms here end up in stores all over the world.

Say It in French

France's 60 million people are united by a common language, French. Like English and many other languages, the French language has roots in Latin. Try these simple French phrases.

Hello
Bonjour (bohn·ZHOOR)

Good-bye
Au revoir (oh reh·VWAH)

My name is ______.
Je m'appelle (zhuh mah·PELL) ______.

PATRICK SHEANDELL O'CARROLL/GETTY IMAGES

CHAPTER 10

Europe Today

Essential Question

Human-Environment Interaction Europe is one of the economic powerhouses of the world, home to many large companies that sell goods in the United States. Europe is also an important market for goods and services produced in North America, such as movies and computer programs. What factors help make a region an important world economic center?

BIG Ideas

Chapter Audio

Russians relaxing on May Day holiday, St. Petersburg

Section 1: Northern Europe

BIG IDEA Geographers organize the Earth into regions that share common characteristics. The countries of northern Europe have diverse economies.

Section 2: Europe's Heartland

BIG IDEA People's actions can change the physical environment. The countries of Europe's heartland are agricultural and manufacturing centers.

Section 3: Southern Europe

BIG IDEA Places reflect the relationship between humans and the physical environment. Land and water influence how people live in southern Europe.

Section 4: Eastern Europe

BIG IDEA Geography is used to interpret the past, understand the present, and plan for the future. Eastern Europe is struggling to rebuild.

Section 5: Russia

BIG IDEA Culture groups shape human systems. Russia is undergoing major changes.

Organizing Information Make this Foldable to help you organize information about the countries of Europe today.

Step 1 Place two 11 x 17 pieces of paper together.

Step 2 Fold the papers in half to form a booklet.

Step 3 Label your booklet as shown.

Reading and Writing As you read the chapter, take notes about each European country. Use your notes to write five quiz questions.

Visit glencoe.com and enter QuickPass™ code GA6EOW6225c10 for Chapter 10 resources.

Guide to Reading

BIG Idea

Geographers organize the Earth into regions that share common characteristics.

Content Vocabulary

- constitutional monarchy *(p. 286)*
- parliamentary democracy *(p. 287)*
- peat *(p. 289)*
- bog *(p. 289)*
- productivity *(p. 289)*
- geyser *(p. 291)*
- fjord *(p. 291)*
- geothermal energy *(p. 291)*

Academic Vocabulary

- differentiate *(p. 285)*
- document *(p. 286)*
- vary *(p. 290)*

Reading Strategy

Organizing Information Use a graphic organizer like the one below to organize key facts about the people and cultures of northern Europe.

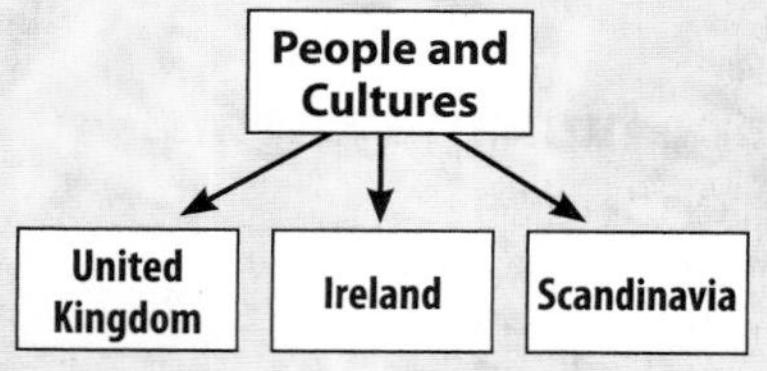

Northern Europe

Picture This Iceland's huge chunks of moving ice are centuries old. Iceland, however, is not a bitter cold wasteland. It has a relatively mild climate even though it is near the Arctic Circle. The people of Iceland have adjusted to living in this climate and have made efficient use of the country's resources. Learn more about Iceland and other countries of northern Europe by reading Section 1.

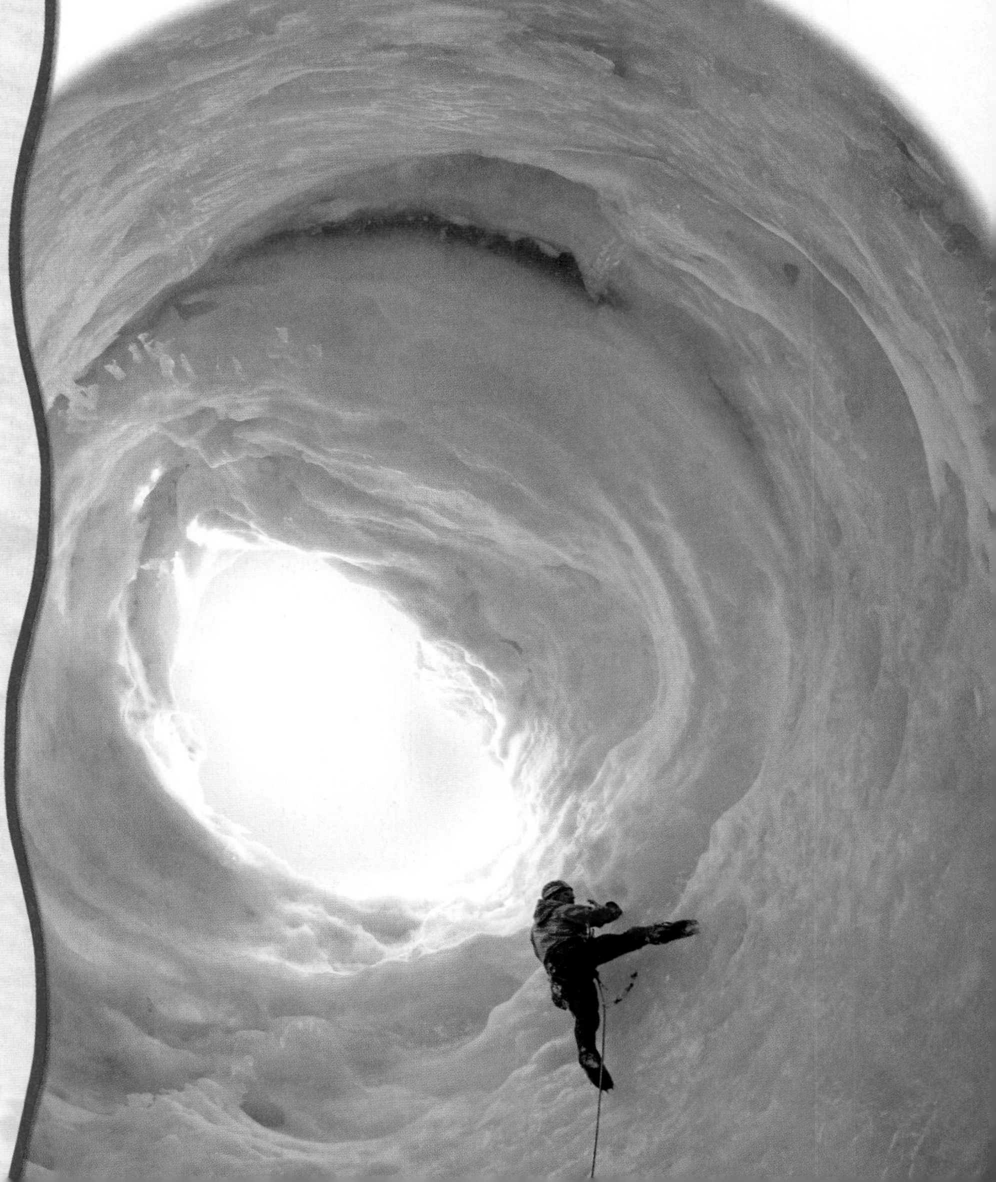

▼ A glacial wall in Iceland

The United Kingdom

Main Idea **Once the center of a worldwide empire, the United Kingdom has had a great impact on the rest of the world.**

Geography and You Have you ever seen a picture of Big Ben, the large clock tower located in London? Big Ben is a symbol of the United Kingdom. Read to find out more about this country in the North Atlantic.

It is easy to be confused by the different names for the island nation off the northwest coast of mainland Europe. People sometimes call it Great Britain, the British Isles, or simply England. The true name, though, is the *United Kingdom of Great Britain and Northern Ireland,* or the *United Kingdom.*

The country includes four separate regions, which you can see in **Figure 1.** Three of them—England, Scotland, and Wales—make up the island of Great Britain. The fourth region, Northern Ireland, occupies a corner of the nearby island of Ireland. (The rest of that island is a completely independent country known as the Republic of Ireland.)

All the people of the United Kingdom can be described as British. Sometimes, though, people **differentiate** among them by referring to the English, the Scots, the Welsh, or the Irish.

The Land

Great Britain is separated from the rest of Europe by the English Channel. Historically, this body of water both connected and protected the British. They were close enough to the mainland to share in European culture. At the same time, they were far enough away to be largely safe from foreign invasions and free to develop their own government and economy.

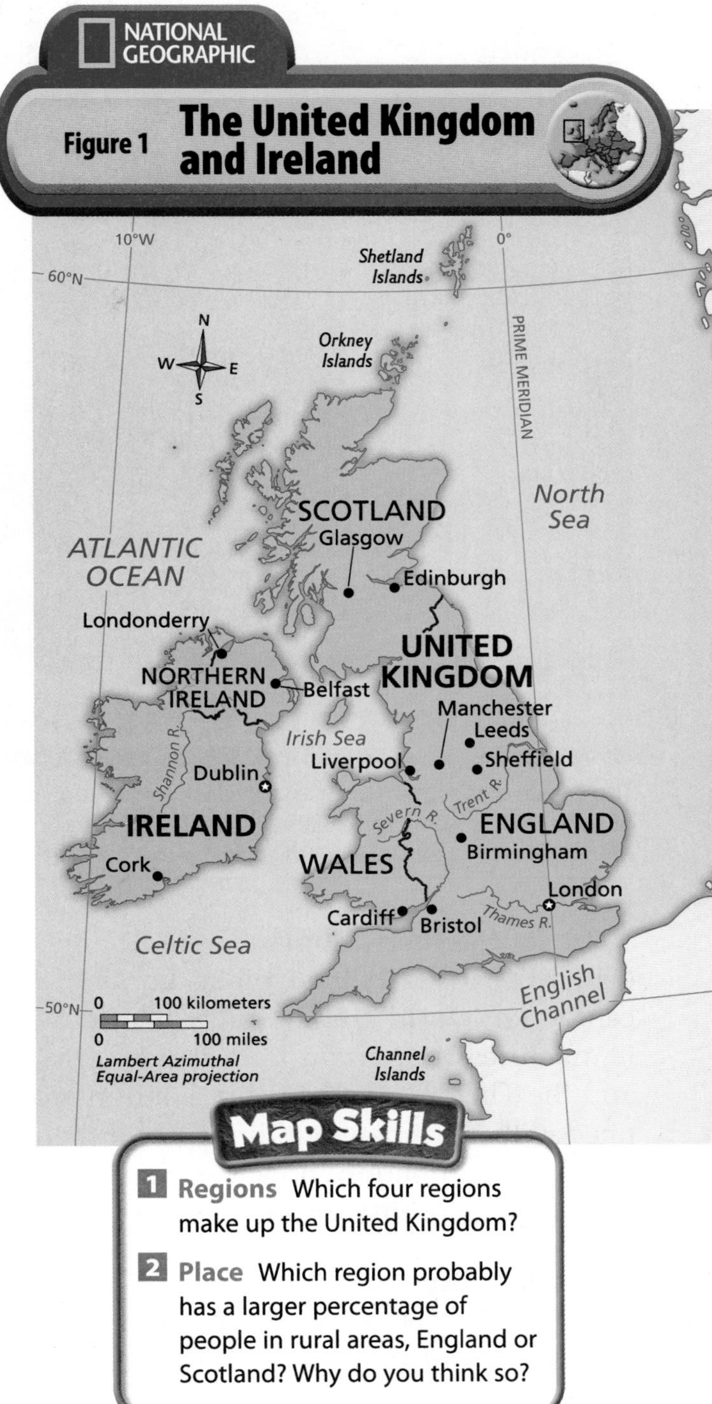

Figure 1 **The United Kingdom and Ireland**

Map Skills

1. **Regions** Which four regions make up the United Kingdom?
2. **Place** Which region probably has a larger percentage of people in rural areas, England or Scotland? Why do you think so?

Rolling fertile plains cover the southern and eastern areas of England. These plains support productive farms. Rough highlands and mountains are found to the north and west in Scotland and Wales. Poor soil and a cold climate make farming difficult in these areas, but many people herd sheep.

Government in the United Kingdom

The Palace of Westminster, with the clock tower known as Big Ben, lies in the heart of London. It is home to Parliament, the lawmaking body of the United Kingdom.
Place **How did the United Kingdom become a parliamentary democracy?**

In southeastern England, the Thames (TEHMZ) River helped make London a center for world trade. Today, shipping is much less important than it once was, and the Thames riverbanks in London are lined with apartment buildings rather than warehouses. London, however, remains a world center of finance and business.

The Economy

More than 250 years ago, British inventors and scientists sparked the Industrial Revolution. Today, the United Kingdom is still a major industrial and trading country. Manufactured goods and machinery are its leading exports. New computer and electronics industries, however, are gradually replacing these older industries. Service industries, such as banking and health care, are now a major part of the economy.

Coal once powered the British economy, but oil and natural gas are now the leading energy sources. These fossil fuels come from fields beneath the North Sea. These oil and gas fields meet most of the United Kingdom's energy needs. They also provide fuel exports that give the country a valuable source of income.

Government

The government of the United Kingdom is a **constitutional monarchy.** A king or queen serves as head of state and takes part in ceremonies, but elected officials actively run the government.

The British trace the roots of this form of government to the early 1200s. At that time, nobles forced King John of England to sign the Magna Carta, a **document** that took away some of the king's powers. For example, the king could no longer collect taxes unless a group of nobles agreed. Also, people accused of crimes had a right to fair trials by their peers, or equals.

Gradually, a lawmaking body called Parliament arose. In 1628 Parliament decided that King Charles I had misused his power. It forced him to sign the Petition of Right, which said that taxes could be enacted only if Parliament approved. In addition, the king could not imprison people unless they were convicted of a crime. As time passed, more limits were placed on the ruler's authority. The English Bill of Rights, passed in 1689, gave Parliament the power to tax and stated that monarchs could not suspend the laws or form their own armies. That document later helped shape the thinking of the men who wrote the U.S. Constitution.

Today, the United Kingdom is a **parliamentary democracy** as well as a constitutional monarchy. Voters elect members of Parliament, and the leader of the party with the most elected officials becomes prime minister, or head of the government. The prime minister can propose new laws, but only Parliament can put them into action. The prime minister must appear in Parliament regularly to explain and defend his or her decisions. Parliament also has the power to force the prime minister out of office and require new elections. This is a power the U.S. Congress does not have over the U.S. president.

Scotland, Wales, and Northern Ireland have regional legislatures that have control over matters such as health care and education. The Scottish Parliament even has the power to raise or lower taxes in Scotland.

The People

With more than 60 million people, the United Kingdom is the third-most-populous country in Europe. Nearly 9 of every 10 people live in cities. London is by far the largest city, with some 7.6 million residents.

The British people speak English, although Welsh and Scottish Gaelic (GAY·lihk) are spoken in some areas. Most people in the United Kingdom are Protestant Christians. Immigrants from South Asia, Africa, and the Caribbean area, however, practice religions such as Islam, Sikhism, and Hinduism.

In the 1700s and 1800s, when the United Kingdom had a powerful empire, British culture spread to many lands. As a result, the British sport of cricket is now played in Australia, South Asia, and the Caribbean. The English language is spoken in the United States, Canada, South Africa, and a number of other countries. Britain's rich literature of poems, plays, and novels is enjoyed worldwide, too.

Reading Check **Determining Cause and Effect** How has the location of the United Kingdom shaped its history?

Cricket: A British Sport

NATIONAL GEOGRAPHIC

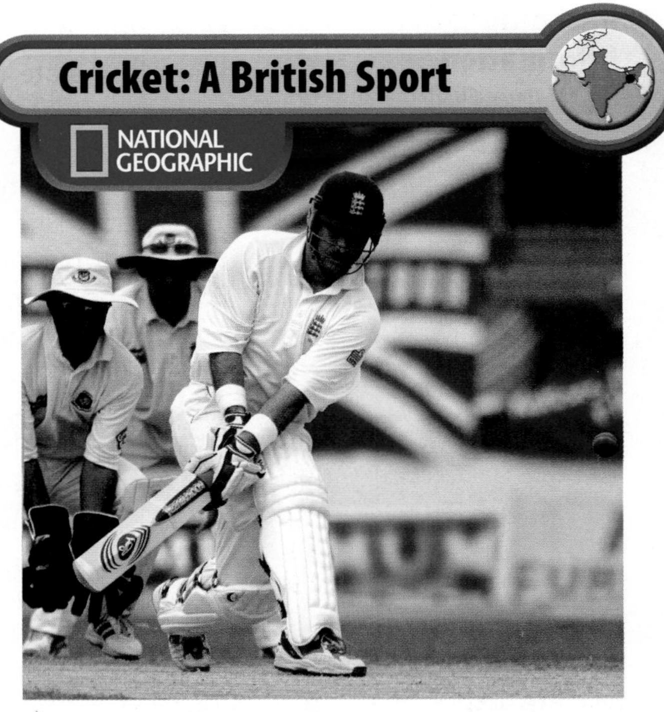

A batsman, or player, hits the ball in a cricket match between England and the South Asian country of Bangladesh. ***Movement*** **How did British sports and culture spread to other lands?**

Charles Dickens
(1812–1870)

One of Britain's most famous novelists, Charles Dickens, had a difficult childhood because of family financial problems. As a result, Dickens developed a deep sympathy for the lower classes and for the young children who sometimes suffered from society's strict rules. These feelings are evident in many of his books.

Background Information

In *Hard Times,* Charles Dickens explores the problems raised by the Industrial Revolution. His book harshly criticizes the people who promoted this new way of working and the effects it had on the environment. In this passage, Dickens describes an industrial city, which he names Coketown.

Reader's Dictionary

interminable: unending

melancholy: sad

workful: useful

infirmary: hospital

dearest: for the highest price

HARD TIMES

By Charles Dickens

It was a town of red brick, or of brick that would have been red if the smoke and ashes had allowed it; but as matters stood it was a town of unnatural red and black. . . .

It was a town of machinery and tall chimneys, out of which **interminable** serpents of smoke trailed themselves for ever and ever, and never got uncoiled.

It had a black canal in it, and a river that ran purple with ill-smelling dye, and vast piles of buildings full of windows where there was a rattling and a trembling all day long, and where the piston of the steam-engine worked monotonously up and down, like the head of an elephant in a state of **melancholy** madness. It contained several large streets all very like one another, and many small streets still more like one another inhabited by people equally like one another, who all went in and out at the same hours, with the same sound upon the same pavements, to do the same work, and to whom every day was the same as yesterday and to-morrow, and every year the counterpart [duplicate] of the last and the next. . . .

You saw nothing in Coketown but what was severely **workful**. . . . All the public inscriptions in the town were painted alike, in severe characters of black and white. The jail might have been the **infirmary,** the infirmary might have been the jail, the townhall might have been either, or both, or anything else. . . . What you couldn't state in figures, or show to be purchasable in the cheapest market and salable in the **dearest,** was not [to be found there], and never should be. . . .

From: *Hard Times,* Charles Dickens, New York Books, Inc., n.d.

Analyzing Literature

1. **Making Inferences** How would you describe Coketown?
2. **Read to Write** Suppose you were a person who moved from a farm to work in a factory in Coketown. Write a letter to a family member that contrasts life on the farm with life in the city.

The Republic of Ireland

Main Idea Ireland is growing economically, but a territorial dispute remains unsettled.

Geography and You Why do you think Ireland is called the Emerald Isle? Read to find out about Ireland and its resources.

When people speak of Ireland, they usually mean the Republic of Ireland. This is the Catholic country that occupies the southern five-sixths of the island of Ireland. The country won its independence from the United Kingdom in 1922. The British, meanwhile, keep control of Northern Ireland, where most people are Protestants.

The Land

Ireland has the shape of a shallow bowl. The interior is a lowland plain with gently rolling hills. The coastal areas are rocky highlands and towering cliffs.

Ireland's regular rainfall produces lush, green fields. The landscape stays so green year-round that the country is nicknamed the Emerald Isle. Low-lying areas are rich in **peat,** or plants that have partly decayed in water. Peat is dug from **bogs,** or low swampy lands. It is then dried and can be burned for fuel.

The Economy

Irish farmers raise sheep and cattle and grow vegetables such as sugar beets and potatoes. Potatoes were Ireland's chief food in the 1800s. When disease destroyed the potato crop in the 1840s, more than one million people died. Another million left for the United States and other countries.

Today, manufacturing employs more of Ireland's people than farming does.

NATIONAL GEOGRAPHIC

Irish High-Tech Industry

Irish workers make computer parts in a laboratory "clean room." ***Place*** **How has Ireland's economy changed in recent years?**

The Irish work in industries that produce clothing, pharmaceuticals, and computer equipment. In recent years, the increased productivity of Irish workers has helped Ireland's economy. **Productivity** is a measure of how much work a person does in a specific amount of time. When workers produce more goods, companies earn higher profits and the workers earn higher incomes.

The People

The Irish trace their ancestry to the Celts, who settled the island hundreds of years ago. Irish Gaelic, a Celtic language, and English are Ireland's two languages. About 60 percent of the Irish live in cities or towns. Nearly one-third live in Dublin, the capital.

The Irish are very proud of their culture. Irish music and folk dancing are performed around the world. Of all the arts, however, the Irish have had their greatest influence on literature. Playwright George Bernard Shaw, poet William Butler Yeats, and novelist James Joyce are some of Ireland's best-known writers.

Conflict Over Northern Ireland

The Irish are also strong Catholics, and many of their Catholic neighbors in Northern Ireland would like to unite with them. However, most Protestants in Northern Ireland—who are the dominant group there—wish to remain part of the United Kingdom. This dispute over Northern Ireland has led to violence, especially from the 1960s to the 1990s. In 1998 leaders of the United Kingdom and the Republic of Ireland met with leaders of both sides in Northern Ireland. They signed an agreement to end the violence. In 2007 the heads of Northern Ireland's political parties agreed to share power in a new regional government.

Reading Check **Identifying Cause and Effect** What happened as a result of the potato crop failure in the 1840s?

Irish Folk Dance

NATIONAL GEOGRAPHIC

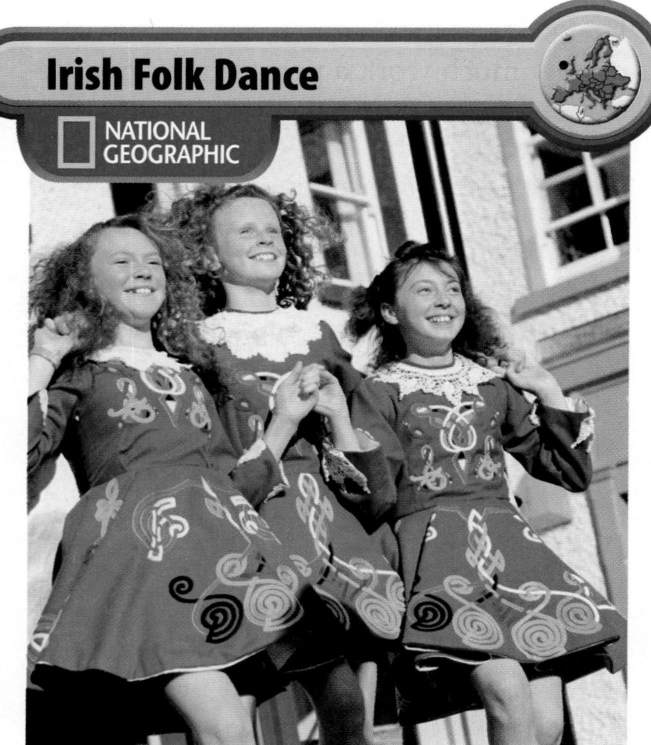

▲ The féis (FESH) is a celebration of Irish culture that includes dances such as the jig, reel, and hornpipe. ***Place*** **To whom do the Irish trace their ancestry?**

Scandinavia

Main Idea **The Scandinavian countries have similar cultures and high standards of living.**

Geography and You How would you like to live in a place where the sun never sets in midsummer? The Land of the Midnight Sun lies in the far north of Europe. Read on to see how the people there, known as Scandinavians, adapt to their environment.

Scandinavia, the northernmost part of Europe, is made up of five nations: Norway, Sweden, Finland, Denmark, and Iceland. These countries have related histories and, except for Finland, share similar cultures. They also have standards of living that are among the world's highest.

The Land

Although Scandinavia lies north, warm winds from the North Atlantic Current give its southern and western areas a relatively mild climate. Central Scandinavia has long, cold winters and short, warm summers. The northernmost part of Scandinavia near the Arctic Circle, however, has a very cold climate. Because this rugged area is so far north, there are summer days when the sun never sets. Many people have to darken their windows to sleep. In midwinter, though, these same people may battle depression, because there are days when the sun never rises.

Scandinavia's physical landscape is quite **varied** because of its large size. Many islands dot the jagged coastlines. Lowland plains stretch over Denmark and the southern part of Sweden and Finland. Mountains form a backbone along the border of Norway and Sweden. Forests and lakes cover much of Sweden and Finland. In the far north, above the Arctic Circle, the land is barren tundra that remains frozen for most of the year.

Two countries—Iceland and Norway—have special features. The island of Iceland sits in an area of the North Atlantic Ocean where two of Earth's tectonic plates meet. The two plates are pulling away from each other, allowing hot magma to rise to the surface. This creates hot springs and **geysers** (GY·zuhrs), which are springs that shoot hot water and steam into the air. Iceland also has about 200 volcanoes, though many are not active.

Norway, meanwhile, is known for its many beautiful **fjords** (fee·AWRDS), or narrow inlets of the sea. Steep cliffs or slopes surround the fjords, which were carved by glaciers long ago. Fjords provide inland waterways that supply fish for food and export.

Hot Lake in Iceland

People in Iceland swim in a human-made lake. The lake's warm water comes from the nearby plant, which produces energy from hot springs. ***Place*** **Why are hot springs numerous in Iceland?**

The Economies

The countries of Scandinavia are wealthy and prosperous. Their economies are based on a mix of agriculture, manufacturing, and service industries. Although farmland is limited, most Scandinavian countries produce most of the food they need. Fishing is an important industry, especially in Norway and Iceland.

For energy, Norway relies on its own oil and natural gas, taken from fields under the North Sea. Iceland taps the molten rock beneath its surface to make **geothermal energy.** This is electricity produced by natural underground sources of steam. Iceland also uses hydroelectric power. Finland takes advantage of its fast-running rivers to generate hydroelectric power as well. Sweden uses a combination of nuclear power and oil.

Some Scandinavian countries have abundant mineral and forest resources that support various industries. Sweden has reserves of iron ore that it uses to produce steel for a variety of products, including cars such as Saabs and Volvos. Shipbuilding is important in Finland and Denmark, as are wood and wood product industries in Finland and Sweden.

Denmark plays an important role in world trade. Copenhagen, its capital, sits at the entrance to the Baltic Sea. The largest ships cannot enter that sea because it is not deep enough for them. As a result, many ships stop in Copenhagen, where workers transfer cargoes to other vessels.

People and Culture

Most of the Scandinavian countries are less densely settled than other European countries. Large parts of Scandinavia are located in the cold north or are too mountainous to attract many people. Only Denmark, the smallest of the five countries, has a high population density. Denmark has a mild climate and relatively flat land that supports much agriculture.

The peoples of Norway, Sweden, Denmark, and Iceland share ethnic ties and speak related languages. They mostly descend from Germanic peoples who settled Scandinavia thousands of years ago. The ancestors of Finland's people, however, probably came from what is now Siberia in Russia. As a result, the Finnish language and culture differ from those of the other Scandinavian countries. Still, Finland shares close historic and religious links to the rest of Scandinavia. For example, most Finns—like most other Scandinavians—belong to the Protestant Lutheran Church.

During the Middle Ages, Scandinavian sailors and traders known as Vikings raided areas of western Europe and explored the North Atlantic Ocean, even reaching America. They also laid the foundation of the modern nations of Denmark, Norway, Sweden, and Iceland. For several hundred years, Sweden ruled its neighbor, Finland. Finland later was controlled by Russia for many years before gaining independence.

Today, Denmark, Norway, and Sweden are constitutional monarchies with governments similar to that of the United Kingdom. Finland and Iceland are republics with elected presidents. Iceland's parliament, the Althing, first met in A.D. 930, making it one of the oldest surviving legislatures in the world.

The Scandinavian countries take pride in providing extensive services to their citizens. As welfare states, they not only help the needy, but they also offer health care, child care, elder care, and retirement benefits to all. In return for these services, the people pay some of the highest taxes in the world.

Reading Check **Identifying** What energy resources are found in Scandinavia?

Section Review

Vocabulary

1. **Explain** the meaning of:
   - **a.** constitutional monarchy
   - **b.** parliamentary democracy
   - **c.** peat
   - **d.** bog
   - **e.** productivity
   - **f.** geyser
   - **g.** fjord
   - **h.** geothermal energy

Main Ideas

2. **Summarizing** Use a graphic organizer like the one below to summarize important details about the United Kingdom's government, its history, and how it has influenced governments around the world.

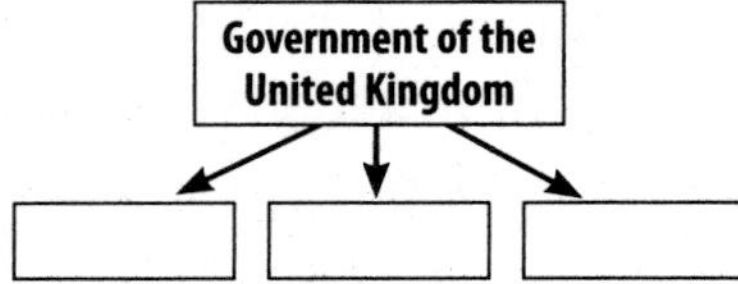

3. **Explaining** Why is the island of Ireland divided, and how has that led to conflict?
4. **Making Generalizations** What do the Scandinavian countries have in common?

Critical Thinking

5. **BIG Idea** Why are the United Kingdom, Ireland, and the countries of Scandinavia considered a subregion of Europe?
6. **Challenge** How are the constitutional monarchies of northern Europe similar to the government of the United States? How are they different?

Writing About Geography

7. **Expository Writing** Write a paragraph comparing the economies of the countries of northern Europe.

Guide to Reading

BIG Idea

People's actions can change the physical environment.

Content Vocabulary

- specialization *(p. 294)*
- high-technology industry *(p. 294)*
- bilingual *(p. 296)*
- polder *(p. 296)*
- multinational company *(p. 296)*
- reunification *(p. 300)*
- neutrality *(p. 300)*

Academic Vocabulary

- rely *(p. 294)*
- invest *(p. 299)*

Reading Strategy

Comparing and Contrasting
Use a Venn diagram like the one below to compare and contrast two countries in Europe's heartland.

SECTION 2

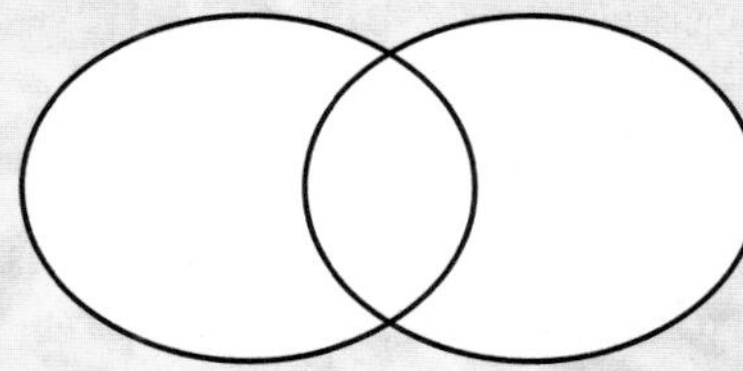

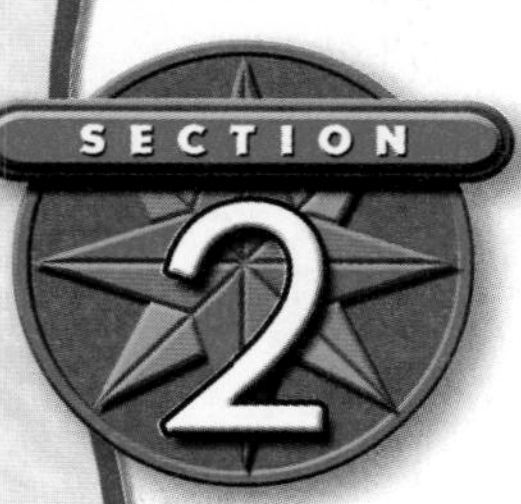

Europe's Heartland

Section Audio   Spotlight Video

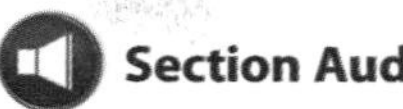

Picture This Mont Blanc, near the French-Italian border, is the highest point in Europe. Glacial hazards and frequent avalanches make hiking and skiing in this area dangerous. Torchlight parades are held to honor those who have lost their lives on the mountain. Mountains in Europe influence how and where people live. Read this section to learn how major landforms affect people living in the heartland of Europe.

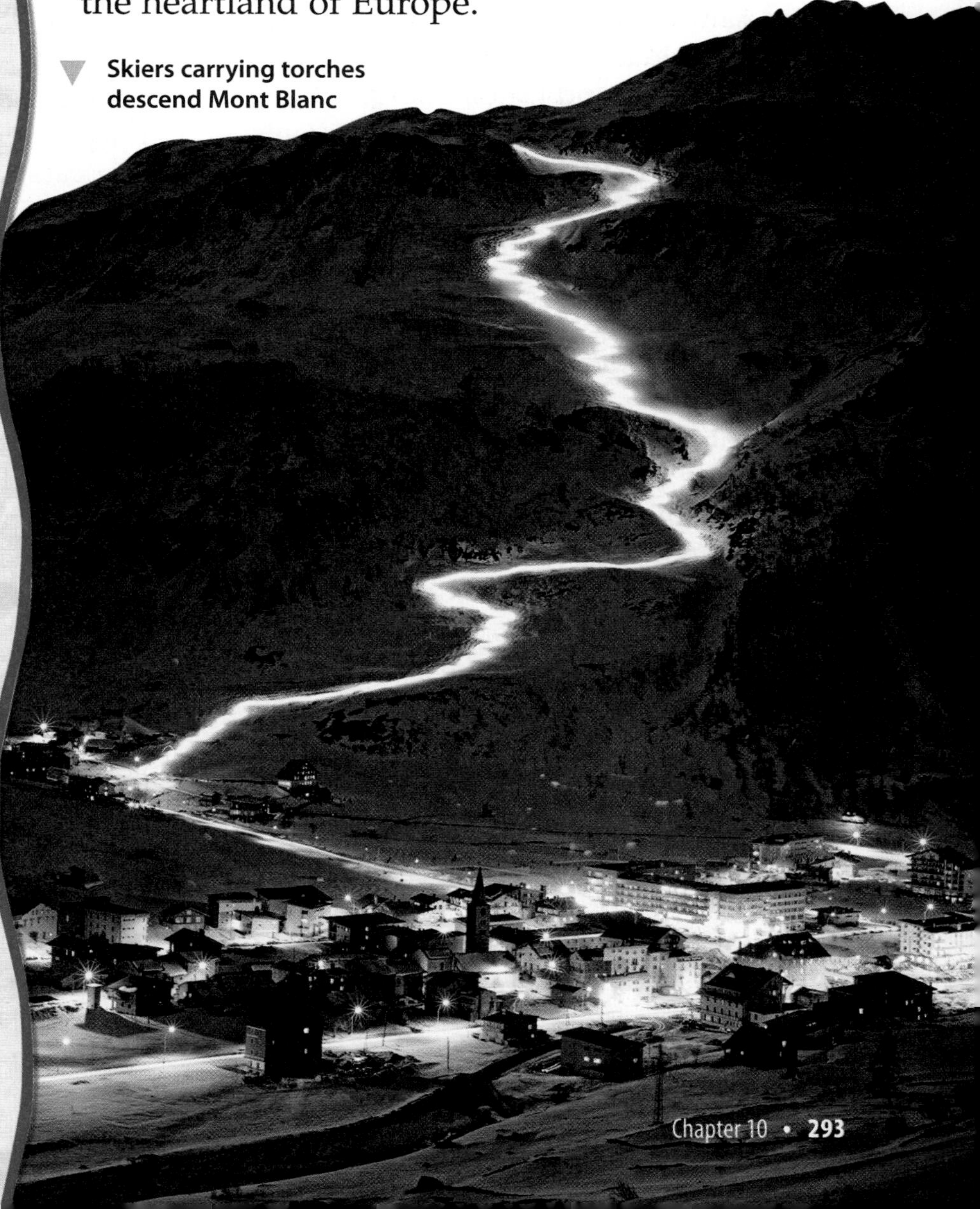

▼ Skiers carrying torches descend Mont Blanc

France and the Benelux Countries

Main Idea **France and the Benelux countries are important cultural, agricultural, and manufacturing centers of Europe.**

Geography and You When you think of France, perhaps you picture the Eiffel Tower in Paris. There is, of course, much more to the country, as you will read.

France is in the heart of western Europe. Its three small neighbors to the northeast are known as the Benelux countries. The group name comes from the first syllables of the individual country names—*Be*lgium, the *Ne*therlands, and *Lux*embourg.

France's Land and Economy

France is the largest country in western Europe. It is slightly smaller than Texas. The landscape in France varies widely. Most of northern France is part of the vast Northern European Plain. In the south, high mountain ranges separate the country from Spain, Italy, and Switzerland. Rivers, such as the Seine (SAYN) and the Loire (LWAHR), link France's different regions.

Most of France has a mild or warm climate and rich soil that is ideal for farming. France's agriculture is characterized by **specialization**. This means focusing efforts on certain activities to make the best use of resources. One area of specialization for the French is growing grapes and making wines. Farmers also use the milk of dairy cattle and sheep to produce about 250 kinds of world-famous cheese. France sells these cheeses and other food products to countries that cannot produce them on their own. In turn, France imports goods that it cannot easily make.

Louvre Museum, Paris

NATIONAL GEOGRAPHIC

The Louvre, in Paris, houses some of the world's most famous paintings and sculptures. ***Place*** **What other attractions in France draw tourists?**

France **relies** on industry as well as agriculture. Workers in traditional industries make cars and trucks, chemicals, textiles, and processed foods. France also has new **high-technology industries**, which include making computers and other products that require sophisticated engineering. Tourism is an important industry in France. It provides jobs to about 1 in 12 French workers. Millions of people come each year to visit Paris, France's vibrant capital. Other tourists vacation on sunny Mediterranean beaches, ski in the snowy Alps, and tour historic castles called châteaux (sha·TOHZ).

France's People and Culture

Most French trace their ancestry to the Celts, Romans, and Germanic peoples of early Europe. The majority speak French and consider themselves to be Roman Catholic. Islam is France's second religion, because so many people have migrated from Muslim countries in Africa.

Most of France's 60.7 million people live in urban areas. Almost 10 million make their homes in Paris, one of Europe's largest cities.

There, people can enjoy museums, universities, fine restaurants, and charming cafes. The Seine River and landmarks like the Eiffel Tower and Notre Dame Cathedral add to the city's beauty.

The French take great pride in their culture, which has greatly influenced the Western world. French cooking and French fashion are admired far and wide. France also boasts famous philosophers, writers, artists, composers, and film directors.

The French Revolution of the late 1700s also influenced the Western world. It brought about the decline of powerful monarchies and the rise of democracies. Today France is a democratic republic with both a president, elected by the people, and a prime minister, appointed by the president. The president has a great deal of power and can even dismiss the legislature, forcing new elections to be held.

The Benelux Countries

The small Benelux countries—Belgium, the Netherlands, and Luxembourg—have much in common. Their lands are low, flat, and densely populated. Most people live in cities, work in businesses or factories, and enjoy a high standard of living. All three nations are also parliamentary democracies with monarchs as heads of state.

Belgium has long been a trade and manufacturing center. With relatively few natural resources of its own, the country imports the raw materials to make and export vehicles, chemicals, and textiles.

TIME GLOBAL CITIZENS

NAME: THIERRY HENRY **HOME COUNTRY:** France

ACHIEVEMENT: This soccer player helped power the French national team to years of success. Now Henry is using his hero status on the soccer field to fight racism in European society. Henry has been the target of racist slurs and has witnessed racial abuse by players and fans at European sporting events. So in January 2005, Henry launched the Stand Up Speak Up campaign to fight racism. In one year, Henry raised nearly $6 million to be distributed to groups in Europe dedicated to fighting racism. The funds also support teen athletic groups that emphasize sportsmanship and respect for others.

Henry speaks out against racism at sporting events.

EDDIE KEOGH/REUTERS PHOTO ARCHIVE/NEWSCOM; (INSET) GETTY IMAGES FOR NIKE

QUOTE: "I want to be able to watch football [soccer] on TV or attend a match and not hear a single racist insult. That's what I'd like to do for future generations of players."

CITIZENS IN ACTION Why might some people respect the views of athletes and celebrities more than those of other citizens? How should athletes handle this "power"?

Most Belgians live in crowded urban areas. Antwerp is a busy port and the center of the world diamond industry. Brussels is the capital and headquarters of the European Union (EU).

Belgium is made up of three regions—Flanders, Wallonia, and Brussels. In Flanders, to the north and west of Brussels, most people speak Dutch and are known as Flemings. In Wallonia, the areas south and east of Brussels, most people speak French and are known as Walloons. The population of the Brussels region comes from both language groups. As a result, the Brussels region is officially **bilingual,** using two languages. While each region practices self-rule, tensions sometimes arise between Flemings and Walloons.

NATIONAL GEOGRAPHIC

Antwerp's Diamond Trade

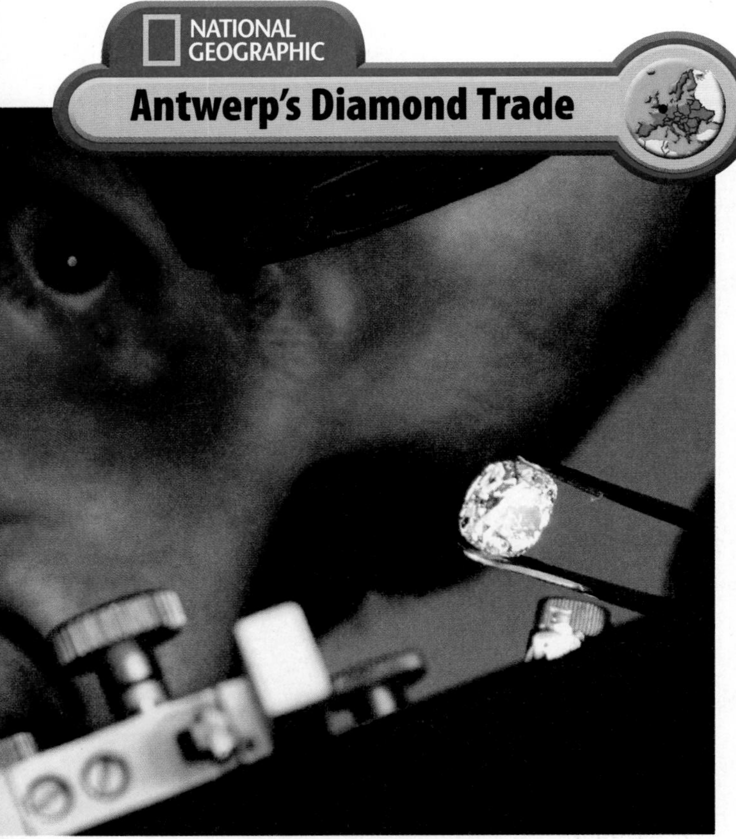

▲ Antwerp has been a center of the world's diamond trade for more than 500 years. Some $20 billion in diamond sales occur there annually. ***Movement*** **What goods does Belgium export?**

To the north of Belgium is the Netherlands, whose people are known as the Dutch. About 25 percent of the Netherlands lies below sea level. Without defenses against the sea, high tides would flood much of the country. The Dutch have built dikes, or banks of soil, to control and confine the sea as seen in **Figure 2.** They drain and pump the wetlands dry. Once run by windmills, pumps are now driven by steam or electricity. The drained lands, called **polders,** have rich farming soil.

About 90 percent of the Dutch live in cities and towns. Amsterdam is the capital and largest city. Living in a densely populated country, the Dutch make good use of their space. Houses are narrow but tall, and apartments are often built on canals and over highways. The Dutch work in service industries, manufacturing, and trade. The major exports of the Netherlands are cheese, vegetables, and flowers. Acres and acres of tulip fields bloom in the spring, and each year the Dutch export about two million tulip bulbs.

Southeast of Belgium lies Luxembourg, one of Europe's smallest countries. Centrally located in Europe, Luxembourg thrives as a center of trade and finance. Many **multinational companies,** or firms that do business in several countries, have their headquarters here. The people of Luxembourg have a mixed French and German background.

Challenges

France and the Benelux countries are challenged by population changes. First, their populations are aging. An aging population puts pressure on workers who must pay taxes to provide retirement and health care benefits for older people. Second, France and the Benelux countries have fairly large African and Asian minority

See StudentWorks™ Plus or glencoe.com.

Figure 2 **Areas of the Netherlands Reclaimed From the Sea**

Windmills in the Netherlands

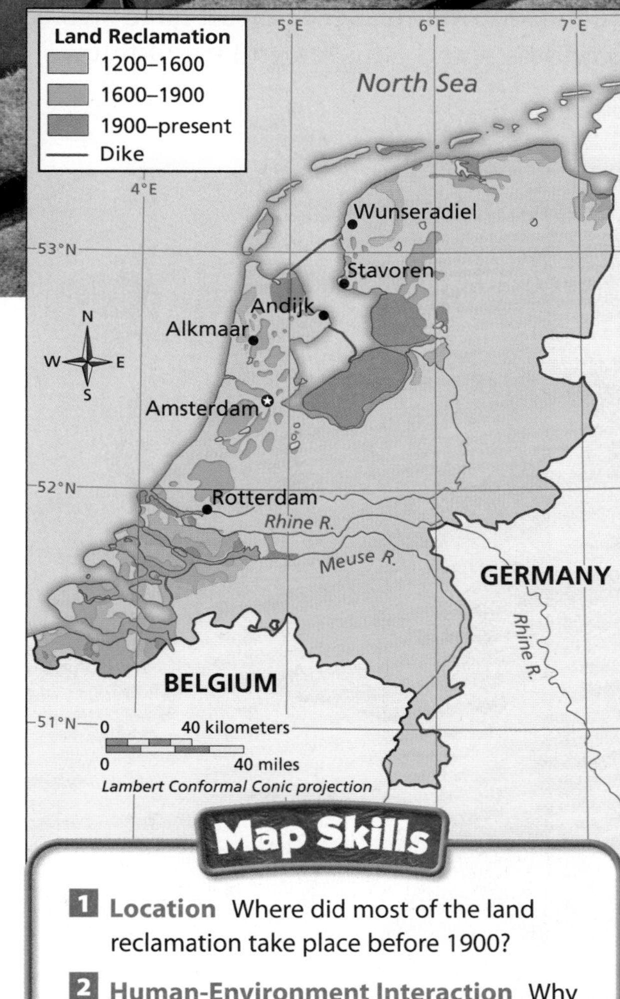

Map Skills

1. **Location** Where did most of the land reclamation take place before 1900?
2. **Human-Environment Interaction** Why did the Dutch reclaim land from the sea?

populations. Some people in the majority culture fear that many in these groups appear unwilling to accept European culture and customs. However, many members of minority groups live in crowded neighborhoods with poor schools, high unemployment, and little contact with the majority culture. In 2005 frustration among North Africans in France boiled over into almost three weeks of rioting. French government leaders have vowed to fight discrimination and improve conditions in ethnic communities.

Reading Check **Explaining** How does France's physical geography contribute to its agriculture?

Germany and the Alpine Countries

Main Idea **Germany, Switzerland, and Austria are known for their mountain scenery and prosperous economies.**

Geography and You Have you ever found yourself working alongside someone you used to compete against? Germans are in that position now that the two halves of their country are reunited. Read to learn more.

Germany and the Alpine countries—Switzerland, Austria, and Liechtenstein—lie in Central Europe. They all have strong economies and a high standard of living.

German Clock Maker

▲ Germany's Black Forest region is famous for its finely crafted clocks, including cuckoo clocks. ***Place*** **Describe Germany's industry and agriculture today.**

Germany's Land

A large country encircled by nine other nations, Germany sits snugly in the heart of Europe. The flat Northern European Plain extends across northern Germany. Rocky highlands, some of which contain rich coal deposits, cover the central part of the country. The majestic Alps rise in the far south. The Alps are famous for their beauty, but many forests on the lower slopes of these mountains are threatened by acid rain.

Rivers have been vital to Germany's economic growth. They are used to transport raw materials to factories and to carry manufactured goods to market. The Danube River, one of Europe's most important waterways, begins in the Black Forest and winds eastward across southern Germany. Another river, the Elbe, flows from the central highlands to the North Sea. Hamburg, Germany's largest port city, is located on the Elbe River.

The most important of Germany's rivers—the Rhine—actually begins in the Swiss Alps. It then passes through Germany and the Netherlands before spilling into the North Sea. The Rhine is long and deep, allowing oceangoing ships to travel far inland.

History and Government

Germany's central location in Europe has long made it a crossroads for peoples, ideas, and armies. For centuries, Germany was a collection of states that were deeply involved in Europe's wars and religious struggles. In 1871 these states joined together to form the modern nation of Germany.

During the 1900s, Germany's efforts to dominate Europe helped spark two world wars. Allied countries—the United States, the Soviet Union, the United Kingdom, and France—defeated Germany in World War II.

In 1945 the Allies divided Germany into four zones of occupation. The Soviet zone later became Communist-ruled East Germany. The three other zones, controlled by the United States, the United Kingdom, and France, became democratic West Germany. After the collapse of communism, the two parts of Germany were reunited in 1990.

Today, Germany—like the United States—is a federal republic. This means that the national government and state governments share power. An elected president serves as Germany's head of state, but he or she performs only ceremonial duties. The country's chancellor, chosen by parliament, is the real head of government.

Germany's People

Germany has the largest population in the European Union—82.5 million. Nearly 90 percent of the people live in urban areas. The largest city, and the nation's capital, is Berlin. With many museums, concert halls, and theaters, Berlin is a cultural center as well as the seat of government. Germans are proud to have produced many brilliant thinkers and writers, as well as composers such as Johann Sebastian Bach and Ludwig van Beethoven.

About 90 percent of the country's people are native Germans, and German is the main language. Most of the rest of the population has immigrated from eastern Europe and Turkey. These immigrants came to Germany to find work or to escape political troubles in their homelands. The newcomers include many Muslims and Jews, but most Germans are Protestant or Catholic.

The Economy

Today, Germany is a global economic power and a leader in the European Union. This is due in part to Germany's highly productive agriculture. In the river valleys and plains areas, the fertile land and mild climate are well suited for farming. Germany produces enough food to feed its people and export its surplus.

Germany's Auto Industry

New cars are placed in a huge storage tower near an automobile plant in Wolfsburg, Germany. ***Place*** **What role does Germany have in the global economy?**

It is industry, though, that is most responsible for Germany's strong economy. The country is a leading producer of steel, chemicals, cars, and electrical equipment. During the late 1900s, many Western industrialized countries experienced a decline in manufacturing. In Germany, however, the decrease was not dramatic. German firms had **invested** money to research and develop desirable, competitive products.

One of Germany's economic challenges has come as a result of **reunification,** when East and West Germany united under one government in 1990. At the time, workers in East Germany had less experience and less training in modern technology than workers in West Germany. Old and inefficient factories in the east could not compete with the more advanced industries in the west. Many businesses closed, and economic activities in the eastern part of Germany continue to lag behind those in the prosperous west.

The Alpine Countries

The Alpine countries take their name from the Alps of central Europe. These mountainous countries include Switzerland, Austria, and Liechtenstein. Liechtenstein is a tiny country of only 62 square miles (161 sq. km)—smaller than Washington, D.C. The whole population—about 40,000 people—would not even fill a major league baseball stadium.

Switzerland is also a small country, but it is much bigger than Liechtenstein and far more important internationally. The few travel routes that cut through the Alps lie in Switzerland. So for centuries, the Swiss have been "gatekeepers" between northern and southern Europe. That role helped Switzerland decide long ago to practice **neutrality,** or refusal to take sides in wars. As a result, for more than 700 years the Swiss have enjoyed a stable democratic government, even when fighting has raged around them. Today many international organizations, such as the International Red Cross, are based in the Swiss city of Geneva.

Switzerland's geography also affected the growth of individual communities. The rugged mountains isolated groups of people from one another. As a result, each town and city treasures its unique traditions and independence. Today the people of Switzerland represent many different ethnic groups and religions. The country also has not one but four national languages: German, French, and Italian—which are the native tongues of Switzerland's neighbors—and Romansch. Most Swiss speak German, and many speak more than one language.

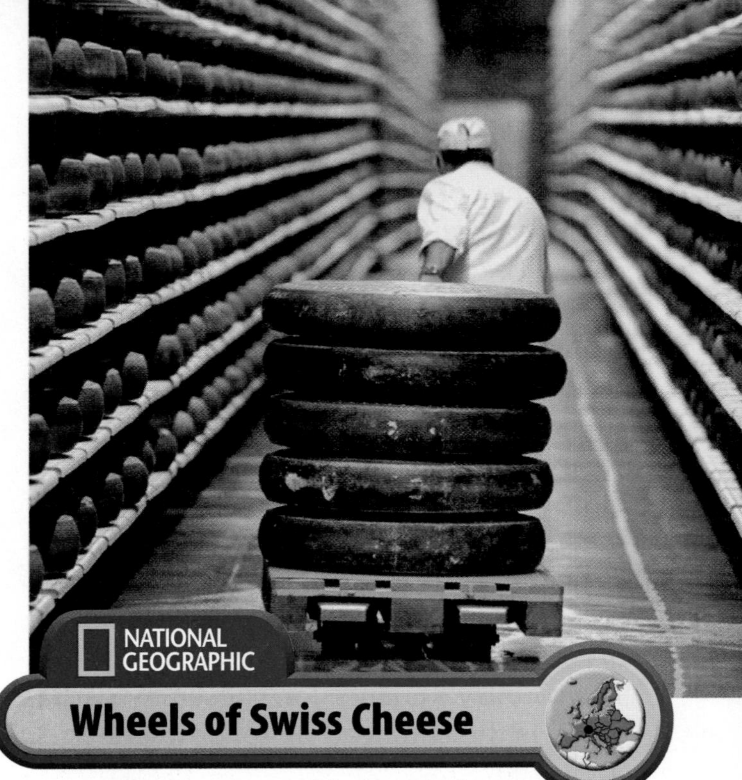

Wheels of Swiss Cheese

Fine cheeses may be aged for years before they are ready to eat. Switzerland exports more than 50,000 tons of cheese each year. ***Place*** **How did Switzerland's geography affect its communities?**

Although it has few natural resources, Switzerland is a thriving industrial nation. Dams on Switzerland's rivers produce great amounts of hydroelectric power for industries and homes. Using imported materials, Swiss workers make high-quality electronic equipment, chemicals, and other goods. The country is also known for its fine clocks and watches, excellent chocolate and cheeses, and its multipurpose Swiss army knives. A large part of the Swiss economy is dependent upon its banking and other financial services. Because Switzerland's neutrality is honored by other countries, people from around the world consider Swiss banks to be safe and secure.

East of Switzerland is landlocked Austria. The Alps cover the western three-quarters of Austria, so there is little good farmland. The beautiful mountain scenery does, however, attract many skiers and tourists. The mountains also provide valuable timber and iron ore and, as in Switzerland, fast-moving rivers generate hydroelectric power. With these resources, Austria's factories produce machinery, chemicals, metals, and vehicles. Austria also has strong banking and insurance industries.

The people of Austria mainly speak German and are Roman Catholic. Most Austrians live in cities and towns. Vienna, on the Danube River, is the capital and largest city, and about one-fifth of Austrians live there. Before World War I, Vienna was the heart of the vast Austro-Hungarian Empire that covered much of central and southeastern Europe. Vienna was also a center of culture and learning. Some of the world's greatest composers, including Wolfgang Amadeus Mozart, lived or performed in Vienna. The city's concert halls, historic palaces, and churches continue to draw music lovers and other visitors today.

Reading Check **Contrasting** How do the economies of the western and eastern parts of Germany differ?

Section 2 Review

Vocabulary

1. **Explain** the significance of the following terms:
   - a. specialization
   - b. high-technology industry
   - c. bilingual
   - d. polder
   - e. multinational company
   - f. reunification
   - g. neutrality

Main Ideas

2. **Explaining** How has French culture influenced the world?
3. **Analyzing** Draw a Venn diagram to analyze how agriculture is similar and different in France and Germany.

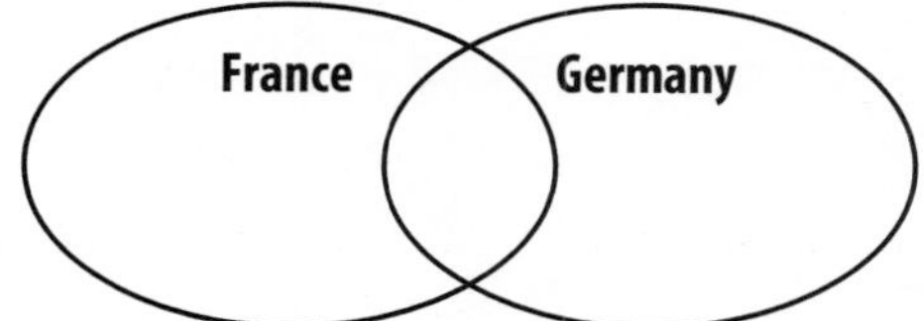

Critical Thinking

4. **Making Generalizations** How does specialization in French agriculture and food production lead to interdependence with other countries?
5. **BIG Idea** Give three examples of how people in this part of Europe have changed the environment. Explain if you think those changes are positive or negative.
6. **Challenge** Do you think the economic successes of the countries of Europe's heartland can continue in the future? Explain your answer fully.

Writing About Geography

7. **Persuasive Writing** Write a letter to a friend trying to persuade him or her to visit a specific country in Europe's heartland with you. Describe why that country interests you.

Guide to Reading

BIG Idea

Places reflect the relationship between humans and the physical environment.

Content Vocabulary

- dry farming *(p. 303)*
- autonomy *(p. 303)*
- subsidy *(p. 304)*

Academic Vocabulary

- similar *(p. 303)*
- militant *(p. 304)*

Reading Strategy

Making Generalizations Use a diagram like the one below to write three characteristics shared by the countries in this region.

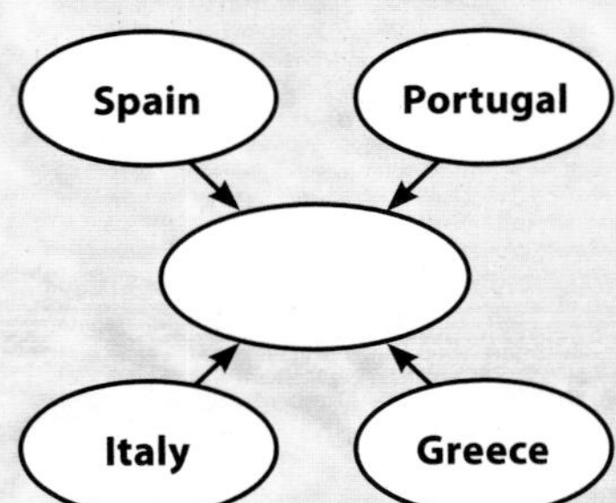

Southern Europe

Picture This Lunchtime lineup! Visit Antiparos, Greece, and you are likely to see octopuses draped over fishing lines to dry in preparation for a later meal. The boneless octopus has a parrot-like beak, a doughnut-shaped brain, eight arms, three hearts, and—it can change colors. Octopuses thrive in the clear, blue waters of the Mediterranean Sea. The sea and the lands surrounding it have supported numerous cultures. Read this section to learn about today's cultures of southern, or Mediterranean, Europe.

Octopuses drying on line, Antiparos, Greece

Spain and Portugal

Main Idea **Spain and Portugal are young democracies with growing economies.**

Geography and You Can you imagine being chased by bulls down the main streets of your hometown? People in Pamplona, Spain, do this every year as part of a summer festival. Keep reading to discover more about colorful Spain and its neighbor, Portugal.

Spain and Portugal occupy the Iberian Peninsula in southwestern Europe. They share it with the tiny nation of Andorra, nestled in the Pyrenees Mountains.

Spain

Most of Spain is covered by the Meseta, a dry plateau surrounded by mountain ranges. The reddish-yellow soil there tends to be poor, and rain is scarce. However, crops such as wheat and vegetables are grown by **dry farming.** This technique does not depend on irrigation. Instead the land is left unplanted every few years so that it can store moisture.

Farming is easier in other parts of the country. Northwestern Spain, which borders the Atlantic Ocean, has mild temperatures and plenty of rain. Southern Spain, which borders the Mediterranean Sea, has wet winters and dry summers. In this area, farmers use irrigation to grow citrus fruits, olives, and grapes—Spain's leading agricultural products.

In the late 1900s, Spain's manufacturing and service industries grew rapidly. Today they dominate the economy. Spanish workers produce processed foods, clothing, footwear, steel, and cars. Spain also benefits greatly from tourism. The country's attractions include castles, cathedrals, and sunny Mediterranean beaches. Tourists also enjoy Spain's cultural traditions, such as bullfighting and flamenco dancing.

NATIONAL GEOGRAPHIC

Spanish Resort

Vacationers enjoy a beautiful beach in Mallorca, a popular resort island off Spain's Mediterranean coast. ***Human-Environment Interaction*** **Besides tourism, what are Spain's other major industries?**

Most of Spain's people speak Castilian Spanish, the country's official language. Some regions of Spain, however, are home to distinct groups with their own languages. The people of Catalonia, in the northeast, speak Catalan, which is **similar** to an old language of southern France. In the Pyrenees, the Basques speak Euskera, a language unrelated to any other in the world.

After years of rule by a dictator, Spain became a democracy in the late 1970s. In recent times, Spain's democratic government has given the different regions of Spain greater **autonomy,** or self-rule. In the Basque region, though, many people want to be completely separate from Spain. Some Basque separatists have used terrorism to try to achieve this goal.

Harvesting Cork

The bark of a cork oak is stripped and then cut and shaped into corks for bottles (inset). The trees will grow new bark within 10 years. ***Place*** **How have subsidies from the European Union impacted agriculture in Portugal?**

Most of Spain's 43.5 million people live in urban areas. The main cities are Madrid, the capital, and Barcelona, the leading seaport and industrial center. The cities of Seville, Granada, and Córdoba, in the south, show the influence of the Muslims who ruled Spain for much of the Middle Ages.

Most people in Spain today are Roman Catholic. A large number of Muslims from North Africa have migrated to Spain in recent years. Tensions have sometimes developed between the Spanish population and Muslim immigrants. Spain was shaken in 2004 when terrorist attacks by suspected Muslim **militants** killed 191 people on Madrid trains.

Portugal

Spain's smaller neighbor to the west is Portugal. Most of Portugal's land is a low coastal plain split in half by the Tagus River. In both the north and the south, people grow a variety of crops. The most important are grapes used for wine making and oak trees that provide cork. Most Portuguese live in small villages on the coast, near the cities of Lisbon and Porto. Many people earn a living there by fishing in the Atlantic Ocean.

Closeness to the ocean helped Portugal become a sea power during the 1500s. The Portuguese built an empire that included Brazil and parts of Asia and Africa. Today Portugal has a democratic government, and its shaky economy is growing stronger with the help of subsidies from the European Union. **Subsidies** are special payments a government makes to support a group or industry. With this help, manufacturing and service industries have become more important than agriculture to Portugal's economy.

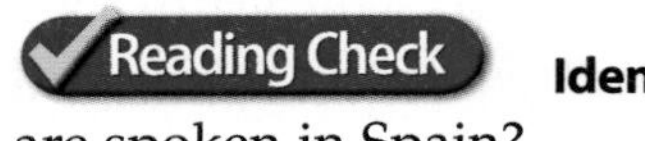

Identifying What languages are spoken in Spain?

Italy

Main Idea **Italy's north and south form two distinct economic regions.**

Geography and You Do you have a favorite Italian food? When people think of Italy, they often think of delicious pasta. Read to learn what else the country produces.

Italy juts out from Europe into the Mediterranean Sea. The mainland looks like a boot about to kick a triangular football. The "football" is Sicily (SIH·suh·lee), an island that is also part of the country.

In Italy's north, the Alps tower over the broad Lombardy plain. In central and southern areas, the Apennine Mountains form a backbone that stretches into Sicily. Volcanoes also dot the landscape. Throughout history, southern Italy has experienced volcanic eruptions and earthquakes.

The Economy

Since the mid-1900s, Italy has changed from a mainly agricultural country into a leading industrial economy. Most of this growth has taken place in northern Italy. Workers in northern manufacturing cities, such as Milan, Turin, and Genoa, produce cars, technical instruments, appliances, clothing, and high-quality goods. The north's fertile Po River valley is also the country's richest farming region. Farmers there raise livestock and grow grapes, olives, and other crops.

Southern Italy is poorer and less industrialized than northern Italy. Much of the terrain is mountainous, with limited mineral deposits, poor land for farming and grazing, and few navigable rivers. As a result, unemployment is high. Unemployment has led many southern Italians to seek a better life in northern Italy or other parts of Europe.

The People

About 90 percent of Italy's 58.7 million people live in urban areas. In the cities, modern life is mingled with the past. Rome, Italy's largest city, was once the center of the Roman Empire. Today, Rome is Italy's capital and home to the country's democratic republic form of government.

The people of Italy speak Italian, and nearly all are Roman Catholic. In fact, the Roman Catholic Church is based in Rome. The Church rules tiny Vatican City, where the pope and other Church leaders live and work. Although Vatican City is within Rome's boundaries, it is an independent country—the smallest in the world.

Reading Check **Explaining** How do the economies of northern and southern Italy differ?

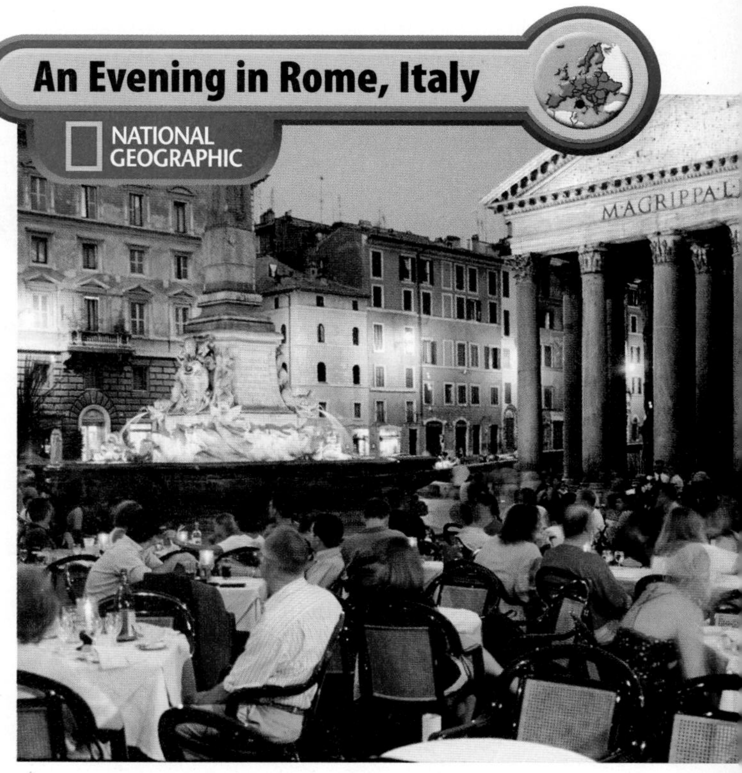

People dine at an outdoor restaurant near the Pantheon, a public building built by the ancient Romans. ***Place*** **What percentage of Italy's people live in urban areas?**

Greece

Main Idea Mountains, seas, and islands have shaped Greece's people and economy.

Geography and You Do you ever go boating or fishing? You will understand why these are popular activities for the Greeks when you read about Greece's geography.

East of Italy, Greece extends from the Balkan Peninsula into the Mediterranean Sea. The country includes not only a mainland, but about 2,000 islands. Like other Mediterranean areas, Greece is often shaken by earthquakes.

Because of mountains and poor, stony soil, agriculture plays a declining role in the Greek economy. In the highlands, people raise sheep and goats. On farms in plains and valleys, farmers grow wheat, olives, and other crops. In recent decades, Greece has developed new industries, such as textiles, footwear, and chemicals. Shipping is a major business. Greece has one of the world's largest shipping fleets, including oil tankers, cargo ships, and passenger vessels. Tourism is another key industry. Each year millions of tourists come to visit historic sites such as the Parthenon, an ancient temple in the city of Athens.

About 60 percent of Greeks are urban dwellers. Nearly a third live in or around Athens, the capital. The Greeks speak a form of Greek similar to that spoken in ancient times. Most of them are Greek Orthodox Christian. Today, Greece is a democratic republic and a member of the European Union.

Reading Check **Explaining** How has geography affected the way Greeks earn a living?

Section 3 Review

Vocabulary

1. **Define** *dry farming, autonomy,* and *subsidy,* and use each word in a sentence.

Main Ideas

2. **Explaining** How did Portugal benefit from joining the EU?
3. **Identifying** Create a graphic organizer like the one below to identify Italy's agricultural and industrial products.

4. **Comparing and Contrasting** How is Greece similar to and different from the other countries of southern Europe?

Critical Thinking

5. **BIG Idea** Write two generalizations describing the connection between the physical geography of southern Europe and the lives of the region's people.
6. **Challenge** Write a paragraph explaining how countries in southern Europe have worked to improve their economies.

Writing About Geography

7. **Descriptive Writing** Write the text for a travel brochure that encourages visitors to take a cruise that stops in the countries of southern Europe. Describe the landscapes, cities, and activities that visitors could see in those countries.

TIME PERSPECTIVES

EXPLORING WORLD ISSUES

WHOSE EUROPE IS IT?

As millions of immigrants relocate to Europe, the region's democracies struggle to redefine themselves.

Muslim immigrants gather on Westminster Bridge in London.

People in the United States, a nation formed by immigrants from around the world, understand the concept "out of many, one." Today, the countries of Europe are struggling to comprehend the idea too. For more than 60 years, millions of immigrants—many of them Muslims—have emigrated to some of Europe's oldest democracies.

It has not been easy to get so many different people to respect each other and live together in harmony. In recent years, cultural and religious clashes have developed as immigrants and Europeans struggle to understand each other. As that work continues, there is no doubt that the struggle will have an enormous impact on Europe's future.

In a restaurant in Paris, a Muslim immigrant and a woman born in France work together.

THE NEW MULTICULTURAL EUROPE

From Paris to Amsterdam and Brussels to Berlin, Europe is changing. Not long ago, most citizens of European countries shared certain characteristics. They were mostly all born in Europe, and the majority of them were white and Christian. These similarities helped create a **national identity** for countries like France, Great Britain, and Germany.

After World War II, many of Europe's immigrants were from countries that had been European colonies, like Algeria, India, and Pakistan. Friendly immigration policies following World War II welcomed the newcomers. Governments also established favorable labor policies in the 1960s that were designed to bring much-needed foreign workers to Europe.

But in recent years, the population of Europe has become more diverse. Millions of immigrants, many of them Muslims from North Africa, Turkey, and Southwest Asia, have left their homelands to start new lives in European nations.

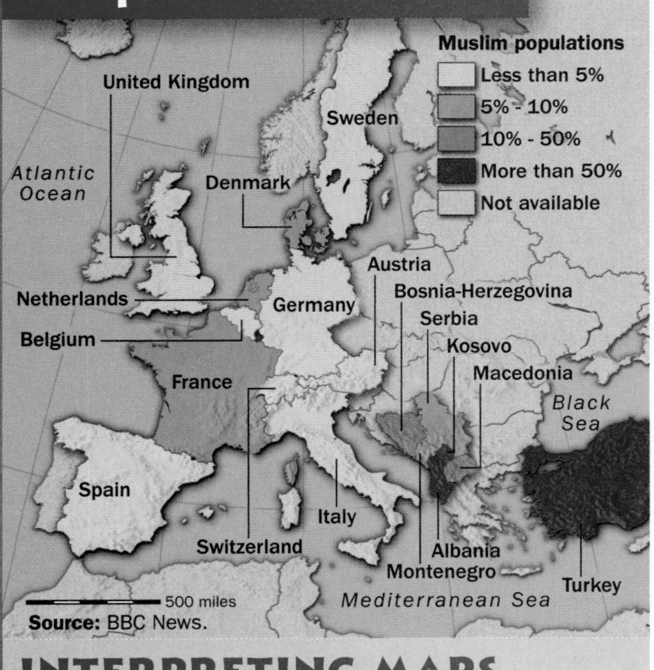

INTERPRETING MAPS

Categorizing Which countries have the largest Muslim populations?

Creating a New Identity

The number of immigrants living in Europe has greatly increased. In 2006, for example, there were about 7 million non-Germans living in Germany. Many of these immigrants are from Turkey. The large population of immigrants and their offspring have transformed and challenged traditional European beliefs.

Europe's immigrant **populations**, or groups of people, often view the world differently from people who were born in Europe. Many of the differences deal with culture, religious freedom, and the rights of women. At times, these different perceptions have caused conflict and bad feelings between Europe's older populations and its new ones. "We feel unwelcome," said a Muslim immigrant in Denmark. Some of the conflicts have been violent and have had a global impact.

Many Turks support their country's proposed admission to the European Union.

AP PHOTO

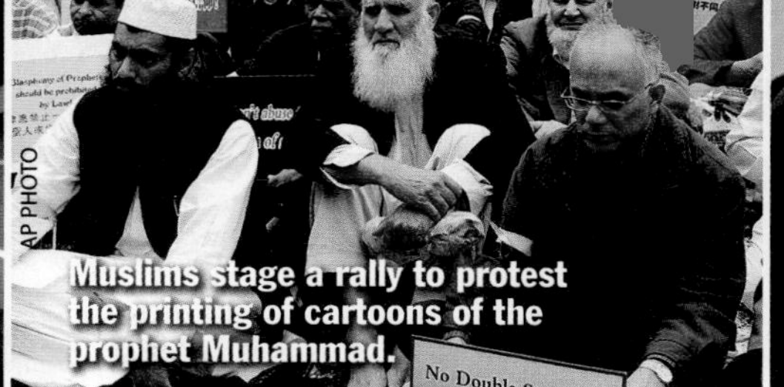

AP PHOTO

Muslims stage a rally to protest the printing of cartoons of the prophet Muhammad.

Danish Prime Minister Fogh Rasmussen, center, discusses the cartoons with a Pakistani diplomat.

AP PHOTO

When Cultures Collide

Early in 2006, Muslims around the world protested cartoons that were published in Europe. The cartoons showed the Muslim religion's prophet Muhammad in a negative way. They were first published in a newspaper in Denmark and later reprinted in various papers throughout Europe.

Muslims across Europe and the world were angry. They thought the cartoons were disrespectful of their religion, **Islam**. This is because Islam does not allow the publication of any images of Muhammad.

Religion and a Free Press

Anger over the cartoons led thousands of Muslims to protest worldwide. Angry protestors marched in several European cities, including London and Copenhagen. Demonstrations were also held throughout Southwest Asia. Many of the protests turned violent as demonstrators burned Danish flags and set fire to Denmark's embassy in Beirut, Lebanon. The riots killed at least 11 people in Afghanistan.

Denmark's prime minister, Anders Fogh Rasmussen, called the protests a global crisis and called for "calm and steadiness." But Fogh Rasmussen would not apologize for what the newspapers did. Like many European leaders and citizens, Fogh Rasmussen believed in the right of a free press. He defended the newspaper's right to print the cartoons of Muhammad even if their publication caused controversy and protest.

A Search for Common Ground

Learning to live with—and absorb—new ethnic groups is one of the greatest challenges facing Europe. Some experts believe that Turkey's proposed admission to the European Union, or the EU, may help bridge the gap between Muslims and traditional Europeans. Turkey would be the first Muslim country in the EU, a group of European nations that have joined together to solve common problems and create economic opportunities.

Experts believe that the European nations will have to learn to compromise and be tolerant of the cultural and religious differences of all of their citizens. Learning how to do that will be a challenge in a multiethnic Europe.

EXPLORING THE ISSUE

1. **Comparing** How were the opinions of Muslim immigrants and European-born citizens different concerning publishing the cartoons of Muhammad?

2. **Making Inferences** How might Turkey's admission into the EU change the way citizens born in Europe view Muslim immigrants?

FRANCE'S CLASH OVER SYMBOLS

In January 2004, thousands of Muslim women and men in France took to the streets of Paris to send a message to the French government. Marching hand in hand, many of the women wore head scarves. Some covered their hair with the French flag.

The protesters were angry over a proposed French law. If passed, the law would stop students from wearing head scarves and other noticeable religious symbols in public schools. French president Jacques Chirac (ZHAHK shee•RAHK) proposed the ban on the head scarves, called ***hijab*** (HEH•JAB), worn by Muslim women and girls. Chirac said the ban was created to make sure French children are not exposed to differences that will "drive people apart." Some Jewish and Christian religious symbols were also included in the proposed ban.

A Heated Debate

Despite the protests, the French government voted the bill into law in 2005. The law continued to be controversial. There are about 5 million Muslims in France, nearly 8 percent of the country's population. Critics of the law say wearing a head scarf in school is a personal choice and a basic right. "The government should not be in the business of telling a woman how to dress," said Salam Al-Marayati, of the Muslim Public Affairs Council.

French officials say the law is not directed against any religion. "The idea is to keep the influence of religion away from public schools," said one French diplomat. "A teacher does not have to know whether students are Muslim, Christian, Jewish, or whatever."

Soon after the ban went into effect, some French Muslims who arrived at school wearing scarves pushed them off their heads when they entered the school grounds. Will cultural differences continue to divide Europe's people? That question remains to be answered by European nations as their populations become more diverse.

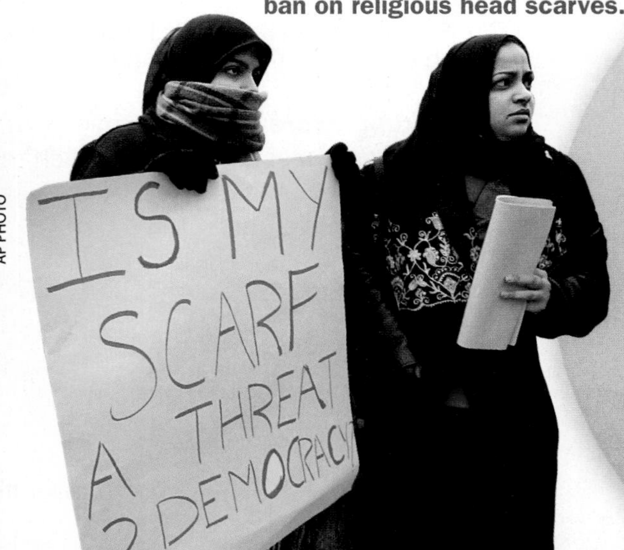

Muslim women protest France's ban on religious head scarves.

AP PHOTO

EXPLORING THE ISSUE

1. **Predicting** How might the ban on head scarves impact the French government's relations with Muslim countries around the world?

2. **Making Inferences** Why do you think France's law banning *hijab* also forbids the wearing of other religious symbols?

The EU flag

REVIEW AND ASSESS

UNDERSTANDING THE ISSUE

1 **Making Connections** What might be some reasons that people leave their homeland to live in another country?

2 **Writing to Inform** Write a short article describing the protests of cartoons about Muhammad. Include information about demonstrations around the world.

3 **Writing to Persuade** Write a letter to a friend in Denmark. Convince your friend that newspapers did or did not have the right to publish the cartoons of Muhammad.

INTERNET RESEARCH ACTIVITIES

4 Use Internet resources to find information about the European Union. Read about the EU's three main governing organizations. Choose one and write a brief description of it in your own words.

5 With your teacher's help, use Internet resources to find information about a former European colony such as India, Algeria, or Hong Kong. Read about how the colony was formed and the relationship it had with the colonizing country. Why do you think immigrants from former colonies might want to live in Europe? Write your answer in a 250-word essay.

BEYOND THE CLASSROOM

6 **Research the history of immigration in the United States during the early 1900s.** What were some of the challenges immigrants faced as they settled in the U.S.? Write your answer in an article appropriate for a school newspaper.

7 **Debate the issue.** Debate this resolution: "Wearing a religious head scarf in school is a personal choice and a basic right." A panel of student judges should decide which team has the most compelling arguments.

How the European Union Grew

For nearly 60 years, European nations have been forming an ever-closer economic and political union. Here's a look at the steps they have taken along the way.

- **1948** The Council of Europe is established, creating a forum for Europe's leaders to discuss ways to work together.
- **1951** France, Germany, Italy, the Netherlands, Belgium, and Luxembourg unite their coal and steel industries.
- **1957** The European Economic Community is formed. The EEC is the first step toward a common economic market.
- **1967** EEC merges with other European organizations to form the European Community (EC).
- **1973** The United Kingdom, Denmark, and Ireland join the EC.
- **1981** Greece becomes the EC's tenth member.
- **1991** The Maastricht Treaty creates plans for a common currency and for cooperation in foreign affairs.
- **2002** Most EU members agree to use a common currency, the euro. Britain, Sweden, and Denmark refuse.
- **2004** The EU admits ten new member nations. EU leaders sign a new constitution for Europe. A year later, voters in France and the Netherlands reject it.

Building Time Line Reading Skills

1. **Analyzing Information** How many years does this time line cover? When did Greece join the EC?

2. **Making Inferences** Why do you think European nations cooperated economically before they worked together politically?

Guide to Reading

BIG Idea

Geography is used to interpret the past, understand the present, and plan for the future.

Content Vocabulary

- command economy *(p. 313)*
- market economy *(p. 314)*
- potash *(p. 314)*
- ethnic cleansing *(p. 320)*

Academic Vocabulary

- income *(p. 314)*
- medical *(p. 320)*

Reading Strategy

Summarizing Use a chart like the one below to summarize key facts about each group of countries.

Country Groups	Key Facts
Poland, Belarus, Baltic Republics	
Czech Republic, Slovakia, Hungary	
Countries of Southeastern Europe	

Eastern Europe

Section Audio

Spotlight Video

Picture This Show your colors! A young person in Kyiv (Kiev), Ukraine, shows his support for the new government of the Orange Revolution. The Orange Revolution took place during the 2004 presidential elections. Orange was the color of the victorious political party. The party chose orange to represent the change in Ukraine's government. Orange represents the changing color of the leaves in autumn—a process that is peaceful and unstoppable. Read this section to learn more about life in eastern Europe today.

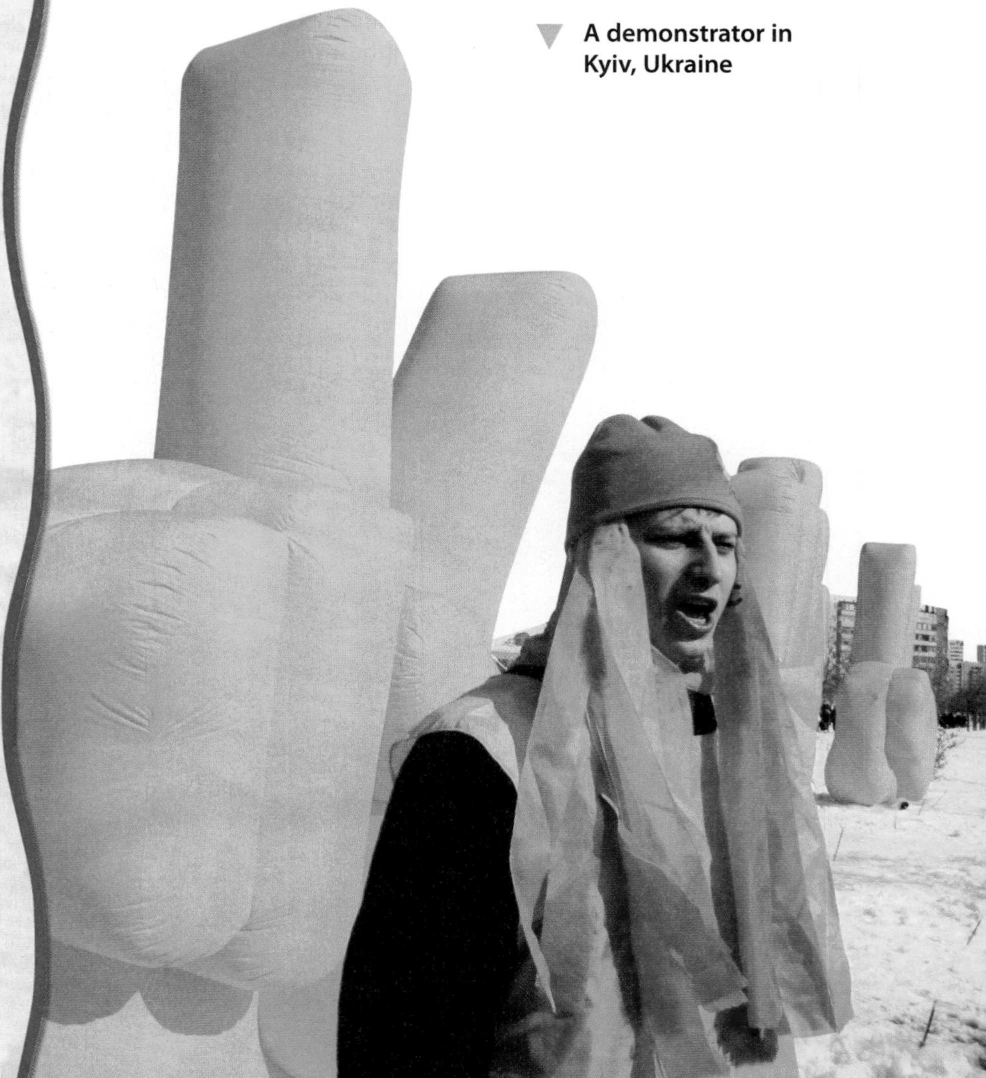

▼ A demonstrator in Kyiv, Ukraine

Poland, Belarus, and the Baltic Republics

Main Idea Poland and the Baltic Republics have become democratic, while Belarus is still influenced by its Communist past.

Geography and You How do you feel when someone orders you to do something? The people of Poland, Belarus, and the Baltic states were all under foreign control at one time. Read what happened to these countries.

Poland, Belarus, and the three Baltic Republics—Lithuania, Latvia, and Estonia—are located in northeastern Europe on or near the Baltic Sea. Although they are neighboring countries, they have distinct histories and cultures.

Poland's Land and History

The sizable country of Poland lies east of Germany. The Carpathian Mountains and other highlands rise on its southern and western edges. Most of Poland, however, is a fertile lowland plain, and the majority of its people live there.

Throughout Poland's history, the largely flat landscape made the country an easy target for invading armies. By the 1800s, Poland had fallen victim to stronger neighbors—Germany, Russia, and Austria.

Poland established its independence again after World War I. But in 1939, German troops once more attacked the country, starting World War II. Poles suffered greatly during the war. Warsaw, the capital, was bombed to ashes.

Struggle for Freedom

After World War II, a Communist government came to power in Poland. Its leaders set up a **command economy,** in which the government decided what, how, and for whom goods would be produced. Poland's postwar government wanted heavy industry and military goods, so few products were made for consumers. This led to food shortages, causing Poland's people to become dissatisfied and demand huge changes.

The Poles wanted a better life, complete with political liberties and religious freedom. Deeply Roman Catholic, most Poles rejoiced when a Polish church leader was chosen to be the head of the Roman Catholic Church in 1978. Pope John Paul II not only stirred national pride in Poland, but he also encouraged the Poles to resist Communist rule.

In the 1980s, Polish workers and farmers formed Solidarity, a labor group that supported peaceful democratic change. Communist leaders finally allowed free elections in 1989 that brought about a democracy.

NATIONAL GEOGRAPHIC

Auschwitz Memorial

Auschwitz was a World War II German prison camp located in Poland. At the camp's entrance was a sign in German that read "Work Sets You Free." Today the camp is a memorial to those who suffered there. ***Movement*** **Why was it easy for armies to invade Poland?**

Social Studies ONLINE

Student Web Activity Visit glencoe.com and complete the Chapter 10 Web Activity about Poland.

This event helped bring about the fall of Communist governments that had long ruled in eastern Europe.

Poland Today

Poland's democratic leaders quickly moved Poland toward a **market economy.** In this system, individuals and businesses make the decisions about how they will use resources and what goods and services to make.

Economic change caused great hardship at first, and many people lost their jobs. Within a few years, however, the economy began to improve. Agriculture remains important, with Poland among the world's top producers of rye and potatoes. Industries, however, are growing. As Poland's economy changes, more people are moving from rural areas to cities, such as Warsaw and Kraków.

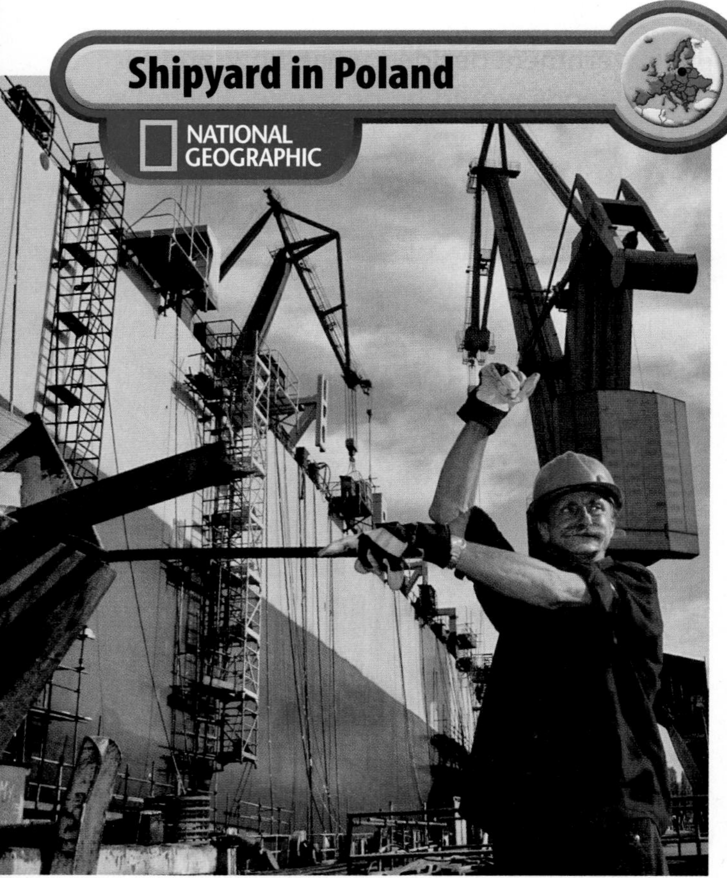

This shipyard in Gdansk, Poland, was the birthplace of the labor group Solidarity in the 1980s. Shipbuilding is still an important industry in Poland today. ***Place*** **What was Solidarity? What was its goal?**

Belarus

East of Poland is Belarus, which also is covered by a lowland plain. Belarus was once part of the Soviet Union, and it still has close ties to Russia. Its leaders favor strong government and a command economy.

Belarus has few resources other than **potash,** a mineral used in making fertilizer. Industries include processing fertilizer and manufacturing trucks, radios, televisions, and bicycles. Government-controlled farms produce vegetables, grain, and other crops.

Most people in Belarus are Eastern Orthodox Slavs. Two-thirds live in cities, such as Minsk, the capital.

The Baltic Republics

The small countries of Lithuania, Latvia, and Estonia lie on the shores of the Baltic Sea. Until 1991, the Baltic Republics were part of the Soviet Union. Today, all three countries have large Russian minority populations. Most people in Estonia and Latvia are Protestant, while Roman Catholics make up the majority in Lithuania.

All three Baltic Republics have seen strong economic growth since the mid-1990s. Their economies are based on dairy farming, beef production, fishing, and shipbuilding. Estonia has done especially well, and its people have the Baltic group's highest average **incomes.** Estonia's major export is telecommunications equipment.

Reading Check **Comparing and Contrasting** What do the Baltic Republics, Belarus, and Poland have in common? How are they different?

Map Skills

1. **Location** What four language families are found in France?
2. **Regions** Why is the Romance language family dominant in southern Europe?

The Czech Republic, Slovakia, and Hungary

Main Idea **The Czech Republic, Slovakia, and Hungary share common histories but have distinct cultures.**

Geography and You Have you ever ended a close friendship? The Czech and Slovak people shared a country for 75 years, but they divided it into two in 1993. Read to learn about their separate nations and their neighbor, Hungary.

In the center of eastern Europe are three landlocked countries: the Czech (CHEHK) Republic, Slovakia, and Hungary. All three were once under Communist rule, but they are now independent democracies.

NATIONAL GEOGRAPHIC

Old and New in Prague

A teenager in Prague, the Czech Republic, talks on her cell phone as she strolls through the city's historic area. ***Regions*** **How does the Czech standard of living compare to that in other eastern European countries?**

The Czech Republic

The Czech Republic has a landscape of rolling hills, lowlands, and plains bordered by mountains. Most of the country's people live in cities, such as Prague (PRAHG), the capital. Prague is known for its beautiful historic buildings and monuments.

The Czech people descend from Slavic groups that settled the area in the A.D. 400s and 500s. By A.D. 900, the Czechs had their own kingdom, which became part of Austria's empire in the 1500s. After Austria's defeat in World War I, the Czechs and their Slovak neighbors united to create an independent country.

Czechoslovakia (CHEHK·uh·sloh·VAHK·ee·uh) lasted from 1918 until 1993. In that year, the Czechs and Slovaks decided to settle ongoing disagreements by splitting into the Czech Republic and Slovakia. Today the Czech Republic is a parliamentary democracy.

The Czechs enjoy a high standard of living compared to other eastern Europeans. Although Communists controlled the government for years, the Czechs rapidly moved from a command economy to a free market economy in the 1990s. Today, large fertile areas make the Czech Republic a major agricultural producer. Manufacturing, however, forms the backbone of the country's economy. Factories produce machinery, vehicles, metals, and textiles. The Czech Republic is also known for its fine crystal and beer. Unfortunately, the country's high level of industrialization has caused environmental problems, such as acid rain.

Slovakia

East of the Czech Republic lies its former partner, Slovakia. In northern Slovakia, the Carpathian Mountains dominate the landscape. Rugged peaks, thick forests, and blue lakes make this area a popular vacation spot. In the south, vineyards and farms spread across fertile lowlands near the Danube River.

Independent since 1993, Slovakia is a democracy today. The Slovaks, however, have moved more slowly to a free market economy than the Czechs have. Slovakia has fewer factories than the Czech Republic, and the country is much less industrialized.

The Slovaks also have a language and culture different from the Czechs. While most Czechs are nonpracticing Catholics or are not religious at all, most Slovaks are devout Catholics. Nearly 60 percent of Slovaks live in towns and cities. Bratislava, on the Danube River, is Slovakia's capital.

Hungary

Hungary is located on a large lowland area south of Slovakia and east of Austria. The capital city, Budapest, straddles Hungary's most important waterway, the Danube River.

The Hungarians are not related to the Slavic and Germanic peoples who live in most of eastern Europe, and the language spoken in Hungary is unique (see **Figure 3**). Their ancestors are the Magyars, who moved into the area from Central Asia about a thousand years ago. Like the Czechs and Slovaks, though, the Hungarians were once part of the Austro-Hungarian Empire. Later, after becoming an independent nation, Hungary too was led by Communists. Today it is a democracy headed by a president.

Hungary has few natural resources besides its fertile land, which is valuable for farming. By importing the necessary raw materials, though, the country began to industrialize after World War II. Today Hungary is an exporter of chemicals, food products, and other goods.

Reading Check **Explaining** Why did Czechoslovakia split into two countries?

Countries of Southeastern Europe

Main Idea **Because of limited natural resources, political upheaval, and ethnic conflict, many countries in southeastern Europe face challenges.**

Geography and You Do you adapt easily to change? The countries of southeastern Europe have been through major political and economic changes in recent times. Read to find out how they have responded.

A number of countries are clustered in southeastern Europe. Ukraine lies north of the Black Sea. Romania, Moldova, and Bulgaria are also on or close to the shores of the Black Sea. Their neighbors on the Balkan Peninsula include Albania, Slovenia, Croatia, Bosnia and Herzegovina, Serbia, Montenegro, Kosovo, and Macedonia.

Workers harvest hay on a farm in western Ukraine, an area known for its productive agriculture. ***Human-Environment Interaction*** **What food crops are harvested in Ukraine?**

With the exception of Albania, these are young countries with newly drawn borders. It is not surprising, then, that many of them are struggling for economic stability.

Ukraine

Slightly smaller than Texas, Ukraine is one of the largest countries in all of Europe. It lies on a lowland plain with the Carpathian Mountains rising along its southwestern border. The most important waterway, the Dnieper (NEE·puhr) River, has been made navigable to allow the shipping of goods.

The Dnieper River divides Ukraine into two regions. To the west, the lowland steppes have rich, black soil that is ideal for farming. Farmers in this "breadbasket of Europe" grow grains, fruits, and vegetables and raise cattle and sheep. The people living here are of Ukrainian descent. To the east of the Dnieper lies a plains area that has coal and iron ore deposits. Heavily industrialized, this eastern area produces cars, ships, locomotives, and airplanes. Many of the people in eastern Ukraine are of Russian descent.

Ukraine was one of the original republics in the Soviet Union, but it became an independent nation after the Soviet Union dissolved in 1991. Since then, ethnic divisions have grown sharper. Ethnic Ukrainians in the west want to link the country to western Europe and join the European Union. Ethnic Russians in the east want closer ties to Russia.

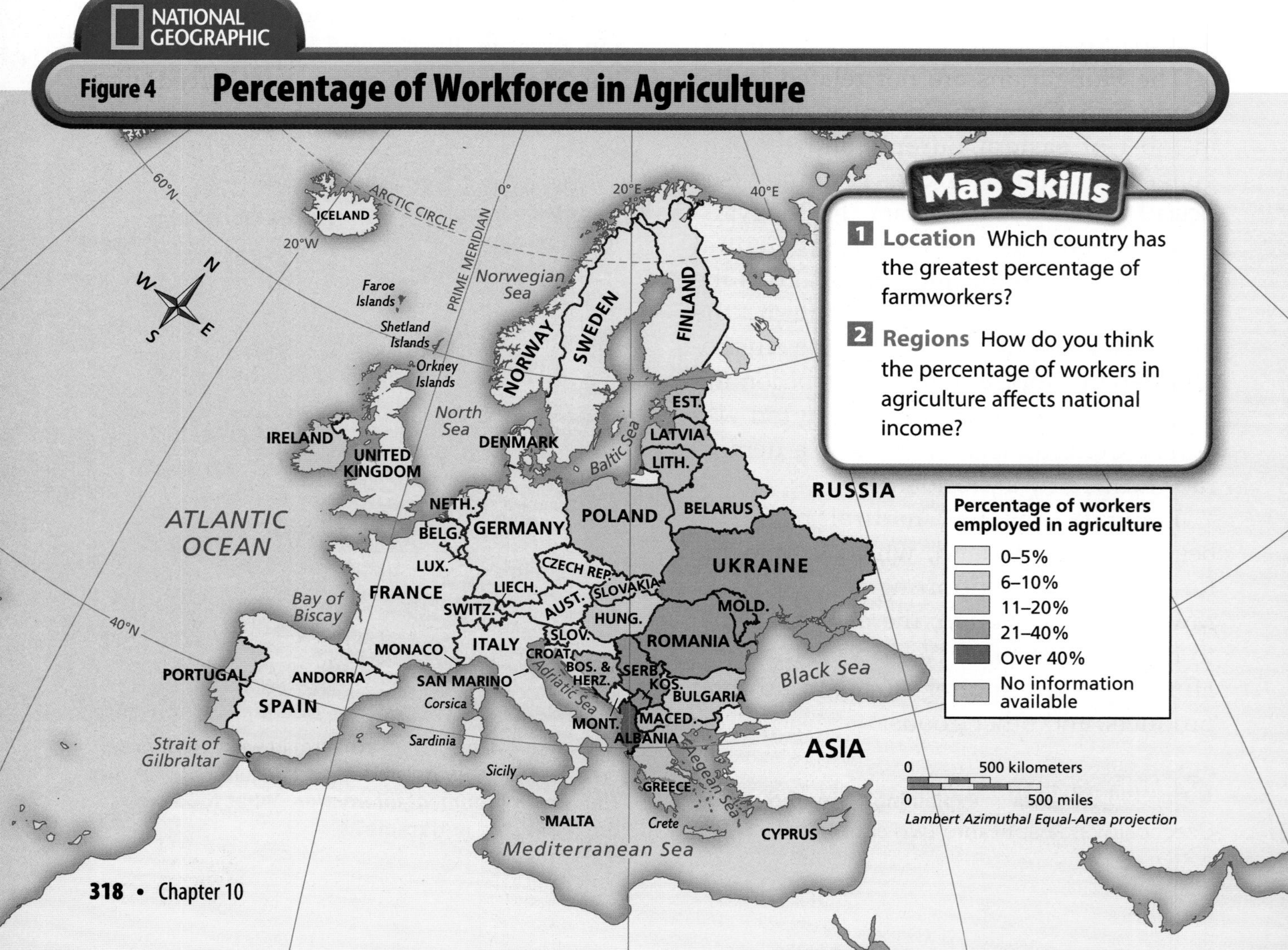

Romania and Moldova

Unlike other eastern European countries, which ended Communist rule peacefully, Romania drove out the Communists in a bloody revolt in 1989. Soon after, the country fell into a deep economic slump. Romania has a wealth of natural resources, however, and the country is now rebounding. Thanks to deposits of coal, petroleum, and natural gas, industry output is growing. Bucharest (BOO·kuh·REHST), the capital, is the major economic and commercial center in the country. Farming also contributes to the economy, and many Romanians are employed in agriculture, as shown in **Figure 4.** Farmers here grow grains, grapes, and other crops.

As the name *Romania* suggests, the Romans once ruled this region and influenced its culture. The Romanian language, for example, is based on the Latin spoken in ancient Rome. In religion, though, Romanians take after their Slavic neighbors. Many are Eastern Orthodox Christian.

Moldova is a small, landlocked country sandwiched between Ukraine on the east and Romania on the west. Moldova's people are mainly Romanian, but Ukrainians and Russians also make up part of the population. Moldova's farms are productive as a result of its fertile soil. Because there are few mineral resources and limited industry, however, Moldova ranks as Europe's poorest country.

Bulgaria

Bulgaria lies south of Romania. It is a mountainous country, but people farm in the fertile river valleys between the peaks. Manufacturing employs many people in Sofia, the capital, and other cities. Tourism is growing as visitors seek out Bulgaria's scenic resorts on the Black Sea.

Most of Bulgaria's 7.7 million people trace their ancestry to the Slavs, Turks, and other groups from Central Asia. Most Bulgarians are Eastern Orthodox Christian. A sizable minority are Muslim.

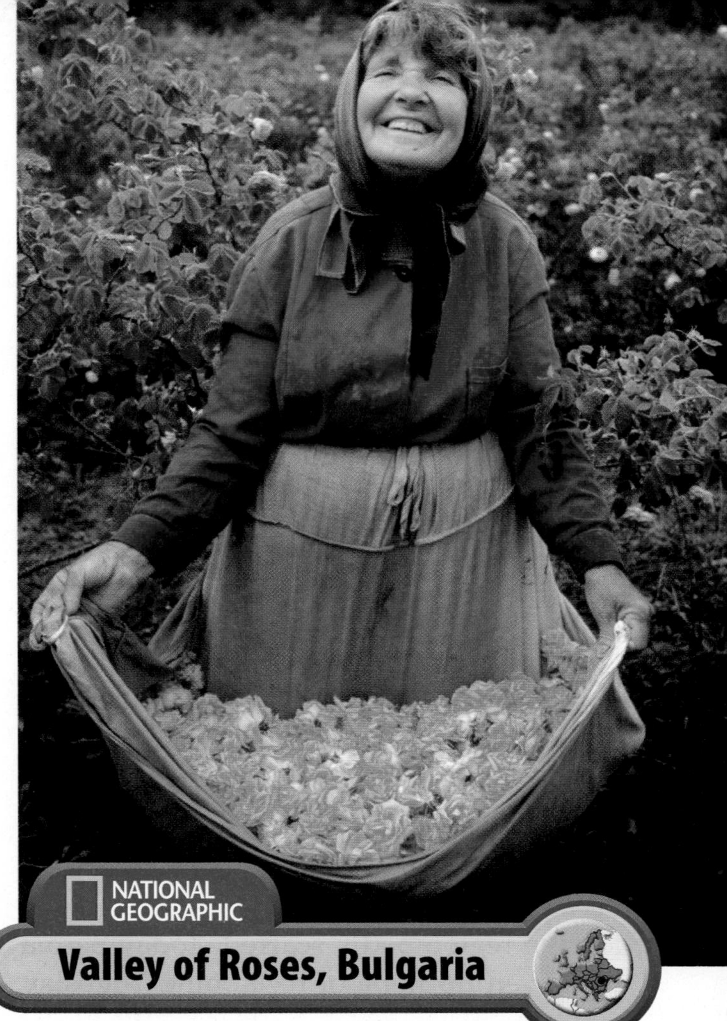

NATIONAL GEOGRAPHIC

Valley of Roses, Bulgaria

A worker holds an apron full of rose blooms gathered at a farm in Bulgaria's famous Valley of Roses. ***Place*** **What are Bulgaria's major economic activities?**

Other Balkan States

To the south and west of Bulgaria, a number of other countries crowd the Balkan Peninsula. Albania, on the Adriatic Sea, is the only country in Europe with a majority Muslim population. It is also unique because farmers outnumber factory workers. With its economy still heavily agricultural, Albania is one of the poorest countries in Europe.

Other Balkan countries include Slovenia, Croatia, Bosnia and Herzegovina, Macedonia, Serbia, Montenegro, and Kosovo.

None of these nations were even on the map until the 1990s. Before then, they were all part of a Communist country called Yugoslavia.

When communism collapsed in Eastern Europe, the different ethnic groups of Yugoslavia struggled for power. In the early 1990s, four parts of the country—Slovenia, Croatia, Bosnia and Herzegovina, and Macedonia—declared their independence. Meanwhile, another strong part, Serbia, wanted to keep Yugoslavia together under Serbian rule. Serbia's leader used force to try to build power.

The heaviest fighting took place in Bosnia and Herzegovina. There, Serbs carried out **ethnic cleansing**—removing or killing an entire ethnic group—against the Bosnian population. Many people died or became refugees. This and other conflicts left the region badly scarred. Today Serbia has given up hope of reclaiming Yugoslav lands. Montenegro and Kosovo split away from Serbia, and where Yugoslavia once was, there are now seven separate nations.

These Balkan countries were relatively poor during Communist rule, and they continue to be among the poorest in Europe. The mountainous landscape of the Balkan Peninsula makes farming difficult, and there are few natural resources to support economic growth. Ethnic conflict has added to these problems.

Despite these challenges, some countries are moving forward. Slovenia has experienced steady economic growth since it gained independence. Slovenian industries produce machinery, appliances, vehicles, and **medical** supplies. Croatia's economy has also improved, although not as much as Slovenia's.

Reading Check **Explaining** Why have conflicts been fought in the Balkan Peninsula?

Section 4 Review

Vocabulary

1. **Explain** the differences between *command economy* and *market economy*. Define *potash* and *ethnic cleansing*.

Main Ideas

2. **Sequencing** List the events that led to democracy in Poland.
3. **Comparing** Create a Venn diagram like the one below to compare the Czech Republic and Slovakia.

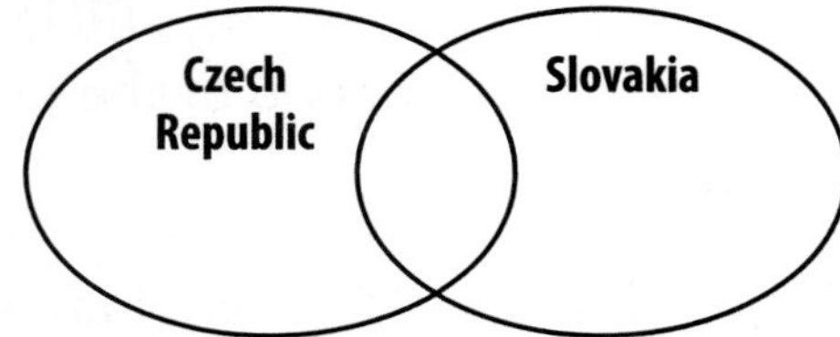

4. **Explaining** Why are many of the countries of southeastern Europe struggling for economic success?

Critical Thinking

5. **BIG Idea** How have eastern Europe's history and physical geography led to differences between that region and other parts of Europe today?
6. **Challenge** Based on what you have read, what do you think will happen politically in Ukraine over the next few years? Why?

Writing About Geography

7. **Using Your FOLDABLES** Use your Foldable to write a paragraph comparing and contrasting conditions in two countries in eastern Europe.

Russia

Guide to Reading

BIG Idea

Culture groups shape human systems.

Content Vocabulary

- privatization *(p. 322)*
- pensioner *(p. 322)*
- heavy industry *(p. 323)*
- light industry *(p.323)*
- oligarch *(p. 324)*
- separatist movement *(p. 324)*

Academic Vocabulary

- comprise *(p. 322)*
- prior *(p. 323)*
- volume *(p. 323)*
- unify *(p. 324)*

Reading Strategy

Analyzing Information Use a diagram like the one below to identify the changes, both positive and negative, that have resulted from Russia's switch to a free market economy.

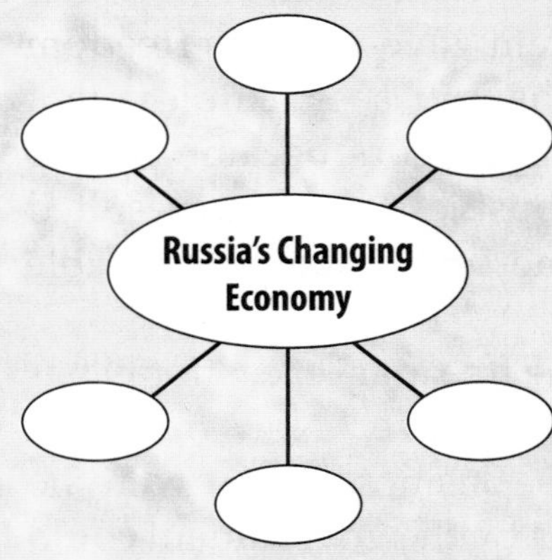

Section Audio

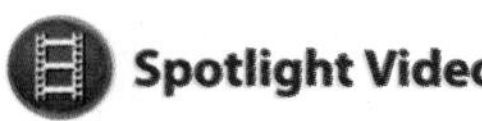
Spotlight Video

Picture This What do you think is the most popular possession in Russia? A car? A computer? No, it is most likely a cell phone. The popularity of cell phones has skyrocketed in Russia. Russia has a growing middle class with money to spend. Young business-savvy entrepreneurs are starting companies that provide trendy and modern products—like cell phones—to this middle class. As the number of cell phone businesses has increased, so has cell phone use. It is estimated that in 1996, only 10,000 people in Moscow owned cell phones, which cost about $2,000 each! Now 80 million Russians, or about 60 percent of the population, own cell phones, which cost about $100 each. The economy is just one part of Russia that is changing. Read on to learn more about modern Russia's challenges.

▼ Most popular possession in Russia

Russia's New Economy

Main Idea **The fall of communism led to great changes in Russia.**

Geography and You Can you imagine having to completely change your way of life? Read to learn how Russians faced that situation in the early 1990s.

When communism fell in 1991, Russia had to build a new government and economy. Russia is still adjusting to the effects of these changes.

NATIONAL GEOGRAPHIC

Voting in Russia

Voters in Russia today can choose from many political parties and groups. ***Regions*** **How are the governments of Russia and the United States similar and different?**

Political and Economic Changes

Russia's official name is the Russian Federation. This name reflects the fact that Russia **comprises,** or is made up of, many different regions or territories. Russia has many ethnic groups and many languages. Russians are the dominant group, though, and Russian is the main language.

Like the United States, Russia is a federal republic. That means power is divided between national and regional governments. How the two levels of government share power is less clearly defined than in the United States, though. Another difference appears within the national government. In the United States, the president and Congress share power. In Russia, the president has much more power than the lawmaking body.

Russia's constitution promises to protect such rights as free speech and freedom of the press. In practice, however, the government limits some of these rights. For example, it limits the means by which critics can express their views.

In the days of the Soviet Union, Russia had a command economy. With the collapse of communism, it adopted a market economy. To make this change, the government introduced **privatization** (PRY·vuh·tuh·ZAY·shuhn). This is the transfer of ownership of businesses from the government to individuals. Companies now had to compete against each other.

The new system gave workers freedom to quit their jobs and seek employment elsewhere. Entrepreneurs became free to start their own businesses. It also resulted in more consumer goods being available to people.

The shift to the free market economy has not gone easily, however. New freedoms meant new risks. Businesses that were no longer supported by the government could fail, and workers could lose their jobs. Many people suffered. Some had to take second jobs. The government also dropped price controls. This change hurt **pensioners** (PEHN·shuhn·huhrs), however. Pensioners are people who receive regular payments from the government because they are too old or too sick to work. Because the amount of these payments is usually fixed, or unchanging, people could not afford higher prices for basic items like food.

Russia's Economic Regions

Moscow is Russia's most important economic region and the nation's political, economic, and transportation center. **Prior** to the fall of communism, most of Russia's factories focused on **heavy industry**, or the production of goods such as machinery, mining equipment, and steel. In recent years, many factories shifted to **light industry**, or the production of consumer goods, such as clothing and household products. High technology and electronics industries have also developed in Moscow.

The Baltic region is located in northwestern Russia and includes the city of St. Petersburg. Once Russia's capital, St. Petersburg is a major port and an industrial and cultural center. A high **volume,** or amount, of goods passes through its port. Factories there make machinery, ships, automobiles, and other items. Well-known for its palaces and churches, St. Petersburg attracts thousands of tourists from around the world each year.

Kaliningrad is another major Russian port on the Baltic Sea. It lies on a small piece of land between Poland and Lithuania and is isolated from the rest of Russia. Goods shipped to Kaliningrad must cross other countries to reach the nearest part of inland Russia. The city is important to Russia, though. It is Russia's only port on the Baltic Sea that stays ice-free all year.

The Volga region, south of Moscow, is a major center of farming. The Volga River is vital to this economic activity. This 2,300-mile (3,701-km) waterway carries nearly half of Russia's river traffic. The Volga River also supplies water for hydroelectric power and for irrigation. Farmers in the region grow wheat, sugar beets, and other crops.

The Urals region is a major source of mineral resources. The Ural Mountains contain copper, gold, lead, nickel, and bauxite, as well as energy resources.

Siberia's rugged landscape and cold climate make it difficult to take advantage of its many resources. Yet the region holds valuable deposits of iron ore, uranium, gold, coal, and timber. Since resources in other parts of the world are being used up, Russia may be able to benefit in the future from tapping into these riches.

Russia's regions differ greatly in terms of how well off the people are. Incomes are much higher in Moscow compared to other cities and areas of the country. Incomes are far lower in the southern and central parts of Russia than in the western regions.

Reading Check **Categorizing** Which economic regions are important for manufacturing? For agriculture?

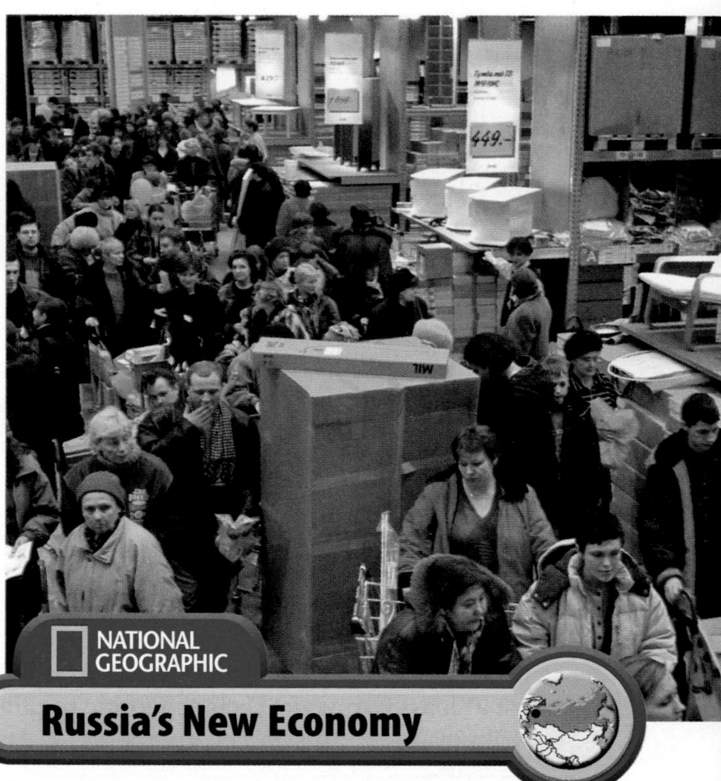

Russia's New Economy

Large discount stores are opening in Russia as the economy grows and people have more money to spend on consumer goods. ***Place*** **In what parts of Russia are incomes lowest?**

Russia's Challenges

Main Idea **Russians face several challenges in the future.**

Geography and You Do you think a country needs strong leaders to solve problems? Can leaders be too strong? Read to learn about growing challenges to Russia's new government and economy.

Becoming democratic has not been easy for Russia. Vladimir Putin, who became president in 1999, greatly expanded the power of the president. Some people worried that his actions made that office too strong. In 2008, a Putin ally named Dmitry Medvedev won election as president. Critics said the election was neither free nor democratic.

Another challenge is the rise of **oligarchs** (AH·luh·garhrks). An oligarch is a member of a small group of rulers that holds great power. Putin acted to limit the power of the oligarchs, but these actions also gave the government more power.

Another challenge is to extend prosperity to all people. As you have read, Russia's regions differ greatly in their economic success. Even in regions that are economically advanced, such as Moscow, some people have fallen into poverty.

Finally, Russia faces a challenge in its effort to **unify,** or bring together, the country. Members of some ethnic groups have formed **separatist movements**, campaigns to break away from the national government and form independent countries. One of the most violent of these movements began in Chechnya, a Muslim region in southern Russia. Fighting there has dragged on for years.

Reading Check **Identifying** Identify and describe two challenges to Russia's government.

Section 5 Review

Vocabulary

1. **Explain** the significance of:
   - **a.** privatization
   - **b.** pensioner
   - **c.** heavy industry
   - **e.** light industry
   - **f.** oligarch
   - **g.** separatist movement

Main Ideas

2. **Describing** Describe some of the freedoms the Russian people gained after the fall of communism.
3. **Explaining** Create a chart like the one below to list at least two ways each economic region contributes to the Russian economy.

Region	Contribution

Critical Thinking

4. **Analyzing Information** Why have some Russians been unhappy about Russia's economic changes?
5. **Comparing and Contrasting** Compare and contrast the cities of Moscow and St. Petersburg in terms of location and economic activity.
6. **BIG Idea** What factors create challenges to Russian unity?

Writing About Geography

7. **Persuasive Writing** Write an editorial to support or oppose the changes that the new democratic Russian government made after the fall of communism.

Visual Summary

Northern Europe

- The United Kingdom is a major industrial and trading country.
- The Republic of Ireland's economy is becoming more industrial.
- Fishing is an important industry in the Scandinavian countries.

Members of the British royal family

France and the Benelux Countries

- France is a world center of art, learning, and culture.
- The Benelux countries are low, flat, and densely populated.

Europe at night

Schoolgirls in France

Germany and the Alpine Countries

- Rivers have been vital to Germany's economic growth.
- Germany is an economic power and a leader in the European Union.
- The Alps dominate Switzerland, Austria, and Liechtenstein.

Southern Europe

- Spain's historic sites and sunny beaches attract many tourists.
- Most of Italy's industry lies in the northern part of the country.
- Greece consists of a mountainous mainland and more than 2,000 islands.

Eastern Europe

- Poland is a large country with northern plains and southern highlands.
- The Danube River flows through Budapest, Hungary's historic capital.
- Ukrainians disagree on whether to strengthen ties to western Europe or to Russia.
- Ethnic conflict has torn apart Balkan countries in recent years.

Industry in eastern Europe

Russia

- The move toward democracy and a market economy has benefited some Russians while bringing hardships to others.
- Moscow is central to Russia's economy but other regions have important resources and products.

Study anywhere, anytime! Download quizzes and flash cards to your PDA from glencoe.com.

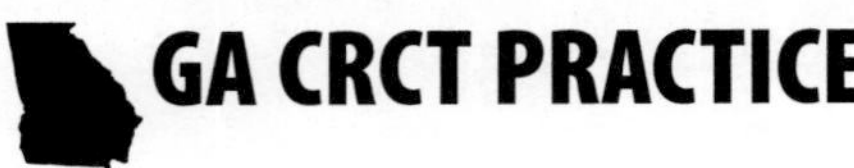

GA CRCT PRACTICE

TEST-TAKING TIP

Consider carefully before changing your answer to a multiple-answer test question. Unless you misread the question, your first answer choice is often correct.

Directions: Choose the best answer for each question.

1 **How are the governments of Germany and the United Kingdom similar?**

A Germany's chancellor and the United Kingdom's prime minister perform only ceremonial duties.
B Germany's chancellor and the United Kingdom's prime minister are determined by their parliaments.
C Voters elect Germany's chancellor and the United Kingdom's prime minister.
D National government and state governments in Germany and the United Kingdom share power equally.

2 **In which country are Catholicism and Islam the major religions?**

A Italy
B Greece
C France
D Ireland

3 **What effect do natural resources have on the economies of Scandinavian countries?**

A They have abundant resources that support a variety of industries.
B They have very few natural resources, so they must import many goods.
C The countries are running out of money because they have used almost all of their natural resources.
D The small supply of natural resources has forced many Scandinavians to leave their homelands, shrinking the region's economies.

4 **The Brussels region of Belgium has two official languages: Dutch and French. What word is used to describe this region?**

A bilateral
B equal
C double meaning
D bilingual

5 **Why do most people live in northern Italy rather than southern Italy?**

A They are not allowed to own property in southern Italy until the age of 30.
B The mountains are good for farming and livestock grazing.
C Most Italians want to live closer to the Alps to play winter sports.
D The land is more fertile, and the economy is stronger.

6 **Where has conflict erupted between Catholics and Protestants?**

A Finland
B Sweden
C Iceland
D Northern Ireland

7 **Why is Kaliningrad important to Russia?**

A It attracts tourists from around the world, which boosts the economy.
B It is the only warm water port on the Baltic Sea.
C It was once Russia's capital and has many historic landmarks.
D It is the central location for Russia's armed forces.

8 **To change from a command economy to a market economy, Russia transferred ownership of businesses from the government to individuals. What word describes this process?**

A training
B pensioners
C privatization
D profit sharing

9 **Look at the map and answer the questions that follow.**

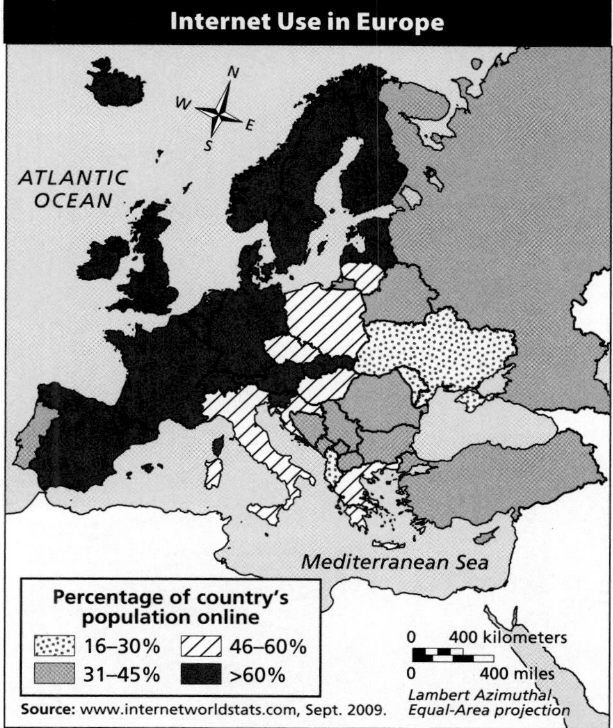

Which of the following countries has the lowest percentage of residents online?

A Ukraine
B Czech Republic
C Bulgaria
D Poland

10 **Which of the following countries has the highest percentage of residents online?**

A Greece
B Hungary
C Iceland
D Portugal

11 **In general, where in Europe are most people online?**

A Southern Europe
B Northern and Western Europe
C Eastern Europe
D the Balkan countries

12 **Read the document and answer the questions that follow.**

> *The EU [European Union] views enlargement [expansion]as a historic opportunity to help in the transformation of the countries involved, extending peace, stability, prosperity, democracy, human rights and the rule of law throughout Europe. The carefully managed process of enlargement is one of the EU's most powerful policy tools that has helped to transform the countries of Central and Eastern Europe into more modern, functioning democracies.*
>
> —from "European Union Enlargement," CRS Report for Congress, Congressional Research Service, 2006

According to this report, how does the European Union view its own expansion?

A It is a way to collect taxes from more countries.
B It is necessary so that member countries do not become colonies of other nations.
C It is a way to create a single banking system throughout Europe.
D It is an extraordinary opportunity to transform the countries that have been admitted to the union.

13 **How does the European Union's expansion affect Europe?**

A It stops disagreements and wars between countries.
B It donates money to improve the economies of European countries.
C It helps change countries into better places to live and work.
D It creates a central government for all member countries.

For additional test practice, use Self-Check Quizzes—Chapter 10 at glencoe.com.

Need Extra Help?

If You Missed Questions...	1	2	3	4	5	6	7	8	9	10	11	12	13
Go to Page...	287	294	291	296	305	290	323	322	26	26	26	296	296

UNIT 4

Australia

CHAPTER 11
Geography and History of Australia

CHAPTER 12
Australia Today

Sydney, Australia

NATIONAL GEOGRAPHIC

NGS ONLINE For more information about the region, see www.nationalgeographic.com/education.

Regional Atlas

Australia

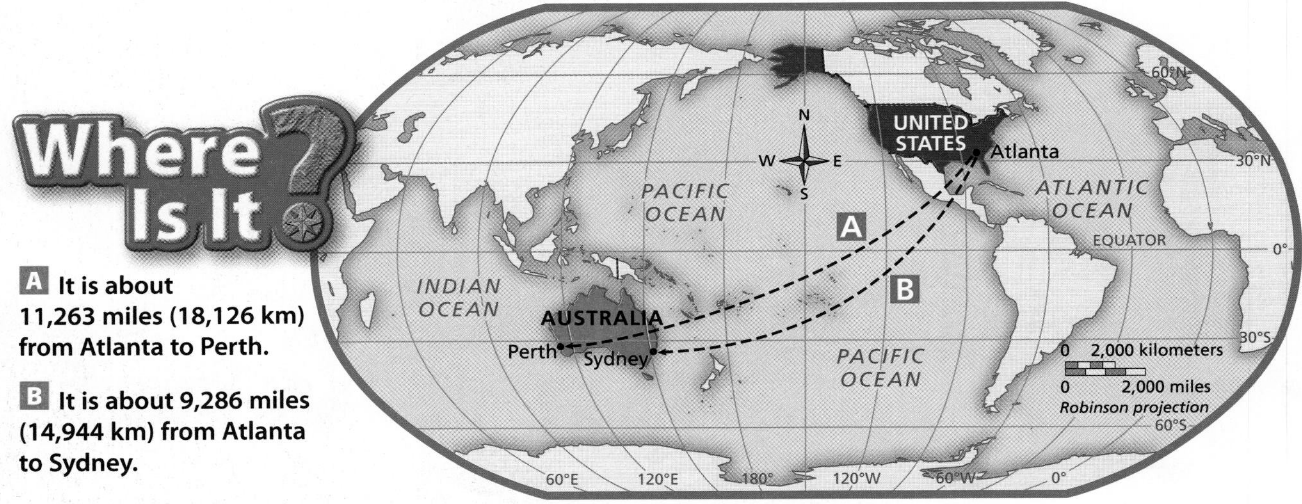

A It is about 11,263 miles (18,126 km) from Atlanta to Perth.

B It is about 9,286 miles (14,944 km) from Atlanta to Sydney.

With an area of 3.0 million square miles (7.8 million sq. km), Australia is slightly smaller than the continental United States. Its population, however, at only about 20 million, is much smaller than that of the United States.

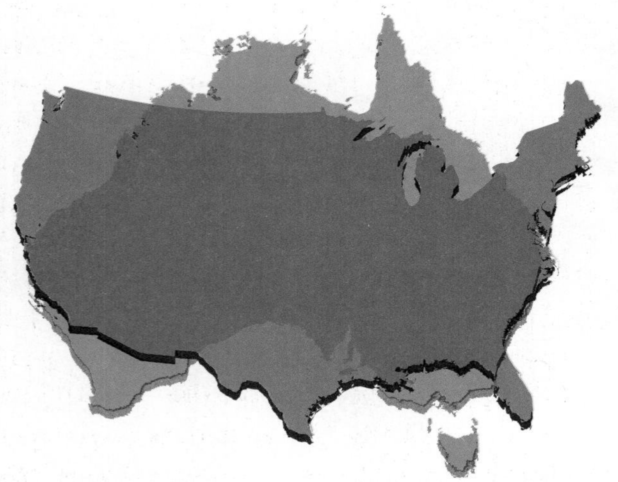

Comparing Population

United States and Australia

United States	🚹🚹🚹🚹🚹🚹🚹🚹🚹🚹
Australia	🚹

🚹 = 30,000,000

Source: *World Population Data Sheet*, 2005.

GEO Fast Facts

Largest Lake

Lake Eyre 3,600 sq. mi. (9,324 sq. km)

Largest Coral Reef

Great Barrier Reef 1,250 mi. (2,011 km) long

Longest River

Darling River 1,702 mi. (2,739 km) long

Highest Point

Mount Kosciuszko 7,310 ft. (2,228 m) high

UNIT 4

Regional Atlas

Australia

PHYSICAL

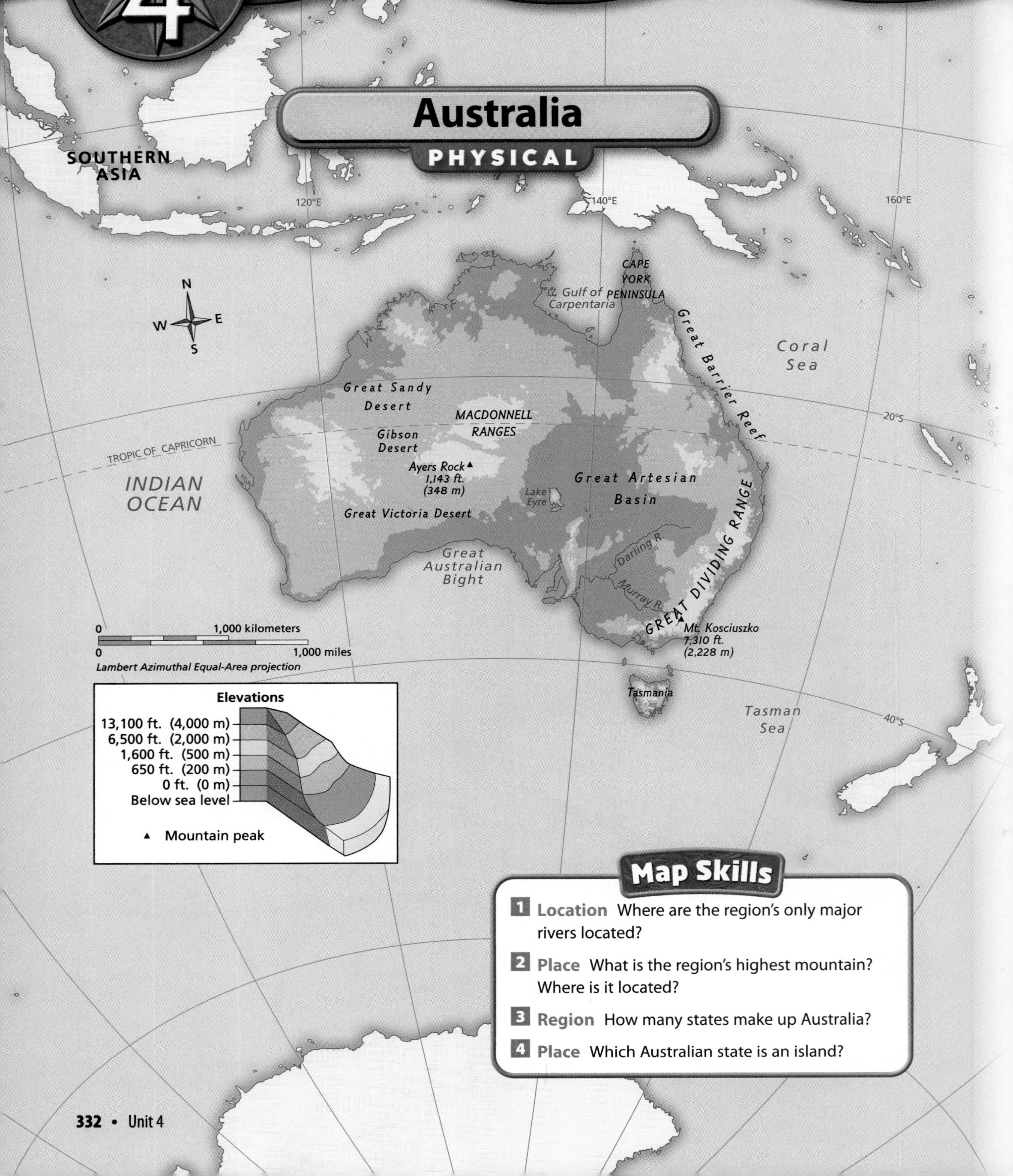

Map Skills

1. **Location** Where are the region's only major rivers located?
2. **Place** What is the region's highest mountain? Where is it located?
3. **Region** How many states make up Australia?
4. **Place** Which Australian state is an island?

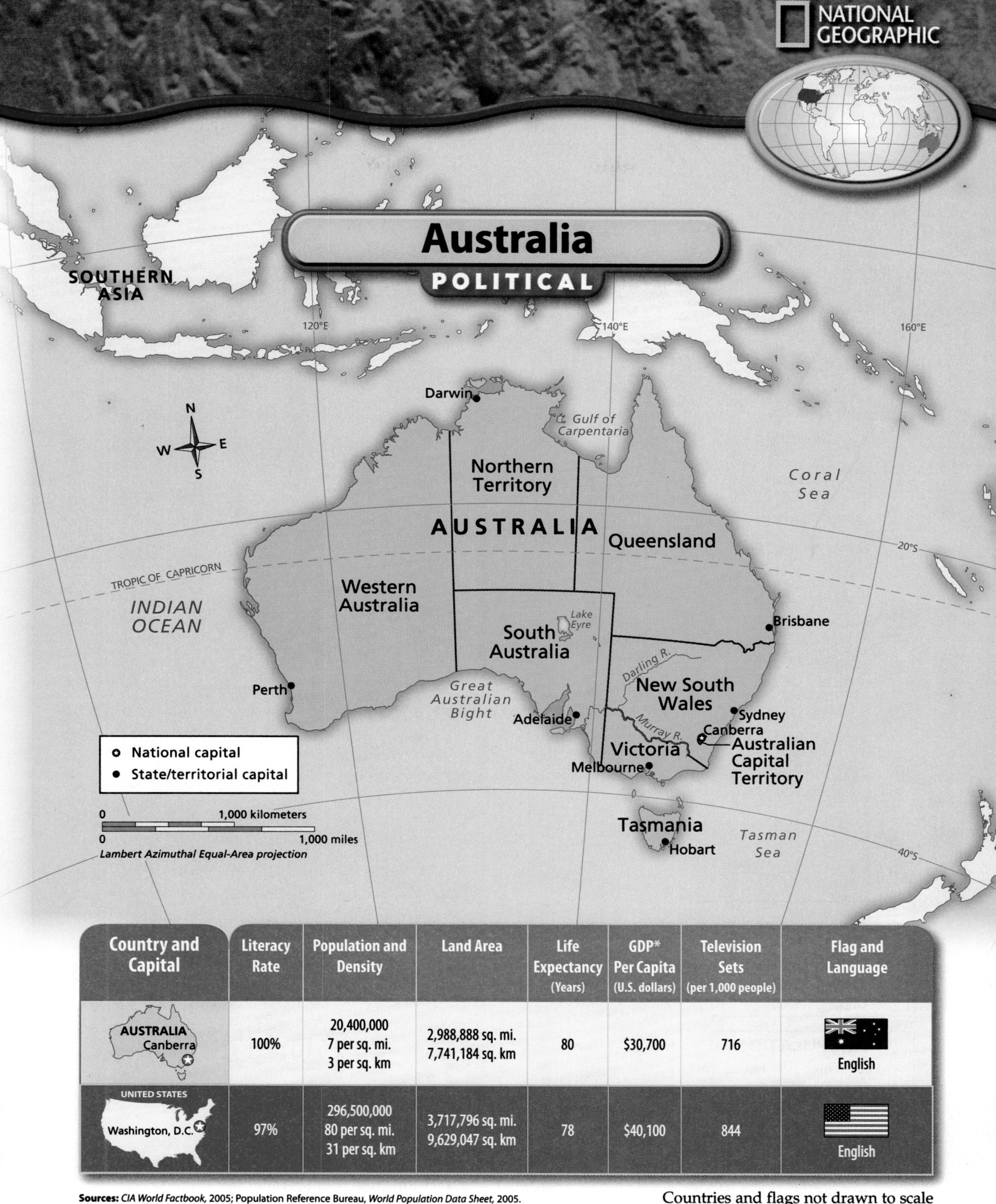

Country and Capital	Literacy Rate	Population and Density	Land Area	Life Expectancy (Years)	GDP* Per Capita (U.S. dollars)	Television Sets (per 1,000 people)	Flag and Language
AUSTRALIA Canberra	100%	20,400,000 7 per sq. mi. 3 per sq. km	2,988,888 sq. mi. 7,741,184 sq. km	80	$30,700	716	English
UNITED STATES Washington, D.C.	97%	296,500,000 80 per sq. mi. 31 per sq. km	3,717,796 sq. mi. 9,629,047 sq. km	78	$40,100	844	English

Sources: *CIA World Factbook*, 2005; Population Reference Bureau, *World Population Data Sheet*, 2005.

Countries and flags not drawn to scale

*Gross Domestic Product

For more country facts, go to the **Nations of the World Atlas** at glencoe.com.

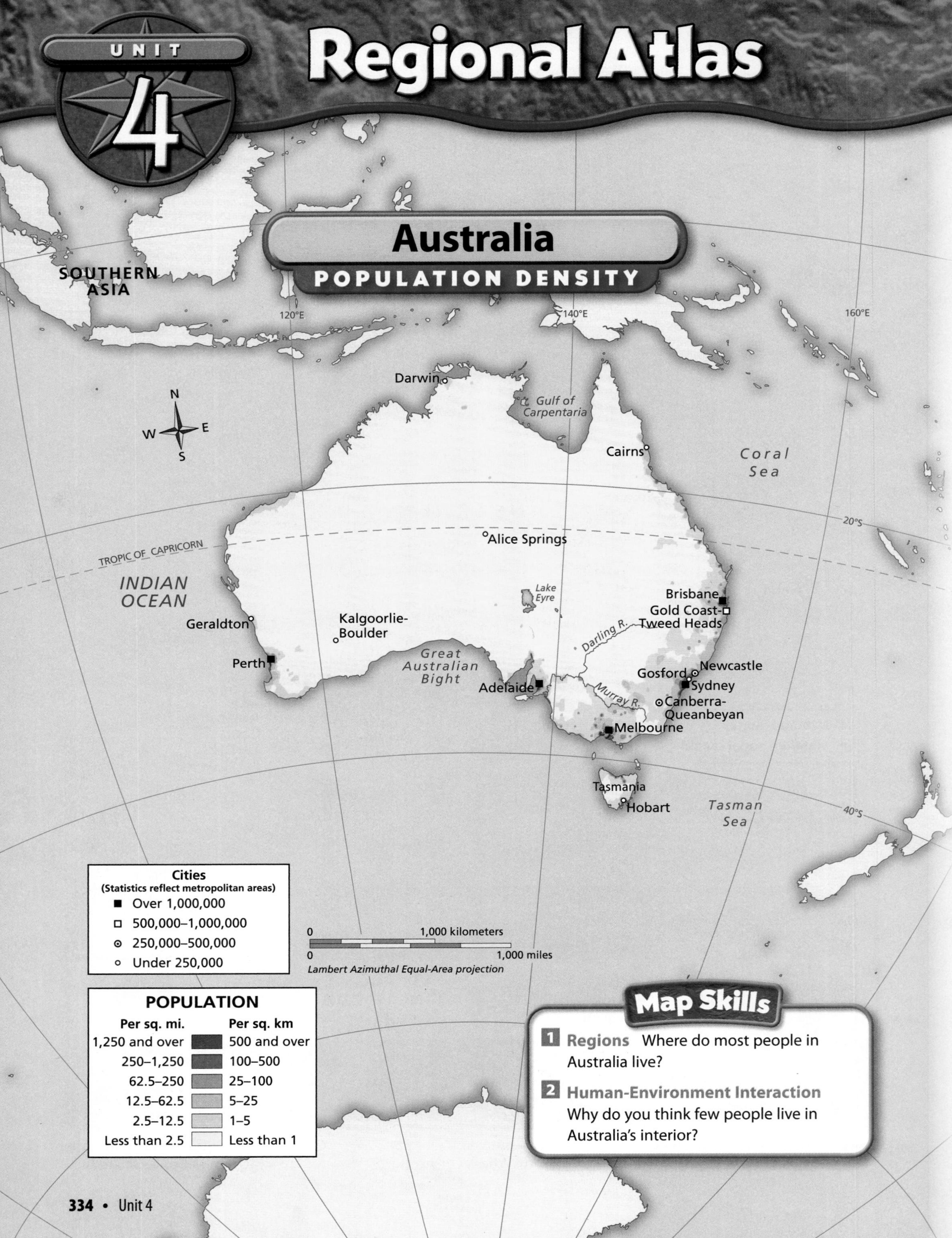

Map Skills

1. **Regions** Where do most people in Australia live?
2. **Human-Environment Interaction** Why do you think few people live in Australia's interior?

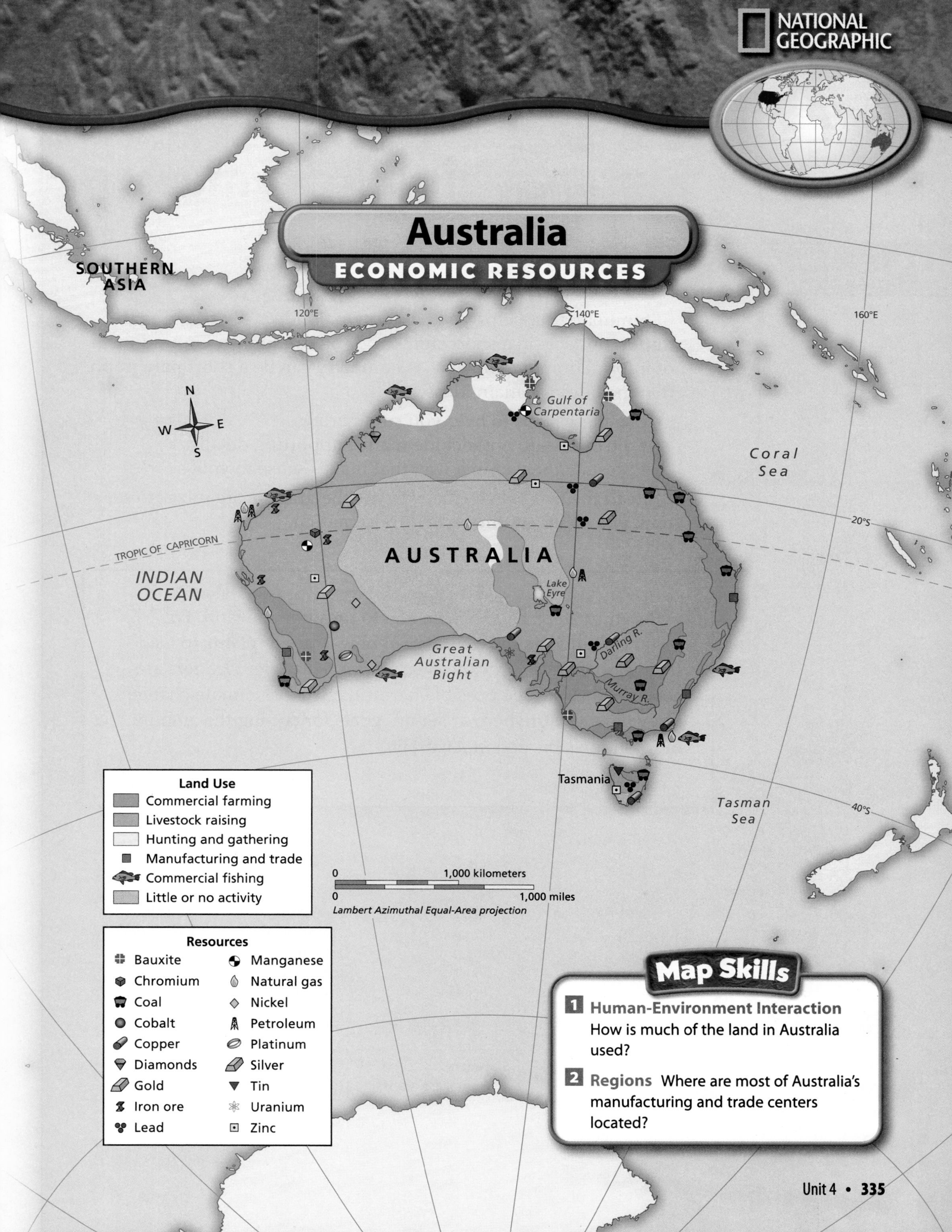

Map Skills

1. **Human-Environment Interaction** How is much of the land in Australia used?
2. **Regions** Where are most of Australia's manufacturing and trade centers located?

Reading Social Studies

Summarizing Information

Learn It!

Summarizing helps you focus on main ideas. By restating the important facts in a short summary, you can reduce the amount of information to remember. A summary can be a short paragraph that includes the main ideas.

Use these steps to help you summarize:

- Be brief—do not include many supporting details.
- Restate the text in a way that makes sense to you.

Read the text below. Then review the graphic organizer to see how you could summarize the information.

> Recently, steps have been taken to preserve the land. For instance, ranchers have cultivated new types of plants to feed their herds and to prevent overgrazing. Australian leaders are concerned about the possible harmful effects of climate change. They have **established,** or set up, goals for cutting the amount of fossil fuels burned in Australia.
>
> *—from page 368*

Fact: Australians are taking steps to preserve their land.

Fact: Australian ranchers are attempting to prevent overgrazing of land.

Fact: Australians are reducing the amount of fossil fuels that are burned.

Summary: Australians are taking action to protect the environment.

Reading Tip

As you read and summarize in your own words, try not to change the author's original meanings or ideas.

2 Practice It!

Read the following paragraph from this unit.
- Draw an organizer like the one shown below.
- Write the main facts from the paragraph in the top boxes.
- Write a summary of the paragraph in the bottom box.

Read to Write Activity

Read the section "Australia's Resources" on page 343 of your text and summarize its information. Be sure that you do not use the author's words. Paraphrase the ideas in your own words.

Early Aborigines were semi-nomadic hunters and gatherers. They traveled across the Australian landscape in small groups. To survive, they became skilled at identifying plants that could be eaten and at tracking animals. They also learned to locate water in the continent's dry environment.

—*from page 347*

Aborigine man

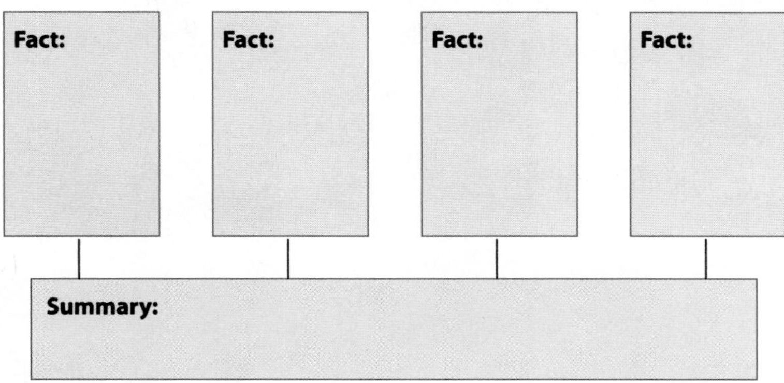

3 Apply It!

With a partner, choose a section to summarize. After each of you summarizes the section on your own, exchange your papers and check to see if the summaries are complete. Note whether any important ideas are missing. Return your summaries to each other and make the changes. Use your summaries to help you study for assessment.

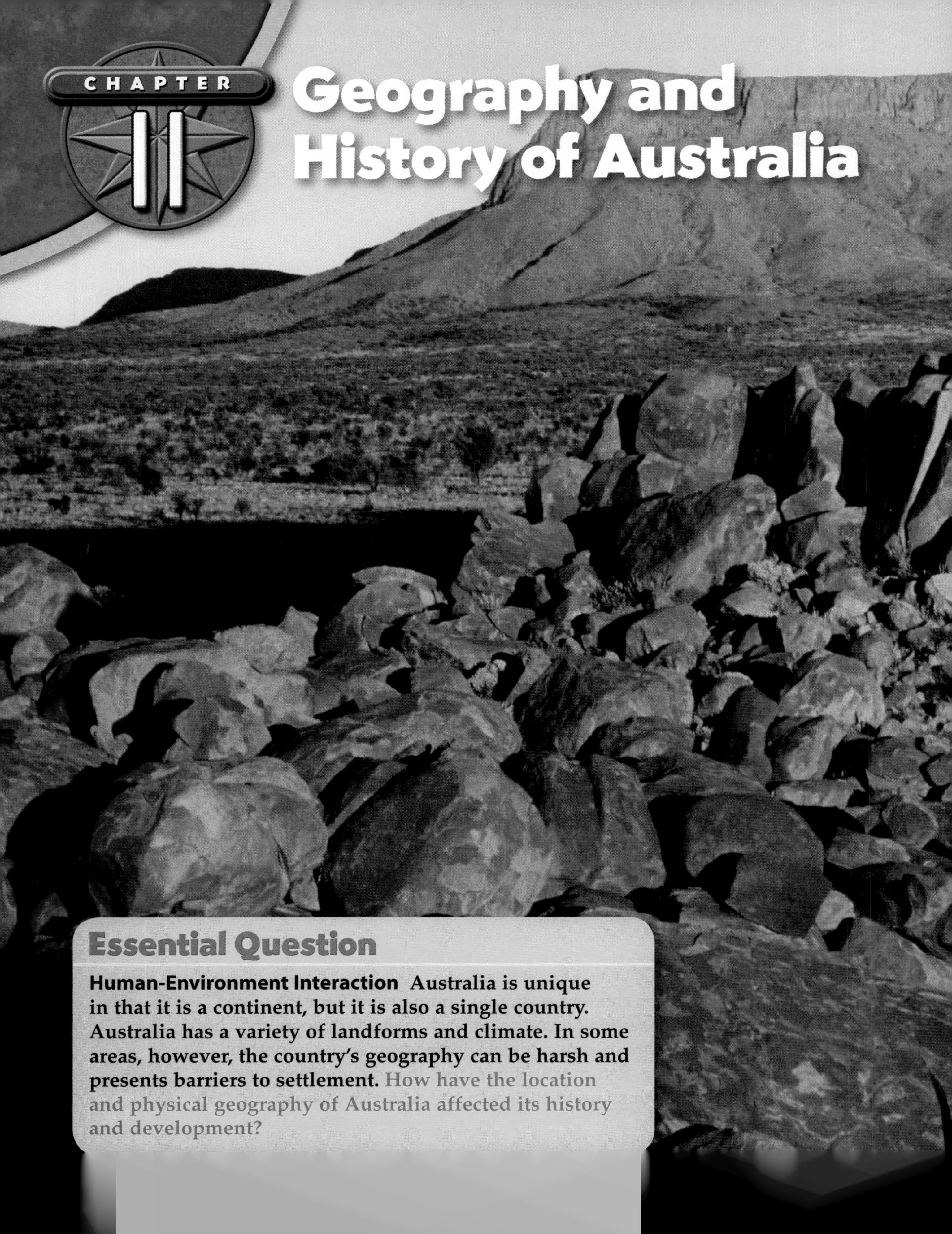

CHAPTER 11

Geography and History of Australia

Essential Question

Human-Environment Interaction Australia is unique in that it is a continent, but it is also a single country. Australia has a variety of landforms and climate. In some areas, however, the country's geography can be harsh and presents barriers to settlement. How have the location and physical geography of Australia affected its history and development?

Chapter Audio

Desert landscape, central Australia

Section 1: Physical Geography and Climate

BIG IDEA Places reflect the relationship between humans and the physical environment. The landforms and climate of Australia influence patterns of settlement and ways of life.

Section 2: History and Government

BIG IDEA Culture groups shape human systems. The people who have settled Australia shaped the nation's history and government.

FOLDABLES™ Study Organizer

Summarizing Information Make this Foldable to help you organize information about the physical geography, history, and government of Australia.

Step 1 Fold the bottom edge of a piece of paper up 2 inches to create a flap.

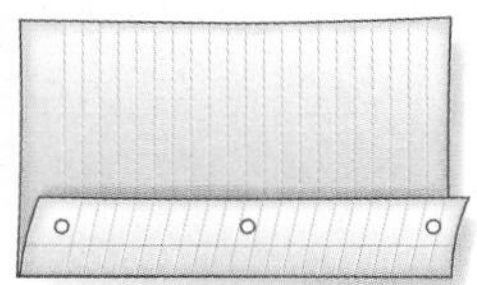

Step 2 Fold into thirds.

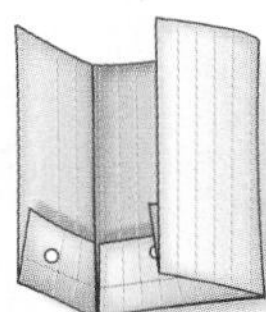

Step 3 Glue to form pockets and label as shown. Use pockets to hold notes taken on slips of paper.

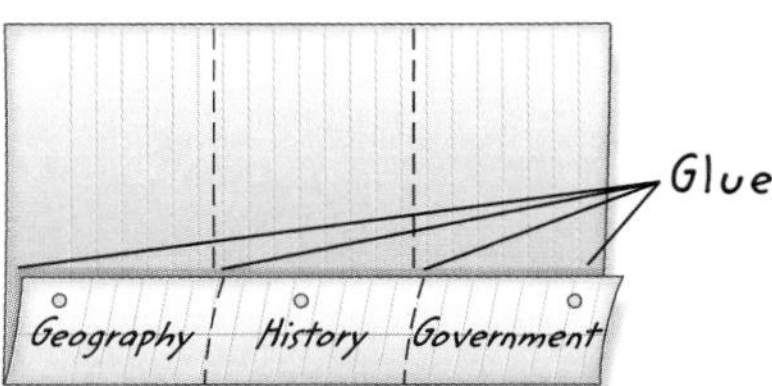

Reading and Writing As you read the chapter, take notes on slips of paper. Place each note in the correct pocket of your Foldable. Use your notes to write a short summary of the geography, history, or government of Australia.

Visit glencoe.com and enter QuickPass™ code GA6EOW6225c11 for Chapter 11 resources.

Guide to Reading

Physical Geography and Climate

Section Audio

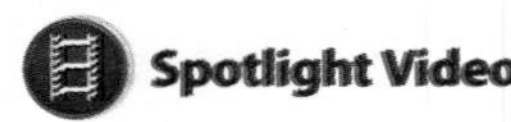
Spotlight Video

BIG Idea

Places reflect the relationship between humans and the physical environment.

Content Vocabulary

- outback *(p. 341)*
- coral reef *(p. 341)*
- eucalyptus *(p. 342)*
- marsupial *(p. 343)*

Academic Vocabulary

- adjacent *(p. 341)*
- accurate *(p. 341)*
- distort *(p. 342)*
- sufficient *(p. 342)*

Reading Strategy

Analyzing Information Use a chart like the one below to list key facts about Australia's land, climate, and resources.

Australia's Land	Australia's Climate	Australia's Resources

Picture This Catch the wave! There's no need to rush, though—this wave has been here for more than 2.7 billion years, and it is not going anywhere soon. The "wave" is actually a granite cliff face near Hyden, Australia. Weathering and erosion have undercut the cliff base, leaving a rounded overhang. As you read this section, you will learn more about the spectacular landforms of Australia.

Wave Rock

Land and Climate

Main Idea **Much of Australia is flat and dry.**

Geography and You Have you ever seen beautiful tropical fish swimming on a coral reef? The world's largest coral reef lies off Australia's northeast coast. Read to learn more about it and other physical features of this unique nation.

Australia, the sixth-largest country in the world, is also the world's smallest continent. Australia lies separate from other continents. As a result, many of its plants and animals are found nowhere else.

Landforms of Australia

Australia is mostly flat. In fact, it has a lower elevation than all the other continents. It also has low relief, meaning there are few differences in the elevations of **adjacent,** or neighboring, areas. Only a small fraction of the land is over 2,000 feet (610 m) high. The highest point, Mt. Kosciuszko, reaches to only 7,310 feet (2,288 m).

Narrow plains along the southern and southeastern coasts have the country's best farmland. They are also home to much of its population. Two major rivers, the Murray and the Darling, drain these areas.

A ridge of highlands called the Great Dividing Range stretches along eastern Australia. It runs from the Cape York Peninsula to the island of Tasmania, which belongs to Australia. From the east, the Great Dividing Range looks like mountains. It is more **accurately,** or correctly, an escarpment. An escarpment is the edge of a plateau that sharply drops to lowlands below.

To the west of the range, the land gradually blends into the **outback.** The outback is a vast area of plains and plateaus that is mostly flat and dry. It is also dotted with isolated, heavily eroded masses of rock that rise above the lowlands. Ayers Rock is one of these massive rocks. Also called Uluru, this rock is sacred to the Aborigines (A·buh·RIHJ·neez), the first people to settle Australia. The rock, made of sandstone, appears to change color during the day, depending on how the sun's light strikes it.

Deserts, such as the Great Victoria Desert, cover much of western Australia. Large sand dunes that change shape in the wind are common in these deserts.

Off Australia's northeastern coast, in the Coral Sea, lies the Great Barrier Reef. This natural wonder is the world's largest **coral reef,** a structure formed by the skeletons of small sea animals. Its colorful formations stretch about 1,250 miles (2,011 km).

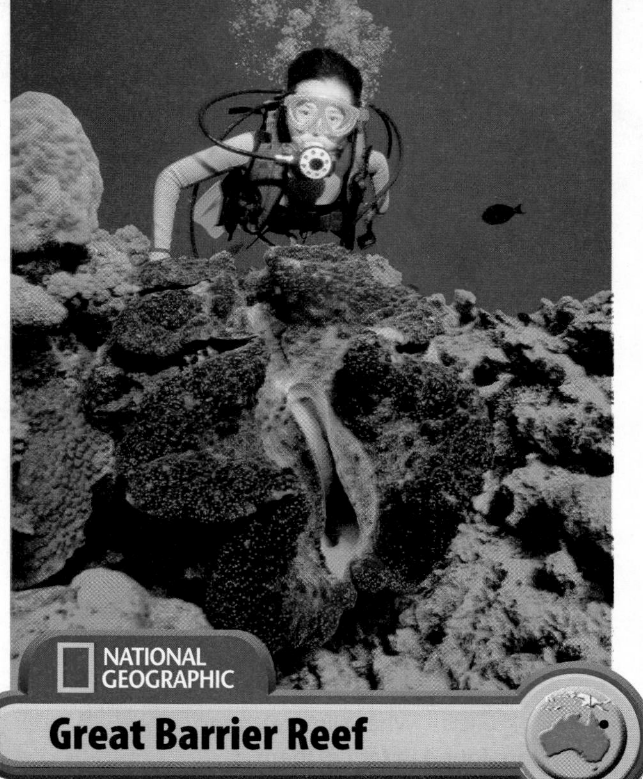

Great Barrier Reef

The Great Barrier Reef is home to many creatures like this giant clam. Giant clams can live for 70 years and grow to be more than 3 feet (1 m) long.
Location **Where is the Great Barrier Reef located?**

Student Web Activity Visit glencoe.com and complete the Chapter 11 Web Activity about the Great Barrier Reef.

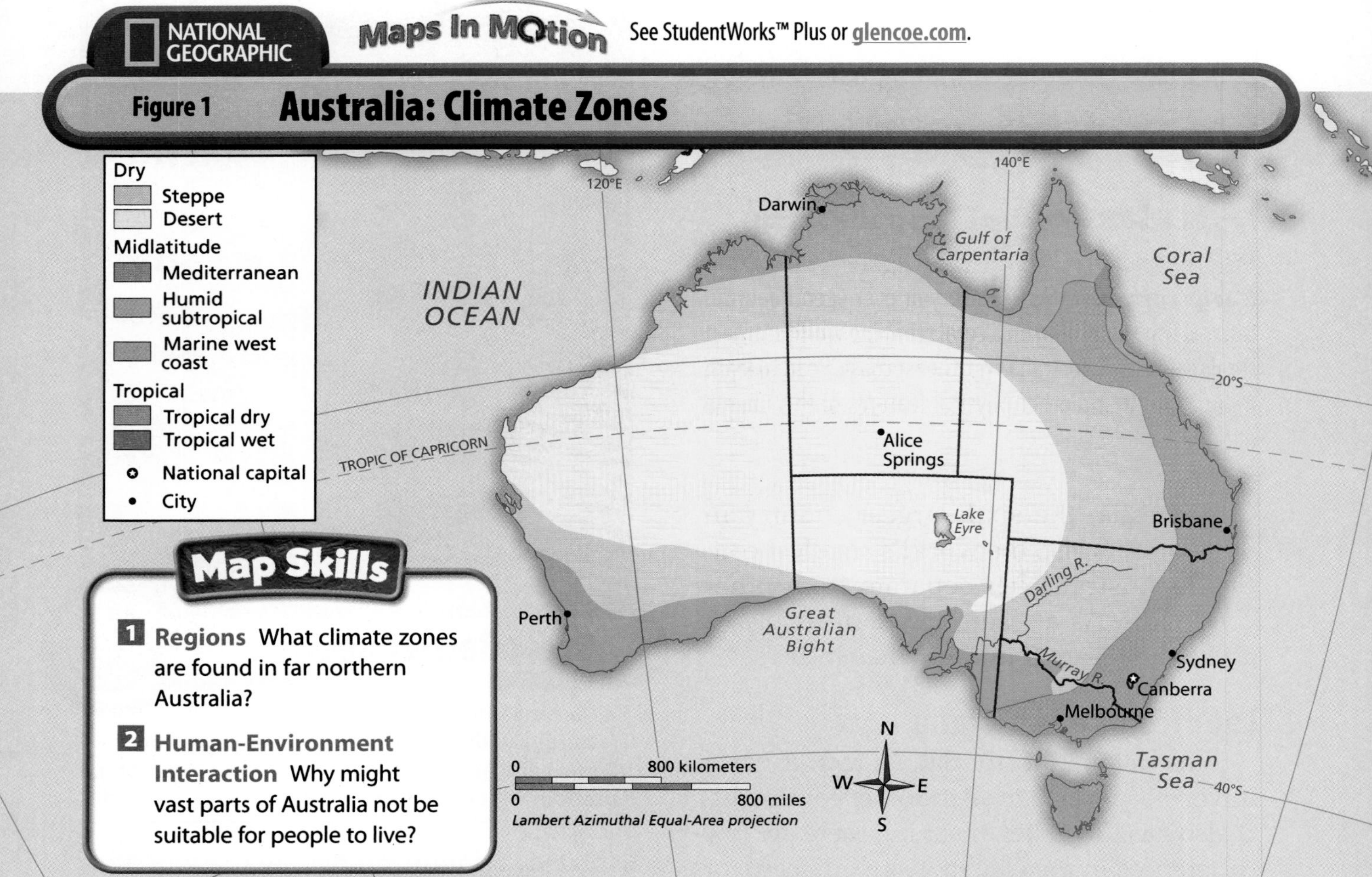

Climate Zones

Australia is a mainly dry continent. Although moist winds blowing off the ocean drop rain on the coasts, little rainfall reaches the vast interior. As a result, about one-third of Australia is desert, and another third is partly dry steppe.

Some deserts receive no more than 8 inches (20 cm) of rain a year. These averages may **distort,** or present a misleading impression of normal climate patterns. Rainfall can be well below the average in any year. In fact, rain may not fall at all for long periods of time. When rains do come to Australia's interior, they often arrive in heavy bursts that cause floods. High temperatures then quickly evaporate the water.

The plants of Australia are suited to these conditions. **Eucalyptus** (yoo·kuh·LIHP·tuhs) trees, for example, are native to Australia. Their thick, leathery leaves—the favorite food of koalas—prevent moisture loss and can survive rushing floodwaters. Other plants send long roots deep into the earth to find water during the dry season.

As **Figure 1** shows, Australia has a number of climates. Part of the southeastern coast has a marine west coast climate. Summers here are warm, and winters are cool and rainy. Most people live in this area.

Southern and western Australia have a Mediterranean climate of warm summers and mild winters. In these areas, rainfall is **sufficient,** or enough, for raising crops. The far north has a tropical dry, or savanna, climate. Temperatures are warm year round, with dry winters and hot, humid summers.

Reading Check **Explaining** Why is much of Australia hot and dry?

Australia's Resources

Main Idea **Australia is rich in resources.**

Geography and You You have probably seen photographs of the Australian outback. Read to discover the resources found there, including unusual wildlife that live in the region.

Australia is a leading producer of iron ore, zinc, lead, and bauxite. Some of these metals are used by industry in Australia. Much, though, is exported. Other minerals there include uranium, nickel, and copper.

Not much more than thirty years ago, western Australia was found to have large deposits of diamonds. Today, Australia is one of the world's top producers of diamonds. Australia is also a source of beautiful gems, such as opals and sapphires, as well as gold and silver.

Australia's oil reserves supply much of its need for oil. However, a large amount of oil must still be imported. Australia also has abundant coal reserves, but some people object to burning coal, which can hurt the environment.

Hydroelectric power is not a good option in Australia. The country has few rivers, and most do not run fast enough for this purpose. Australia might be able to obtain power from the wind and the sun. It still does not have much of the needed equipment to do this, however.

Because Australia is far from most other land masses, it has long been isolated. As a result, some of its plants and animals are not found anywhere else in the world. Two well-known Australian animals are kangaroos and koalas. Both are **marsupials,** or mammals that carry their young in a pouch.

Reading Check **Explaining** Why is little hydroelectric power created in Australia?

Section Review

Vocabulary

1. **Explain** the significance of
   a. outback
   b. coral reef
   c. eucalyptus
   d. marsupial

Main Ideas

2. **Summarizing** Use a diagram like the one below to list and describe three features of Australia's outback.

3. **Categorizing** Categorize and identify the resources found in Australia.

Critical Thinking

4. **BIG Idea** How do landforms and climate affect where most Australians live?
5. **Determining Cause and Effect** Why does this region have unique types of animals?
6. **Challenge** Considering Australia's energy resources, what would you do to meet the nation's energy needs if you were the leader of the country?

Writing About Geography

7. **Using Your FOLDABLES™** Use your Foldable to write three entries from the diary of a traveler crossing different regions of Australia.

Ayers Rock (Uluru): Should Climbing It Be Banned?

Ayers Rock is a red sandstone formation in Australia's central desert. Many tourists visit and climb the rock, which is as high as a 95-story building.

The Aborigines own Ayers Rock, which they call Uluru. They view Uluru as sacred and ask people to show respect by not climbing it. They also warn about the dangers that climbing poses to climbers and the environment alike.

Some people agree and want the Australian government to ban tourists from climbing the site. Others believe that a ban would keep people from enjoying a unique experience of nature and would reduce tourism to the area.

Banning

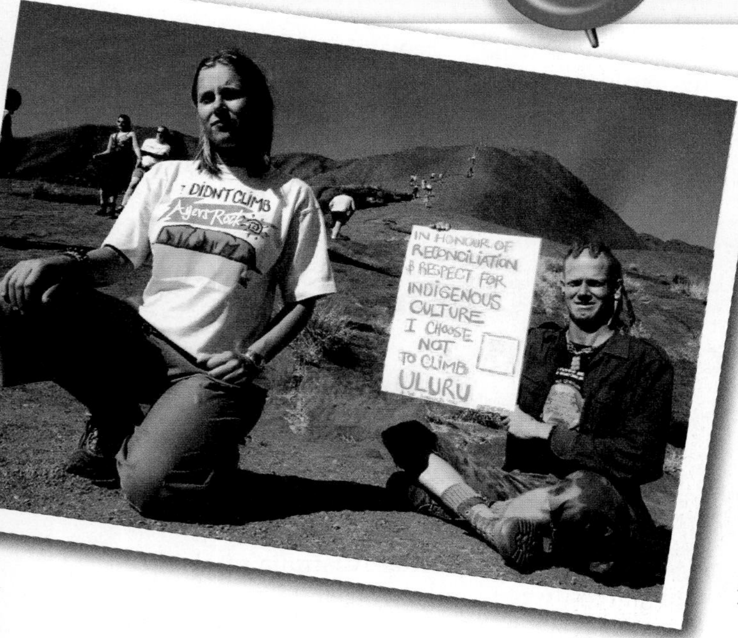

It is very steep, very slippery, strenuous. It's higher than the Eiffel Tower, so up until 2000 more than 30 people had died on the climb. We still have over a dozen injuries and incidents every year.

[There are] erosion concerns and there are no toilets on the top of the rock. So human behaviour up there means that we get run-off fouling [polluting] water holes, and having impacts on plants and animals and the health of Aboriginal kids who play in those water holes. And culturally, Uluru is very significant to traditional owners.

—Peter Cochrane,
Director of National Parks, Australia

Against Banning

With Australian tourism facing a big downturn due to the global financial crisis, I can't believe the Government would even think about doing something like this, that will turn away tourists from one of our most visited attractions.

Younger tourists in particular will not want to make the trek . . . just to look at the Rock. They want to take away photos of themselves on top of it, to show to their family and friends. It is an achievement to climb such a well-known icon. . . .

I call on [Prime Minister Kevin Rudd] to announce that Ayers Rock will remain open to all who wish to climb it.

—Australian senator Ian Macdonald,
Opposition Spokesperson for Northern Australia

You Be the Geographer

1. **Explaining** Why do some people oppose climbing Ayers Rock (Uluru)?
2. **Critical Thinking** What do the supporters of climbing fear will happen if climbing the rock is banned?
3. **Read to Write** Write a paragraph stating your opinion about whether tourists should have unlimited access to heritage sites, such as Ayers Rock (Uluru).

Guide to Reading

BIG Idea

Culture groups shape human systems.

Content Vocabulary

- clan *(p. 347)*
- boomerang *(p. 347)*
- penal colony *(p. 348)*
- suffrage *(p. 349)*

Academic Vocabulary

- acquire *(p. 348)*
- prime *(p. 348)*

Reading Strategy

Summarizing Use a chart like the one below to organize key facts about the three periods of Australia's history.

Australia's History		
First Peoples	Colony	Nation

History and Government

 Section Audio  Spotlight Video

Picture This Future rodeo cowboys in Australia practice their skills using an empty steel drum suspended on a rope. A rodeo rider must ride an angry bull or a bucking horse for at least eight seconds. Falling off before the eight seconds is up results in a score of zero. During outback rodeos, Aborigines and Australians of European descent gather to compete in a variety of events. Read this section to learn more about the history of the people of Australia.

Rodeo practice in western Australia

The History of Australia

Main Idea **A mix of people have settled Australia.**

Geography and You What role did European explorers and settlers play in the history of the Americas? Read to find out how Europeans also explored and settled Australia.

Some 40,000 years ago, the Earth was undergoing a period known as an Ice Age. At the time, temperatures were lower than they are now, and much more of Earth's water was trapped in ice. As a result, water levels of the oceans were lower, exposing more land. In this time, peoples from Southeast Asia came, either by land or by boat, to Australia. Several thousand years later, the Ice Age ended. Ocean levels rose when the ice melted, and the people in Australia were cut off from the rest of the world. The people now called Aborigines are descendants of these first people.

Australia's Aborigines

At the time of the arrival of the first Europeans, Australia's Aborigines lived in more than 600 **clans.** Clans are large groups of people with shared ancestors. The Aborigines lived in many different environments. Each clan developed a way of life suited to its surroundings—from lush forest areas to the dry outback. Each group had its own area in which it lived. Natural boundaries, such as bodies of water or rock outcroppings, separated the territories. The Aborigines greatly respected the land, and they sought to sustain their environment.

Early Aborigines were semi-nomadic hunters and gatherers. They traveled across the Australian landscape in small groups.

Aboriginal Heritage

Australia's Aborigines have kept their cultural heritage alive by passing down their language, arts, and rituals through generations. ***Place*** **How did the Aborigines survive in Australia's harsh climates?**

To survive, they became skilled at identifying plants that could be eaten and at tracking animals. They also learned to locate water in the continent's dry environment.

To hunt small animals, the Aborigines developed a special weapon called a **boomerang.** A boomerang is a flat, bent, wooden tool that hunters throw to stun prey. If this weapon misses its target, the bend in the wood makes it sail back to the hunter.

The religion of the Aborigines focuses on the relationship of people to nature. The Aborigines believe that powerful spirits created the land and that their role as a people is to care for the land. Ancient rock paintings and stories tell much about their early history. Music, song, and dance are important to the Aborigines. A long, hollow tubelike wind instrument called the didgeridoo is often played at ceremonies.

The Arrival of Europeans

From the 1500s to the 1800s, Europeans from various countries explored the South Pacific and the lands within this vast stretch of ocean. Europe's nations soon began to **acquire,** or obtain, parts of the region as colonies.

One of the first Europeans to approach Australia was the Dutch explorer Abel Tasman. In 1642, he explored the island of Tasmania, which is today named for him. Perhaps the most well known explorer, though, was the British sailor Captain James Cook. He made three voyages to the region between 1768 and 1779. Cook visited several Pacific islands and produced amazingly accurate maps of the area. He also claimed eastern Australia for Great Britain.

The British government at first used Australia as a **penal colony.** A penal colony is a place where prisoners are sent to create settlements and serve out their sentences. Many of the convicts sent to Australia during this time had been imprisoned for only minor crimes. The first convicts arrived in early 1788 in a group of six ships known as the First Fleet. These ships carried nearly 1,000 settlers. Between 1788 and 1868, about 160,000 convicts were taken to Australia. Once they served their sentences, most stayed in the new land.

By the mid-1800s, the British government stopped sending convicts to Australia. Many free British settlers began migrating to the faraway land, hoping to obtain inexpensive land and prosper.

Settlers stayed along the coasts at first. Gradually, they moved farther inland. Many of them began to farm, growing wheat. Ranchers soon realized that conditions made Australia a **prime,** or very attractive, land for raising sheep that produced a fine wool. Wool exports became a major part of the economy.

The discovery of minerals also boosted the economy. Copper was the first metal found. The discovery of gold in 1851 led to a rush of settlers and greatly increased Australia's population. By 1861, the European population had passed 1 million.

When Captain Cook landed in Australia, about 300,000 Aborigines lived there. Relations between the Aborigines and settlers were mostly peaceful. As the Europeans took more land, however, the Aborigines were forced to defend their traditional grounds. Because they fought with spears and other primitive weapons, the Aborigines were easily defeated by the rifle-carrying Europeans. To make matters worse, the Aborigines had no resistance to European diseases. By the late 1800s, warfare and illness cut the number of Aborigines to about 80,000.

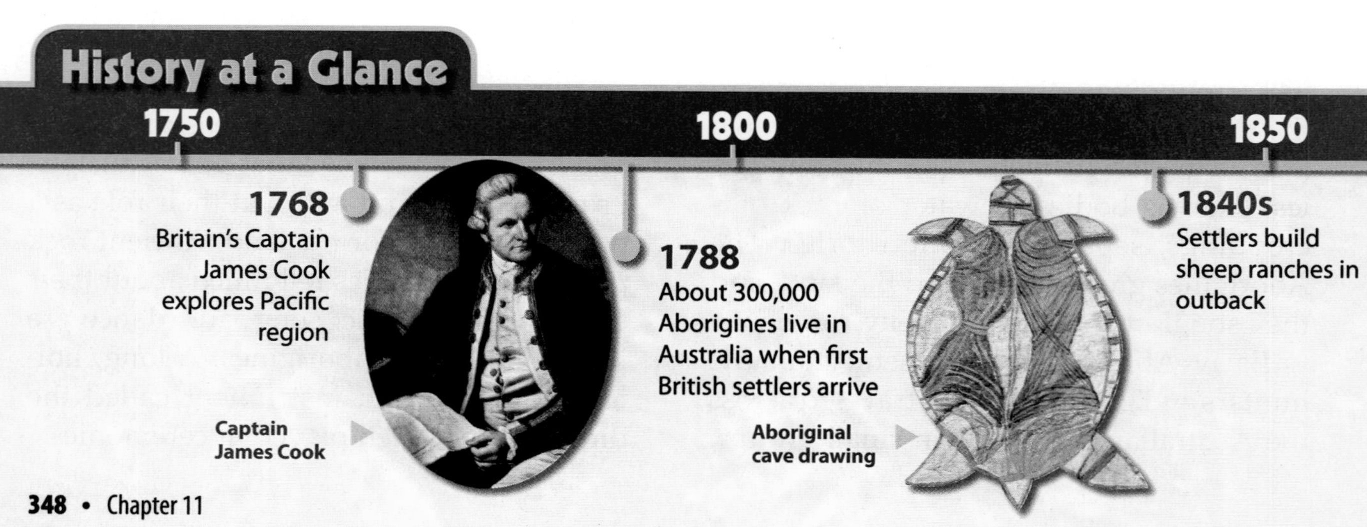

Captain James Cook

Aboriginal cave drawing

From Colony to Nation

In the 1800s, Australia was split into six separate colonies. Each had its own legislature to make laws for the people within its boundaries. In other parts of the world, voting was typically limited to property owners. In Australia, though, all men had the right to vote.

By the late 1800s, more and more settlers were arriving in Australia. The wool industry continued to grow, as did ranching. These industries were helped by the spread of railroads into the interior. Trains could carry wool and cattle from rural areas to markets in the cities.

Beginning in the mid-1800s, many Australians sought to unite the colonies and gain independence. In 1901, Australia peacefully became free of British rule. All the colonies were organized into one unified nation known as the Commonwealth of Australia. Women won **suffrage**, or the right to vote, the following year. Aborigines, however, did not have the rights of citizens. Also, Australia had laws that favored immigrants from Europe and kept out people from other regions.

As part of the British Empire, Australia sent troops to fight with Britain in World War I. Thousands died in the battle of Gallipoli, in Turkey. Australians still pay respect to those who fell on the anniversary of the first day of this battle each year.

During World War II, Australia was threatened when Japanese troops reached as far south as nearby New Guinea. Australian soldiers joined with British and American forces to defeat the Japanese. The war was the beginning of close ties between Australia and the United States, which still exist today.

Modern Australia

During World War II, Australia's economy shifted to a greater emphasis on manufacturing. This move helped lead to greater prosperity after the war. In the late 1900s, Australia's economy continued to grow, and the people of Australia enjoyed an increased standard of living.

The late 1900s saw other changes. Australia built closer economic ties with Asian countries. These ties helped convince Australians to allow Asians and other non-Europeans to settle in Australia. The lives of Aborigines changed as well. Their population grew, and in 1962, Aborigines finally gained the right to vote.

Reading Check **Summarizing** What part did James Cook play in making Australia a British colony?

Sydney Opera House, Sydney, Australia

The Government of Australia

Main Idea **The government of Australia has a federal system that divides power.**

Geography and You Would you want someone who lives far from you to make all the laws you have to follow? Read to learn how Australians solved the problem of governing a large country.

Australia won freedom from British rule peacefully during the early 1900s. Many countries at that time had a unitary government. That is, the national government had most of the power and controlled local governments. Because of Australia's large size, its people wanted to keep some power at the local level.

As a result, Australians chose a federal system of government like that of the United States and Canada. In a federal system, the power to make and enforce laws is divided between the national government and the states and territories. Australia today has 6 states and 2 territories. While the national government makes laws for the entire nation, officials in state and territorial governments make laws for the people who live in their areas.

Australia also is a parliamentary democracy. Voters elect representatives to a national law-making body called Parliament. Like the U.S. Congress, Australia's Parliament has two parts: a Senate and a House of Representatives. The 76 members of Australia's Senate are evenly divided among the states, with the territories having 2 senators each. The House of Representatives is made up of 150 members from around the country. Each member represents the same number of people.

In Australia, a prime minister runs the national government. He or she is chosen from the political party with the most seats in the House of Representatives.

Reading Check **Identifying** What is the title for the leader of Australia's government?

Section 2 Review

Vocabulary

1. **Explain** the meaning of *clan, boomerang, penal colony,* and *suffrage* by using each word in a sentence.

Main Ideas

2. **Explaining** How did the first people arrive in Australia?
3. **Summarizing** Use a diagram like the one below to identify key events in the historical development of Australia.

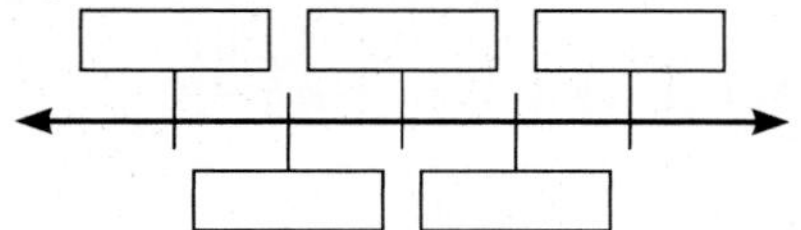

Critical Thinking

4. **Analyzing Information** Why did clans living in different parts of Australia need to follow different ways of life?
5. **Challenge** How do the rights of Australians in the 1800s compare to their rights today?
6. **BIG Idea** How does the government of Australia reflect the nation's history?

Writing About Geography

7. **Expository Writing** Write a short essay describing the growth of Australia following the arrival of Europeans in 1788.

Visual Summary

Geography of Australia

- Australia is mainly flat with low relief. Much of the interior is covered by deserts.
- The Great Barrier Reef is the largest coral reef in the world.
- Australia has mainly warm, dry climates. The country's coasts have more moderate temperatures and receive more rainfall than inland areas.

Resources

- Australia is rich in mineral resources.
- Australia has some oil and large deposits of coal. Wind and solar energy are not widely developed.
- Because Australia remained isolated for a long period, it has many unique plants and animals.

Climbing a mountain ash

Australia's History

- Hunters from Southeast Asia settled Australia about 40,000 years ago.
- Australia's Aborigines were hunter-gatherers and greatly respected the land on which they lived.
- Europeans explored Australia from the 1500s to the 1800s and began settling it in the late 1700s.
- Warfare and disease caused Aborigine populations to decline.
- Australia gained independence in 1901.
- In the late 1900s, Australia built a prosperous, developed economy.

Australia's Government

- Australia has a federal government, with power shared by the states and the national government.
- Australia is a parliamentary democracy, led by the prime minister, who is chosen from the majority party in Parliament.

Aborigine woman voting

Kalgoorlie gold mine, Australia

STUDY TO GO Study anywhere, anytime! Download quizzes and flash cards to your PDA from glencoe.com.

CHAPTER 11 ASSESSMENT

TEST-TAKING TIP

Do not wait until the last minute to prepare for a test. Make sure you ask questions in class after you have studied, but before you take the test.

Directions: Choose the best answer for each question.

1 **What do Australians call the enormous interior of their country?**

A highlands
B escarpment
C geyser
D outback

2 **Why is most of Australia dry?**

A The average annual temperature is about 95 degrees.
B Almost all of Australia's lands are deserts.
C The winds drop most of the rain along the continent's coastlines.
D The types of winds that blow near Australia rarely carry moisture.

3 **Australia is one of the world's top producers of which of the following precious materials?**

A pearls
B diamonds
C emeralds
D rubies

4 **Why are some plants and animals in Australia found nowhere else in the world?**

A The species died out everywhere except in Australia.
B They are so new that they have not had time to spread to the rest of the world.
C There are no other continents nearby.
D Climates in other parts of the world cannot support these plants and animals.

5 **From where did Australia's first settlers arrive over 40,000 years ago?**

A New Zealand
B Southeast Asia
C South America
D Europe

6 **In what type of setting did the early Aborigines live?**

A in tents
B in clans
C in one large group
D in a settlement similar to a city

7 **Why did Australia's population quickly increase beginning in 1851?**

A Ships with new convicts arrived.
B New jobs were created with the ranching industry.
C The birth rate unexpectedly increased.
D Gold was discovered.

8 **How is Australia's government similar to Canada's?**

A A prime minister runs the federal government.
B The British queen runs the federal government.
C A president runs the federal government.
D Each state has its own government and head official.

9 **Which of the following is the law-making body of Australia?**

A General Assembly
B the Senate
C Parliament
D Congress

10 **Look at the map.**

Australia's Vegetation

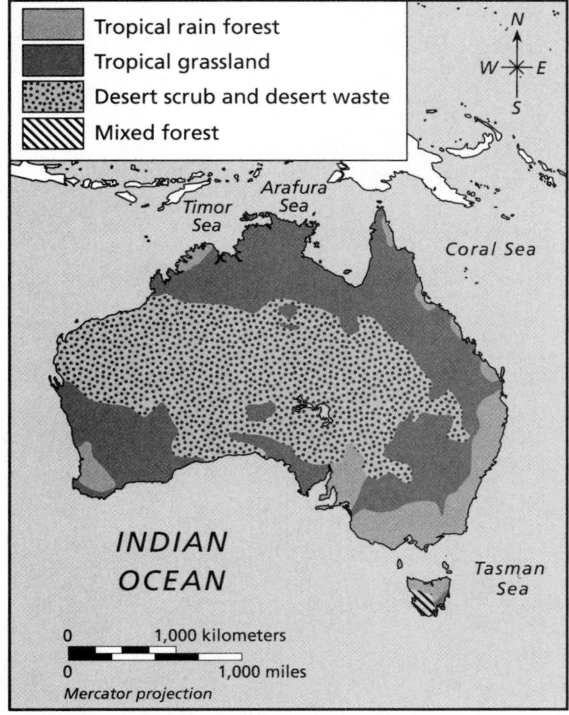

What kind of vegetation covers most of central Australia?

A tropical rain forest
B mixed forest
C desert scrub
D tropical grassland

11 **Why do you think early explorers, who approached from the west, were hesitant to settle Australia?**

A The first land they saw was desert or tropical grassland.
B Since they could not see beyond the coast, explorers thought the area was too small to be settled.
C Native people attacked the explorers with advanced weapons.
D They believed enemies were hiding in the thick coastal forests.

12 **Read the document and answer the questions that follow.**

After discovering Australia in April 1770, Captain James Cook sailed up the east coast. He and his crew often saw small groups of Aborigines along the water's edge.

> May 6. *No sort of cloathing* [clothing] *or ornaments were ever seen by any of us upon any one of them or in or about any of their hutts* [huts], *from which I conclude that they never wear any. Some we saw that had their faces and bodies painted with a sort of white paint or Pigment. Altho I have said that shell fish is their chief support yet they catch other sorts of fish some of which we found roasting on the fire the first time we landed, some of these they strike with gigs* [spears] *and others they catch with hook and line. . . . However we could know but very little of their customs as we never were able to form any connections with them, they had not so much as touch'd the things we had left in their hutts on purpose for them to take away.*
>
> —The Explorations of Captain James Cook in the Pacific

How does Captain Cook describe the people of Australia?

A Their skin was naturally white.
B They did not wear clothing or jewelry.
C They lived in small grass huts.
D They used traps to hunt small animals for food.

13 **What is the MOST LIKELY reason the people did not touch the items that Captain Cook and his crew left for them?**

A They were afraid and not sure what the items were.
B They already had the items and did not need any more.
C They wanted to show Captain Cook they did not like him.
D They wanted their enemies to take the items.

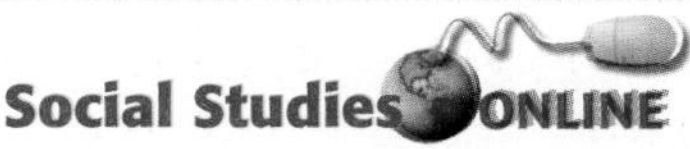

For additional test practice, use Self-Check Quizzes—Chapter 11 at glencoe.com.

Need Extra Help?

If You Missed Questions...	1	2	3	4	5	6	7	8	9	10	11	12	13
Go to Page...	341	342	343	343	347	347	348	350	350	342	342	347	347

CHAPTER 12

Australia Today

Essential Question

Place Australia today has a great variety of peoples and cultures. The continent's original inhabitants, the Aborigines, have managed to keep elements of their ancient culture alive. More recently, new arrivals from other lands have changed the cultural mix. With a healthy economy, Australia holds great promise for its residents. How does the mix of people and cultures make Australia unique?

BIG Ideas

Section 1: Culture and Lifestyles

BIG IDEA Culture groups shape human systems. Australians come from many different backgrounds. Most live along the coasts in cities, but some live in the country's hot interior. Tensions still exist over the issue of land claims by the country's native Aborigines.

Section 2: Challenges for Australia

BIG IDEA People's actions can change the physical environment. Australia has a successful economy. Economic activities range from ranching and mining to high-tech industries and tourism. Some concerns do exist about Australia's environment, however.

FOLDABLES™ Study Organizer

Categorizing Information Make this Foldable to help you summarize information about Australia today.

Step 1 Fold two sheets of paper on top of one another about 1 inch apart.

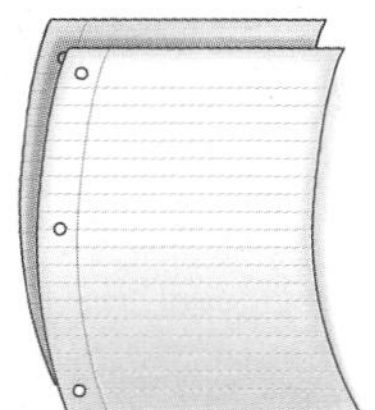

Step 2 Fold the paper to form 4 equal tabs.

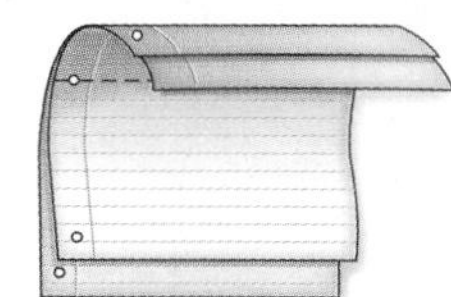

Step 3 Staple the sheets, and label each tab as shown.

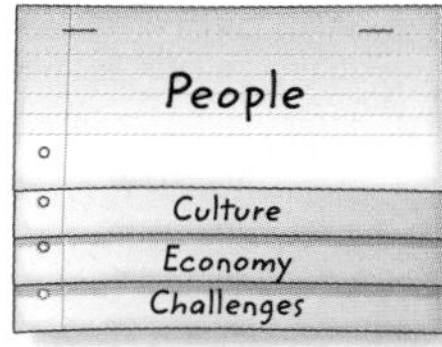

Reading and Writing
After you have finished taking notes in your Foldable, write a short essay describing one aspect of Australia today, either its people, culture, economy, or the challenges faced by Australians.

Visit glencoe.com and enter QuickPass™ code GA6EOW6225c12 for Chapter 12 resources.

Guide to Reading

BIG Idea

Culture groups shape human systems.

Content Vocabulary

- bush *(p. 357)*
- station *(p. 357)*
- lawsuit *(p. 359)*

Academic Vocabulary

- sustain *(p. 357)*
- consist *(p. 360)*
- generation *(p. 360)*

Reading Strategy

Making Generalizations Use a diagram like the one below. Write three important facts about Australia's people, culture, and daily life in the smaller boxes. Then, in the larger box, write a generalization that you can draw from those facts.

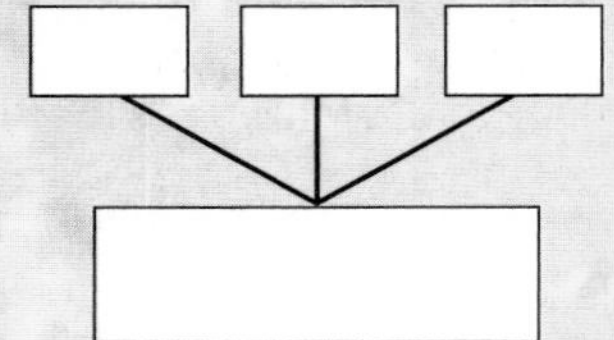

Cultures and Lifestyles

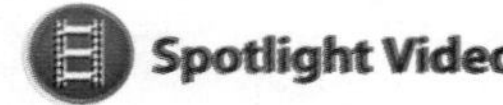

Picture This It is so hot on an Australian beach, you could fry an egg! Well, a fiberglass egg, that is. The artist who created this sculpture was inspired by people who lounge on Australian beaches, hoping for a bronze tan. The sculpture is part of a popular event in Sydney that celebrates the summer lifestyles of Australians. Sculptors from around the world, as well as from Australia, contribute more than 100 works of art to the beach display. Other sculptures have included a pair of oversized sunglasses. Read this section to learn more about the culture and lifestyles of the people of Australia.

▼ Celebrating Australian summers

Australia's People

Main Idea **Australia has an increasingly varied population.**

Geography and You Have you ever traveled a great distance without seeing any signs of human life? Read to learn about an area of Australia where one can travel 100 miles (161 km) without seeing another human being.

Australia has about 20.6 million people. They are not evenly spread out through Australia's vast territory, however. Much of the land is too dry or remote to **sustain,** or support, settlements. As a result, people tend to concentrate in just a few areas. Most Australians live in coastal areas that have a mild climate, fertile soil, and access to the ocean.

Urban and Rural Life

About 83 percent of Australia's people live in cities. The largest cities are in the southeast. Sydney has more than 4.1 million people, and Melbourne has more than 3.5 million. The cities of Brisbane, Perth, and Adelaide each have more than 1 million people. These cities are thriving commercial centers with modern buildings and transportation systems.

A small number of Australians live in rural areas, or the **bush.** Some of them work on cattle or sheep ranches, which Australians call **stations.** Others farm or work in mining camps. Because the outback is so large, settlements there are usually far apart.

More than 90 percent of Australia's population is of European descent. The largest groups are people of English, Irish, and Scottish ancestry. Other large groups include people of Italian and German heritage. Large numbers of immigrants have come to Australia from China, India, and other Asian countries in recent decades. People of Asian descent now make up about 6 percent of Australia's population. Aborigines make up less than 3 percent of Australia's people. Their numbers have risen sharply in the last few decades. English is the country's official language, though many different Aboriginal languages are still spoken.

Nearly two-thirds of Australia's people are Christians. Catholics form the largest part of this group. The arrival of Asian immigrants has increased the number of Buddhists and Muslims in recent decades.

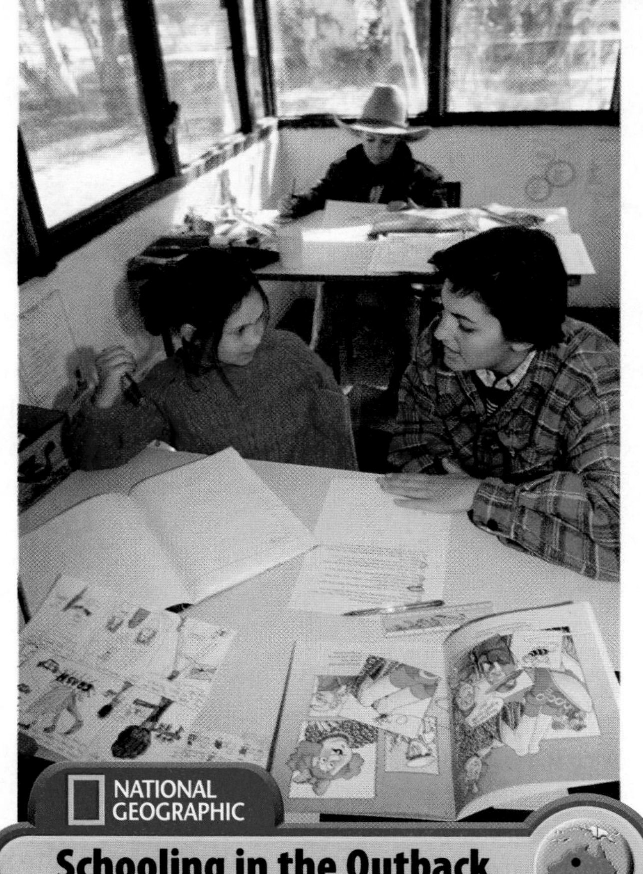

NATIONAL GEOGRAPHIC

Schooling in the Outback

Because ranches in Australia's outback are large and far apart, children often attend school in small classrooms on the ranch. ***Location*** **Where do most of Australia's people live?**

Social Studies ONLINE

Student Web Activity Visit glencoe.com and complete the Chapter 12 Web Activity about the Aborigines.

Garry Disher
(1949–)

Australian author Garry Disher grew up on a wheat and sheep farm that his family owned for generations. His stories capture the experience of living and working in north central Australia. Disher has won several awards for his work, including Australia's Children's Book of the Year Award in 1993 for *The Bamboo Flute.*

Background Information

The Bamboo Flute takes place in 1932. At that time, Australia was struggling with economic problems and a drought. Life was especially difficult for farmers and ranchers.

Reader's Dictionary

quarreling: arguing

paddock: an enclosed area for livestock

sodden: soaked through

THE BAMBOO FLUTE

By Garry Disher

There was once music in our lives, but I can feel it slipping away. Men are tramping the dusty roads, asking for work, a sandwich, a cup of tea. My father is bitter and my mother is sad. I have no brothers, no sisters, no after-school friends. The days are long. No one has time for music.

That's why I dream it.

I'm dreaming it now.

I'm dreaming a violin note, threading it through the **quarreling** cries of the dawn birds outside my window. . . .

The soft light of dawn is leaking through the gaps in the curtain. Five o'clock. I swing my feet on to the floor, drag on my clothes and boots, and leave the house.

My father is waiting for me at the **paddock** gate, his forearms on the top rail. . . .

He opens the gate and I follow him into the paddock. The grass is dewy this morning. Soon my boots feel lumpy and **sodden.**

The cows are in the farthest corner, of course. I watch my father tip back his throat and let out a whistle. . . .

Sometimes the cows respond, sometimes they don't. This time they don't, so we set out to fetch them. . . .

Milking is just one of the tasks in my endless day. After breakfast, there's a one-hour walk to school. Lessons, lunch, lessons—and rapped [tapped] knuckles when I fall asleep at my desk. Then the long walk home. Chop the firewood. Collect the eggs. Weed the vegetable patch. Homework. Teatime. Bedtime.

So I dream. Who wouldn't?

Analyzing Literature

1. **Making Inferences** Why does the boy say he can feel the music "slipping away"?
2. **Read to Write** Rewrite the passage above from the perspective of the father. Describe his thoughts and feelings.

Australia's Aborigines

Many Aborigines still hold to traditional ways and beliefs. The Aborigines believe in the idea of Dreamtime, the time long ago when they say wandering spirits created the world. They believe that all natural things—rocks, trees, plants, animals, and humans—have a spirit and are related to one another.

One of the major challenges facing Australians today involves the Aborigines. For years, Aborigines suffered discrimination from white Australians. Recently the government has tried to improve conditions for the Aborigines, but problems still exist. For example, Aborigines tend to receive less education than white Australians. Because they have a lower literacy rate, they also tend to work in lower-paying jobs and suffer more from poverty and poor health care.

In recent years, Aborigines have pushed more forcefully for their rights. In the late 1980s, a group of Aborigines tried to block mining on land they said belonged to their people. To do this, they filed a **lawsuit**, or a legal action in court intended to address a problem. In 1992 a court ruled that the Aborigines did indeed control the land and had the right to request that the mining be stopped. Later decisions in other cases extended Aborigines' control over land being used for sheep ranches and other activities.

These decisions opened the possibility that Aborigines could claim much of Australia's land. Other groups worried that they might lose their land to such claims. The government is trying to find a way to balance the claims of Aborigines and those of other landowners.

Reading Check **Describing** Describe Australia's urban/rural population pattern.

Australia's Culture and Daily Life

Main Idea Lifestyles in Australia reflect the cultures of its varied settlers, as well as that of the native Aborigines.

Geography and You Do people in your community have similar backgrounds, or are they different? How do their backgrounds affect local culture? Read to find out about the culture and daily life in Australia.

For hundreds of years, European traditions dominated the culture of Australia. Recently, Asian influences have grown, and Aboriginal culture has been revived. All these groups have an impact on the arts and daily life in Australia.

The arts in Australia draw from the past as well as the present. The Aborigines created paintings on rock and bark to tell about the relationship of humans to nature. They also use music and dance to celebrate their communities.

Melbourne, Australia

NATIONAL GEOGRAPHIC

Residents in Australia's large cities enjoy many conveniences, such as Melbourne's library, visible behind the sculpture in the foreground. ***Place*** **What area's traditions have dominated Australian culture?**

The land has also been a theme of much art created by Australians of European descent. Many novelists and artists have written and painted works inspired by the vast outback. Others focused on life in Australia's growing cities.

Architecture in Australia tended to mimic the styles of Britain until the late 1900s. In 1973, the Sydney Opera House opened. This new building won worldwide praise for its bold, modern design.

Australian films and filmmakers have also gained fame in recent years. Actor Hugh Jackman was born and raised in Australia. Nicole Kidman, born in the United States, grew up in and studied acting in Australia.

Most Australians of European descent live in nuclear families—parents and children only. Aboriginal communities **consist** of, or are made up of, several extended families. Extended families have relatives from three or four **generations,** or groups of people of about the same age, living together. Extended families often include grandparents as well as parents and children.

Australians enjoy many different types of outdoor sports. Two popular team sports are borrowed from other lands. Cricket, a game played with a bat and a ball, came from Britain. Australian national teams have won two world championships in this sport. Australian rules football is based on a version of football played in the British Isles. Other popular sports include swimming, horseback riding, and tennis.

Reading Check **Describing** Describe the impact of the country's landscape on Australia's arts.

Section 1 Review

Vocabulary

1. **Explain** the significance of
   - **a.** bush
   - **b.** station
   - **c.** lawsuit

Main Ideas

2. **Comparing and Contrasting** Use a Venn diagram like the one below to compare the lives of Aborigines and Australians of European descent.

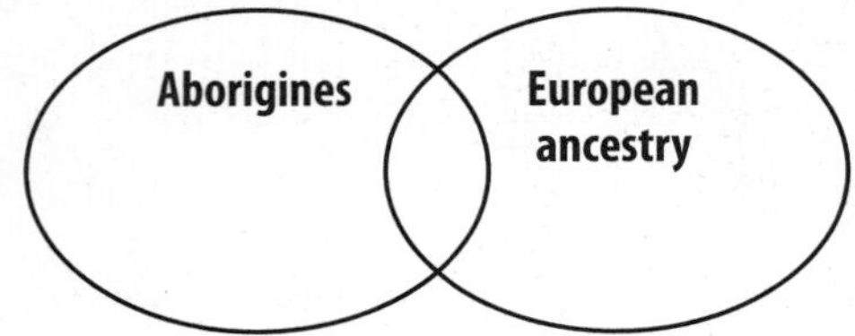

3. **Explaining** What issues have Australia's Aborigines faced in the past and continue to face today?

Critical Thinking

4. BIG Idea Why are the English language and Christianity dominant in Australia?
5. **Analyzing** Where do most of Australia's people live? Why?
6. **Challenge** How are European influences reflected in the lifestyles of the people of Australia?

Writing About Geography

7. **Persuasive Writing** Write an advertisement that the government of Australia could use to attract immigrants. Be sure to describe the benefits of moving to Australia.

TIME PERSPECTIVES

EXPLORING WORLD ISSUES

SAVING THEIR TREASURES

After years of neglect, New Zealand and Australia are working to preserve important cultures and natural resources.

A Maori and a New Zealander of European ancestry exchange a traditional Maori greeting.

New Zealand and Australia are nations with different ethnic groups—each group with its own rich culture and traditions. For nearly two centuries, European settlers and their descendants and local people—the Maori in New Zealand and the Aborigines in Australia—have lived side by side. But the groups have often struggled to accept and respect their differences.

Today, the two countries are working to preserve the cultures of each ethnic group and to work out their differences. Schools are teaching the language and traditions of local cultures. Governments are creating jobs for people. In addition to safeguarding cultural resources, Australia is working to save natural resources, such as the Great Barrier Reef. All threatened resources are treasures worth preserving.

MIKE POWELL/GETTY IMAGES

A Maori warrior wears the traditional dress.

A LONG STRUGGLE FOR RESPECT

For Angeline Greensill, the town of Raglan on New Zealand's North Island isn't just the place where she was born. The coastal town is also a link to her ancestors. She believes it is the home of Maori spirits who live on its green hills and sandy beaches. Greensill is a **Maori**, a native New Zealander. She and her family are members of the Tainui tribe, one of dozens of Maori ***iwis***, or tribes.

The Maori were the first people to reach New Zealand. Beginning around A.D. 600, they arrived in big canoes from islands in the Pacific Ocean and built a rich culture. They were primarily warriors who expressed themselves through songs, woodcarving, and tattooing. The Maori felt a deep connection to nature, their ancestors, and the land. "The earth is our mother," Greensill explained. "When we die, we go back to it."

A Battle to Survive

For nearly two hundred years, the Maori have been struggling to hold on to their culture and sacred land. In the 1820s, settlers from Great Britain began arriving in New Zealand in large numbers. Most settlers did not value Maori culture or their land rights. They moved onto Maori land and paid little or nothing for it. The Maori who tried to protect their land were often forced off it.

Most British were **ethnocentric**, or convinced their way of life was better than that of any other group. They believed the Maori would be better off if they gave up their traditional ways.

Maori Tribal Lands

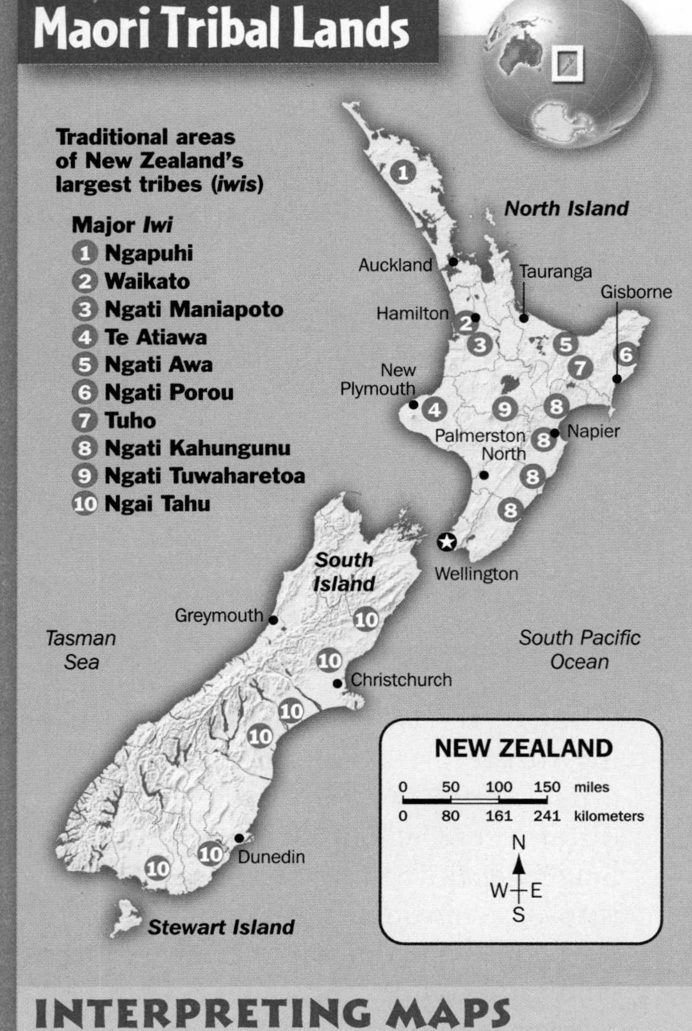

INTERPRETING MAPS

Identifying Which tribe settled the farthest north on North Island?

About 200 years ago, New Zealand was home to dozens of *iwis*, or tribes. The map shows where the largest tribes were located.

Children learn the Maori language at a school in New Zealand.

PAUL A. SOUDERS/CORBIS

Protestors at a rally demand fair treatment for the Maori.

NEIL RABINOWITZ/CORBIS

Keisha Castle-Hughes stars in *Whale Rider*, a movie about a Maori girl.

NEW ZEALAND FILM COMM/THE KOBAL COLLECTION

Broken Promises

In 1840 the colonial British and Maori tribal chiefs signed the **Treaty of Waitangi**. The treaty became New Zealand's founding document, much like the U.S. Declaration of Independence. In return for the right to rule New Zealand, the British promised to protect Maori land rights.

Over the next 150 years, however, the Maori lost control of most of their territory. Maori tribal chiefs sold some of it, but much of the land was taken by the government or illegally fenced off by British farmers. "The Maori started with 66 million acres," Greensill said. "By 1975, we had about 4 million."

Australia's Similar Mistakes

Australia's treatment of its original people, the **Aborigines**, resembles the treatment of the Maori in New Zealand. For 40,000 years the Aborigines lived throughout Australia. In 1788 British settlers arrived and immediately began to drive the Aborigines off their sacred tribal land. Many Aborigines who resisted the British were killed.

Righting Wrongs

How do you solve problems that began centuries ago? In recent years, New Zealand's government has been working to "close the gap" between its Maori citizens and those of European ancestry. To help keep Maori culture alive, schools are teaching the Maori language and traditions. The government is also working to provide the Maori with adequate jobs, health care, and housing. Since 2004, the Maori political party has represented the tribes in New Zealand's parliament.

The land ownership issue, however, has been difficult to resolve. The government cannot return land to the Maori without affecting the people who currently live on it. To address the land issues, the Waitangi Tribunal was established in 1975 to hear Maori land rights grievances. By June 2005, more than 1,200 Maori claims of land ownership had been registered with the tribunal. Some *iwis* have had their land returned, whereas others have been paid for land that they were forced to give up.

There is still a lot of work to be done, but by 2006, the gap between New Zealand's ethnic groups seemed a little smaller. "The future is looking good," Greensill said. "Maori people have a sense of awakening."

EXPLORING THE ISSUE

1. **Summarizing** What happened after the Treaty of Waitangi was signed?
2. **Making Inferences** How might the Waitangi Tribunal and the Maori political party help New Zealand's government create fair land rights policies?

SAVING AUSTRALIAN TREASURES

Ancient cultures are not the only endangered treasures in the South Pacific. In Australia, global warming is threatening a fragile ecosystem. The country's Great Barrier Reef is a chain of 2,900 coral reefs that stretches 1,240 miles (1,995 km) along the east coast. The giant ocean reef is home to thousands of fish, plants, and other marine life.

In recent years, some scientists believe that global warming is threatening to destroy the reef. As global warming heats the ocean's surface, a deadly situation called coral bleaching occurs. Coral contains tiny algae, or water plants, that give coral its vibrant color. Coral also uses the algae to create its food. At high temperatures, though, coral releases the algae. Without it, coral loses its beautiful color and dies. When the coral dies, so do many of the animals and plants that live in the reef. To save the aquatic ecosystem, Australia's government is studying ways to help the reef adapt to warmer waters.

REUTERS/WILL BURGESS

An animal rights activist protests the killing of kangaroos.

Human activity and pollution from fishermen and tourists have also done enormous damage to the reef. To decrease their impact, "no-take zones" were set up in 2004. No fishing or coral collecting is allowed in the zones.

Kangaroos Everywhere

Another **icon**, or symbol, of Australia is in danger of being damaged by human activity: the kangaroo. With 50 million of the pouched marsupials bouncing around, Australia's kangaroo population is immense. As they search for food, kangaroos often destroy farmland and cause car crashes. To control the kangaroo population, Australia's government permits a certain amount to be hunted.

Animal rights groups, however, are working to protect the kangaroos. They propose establishing safe places where tourists can view kangaroos in their natural habitat. "We want to promote kangaroos as part of the tourism industry," said one activist.

EXPLORING THE ISSUE

1. **Determining Cause and Effect** How might establishing "no-take zones" help preserve Australia's Great Barrier Reef?
2. **Explaining** Why might the creation of "safe places" for kangaroos help increase tourism in parts of Australia?

Tourists wade in the waters at the Great Barrier Reef.

REVIEW AND ASSESS

UNDERSTANDING THE ISSUE

1 **Making Connections** How did the Treaty of Waitangi fail to protect the rights of New Zealand's Maori tribes? How did British settlers' ethnocentric attitudes affect their relations with the Maori?

2 **Writing to Inform** Write a short article describing how Maori tribes lost their land to British settlers. Be sure to include the history of the Treaty of Waitangi.

3 **Writing to Persuade** Write a paragraph that starts with this sentence: Preserving the Great Barrier Reef is important because . . .

INTERNET RESEARCH ACTIVITIES

4 With your teacher's help, use Internet resources to learn more about Maori culture. Read about the history of the Maori language and the purpose of the Maori Language Commission. How important is language to a culture's survival? Write a short essay answering that question, using facts you find in your search.

5 Go to the Web site of the Great Barrier Reef Marine Park, www.gbrmpa.gov.au/. Click on the "Conservation, Heritage and Indigenous Partnerships" link. Read about the work being done to protect the many species and habitats found on the reef. Present your findings to your classmates.

BEYOND THE CLASSROOM

6 **Work in groups** to develop ways young people can learn about the culture and traditions of ethnic groups in your community. Write your suggestions on a poster. Include the names of social organizations that teach groups how to overcome the differences that exist between them. Bring the poster to class and display it.

7 **Visit your school or local library** to find books and articles on the impact of global warming on the Earth. Besides the Great Barrier Reef, research other ecosystems and species that are threatened by climate change. Discuss your findings with your friends and classmates.

A Natural Tourist Attraction

Human activity has had a huge effect on Australia's Great Barrier Reef. Here is a look at the number of tourists who have visited the fragile ecosystem in recent years.

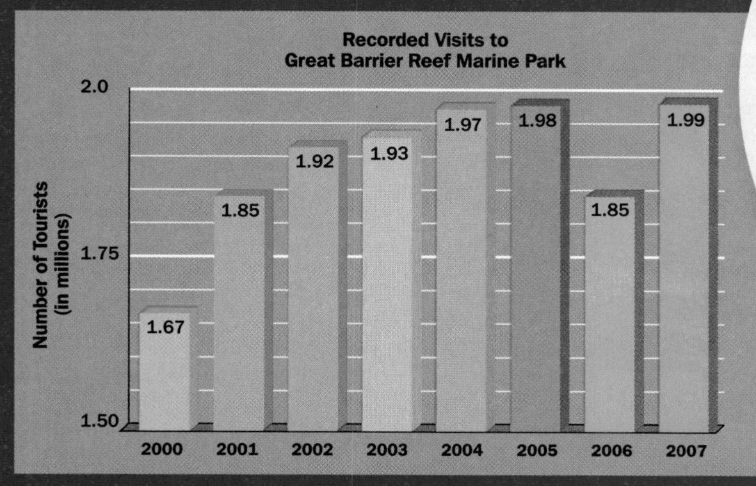

Source: Great Barrier Reef Marine Park Authority.

Building Chart Reading Skills

1. **Analyzing Information** How many more tourists visited the Great Barrier Reef Marine Park in 2007 than in 2000?
2. **Predicting** How might the increase in tourism to the Great Barrier Reef impact this fragile ecosystem?

Guide to Reading

BIG Idea

People's actions can change the physical environment.

Content Vocabulary

- merino *(p. 367)*
- pasture *(p. 368)*
- habitat *(p. 368)*

Academic Vocabulary

- extract *(p. 367)*
- establish *(p. 368)*

Reading Strategy

Organizing Use a format like the one below to make an outline of the section. Write each main heading on a line with a Roman numeral, then list important facts below it.

I. First Main Heading
  A. Key fact 1
  B. Key fact 2
II. Second Main Heading
  A. Key fact 1
  B. Key fact 2

Challenges for Australia

Picture This Australians love to spend time outdoors! Each year, Australians of all ages gather at beaches around the country to participate in surfing and swimming competitions. Young surfers also learn how to avoid hazardous ocean currents and dangerous animals. Australia is home to a number of species of plants and animals that do not exist anywhere else on earth. Many Australians are concerned about protecting their unique environment. Read this section to learn more about the challenges Australians face today.

Competition at children's surf carnival, Australia

Australia's Economy

Main Idea **Australia has a strong economy and its people have a generally high standard of living.**

Geography and You What types of products, agricultural or industrial, do businesses in your area produce? Read to learn what products Australia specializes in.

Australia has a mixed economy. Most businesses are owned privately, though the government plays a role in economic matters. It regulates businesses and provides all people with health care.

In recent years, Australia's economy has grown closer to those of Asian countries. Trade with China and other Asian nations has increased greatly. Trade with the United Kingdom, however, has dropped somewhat. In recent years, Australia's economy—based on its currency, the Australian dollar—has gained by cutting barriers to trade. More trade has led to greater prosperity.

Australia has a high literacy rate—nearly all of its people can read. A successful education system also aids the economy. Australian workers tend to hold good jobs with good salaries and are generally productive workers. They therefore enjoy a relatively high standard of living.

Australia's prosperous economy is partly based on the export of mineral and energy resources **extracted,** or removed, from the earth. These riches include coal, iron ore, gold, bauxite, oil, and natural gas. Other exports include gems, zinc, and lead. China and Japan purchase large amounts of these Australian resources. The mining industry holds great promise for Australia.

Australia's dry climate and poor soils limit farming. Irrigation, however, allows farmers to grow grains, cotton, sugarcane, fruits, and vegetables. The main agricultural activity, though, is raising cattle and sheep. Australia is a major exporter of wool, lamb, beef, and cattle hides. Many sheep raised in the country are **merinos**, a breed of sheep known for its fine wool.

In the mid-1900s, manufacturing became an important part of Australia's economy. Many factories there continue to produce processed foods, cars and trucks, cloth, and chemicals. Entrepreneurs involved in high-technology industries, service industries, and tourism also play a large role in the economy. Most of Australia's industries are located near Sydney and Melbourne.

Reading Check **Identifying** What is Australia's main agricultural activity?

Graphs In MOtion See StudentWorks™ Plus or glencoe.com.

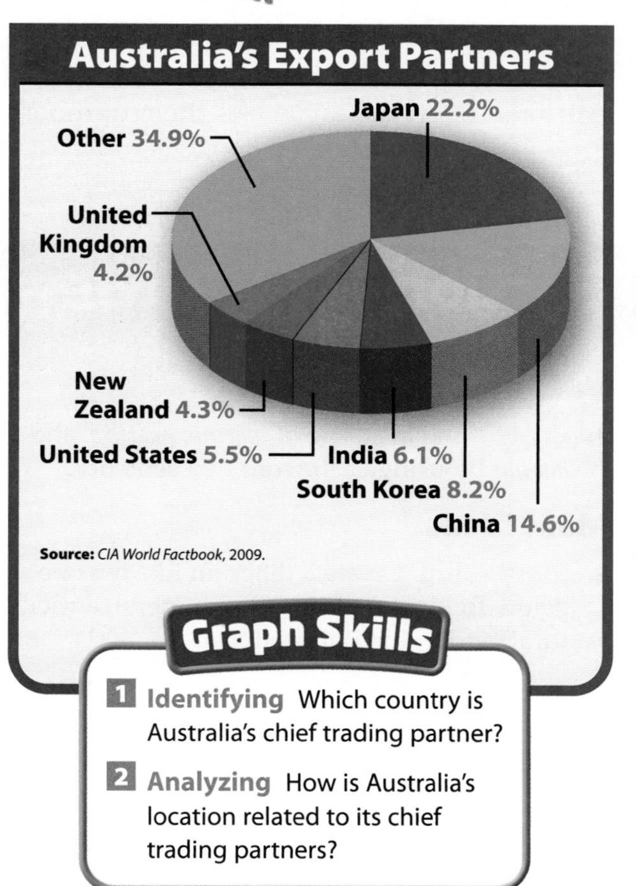

Australia's Challenges

Main Idea **Australia has a strong economy, but economic growth has created challenges for the environment.**

Geography and You Could introducing a new species of toad hurt the environment? Read to learn about Australia's environmental challenges.

Some economic activities have damaged Australia's land. Many trees have been cut down to provide more pasture for sheep. **Pasture** is the grasses and other plants that are feed for grazing animals. These actions, along with overgrazing by sheep and cattle, have removed plants and grasses that hold the soil. As a result, winds have blown away much of the topsoil.

In addition, Australia's native wildlife has been threatened by animals that settlers have brought into the country. In some cases, these animals have thrived in their new **habitats,** or living areas. As their numbers rose, native animals suffered. For instance, Hawaiian cane toads were introduced to eat insects that damage sugarcane crops. Unfortunately, the toads did not eat the insects. Their skin, however, contains poisons that kill other animals that eat the toads.

In some areas, mining operations have caused environmental problems. Also, coal is used to produce much of Australia's electricity. Many people worry about the pollution caused by burning coal.

Recently, steps have been taken to preserve the land. For instance, ranchers have cultivated new types of plants to feed their herds and to prevent overgrazing. Australian leaders are concerned about the possible harmful effects of climate change. They have **established,** or set up, goals for cutting the amount of fossil fuels burned in Australia.

Reading Check **Understanding Cause and Effect** Why was the Hawaiian cane toad introduced into Australia? What was the result?

Section 2 Review

Vocabulary

1. **Explain** the meaning of *merino, pasture,* and *habitat* by using each word in a sentence.

Main Ideas

2. **Identifying** Create a diagram like the one below to identify Australia's mineral, agricultural, and industrial products.

Mineral	Agricultural	Industrial

3. **Describing** Describe how Australia's trading partners have changed over the years.

Critical Thinking

4. **Analyzing** How do some of Australia's main exports depend on the country's land?
5. **BIG Idea** What economic activities pose challenges to the environment in Australia?
6. **Challenge** Do you think Australia will continue to be economically successful in the future? Explain your answer.

Writing About Geography

7. **Using Your FOLDABLES** Use your Foldable to write a paragraph explaining how Australia's economy or environment has changed in recent years.

Visual Summary

People of Australia

- Most of Australia's people are of European descent. The number of people of Asian and Aboriginal backgrounds has grown in recent years.
- Most of Australia's people live in cities near the coasts.
- The chief language and religions of Australia reflect European culture.
- The Aborigines still face problems in Australian society.

Sydney, Australia

Culture of Australia

- The arts and culture of the Aborigines go back thousands of years and are enjoying a modern revival.
- Australia's land has long served as a theme in the country's literature and art.
- Australia's film industry has grown in importance.

Exhibit of Aboriginal art

Daily Life

- Australians of European descent tend to live in nuclear families, while Aborigines often live in extended families.
- Australians enjoy a variety of outdoor sports, many of which came from Europe.

Cross-country bicycle race, Canberra, Australia

Economy

- Australia has a prosperous mixed economy dependent on trade.
- In recent years, Asian countries have become Australia's chief trading partners.
- Australia exports many minerals, including coal, iron ore, bauxite, gold, oil, and natural gas.
- The cattle and sheep industries are very important to Australia's economy.
- Manufacturing, services, and tourism are growing in economic importance.

Farmer feeding cattle near Brisbane, Australia

Environment

- Mining and ranching have caused some damage to the environment.
- Animals introduced from other lands are sometimes harmful to native animals.
- Australians are taking steps to protect the environment.

Study anywhere, anytime! Download quizzes and flash cards to your PDA from **glencoe.com**.

CHAPTER 12 ASSESSMENT

TEST-TAKING TIP

On a multiple-choice test, several answers may apply. Remember, however, that you are looking for the best answer.

Directions: Choose the best answer for each question.

1 **What type of economy does the following statement describe? Most businesses are privately owned in Australia, but they are regulated by the government.**

A mixed
B traditional
C command
D market

2 **Why is the mining industry expected to contribute to Australia's future economic growth?**

A Australia will have to rely on mining because it is losing money in the agriculture and manufacturing industries.
B Many of the country's unemployed workers are being trained as miners.
C Australia has a variety of mineral and energy resources that other countries need.
D Australian scientists have found a way to renew the declining supply of mineral and energy resources.

3 **How does Australia's literacy rate MOST LIKELY affect the country's standard of living?**

A Its high literacy rate means that most citizens move to other countries for better jobs, decreasing the standard of living in Australia.
B Its low literacy rate means most citizens work in jobs that require little education, lowering Australia's standard of living.
C Its high literacy rate means that its citizens have higher-paying jobs, increasing the standard of living.
D Its high literacy rate means there are too many educated people for the number of available jobs, so unemployment is high and the standard of living is low.

4 **What percentage of Australia's citizens are European descendants?**

A 50 percent
B 90 percent
C 80 percent
D 30 percent

5 **Why do most Australians live along the coasts?**

A There are no transportation routes to the interior region of the country.
B The mild temperatures and fertile soil provide comfortable living conditions and good farming conditions.
C Most of Australia's mineral resources are located along its coasts.
D People cannot live anywhere else because mountains prevent them from moving inland.

6 **Which of the following statements best describes the current situation of the Aborigines?**

A They receive more education than white Australians.
B They are not allowed to vote or own property.
C They own most of the land in Australia.
D They suffer more from poverty and poor health care.

7 **How do cattle and sheep farmers contribute to Australia's economic growth?**

A They export the meat, sheep's wool, and cattle hides to other countries.
B They make clothing from the sheep's wool and cattle hides to export.
C They sell the milk and other dairy products to developing countries.
D They only sell the meat and other products to Australians.

8 **Which of the following statements is most accurate?**

A Most of Australia's trade is with the United Kingdom.
B Australia's trade with Asian countries has greatly increased in recent years.
C Australia's main exports are fruits and grains.
D Australia's economy depends on its banking industry.

9 **Look at the chart and answer the questions that follow.**

Religious Membership of Australians	
Religion	**Percent**
Catholic	25.8
Anglican (the English Church)	18.7
Other Christian	16.6
Eastern Orthodox	2.7
Buddhist	2.1
Muslim	1.7
Unspecified or other	13.7
None	18.7
Source: www.cia.gov, *The World Factbook*, 2009.	

Which group has the largest membership of Australians?

A Anglican
B Buddhist
C Catholic
D Eastern Orthodox

10 **According to the chart, what percentage of Australians do not practice a religion?**

A 18.7 percent
B 13.7 percent
C 16.6 percent
D 1.7 percent

11 **Why are most Australians Christians?**

A Christianity is the most popular religion worldwide.
B Europeans brought their religious beliefs with them when they settled in Australia.
C Australia is geographically closer to the birthplace of Christianity than it is to the birthplace of any other religion.
D The leaders of other religions have left Australia in recent years.

12 **Read the document and answer the questions that follow.**

The following Australian government report describes the lasting effect of European colonization on the health of the Aborigines.

The Health and Welfare of Australia's Aboriginal and Torres Strait Islander Peoples, 2003

The diseases and conditions examined . . . include circulatory system diseases, diabetes, . . . kidney disease, cancer, respiratory diseases, communicable diseases, injury and poisoning, vision and hearing problems, oral health and mental health. For most of these conditions Indigenous peoples [Aborigines] had higher prevalence [occurrence] rates, higher hospitalisation rates and higher death rates than non-Indigenous Australians. Moreover, some of the chronic [long-lasting] diseases described here are diagnosed at a younger age in Indigenous persons than non-Indigenous persons, resulting in a lower quality of life at younger ages and premature mortality [death].

—Australian Institute of Health and Welfare

According to the document, what do many Aborigines suffer from?

A diseases that affect only the respiratory system
B allergies caused by pollution
C nervous system diseases
D a wide range of diseases and medical conditions

13 **What is the MOST LIKELY reason these diseases occur often in Aborigines?**

A They live in old, overcrowded housing.
B They receive poor education and medical care.
C They have weak immune systems inherited from their ancestors.
D They work dangerous jobs that other Australians refuse.

For additional test practice, use Self-Check Quizzes—Chapter 12 at glencoe.com.

Need Extra Help?

If You Missed Questions...	1	2	3	4	5	6	7	8	9	10	11	12	13
Go to Page...	367	367	367	357	357	359	367	367	357	357	357	359	359

Appendix

Contents

What Is an Appendix?

What Is an Appendix?

An appendix is the additional material you often find at the end of books. The following information will help you learn how to use the Appendix in *Georgia's Exploring Our World: People, Places, and Cultures.*

Personal Finance Handbook

The Personal Finance Handbook introduces money management skills. You will learn about saving, spending, and investing.

Skills Handbook

The Skills Handbook offers you information and practice using critical thinking and social studies skills. Mastering these skills will help you in all your courses.

Gazetteer

The Gazetteer (GA·zuh·TIHR) is a geographical dictionary. It lists many of the world's largest countries, cities, and important geographic features. Each entry also includes a page number telling where the place is shown on a map in the textbook.

English-Spanish Glossary

A glossary is a list of important or difficult terms found in a textbook. The glossary gives a definition of each term as it is used in the book. The glossary also includes page numbers telling you where in the book the term is used. Since words may have additional meanings, you may wish to use a dictionary to find other uses for them.

In *Georgia's Exploring Our World: People, Places, and Cultures,* the Spanish glossary is included with the English glossary. The Spanish term is located directly across from the English term. A Spanish glossary is especially important to bilingual students, or those Spanish-speaking students who are learning the English language.

Index

The Index is an alphabetical listing that includes the subjects of the book and the page numbers where those subjects can be found. The index in this book also lets you know that certain pages contain maps, graphs, photos, or paintings about the subject.

Acknowledgments

This section lists photo credits and literary credits for the book. You can look at this section to find out where the publisher obtained the permission to use a photograph or to use excerpts from other books.

Test Yourself

Find the answers to these questions by using the Appendix on the following pages.

1. What does *famine* mean?
2. Where did you find what the word *famine* means?
3. What is the Spanish word for *availability?*
4. What skill is discussed on page 392?
5. What are the latitude and longitude of Moscow?
6. On what pages can you find information about the government of the United Kingdom?

Personal Finance Handbook

Contents

Money Management: Income

Why Salaries Differ

A salary is the amount of money a person is paid for doing his or her job. People earn different salaries for a variety of reasons. Sometimes it's due to the type of industry in which they work; other times it's because of where their job is located. One of the most important factors that influences a person's salary is the amount of education he or she has achieved.

The chart below shows how much a person's weekly income is directly affected by the level of education achieved.

Average Weekly Income (in Dollars)	Level of Education Achieved
1,555	Doctoral degree
1,228	Master's degree
978	Bachelor's degree
736	Associate degree
645	Some college, no degree
591	High school graduate
426	Less than a high school diploma

Source: *Bureau of Labor Statistics, Current Population Survey,* 2008.

Most people would like to work in a career that is interesting and financially rewarding. Sometimes, however, this is difficult to achieve. To plan for your future career, you should consider your skills, interests, and the amount of money you would like to earn.

For example, you might like to play basketball, but you may not have all the skills needed to become a professional basketball player. You should think about the skills you do have when you consider a career. If you are good at math, for instance, you might think about working in computer science, engineering, or accounting.

Analyzing Economics

1. **Calculating** What is the difference in average weekly income between a high school graduate and a person with a bachelor's degree?
2. **Making Generalizations** Describe how income is directly affected by the level of education a person has achieved.

Money Management: Income

Two Types of Income

As you grow older and find a job, you will earn an income. You have the right to spend your income on whatever you want. Like most people, however, you must make choices about buying the things you *need* versus buying the things you *want.*

Before you receive your paycheck, taxes for federal and local governments are usually deducted, or subtracted, from it. The money that people earn before taxes are paid is called **gross pay.** Once taxes are subtracted from their gross pay, people are left with their **net pay.** Net pay is known as **disposable income.** This income is used to pay for things you need such as clothing, food, or utility bills.

After these expenses are paid, the remaining money is known as **discretionary income.** Discretionary income is used to pay for goods and services that people *want* rather than what they *need.*

The charts below reflect disposable income and discretionary income. Chart #1 is an employee's paycheck stub. Chart #2 lists the expenses that the employee must pay each month.

Chart #1

	Amount
Gross Pay	$1,041.60
Federal Income	–$82.19
Social Security Tax	–$64.59
Medicare Tax	–$15.11
State Income Tax	–$34.27
City Income Tax	–$3.14
Net Pay	$842.30

Chart #2

Expenses	Monthly Cost
Rent	$350
Food	$170
Clothing	$50
Electricity	$65
Telephone	$25
Total	$660

Analyzing Economics

1. **Calculating** In Chart #1, how much disposable income does the employee have each month? Using both charts, how much discretionary income does the person have?
2. **Analyzing** Which type of income would you use to pay for a car? A medical bill? Dinner at a restaurant?

Money Management: Spending

Personal Finance Handbook

Everyone Pays Opportunity Costs

When we choose to do one thing over another, we make a **trade-off.** We choose to give up one thing in order to get something else. An example of a trade-off might be if you studied for a test instead of attending a soccer game with friends. You give up your time to visit and have fun with your friends in order to earn a passing grade.

When we make a trade-off, we pay an **opportunity cost.** Opportunity cost is the cost of the next best use of your time or money when you choose to do one thing rather than another.

Everyone pays opportunity costs. Every time you spend money, you give up the chance to buy something else. For example, Sandy earns $80 a week at her part-time job. This week she has two ways she could spend her money: a brake repair that her car needs immediately or dinner with her friends.

Below is a decision-making chart that Sandy created to help her decide how she should spend her money.

Problem	Possible Solutions	Consequences of Choices
Should I spend my money on my car that needs a brake repair or go out for a nice dinner with friends?	**1. Pay $75 for brake repair and go to dinner with friends another time** **2. Spend money on dinner and wait to get a brake repair**	**1. My car is safe to drive, but I won't be able to have fun at dinner with my friends.** **2. I will have fun with friends, but I will not be able to drive my car because it is unsafe.**

To make a decision using a chart like the one above, you would:

- identify the problem;
- list the possible solutions to be made and their consequences;
- evaluate each choice by its consequences; and
- make a decision.

Analyzing Economics

1. **Evaluating** How should Sandy spend her $80?
2. **Explaining** Based on your answer to Question 1, what are her opportunity costs?

Money Management: Spending

Long-Term Goals and Buying Decisions

Long-term goals, such as buying a computer or paying for a college education, are important to remember when you make everyday buying decisions. How can you stay focused on your long-term goals when you are tempted to spend your money today?

In order to understand how you are spending your money, track your expenses. Make a list of all the items that you buy for several weeks. Then you can analyze your spending habits.

Next, use your list to create a budget like the one below. A budget identifies how much money you can spend based upon how much income you earn. For example, a student makes $40 a week at a steady job. The budget below reflects how the student spends that income each week.

Expenses	Weekly Cost
Entertainment	**$10**
Clothing	**$10**
School lunches	**$12**
Gifts	**$3**
Savings (long-term goal)	**$5**
Total	**$40**

You can adjust your budget by changing your spending habits. If you spend less money in one or more categories, you might use this money to help you reach your long-term goals more quickly.

Analyzing Economics

1. **Identifying** Using the budget above, which category would be the most difficult to cut spending in?
2. **Calculating** Think about your own expenses. Create a budget that shows how you would spend your money if you made $40 every week.

Money Management: Credit

Cash or Credit?

When people use credit cards, they are able to make purchases without paying cash. They are borrowing money from the bank that issued the card so they can immediately purchase items. Then they will repay that money later.

Credit cards have advantages and disadvantages.

Advantages	Disadvantages
• Buy items now • No need to carry cash • Creates a record of purchases • Combines bills into one payment	• Interest charges increase the item's cost • Might lose track of your spending • Can lead to impulse buying

A credit card company charges you a fee called **interest** for loaning you their money. Interest is based on the amount of money you borrowed, and is usually a percentage. The interest rate is called the **annual percentage rate (APR).**

If you immediately pay back the entire amount you borrowed, you pay $0 in interest. However, if you delay making a payment, you might owe interest. For example, let's say you used your credit card to buy a $50 pair of shoes, and the credit card company charges a 21.0 percent APR.

Multiply the price of the shoes by the APR:	$50.00 x 21.0 percent = $10.50
Add the amount of interest to your original purchase:	$50.00 + $10.50 = $60.50
Final cost of shoes:	$60.50

Should you pay for an item with a credit card or cash? Ask yourself the following questions.

- Do I really need this item? Can I buy it later?
- If I pay cash, what will I give up that I could use the cash for?
- Can I afford to pay back the amount I owe on the credit card?

Analyzing Economics

1. **Describing** How could a person avoid credit card debt?
2. **Analyzing** Why might consumers hesitate to use credit cards if people are losing their jobs throughout the country?

Money Management: Savings

How Your Savings Helps the Economy

Do you dream of owning a car? Going to college? One way to pay for these things is by saving your money. To **save** means to set aside part of your income so you have it to use later.

If you save your money in a box or a drawer, you are the only one who benefits. However, if you save your money in a bank, the whole community benefits. When people or businesses ask a bank for a loan, bank officials loan them the money from savings accounts. The people who borrow the money agree to pay it back with interest.

Follow the diagram below that shows what happens to your money when you deposit it in a bank.

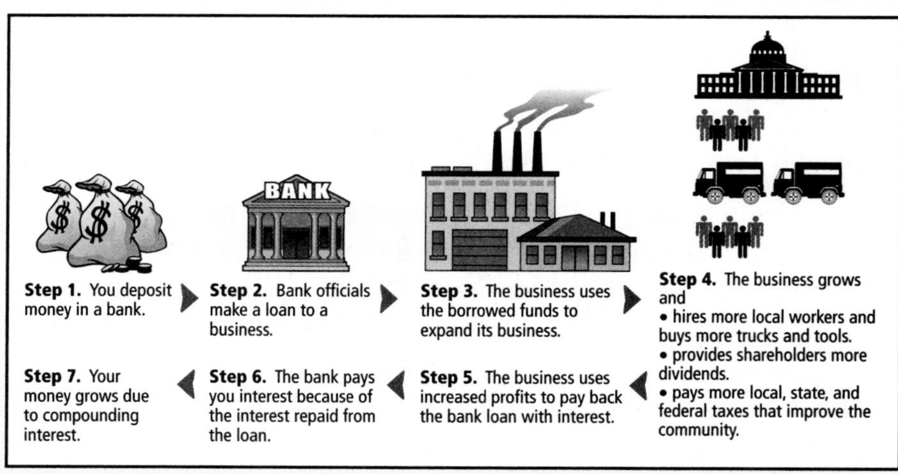

Some savings accounts earn **compounded interest.** This means that when the bank calculates the interest it owes you, it determines the amount based on the entire amount of money you have in your account—including the interest you've already earned. This type of account allows you to make even more money than you started with.

Analyzing Economics

1. **Identifying** Using the illustration above, what does the business use to repay the loan plus interest?
2. **Analyzing** What should you consider before you decide how much money to save?

Money Management: Investing

Investing

What will you do with money you earn from your jobs? How will you plan to buy a car or a house? Most people try to save their money for future needs. By investing, however, people not only save their money, but they can also earn additional money to achieve their financial goals. People can earn **interest,** or a payment for lending their money, on funds they save and invest.

Look at the chart below to see the different ways people save and invest.

Ways to Save and Invest	
Certificates of Deposit	When you buy a **certificate of deposit (CD)**, you promise to keep your money in the bank for a certain amount of time. The money in your account earns interest.
Stocks	When you buy **stock** in a company, you become one of its owners. The more stocks you buy, the more of the company you own.
Bonds	When you buy a **bond**, you are lending your money to a company. The company promises to return your money plus pay you interest on a specific date in the future. City, state, and federal governments also sell bonds.
Mutual Funds	When you invest in a **mutual fund**, a financial expert combines your money with the money of other investors. The entire amount is used to buy a variety of stocks and bonds. The stocks and bonds are then put into a fund called a mutual fund.

Analyzing Economics

1. **Contrasting** What is the difference between a stock and a bond?
2. **Explaining** What might be an advantage of investing your money in many different types of stocks and bonds?

Skills Handbook

Contents

Interpreting Political Cartoons

Why Learn This Skill?

Political cartoons express opinions through art. The cartoons appear in newspapers, magazines, books, and on the Internet. Political cartoons usually focus on public figures, political events, or economic or social conditions. This type of art can give you a summary of an event or circumstance, along with the artist's opinion, in an entertaining way.

1 Learn It!

Follow these steps to interpret political cartoons:

- Read the title, caption, or conversation balloons. They help you identify the subject of the cartoon.
- Identify the characters or people in the cartoon. They may be caricatures, or unrealistic drawings that exaggerate the characters' physical features.
- Identify any symbols. Symbols are objects that stand for something else. An example is the American flag, which is a symbol of our country. Commonly recognized symbols may not be labeled. Unusual symbols might be labeled.
- Examine the actions in the cartoon—what is happening and why?
- Identify the cartoonist's purpose. What statement or idea is he or she trying to express? Decide if the cartoonist wants to persuade, criticize, or just make people think.

2 Practice It!

On a separate sheet of paper, answer these questions about the political cartoon below.

1. What is the subject of the cartoon?

2. What words give clues to the meaning of the cartoon?

3. What item seems out of place?

4. What message do you think the cartoonist is trying to send?

3 Apply It!

Bring a newsmagazine to class. With a partner, analyze the message in each political cartoon you find in the magazine.

Predicting

Why Learn This Skill?

You have probably read about people making difficult decisions based on something they think *might* happen. You will have a better understanding of why people make certain choices when you consider the factors that influenced their decisions.

1 Learn It!

As you read a paragraph or section in your book, think about what might happen next. What you think will happen is your *prediction*. A prediction does not have a correct or incorrect answer. A prediction is an educated guess of what might happen next based on facts.

To make a prediction, ask yourself:

- What happened in this paragraph or section?
- What prior knowledge do I have about the information in the text?
- What similar circumstances do I know of?
- What do I think might happen next?
- Test your prediction: read further to see if you were correct.

▲ Aztec shield

2 Practice It!

To practice the skill, read the following paragraphs about the Aztec Empire. Then answer the questions.

In the late 1400s and early 1500s, Spanish explorers arrived in the Americas. They were greatly impressed by the magnificent cities and the great riches of the Native Americans.

In 1519 a Spanish army led by Hernán Cortés landed on Mexico's Gulf coast. He and about 600 soldiers marched to Tenochtitlán, which they had heard was filled with gold.

1. Choose the outcome that is most likely to occur between the Native Americans and the Spaniards.
   a. The Spaniards will conquer the Native Americans.
   b. The Native Americans will conquer the Spaniards.
   c. The two groups will become friends.
2. What clues in the text help you make your prediction?

3 Apply It!

Watch a television show or a movie. Halfway through the show, write down your prediction of how it will end. At the end of the show, check your prediction. Were you correct? What clues did you use to make your prediction?

Analyzing Library and Research Resources

Why Learn This Skill?

Imagine that your teacher asked you to write a report about the physical geography of Australia using library or Internet resources. Knowing how to choose sources that contain accurate information will help you save time in the library or on the Internet. You will also be able to write a better report.

1 Learn It!

Not all sources will be useful for your report on Australia's physical geography. Even some sources that involve topics about Australia will not always provide the information you want. In analyzing sources for your research project, choose items that are nonfiction and that contain the most information about your topic.

When choosing research resources, ask these questions:

- Is the information up-to-date?
- Does a book's index have several page references listed for the topic?
- Is the research written in a way that is easy to understand?
- Are there helpful illustrations and photos?

2 Practice It!

Look at the following list of sources. Which would be most helpful in writing a report on the physical geography of Australia? Explain your choices.

(1) A current travel guide to Australia

(2) A book about Australia's landforms and climates

(3) A children's storybook about an Australian kangaroo

(4) A student's notes on the Internet about a family trip to Australia

(5) A study of the rise and fall of the British Empire

(6) A Web site with physical maps of Australia

(7) A book about Australian government

(8) A geographical dictionary

3 Apply It!

Go to your local library or use the Internet to create a bibliography of sources you might use to write a report on the physical geography of Australia. Explain why you chose each source.

Uluru (Ayers Rock) in central Australia

Interpreting a Chart

Why Learn This Skill?

To make learning easier, you can organize information into groups of related facts and ideas. One way to organize information is with a chart. A chart presents written or numerical information in columns and rows. It helps you to remember and compare information more easily.

Learn It!

To organize information in a chart, follow these steps:

- Decide what information you must organize.
- Identify several major categories of ideas or facts about the topic, and use these categories as column headings.
- Find information that fits into each category, and write those facts or ideas under the appropriate column heading.

2 Practice It!

On a separate sheet of paper, answer the following questions using the chart at the bottom of this page.

1. What type of information does the chart contain?
2. What other related information appears in the chart?
3. Canada also exports clothing and beverages to the United States. Is it necessary to create a new chart to show this information?

3 Apply It!

Create a chart to track your school assignments. Work with five areas of information: Subject, Assignment, Description, Due Date, and Date Completed. Be sure to keep your chart up-to-date.

U.S. International Trade

	Japan	United Kingdom	Canada
Exports to U.S.	**Engines, rubber goods, cars, trucks, buses**	**Dairy products, beverages, petroleum products**	**Wheat, minerals, paper, mining machines**
Value of Exports to U.S.	**$138 billion**	**$51.1 billion**	**$287.9 billion**
Imports from U.S.	**Meat, fish, sugar, tobacco, coffee**	**Fruit, tobacco, electrical equipment**	**Fish, sugar, metals, clothing**
Value of Imports from U.S.	**$55.4 billion**	**$38.6 billion**	**$211.3 billion**

Source: *CIA World Factbook*, 2006; *United States Census Bureau, Foreign Trade Statistics*, 2005.

Making Comparisons

Why Learn This Skill?

Suppose you want to buy a portable CD player, and you must choose among three models. To make this decision, you would probably compare various features of the three models, such as price, sound quality, size, and so on. After you compare the models, you will choose the one that is best for you. In your studies of world geography, you must often compare countries of the world to identify patterns, make predictions, or make generalizations about regions.

Learn It!

When making comparisons, you identify and examine two or more places, peoples, economies, or forms of government. Then you identify any similarities between two topics, or ways the two topics are alike.

When making comparisons, apply the following steps:

- Decide what topics to compare. Clue words such as *also, as well as, like, same as,* and *similar to* can help you identify when topics are being compared.
- Read the information about each topic carefully.
- Identify what information is similar for both topics.

Practice It!

To practice the skill, analyze the information in the chart at the bottom of this page. Then answer these questions.

1. What countries are being compared?
2. What categories for each country are being compared?
3. In what ways are the United States and the United Kingdom similar?
4. Suppose you wanted to compare the two countries in more detail. What other categories might you use?

Apply It!

Think about two sports that are played at your school. Make a chart comparing categories such as where the games are played, who plays them, what equipment is used, and so on.

The United States and the United Kingdom

	United States	United Kingdom
Location	North America	Europe
Language	English	English
Form of Government	Federal republic	Constitutional monarchy
Popular Sports	Baseball, football, basketball	Soccer, rugby, cricket
Popular Foods	Hamburgers, hot dogs	Fish and chips, roast beef

Analyzing Primary Sources

Skills Handbook

Why Learn This Skill?

People who study history examine pieces of evidence to reconstruct events. These types of evidence—both written and illustrated—are called *primary sources*. Examining primary sources can help you understand the history of a place.

 Learn It!

Primary sources are firsthand accounts that describe a historical event or time period. They can include letters, diaries, photographs and pictures, news articles, legal documents, stories, literature, and artwork.

Ask yourself the following questions when analyzing primary sources:

- What is the primary source?
- Who created it?
- Where is it from?
- When was it created?
- What does it reveal about the topic I am studying?

 Practice It!

The following primary source is from *The Log of Christopher Columbus*. Christopher Columbus reached the new world on October 12, 1492. Columbus's entry explains what occurred when he and his shipmates encountered Native Americans. Read the entry, and then answer the questions that follow.

> *October 12:*
>
> *The people here called this island* Guanahani *in their language, and their speech is very fluent [easily flowing], although I do not understand any of it. They are friendly . . . people who [bear] no arms except for small spears, and they have no iron. I showed one my sword, and through ignorance he grabbed it by the blade and cut himself. . . .*
>
> *. . . They traded and gave everything they had with good will, but it seems to me that they have very little and are poor in everything. . . .*
>
> *This afternoon the people of San Salvador came swimming to our ships and in boats made from one log. They brought us parrots, balls of cotton thread, spears, and many other things. . . . For these items we swapped them little glass beads and hawks' bells.*
>
> —*The Log of Christopher Columbus*

1. Why did Columbus believe that the Native Americans had no knowledge about weapons?
2. Does Columbus fear the Native Americans? Explain.
3. What items did Columbus and his crew exchange with the Native Americans?
4. Why is this reading a primary source?

 Apply It!

Find a primary source from your past, such as a photo, newspaper clipping, or diary entry. Explain to the class what it shows about that time in your life.

Recognizing Bias

Why Learn This Skill?

If you say, "Cats make better pets than dogs," you are stating a bias. A *bias* is an attitude that favors one way of thinking over another. It can prevent you from looking at a situation in a reasonable or truthful way.

1 Learn It!

Most people have feelings and ideas that affect their point of view on a subject. Their viewpoint, or *bias*, influences the way they interpret events. For this reason, an idea that is stated as a fact may really be only an opinion. Recognizing bias will help you judge the accuracy of what you read.

To recognize bias, follow these steps:

- Identify the speaker or writer and examine his or her views. Why did he or she speak or write about a particular issue?
- Look for language that shows emotion or opinion. Look for words such as *all, never, best, worst, might*, or *should*.
- Examine the information for imbalances. Is it written from one point of view? Does it take into consideration other points of view?
- Identify statements of fact. Factual statements usually answer the *who, what, where*, and *when* questions.
- Does the writer use facts to support his or her point of view?

2 Practice It!

Read the following statement about wildlife in Africa, and answer the questions below.

Mountain gorillas live in the misty mountain forests of East Africa. Logging and mining, however, are destroying the forests. Unless the forests are protected, the gorillas will lose their homes and disappear forever. As a concerned African naturalist, I must emphasize that this will be the worst event in Africa's history.

1. What problem is the speaker addressing?
2. What reasons does the speaker give for the loss of the forests?
3. What is the speaker's point of view, or bias?
4. What words give clues as to the speaker's bias?

3 Apply It!

Choose a letter from the editorial page of a newspaper. Summarize the issue being discussed and the writer's bias about the issue. Describe a possible opposing opinion and who might have it and why.

Mountain gorilla

Interpreting a Circle Graph

Why Learn This Skill?

Have you ever watched someone serve pieces of pie? When the pie is cut evenly, everyone's slice is the same size. If one slice is cut a little larger, however, someone else gets a smaller piece. A *circle graph* is like a sliced pie. In fact, a circle graph is also called a pie chart. In a circle graph, the complete circle represents a whole group—or 100 percent. The circle is divided into "slices," or wedge-shaped sections representing parts of the whole.

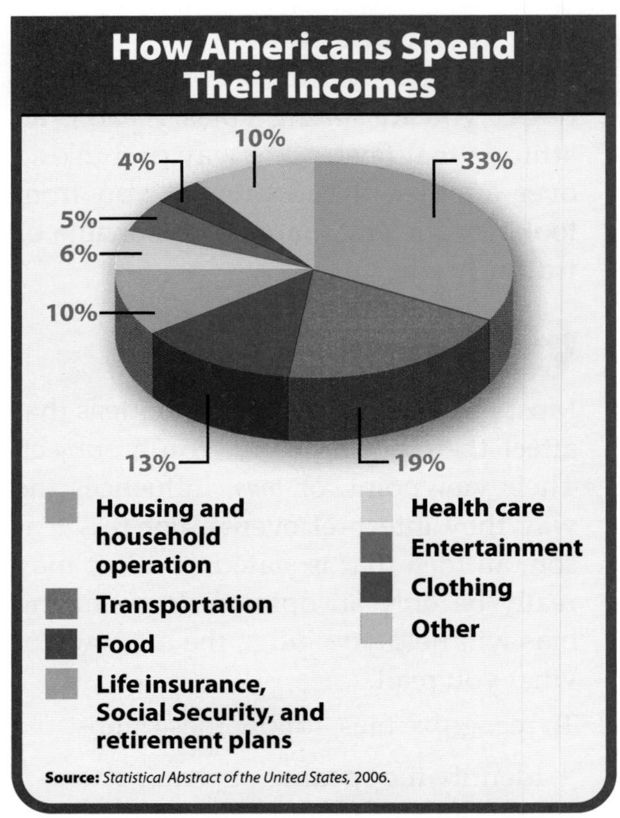

1 Learn It!

To read and interpret a circle graph, follow these steps:

- Read the title of the circle graph to find the subject.
- Study the labels or the key to see what each "slice" represents.
- Compare the sizes of the circle slices.

2 Practice It!

Study the circle graph on this page, and answer the following questions.

1. What is the subject of the circle graph?
2. On what do Americans spend most of their incomes?
3. On what do Americans spend the least portion of their incomes?
4. What is the total percentage of income spent on transportation and food?

3 Apply It!

Quiz 10 friends about the capitals of India, Pakistan, and Bangladesh. Create a circle graph showing what percentage knew (a) all three capitals; (b) two capitals; (c) one capital; or (d) no capitals.

Sequencing Events

Why Learn This Skill?

Have you ever had to remember events and their dates in the order in which they happened? *Sequencing* means listing facts in the correct order that they occurred. A time line helps you do this. A time line is a diagram that shows how dates and events relate to one another. The years are evenly spaced along most time lines. Events on time lines are described beside the date on which they occurred.

Learn It!

To understand how to sequence events, follow these steps:

- As you read, look for dates or clue words that hint at chronological order, such as *in 2006, the late 1900s, first, then, finally,* and *after*.
- To read a time line, find the dates on the opposite ends of the time line. These dates show the range of time that is covered.
- Note the equal spacing between dates on the time line.
- Study the order of events.
- Look to see how the events relate to one another.

Practice It!

Examine the time line on this page and answer the following questions.

1. When does the time line begin? When does it end?
2. What major event happened in the late 1700s?
3. Did the Civil War begin before or after the United States entered World War I?
4. During what decade did the Cold War end?

Apply It!

List key events from one of the chapters in your textbook that covers the history of a region. Create a time line that lists these events in the order they occurred.

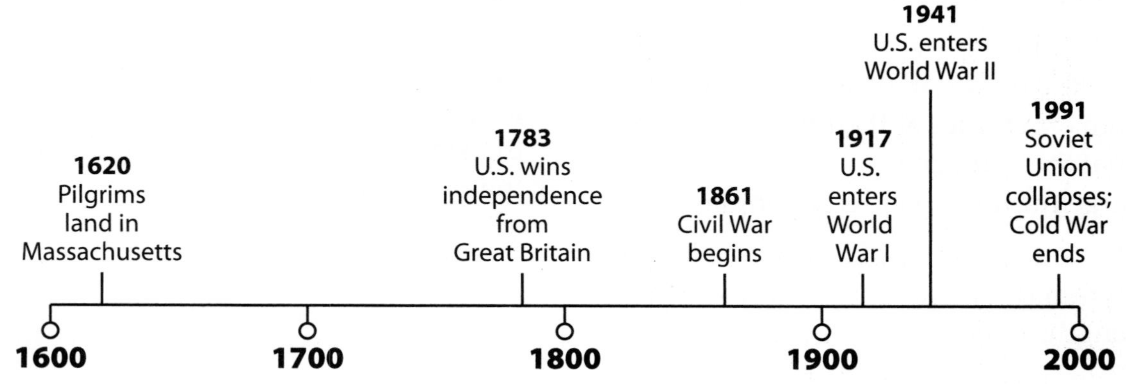

Skills Handbook

Interpreting a Population Pyramid

Why Learn This Skill?

A population pyramid shows a country's population by age and gender. Geographers use population pyramids to plan for a country's future needs.

1 Learn It!

A population pyramid is two bar graphs. These bar graphs show the number of males and females living in a region. The number of males and females is given as a percentage along the bottom of the graph. The age range for each group is listed along the left side of the graph.

To interpret population pyramids, follow these steps:

- Look at the bar graphs for the male and female groups.
- Identify, for each group, the bars that indicate the largest percentage and the smallest percentage.
- Find the age range for these groups.
- If a country's population is *growing*, the pyramid will be large at the bottom. This shows that the country's population has a large number of children and young people.
- If a country's population is *declining*, the pyramid will be narrow at the bottom and wider at the top. This means that the country's population has a large number of elderly people.
- If a country's population is *stable*, the pyramid will have bars with similar lengths over several age ranges.

2 Practice It!

Study the 2007 population pyramid for Spain shown below, then answer the following questions.

1. Which age group makes up the largest portion of Spain's population?
2. Does it appear that Spanish men or Spanish women live longer? Explain.
3. What does the shape of the pyramid tell you about Spain's population?

Spain's Population by Age and Sex

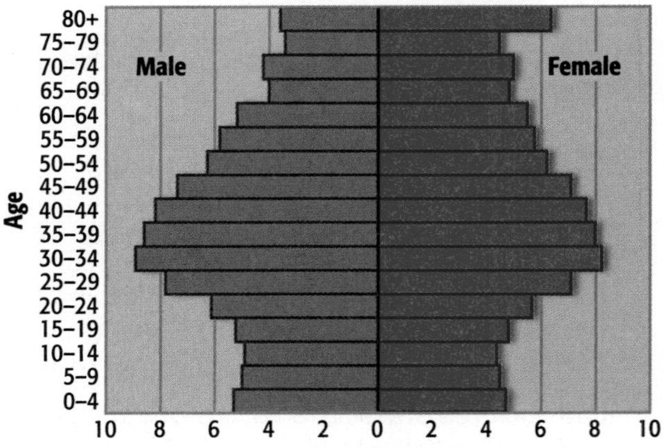

Source: *U.S. Census Bureau, International Data Base.*

3 Apply It!

Find the population pyramids for two countries at www.census.gov/ipc/www/idb/. Then write a paragraph to describe the similarities and differences between their populations.

Gazetteer

Gazetteer

A gazetteer (GA•zuh•TIHR) is a geographic index or dictionary. It shows latitude and longitude for cities and certain other places. Latitude and longitude are shown in this way: 48°N 2°E, or 48 degrees north latitude and two degrees east longitude. This Gazetteer lists many important geographic features and most of the world's largest independent countries and their capitals. The page numbers tell where each entry can be found on a map in this book. As an aid to pronunciation, most entries are spelled phonetically.

Abidjan [AH•bee•JAHN] Capital of Côte d'Ivoire. 5°N 4°W (p. RA22)

Abu Dhabi [AH•boo DAH•bee] Capital of the United Arab Emirates. 24°N 54°E (p. RA24)

Abuja [ah•BOO•jah] Capital of Nigeria. 8°N 9°E (p. RA22)

Accra [ah•KRUH] Capital of Ghana. 6°N 0° longitude (p. RA22)

Addis Ababa [AHD•dihs AH•bah•BAH] Capital of Ethiopia. 9°N 39°E (p. RA22)

Adriatic [AY•dree•A•tihk] **Sea** Arm of the Mediterranean Sea between the Balkan Peninsula and Italy. (p. RA20)

Afghanistan [af•GA•nuh•STAN] Central Asian country west of Pakistan. (p. RA25)

Albania [al•BAY•nee•uh] Country on the Adriatic Sea, south of Serbia. (p. RA18)

Algeria [al•JIHR•ee•uh] North African country east of Morocco. (p. RA22)

Algiers [al•JIHRZ] Capital of Algeria. 37°N 3°E (p. RA22)

Alps [ALPS] Mountain ranges extending through central Europe. (p. RA20)

Amazon [A•muh•ZAHN] **River** Largest river in the world by volume and second-largest in length. (p. RA17)

Amman [a•MAHN] Capital of Jordan. 32°N 36°E (p. RA24)

Amsterdam [AHM•stuhr•DAHM] Capital of the Netherlands. 52°N 5°E (p. RA18)

Andes [AN•DEEZ] Mountain system extending north and south along the western side of South America. (p. RA17)

Andorra [an•DAWR•uh] Small country in southern Europe between France and Spain. 43°N 2°E (p. RA18)

Angola [ang•GOH•luh] Southern African country north of Namibia. (p. RA22)

Ankara [AHNG•kuh•ruh] Capital of Turkey. 40°N 33°E (p. RA24)

Antananarivo [AHN•tah•NAH•nah•REE•voh] Capital of Madagascar. 19°S 48°E (p. RA22)

Arabian [uh•RAY•bee•uhn] **Peninsula** Large peninsula extending into the Arabian Sea. (p. RA25)

Argentina [AHR•juhn•TEE•nuh] South American country east of Chile. (p. RA16)

Armenia [ahr•MEE•nee•uh] European-Asian country between the Black and Caspian Seas. 40°N 45°E (p. RA26)

Ashkhabad [AHSH•gah•BAHD] Capital of Turkmenistan. 38°N 58°E (p. RA25)

Asmara [az•MAHR•uh] Capital of Eritrea. 16°N 39°E (p. RA22)

Astana Capital of Kazakhstan. 51°N 72°E (p. RA26)

Asunción [ah•SOON•see•OHN] Capital of Paraguay. 25°S 58°W (p. RA16)

Athens Capital of Greece. 38°N 24°E (p. RA19)

Atlas [AT•luhs] **Mountains** Mountain range on the northern edge of the Sahara. (p. RA23)

Australia [aw•STRAYL•yuh] Country and continent in Southern Hemisphere. (p. RA30)

Austria [AWS•tree•uh] Western European country east of Switzerland and south of Germany and the Czech Republic. (p. RA18)

Azerbaijan [A•zuhr•BY•JAHN] European-Asian country on the Caspian Sea. (p. RA25)

Baghdad Capital of Iraq. 33°N 44°E (p. RA25)

Bahamas [buh•HAH•muhz] Country made up of many islands between Cuba and the United States. (p. RA15)

Bahrain [bah•RAYN] Country located on the Persian Gulf. 26°N 51°E (p. RA25)

Baku [bah•KOO] Capital of Azerbaijan. 40°N 50°E (p. RA25)

Balkan [BAWL•kuhn] **Peninsula** Peninsula in southeastern Europe. (p. RA21)

Baltic [BAWL•tihk] **Sea** Sea in northern Europe that is connected to the North Sea. (p. RA20)

Bamako [BAH•mah•KOH] Capital of Mali. 13°N 8°W (p. RA22)

Bangkok [BANG•KAHK] Capital of Thailand. 14°N 100°E (p. RA27)

Bangladesh [BAHNG•gluh•DEHSH] South Asian country bordered by India and Myanmar. (p. RA27)

Bangui [BAHNG•GEE] Capital of the Central African Republic. 4°N 19°E (p. RA22)

Banjul [BAHN•JOOL] Capital of Gambia. 13°N 17°W (p. RA22)

Barbados [bahr•BAY•duhs] Island country between the Atlantic Ocean and the Caribbean Sea. 14°N 59°W (p. RA15)
Beijing [BAY•JIHNG] Capital of China. 40°N 116°E (p. RA27)
Beirut [bay•ROOT] Capital of Lebanon. 34°N 36°E (p. RA24)
Belarus [BEE•luh•ROOS] Eastern European country west of Russia. 54°N 28°E (p. RA19)
Belgium [BEHL•juhm] Western European country south of the Netherlands. (p. RA18)
Belgrade [BEHL•GRAYD] Capital of Serbia. 45°N 21°E (p. RA19)
Belize [buh•LEEZ] Central American country east of Guatemala. (p. RA14)
Belmopan [BEHL•moh•PAHN] Capital of Belize. 17°N 89°W (p. RA14)
Benin [buh•NEEN] West African country west of Nigeria. (p. RA22)
Berlin [behr•LEEN] Capital of Germany. 53°N 13°E (p. RA18)
Bern Capital of Switzerland. 47°N 7°E (p. RA18)
Bhutan [boo•TAHN] South Asian country northeast of India. (p. RA27)
Bishkek [bihsh•KEHK] Capital of Kyrgyzstan. 43°N 75°E (p. RA26)
Bissau [bihs•SOW] Capital of Guinea-Bissau. 12°N 16°W (p. RA22)
Black Sea Large sea between Europe and Asia. (p. RA21)
Bloemfontein [BLOOM•FAHN•TAYN] Judicial capital of South Africa. 26°E 29°S (p. RA22)
Bogotá [BOH•goh•TAH] Capital of Colombia. 5°N 74°W (p. RA16)
Bolivia [buh•LIHV•ee•uh] Country in the central part of South America, north of Argentina. (p. RA16)
Bosnia and Herzegovina [BAHZ•nee•uh HEHRT•seh•GAW•vee•nuh] Southeastern European country bordered by Croatia, Serbia, and Montenegro. (p. RA18)
Botswana [bawt•SWAH•nah] Southern African country north of the Republic of South Africa. (p. RA22)
Brasília [brah•ZEEL•yuh] Capital of Brazil. 16°S 48°W (p. RA16)
Bratislava [BRAH•tih•SLAH•vuh] Capital of Slovakia. 48°N 17°E (p. RA18)
Brazil [bruh•ZIHL] Largest country in South America. (p. RA16)
Brazzaville [BRAH•zuh•VEEL] Capital of Congo. 4°S 15°E (p. RA22)
Brunei [bru•NY] Southeast Asian country on northern coast of the island of Borneo. (p. RA27)
Brussels [BRUH•suhlz] Capital of Belgium. 51°N 4°E (p. RA18)
Bucharest [BOO•kuh•REHST] Capital of Romania. 44°N 26°E (p. RA19)
Budapest [BOO•duh•PEHST] Capital of Hungary. 48°N 19°E (p. RA18)
Buenos Aires [BWAY•nuhs AR•eez] Capital of Argentina. 34°S 58°W (p. RA16)
Bujumbura [BOO•juhm•BUR•uh] Capital of Burundi. 3°S 29°E (p. RA22)
Bulgaria [BUHL•GAR•ee•uh] Southeastern European country south of Romania. (p. RA19)
Burkina Faso [bur•KEE•nuh FAH•soh] West African country south of Mali. (p. RA22)
Burundi [bu•ROON•dee] East African country at the northern end of Lake Tanganyika. 3°S 30°E (p. RA22)

Cairo [KY•ROH] Capital of Egypt. 31°N 32°E (p. RA24)
Cambodia [kam•BOH•dee•uh] Southeast Asian country south of Thailand and Laos. (p. RA27)
Cameroon [KA•muh•ROON] Central African country on the northeast shore of the Gulf of Guinea. (p. RA22)
Canada [KA•nuh•duh] Northernmost country in North America. (p. RA6)
Canberra [KAN•BEHR•uh] Capital of Australia. 35°S 149°E (p. RA30)
Cape Town Legislative capital of the Republic of South Africa. 34°S 18°E (p. RA22)
Cape Verde [VUHRD] Island country off the coast of western Africa in the Atlantic Ocean. 15°N 24°W (p. RA22)
Caracas [kah•RAH•kahs] Capital of Venezuela. 11°N 67°W (p. RA16)
Caribbean [KAR•uh•BEE•uhn] **Islands** Islands in the Caribbean Sea between North America and South America, also known as West Indies. (p. RA15)
Caribbean Sea Part of the Atlantic Ocean bordered by the West Indies, South America, and Central America. (p. RA15)
Caspian [KAS•pee•uhn] **Sea** Salt lake between Europe and Asia that is the world's largest inland body of water. (p. RA21)
Caucasus [KAW•kuh•suhs] **Mountains** Mountain range between the Black and Caspian Seas. (p. RA21)
Central African Republic Central African country south of Chad. (p. RA22)
Chad [CHAD] Country west of Sudan in the African Sahel. (p. RA22)
Chang Jiang [CHAHNG jee•AHNG] Principal river of China that begins in Tibet and flows into the East China Sea near Shanghai; also known as the Yangtze River. (p. RA29)
Chile [CHEE•lay] South American country west of Argentina. (p. RA16)
China [CHY•nuh] Country in eastern and central Asia, known officially as the People's Republic of China. (p. RA27)
Chişinău [KEE•shee•NOW] Capital of Moldova. 47°N 29°E (p. RA19)
Colombia [kuh•LUHM•bee•uh] South American country west of Venezuela. (p. RA16)

Colombo [kuh•LUHM•boh] Capital of Sri Lanka. 7°N 80°E (p. RA26)
Comoros [KAH•muh•ROHZ] Small island country in Indian Ocean between the island of Madagascar and the southeast African mainland. 13°S 43°E (p. RA22)
Conakry [KAH•nuh•kree] Capital of Guinea. 10°N 14°W (p. RA22)
Congo [KAHNG•goh] Central African country east of the Democratic Republic of the Congo. 3°S 14°E (p. RA22)
Congo, Democratic Republic of the Central African country north of Zambia and Angola. 1°S 22°E (p. RA22)
Copenhagen [KOH•puhn•HAY•guhn] Capital of Denmark. 56°N 12°E (p. RA18)
Costa Rica [KAWS•tah REE•kah] Central American country south of Nicaragua. (p. RA15)
Côte d'Ivoire [KOHT dee•VWAHR] West African country south of Mali. (p. RA22)
Croatia [kroh•AY•shuh] Southeastern European country on the Adriatic Sea. (p. RA18)
Cuba [KYOO•buh] Island country in the Caribbean Sea. (p. RA15)
Cyprus [SY•pruhs] Island country in the eastern Mediterranean Sea, south of Turkey. (p. RA19)
Czech [CHEHK] **Republic** Eastern European country north of Austria. (p. RA18)

Dakar [dah•KAHR] Capital of Senegal. 15°N 17°W (p. RA22)
Damascus [duh•MAS•kuhs] Capital of Syria. 34°N 36°E (p. RA24)
Dar es Salaam [DAHR EHS sah•LAHM] Commercial capital of Tanzania. 7°S 39°E (p. RA22)
Denmark Northern European country between the Baltic and North Seas. (p. RA18)
Dhaka [DA•kuh] Capital of Bangladesh. 24°N 90°E (p. RA27)
Djibouti [jih•BOO•tee] East African country on the Gulf of Aden. 12°N 43°E (p. RA22)
Dodoma [doh•DOH•mah] Political capital of Tanzania. 6°S 36°E (p. RA22)
Doha [DOH•huh] Capital of Qatar. 25°N 51°E (p. RA25)
Dominican [duh•MIH•nih•kuhn] **Republic** Country in the Caribbean Sea on the eastern part of the island of Hispaniola. (p. RA15)
Dublin [DUH•blihn] Capital of Ireland. 53°N 6°W (p. RA18)
Dushanbe [doo•SHAM•buh] Capital of Tajikistan. 39°N 69°E (p. RA25)

East Timor [TEE•MOHR] Previous province of Indonesia, now under UN administration. 10°S 127°E (p. RA27)
Ecuador [EH•kwuh•dawr] South American country southwest of Colombia. (p. RA16)
Egypt [EE•jihpt] North African country on the Mediterranean Sea. (p. RA24)
El Salvador [ehl SAL•vuh•dawr] Central American country southwest of Honduras. (p. RA14)
Equatorial Guinea [EE•kwuh•TOHR•ee•uhl GIH•nee] Central African country south of Cameroon. (p. RA22)
Eritrea [EHR•uh•TREE•uh] East African country north of Ethiopia. (p. RA22)
Estonia [eh•STOH•nee•uh] Eastern European country on the Baltic Sea. (p. RA19)
Ethiopia [EE•thee•OH•pee•uh] East African country north of Somalia and Kenya. (p. RA22)
Euphrates [yu•FRAY•teez] **River** River in southwestern Asia that flows through Syria and Iraq and joins the Tigris River. (p. RA25)

Fiji [FEE•jee] **Islands** Country comprised of an island group in the southwest Pacific Ocean. 19°S 175°E (p. RA30)
Finland [FIHN•luhnd] Northern European country east of Sweden. (p. RA19)
France [FRANS] Western European country south of the United Kingdom. (p. RA18)
Freetown Capital of Sierra Leone. (p. RA22)
French Guiana [gee•A•nuh] French-owned territory in northern South America. (p. RA16)

Gabon [ga•BOHN] Central African country on the Atlantic Ocean. (p. RA22)
Gaborone [GAH•boh•ROH•nay] Capital of Botswana. (p. RA22)
Gambia [GAM•bee•uh] West African country along the Gambia River. (p. RA22)
Georgetown [JAWRJ•TOWN] Capital of Guyana. 8°N 58°W (p. RA16)
Georgia [JAWR•juh] European-Asian country bordering the Black Sea south of Russia. (p. RA26)
Germany [JUHR•muh•nee] Western European country south of Denmark, officially called the Federal Republic of Germany. (p. RA18)
Ghana [GAH•nuh] West African country on the Gulf of Guinea. (p. RA22)
Great Plains The continental slope extending through the United States and Canada. (p. RA7)
Greece [GREES] Southern European country on the Balkan Peninsula. (p. RA19)
Greenland [GREEN•luhnd] Island in northwestern Atlantic Ocean and the largest island in the world. (p. RA6)
Guatemala [GWAH•tay•MAH•lah] Central American country south of Mexico. (p. RA14)

Guatemala Capital of Guatemala. 15°N 91°W (p. RA14)

Guinea [GIH•nee] West African country on the Atlantic coast. (p. RA22)

Guinea-Bissau [GIH•nee bih•SOW] West African country on the Atlantic coast. (p. RA22)

Gulf of Mexico Gulf on part of the southern coast of North America. (p. RA7)

Guyana [gy•AH•nuh] South American country between Venezuela and Suriname. (p. RA16)

Haiti [HAY•tee] Country in the Caribbean Sea on the western part of the island of Hispaniola. (p. RA15)

Hanoi [ha•NOY] Capital of Vietnam. 21°N 106°E (p. RA27)

Harare [hah•RAH•RAY] Capital of Zimbabwe. 18°S 31°E (p. RA22)

Havana [huh•VA•nuh] Capital of Cuba. 23°N 82°W (p. RA15)

Helsinki [HEHL•SIHNG•kee] Capital of Finland. 60°N 24°E (p. RA19)

Himalaya [HI•muh•LAY•uh] Mountain ranges in southern Asia, bordering the Indian subcontinent on the north. (p. RA28)

Honduras [hahn•DUR•uhs] Central American country on the Caribbean Sea. (p. RA14)

Hong Kong Port and industrial center in southern China. 22°N 115°E (p. RA27)

Huang He [HWAHNG HUH] River in northern and eastern China, also known as the Yellow River. (p. RA29)

Hungary [HUHNG•guh•ree] Eastern European country south of Slovakia. (p. RA18)

Iberian [eye•BIHR•ee•uhn] **Peninsula** Peninsula in southwest Europe, occupied by Spain and Portugal. (p. RA20)

Iceland Island country between the North Atlantic and Arctic Oceans. (p. RA18)

India [IHN•dee•uh] South Asian country south of China and Nepal. (p. RA26)

Indonesia [IHN•duh•NEE•zhuh] Southeast Asian island country known as the Republic of Indonesia. (p. RA27)

Indus [IHN•duhs] **River** River in Asia that begins in Tibet and flows through Pakistan to the Arabian Sea. (p. RA28)

Iran [ih•RAN] Southwest Asian country that was formerly named Persia. (p. RA25)

Iraq [ih•RAHK] Southwest Asian country west of Iran. (p. RA25)

Ireland [EYER•luhnd] Island west of Great Britain occupied by the Republic of Ireland and Northern Ireland. (p. RA18)

Islamabad [ihs•LAH•muh•BAHD] Capital of Pakistan. 34°N 73°E (p. RA26)

Israel [IHZ•ree•uhl] Southwest Asian country south of Lebanon. (p. RA24)

Italy [IHT•uhl•ee] Southern European country south of Switzerland and east of France. (p. RA18)

Jakarta [juh•KAHR•tuh] Capital of Indonesia. 6°S 107°E (p. RA27)

Jamaica [juh•MAY•kuh] Island country in the Caribbean Sea. (p. RA15)

Japan [juh•PAN] East Asian country consisting of the four large islands of Hokkaido, Honshu, Shikoku, and Kyushu, plus thousands of small islands. (p. RA27)

Jerusalem [juh•ROO•suh•luhm] Capital of Israel and a holy city for Christians, Jews, and Muslims. 32°N 35°E (p. RA24)

Jordan [JAWRD•uhn] Southwest Asian country south of Syria. (p. RA24)

Kabul [KAH•buhl] Capital of Afghanistan. 35°N 69°E (p. RA25)

Kampala [kahm•PAH•lah] Capital of Uganda. 0° latitude 32°E (p. RA22)

Kathmandu [KAT•MAN•DOO] Capital of Nepal. 28°N 85°E (p. RA26)

Kazakhstan [kuh•ZAHK•STAHN] Large Asian country south of Russia and bordering the Caspian Sea. (p. RA26)

Kenya [KEHN•yuh] East African country south of Ethiopia. (p. RA22)

Khartoum [kahr•TOOM] Capital of Sudan. 16°N 33°E (p. RA22)

Kigali [kee•GAH•lee] Capital of Rwanda. 2°S 30°E (p. RA22)

Kingston [KIHNG•stuhn] Capital of Jamaica. 18°N 77°W (p. RA15)

Kinshasa [kihn•SHAH•suh] Capital of the Democratic Republic of the Congo. 4°S 15°E (p. RA22)

Kuala Lumpur [KWAH•luh LUM•PUR] Capital of Malaysia. 3°N 102°E (p. RA27)

Kuwait [ku•WAYT] Country on the Persian Gulf between Saudi Arabia and Iraq. (p. RA25)

Kyiv [KEE•ihf] Capital of Ukraine. 50°N 31°E (p. RA19)

Kyrgyzstan [KIHR•gih•STAN] Central Asian country on China's western border. (p. RA26)

Laos [LOWS] Southeast Asian country south of China and west of Vietnam. (p. RA27)

Gazetteer

La Paz [lah PAHS] Administrative capital of Bolivia, and the highest capital in the world. 17°S 68°W (p. RA16)
Latvia [LAT•vee•uh] Eastern European country west of Russia on the Baltic Sea. (p. RA19)
Lebanon [LEH•buh•nuhn] Country south of Syria on the Mediterranean Sea. (p. RA24)
Lesotho [luh•SOH•TOH] Southern African country within the borders of the Republic of South Africa. (p. RA22)
Liberia [ly•BIHR•ee•uh] West African country south of Guinea. (p. RA22)
Libreville [LEE•bruh•VIHL] Capital of Gabon. 1°N 9°E (p. RA22)
Libya [LIH•bee•uh] North African country west of Egypt on the Mediterranean Sea. (p. RA22)
Liechtenstein [LIHKT•uhn•SHTYN] Small country in central Europe between Switzerland and Austria. 47°N 10°E (p. RA18)
Lilongwe [lih•LAWNG•GWAY] Capital of Malawi. 14°S 34°E (p. RA22)
Lima [LEE•mah] Capital of Peru. 12°S 77°W (p. RA16)
Lisbon [LIHZ•buhn] Capital of Portugal. 39°N 9°W (p. RA18)
Lithuania [LIH•thuh•WAY•nee•uh] Eastern European country northwest of Belarus on the Baltic Sea. (p. RA21)
Ljubljana [lee•oo•blee•AH•nuh] Capital of Slovenia. 46°N 14°E (p. RA18)
Lomé [loh•MAY] Capital of Togo. 6°N 1°E (p. RA22)
London Capital of the United Kingdom, on the Thames River. 52°N 0° longitude (p. RA18)
Luanda [lu•AHN•duh] Capital of Angola. 9°S 13°E (p. RA22)
Lusaka [loo•SAH•kah] Capital of Zambia. 15°S 28°E (p. RA22)
Luxembourg [LUHK•suhm•BUHRG] Small European country bordered by France, Belgium, and Germany. 50°N 7°E (p. RA18)

Macao [muh•KOW] Port in southern China. 22°N 113°E (p. RA27)
Macedonia [MA•suh•DOH•nee•uh] Southeastern European country north of Greece. (p. RA19). Macedonia also refers to a geographic region covering northern Greece, the country Macedonia, and part of Bulgaria.
Madagascar [MA•duh•GAS•kuhr] Island in the Indian Ocean off the southeastern coast of Africa. (p. RA22)
Madrid Capital of Spain. 41°N 4°W (p. RA18)
Malabo [mah•LAH•boh] Capital of Equatorial Guinea. 4°N 9°E (p. RA22)
Malawi [mah•LAH•wee] Southern African country south of Tanzania and east of Zambia. (p. RA22)
Malaysia [muh•LAY•zhuh] Southeast Asian country with land on the Malay Peninsula and on the island of Borneo. (p. RA27)
Maldives [MAWL•DEEVZ] Island country southwest of India in the Indian Ocean. (p. RA26)
Mali [MAH•lee] West African country east of Mauritania. (p. RA22)
Managua [mah•NAH•gwah] Capital of Nicaragua. (p. RA15)
Manila [muh•NIH•luh] Capital of the Philippines. 15°N 121°E (p. RA27)
Maputo [mah•POO•toh] Capital of Mozambique. 26°S 33°E (p. RA22)
Maseru [MA•zuh•ROO] Capital of Lesotho. 29°S 27°E (p. RA22)
Masqat [MUHS•KAHT] Capital of Oman. 23°N 59°E (p. RA25)
Mauritania [MAWR•uh•TAY•nee•uh] West African country north of Senegal. (p. RA22)
Mauritius [maw•RIH•shuhs] Island country in the Indian Ocean east of Madagascar. 21°S 58°E (p. RA3)
Mbabane [uhm•bah•BAH•nay] Capital of Swaziland. 26°S 31°E (p. RA22)
Mediterranean [MEH•duh•tuh•RAY•nee•uhn] **Sea** Large inland sea surrounded by Europe, Asia, and Africa. (p. RA20)
Mekong [MAY•KAWNG] **River** River in southeastern Asia that begins in Tibet and empties into the South China Sea. (p. RA29)
Mexico [MEHK•sih•KOH] North American country south of the United States. (p. RA14)
Mexico City Capital of Mexico. 19°N 99°W (p. RA14)
Minsk [MIHNSK] Capital of Belarus. 54°N 28°E (p. RA19)
Mississippi [MIH•suh•SIH•pee] **River** Large river system in the central United States that flows southward into the Gulf of Mexico. (p. RA11)
Mogadishu [MOH•guh•DEE•SHOO] Capital of Somalia. 2°N 45°E (p. RA22)
Moldova [mawl•DAW•vuh] Small European country between Ukraine and Romania. (p. RA19)
Monaco [MAH•nuh•KOH] Small country in southern Europe on the French Mediterranean coast. 44°N 8°E (p. RA18)
Mongolia [mahn•GOHL•yuh] Country in Asia between Russia and China. (p. RA23)
Monrovia [muhn•ROH•vee•uh] Capital of Liberia. 6°N 11°W (p. RA22)
Monetenegro [MAHN•tuh•NEE•groh] Eastern European country. (p. RA18)
Montevideo [MAHN•tuh•vuh•DAY•OH] Capital of Uruguay. 35°S 56°W (p. RA16)
Morocco [muh•RAH•KOH] North African country on the Mediterranean Sea and the Atlantic Ocean. (p. RA22)
Moscow [MAHS•KOW] Capital of Russia. 56°N 38°E (p. RA19)

Gazetteer

Mount Everest [EHV•ruhst] Highest mountain in the world, in the Himalaya between Nepal and Tibet. (p. RA28)

Mozambique [MOH•zahm•BEEK] Southern African country south of Tanzania. (p. RA22)

Myanmar [MYAHN•MAHR] Southeast Asian country south of China and India, formerly called Burma. (p. RA27)

Nairobi [ny•ROH•bee] Capital of Kenya. 1°S 37°E (p. RA22)

Namibia [nuh•MIH•bee•uh] Southern African country south of Angola on the Atlantic Ocean. 20°S 16°E (p. RA22)

Nassau [NA•SAW] Capital of the Bahamas. 25°N 77°W (p. RA15)

N'Djamena [uhn•jah•MAY•nah] Capital of Chad. 12°N 15°E (p. RA22)

Nepal [NAY•PAHL] Mountain country between India and China. (p. RA26)

Netherlands [NEH•thuhr•lundz] Western European country north of Belgium. (p. RA18)

New Delhi [NOO DEH•lee] Capital of India. 29°N 77°E (p. RA26)

New Zealand [NOO ZEE•luhnd] Major island country southeast of Australia in the South Pacific. (p. RA30)

Niamey [nee•AHM•ay] Capital of Niger. 14°N 2°E (p. RA22)

Nicaragua [NIH•kuh•RAH•gwuh] Central American country south of Honduras. (p. RA15)

Nicosia [NIH•kuh•SEE•uh] Capital of Cyprus. 35°N 33°E (p. RA19)

Niger [NY•juhr] West African country north of Nigeria. (p. RA22)

Nigeria [ny•JIHR•ee•uh] West African country along the Gulf of Guinea. (p. RA22)

Nile [NYL] **River** Longest river in the world, flowing north through eastern Africa. (p. RA23)

North Korea [kuh•REE•uh] East Asian country in the northernmost part of the Korean Peninsula. (p. RA27)

Norway [NAWR•WAY] Northern European country on the Scandinavian peninsula. (p. RA18)

Nouakchott [nu•AHK•SHAHT] Capital of Mauritania. 18°N 16°W (p. RA22)

Oman [oh•MAHN] Country on the Arabian Sea and the Gulf of Oman. (p. RA25)

Oslo [AHZ•loh] Capital of Norway. 60°N 11°E (p. RA18)

Ottawa [AH•tuh•wuh] Capital of Canada. 45°N 76°W (p. RA13)

Ouagadougou [WAH•gah•DOO•goo] Capital of Burkina Faso. 12°N 2°W (p. RA22)

Pakistan [PA•kih•STAN] South Asian country northwest of India on the Arabian Sea. (p. RA26)

Palau [puh•LOW) Island country in the Pacific Ocean. 7°N 135°E (p. RA30)

Panama [PA•nuh•MAH] Central American country on the Isthmus of Panama. (p. RA15)

Panama Capital of Panama. 9°N 79°W (p. RA15)

Papua New Guinea [PA•pyu•wuh NOO GIH•nee] Island country in the Pacific Ocean north of Australia. 7°S 142°E (p. RA30)

Paraguay [PAR•uh•GWY] South American country northeast of Argentina. (p. RA16)

Paramaribo [PAH•rah•MAH•ree•boh] Capital of Suriname. 6°N 55°W (p. RA16)

Paris Capital of France. 49°N 2°E (p. RA18)

Persian [PUHR•zhuhn] **Gulf** Arm of the Arabian Sea between Iran and Saudi Arabia. (p. RA25)

Peru [puh•ROO] South American country south of Ecuador and Colombia. (p. RA16)

Philippines [FIH•luh•PEENZ] Island country in the Pacific Ocean southeast of China. (p. RA27)

Phnom Penh [puh•NAWM PEHN] Capital of Cambodia. 12°N 106°E (p. RA27)

Poland [POH•luhnd] Eastern European country on the Baltic Sea. (p. RA18)

Port-au-Prince [POHRT•oh•PRIHNS] Capital of Haiti. 19°N 72°W (p. RA15)

Port Moresby [MOHRZ•bee] Capital of Papua New Guinea. 10°S 147°E (p. RA30)

Port-of-Spain [SPAYN] Capital of Trinidad and Tobago. 11°N 62°W (p. RA15)

Porto-Novo [POHR•toh•NOH•voh] Capital of Benin. 7°N 3°E (p. RA22)

Portugal [POHR•chih•guhl] Country west of Spain on the Iberian Peninsula. (p. RA18)

Prague [PRAHG] Capital of the Czech Republic. 51°N 15°E (p. RA18)

Puerto Rico [PWEHR•toh REE•koh] Island in the Caribbean Sea; U.S. Commonwealth. (p. RA15)

P'yŏngyang [pee•AWNG•YAHNG] Capital of North Korea. 39°N 126°E (p. RA27)

Qatar [KAH•tuhr] Country on the southwestern shore of the Persian Gulf. (p. RA25)

Quito [KEE•toh] Capital of Ecuador. 0° latitude 79°W (p. RA16)

Rabat [ruh•BAHT] Capital of Morocco. 34°N 7°W (p. RA22)

Reykjavík [RAY•kyah•VEEK] Capital of Iceland. 64°N 22°W (p. RA18)

Rhine [RYN] **River** River in western Europe that flows into the North Sea. (p. RA20)
Riga [REE•guh] Capital of Latvia. 57°N 24°E (p. RA19)
Rio Grande [REE•oh GRAND] River that forms part of the boundary between the United States and Mexico. (p. RA10)
Riyadh [ree•YAHD] Capital of Saudi Arabia. 25°N 47°E (p. RA25)
Rocky Mountains Mountain system in western North America. (p. RA7)
Romania [ru•MAY•nee•uh] Eastern European country east of Hungary. (p. RA19)
Rome Capital of Italy. 42°N 13°E (p. RA18)
Russia [RUH•shuh] Largest country in the world, covering parts of Europe and Asia. (pp. RA19, RA27)
Rwanda [ruh•WAHN•duh] East African country south of Uganda. 2°S 30°E (p. RA22)

Sahara [suh•HAR•uh] Desert region in northern Africa that is the largest hot desert in the world. (p. RA23)
Saint Lawrence [LAWR•uhns] **River** River that flows from Lake Ontario to the Atlantic Ocean and forms part of the boundary between the United States and Canada. (p. RA13)
Sanaa [sahn•AH] Capital of Yemen. 15°N 44°E (p. RA25)
San José [SAN hoh•ZAY] Capital of Costa Rica. 10°N 84°W (p. RA15)
San Marino [SAN muh•REE•noh] Small European country located on the Italian Peninsula. 44°N 13°E (p. RA18)
San Salvador [SAN SAL•vuh•DAWR] Capital of El Salvador. 14°N 89°W (p. RA14)
Santiago [SAN•tee•AH•goh] Capital of Chile. 33°S 71°W (p. RA16)
Santo Domingo [SAN•toh duh•MIHNG•goh] Capital of the Dominican Republic. 19°N 70°W (p. RA15)
São Tomé and Príncipe [sow too•MAY PREEN•see•pee] Small island country in the Gulf of Guinea off the coast of central Africa. 1°N 7°E (p. RA22)
Sarajevo [SAR•uh•YAY•voh] Capital of Bosnia and Herzegovina. 43°N 18°E (p. RA18)
Saudi Arabia [SOW•dee uh•RAY•bee•uh] Country on the Arabian Peninsula. (p. RA25)
Senegal [SEH•nih•GAWL] West African country on the Atlantic coast. (p. RA22)
Seoul [SOHL] Capital of South Korea. 38°N 127°E (p. RA27)
Serbia [SUHR•bee•uh] Eastern European country south of Hungary. (p. RA18)
Seychelles [say•SHEHL] Small island country in the Indian Ocean off eastern Africa. 6°S 56°E (p. RA22)
Sierra Leone [see•EHR•uh lee•OHN] West African country south of Guinea. (p. RA22)
Singapore [SIHNG•uh•POHR] Southeast Asian island country near tip of the Malay Peninsula. (p. RA27)
Skopje [SKAW•PYAY] Capital of the country of Macedonia. 42°N 21°E (p. RA19)
Slovakia [sloh•VAH•kee•uh] Eastern European country south of Poland. (p. RA18)
Slovenia [sloh•VEE•nee•uh] Southeastern European country south of Austria on the Adriatic Sea. (p. RA18)
Sofia [SOH•fee•uh] Capital of Bulgaria. 43°N 23°E (p. RA19)
Solomon [SAH•luh•muhn] **Islands** Island country in the Pacific Ocean northeast of Australia. (p. RA30)
Somalia [soh•MAH•lee•uh] East African country on the Gulf of Aden and the Indian Ocean. (p. RA22)
South Africa [A•frih•kuh] Country at the southern tip of Africa, officially the Republic of South Africa. (p. RA22)
South Korea [kuh•REE•uh] East Asian country on the Korean Peninsula between the Yellow Sea and the Sea of Japan. (p. RA27)
Spain [SPAYN] Southern European country on the Iberian Peninsula. (p. RA18)
Sri Lanka [SREE LAHNG•kuh] Country in the Indian Ocean south of India, formerly called Ceylon. (p. RA26)
Stockholm [STAHK•HOHLM] Capital of Sweden. 59°N 18°E (p. RA18)
Sucre [SOO•kray] Constitutional capital of Bolivia. 19°S 65°W (p. RA16)
Sudan [soo•DAN] East African country south of Egypt. (p. RA22)
Suriname [SUR•uh•NAH•muh] South American country between Guyana and French Guiana. (p. RA16)
Suva [SOO•vah] Capital of the Fiji Islands. 18°S 177°E (p. RA30)
Swaziland [SWAH•zee•land] Southern African country west of Mozambique, almost entirely within the Republic of South Africa. (p. RA22)
Sweden Northern European country on the eastern side of the Scandinavian peninsula. (p. RA18)
Switzerland [SWIHT•suhr•luhnd] European country in the Alps south of Germany. (p. RA18)
Syria [SIHR•ee•uh] Southwest Asian country on the east side of the Mediterranean Sea. (p. RA24)

Taipei [TY•PAY] Capital of Taiwan. 25°N 122°E (p. RA27)
Taiwan [TY•WAHN] Island country off the southeast coast of China; the seat of the Chinese Nationalist government. (p. RA27)
Tajikistan [tah•JIH•kih•STAN] Central Asian country east of Turkmenistan. (p. RA26)

Gazetteer

Tallinn [TA•luhn] Capital of Estonia. 59°N 25°E (p. RA19)

Tanzania [TAN•zuh•NEE•uh] East African country south of Kenya. (p. RA22)

Tashkent [tash•KEHNT] Capital of Uzbekistan. 41°N 69°E (p. RA26)

Tbilisi [tuh•bih•LEE•see] Capital of the Republic of Georgia. 42°N 45°E (p. RA26)

Tegucigalpa [tay•GOO•see•GAHL•pah] Capital of Honduras. 14°N 87°W (p. RA14)

Tehran [TAY•uh•RAN] Capital of Iran. 36°N 52°E (p. RA25)

Thailand [TY•LAND] Southeast Asian country east of Myanmar. 17°N 101°E (p. RA27)

Thimphu [thihm•POO] Capital of Bhutan. 28°N 90°E (p. RA27)

Tigris [TY•gruhs] **River** River in southeastern Turkey and Iraq that merges with the Euphrates River. (p. RA25)

Tiranë [tih•RAH•nuh] Capital of Albania. 42°N 20°E (p. RA18)

Togo [TOH•goh] West African country between Benin and Ghana on the Gulf of Guinea. (p. RA22)

Tokyo [TOH•kee•OH] Capital of Japan. 36°N 140°E (p. RA27)

Trinidad and Tobago [TRIH•nuh•DAD tuh•BAY•goh] Island country near Venezuela between the Atlantic Ocean and the Caribbean Sea. (p. RA15)

Tripoli [TRIH•puh•lee] Capital of Libya. 33°N 13°E (p. RA22)

Tshwane [ch•WAH•nay] Executive capital of South Africa. 26°S 28°E (p. RA22)

Tunis [TOO•nuhs] Capital of Tunisia. 37°N 10°E (p. RA22)

Tunisia [too•NEE•zhuh] North African country on the Mediterranean Sea between Libya and Algeria. (p. RA22)

Turkey [TUHR•kee] Country in southeastern Europe and western Asia. (p. RA24)

Turkmenistan [tuhrk•MEH•nuh•STAN] Central Asian country on the Caspian Sea. (p. RA25)

Uganda [yoo•GAHN•dah] East African country south of Sudan. (p. RA22)

Ukraine [yoo•KRAYN] Eastern European country west of Russia on the Black Sea. (p. RA25)

Ulaanbaatar [OO•LAHN•BAH•TAWR] Capital of Mongolia. 48°N 107°E (p. RA27)

United Arab Emirates [EH•muh•ruhts] Country made up of seven states on the eastern side of the Arabian Peninsula. (p. RA25)

United Kingdom Western European island country made up of England, Scotland, Wales, and Northern Ireland. (p. RA18)

United States of America Country in North America made up of 50 states, mostly between Canada and Mexico. (p. RA8)

Uruguay [YUR•uh•GWAY] South American country south of Brazil on the Atlantic Ocean. (p. RA16)

Uzbekistan [UZ•BEH•kih•STAN] Central Asian country south of Kazakhstan. (p. RA25)

Vanuatu [VAN•WAH•TOO] Country made up of islands in the Pacific Ocean east of Australia. (p. RA30)

Vatican [VA•tih•kuhn] **City** Headquarters of the Roman Catholic Church, located in the city of Rome in Italy. 42°N 13°E (p. RA18)

Venezuela [VEH•nuh•ZWAY•luh] South American country on the Caribbean Sea between Colombia and Guyana. (p. RA16)

Vienna [vee•EH•nuh] Capital of Austria. 48°N 16°E (p. RA18)

Vientiane [vyehn•TYAHN] Capital of Laos. 18°N 103°E (p. RA27)

Vietnam [vee•EHT•NAHM] Southeast Asian country east of Laos and Cambodia. (p. RA27)

Vilnius [VIL•nee•uhs] Capital of Lithuania. 55°N 25°E (p. RA19)

Warsaw Capital of Poland. 52°N 21°E (p. RA19)

Washington, D.C. Capital of the United States, in the District of Columbia. 39°N 77°W (p. RA8)

Wellington [WEH•lihng•tuhn] Capital of New Zealand. 41°S 175°E (p. RA30)

West Indies Caribbean islands between North America and South America. (p. RA15)

Windhoek [VIHNT•HUK] Capital of Namibia. 22°S 17°E (p. RA22)

Yamoussoukro [YAH•moo•SOO•kroh] Second capital of Côte d'Ivoire. 7°N 6°W (p. RA22)

Yangon [YAHNG•GOHN] City in Myanmar; formerly called Rangoon. 17°N 96°E (p. RA27)

Yaoundé [yown•DAY] Capital of Cameroon. 4°N 12°E (p. RA22)

Yemen [YEH•muhn] Country south of Saudi Arabia on the Arabian Peninsula. (p. RA25)

Yerevan [YEHR•uh•VAHN] Capital of Armenia. 40°N 44°E (p. RA25)

Zagreb [ZAH•GREHB] Capital of Croatia. 46°N 16°E (p. RA18)

Zambia [ZAM•bee•uh] Southern African country north of Zimbabwe. (p. RA22)

Zimbabwe [zihm•BAH•bway] Southern African country northeast of Botswana. (p. RA22)

Glossary/Glosario

- Content vocabulary are words that relate to geography content. They are **boldfaced** and highlighted yellow in your text.
- Words below that have an asterisk (*) are academic vocabulary. They help you understand your school subjects and are **boldfaced** in your text.

English

absolute location exact spot where a place is found (p. 15)

***access** a way or means of approach (p. 231)

***accumulate** to increase in amount (p. 48)

***accurate** exact (p. 341)

acid rain chemicals from air pollution that combine with precipitation (pp. 64, 202)

***acquire** to get (p. 348)

***adapt** change (p. 191)

***adjacent** next to or near (p. 341)

***affect** to influence, or produce an effect upon (p. 231)

***alter** to change (p. 57)

altitude height above sea level (p. 131)

aquifer underground layer of rock through which water flows (p. 52)

archipelago group of islands (p. 123)

***assemble** put together (p. 165)

atmosphere layer of oxygen and other gases that surrounds Earth (p. 36)

***attitudes** a particular feeling or way of thinking about something (p. 272)

***authority** power or influence over others (p. 260)

autonomy having independence from another country (p. 303)

***availability** state of being easy or possible to get or use (p. 52)

axis imaginary line that passes through the center of Earth from the North Pole to the South Pole (p. 36)

Español

ubicación absoluta punto exacto donde se encuentra un lugar (pág. 15)

***acceso** manera o medio de acercamiento (pág. 231)

***acumular** aumentar en cantidad (pág. 48)

***preciso** exacto (pág. 341)

lluvia ácida sustancias químicas producto de la contaminación ambiental que se mezclan con las precipitaciones (págs. 64, 202)

***adquirir** conseguir (pág. 348)

***adaptar** cambiar (pág. 191)

***adyacente** junto a o cerca de (pág. 341)

***afectar** influir o producir un efecto en algo o alguien (pág. 231)

***alterar** cambiar (pág. 57)

altitud altura sobre el nivel del mar (pág. 131)

acuífero capa de roca subterránea a través de la que fluye agua (pág. 52)

archipiélago groupo de islas (pág. 123)

***reunir** juntar (pág. 165)

atmósfera capa de oxígeno y otros gases que rodean la Tierra (pág. 36)

***actitudes** sentimientos o maneras de pensar particulares respecto de algo (pág. 272)

***autoridad** poder o influencia sobre los demás (pág. 260)

autonomía ser independiente de otro país (pág. 303)

***disponibilidad** fácil o posible de obtener o usar (pág. 52)

eje línea imaginaria que atraviesa el centro de la Tierra desde el Polo Norte al Polo Sur (pág. 36)

B

ban legally block (p. 145)

prohibir impedir legalmente (pág. 145)

***benefit** something that does good to a person or thing (p. 231)

***beneficio** bien que se hace a una persona o cosa (pág. 231)

bilingual accepting two official languages; able to speak two languages (pp. 196, 296)

bilingüe que acepta dos idiomas oficiales, que puede hablar dos idiomas (págs. 196, 296)

biodiversity variety of plants and animals living on the planet (p. 66)

biodiversidad variedad de plantas y animales que viven en el planeta (pág. 66)

biome area that includes particular kinds of plants and animals adapted to conditions there (p. 60)

bioma área que incluye clases particulares de plantas y animales adaptadas a las condiciones del área (pág. 60)

birthrate number of children born each year for every 1,000 people (p. 73)

índice de natalidad cantidad de niños nacidos por año cada 1,000 personas (pág. 73)

bog low swampy area (p. 289)

ciénaga zona pantanosa y baja (pág. 289)

***bonds** a uniting or binding force or influence (p. 269)

***lazos** fuerza influyente que une o vincula (pág. 269)

boomerang flat, bent wooden tool of the Australian Aborigines that is thrown to stun prey when it strikes them and that sails back to the hunter if it misses its target (p. 347)

bumerán arma de madera curva y plana de los aborígenes australianos, que se arroja para golpear y aturdir a la presa y que regresa al cazador si no da en el blanco (pág. 347)

bush rural areas in Australia (p. 357)

monte zonas rurales de Australia (pág. 357)

C

canopy umbrella-like covering formed by the tops of trees in a rain forest (p. 130)

bóveda de follaje cubierta en forma de sombrilla, formada por las copas de los árboles en una selva tropical (pág. 130)

carnival large festival held each spring in countries in Latin America on the last day before the Christian holy period called Lent (p. 154)

carnaval gran festival que se realiza cada primavera en países de América Latina el día antes del período sagrado cristiano llamado Cuaresma (pág. 154)

cash crop farm product grown for export (p. 141)

cultivo comercial producto agrícola cultivado para la exportación (pág. 141)

caudillo Latin American ruler, often a military officer or wealthy individual ruling as a dictator (p. 143)

caudillo gobernante latinoamericano, a menudo un oficial militar o un hombre rico que gobierna como dictador (pág. 143)

century a period of 100 years (p. 16)

siglo período de cien años (pág. 16)

city-state independent political unit that includes a city and the surrounding area (p. 255)

ciudad-estado unidad política independiente que incluye una ciudad y el área circundante (pág. 255)

civilization highly developed culture (p. 86)

civilización cultura con un alto desarrollo (pág. 86)

clan large group of people who have a common ancestor in the far past (p. 347)

clan grupo extenso de personas que tienen un ancestro en común en el pasado lejano (pág. 347)

classical referring to the civilizations of ancient Greece and Rome (p. 255)

clásico referente a las civilizaciones de la Grecia y Roma antiguas (pág. 255)

climate pattern of weather that takes place in an area over many years (p. 56)

clima conjunto de condiciones atmosféricas que ocurren en una zona durante muchos años (pág. 56)

climate zone areas that have similar patterns of temperature and rainfall, and may have similar vegetation (p. 59)

zona climática áreas que tienen patrones similares de temperatura y precipitaciones, y pueden tener vegetación similar (pág. 59)

Cold War period from about 1947 until 1991 when the United States and the Soviet Union engaged in a political struggle for world influence but did not fight each other (p. 263)

Guerra Fría período desde 1947 hasta 1991, cuando los Estados Unidos y la Unión Soviética se involucraron en una lucha política para influir en el mundo pero sin combatir entre sí (pág. 263)

collection part of the water cycle; process by which streams and rivers carry water that has fallen to the earth back to the oceans (p. 54)

escurrimiento parte del ciclo del agua; proceso en el que los ríos y arroyos llevan el agua que cayó a la tierra, de regreso a los océanos (pág. 54)

colony overseas settlement tied to a parent country (p. 194)

colonia asentamiento en el extranjero unido a un país madre (pág. 194)

command economy economic system in which the government decides how resources are used and what goods and services are produced (pp. 170, 313)

economía de mando sistema económico en el que el gobierno decide cómo se usan los recursos y qué bienes y servicios se producen (págs. 170, 313)

***comment** to talk about (p. 154)

***comentar** hablar sobre algo (pág. 154)

commonwealth self-governing territory (p. 170)

mancomunidad territorio que se autogobierna (pág. 170)

communist state country whose government has strong control over the economy and society as a whole (pp. 145, 262)

estado comunista país cuyo gobierno tiene un fuerte control de la economía y la sociedad como un todo (págs. 145, 262)

***complex** highly developed (p. 140)

***complejo** altamente desarrollado (pág. 140)

***comprise** to be made up of (p. 322)

***componer** estar compuesto de (pág. 322)

condensation part of the water cycle; process by which water changes from gas to liquid (p. 54)

condensación parte del ciclo del agua; proceso en el que el agua cambia de la forma gaseosa a la forma líquida (pág. 54)

coniferous referring to evergreen trees that have their seeds in cones (p. 243)

coníferas referente a árboles perennes que guardan sus semillas en conos (pág. 243)

conservation careful use of resources to avoid wasting them (p. 66)

conservación uso cuidadoso de los recursos para evitar su derroche (pág. 66)

***considerable** much (p. 130)

***considerable** mucho (pág. 130)

***consist** made up of (p. 360)

***consistir** compuesto por (pág. 360)

***constant** happening a lot or all the time (p. 47)

***constante** que sucede la mayor parte del o todo el tiempo (pág. 47)

constitutional monarchy form of government in which a monarch is the head of state but elected officials run the government (p. 286)

monarquía constitucional forma de gobierno en la que un monarca es la cabeza del estado pero en el que funcionarios electos controlan el gobierno (pág. 286)

***constrain** to limit (p. 189)

***obligar** limitar (pág. 189)

continent large landmass that rises above an ocean (p. 45)

continente gran masa continental que se alza por encima de un océano (pág. 45)

continental shelf plateau off of a continent that lies under the ocean and stretches for several miles (p. 50)

plataforma continental meseta saliente de un continente que se encuentra bajo el océano y se extiende por varias millas (pág. 50)

coral reef long undersea structure formed by the tiny skeletons of coral, a kind of sea life (p. 341)

arrecife de coral gran estructura submarina formada por los diminutos esqueletos del coral, un tipo de vida marina (pág. 341)

core area at the center of the Earth, which includes a solid inner core and a hot liquid outer core (p. 45)

núcleo área del centro de la Tierra que incluye un núcleo interno sólido y un núcleo externo de líquido caliente (pág. 45)

crop rotation changing what crops farmers plant in a field from year to year (p. 65)

rotación de cultivos cambio en los cultivos que los agricultores plantan en un campo entre un año y el siguiente (pág. 65)

crust uppermost layer of the Earth (p. 45)

corteza capa superior de la Tierra (pág. 45)

cultural diffusion process of spreading ideas, languages, and customs from one culture to another (p. 87)

difusión cultural proceso de divulgación de ideas, idiomas y costumbres de una cultura a otra (pág. 87)

culture way of life of a group of people who share similar beliefs and customs (p. 83)

cultura estilo de vida de un grupo de personas que comparten creencias y costumbres similares (pág. 83)

culture region area that includes different countries that share similar cultural traits (p. 88)

región cultural zona que incluye diferentes países que comparten características culturales similares (pág. 88)

***currency** money (p. 265)

***moneda** dinero (pág. 265)

current steadily flowing stream of water in the ocean (p. 57)

corriente curso de agua que fluye constantemente en el océano (pág. 57)

czar title given to the emperors of Russia's past (p. 260)

zar título que recibían los emperadores de Rusia en el pasado (pág. 260)

death rate number of deaths per year out of every 1,000 people (p. 73)

índice de mortalidad número de muertes por año cada 1,000 personas (pág. 73)

decade a period of 10 years (p. 16)

década período de diez años (pág. 16)

deciduous trees that lose their leaves in the fall (p. 243)

caducifolios árboles que pierden sus hojas en otoño (pág. 243)

default failure to make debt payments that are due to a lender (p. 180)

incumplimiento imposibilidad de realizar los pagos de deuda que se deben a un prestamista (pág. 180)

***define** to describe or establish (p. 50)

***definir** describir o establecer (pág. 50)

deforestation cutting down of forests without replanting new trees (p. 65)

deforestación destrucción de bosques sin plantar nuevos árboles (pág. 65)

democracy form of limited government in which power rests with the people, and all citizens share in running the government (pp. 85, 255)

democracia forma de gobierno limitado en el que el poder reside en la gente, y en el que todos los ciudadanos comparten la gestión del gobierno (págs. 85, 255)

developed country country with an economy that has a mix of agriculture, a great deal of manufacturing, and service industries and that is very productive and provides its people with a high standard of living (p. 94)

país desarrollado país con una economía que combina agricultura, manufacturas e industrias de servicio; es muy productivo y proporciona a sus habitantes un nivel de vida alto (pág. 94)

developing country country that has limited industry, where agriculture remains important, incomes are generally low (p. 94)

país en vías de desarrollo país que posee una industria limitada, en el que la agricultura sigue siendo importante y los ingresos son, en general, bajos (pág. 94)

dialect local form of a language that may have a distinct vocabulary and pronunciation (p. 84)

dialecto forma local de un idioma que puede tener un vocabulario y una pronunciación diferentes (pág. 84)

dictatorship form of government in which a leader rules by force and typically limits citizens' freedoms (p. 86)

dictadura forma de gobierno en el que un líder gobierna por la fuerza y, por lo general, limita las libertades de los ciudadanos (pág. 86)

***differentiate** to make or become different in some way (p. 285)

***distinguir, diferenciar** hacer o volver diferente de algún modo (pág. 285)

***distort** to present in a manner that is misleading (p. 342)

***distorsionar** presentar de forma engañosa (pág. 342)

***distribute** to spread out (p. 56)

***distribuir** dispersar (pág. 56)

divide the high point in a landmass that determines the direction rivers flow (p. 190)

divisoria de aguas punto alto de una masa continental que determina la dirección en la que fluye un río (pág. 190)

***document** an important paper (p. 286)

***documento** papel importante (pág. 286)

***dominant** having controlling influence over others (p. 256)

***dominante** que posee influencia controladora sobre los demás (pág. 256)

dominion self-governing country in the British Empire (p. 195)

dominio país con gobierno propio en el Imperio Británico (pág. 195)

dry farming agriculture that conserves water and uses crops and growing methods suited to semiarid environments (p. 303)

agricultura de secano agricultura que conserva el agua y usa cultivos y métodos de crecimiento apropiados para medios semiáridos (pág. 303)

earthquake sudden and violent movement of the Earth's crust that shakes the land, and can cause great damage (p. 47)

terremoto movimiento sorpresivo y violento de la corteza terrestre que sacude la tierra y puede ocasionar grandes daños (pág. 47)

economic system system that sets rules for deciding what goods and services to produce, how to produce them, and who will receive them (p. 94)

sistema económico sistema que establece las reglas que deciden qué bienes y servicios se producen, cómo producirlos y quién los recibirá (pág. 94)

***economy** way of producing goods (p. 195)

***economía** modo de producción de bienes (pág. 195)

ecosystem place shared by plants and animals that depend on one another for survival (p. 66)

ecosistema lugar compartido por plantas y animales que dependen unos de otros para sobrevivir (pág. 66)

***element** part of something larger (p. 149)

***elemento** parte de algo más grande (pág. 149)

***eliminate** to remove or get rid of (p. 263)

***eliminar** quitar o deshacerse de (pág. 263)

El Niño weather phenomenon marked by very heavy rains in western South America, often causing flooding; reduced rainfall in Southern Asia, Australia, and Africa; and severe storms in North America; opposite of **La Niña** (p. 58)

El Niño fenómeno meteorológico caracterizado por lluvias muy fuertes en la parte occidental de América del Sur, que suelen provocar inundaciones; lluvias reducidas en el sur de Asia, Australia y África, y grandes tormentas en América del Norte; opuesto de **La Niña** (pág. 58)

emigrate to leave a country and move to another (p. 75)

emperor all-powerful ruler (p. 257)

empire collection of different territories united under the rule of one government (p. 140)

environment natural surroundings of people (p. 15)

equinox either of the days in spring and fall in which the noon sun is overhead at the Equator and day and night are of equal length in both the Northern and Southern Hemispheres (p. 38)

erosion process by which weathered bits of rock are moved elsewhere by water, wind, or ice (p. 48)

escarpment steep cliff at the edge of a plateau with a lowland area below (p. 124)

***establish** to set up (p. 368)

estuary an area where river currents and ocean tides meet (p. 124)

ethnic cleansing forcing people from one ethnic or religious group to leave an area so that it can be used by another group (p. 320)

ethnic group people with a common language, history, religion, and some physical traits (pp. 84, 269)

eucalyptus tree found only in Australia and nearby islands that is well suited to dry conditions, with leathery leaves, deep roots, and ability to survive when rivers flood (p. 342)

evaporation part of the water cycle; process by which water changes from liquid to gas (p. 53)

export to sell goods or resources to other countries (p. 95)

***extract** to remove (p. 367)

emigrar dejar un país y mudarse a otro (pág. 75)

emperador gobernante todopoderoso (pág. 257)

imperio conjunto de diferentes territorios unidos bajo el control de un gobierno (pág. 140)

medio ambiente entorno natural de las personas (pág. 15)

equinoccio cualquier de los días en primavera y otoño cuando el sol del mediodía está sobre el Ecuador y el día y la noche tienen igual duración en los hemisferios Sur y Norte (pág. 38)

erosión proceso por el que trozos de roca expuestos a la intemperie se mueven a otros sitios con el agua, el viento o el hielo (pág. 48)

escarpadura acantilado en gran pendiente en el borde de una meseta con una área de tierra baja debajo (pág. 124)

***establecer** formar (pág. 368)

estuario área donde las corrientes del río y la mareas del océano se encuentran (pág. 124)

limpieza étnica forzar a la gente de un grupo étnico o religioso a abandonar un área para que la use otro grupo (pág. 320)

grupo étnico personas con idioma, historia, religión y ciertas características físicas en común (págs. 84, 269)

eucalipto árbol que se encuentra solamente en Australia y las islas cercanas y que está bien adaptado a condiciones secas, con hojas coriáceas, raíces profundas y capacidad de sobrevivir con las inundaciones de los ríos (pág. 342)

evaporación parte del ciclo del agua; proceso en el que el agua cambia de la forma líquida a la forma gaseosa (pág. 53)

exportar vender bienes o recursos a otros países (pág. 95)

***extraer** quitar (pág. 367)

***facilitate** to make possible (p. 129)

famine severe lack of food (p. 73)

fault crack in the Earth's crust where two tectonic plates meet; prone to earthquakes (p. 47)

favela an overcrowded city slum in Brazil (p. 177)

***facilitar** hacer posible (pág. 129)

hambruna falta grave de alimentos (pág. 73)

falla fractura en la corteza terrestre donde se unen dos placas tectónicas, propensa a los terremotos (pág. 47)

favela barrio pobre y superpoblado de una ciudad en Brasil (pág. 177)

***feature** a part or detail that stands out (p. 242)

***característica** parte o detalle que se destaca (pág. 242)

federalism form of government in which power is divided between the federal, or national, government and the state governments (p. 196)

federalismo forma de gobierno en el que el poder está dividido entre el gobierno federal, o nacional, y los estados (pág. 196)

***fee** payment (p. 169)

***cargo** pagos (pág. 169)

fertility rate average number of children born to each woman (p. 269)

tasa de fertilidad cantidad de niños nacidos de cada mujer (pág. 269)

feudalism political and social system in which kings gave land to nobles in exchange for the nobles' promise to serve them; those nobles provided military service as knights for the king (p. 258)

feudalismo sistema político y social en el que los reyes entregaban tierras a los nobles a cambio de su promesa de servirlos; dichos nobles brindaban servicio militar como caballeros del rey (pág. 258)

***finance** provide funds or capital (p. 95)

***financiar** proporcionar fondos o capital (pág. 95)

***finite** limited in supply (p. 93)

***finito** limitado en el suministro (pág. 93)

fjord narrow, U-shaped coastal valley with steep sides formed by the action of glaciers (p. 291)

fiordo valle costero angosto y en forma de U con laderas abruptas que se formó por la acción de los glaciares (pág. 291)

fossil fuel oil, natural gas, or coal, which are an important part of the world's energy supply (p. 235)

combustibles fósiles petróleo, gas natural o carbón, que son una parte importante del suministro de la energía del mundo (pág. 235)

free market type of economy in which people are free to buy, produce, and sell with limited government involvement (p. 199)

mercado libre tipo de economía en el que las personas son libres para comprar, producir y vender con participación limitada del gobierno (pág. 199)

free trade removal of trade restrictions so that goods flow freely among countries (p. 96)

libre comercio eliminación de restricciones comerciales de modo que los bienes circulen libremente entre los países (pág. 96)

gasohol human-made fuel produced from mixing gasoline and alcohol made from sugarcane (p. 125)

gasohol combustible fabricado por el ser humano, producto de la mezcla de gasolina y alcohol hecho de caña de azúcar (pág. 125)

gaucho cowhand in Argentina (p. 179)

gaucho vaqueros de Argentina (pág. 179)

***generate** make (p. 197)

***generar** hacer (pág. 197)

generation groups of people about the same age (p. 360)

generación grupos de personas de aproximadamente la misma edad (pág. 360)

Geographic Information Systems (GIS) combination of computer hardware and software used to gather, store, and analyze geographic information and then display it on a screen (p. 17)

Sistemas de Información Geográfica (GIS) combinación de hardware y software para obtener, almacenar y analizar información geográfica y luego exhibirla en una pantalla (pág. 17)

geography study of the Earth and its people (p. 15)

geografía estudio de la Tierra y sus habitantes (pág. 15)

geothermal energy electricity produced by natural underground sources of steam (p. 291)

energía geotérmica electricidad producida por fuentes de vapor subterráneas naturales (pág. 291)

geyser spring of water heated by molten rock inside the Earth that, from time to time, shoots hot water into the air (p. 291)

géiser fuente de agua calentada por roca derretida dentro de la Tierra que de vez en cuando lanza agua caliente al aire (pág. 291)

glacier giant sheets of ice (p. 190)

glaciar capas gigantes de hielo (pág. 190)

globalization development of a worldwide culture with an interdependent economy (p. 89)

globalización desarrollo de una cultura amplia mundial con una economía interdependiente (pág. 89)

Global Positioning System (GPS) group of satellites that uses radio signals to determine the exact location of places on Earth (p. 17)

Sistema de Posicionamiento Global (GPS) grupos de satélites que envían señales de radio que registran la ubicación exacta de cada lugar en la Tierra (pág. 17)

greenhouse effect buildup of certain gases in the Earth's atmosphere that, like a greenhouse, retain the sun's warmth (p. 64)

efecto invernadero acumulación de ciertos gases en la atmósfera de la Tierra que, al igual que un invernadero, retienen el calor del Sol (pág. 64)

gross domestic product (GDP) total dollar value of all goods and services produced in a single year (p. 95)

producto bruto interno (PBI) valor total en dólares de todos los bienes y servicios producidos en un año (pág. 95)

groundwater water that filters through the soil into the ground (p. 52)

agua subterránea agua que se filtra a través del suelo hacia las profundidades (pág. 52)

habitat type of environment in which a particular animal species lives (p. 368)

hábitat tipo de medio ambiente en donde vive una especie particular de animal (pág. 368)

heavy industry manufacture of goods such as machinery, mining equipment, and steel (p. 323)

industria pesada fabricación de bienes como maquinarias, equipo de minería y acero (pág. 323)

hieroglyphics system of writing that uses small pictures to represent sounds or words (p. 139)

jeroglíficos sistema de escritura que usa pequeños dibujos para representar sonidos o palabras (pág. 139)

high-technology industry areas of business that include making computers and other products with sophisticated engineering (p. 294)

industria de alta tecnología áreas de negocios que incluyen la creación de computadoras y otros productos con ingeniería sofisticada (pág. 294)

Holocaust mass killing of 6 million European Jews by Germany's Nazi leaders during World War II (p. 263)

Holocausto asesinato masivo de 6 millones de judíos europeos por parte de los líderes nazis de Alemania durante la Segunda Guerra Mundial (pág. 263)

***identical** exactly the same (p. 38)

***idéntico** exactamente lo mismo (pág. 38)

***impact** effect (p. 237)

***impacto** efecto (pág. 237)

import to buy resources or goods from other countries (p. 95)

importar comprar bienes o recursos a otros países (pág. 95)

***income** earned money (p. 314)

***ingreso** dinero ganado (pág. 314)

indigenous people descended from an area's first inhabitants (p. 196)

indígenas pueblo descendiente de los primeros habitantes de un área (pág. 196)

infrastructure system of roads and railroads that allows the transport of materials (p. 237)

infraestructura sistema de carreteras y vías férreas que permiten el transporte de materiales (pág. 237)

***inhibit** to limit (p. 237)

***inhibir** limitar (pág. 237)

interdependence condition that exists when countries rely on each other for ideas, goods, services, and markets (p. 96)

interdependencia condición que existe cuando los países dependen uno del otro para obtener ideas, bienes, servicios y mercados (pág. 96)

***internal** existing or taking place within (p. 75)

***interno** que existe o sucede dentro de (pág. 75)

***invest** to lay out money so as to return a profit (p. 299)

***invertir** colocar dinero de manera de obtener una ganancia (pág. 299)

irrigation process of collecting water and distributing it to crops (p. 66)

irrigación proceso de recolección de agua y su distribución en los cultivos (pág. 66)

***issue** problem (p. 178)

***asunto** problema (pág. 178)

isthmus narrow stretch of land connecting two larger land areas (p. 123)

istmo extensión estrecha de tierra que conecta dos masas de tierra más grandes (pág. 123)

jade shiny stone that comes in many shades of green (p. 139)

jade piedra brillante de varios tonos de verde (pág. 139)

landlocked having no border with ocean or sea (p. 231)

sin salida al mar que no posee fronteras al mar o al océano (pág. 231)

La Niña weather phenomenon marked by unusually cool waters in the eastern Pacific and low amounts of rainfall there and heavier rains—and a greater chance of typhoons—in the western Pacific; opposite of **El Niño** (p. 58)

La Niña fenómeno meteorológico caracterizado por aguas inusualmente frías y bajas cantidades de lluvia en el este del Pacífico, y fuertes lluvias (y una mayor posibilidad de tifones) en el oeste del Pacífico; opuesto de **El Niño** (pág. 58)

lawsuit legal action in which people ask for relief from some damage done to them by someone else (p. 359)

pleito acción legal en la que las personas exigen pago por algún daño que alguien les hizo (pág. 359)

***layer** a thickness or fold (p. 64)

***capa** grosor o doblez (pág. 64)

leap year year with 366 days, which happens every fourth year to make calendars match Earth's movement around the sun (p. 36)

año bisiesto año con 366 días, que ocurre cada cuatro años para hacer que los calendarios coincidan con el movimiento de la Tierra alrededor del Sol (pág. 36)

light industry manufacture of consumer goods such as clothing, shoes, furniture, and household products (p. 323)

industria liviana fabricación de bienes de consumo como ropas, calzado, muebles y productos para la casa (pág. 323)

literacy rate percentage of people who can read and write (p. 169)

tasa de alfabetización porcentaje de personas que saben leer y escribir (pág. 169)

Llanos tropical grasslands that stretch through eastern Colombia and Venezuela (p. 124)

llanos praderas tropicales que se extienden a través del este de Colombia y Venezuela (pág. 124)

local wind wind pattern typical of a small area (p. 59)

viento local patrón de viento típico de un área pequeña (pág. 59)

Glossary/Glosario

magma hot melted rock inside the Earth that flows to the surface when a volcano erupts (p. 45)

***maintain** to keep up (p. 178)

maize corn (p. 139)

***major** to be great in size or impact (p. 241)

mantle Earth's thickest layer, found between the core and the crust (p. 45)

maquiladora a foreign-owned factory in Mexico where workers assemble parts made in other countries (p. 165)

market economy economic system in which individuals make the decisions about how resources are used and what goods and services to provide (p. 314)

marsupial mammals that carry their young in a pouch (p. 343)

***medical** relating to the science or practice of medicine (p. 320)

merino breed of sheep known for especially fine wool (p. 367)

mestizo in Latin America, a person of mixed Native American and European heritage (p. 151)

migrant worker person who earns a living by temporarily moving to a place separate from his or her home in order to work (p. 166)

migration movement of people (p. 149)

***militant** person who uses war or violence to accomplish goals (p. 304)

millennium a period of 1,000 years (p. 16)

mistral cold, dry winter wind from the north that strikes southern France (p. 245)

monarchy government led by king or queen who inherited power by being born into ruling family (p. 86)

multinational company company that has locations in more than one country (p. 296)

mural large painting on a wall (p. 154)

magma roca caliente y derretida dentro de la Tierra que fluye a la superficie durante la erupción de un volcán (pág. 45)

***mantener** conservar (pág. 178)

maíz mazorca y grano (pág. 139)

***principal** grande en tamaño o impacto (pág. 241)

manto capa más gruesa de la Tierra que se encuentra entre el núcleo y la corteza (pág. 45)

maquiladora fábrica de propiedad extranjera en México donde los trabajadores montan piezas hechas en otros países (pág. 165)

economía de mercado sistema económico en el que las personas toman las decisiones sobre cómo se usan los recursos y qué bienes y servicios se proveen (pág. 314)

marsupial mamíferos que llevan a sus crías en una bolsa (pág. 343)

***médico** relativo a la ciencia o la práctica de la medicina (pág. 320)

merino raza de ovejas conocidas por su lana particularmente fina (pág. 367)

mestizo en América Latina, persona de herencia mixta de nativos americanos y europeos (pág. 151)

trabajador migratorio persona que se gana la vida mudándose temporalmente a un sitio alejado de su hogar para poder trabajar (pág. 166)

migración movimiento de personas (pág. 149)

***militante** persona que usa la guerra o la violencia para lograr objetivos (pág. 304)

milenio período de 1000 años (pág. 16)

mistral viento invernal, frío y seco, que llega al sur de Francia desde el norte (pág. 245)

monarquía gobierno conducido por un rey o una reina que heredaron el poder al nacer dentro de la familia reinante (pág. 86)

compañía multinacional empresa que tiene ubicaciones en más de un país (pág. 296)

mural pintura grande sobre una pared (pág. 154)

national debt money owed by the government (p. 180)

deuda nacional dinero que el gobierno debe (pág. 180)

nationalism feelings of affection and loyalty towards one's country (p. 275)

nacionalismo sentimiento de afecto y lealtad hacia el propio país (pág. 275)

natural resource material from the Earth that people use to meet their needs (p. 93)

recurso natural material del planeta Tierra que la gente usa para cubrir sus necesidades (pág. 93)

navigable referring to a body of water wide and deep enough for ships to use (pp. 190, 234)

navegable referente a un cuerpo de agua con anchura y profundidad suficientes para que lo usen barcos (págs. 190, 234)

neutrality refusal to take sides in a war between other countries (p. 300)

neutralidad negativa a tomar posición en una guerra entre otros países (pág. 300)

newly industrialized country country that is creating new manufacturing and business (p. 94)

país recientemente industrializado país que está creando nuevos negocios y manufacturas (pág. 94)

newsprint type of paper used for printing newspapers (p. 200)

papel de periódico tipo de papel usado para imprimir periódicos (pág. 200)

nonrenewable resource natural resource such as a mineral that cannot be replaced (p. 93)

recurso no renovable recurso natural, como un mineral, que no se puede reemplazar (pág. 93)

obsidian hard, black, volcanic glass useful for making weapons (p. 139)

obsidiana vidrio volcánico de color negro y resistente, útil para fabricar armas (pág. 139)

***occur** to be found in (p. 50)

***ocurrir** que se encuentra en algo (pág. 50)

oligarch member of a small ruling group that holds great power (p. 324)

oligarca miembro de un grupo pequeño de gobierno que posee gran poder (pág. 324)

oral tradition passing stories by word of mouth from generation to generation (p. 274)

tradición oral pasar historias de boca en boca de generación en generación (pág. 274)

orbit specific path each planet follows around the sun (p. 35)

órbita trayectoria específica que cada planeta sigue alrededor del Sol (pág. 35)

outback inland areas of Australia west of the Great Dividing Range (p. 341)

outback áreas del interior de Australia al oeste de la Gran Cordillera Divisoria (pág. 341)

Pampas treeless grassland of Argentina and Uruguay (p. 124)

pampas pradera desprovista de árboles en Argentina y Uruguay (pág. 124)

parliamentary democracy form of government in which voters elect representatives to a law-making body called Parliament, and members of Parliament vote for an official called the prime minister to head the government (pp. 195, 287)

democracia parlamentaria forma de gobierno en la que los votantes eligen representantes para un cuerpo que crea las leyes denominado Parlamento, sus miembros votan a un funcionario llamado primer ministro como jefe del gobierno (págs. 195, 287)

***participate** take part in (p. 197)

***participar** tomar parte en (pág. 197)

pass space people can use to travel through a mountain range (p. 233)

paso lugar que la gente puede usar para viajar a través de una cordillera montañosa (pág. 233)

pasture grasses and other plants that are ideal feed for grazing animals (p. 368)

pastura pastos y otras plantas que son el alimento ideal para los animales de pastoreo (pág. 368)

peat plants partly decayed in water which can be dried and burned for fuel (p. 289)

turba plantas parcialmente descompuestas en agua que pueden secarse y usarse como combustible (pág. 289)

penal colony area outside of the home country where prisoners are sent for confinement and punishment (p. 348)

penal en colonia área de detención de prisioneros ubicada en otro país, considerado dependiente o colonía (pág. 348)

pensioner person who receives regular payments from the government because he or she is too old or sick to work (p. 322)

pensionado persona que recibe pagos regulares del gobierno dado que está demasiado anciana o enferma para trabajar (pág. 322)

***period** a portion of time (p. 247)

***período** lapso de tiempo (pág. 247)

permafrost permanently frozen lower layers of soil found in the tundra and subarctic climate zones (p. 247)

permafrost capas de suelo inferiores que están permanentemente congeladas en la tundra y en las zonas de clima ártico (pág. 247)

pesticide powerful chemicals that kill crop-destroying insects (p. 66)

pesticidas fuertes sustancias químicas que matan los insectos que destruyen los cultivos (pág. 66)

***physical** related to natural science (p. 15)

***físico** relativo a las sciencias naturales (pág. 15)

pidgin language language formed by combining parts of several different languages (p. 151)

lengua mixta idioma formado por la combinación de partes de varios idiomas diferentes (pág. 151)

plantation large farm (p. 165)

plantación granja grande (pág. 165)

plate tectonics scientific theory that explains how processes within the Earth form continents and cause their movement (p. 46)

tectónica de placas teoría científica que explica cómo los procesos dentro de la Tierra forman los continentes y causan su movimiento (pág. 46)

plaza public square in Latin American city around which government buildings and major churches were built (p. 163)

plaza lugar público en las ciudades de América Latina alrededor del que se construyeron las iglesias principales y los edificios gubernamentales (pág. 163)

polder reclaimed wetlands that use a system of dikes and pumps to keep out the sea's waters (p. 296)

pólder pantanos recuperados que usan un sistema de diques y bombas para mantener fuera a las aguas marinas (pág. 296)

pope head of the Roman Catholic Church (p. 258)

papa líder de la Iglesia Católica Romana (pág. 258)

population density average number of people living in a square mile or square kilometer (p. 74)

densidad de población cantidad promedio de personas que viven en una milla cuadrada o un kilómetro cuadrado (pág. 74)

potash mineral salt used in making fertilizer (p. 314)

potasa sal mineral usada en la fabricación de fertilizantes (pág. 314)

prairie rolling inland grassland region with fertile soil (p. 189)

pradera región interna de las llanuras, con pastizales ondulantes y tierras fértiles (pág. 189)

precipitation part of the water cycle; process by which water falls to the Earth as, for example, rain or snow (p. 54)

precipitación parte del ciclo del agua; proceso mediante el que el agua cae a la Tierra, por ejemplo, como lluvia o nieve (pág. 54)

prevailing winds wind patterns that are similar over time (p. 57)

vientos predominantes patrones de viento que se mantienen similares con el paso del tiempo (pág. 57)

***primary** main or most important (p. 271)

***primario** principal o más importante (pág. 271)

***prime** very attractive (p. 348)

***excelente** muy atractivo (pág. 348)

***principle** rule or guideline (p. 140)

***principio** regla o pauta (pág. 140)

***prior** earlier in time or order (p. 323)

***precedente** anterior en tiempo u orden (pág. 323)

privatization transfer of ownership of businesses from the government to individuals (p. 322)

privatización transferencia de propiedad de los negocios del gobierno a particulares (pág. 322)

productivity measure of how much work a person produces in a set amount of time (p. 289)

productividad medición de cuánto trabajo produce una persona en una cantidad fija de tiempo (pág. 289)

profit money a business earns after all its expenses are met (p. 199)

ganancia dinero que se gana en un negocio luego de cubrir todos los gastos (pág. 199)

***promote** to put forward (p. 276)

***promover** impulsar (pág. 276)

quota number limit on how many items of a particular product can be imported from a certain nation (p. 95)

cupo límite de la cantidad de artículos de un producto determinado que puede importarse de cierto país (pág. 95)

rain forest dense stand of trees and other growth that receives high amounts of precipitation each year (p. 129)

selva tropical agrupación densa de árboles y otras plantas que reciben grandes cantidades de precipitación cada año (pág. 129)

rain shadow effect of mountains that blocks rain from reaching interior regions (p. 59)

sombra de lluvia efecto de las montañas que impiden que la lluvia alcance regiones interiores (pág. 59)

refugee person who flees to another country to escape persecution or disaster (p. 76)

refugiado persona que huye a otro país para escapar de la persecución o el desastre (pág. 76)

relative location description of where a place is in relation to the features around it (p. 15)

ubicación relativa descripción de dónde está un lugar en relación con las características a su alrededor (pág. 15)

***release** to relieve pressure (p. 45)

***liberar** aliviar la presión (pág. 45)

***reluctant** hesitant (p. 200)

***reacio** indeciso (pág. 200)

***rely** to depend on (p. 294)

***confiar** depender de (pág. 294)

remittance money sent back home by workers who leave their home country to work in other nations (p. 170)

remesa dinero que envían a su hogar los trabajadores que abandonan su país para trabajar en otras naciones (pág. 170)

renewable resource natural resource that can be replaced naturally or grown again (p. 93)

recurso renovable recurso natural que puede reemplazarse o crecer nuevamente de manera natural (pág. 93)

representative democracy form of government in which voters choose leaders who make and enforce the laws (p. 195)

democracia representativa forma de gobierno en el que los votantes eligen a sus líderes para que hagan cumplir las leyes (pág. 195)

republic government in which people choose their leaders (p. 256)

república gobierno en el que las personas eligen a sus líderes (pág. 256)

***reside** live (p. 124)

***residir** vivir (pág. 124)

***restriction** limitation (p. 201)

***restricción** limitación (pág. 201)

reunification the act of being brought back together (p. 300)

reunificación el acto de ser vuelto a reunir (pág. 300)

***reveal** make known (p. 164)

***revelar** dar a conocer (pág. 164)

***reverse** opposite (p. 38)

***reverso** opuesto (pág. 38)

revolution one complete circuit around the sun (p. 36); sweeping change (pp. 145, 261)

rotate to spin on an axis (p. 36)

***route** journey (p. 190)

revolución giro completo alrededor del Sol (pág. 36); cambio radical (págs. 145, 261)

rotar girar sobre su eje (pág. 36)

***travesía** viaje (pág. 190)

S

secular nonreligious (p. 272)

selva Brazilian name for the Amazonian rain forest (p. 177)

separatist movement campaign by members of an ethnic group to break away from the national government and form an independent state (p. 324)

***shift** to change from one to another (p. 169)

***significant** important (p. 37)

***similar** having qualities in common (p. 303)

sirocco hot winds from Africa that blow across southern Europe (p. 245)

smog thick haze of smoke and chemicals (p. 64)

sodium nitrate mineral used in fertilizer and explosives (p. 182)

softwood wood of evergreen trees, often used in buildings or making furniture (p. 236)

solar system planets, along with their moons, asteroids and other bodies, and the sun (p. 35)

specialization focusing on certain economic activities to make the best use of resources (p. 294)

***stable** firmly established; not likely to change suddenly or greatly (p. 143)

station cattle or sheep ranch in rural Australia (p. 357)

stock part ownership in a company (p. 199)

***style** form (p. 154)

subregion smaller area of a region (p. 123)

subsidy special payment made by a government to support a particular group or industry (p. 304)

subsistence farm small plot of land on which a farmer grows only enough food to feed his or her family (p. 165)

secular no religioso (pág. 272)

selva nombre brasilero para los bosques tropicales del Amazonas (pág. 177)

movimiento separatista campaña realizada por los miembros de un grupo étnico para separarse del gobierno nacional y formar un estado independiente (pág. 324)

***alternar** cambiar de una cosa a otra (pág. 169)

***significativo** importante (pág. 37)

***similar** que posee cualidades en común (pág. 303)

siroco vientos calientes de África que soplan atravesando el sur de Europa (pág. 245)

smog neblina espesa, resultado de la combinación de humo y sustancias químicas (pág. 64)

nitrato de sodio mineral que se usa en fertilizantes y explosivos (pág. 182)

madera blanda madera de árboles siempre verdes, que se utiliza comúnmente en edificios o muebles (pág. 236)

sistema solar los planetas y sus lunas, los asteroides y otros cuerpos celestes además del Sol (pág. 35)

especialización concentrarse en ciertas actividades económicas para hacer el mejor uso de recursos (pág. 294)

***estable** establecido con firmeza; sin probabilidades de cambiar repentina o ampliamente (pág. 143)

estación rancho de ovejas o vacas en la zona rural de Australia (pág. 357)

acción parte propietaria en una empresa (pág. 199)

***estilo** forma (pág. 154)

subregión zona más pequeña de una región (pág. 123)

subsidio pago especial hecho por un gobierno para apoyar a un grupo o industria particular (pág. 304)

agricultura de subsistencia parcela de tierra en la cual un granjero cultiva sólo los alimentos suficientes para alimentar a su familia (pág. 165)

***sufficient** enough (p. 342)

suffrage right to vote (p. 349)

summer solstice day that has the most daylight hours and the fewest hours of darkness (p. 37)

***suficiente** bastante (pág. 342)

sufragio derecho al voto (pág. 349)

solsticio de verano día que tiene la mayor cantidad de horas de luz diurna y la menor cantidad de horas de oscuridad (pág. 37)

taiga large coniferous forests (p. 247)

tariff tax added to the price of goods that are imported (pp. 95, 170)

***technique** a method of accomplishing something (p. 65)

***technology** the application of scientific discoveries to practical use (p. 73)

***theme** topic (p. 15)

trade surplus situation that occurs when the value of a country's exports is higher than the value of its imports (p. 201)

***transform** greatly change (p. 141)

***transport** move (p. 123)

trench deep cut in the ocean floor (p. 50)

tributary small river that flows into a larger river (p. 124)

Tropics area between the Tropic of Cancer and the Tropic of Capricorn, which has generally warm temperatures because it receives the direct rays of the sun for much of the year (pp. 38, 129)

taiga grandes bosques coníferos (pág. 247)

tarifa impuesto agregado al precio de los bienes que se importan (págs. 95, 170)

***técnica** un método para lograr algo (pág. 65)

***tecnología** la aplicación de los descubrimientos científicos a un uso práctico (pág. 73)

***tema** tópico (pág. 15)

excedente comercial situación que ocurre cuando el valor de las exportaciones de un país es mayor que el valor de sus importaciones (pág. 201)

***transformar** cambiar mucho (pág. 141)

***transportar** mover (pág. 123)

fosa marina corte profundo en el suelo marino (pág. 50)

tributario río pequeño que fluye dentro de un río más grande (pág. 124)

trópicos área entre el Trópico de Cáncer y el Trópico de Capricornio con temperaturas generalmente cálidas, ya que recibe los rayos directos del Sol durante gran parte del año (págs. 38, 129)

***unify** to unite or bring together (p. 324)

***unique** being the only one of its kind (p. 89)

urban climate weather patterns in cities, including higher temperatures and distinct wind patterns, as compared to nearby rural areas (p. 61)

urbanization growth of cities (pp. 75, 270)

***unificar** unir o juntar (pág. 324)

***exclusivo** ser el único en su tipo (pág. 89)

clima urbano patrones climáticos de las ciudades, incluyendo temperaturas más altas y patrones de vientos distintos, al compararse con áreas rurales cercanas (pág. 61)

urbanización crecimiento de las ciudades (págs. 75, 270)

vaquero Mexican cowhand (p. 164)

vaquero empleado que trabaja con el ganado en México (pág. 164)

***vary** to be different (p. 290)

***variar** ser diferente (pág. 290)

***volume** amount (p. 323)

***volumen** cantidad (pág. 323)

water cycle system in which water moves from the Earth to the air and back to the Earth (p. 53)

ciclo del agua sistema en el que el agua se mueve de la Tierra hacia el aire y luego de vuelta hacia la Tierra (pág. 53)

weather changes in temperature, wind speed and direction, and air moisture that take place over a short period of time (p. 56)

clima cambios en la temperatura, velocidad y dirección del viento, y humedad en el aire que duran un período breve (pág. 56)

weathering process in which rock is broken into smaller pieces by water and ice, chemicals, or even plants (p. 47)

deterioro por exposición proceso por el cual se rompen las rocas en pedazos más pequeños ocasionado por el agua y el hielo, las químicos o hasta los vegetales (pág. 47)

welfare state country where the government is the main provider of support for the sick, needy, and the retired (p. 269)

estado de bienestar país en el que el gobierno es el proveedor principal de ayuda para los enfermos, necesitados y jubilados (pág. 269)

***widespread** scattered or found in a wide area (pp. 86)

***generalizado** que se distribuye o encuentra en un área amplia (pág. 86)

winter solstice day of the year that has the fewest hours of sunlight and the most hours of darkness (p. 38)

solsticio de invierno día del año que tiene la menor cantidad de horas de luz diurna y la mayor cantidad de horas de oscuridad (pág. 38)

Index

c=chart m=map
d=diagram p=photo
g=graph q=quote

Index

Index

Index

Index

Index

Index

Acknowledgments

Text

51 Valentin Rasputin. *Farewell to Matyora.* Trans. Antonina W. Bouis. Evanston, IL: Northwestern University Press. 1991.; **152** "The Hard-Hearted Son" from *Folktales of Mexico,* edited and translated by Americo Paredes. Copyright © 1970 by The University of Chicago. Reprinted by permission of The University of Chicago Press.; **175** From "Debate still rages on 10th anniversary of Quebec's sovereignty referendum" CBC News, October 30, 2005. Reprinted by permission of CBC Radio Canada.; **266** From "Language is the key to integration" an interview with Armin Laschet, by Anna Reimann. Spiegel Online, January 27, 2006. Reprinted by permission.; **267** From "Speaking up for multilingualism" by David Gordon Smith. Expatica Germany, January 26, 2006. Reprinted by permission of Expatica Communications BV, www.expatica.com; **288** Charles Dickens. *Hard Times.* In *The Works of Charles Dickens.* New York: Books, Inc. 1854.; **388** From *The Log of Christopher Columbus,* translation © 1987 by Robert H. Fuson. Reprinted by permission of Amelia Fuson.

Photographs

Cover (tl r)CORBIS, (tc)Alan R. Moller/Getty Images, (c)Bill Bachman/Alamy, (r)CORBIS, (bl)Paul Thompson/Alamy; **v** Paul A. Souders/CORBIS; **vi** Ken Usami/Photodisc Green/Getty Images; **viii** (l)Tim Page/CORBIS, (r)Alfredo Maiquez/Getty Images; **xv** PhotoDisc; **RA38-1** Blaine Harrington III/Corbis; **11** Gunter Marx Photography/CORBIS; **12–13** Keren Su/Getty Images; **14** George Steinmetz/CORBIS; **15** age fotostock/SuperStock; **16** Michael S. Yamashita/CORBIS; **18** (t)ThinkStock/SuperStock, (cl)Janet Foster/Masterfile, (cr)Mark Tomalty/Masterfile, (bl)age fotostock/SuperStock, (br)Jurgen Freund/Nature Picture Library; **20** (t)David Young-Wolff/PhotoEdit, (tc)NOAA/CORBIS, (b)The Photolibrary Wales/Alamy, (bc)Steve Winter/Getty Images; **22** (t)Dorling Kindersley/Getty Images, (b)Steve Skjold/Alamy; **34** NASA; **36** (l)Andrew Parker/Alamy, (r)World Perspectives/Getty Images; **39** (t)Tony West/CORBIS, (cl)imagebroker/Alamy, (cr)Kevin George/Alamy, (b)StockTrek/Getty Images; **42–43** Pawel Wysocki/Getty Images; **44** Arctic-Images/CORBIS; **46** Robert Yager/Getty Images; **48** Susana Raab/Getty Images; **49** Patrick Frilet/Hemis/CORBIS; **50** Walter Geiersperger/CORBIS; **51** (t)Marc Garanger/CORBIS, (b)Wolfgang Kaehler/CORBIS; **52** (l)Vick Fisher/Alamy, (r)Joseph Van Os/Riser/Getty Images; **54** Yves Marcoux/Getty Images; **55** Alejandro Ernesto/epa/CORBIS; **57** John Maier Jr./Argus Fotoarchiv/CORBIS SYGMA; **61** Art Kowalsky/Alamy; **62** Peter Arnold, Inc./Alamy; **63** Ron Watts/Getty Images; **64** Norbert Rosing/National Geographic Image Collection; **67** (t)Chris Harris/Getty Images, (bl)Alessandro della Bella/epa/CORBIS, (br)Greg Stott/Masterfile; **70–71** Ritterbach Ritterbach/Photolibrary; **72** Macduff Everton/CORBIS; **74** (l)Gunter Marx Photography/CORBIS, (r)Pete Ryan/Getty Images; **77** Wayne R. Bilenduke/Getty Images; **78** Jagadeesh NV/Reuters; **79** (tl)REUTERS/Bobby Yip, (tc b)AP Images, (tr)Danita Delimont/Alamy; **80** Gary Hershorn/Reuters; **81** (t)Baldev/CORBIS, (b)Blend/PunchStock; **82** Robert Wagenhoffer/CORBIS; **84** White Fox/Photolibrary; **86** Mary Evans Picture Library; **87** Sergei Karpukhin/Reuters/CORBIS; **89** Danita Delimont/Alamy; **90** Sam Edwards/Getty Images; **90–91** W. Cody/CORBIS; **91** Juan Barreto/AFP/Getty Images; **92** Bert Bostelmann/Getty Images; **95** (l)AP Images, (r)George Pimentel/AP Images; **97** (t)Keith Dannemiller/Alamy, (bl)Justin Kase Zelevenz/Alamy, (br)Philippe Colombi/Getty Images; **100** (t to b)Creatas/SuperStock, AP Images, Jim Zuckerman/CORBIS, Kurt Scholz/SuperStock, Lisa Englebrecht/Danitadelimont.com, Gary Cook/Alamy; **100–101** NASA; **101** (t)Jose Azel/Getty Images, (c)Macduff Everton/CORBIS, (bl)ITAR-TASS/VITALY BELOUSOV/NEWSCOM; **102** AP Images; **102–103** Stone/Getty Images; **105** (t)Daryl Benson/Getty Images, (c)Christian Heeb/Aurora Photos, (bl)Jeff Rotman/Getty Images, (br)Hubert Stadler/CORBIS; **119** Marcelo Sayao/epa/CORBIS; **120–121** Tony Savino/The Image Works; **122** Jeremy Horner/CORBIS; **123** Jon Arnold Images/SuperStock; **124** Kit Houghton/CORBIS; **125** Pete Oxford/Nature Picture Library; **127** (t)Media Bakery, (b)Bridgeman Art Library; **128** David Lyons/National Geographic Image Collection; **130** (l)Tui De Roy/Minden Pictures, (r)Brent Winebrenner/Lonely Planet Images; **133** (tl)SuperStock, (tr)Trevor Smithers ARPS/Alamy, (c)Rodrigo Arangua/AFP/Getty Images, (b)Ernesto Rios Lanz/Sexto Sol/Getty Images; **136–137** Danny Lehman/CORBIS; **138** Carlos Lopez-Barillas/CORBIS; **139** Author's Image/PunchStock; **141** Werner Forman/CORBIS; **142** (l)Charles & Josette Lenars/CORBIS, (r)Brooklyn Museum/CORBIS; **143** (l)Index, Museo de America, Madrid/Bridgeman Art Library, (r)Angelo Cavalli/Getty Images; **144** (l)H.N. Rudd/CORBIS, (r)Jose Fuste Raga/CORBIS; **146** Tim Page/CORBIS; **146–147** Kevin Schafer/Photographer's Choice RF/Getty Images; **147** Alfredo Maiquez/Getty Images; **148** Blaine Harrington III/CORBIS; **149** Tom Cockrem/Lonely Planet Images; **150** Brand X Pictures/PunchStock; **151** (l)Chris Brandis/AP Images, (r)AM Corporation/Alamy; **152** Robert Holmes/CORBIS; **153** GM Photo Images/Alamy; **155** (tl)Danny Lehman/CORBIS, (tr)Mario Algaze/The Image Works, (bl)Alfredo Dagli Orti/The Art Archive/CORBIS, (br)Adriano Machado/Reuters/CORBIS; **158** Adriana Zehbrauskas/Polaris; **159** (l)Adriana Zehbrauskas/Polaris, (tr)Danita Delimont/Alamy, (cr)Ken Welsh/age fotostock, (br)Luc Novovitch/Alamy; **160–161** Chad Ehlers/Getty Images; **162** Lynsey Addario/CORBIS; **163** World Pictures/Alamy; **164** Danita Delimont/Alamy; **165** Danny Lehman/CORBIS; **167** Oswaldo Rivas/Reuters/CORBIS; **168** (l)Mark Godfrey copyright 2004 The Nature Conservancy, (r)Courtesy Marie Claire Paiz; **169** Alejandro Ernesto/epa/CORBIS; **171** Dolores Ochoa/AP Images; **172** Peter Arnold, Inc./Alamy; **173** (tl)World Picture Library/Alamy, (tc)AP Photo/Alberto Cesar-Greenpeace/HO, (tr)Sue Cunningham Photographic/Alamy, (b)Reuters/Carlos Barria; **174** Reuters/Jamil Bittar; **175** Reuters/Paulo Whitaker; **176** Roger Ressmeyer/CORBIS; **177** Paulo Whitaker/Reuters/Landov; **179** Vanderlei Almeida/AFP/Getty Images; **180** Eduardo De Baia/AP Images; **181** Eliseo Fernandez/Reuters/CORBIS; **183** (t)Marcelo Sayao/epa/CORBIS, (cl)Marco Ugarte/AP Images, (cr)Juan Barreto/AFP/Getty Images, (b)Jeff Greenberg/age fotostock; **186–187** Gunter Marx Photography/CORBIS; **188** Bill Brooks/Alamy; **189** Philip & Karen Smith/SuperStock; **193** Peter Gridley/Getty Images; **194** Mary Evans Picture Library; **195** Rogerio Barbosa/AFP/Getty Images; **196** Alan Marsh/Getty Images; **198** Barrett & MacKay/Photolibrary; **199** Paul Thompson/Corbis; **201** Jason Kryk/AP Images; **203** (t)Roy Rainford/Robert Harding, (cl)Paul A. Souders/CORBIS, (cr)Adam Pretty/Getty Images, (b)Tim Smith/Getty Images; **206** Aaron Huey/Polaris; **207** (l)Aaron Huey/Polaris, (tcr)Melanie Acevedo, (tr)Ryan Remiorz/AP Images, (bcr)Roy Morsch/age fotostock, (br)Purestock/Alamy; **208–209** Roberto Gerometta/Lonely Planet Images; **211** (t)Anthony West/CORBIS, (bl)Konstantin Mikhailov/Nature Picture Library, (bc)Tkachev Andrei/ITAR-TASS/Landov, (br)age fotostock/SuperStock; **225** Nicole Duplaix/National Geographic Image Collection/Getty Images; **227** Tim Graham/Getty Images; **228–229** Richard Nebesky/Lonely Planet Images; **230** Emile Luider/Getty Images; **231** age fotostock/SuperStock; **232** (l)Chase Jarvis/Getty Images, (r)Jon Arnold/SuperStock; **233** Christian Steinhausen/Getty Images; **234** Walter Geiersperger/CORBIS; **236** age fotostock/SuperStock; **237** (l)Ben Osborne/Getty Images, (r)Andra Maslennikov/Peter Arnold, Inc.; **239** Sergei Supinsky/AFP/Getty Images; **240** Rashid Salikhov/EPA/epa/CORBIS; **244** Raymond Gehman/CORBIS; **245** George Simhoni/Masterfile; **247** B. & C. Alexander/Photo Researchers; **249** (t)John Garrett/CORBIS, (cl)age fotostock/SuperStock, (cr)age fotostock/SuperStock, (b)Asgeir Helgestad/Nature Picture Library; **252–253** Hubert Stadler/CORBIS; **254** David Tomlinson/Lonely Planet Images; **255** Ted Spiegel/CORBIS; **257** (l)Matt Houston/AP Images, (r)Royalty-Free/CORBIS; **258** C. Steve Vidler/eStock Photo; **259** National Gallery Collection, By kind permission of the Trustees of the National Gallery, London/CORBIS; **260** (l)Scala/Art Resource, NY, (r)Royalty Free/Getty Images; **261** (l)Ashmolean Museum, University of Oxford, UK/Bridgeman Art Library, (r)Réunion des Musées Nationaux/Art Resource, NY; **262** Time & Life Pictures/Getty Images; **263** Central Press/Getty Images; **266** Homer Sykes/Alamy; **266–267** Royalty-Free/CORBIS; **267** Robert Fried Photography; **268** Jeff Morgan/Alamy; **269** Gideon Mendel/CORBIS; **270** Michel Euler/AP Images; **271** Simeone Huber/Getty Images; **272** Daniel Mihailescu/AFP/Getty Images; **274** Steve Vidler/SuperStock; **275** (l)Igor Akimov/ITAR-TASS/Landov, (r)Topham/The Image Works; **277** (t)Art Resource, NY, (cl)The Art Archive, (cr)Jonathan Smith/Lonely Planet Images, (b)Masterfile; **280** Richard Harbus/Polaris; **281** (l)Richard Harbus/Polaris, (tr)Steven Mark Needham/Picturearts/Newscom, (cr)Franck Fife/AFP/Newscom, (br)Patrick Sheandell O'Carroll/Getty Images; **282–283** Belinsky Yuri/ITAR-TASS/CORBIS; **284** The Image Bank/Getty Images; **286** Manfred Gottschalk/Lonely Planet Images; **287** Jayanta Shaw/Reuters/CORBIS; **288** (l)General Photographic Agency/Getty Images, (r)Mary Evans Picture Library/The Image Works; **289** Gideon Mendel/CORBIS; **290** scenicireland.com/Christopher Hill Photographic/Alamy; **291** Palmi Gudmundsson/Getty Images; **293** George F. Mobley/National Geographic Image Collection; **294** Jack Dabaghian/Reuters/CORBIS; **295** (l)Eddie Koegh/Reuters Photo Archive/Newscom, (r)Getty Images for Nike; **296** Reuters/Luis D'Orey; **297** K.M. Westermann/CORBIS; **298** Winfried Rothermel/AP Images; **299** Christian Charisius/Reuters/CORBIS; **300** Martin Ruetschi/epa/CORBIS; **302** Taxi/Getty Images; **303** age fotostock/SuperStock; **304** (inset)Charles O'Rear/CORBIS, (bkgd)Jose Manuel Ribeiro/Reuters/Landov; **305** Peter Adams/Getty Images; **307** Brian Atkinson/Alamy; **308** Jack Naegelen/Reuters/CORBIS; **309 310** AP Images; **312** Sergei Supinsky/AFP/Getty Images; **313** Fabrizio Bensch/Reuters; **314** Katarina Stoltz/Reuters/CORBIS; **316** Sean Gallup/Newsmakers/Getty Images; **317** Peter Turnley/CORBIS; **319** Robb Kendrick/Getty Images; **321** Richard Nowitz/National Geographic Image Collection; **322** Ivan Sekretarev/AP Images; **323** AP Images; **325** (t)Alain Nogues/CORBIS; **325** (cl)Tim Graham/Getty Images, (cr)Bob Stern/The Image Works, (b)Goddard Space Flight Center, Scientific Visualization Studio/NASA; **328–329** R. Wallace/Stock Photos/zefa/CORBIS; **331** (tl)R. Ian Lloyd/Masterfile, (tr)Fred Bavendam/Minden Pictures, (bl)Michael & Patricia Fogden/CORBIS, (br)Pawel Toczynski/photolibrary; **337** Oliver Gerhard/Photolibrary; **338–339** Frans Lanting/Corbis; **340** Chris Mellor/Lonely Planet Images; **341** Ken Usami/Photodisc Green/Getty Images; **344** John Van Hasselt/CORBIS SYGMA; **344–345** Marc Romanelli/Getty Images; **345** John Van Hasselt/CORBIS SYGMA; **346** Richard I'Anson/Lonely Planet Images; **347** Oliver Gerhard/Photolibrary; **348** (l)Mary Evans/AISA Media, (r)SuperStock; **349** age fotostock/SuperStock; **351** (t)Bill Hatcher/National Geographic/Getty Images, (c)John Van Hasselt/Corbis, (b)age fotostock/SuperStock; **354–355** Bill Bachman/Wild Light; **356** Will Burgess/Reuters/CORBIS; **357** Bill Bachman/Alamy; **358** (t)Wallace-Crabbe/National Library of Australia, (b)CORBIS; **359** Richard Nebesky/Lonely Planet Images; **361 362** Mike Powell/Getty Images; **363** (l)Paul A. Souders/CORBIS, (c)Neil Rabinowitz/CORBIS, (r)New Zealand Film Comm./The Kobal Collection; **364** Reuters/Will Burgess; **365** Dave G. Houser/Post-Houser Stock/CORBIS; **366** Paul Beinssen/Lonely Planet Images; **369** (t)Axiom Photographic Limited/SuperStock, (cl)Chris McGrath/Getty Images, (cr)Heather Faulkner/AFP/Getty Images, (b)Stefan Postles/Getty Images; **372** Wade Eakle/Lonely Planet Images; **374** through **381** Don Farrall/Getty Images; **383** Jerry Barnett; **384** Museum für Völkerkunde, Wien oder MVK, Wien; **385** Larry Williams/CORBIS; **389** Michael Nichols/National Geographic Image Collection.